THE UK AND EUROPEAN HUMAN RIGHTS

The UK's engagement with the legal protection of human rights at a European level has been, at varying stages, pioneering, sceptical and antagonistic. The UK government, media and public opinion have all at times expressed concerns about the growing influence of European human rights law, particularly in the controversial contexts of prisoner voting and deportation of suspected terrorists as well as in the context of British military action abroad. British politicians and judges have also, however, played important roles in drafting, implementing and interpreting the European Convention on Human Rights. Its incorporation into domestic law in the Human Rights Act 1998 intensified the ongoing debate about the UK's international and regional human rights commitments. Furthermore, the increasing importance of the European Union in the human rights sphere has added another layer to the relationship and highlights the complex relationship(s) between the UK government, the Westminster Parliament and judges in the UK, Strasbourg and Luxembourg.

The UK and European Human Rights

A Strained Relationship?

Edited by
Katja S Ziegler
Elizabeth Wicks
and
Loveday Hodson

·HART·
PUBLISHING
OXFORD AND PORTLAND, OREGON
2015

Hart Publishing

An imprint of Bloomsbury Publishing Plc

Hart Publishing Ltd	Bloomsbury Publishing Plc
Kemp House	50 Bedford Square
Chawley Park	London
Cumnor Hill	WC1B 3DP
Oxford OX2 9PH	UK
UK	

www.hartpub.co.uk
www.bloomsbury.com

Published in North America (US and Canada) by
Hart Publishing
c/o International Specialized Book Services
920 NE 58th Avenue, Suite 300
Portland, OR 97213-3786
USA

www.isbs.com

**HART PUBLISHING, the Hart/Stag logo, BLOOMSBURY and the
Diana logo are trademarks of Bloomsbury Publishing Plc**

British Library Cataloguing-in-Publication Data
A catalogue record for this book is available from the British Library.

ISBN: 978-1-84946-795-7

Typeset by Compuscript Ltd, Shannon
Printed and bound in Great Britain by
Lightning Source UK Ltd

To find out more about our authors and books visit www.hartpublishing.co.uk. Here you will
find extracts, author information, details of forthcoming events and the option to sign up for our
newsletters.

Foreword

ANTHONY W BRADLEY

In the Preamble to the UN Charter, signed in June 1945, representatives of the assembled nations in San Francisco expressed their determination to 'reaffirm faith in fundamental human rights, in the dignity and worth of the human person, in the equal rights of men and women and of nations large and small'. In 1951, the United Kingdom was the first country to ratify the European Convention on Human Rights (ECHR), from which was to develop an elaborate judicial system for enabling fundamental rights to have practical effect in Europe. The Convention has proved to be an essential complement to the growth of European economic integration.

In April 2012, during a conference summoned by the UK government, the 47 States that are now party to the ECHR adopted the Brighton Declaration, which reaffirmed these States' 'deep and abiding commitment to the Convention and to the fulfilment of their obligation ... to secure to everyone within their jurisdiction the rights and freedoms defined in the Convention'. But in October 2014, the Conservative Party, the major partner in the UK's coalition government, published proposals that were intended to diminish and possibly to eliminate entirely British participation in what had in the years since 1945 become a significant aspect of international relations.[1] That significance had been extended when the fall of the Berlin Wall enabled States in Eastern Europe to adhere to the Convention and join the Council of Europe.

It would be unrealistic to imagine any country in which the advances made in the protection of human rights could be achieved at no cost. In his masterly study of the rise of human rights in Europe, entitled *Human Rights and the End of Empire*,[2] the late Professor Brian Simpson examined Britain's role in the genesis of the ECHR. We can see clearly now how, after 1945, the UK's imperial past eventually gave way to a European present. But, simply as a question of the UK's future in the world, many (including myself) find it difficult to envisage what that future might be if the UK were to seek to withdraw from Europe. And there can be no future for the UK in Europe if the extremist call for withdrawal from European human rights is heard and acted upon.

Nevertheless, if such a call is to become more strident, we need to understand what the causes of the present 'strained relationship' between Britain and the Strasbourg Court may be: some of these causes are deep-seated and inherent in any system for protecting human rights, while others are more local or ephemeral.

---

[1] *Protecting Human Rights in the UK: The Conservatives' Proposals for Changing Britain's Human Rights Laws* (2012).
[2] AWB Simpson, *Human Rights and the End of Empire: Britain and the Genesis of the European Convention* (Oxford, Oxford University Press, 2001).

And this relationship in respect of human rights must be seen alongside the range of problems faced by government and democracy that arise from the European economic system.

The present volume does not offer a single route-map for action that will resolve all current difficulties. But it does bring together a rich body of interrelated studies that cast light from different perspectives on the many questions that arise in adjusting the historical unwritten, 'political' constitution of the UK to the current need for 'legal' protection of human rights in a changing Europe. The starting point for debating protection for human rights has long ceased to be the patronising observation of AV Dicey that 'most foreign constitution-makers have begun with declarations of rights. For this they have often been in nowise to blame'—or his exaggerated claim that 'the Habeas Corpus Acts declare no principle and define no rights, but they are for practical purposes worth a hundred constitutional articles guaranteeing individual liberty'.[3] But Dicey's stress on the sovereignty of Parliament is still influential in both the 'legal' and the 'political' constitutions of the UK: this can clearly be seen in the elaborate crafting of the Human Rights Act 1998.

Inevitably, if there is to be greater legal protection of human rights in the UK, this will add to the authority that is exercised by the civil and criminal courts: in a world in which many politicians seem not to be deserving of great respect, and in which vociferous sections of the press have ridden roughshod over the law to stimulate public curiosity, we should not be aghast at an extended role for the judges. Nor is it surprising if the constitutional doctrine of 'rule of law' thereby gains substance, as public discourse moves into a new plane, with judges in both national and international courts being required to consider what the law should be as well as exercising their traditional role of deciding on the law as it now is.

The chapters in this volume that examine Britain's relationship with Europe reveal the formidable nature of the questions that arise. These include the division of authority over fundamental rights in the UK between government, Parliament and the courts, to which must be added the competing role of European institutions and the emergence of a devolved UK landscape. Issues of legitimacy, sovereignty and juristic methodology inevitably arise from attempts to determine the essence of fundamental rights in a changing world. Such questions need to be considered in a comparative context. The experiences of Austria, France, Germany and Italy demonstrate subtle ways in which national institutions may adjust to the 'incoming tide' of European protection for human rights; the contrasting story of events in Russia emphasises the value of that cause, rather than illustrating its futility.

Given the expert knowledge of the contributors and the care the editors of the book have taken, there is no need for even a metaphorical bottle of champagne to be broken on its bows as it is launched. But we should all be confident that the issues addressed in these pages can be resolved in a way that both benefits the governance of the United Kingdom and of Europe and makes more effective the protection of human rights for the people of Europe.

1 May 2015

---

[3] AV Dicey, *Law of the Constitution*, 10th edn (ed ECS Wade) (Houndmills, Macmillan, 1959) 198, 199.

Table of Contents

List of Contributors

Ed Bates

Dr Ed Bates is a Senior Lecturer in Law at the University of Leicester. His recent work includes 'Analysing the Prisoner Voting Saga and the British Challenge to Strasbourg' (2014) 14 *Human Rights Law Review* 503. He is a co-author of Harris, O'Boyle and Warbrick, *The Law of the European Convention on Human Rights* (Oxford University Press, 2014) and the author of *The Evolution of the European Convention on Human Rights* (Oxford University Press, 2010).

Bill Bowring

Professor Bill Bowring is an expert on human rights and Russian law. He was appointed Professor of Law at Birkbeck College, University of London in September 2006 and is a practising barrister at Field Court Chambers in Gray's Inn. He previously taught at the University of East London, Essex University and London Metropolitan University. In 2003 Bill founded and is currently Chair of the European Human Rights Advocacy Centre (EHRAC), which, in partnership with the Russian NGO Memorial and the Bar Human Rights Committee, is assisting with many cases against Russia and other former Soviet Union (FSU) countries before the European Court of Human Rights (ECtHR). As a barrister, he has represented applicants before the ECtHR in cases against Armenia, Azerbaijan, Estonia, Georgia, Latvia, Russia and Turkey. Bill has acted as expert for the Council of Europe on human and minority rights issues, and works as a trainer and expert for the Council, the European Union, the UN, Amnesty International and others. He has over 90 publications to his name on the topics of international law, human rights, minority rights and Russian law. His latest book is *Law, Rights and Ideology in Russia: Landmarks in the Destiny of a Great Power* (Routledge, 2013). Bill speaks fluent Russian and has been travelling to Russia and FSU since 1983.

Anthony W Bradley

Anthony Bradley is Professor emeritus of Constitutional Law, University of Edinburgh, and a Research Fellow at the Institute of European and Comparative Law, University of Oxford. He formerly practised as a barrister, being appointed QC (Hon) in 2011. From 2002 to 2005 he was legal adviser to the House of Lords Committee on the Constitution; from 2003 to 2010 he was a UK member of the European Commission for Democracy through Law ('Venice Commission'); and from 2004 to 2007 he was a vice-president of the International Association of Constitutional Law. His publications include (with Keith Ewing) *Constitutional and Administrative Law*, 16th edn (London, Pearson, 2015), and (with Mark Janis and Richard Kay), *European Human Rights Law: Text and Materials*, 3rd edn (Oxford, Oxford University Press, 2008). Other publications are (with S Fraser Butlin) 'The Human Rights Act and Judicial Review' in M Supperstone, J Goudie and P Walker (eds),

Judicial Review, 5th edn (London, Butterworths, 2014); and 'The Sovereignty of Parliament: Form or Substance?' in J Jowell and D Oliver (eds), *The Changing Constitution*, 7th edn (Oxford, Oxford University Press, 2007).

Olga Chernishova

Dr Olga Chernishova graduated in law from the Moscow State Lomonosov University in 1995. She obtained an LLM in comparative constitutional law from the Central European University, Budapest (1995) and a PhD in law from the Moscow State Legal Academy (2005). She has been working as a lawyer since 1999, and since 2006 has been head of a legal division at the Registry of the European Court of Human Rights. She has authored over 20 publications on the European Court's practice and its organisation and reform, the rapport between Russian constitutional law and international human rights law, and the situation of refugees and foreign nationals in Russia.

Richard Clayton

Richard Clayton QC practices at 4–5 Grays Inn Square and Kings Chambers. He undertakes a wide range of advisory and litigation public law work, including community care and mental health, education, health care, human rights, local government vires and finance, constitutional and standards issues, education, planning and environmental cases, Privy Council and international constitutional work, and public procurement. He has been the UK representative to the Venice Commission, the Council of Europe's advisory body on constitutional law, since 2010 and has recently been re-appointed until 2018. Richard is a former Chairman of the Constitutional and Administrative Law Bar Association, and a former Vice Chair of Liberty, and has been an Associate Fellow at the Centre for Public Law at Cambridge University since 2001. He is the author of a number of books including Clayton and Tomlinson, *The Law of Human Rights* (Oxford, Oxford University Press, 2nd edn 2009), which has been cited in the House of Lords and Supreme Court about 40 times and regularly contributes to academic journals such as *Public Law*. Richard is ranked in Chambers Directory and the Legal 500 as a Leading Silk in Public Law, Human Rights and Local Government Law.

Brice Dickson

Brice Dickson is Professor of International and Comparative Law at Queen's University Belfast and a former Chief Commissioner of the Northern Ireland Human Rights Commission. He is the author of *The European Convention on Human Rights and the Conflict in Northern Ireland* (Oxford, Oxford University Press, 2010) and of *Human Rights and the United Kingdom Supreme Court* (Oxford, Oxford University Press, 2013). With the help of a Leverhulme Research Fellowship he is currently working on a study of the Supreme Court of Ireland.

Alice Donald

Dr Alice Donald is a Senior Lecturer in the Department of Law and Politics, Middlesex University. Her socio-legal research focuses on the implementation and impact of human rights law, particularly in the UK and Europe. She is currently working on a book entitled *Parliaments and the European Court of Human Rights* (co-authored with Philip Leach) (Oxford University Press, forthcoming 2016).

Alice has published widely on human rights, including on the relationship between the UK and the Convention system; the possible development of a bill of rights for the UK; and the interaction between human rights, equality and religion or belief. She previously worked as a commissioner, editor and broadcast journalist in the BBC World Service (1991–2005).

Sionaidh Douglas-Scott

Sionaidh Douglas-Scott is Professor of European and Human Rights Law at the University of Oxford. Before Oxford, she was Professor of Law at King's College London. She works primarily in the field of EU public law and legal and social theory, specialising, in particular, in EU human rights law. She is the author of the monograph *Constitutional Law of the EU* (London, Longman, 2002), and has published widely on EU human rights law. She has held visiting posts at various institutions, including the University of Bonn, where she was visiting Jean Monnet professor. Since 1993, she has co-taught and developed a course on comparative US and EU human rights law with Justice Anthony Kennedy of the US Supreme Court at the Salzburg Forum for International Studies. Her current projects include a monograph on European human rights law, and she is co-editing a research handbook on the European Union and human rights. Professor Douglas-Scott has recently completed a monograph, *Law After Modernity* (Oxford, Hart Publishing, 2013), which explores on a more abstract level many of the issues of pluralism, justice and human rights that can be found in her work on the EU, and, unusually for a work of legal theory, is illustrated with various images and artistic works.

Helen Fenwick

Helen Fenwick is Professor of Law at Durham University, and a Human Rights Consultant to Doughty Street Chambers in London, one of a group of chambers specialising in human rights litigation. She was Joint Director of the University of Durham Human Rights Centre until 2012. She specialises in human rights, the European Convention on Human Rights, counter-terrorist law and policy, public protest, media law and the Human Rights Act. She is the author of *Civil Rights: New Labour, Freedom and the Human Rights Act* (London, Longman/Pearson, 2000); *Media Freedom under the Human Rights Act* (Oxford, Oxford University Press, 2006, with G Phillipson); *Text, Cases and Materials on Public Law and Human Rights*, 3rd edn (Oxford, Routledge, 2010, with G Phillipson); *Civil Liberties and Human Rights*, 4th edn (Oxford, Routledge, 2007); and *Halsbury's Laws* 5th Edition (2013) Volume 88A Parts 1 and 2 (Part 2 with Stephen Cragg QC) 'Rights and Freedoms'. She has recently given a number of papers at international conferences on human rights and terrorism, and has published a number of pieces on that subject in the *Modern Law Review*, *Current Legal Problems*, *Public Law* and the *McGill Law Journal*. She has also contributed to edited collections in that field, including *Global Terrorism*, 2nd edn (Cambridge, Cambridge University Press, 2012, ed V Ramraj, M Hor, K Roach).

Lieve Gies

Dr Lieve Gies is a Senior Lecturer in the Department of Media and Communication at the University of Leicester. Her main research interests are in the area of media representations of the law. She is author of *Mediating Human Rights: Media, Culture and Human Rights Law* (Abingdon, Routledge-Cavendish 2014).

Paul Gragl

Dr Paul Gragl is a Lecturer in Law at Queen Mary, University of London. He is the author of *The Accession of the European Union to the European Convention on Human Rights* (Oxford, Hart Publishing, 2013), the very first monograph on this topic, and has published widely in the area of European human rights law. Beyond human rights, he has a research interest in the relationship between international and domestic law, and is currently working on a book in which he applies Hans Kelsen's *Pure Theory of Law* in order to describe and theorise the normative correlation between public international law and the law of the European Union.

Constance Grewe

Constance Grewe was a Professor at Robert Schuman University, Strasbourg between 1997 and 2011. From 2003–06 she acted as Vice-President of research at the University of Strasbourg. Since September 2004 she has been a Judge of the Constitutional Court of Bosnia and Herzegovina. Previously she was a professor at the Universities of Chambéry and Caen. Her research and publishing interests lie in the areas of comparative constitutional law, especially fundamental rights, constitutional justice and German constitutional law, as well as interactions between international/European and domestic law, especially ECHR law, the circulation of 'legal models', and fundamental rights in the EU. She is on the editorial advisory boards of *Europäische Grundrechte Zeitschrift* (EuGRZ) and *Revue française de droit constitutionnel* (RFDC). She has received, amongst others, the following distinctions: Decoration for Services to Education (Palmes académiques) (2001), Legion of Honour: Chevalier (2002), Research Award of the Humboldt Foundation (2008), and an honorary doctorate from the University of Basel.

Loveday Hodson

Dr Loveday Hodson is a Senior Lecturer in Law at the University of Leicester. Her research interest lies particularly in the area of LGBT family rights in international law, and she has published a number of academic articles and NGO reports on this subject. She also writes on international human rights law and social movements. In 2011 she published a monograph with Hart Publishing, *NGOs and the Struggle for Human Rights in Europe*. Loveday is also the co-convenor of the European Society of International Law's interest group on Feminism and International Law.

The Rt Hon the Lord Kerr of Tonaghmore

Lord Kerr was appointed a judge of the High Court of Northern Ireland in 1993. He served as Commercial judge until taking over the judicial review portfolio in 1995. He has sat as an ad hoc judge at the European Court of Human Rights in Strasbourg. He is a past chairman of the Mental Health Commission for Northern Ireland and of the Distinction and Meritorious Service Awards Committee, which determines the remuneration of senior medical consultants in the National Health Service. In 1999 he was an Eisenhower Fellow. From October 2003 until 2004 he was President of the Medico-Legal Society. He was a member of the Judicial Studies Board until his appointment as Lord Chief Justice. He was also Chairman of the Northern Ireland Judicial Appointments Commission. He became Lord Chief Justice of Northern Ireland on 12 January 2004 and remained in that position until his appointment as a Lord of Appeal in Ordinary on 29 June 2009. He became a Justice of the Supreme Court in October 2009.

Luis López Guerra

Judge López Guerra was appointed to the European Court of Human Rights in February 2008. He holds degrees in law and political science from Complutense University, a Master of Arts in Political Science (Michigan State University), and was awarded a doctorate in Law by Complutense University in 1975. In 1978 he was appointed Professor of Constitutional Law at Extremadura University (1979–95). From 1986–95 he was a Judge at the Constitutional Court of Spain and from 1995–2008 was Professor of Constitutional Law at Universidad Carlos III. He was Vice-President of the General Council of the Judiciary from 1996–2001. Between 2004 and 2007 he was Secretary of State for Justice. He has been awarded academic scholarships by the Fulbright Commission, the March Foundation and the Deutscher Akademischer Austauschdienst. He is author of numerous publications on constitutional law, including *Derecho constitucional*, 9th edn (Valencia, Tirant lo Blanch, 2013), *Introducción al derecho constitucional* (Valencia, Tirant lo Blanch, 1994), *El poder judicial en el estado constitucional* (Lima, Palestra Editores, 2001) and *Las sentencias básicas del tribunal constitucional*, 3rd edn (Madrid, Boletin Oficial del Estado, 2008).

Paul Mahoney

Judge Paul Mahoney has been the UK judge at the European Court of Human Rights (Strasbourg) since November 2012. Between 2005 and 2011 he was President of the European Union Civil Service Tribunal, a specialist first-instance chamber of the Court of Justice of the European Union (Luxembourg). Prior to that, he spent the greater part of his career in the Registry of the Strasbourg Court, beginning as a case-lawyer in 1974 working on the case of *Golder v UK* and ending as Registrar of the Court between 2001 and 2005, with a three-year break in the 1990s as Head of Personnel of the Council of Europe (Strasbourg). His early career was as a lecturer (in Roman law and tort) at University College London, followed by two years of practice as a barrister in London until 1974. He has law degrees from the University of Oxford and University College London, and was awarded an honorary doctorate by the Aristotle University of Thessaloniki in 2011. He is co-editor of three books on international human rights law and the author of various articles on European civil service law and the European Convention on Human Rights. He served as associate editor of the *Human Rights Law Journal* from 1980 until 2012.

David Mead

David Mead is Professor of UK Human Rights Law in the Law School at the University of East Anglia. While his primary research interest is public order, protest and policing (he is the author of *The New Law of Peaceful Protest* (Oxford, Hart Publishing, 2010) and numerous articles since the mid-1990s), he has written on the Human Rights Act and on the modalities of human rights protection generally both in journals such as *Public Law* and in forums such as the UKCLA's blog. His own occasional blog is ProtestMatters and he tweets as @seethingmead.

Andreas Th Müller

Andreas Th Müller is Assistant Professor in the Department of European Law and Public International Law at the University of Innsbruck, Austria. He is visiting professor at the University of Alcalá de Henares, Spain and the Universidad Panamericana, Mexico City. In 2009/10 he was law clerk at the International Court of Justice for Judges Abdul G Koroma (Sierra Leone) and Bruno Simma (Germany). Since 2010, he has been permanent reviewer for the *Vienna Journal on International Constitutional Law*. Recent publications include: *Islam and International Law: Engaging Self-Centrism from a Plurality of Perspectives* (Leiden, Brill, 2013, with Marie-Luisa Frick); 'Exercise and Limits of Jurisdiction' (with Bruno Simma) in James Crawford and Martti Koskenniemi (eds), *The Cambridge Companion to International Law* (Cambridge, Cambridge University Press 2012); and 'Elements of Supranationality in the Law of International Organizations' (with Werner Schroeder) in Ulrich Fastenrath et al (eds), *From Bilateralism to Community Interest: Essays in Honour of Bruno Simma* (Oxford, Oxford University Press, 2011).

Mark Ockelton

Mark Ockelton is Vice President of the Upper Tribunal, a Recorder and Deputy High Court Judge, Deputy International Course Director at the Judicial College, and a Bencher of Lincoln's Inn. After being called to the Bar in 1977 he was a University Lecturer and Senior Lecturer at the University of Leeds, with visiting posts in France and the USA, before taking a full-time judicial post in 1996.

Noreen O'Meara

Dr Noreen O'Meara is a Lecturer in Law at the University of Surrey. Noreen read for her undergraduate degree at the University of Cambridge, completed an LLM (Public Law) at University College London, and was awarded a PhD by Queen Mary, University of London on the topic of evolving judicial dialogue between highest national courts and the Court of Justice of the European Union (CJEU). She has completed advanced legal studies at the European University Institute, Florence and the Université Paris-1 (Panthéon-Sorbonne), and spent time in practice at the European Commission (Legal Service) and CJEU following her call to the Bar (Inner Temple). Her research focuses, in particular, on relationships between national courts and the CJEU and the European Court of Human Rights respectively, on the evolving EU-ECHR interface, and on the reform of judicial institutions.

Clare Ovey

Clare Ovey is a Head of Division at the Registry of the European Court of Human Rights in Strasbourg. She is also co-author (with B Rainey and L Wicks) of the sixth edition of *Jacobs, White and Ovey: The European Convention on Human Rights* (Oxford, Oxford University Press, 2014).

Oreste Pollicino

Oreste Pollicino is Associate Professor of Comparative Public Law and Information and Internet Law at Bocconi University, Milan (Italy). He is editor of the *International Journal of Communications Law and Policy* as well as the founder of two leading Italian blogs, medialaws.eu and dirritticomparati.it. His research interests lie in the field of European and comparative constitutional law as well as media and internet law.

Julia Rackow

Julia Rackow is a doctoral student in international law at Humboldt University in Berlin and works as a solicitor/barrister (Rechtsanwältin) in public law. She studied law in Berlin, where she also completed her legal training. She received the Certificate of Transnational Law from the University of Geneva and a Masters in Human Rights, Democracy and International Justice from the University of Valencia.

Robert Uerpmann-Wittzack

Robert Uerpmann-Wittzack is Professor of Public and International Law at the University of Regensburg. He studied law in Berlin, Tübingen and Aix-en-Provence, where he passed the Maîtrise en droit in 1988. He defended his doctoral thesis on the influence of the European Convention on Human Rights on German jurisprudence in 1992 and completed his Habilitation thesis on the legal notion of public interest in 1999. Major publications relate to the international protection of human rights and to the relationship between international, European and domestic law. Robert Uerpmann-Wittzack is a member of the Regensburg Research Group on Information Society Law founded in 2002, and he has been a co-editor of the German international law journal *Archiv des Völkerrechts* since 2007.

Elizabeth Wicks

Elizabeth Wicks is Professor of Human Rights Law at the University of Leicester, with a particular interest in human rights in healthcare. Publications include *The Evolution of a Constitution: Eight Key Moments in British Constitutional History* (Oxford, Hart Publishing, 2006); *Human Rights and Healthcare* (Oxford, Hart Publishing, 2007); and *The Right to Life and Conflicting Interests* (Oxford, Oxford University Press, 2010). She is a co-author (with B Rainey and C Ovey) of the sixth edition of *Jacobs, White and Ovey: The European Convention on Human Rights* (Oxford, Oxford University Press, 2014). She is a member of the Centre for European Law and Internationalisation and the Midlands Medical Law Consortium. Current research interests include faith and belief in end of life decision-making; the position of suicide under the ECHR; and state interest in issues of bodily autonomy.

Katja S Ziegler

Katja S Ziegler is Sir Robert Jennings Professor of International Law at the University of Leicester and Director of the Centre for European Law and Internationalisation (CELI). Previously she was a Lecturer, then Reader at the University of Oxford (2002–12). Her current research concerns the constitutionalisation and intersection of legal orders in an international, European and comparative law context, in particular by human rights; and limits on executive power to resort to military force in constitutional and international law. Recent publications include 'The Relationship between EU Law and International Law' in Dennis Patterson and Anna Södersten (eds), *Blackwell Companion for European Union Law and International Law* (Hoboken, NJ, Wiley-Blackwell, forthcoming, 2015); *The Evolution of Fundamental*

Rights Charters and Case Law: A Comparison of the European and the United Nations Systems (together with L Lazarus, N Ghanea and C Costello (European Parliament, Directorate General for Internal Policies 2011)); 'International Law and EU Law: Between Asymmetric Constitutionalism and Fragmentation' in Alexander Orakhelashvili (ed), *Research Handbook on the Theory of International Law* (Cheltenham, Edwards Elgar, 2011), chapter 10, 268–327.

Reuven (Ruvi) Ziegler
Dr Ruvi Ziegler is a Lecturer in Law at the University of Reading School of Law, where he is a member of the Global Law at Reading (GLAR) research group (specialising in human rights, international humanitarian law and international refugee law). He is Editor-in-Chief of a Working Paper Series, *Refugee Law Initiative* (School of Advanced Study, University of London). He is a Research Associate at the Refugee Studies Centre, University of Oxford, and an Academic visitor at its Faculty of Law. He is also a researcher at the Israel Democracy Institute (analysing the treatment of African asylum seekers in Israel as part of the Constitutional Principles project). Previously, he was a visiting researcher at Harvard Law School (affiliated with its Immigration and Refugee Clinic and with the Human Rights Program), a tutor in public international law at the University of Oxford, and a legal advising officer at the Israel Defence Forces' Legal Counselor's Office (mandatory military service). He holds DPhil, MPhil and BCL degrees from the University of Oxford; an LLM with specialisation in public law from Hebrew University; and a joint LLB and BA from the University of Haifa.

Introduction

1

The UK and European Human Rights: A Strained Relationship?

KATJA S ZIEGLER, ELIZABETH WICKS AND LOVEDAY HODSON

> Where, after all, do universal human rights begin? In small places, close to home—
> so close and so small that they cannot be seen on any maps of the world. Yet they
> are the world of the individual person; the neighbourhood he lives in; the school or
> college he attends; the factory, farm or office where he works. Such are the places
> where every man, woman and child seeks equal justice, equal opportunity, equal
> dignity without discrimination. Unless these rights have meaning there, they have
> little meaning anywhere. Without concerned citizen action to uphold them close to
> home, we shall look in vain for progress in the larger world.[1]

THE RELATIONSHIP BETWEEN the UK and the European systems regarding the protection of human rights has become ever more contentious. The debates about prisoner voting, detention and deportation of suspected terrorists (and the absolute nature of Article 3 of the European Convention on Human Rights (ECHR) in this context), immigration decisions and courts passing judgments in the context of British military action abroad are paradigmatic.

Historically, the UK's engagement with the legal protection of human rights at a European level has been, at varying stages, pioneering, sceptical and antagonistic. British politicians and judges have played important roles in drafting, implementing and interpreting the ECHR. However, the UK government, media and public opinion have all at times expressed concern at the growing influence of European human rights law, not only but particularly in controversial contexts. It is one aim of this book to enquire into the reasons behind such concerns.

I. THE COMPLEXITY OF THE 'STRAINED' RELATIONSHIP

When enquiring into those reasons, one thing that is immediately striking is the complexity of the 'strained' relationship—or even relationships—involved. The

---

[1] Eleanor Roosevelt, 'In Our Hands', speech delivered on the occasion of the 10th anniversary of the Universal Declaration of Human Rights 1958; E Roosevelt, *The Great Question* (New York, United Nations, 1958).

incorporation of the ECHR into domestic law by the Human Rights Act 1998 (HRA) intensified the ongoing debates about the UK's international and regional human rights commitments. The HRA may have been designed to 'bring rights home', but it also highlights the complex relationship(s) between the UK government, the Westminster Parliament and judges in the UK, both amongst themselves and with Strasbourg.

Furthermore, the different layers of European human rights (and the respective, potentially different substantive standards they lay down) and their relationship with domestic rights make the relationship more complex. The increasing importance of the European Union (EU) in the human rights sphere has added another dimension to the topic. European human rights can no longer be considered solely by reference to the ECHR, for several reasons. The very substance and content of European human rights is shaped by cross-referencing and cross-fertilisation of the two European courts; and the Member States/States Parties provide a formal link between the systems in the 'two Europes' which influences the relationship between the States and the respective courts. Furthermore, the ECHR (in particular through its domestic incorporation by the HRA) and EU human rights may be applicable concurrently in the same case. This may not only lead to forum shopping at the European level, where the same rights are interpreted differently,[2] but might also give rise to different remedies available at national law.[3] Therefore, the relationship between the UK and EU human rights (in particular the EU Charter of Fundamental Rights (EUCFR) and the possible accession of the EU to the ECHR) is considered alongside the issue of its relationship with Strasbourg, and it will be explored whether it is a separate issue or a connected one.

Beyond the legal dimension, the relationship is also influenced by the wider society in which European human rights operate. This book furthermore explores the relationship from the perspective of debates and perceptions among the general public and media.

II. WHY THE 'STRAIN'?

'Strains' in the relationship between a State and an international monitoring body can occasionally be expected as being in the very nature of that relationship. However, such strains seem to have become an ongoing theme in the UK–Strasbourg relationship, with heated language often being used. At least that is the impression one gets from political and public discourse in the UK, which has culminated so far in the announcement in October 2014 of Conservative plans to dramatically change the human rights landscape in the UK by proposing to replace the HRA with a

---

[2] *cf* Case C-60/00 *Mary Carpenter v Secretary of State for the Home Department* [2002] ECR I-6279.

[3] The Court of Appeal's judgment in *Benkharbouche v Embassy of the Republic of Sudan and Janah v Libya* [2015] EWCA Civ 33 is a case in point: the Court of Appeal issues a declaration of incompatibility of a provision of the relevant statute (the State Immunity Act 1978) with Art 6 ECHR under the HRA, but is able to disapply the same statutory provision as violating Art 47 EUCFR, EU law providing a more far-reaching remedy.

British bill of rights and responsibilities.[4] This proposal is perceived to be a priority for the new Conservative majority government elected in May 2015.[5] While it is not the aim of this book to analyse the proposal per se, it usefully highlights some of the wider themes and debates taken up by this work, some of which were on the table long before the latest proposal was put on the agenda. In particular, these include the following:

A. Misconceptions about the function of international human rights instruments, including the ECHR, as an external control and safeguard: the expressed intention in the Conservative Party's proposals to make the role of the European Court of Human Rights (ECtHR) advisory only, that is, non-binding, would run against the object and purpose of the ECHR (and thus would also preclude any renegotiation with the other Council of Europe Member States).
B. Failure to appreciate international human rights as minimum standards.
C. Confusion about the relationship between domestic human rights (in particular the ECHR in conjunction with the HRA) and the ECHR at the international level.
D. Misrepresentations about the nature and strength of the formal link between the UK courts and the ECtHR under the HRA (that is, the section 2 HRA obligation to take Strasbourg judgments into account).
E. Populist misconceptions about who human rights are for, perhaps leading to the proposal to limit them to the 'most serious cases',[6] which itself raises the question of who is to judge this standard.
F. Misrepresentations of the dynamic interpretation of human rights: the undifferentiated criticism that a dynamic interpretation (the 'living instrument' doctrine) is per se reproachable; such misrepresentations also frequently concern the linked question of the relationship between the courts and parliament.

These misconceptions and confusions crystallise around a number of concerns as reasons for the strain: first, there are concerns about 'sovereignty' with two rather distinct manifestations. The concern about *(state) sovereignty* in the UK is a concern about decisions being made elsewhere and imposed on the UK (that is, a concern about 'loss of control' as a nation). The concern about the constitutional principle of *parliamentary sovereignty* is a concern about a transfer of control from Parliament to the courts—at various levels. Secondly, there is a wider *scepticism about rights* and the courts which is partially fuelled by, thirdly, a misconception that rights are foreign (European). The perception that rights are 'foreign' allows for the 'externalisation' and 'instrumentalisation' of rights, with a variety of consequential problems.

---

[4] Conservative Party, *Protecting Human Rights in the UK: The Conservatives' Proposals for Changing Britain's Human Rights Laws* (3 October 2014), 5, www.conservatives.com/~/media/Files/Downloadable%20Files/HUMAN_RIGHTS.pdf.

[5] Nicholas Watt, 'Michael Gove to Proceed with Tories' Plans to Scrap Human Rights Act' *The Guardian* (London, 10 May 2015) www.theguardian.com/politics/2015/may/10/michael-gove-to-proceed-with-tories-plans-to-scrap-human-rights-act.

[6] ibid, 7.

Finally, it may be asked whether the very nature of the debate itself in the UK adds further strain.[7]

The concerns expressed in the public debate are predominantly external ones or directed 'outward', in the sense that they focus on a criticism of the Convention and its application by the ECtHR. However, there is a further set of underlying reasons for rights scepticism which are in reality internal to the UK, in particular the principle of parliamentary sovereignty and the constitutional relationship between the branches of government (especially in relation to the power of the courts vis-a-vis Parliament and the executive). Internal concerns are often not so clearly recognisable as such because they are either linked to or conflated/confused with external concerns: the principle of parliamentary sovereignty is frequently conflated with state sovereignty (although there is a link in the sense that state sovereignty comprises the option to adopt a constitutional principle of parliamentary sovereignty); rights are frequently considered to be European even where they are of domestic origin. As such there appears to be a mismatch between the perceived external nature and the actual internal nature of the concerns. To make things worse, there is a further, intersecting dimension, namely the instrumentalisation of human rights. Human rights may be, in a first step, 'disowned' as foreign (European); and in a second step, their name may be (ab)used and 'scapegoated' in various ways, for example by blaming them for politically inopportune results—a phenomenon which is to the detriment of a human rights culture and which may erode the actual protection of human rights. The proverbial 'case of the cat'[8] may be extreme (or at least so one hopes), but it drives home the point dramatically.

III. RELIEVING THE STRAIN: UNTANGLE—OR *DIVIDE ET IMPERA?*

Against the backdrop of such criticisms and concerns (and their instrumentalisation) which inject strain into the relationship between the UK and European human rights and the ECtHR in particular, this book seeks to untangle and examine that relationship from various perspectives in order to ascertain whether, and to what extent, and in which respects, there is strain within a complex relationship with multiple protagonists and legal standards. In other words, the book's contributors will unpick and assess the actual and perceived strain in the UK's relationship with European human rights. They will untangle the complexities in the relationship that result from a number of factors which may be located at the international (here: European) level itself or at the domestic level, or indeed in the interaction between the levels.

The obvious complexity is the multi-layered dimension of European human rights itself—national–ECHR–EU (and the different sources of human rights within the EU: the EUCFR, the ECHR and general principles of EU law)—and the fact that

[7] For further detail, see below, ch 25, section II.
[8] For further detail and discussion see M Ockelton, 'Article 8 ECHR, the UK and Strasbourg: Compliance, Cooperation or Clash? A Judicial Perspective' (ch 11) and D Mead, '"You Couldn't Make It Up": Some Narratives of the Media's Coverage of Human Rights' (ch 23), this volume.

all of the different levels and sources may interact. The complexity of the picture is part of the concern and heightens more general fears of 'encroachment' of European human rights. It also contributes to the question of the appropriate role for the European system of human rights protection at the national level—and the rules and principles delimiting that role. One aim of the book is therefore to shed light on some of the principles at the European level which have proved to be controversial (such as the international minimum standard, subsidiarity, margin of appreciation, and interpretive methods, in particular dynamic interpretation).

The contributors will also consider and highlight further concerns and the underlying reasons for those concerns which are currently not found at the forefront of the debate. The first is the fact that the 'dual function' of ECHR rights as both international and domestic rights (through the HRA) in the UK, which was intended to keep things simple, in fact adds further complexity. Secondly, there are different players at the State level that indeed may require a differentiated analysis as to the level of strain in the relationship. One may look beyond 'the UK' to its individual component institutions of government and society, and, as part of the latter, the media. Thirdly, the fact that the UK constitution is in an ongoing process of change is also a relevant factor. The UK constitution has already evolved considerably in the past 60-odd years, precisely, but not only, because of its relationship with the 'two Europes' (EU and ECHR). The search for the right balance between the principles of democracy (as represented by parliamentary sovereignty) and the rule of law and the role of the courts is not yet complete and, therefore, is another factor to consider when examining the relationship between 'the UK' and European human rights.

The contributors explore the evolution of legal principles which define the relationship in both its doctrinal and contextual dimensions, enquiring into the factors that shape that relationship. They thus consider instruments and tools under the ECHR (such as subsidiarity, the margin of appreciation and reform initiatives in this regard) as well as approaches explored by UK courts (including the mirror principle).

As part of the enquiry into the reasons for the strain experienced in the UK–ECtHR relationship, the book considers the underlying reasons in the legal regime and then explores two contextual perspectives: first, it compares and contrasts other European States Parties with the ECHR, which may shed light on the reasons for peculiarly British (or not) debates. Many States Parties to the ECHR will at one point or another have experienced severe friction with the ECtHR, similar to the *Hirst*[9] and *Chahal*-to-*Othman*[10] sagas in the UK, on issues which affect the institutional structure or internal organisation of the State or 'national sensitivities' (*Poitrimol v France, Kress v France, Lautsi v Italy, SH v Austria*),[11] which run against well-established principles of the legal order (*Von Hannover v Germany*)[12]

---

[9] *Hirst v UK (No 2)* (2005) 42 EHRR 41 (GC)
[10] *Chahal v UK* (1996) 23 EHRR 413; *Saadi v Italy* (2009) 49 EHRR 30; *Othman v UK* (2012) 55 EHRR 1.
[11] *Poitrimol v France* (1994) 18 EHRR 130; *Kress v France* App no 39594/98, ECHR 2001-VI (GC); *Lautsi v Italy* App no 30814/06, ECHR 2011 (GC); *SH v Austria* App no 57813/00, ECHR 2011 (GC).
[12] *von Hannover v Germany* (2005) 40 EHRR 1.

or populist sentiments (*Gäfgen v Germany*),[13] or which are just plain critical in the light of the circumstances of the case (*Konstantin Markin v Russia, Ananyev v Russia*).[14] What are the reactions to such conflicts in law? What elevates them to a strain in the 'relationship'? Is the level of strain in the UK unique, and do reactions elsewhere appear to be similar to or different from those in the UK? Secondly, a further contextual perspective is added in the final part of the book, which discusses representations of human rights in the UK media.

IV. OVERVIEW

The book is divided into five parts.

A. Part I: Compliance, Cooperation or Clash? The Relationship Between the UK and the ECHR/Strasbourg Court

Part I explores the relationship between the UK and the ECHR and ECtHR as one of compliance, cooperation or clash in relation to general and wider issues of the relationship, including its historic, theoretical, constitutional and legal determinants. Part I is spearheaded by perspectives from two judicial protagonists from the ECtHR and the UK Supreme Court respectively, **Judge Paul Mahoney** and **Lord Kerr**. Both judges stress the two-way, cooperative nature of the relationship, which is described as one of dialogue (both in judicial interaction and extra-judicially) and structured along the lines of the Convention principles of subsidiarity, margin of appreciation and European consensus.

In chapter four, **Ed Bates** provides an overview of the narrative of the UK's position regarding the Convention system over the past 60-odd years in order to bring historical perspective and constitutional context to the friction that currently exists between the UK and Strasbourg. He reminds us that although the UK significantly shaped the ECHR during the drafting process, it was anxious about the compromise in state sovereignty that membership of the Convention entailed at the outset, and that questions regarding the legitimacy of the Court's influence over domestic law have been a recurring theme, even before the current strains, in which an exit scenario is seriously discussed. He places the existing strain in the constitutional context of the UK, suggesting that the debate about strains resulting from Strasbourg's influence as an international court may be based on false premises.

We turn in chapter five to a discussion of recent reforms of the Convention system. **Noreen O'Meara** highlights the reforms that took place following the Brighton High Level Conference (2012) which were intended to reduce the Court's backlog, enhance the quality of the Court's work and make its case law more consistent. She assesses the impact of the reforms through Protocols 15 and 16 to the ECHR.

---

[13] *Gäfgen v Germany* App no 22978/05, ECHR 2010 (GC).
[14] *Konstantin Markin v Russia* (2013) 56 EHRR 8 (GC); *Ananyev v Russia* (2012) 55 EHRR 18.

O'Meara argues that the ECtHR has been willing to engage in the reform process, and receptive to political signals for reform: case law even prior to the entry into force of Protocol 15 reflects a greater mindfulness in the application of the principles. She is more sceptical about the effectiveness of the prospective advisory jurisdiction of Protocol 16.

We then move from history and reform to focus on the approach of one of the protagonists in the relationship in more detail, namely the approach of the English courts to Strasbourg case law. **Richard Clayton** discusses the floor-ceiling problem, or mirror principle, that has occupied English judges for some time. He provides an overview of the searching and meandering approach of the English judges since the entry into force of the HRA until recently (*Nicklinson*).[15] Using the Supreme Court's judgment in *Kennedy v Charity Commission*[16] as a recent example, Clayton asks: 'Should the English courts under the Human Rights Act mirror the Strasbourg case law?' While the UK is bound by the Convention as a floor under international law, he answers the second aspect (ceiling) of the question in the negative because otherwise the distinction between Convention rights as UK statutory rights under the HRA and as international rights under the ECHR would not be maintained.

Remaining with the theme of the relationship between the Convention and the protection of rights in English law, in chapter seven **Brice Dickson** turns to a potential protagonist (but currently only given the role of an extra) when he examines whether the common law would be able to fill the gap, should the HRA be repealed. He argues that the common law as it currently stands would not be able to meet the task. He suggests that human rights currently are not, and never have been, central to the English common law, as was demonstrated by the large number of judgments in Strasbourg holding the UK in violation of the ECHR prior to the entry into force of the HRA in 2000. Dickson concludes that although UK Supreme Court justices recognise the deficiencies in the common law—and also its potential—the common law needs to be developed more systematically in order to ensure that the HRA leaves a lasting legacy.

In chapter eight, the final chapter of Part I, two further protagonists in the relationship enter the stage: the UK Parliament (and the role of parliaments more widely, from a comparative perspective) and the executive. **Alice Donald** discusses the need to involve national parliaments in order to implement judgments of the ECtHR effectively. She focuses particularly on the institutional dimension of implementation through the Joint Committee on Human Rights (JCHR), and its approach, impact, effectiveness and limitations in monitoring the response of the executive to Strasbourg judgments. In the light of the heightened debates within the UK in recent years, Donald points to statistics which reveal a low level of 'defeat' in Strasbourg (2 per cent in the years 1999 and 2010), coupled with a relatively strong implementation record regarding Strasbourg judgments, prima facie suggesting the absence of conflict—yet the UK took an extremely antagonistic stance on the prisoner voting issue. This in itself points to totally different reasons for the strain,

---

[15] *R (Nicklinson) v Ministry of Justice; R (AM) v Director of Public Prosecutions* [2014] UKSC 38.
[16] *Kennedy v Charity Commission* [2014] 2 WLR 808.

lying in specifics of the case rather than the fact of defeat in Strasbourg. Donald also discusses the political dimensions of the implementation process and the difficulties faced by the JCHR (and Parliament as a whole) within the context of the controversies surrounding the UK's relationship with the Convention system. She contrasts in an illuminating way the non-implementation of *Hirst*[17] (prisoner voting) with the implementation of *Marper*[18] (biometric data). Donald concludes that the JCHR's monitoring and scrutiny are of a high standard in a European comparison, yet it is severely limited in terms of its influence over the executive with regard to its response to adverse ECtHR judgments.

B. Part II: Specific Issues of Conflict

Part II illustrates the use of some of the principles of the Convention discussed in Part I, such as subsidiarity, the margin of appreciation and interpretation, by focusing on specific, particularly contentious, issues in the relationship (prisoner voting, immigration, anti-terrorism and public order measures as well as extraterritorial action of the UK). These issues are inextricably linked to the perception of strain in the relationship. By taking an issue-oriented perspective (rather than one that starts from legal principle), the hope is that light will be shed on possible reasons for the strain. It may be noted that as with most human rights cases, and visible from the sample, the violation tends to result from executive action—the statutory regime of prisoner voting is the outlier here, providing a window on some of the reasons for the strained relationship. In chapter nine, **Ruvi Ziegler** provides an overview of the ongoing saga of prisoner voting in the UK since *Hirst v UK*[19] and a critique of what must be considered a light-touch approach by Strasbourg—contrary to public perceptions, given the fundamental nature of the right to vote in a democracy. Ziegler also reveals some of the tensions at the national level, in particular parliamentary sovereignty, a dimension also discussed in Part I.

Helen Fenwick uses the discussion of prisoner voting as a starting point for her analysis, which focuses on the existence (and successes, from a UK perspective) of dialogue and what may be called the implementation of an 'enhanced' subsidiarity by the ECtHR post-Brighton. A less benign description would refer to appeasement in response to pressures from the UK. She focuses on cases where the clash is mainly between the executive in the contentious areas of anti-terrorism and public order measures (*A v UK, Gillan v UK, Austin v UK* with regard to Article 5 ECHR,[20] *Saadi v Italy, Othman v UK, Ahmad v UK* with regard to Article 3 ECHR),[21] but also deals with a clash between Strasbourg and the common law/UK courts in the area of the criminal justice system (*Horncastle v UK*[22] with regard to Article 6

---

[17] *Hirst v UK (No 2)* (n 9).
[18] *S and Marper v UK* (2009) 48 EHRR 50 (GC).
[19] *Hirst v UK (No 2)* (n 9).
[20] *A v UK* (2009) 49 EHRR 29; *Gillan v UK* (2010) 50 EHRR 45; *Austin v UK* (2012) 55 EHRR 14.
[21] *Saadi v Italy* (n 9); *Othman v UK* (n 9); *Ahmad v UK* (2013) 56 EHRR 1.
[22] *Horncastle v UK* App no 4184/10 (16 December 2014).

ECHR). Fenwick points to the tension between the pressures on the ECtHR to avoid head-on-clashes (which may lead to 'enhanced subsidiarity'/appeasement of the States Parties) for the sake of 'rescuing' the European Convention system as an institution per se and the appropriate maintenance of a minimum standard applicable to all States. The two issues are of course linked ...

In chapter eleven, **Mark Ockelton** adds a number of issues to the debate from the perspective of a judge in the special jurisdiction of immigration tribunals in the UK, namely problems related to the application of Article 8 ECHR (assessment of proportionality) and the nature of the judiciary's task and role. Ockelton makes a strong case that the real clash is not one of the rules, but an institutional clash between the executive and UK judges.

Chapter twelve, by **Clare Ovey**, concludes Part II's focus on specific issues of conflict by turning to another 'saga' and contentious issue, that of the extra-territorial application of the Convention in situations of armed conflict, which has to a large extent been fuelled by cases against the UK (such as *Al-Skeini v UK*)[23] and has also triggered domestic controversy directed against UK courts when they implemented the principle, for example in *Smith v MOD*.[24] Ovey traces and analyses the meandering search for a solution by the ECtHR in its post-*Banković*[25] case law and places this in the context of current debates in the UK.

C. Part III: The Interplay of Human Rights in Europe: ECHR, EU and National Human Rights

Part III widens the perspective to include the additional and also contentious layer of EU human rights by focusing on the EU Charter of Fundamental Rights and the relationship between EU and ECHR human rights in the context of the potential accession of the EU to the ECHR (including its impact on the UK), and by providing an example of a largely harmonious *ménage à trois* of the Convention, Charter and national human rights in Austria.

Sionaidh Douglas-Scott opens the discussion by pointing to the scepticism towards the EU Charter of Fundamental Rights in the UK, which culminated in a 2014 recommendation by the House of Commons European Scrutiny Committee to pass legislation to disapply the Charter in the UK (contrary to the principle of supremacy of EU law). Douglas-Scott discusses the sources of scepticism and confusion that exist in respect of the Charter, including within government and the domestic courts, such as confusion about the legal relevance of Protocol 30 to the Treaty of Lisbon (the UK 'opt-out') and its effects in UK law (in particular regarding the social rights contained in the Charter which are a significant cause of the

---

[23] *Al-Skeini v UK* (2011) 53 EHRR 18 (GC).
[24] *Smith v Ministry of Defence* [2013] UKSC 41.
[25] *Banković v Belgium, the Czech Republic, Denmark, France, Germany, Greece, Hungary, Iceland, Italy, Luxembourg, the Netherlands, Norway, Poland, Portugal, Spain, Turkey and the United Kingdom* (2007) 44 EHRR SE5 (GC).

reluctance towards the Charter), and misconceptions about the scope of application of the Charter. Douglas-Scott discusses the bases for such concerns and puts them in context, stressing the primary thrust of the Charter to protect against a potentially overreaching EU and EU law. She thus also highlights some of the contradictions of 'euroscepticism' where it meets 'rights scepticism' even when looking at the EU Charter alone.

In chapter fourteen, **Paul Gragl** shows that such tensions and contradictions are heightened further when we take into account the possible accession of the EU to the ECHR—a process that should limit the powers of the EU by subjecting it to external control (like each EU Member State), by filling gaps in the protection of individuals against EU measures and by unifying the European human rights architecture. Although EU accession to the ECHR would limit the EU and thus should be welcomed by eurosceptics, British scepticism towards the ECHR also fuels scepticism towards EU accession to it, leading to fears of tangling the UK legal order in a 'multi-layered labyrinth of European human rights'[26] and a fear of giving supremacy, in domestic law, to the ECHR over national law via the back door of EU law. Meanwhile, the accession process has been stalled by the Court of Justice of the EU's very own version of rights scepticism in Opinion 2/13,[27] perhaps also echoing the conflict with the ECtHR in some of its Member States. Gragl nevertheless points to the advantages of accession and argues that they significantly outweigh such concerns. It may also be highlighted that the ECHR, via the general principles doctrine, applies in the sphere of EU law, and this provides one rationale for the assimilation of the treatment of both bodies of law—as highlighted by Oreste Pollicino in his critique of the Italian Constitutional Court, discussed further below.

Andreas Th Müller complements the discussion of the concerns about the EU Charter and the interaction of EU law with the ECHR in a post-accession scenario in chapter fifteen. Such concerns result in particular from the operation of EU law within the domestic sphere. Austria, while sharing many similarities with the UK, provides a unique example of a harmonious *ménage à trois*—Convention, Charter and Constitution—within domestic law, following the addition of the Charter to the national fundamental rights protection regime by the Austrian Constitutional Court. As in the UK, the ECHR is closely linked to the domestic protection of human rights in Austria and there is no single bill of rights; in fact there are three different sources of fundamental rights. While on the whole the Austrian approach to both the ECHR and the Charter may be described as particularly 'Europe-friendly', Müller reveals that this may also be the result of a complex institutional relationship, interest and power struggle between the three types of jurisdiction and their respective highest courts (Constitutional Court, Supreme Court, Supreme Administrative Court) which may be activist and use the complex set up to further their own agendas (potentially entailing problems both for the domestic constitutional order and for the European legal orders beyond the issue of protection of rights). The example

---

[26] P Gragl, 'Of Tangled and Truthful Hierarchies: EU Accession to the ECHR and its Possible Impact on the UK's Relationship with European Human Rights' (ch 14), this volume, text around n 20.
[27] Opinion 2/13 of 18 December 2014, (2014) ECR I-0000.

of Austria is not unique in this respect, but it highlights the significance of internal factors, such as inter-institutional relationships as one amongst many determinants of the relationship between European human rights and a particular legal order. The examples of Italy and, to an extent, France, discussed later in the book, provide further illustration.

D. Part IV: Perspectives from Other Jurisdictions: Contrasts and Comparisons with the UK Experience

Part IV aims to explore further the determinants of the relationship between the UK and European human rights by looking beyond the UK's legal perspective on the relationship, providing *comparative perspectives*. Do other Convention States experience similar strain to the UK with regard to controversial issues? What is the situation with regard to implementation of the Convention in general and with regard to controversial issues? What is the state of the relationship more broadly, what is the nature of such criticism, and who are the protagonists? As has already been shown in Part III, the question is in various ways linked to, and embedded in, the various ways in which States have shaped their relationship with EU law. At the extremes, the Convention either occupies a contrasting position to EU law, or benefits from, the generally more powerful status of EU law in the national sphere (via the EU doctrines of supremacy, direct effect and state liability). There are also various intermediate and even conflicting scenarios, relating for example to the specific standards applied by national constitutional courts (as in the example of Austria).

The chapters in Part IV explore the relationship between other States and European human rights and explore differences in human rights cultures, while making connections and drawing contrasts with the UK where possible. It is beyond the scope of a publication such as this to provide a comprehensive comparison of all Council of Europe States with regard to all possible issues. This collection presents necessarily a very selective sample of issues and jurisdictions. The jurisdictions covered are a mixture of long-established and more recent Member States, of those with a long-term relationship with the ECHR (the 'usual suspects': France, Italy, Germany) and relatively recent accessions (in the case of Russia, with only a relatively short experience with the Western tradition of human rights as epitomised by the ECHR), and of States with a more indirect or mediated domestic application of the Convention (through domestic bills of rights) which may be contrasted with the direct application in Austria and the UK. The Austrian example is comparable to the UK in so far as the Convention (in effect) doubles up as a domestic human rights standard and as the domestic protection of human rights in Austria is fragmented, being based on a multiplicity of human rights standards. It can be said, however, that at one time or another each of the States has come into conflict with the Convention with regard to issues of 'national sensitivity'.

The scene for the chapters in Part IV is set in chapter sixteen by **Luis López Guerra**, who provides a general overview of compliance with rulings of the ECtHR, thus linking the debates and strain to the crucial question of compliance: the protection of Convention rights, and the credibility and ultimately the legitimacy of the

Convention system as a whole—insofar as it requires the same (minimum) standards for all Member States—depends on compliance with the Convention and ECtHR rulings. At the same time, the monitoring of compliance, and the execution of judgments, is a process of potentially intense interaction between the national level, the ECtHR and the Council of Europe's Committee of Ministers. Guerra highlights an evolution in the case law of the ECtHR away from providing merely declaratory remedies to being more proactive in giving specific instructions as to the implementation of judgments, both in the individual effects of judgments (*inter partes*) and in their more general dimensions (implementation of judgments beyond the parties to the case). It may be said, on the one hand, that in the present context, more specific remedies are more likely to conflict with traditional institutional structures and national sensitivities and thus may be perceived by the State in question as a greater interference and even raise subsidiarity concerns. On the other hand, particularly in the case of systemic, widespread and large-scale violations, such specific remedies are crucial to making the Convention effective.

The following five chapters turn to the consideration of specific jurisdictions. In chapter seventeen, **Constance Grewe** provides an overview of the judicial implementation of the ECHR in France, pointing to the fact that until 2009 France was one of the States that contributed significantly to the caseload of the ECtHR. This, together with a traditional hostility to judicial review of statutes, fearing a '*gouvernement de juges*', led to an inherent tension between the French courts and the ECtHR which reflects to some extent that experienced by the UK. This tension crystallised around some high-profile cases which required fundamental changes to the French legal order (*Poitrimol* (1993), *Kress* (2001)).[28] Not unlike the UK, France experienced constitutional and institutional difficulties in implementing the Convention, particularly in relation to the division of jurisdiction for constitutional review and conventional review between the Constitutional Council and the ordinary courts. Implementation was helped by the introduction of the priority preliminary ruling procedure on the issue of constitutionality by constitutional amendment in 2008 (*question prioritaire de constitutionnalité*, QPC), which had the effect of improving conventional review by the ordinary courts.

Grewe thus also highlights problems similar to those facing Austria and Italy with implementing the ECHR, namely the dynamics, conflicts (and perhaps also separate agendas) relating to the division of competences between courts of different jurisdiction in France. Adopting a historical perspective on these conflicts, Grewe highlights that, although highly controversial at the time the conflicts first arose, today's perception in France of these cases is that they contributed to an improvement of the law and of human rights protection in France. Thus, what started out as a relationship of conflict may be described as a more harmonious one today (although Grewe also identifies some human rights issues that may well lead to further confrontation in the future). Grewe stresses that conflicts and debates in France were predominantly borne out in a technical or technocratic way rather than entering high-level

---

[28] *Poitrimol v France* (n 11); *Kress v France* (n 11).

political or public debate, while pointing out that weak parliamentary involvement may mean that 'optimal subsidiarity' has not been reached.

In chapter eighteen, **Oreste Pollicino** takes us through the labyrinth of the interaction of Italian law with the Convention and EU law. He outlines a radical change in the Italian Constitutional Court's approach to the ECHR: with two decisions of 2007[29] it established that review for conformity with the ECHR as a substantive standard as interpreted by the ECtHR is part of domestic constitutional review. The Constitutional Court thus goes beyond 'taking into account' Strasbourg jurisprudence, as the UK does under section 2 HRA. However, Pollicino also reveals that, although ECHR-friendly on the face of it, the Constitutional Court has subsequently, in effect, monopolised the application of the Convention, thus protecting the authority of national statutes: it stopped a budding practice, emerging since the end of the 1990s, of ordinary courts using the Convention in order to not apply conflicting national law in individual cases, in other words truly assimilating the reception of EU law and the ECHR. A parallel may be drawn here with the UK, where the limited remedy of a declaration of incompatibility under the HRA has come under fire, but still holds strong.[30] It may be asked whether this new strictness in the approach of the Italian Constitutional Court can be seen against the backdrop of the case of *Lautsi v Italy*,[31] considered to be the 'Italian *Hirst*' by some. Pollicino critically analyses the implications of the Italian Constitutional Court's approach and argues for a similar treatment of the ECHR and EU law on the basis of the special status of the ECHR amongst international treaties.

In chapter nineteen, **Julia Rackow** traces the evolution of the relationship between the German Federal Constitutional Court (FCC) and Strasbourg as one moving from conflict to cooperation. She discusses the approach of the German Federal Constitutional Court (FCC) towards the ECHR and ECtHR from *Von Hannover and Görgülü*[32] to the 2011 *Preventive Detention* case[33] (following *M v Germany* in Strasbourg).[34] Formally the FCC continues to adhere to a dualist approach, under which the Convention is not directly applicable in Germany and hence not the standard of assessment of the FCC, as confirmed by the FCC's *Görgülü* decision (formally, it therefore does not go as far as its Italian counterpart, which does use the Convention as the substantive standard of its constitutional review). However, the FCC appears to have become more cooperative than this might suggest. In the *Preventive Detention* case it imposed a duty on courts, making decisions of the ECtHR a 'factual precedent' (*faktische Präzedenzwirkung*). This applies to all ECtHR decisions, not only those in which Germany is a party. The underlying rationale is to minimise the risk of conflicts with (and breaches of) international law. Rackow considers the ongoing headscarf debate in Germany as an area of both potential future clash and public debate, whilst also concluding that, generally,

---

[29] Decision nos 348/2007 and 349/2007.
[30] *Benkharbouche v Embassy of the Republic of Sudan* and *Janah v Libya* (n 3) para 67.
[31] *Lautsi v Italy* (n 11).
[32] *Görgülü v Germany* App no 74969/01 (26 February 2004).
[33] Entscheidungen des Bundesverfassungsgerichts (BVerfGE), 128, 326.
[34] *M v Germany* (2009) 51 EHRR 976.

criticism of the Strasbourg Court in legal and political circles and amongst the public has tended to be issue oriented rather than fundamentally posing a challenge to the legitimacy of the ECHR or ECtHR. Finally, Rackow reflects on various conclusions regarding the UK–Strasbourg relationship, stressing the conflict-reducing potential of a domestic bill of rights very similar to the ECHR, drafted in the same era, while also pointing to the fact that the mere existence of a bill of rights may not in itself avoid conflict: the wider constitutional culture plays a vital part in the harmonious protection of rights.

The last two chapters of Part IV turn further east to discuss a more recent party to the Convention: Russia. Olga Chernishova and Bill Bowring provide insights into the problems concerning the implementation of the ECHR in Russia, national mechanisms to address (in particular) systemic violations of the Convention, and wider debates about the sovereignty of Russia.

In chapter twenty, **Olga Chernishova** discusses specific mechanisms (including Supreme Court plenary resolutions) and problems concerning the implementation of ECtHR judgments in Russia, in particular pilot judgments relating to systemic violations. While the Supreme Court and Constitutional Court provide a general framework for the implementation of the Convention, and in spite of improvements in this general framework, Chernishova points to remaining concerns about the effective implementation of Article 3 ECHR 'on the ground': in cases concerning pre-trial detention where insufficient safeguards against breaches of Article 3 (resulting from over-crowded conditions and the length of pre-trial detention) exist; in cases concerning the extradition and expulsion of foreign nationals and illegal renditions in breach of interim orders of the ECtHR; and in cases concerning the authorisation of and safeguards around covert police operations.

In chapter twenty-one, **Bill Bowring** provides us with the wider context of historic and recent developments in the legal protection and enforcement of international human rights in Russia, revealing not only historic parallels between the UK and Russia but also similarities with regard to the public and media discourse concerning state sovereignty (including exit scare scenarios). He also discusses complexities resulting from ECHR accession, and why Russia nevertheless wished to join the Council of Europe. Against this backdrop, Bowring considers the case of *Konstantin Markin v Russia*,[35] which could have become as antagonising as *Hirst v UK*,[36] and shows how a 'judicial conversation' between the Russian Constitutional Court and the ECtHR was able to defuse the situation. He also provides a useful illustration of how case law from other jurisdictions is used (or rather misused)—namely the Russian Constitutional Court's attempt to justify a hard line against the ECHR on the basis of one (contentious) reading of the German Constitution Court's *Görgülü* decision.[37] Bowring highlights one of the complexities in Russia's relationship with the ECHR, namely the lack of independence of, and public confidence in, the judiciary, which results in particular from the interaction of the executive with the judiciary.

---

[35] *Konstantin Markin v Russia* (n 14).
[36] *Hirst v UK (No 2)* (n 9).
[37] A similar attempt is made in the Conservative Party's *Protecting Human Rights in the UK* (n 4), which 'decontextualises' and misrepresents the approach of Germany to the ECHR and ECtHR decisions.

E. Part V: The Role of the Media in Shaping the Relationship

Following on from Part IV's rather broad-brush comparative approach, which is intended to tease out the determinants of the relationship between the UK and European human rights, Part V considers one of the possible societal and cultural determinants: the role of the media in shaping debates and human rights culture in the UK. This part stands against the backdrop of ferocious attacks by the media of judgments and judges; deliberate, careless or misleading misreporting; *ad hominem* attacks on judges; and general scapegoating of human rights. The chapters in Part V discuss legal aspects relating to the regulation of the media in light of the tension created by its dual position: it is vulnerable to violations of its rights at the same time as being itself a potential 'perpetrator' of rights violations. We then proceed to an outline of various examples and mechanisms of media reporting in the context of human rights. These illustrations are not just confined to the media per se but also relate to the 'instrumentalisation' or 'externalisation' of rights by those who feed reported material to the media.

The first chapter of Part V, by **Robert Uerpmann-Wittzack**, reflects on legal dimensions, focusing on the protection of the media under the principle of freedom of expression. The rights enjoyed by the media as a 'public watchdog' sometimes create tension with the protection of other rights; this chapter explores media regulation and its supervision by national courts and their supervision by the ECtHR. In order for the media to exercise its 'watchdog' function, it must be able to report on legal developments and criticise the judiciary, and so contribute to public debate about judgments and the judiciary, including the Strasbourg Court itself. But media freedom is limited where it disproportionately interferes with the rights of others, for example under Article 8 ECHR. Striking the balance is in principle a matter to be determined at the domestic level. Because state supervision of the media, including that by the courts, is a sensitive issue, the ECtHR has expressed a preference for self-regulation. Uerpmann-Wittzack argues that as long as domestic authorities take a carefully balanced and effective approach (even if control is in the form of self-regulation), Strasbourg should not intervene. He also reflects on media attacks on the ECtHR, which, in line with the general approach, need to be addressed at national level, not by the ECtHR itself.

The next two chapters turn to the discussion of media representation of human rights in the UK. In chapter twenty-three, **David Mead** looks at empirical evidence concerning newspaper reporting and identifies types of misreporting and its techniques, including selective skew in coverage (omission) as well as four 'sins of commission': giving false or misleading prominence to human rights issues, phrasing (language chosen to report), pre-emption (selective, incomplete and therefore misleading reporting that is not false in itself) and partiality (selectivity in relation to sources, data or evidence). He reflects on narratives that readers might be exposed to (such as the 'conflated Europes', 'the English idyll' (or 'Englishness is best'),[38] 'human rights scapegoating', 'the non-universality of human rights'

---

[38] Mead (ch 23), this volume, text near n 76.

and the 'self-preservation of the media' (for example in the context of privacy), and their wider implications, especially in light of the Conservative governments's plans to repeal the Human Rights Act. Mead concludes that the understanding of human rights protection among large parts of the population in the UK will be greatly at odds with reality and that this will have wide ramifications, in particular since one of the aims of the HRA was to embed a culture of human rights.

Against the backdrop of attacks by British media on the HRA, depicting it as a 'villains' charter', **Lieve Gies** looks at how the British press determine and create perceptions of who is a 'deserving' claimant worthy of compassion. She identifies several factors which influence the approach of the media: the kind of rights abuse—whether classic 'home-grown' civil liberties or contemporary European human rights are engaged; and the presence of a 'politics of pity' which facilitates compassion for victims of human rights violations. She points to the arbitrary and unpredictable nature of such determinations, as well as the power of the media to dramatically shape perceptions and outcomes, for example by choosing to bring a 'distant sufferer' close enough to engender pity.

Part V is also presented as a call for further research. The representation of human rights by the media is an area that merits further empirical and comparative work in the future, in light of the factual complexities of the role of the media: as a subject of human rights (freedom of expression and information) and vulnerable to violations (debate about regulation), and as a 'fourth power' that may affect the exercise of human rights by others and may be acting in conjunction with (as well as against) those in formal positions of power. However, the legal issues resulting from this remain challenging, even if some of the relevant doctrinal concepts are not new, such as the balancing of rights in their liberal and protective functions, the horizontal application of rights, the notion of responsibility, and even the direct obligations of private entities under human rights law which may be broadly linked to the evolving discussion of the role of business and human rights. Finally, the media, as the link between technocratic circles and the wider public, play a crucial role in developing a human rights culture, which is of course one of the aims of the HRA.

In the final chapter of the book we offer our own reflections on the themes discussed in the book and on options for the future in the ongoing debate (which is likely to intensify following the 2015 general election) about the relationship between the UK and European human rights.

* * *

The papers presented in this book are largely the result of an international conference held at the Centre for European Law and Internationalisation at the University of Leicester in May 2014. We are indebted to all participants and innumerable colleagues without whose support the conference and subsequent publication would not have been possible. We would like to acknowledge the kind support of the *Modern Law Review*, the College of Arts, Humanities and Law, and the Law School of the University of Leicester.

Part I

Compliance, Cooperation or Clash?
The Relationship Between the UK and
the ECHR/Strasbourg Court

2

The Relationship Between the Strasbourg Court and the National Courts—As Seen from Strasbourg§

PAUL MAHONEY*

I. INTRODUCTORY REMARKS

IN MANY WAYS the European Court of Human Rights in Strasbourg (ECtHR) is the proverbial ivory tower, cut off from ordinary people in the countries of Europe. In the United Kingdom, for instance, it is a largely unknown and often misunderstood beast. Without forgetting the valuable work of the academic community and non-governmental organisations in making the activities of the ECtHR better known, the most obvious partner for the ECtHR in building bridges with the domestic legal orders affected by its rulings is the national judiciary. National judges and the international Strasbourg judges can influence one another in progressively building up a European 'common law' of human rights under the European Convention of Human Rights (ECHR), a 'common law' workable in practice in all courts throughout the 47 Convention States. From this standpoint, the British experience furnishes just one illustration of a more general phenomenon—albeit representing, the present writer believes, one of the noteworthy examples of national courts loyally playing the game, delivering extremely high-quality judgments going into Convention case law and consciously seeking to make the Convention system successful. In the judicial sphere, therefore, it is difficult to talk of a strained relationship.

In the abstract, there exist various options for regulating the relationship between the ECtHR and the national courts, ranging from a hierarchical approach involving the judicial equivalent of micro-management by the ECtHR to a collaborative approach of what has been called 'judicial dialogue' between international and national judges, with the responsibilities being shared. The impression gained upon reading the Strasbourg case law is that the relationship has been oscillating up

---

§ Sections I and II of this chapter are largely based on a talk given in October 2013 at the Inner Temple and subsequently published in an expanded form as P Mahoney, 'The Relationship between the Strasbourg Court and the National Courts' (2014) 130 *Law Quarterly Review* 568.
* Any views expressed are personal. All websites accessed April 2015.

and down this scale, with the working model not yet definitively settled. How the emphasis will be placed in the future will be one factor shaping the kind of overall system of judicial protection of human rights that we will have in Europe.

The following remarks take as their guiding principle the so-called 'subsidiary' character of the international enforcement machinery set up under the Convention. From the early years of the ECtHR's existence, starting in 1968 with the *Belgian Linguistic case*, which concerned the use of languages in education in Belgian schools, it has been reiterated that the international remedy, by its very nature, is subsidiary to protection of human rights at the national level, with the primary responsibility for implementation of the guaranteed rights and freedoms falling on the national authorities—particularly the courts.[1] The present author shares the conviction of Professor Gertrude Lübbe-Wolff, until recently a member of the German Federal Constitutional Court, that

> the long-term viability and strength of the Convention system depend on a division of labour [between the ECtHR Court and the national courts] based on dialogue and on procedural as well as substantive subsidiarity, ... dialogue between the courts in the exercise of their respective jurisdictions and the principle of subsidiarity [being] interconnected.[2]

II. JUDICIAL DIALOGUE OR EXCHANGE THROUGH JUDGMENTS DELIVERED IN GIVEN CASES

In the present chapter I look at the implications of what is expected of national and international judges with regard to implementation of the Convention from the Strasbourg side of the relationship: how the Strasbourg judges treat rulings by national courts.

The perspective of national judges, namely the treatment that they accord judgments from Strasbourg, represents the other side of the coin. The principal question under this latter head, which is not addressed in the present chapter, is the extent to which national judges should feel bound by ECtHR case law, in general as well as in relation to specific judgments concerning their country. The incidence of ECtHR case law on national judicial decision-making is a matter that will on the whole be regulated by domestic law or judicial practice in each country—in the British case, by section 2(1) of the Human Rights Act 1998, which speaks of the British courts being obliged to 'take into account' any relevant ECtHR case law. Although essential for translating the Convention standards into reality in the legal order of each country, on its specifics the issue of what should be the appropriate status attributed to ECHR case law in domestic law is thus something for national judges to resolve.[3]

---

[1] *Belgian Linguistic case* (merits) (1979–80) 1 EHRR 252, para 10.

[2] G Lübbe-Wolff, 'How Can the European Court of Human Rights Reinforce the Role of National Courts in the Convention System?' (2012) 32 *Human Rights Law Journal* 11, 12.

[3] For discussion of these issues see Lord Kerr, 'The Relationship between the Strasbourg Court and the National Courts—As Seen from the UK Supreme Court' (ch 3) and R Clayton, 'Should the English Courts under the Human Rights Act Mirror the Strasbourg Case Law?' (ch 6), this volume.

To return to the Strasbourg perspective, given the admissibility obligation incumbent on applicants to exhaust domestic remedies, the ECtHR, when reviewing the established facts for compliance with the Convention standards, may well be called upon to go over the same terrain as that previously covered by the national courts, especially if, as in the United Kingdom, the national courts customarily take account of the Convention and its case law in cases raising human rights issues. Does the Convention system therefore entail the ECtHR sitting in appeal on judgments given by national courts, including superior courts such as supreme and constitutional courts?

The answer to that question is the typical lawyerly one of 'yes and no'. The ECtHR has developed a principle of interpretation known as the doctrine of the national margin of appreciation (in ordinary English, a doctrine recognising that an area of discretionary choice of action as to both initial policy and then implementation in individual cases is available to the national authorities in certain contexts when they are regulating the exercise of a Convention right). The result of this principle of interpretation, whenever it enters into play, is that the ECtHR will exercise a degree of judicial self-restraint when reviewing decisions taken by national authorities, in particular rulings by national courts, with the degree of restraint varying according to context.

The doctrine derives from the subsidiary character of the Convention machinery of control. It serves to delineate the dividing line between what, in political democracies, is properly a matter for each community to decide for itself at the local level and what is so fundamental that it entails the same requirement for all countries, whatever the variations in legal traditions and culture. Its effect is to open up or shut down the degree of scrutiny of the Strasbourg judges, depending on whether the national 'margin' of democratic discretion, if any, acknowledged to exist in the context is wide or narrow.[4]

Generally speaking, to quote the former British president of the Strasbourg Court, Sir Nicolas Bratza, 'despite what is sometimes heard, the Court is highly respectful of national courts and their place in the Convention system'.[5] In practice, the closer the analysis of the national courts reflects the European Convention and its case law, the more likely the finding will be that the national courts have remained within the domestic margin of appreciation. There will be less temptation for the ECtHR to engage in micro-management of individual situations or even in reviewing the preceding policy-making and, thus, less inclination to disturb the rulings of the national courts if the national courts are visibly operating domestic remedies with an eye to compliance with Convention standards and case law. In other words, if the procedural aspect of subsidiarity (that is, domestic remedies) can be seen to be working

---

[4] For a very recent authoritative study, see the speech of the current President of the Strasbourg Court delivered in March 2014 at University College London: D Spielmann, 'Whither the Margin of Appreciation?' (2014) 67 *Current Legal Problems* 49. For an early contribution by the present author, see P Mahoney, 'Marvellous Richness of Diversity or Invidious Cultural Relativism?' (1998) 19 *Human Rights Law Journal* 1, the introductory article of a special edition of that journal devoted to 'The Doctrine of the Margin of Appreciation under the European Convention on Human Rights: Its Legitimacy in Theory and Application in Practice', in the section on 'Perceived Principles and Premises'.

[5] Address given at the opening of the judicial year in Strasbourg, 27 January 2012, www.echr.coe.int/ Documents/Speech_20120127_Bratza_JY_ENG.pdf.

well, then its substantive aspect (that is, the extent to which the Strasbourg Court will reach into the Convention merits of judicial decisions taken at the national level) will in turn be positively affected in favour of greater deference being accorded to the decisions of the national courts.

Going further, Sir Nicolas Bratza has added: 'National courts applying themselves the Convention can be highly influential in the way in which the [Strasbourg] Court's own interpretation evolves.'[6] Although there have been and will always be instances of the ECtHR in effect reversing national rulings on human rights issues,[7] many cases coming from the United Kingdom Supreme Court (and its predecessor, the House of Lords), as well as from the highest courts of other countries, have illustrated a 'judicial dialogue' accomplished through successive judgments in decided cases, with the position on both sides progressively evolving in the light of the other's judgments. Usually cited in the British context are the cases of *Horncastle*, decided by the House of Lords in 2009,[8] and *Al-Khawaja*, which came before the Grand Chamber in Strasbourg in 2011 on a rehearing from a pre-*Horncastle* Chamber judgment, where the problem posed was the admissibility of hearsay evidence of a witness who had died.[9]

A first point to make about this two-way adjudicatory traffic that now takes place is that careful review of the Strasbourg case law, as well as of the British precedents on the Convention, by the British courts has made the subsequent assessment of Convention compliance to be carried out by the ECtHR a much easier task than it was before the Human Rights Act came into force in 2000: the analysis situating the Convention issue in the context of the British legal system, which utilises concepts that are alien to many of the Strasbourg judges, is already there and is not infrequently used as the basis for the Strasbourg judgment. The *Diane Pretty* case from 2002 (concerning the right to life and assisted suicide)[10] is often cited as an early example of exemplary national reasoning[11] metamorphosing into Strasbourg reasoning. Careful analysis of the relevant human rights case law by the domestic British courts in *Pretty* clearly helped the ECtHR to develop its own interpretation when the case subsequently came to Strasbourg.[12] This kind of 'borrowing' by the

---

[6] ibid.

[7] For example, *S and Marper v UK* (2009) 48 EHRR 50 (GC) (concerning retention of the applicants' fingerprints and DNA samples after the criminal proceedings against them had ended with an acquittal or been discontinued), where the Grand Chamber of the Strasbourg Court unanimously gave a different reading of Convention law from that arrived at by the UK judges at three levels of jurisdiction (two judges in the Administrative Court, a majority of two to one in the Court of Appeal and a majority of four to one in the House of Lords).

[8] *R v Horncastle* [2009] UKHL 14, [2010] 2 AC 373.

[9] *Al-Khawaja and Tahery v UK* (2012) 54 EHRR 23 (GC). As the latest instalment in this judicial exchange, see the recent judgment in which a chamber applied the Grand Chamber *Al-Khawaja* ratio to the facts of the *Horncastle* case: *Horncastle v UK* App no 4184/10 (16 December 2014).

[10] *Pretty v UK* App no 2346/02, (2002) 35 EHRR 1.

[11] In the instant case, primarily the reasoning of Lord Bingham in the House of Lords (*R (Pretty) v Director of Public Prosecutions and Secretary of State for the Home Department* [2001] UKHL 61, [2002] 1 AC 800), which was quoted verbatim over eight pages in the Strasbourg judgment.

[12] Other cases cited as instances of reasoning of the British courts having influenced the reasoning of the Strasbourg Court include: *Cooper v UK* (2004) 39 EHRR 8 (GC) (concerning the independence and impartiality of courts martial); *O'Halloran and Francis v UK* (2008) 46 EHRR 21 (GC) (concerning the

ECtHR from the national courts has not always been possible, or not to such an extent anyway, in cases where the national courts, particularly the highest courts, deal with human rights issues solely in terms of national law and the national constitution.

Despite such cross-fertilisation, it is fair to say that there is far from any consensus among the Strasbourg judges surrounding the margin of appreciation and its application. One can thus discern, from some Strasbourg judgments and some separate opinions of judges, different philosophies as to the deference to be accorded, or not to be accorded, to the assessment of human rights issues by national courts.

Some Strasbourg judges—and to this point they would seem to be the majority—take the view that if the independent and impartial national courts, which are better acquainted with the democratic society of their country, have properly and fully considered the contested legal measure on the basis of the relevant human rights standards, there will need to be strong reasons for them to substitute their own, different assessment. A firm statement to this effect can, for example, be found in the 2009 decision in the *Countryside Alliance* case, rejecting at the preliminary admissibility stage the challenge mounted against the statutory ban on fox hunting:

> [T]he domestic courts have given the greatest possible scrutiny to the applicants' complaints under the Convention ... The Court also notes that the High Court, the Court of Appeal and the House of Lords (as well as ... the Court of Session ...) were each unanimous in finding that the ban was proportionate for the purpose of the [Convention]. Serious reasons would be required for this Court to depart from the clear findings of those courts. From the applicants' submissions, it can discern no such reasons.[13]

This more deferential approach is especially apparent in cases where two Convention rights are in conflict and there are in effect two (or more) potential Convention victims affected by the proceedings before the ECtHR—that is to say, not only the applicant who is asserting one Convention right in order to contest a national judicial ruling, but also an absent party in the form of the opposing, successful party in the domestic litigation who can be said to be the beneficiary of another Convention right. In the case of *MGN* from 2011,[14] where the publisher of the *Daily Mirror*, invoking its freedom of expression as guaranteed by Article 10 ECHR, complained about the House of Lords' ruling that it had breached Naomi Campbell's privacy by publishing articles and pictures about her drug-addiction treatment, the ECtHR, in finding no violation under this head, was evidently attentive to the manner in which the Law Lords had effected the balancing exercise in arbitrating between the competing interests of the applicant publisher's media freedom under Article 10 and

---

right to remain silent); *N v UK* (2008) 47 EHRR 39 (GC) (concerning the removal to Uganda of a failed asylum seeker suffering from AIDS); and *A v UK* App no 3455/05, ECHR 2009-II (GC) (concerning the validity of derogations in respect of indefinite detention of foreign nationals suspected of involvement in terrorism).

[13] *Friend v UK* (2010) 50 EHRR SE6; *Countryside Alliance v UK* (admissibility decision) (2010) 50 EHRR SE6, para 58—arriving at the same conclusion as the House of Lords that the statutory ban was not incompatible with the requirements of the Convention: *R (Countryside Alliance) v Attorney-General* [2007] UKHL 52, [2008] AC 719.

[14] [2004] UKHL 22, [2004] 2 AC 457.

Naomi Campbell's individual privacy, as safeguarded by her right to respect for her private life under Article 8 ECHR.[15]

This model for the international judicial control to be exercised by the ECtHR could be described as one of judicial review of the legality of democratic action at the national level—something along the lines of judicial control of administrative action carried out by national administrative court judges.

In contrast, other Strasbourg judges, fearful of abdicating their ultimate responsibility for ensuring the observance of the Convention by the Contracting States, are minded to take a less deferential attitude. For them, each case is to be individually considered afresh in Strasbourg on its particular merits; the facts (not only the particular circumstances but perhaps also the underlying legislative or judicial policy) are simply to be measured against the Convention standard, almost as a first-instance court would do; and national courts, including the superior courts, are to be 'corrected' whenever the Strasbourg judges do not have the same view as them as to the assessment of the merits of the human rights issue. In relation to national judicial decisions on individual measures, the margin of appreciation will usually be acknowledged, but it may be that stricter scrutiny will be exercised as to whether the principle of proportionality has been observed by the national authorities—say, as to whether the extradition or expulsion of a given person respects the Convention requirement of proportionality in the particular circumstances. This is the approach tending towards the 'micro-management' model, and is taxed by some commentators as sometimes being over-interventionist.[16] More problematically, as regards charges of Strasbourg review of national policy being too interventionist, the last few months of 2013 saw several senior British judges deliver public speeches in which they doubted the democratic legitimacy of some of the Strasbourg jurisprudence expanding the reach of the Convention into new areas, notably social policy, on the basis of the 'living instrument' doctrine of evolutive interpretation.[17]

This is not the place to address such arguments, which go to the broader issue of the relationship between the power of review of the ECtHR and the democratic processes of the Contracting States,[18] but they do indicate an emerging unease on

---

[15] *MGN Ltd v UK* (2012) 55 EHRR SE9, paras 145–55. The Court did however find a violation of Art 10 on account of the applicant publisher having been required to pay the claimant's costs, including success fees.

[16] See eg M Bossuyt (former President of the Belgian Constitutional Court), 'The Court of Strasbourg Acting as an Asylum Court' (2012) 8 *European Constitutional Law Review* 203.

[17] Lord Sumption, 'The Limits of Law', 27th Azlan Shah Lecture, Kuala Lumpur, 20 November 2013, www.supremecourt.uk/docs/speech-131120.pdf; Sir John Laws, 'The Common Law and Europe', Hamlyn Lectures 2013, Lecture III, 27 November 2013, www.judiciary.gov.uk/wp-content/uploads/JCO/Documents/Speeches/laws-lj-speech-hamlyn-lecture-2013.pdf; Lord Judge, 'Constitutional Change: Unfinished Business', University College London, 4 December 2013, www.ucl.ac.uk/constitution-unit/constitution-unit-news/constitution-unit/research/judicial-independence/lordjudgelecture041213.

[18] As the present author understands it, the criticism concerning the 'living instrument' doctrine is not directed against the existence of evolutive interpretation, which allows variable and changing concepts already contained in the Convention (such as 'private and family life', 'correspondence', 'inhuman or degrading treatment' and so on, where the text of the Convention itself implicitly incorporates the possibility of change as attitudes in democratic society evolve) to be construed in the light of modern-day conditions. The 'living instrument' doctrine originated in American constitutional law before crossing the

the part of some senior national judges, not just British, as to the manner in which the Strasbourg Court is engaging with the national authorities, and for that reason they cannot be ignored.

One unknown that thus lies ahead is whether the present, 'highly respectful' attitude—to use the vocabulary of Sir Nicolas Bratza—of the Strasbourg Court towards national courts when reviewing at international level cases that have been through the mill of the national courts will be maintained, or whether the judges will veer off in another direction.

III. JUDICIAL DIALOGUE THROUGH INFORMAL MEETINGS

As far as the United Kingdom judiciary is concerned, it is knocking on an open door to suggest that the more regular the informal meetings between Strasbourg judges and senior national judges, the more productive actual judicial cooperation through judgments delivered is likely to be. The experience of the present author, both as a registrar and as a judge, and both at the Court of Justice of the European Union in Luxembourg and now at the ECtHR, is that such informal meetings do not take the form of purely diplomatic exchanges of niceties. Eleanor Sharpston, the British Advocate General at the Luxembourg Court, when opening the meeting on the occasion of the annual United Kingdom 'Judicial/Academic' visit to the Court of Justice, speaks of the national contingent being expected to spell out where they feel 'the shoe pinches' as regards the case law coming out of the Luxembourg Court. A small delegation from the ECtHR paid a one-day, intensive working visit to the Supreme Court in March 2014, and senior United Kingdom judges visited Strasbourg in July 2014. These kinds of exchange, which the governments in the Brighton Declaration of April 2012 encouraged the Court to develop,[19] undoubtedly facilitate a cooperative, rather than competitive, national–international relationship in terms of the judicial protection of human rights.

IV. JUDICIAL DIALOGUE THROUGH ADVISORY OPINIONS: PROTOCOL NO 16

In the spring of 2012, the present author, together with Luzius Wildhaber, former president of the ECtHR, and two others,[20] prepared a report on case overload at the ECtHR for the European Law Institute.[21] One of the recommendations made

---

Atlantic, and something like it is found in all legal systems where fundamental rights are constitutionally protected. Rather, the criticism would appear to be directed at a perceived illegitimate use of the doctrine by the ECtHR in some cases so as to aggrandise its law-making interpretive power.

[19] Brighton Declaration (Declaration adopted by the Committee of Ministers of the Council of Europe on 20 April 2012 at the High Level Conference on the Future of the European Court of Human Rights, in Brighton), para 12(a)(i).

[20] Professor Marc Entin (Russia) and Professor Jean-Paul Jacqué (France).

[21] The European Law Institute, based in Vienna, is an independent international non-profit organisation whose stated aim is to improve the quality of European law, support its development and contribute to its proper implementation both on a national and on a European level. See the Institute's website: www.europeanlawinstitute.eu.

in that report was the institution of a mechanism of advisory opinions delivered by the ECtHR at the request of superior national courts. This idea—not a new one by any means—was taken up by the governments both in the Brighton Declaration and now in Protocol No 16 to the Convention, which opened for signature in October 2013. This is an optional protocol. It may never be ratified by the United Kingdom—or, at least, not for many years. Nonetheless, there is a strong belief on the part of a substantial body of Convention-watchers that the advisory opinion mechanism that is foreseen is capable of contributing to the better functioning of the ECHR system at both the national and the international levels and, thus, to the better implementation of human rights in Europe. It could facilitate the task of the national courts while reinforcing the subsidiary character of the international intervention that is represented by the Strasbourg machinery, quite apart, in the long run, from relieving the ECtHR of some of its caseload.

The report prepared for the European Law Institute analysed the prospects for an advisory opinion mechanism as follows:

> As a way of facilitating improved national implementation of Convention rights and thereby eventually reducing the number of applications lodged in Strasbourg, the Working Party saw utility in a system of advisory opinions to be sought from the Court by the highest national courts, so as to 'plug' the national judiciary directly, and in a preventive way, into the Convention machinery of protection, thereby leading over time to a better enforcement of the Convention rights by national judges acting in collaboration with the Strasbourg judges …

> There is no suggestion that any mechanism of advisory opinions should take the place, even in part, of the right of individual petition … [T]he aim pursued is … a long-term one: injection of a dose of advisory opinions would furnish an additional means of shifting—permanently—the primary responsibility for human rights protection on to the national plane by putting in place a channel of dialogue between the Court in Strasbourg and the national courts. In so doing, it would contribute, once such a mechanism had 'taken off', to establishing a better balance than now between national and international protection …

Evidently, the intention cannot, as is the case with preliminary rulings in the legal order of the European Union, be to assure a uniform application of the Convention in all the Convention countries. The advisory opinion given by the Court in Strasbourg would bear on interpretative matters—the elucidation of the principles and values relevant for the application of the Convention standard(s) at issue in the given context of the litigation before the national court—, but the application of the Convention to the particular facts (as regards, for example, the test of necessity, the striking of the fair balance, the principle of proportionality, and so on) would always be for the national court. The decision, whatever way it goes, is therefore a national one and any execution of the judgment is for the national authorities. In this way, the principle of subsidiarity finds a privileged expression. This would be especially so if the procedure were to allow a preliminary exchange between the Strasbourg judges and the national judges before the delivery of the advisory opinion, in order to ensure that the 'right' question is being put. At the close of the national proceedings, the right of individual petition to the Court should always remain available to any disappointed litigant claiming that the advice had not been followed or correctly applied to the facts …

In sum, in the right conditions a mechanism of advisory opinions could represent a long-term investment for securing a better balance between national and international protection of human rights.[22]

V. CONCLUDING REMARKS

Since protection of human rights has to be secured primarily by the national authorities, and in the last resort by the national courts, much of the ultimate success of the Convention system will depend on the quality of the cooperation between the courts in the member countries and the ECtHR. The judicial cooperation in deciding human rights cases that this paper has advocated from the Strasbourg perspective is two-way. On the one side, it should involve the ECtHR's acknowledgement of the national courts' better grasp both of the facts and of the national policy and other issues involved in balancing the respective interests of the community and the individual. On the other side, the closer the analysis of human rights issues by the national courts reflects the standards and case law of the Convention, the greater the deference of the ECtHR towards the rulings of national courts is likely to be.

In sum, a cooperative rather than hierarchical or competitive relationship between national courts and the ECtHR can provide the means for placing the centre of gravity for the judicial protection of human rights firmly and solidly at the national level, thereby enabling the ECtHR to fulfil effectively its limited, subsidiary role in the Convention system as well as minimising the perceived risk of illegitimate incursions by the Court into the democratic life of the member countries.

---

[22] *Statement on Case-Overload at the European Court of Human Rights*, July 2012, prepared by a Working Party of the European Law Institute, paras 56–62, www.europeanlawinstitute.eu/fileadmin/ user_upload/p_eli/Publications/S-1-2012_Statement_on_Case_Overload_at_the_European_Court_of_ Human_Rights.pdf.

3

The Relationship Between the Strasbourg Court and the National Courts—As Seen from the UK Supreme Court[1]

THE RT HON THE LORD KERR OF TONAGHMORE

CONSIDERING THE RELATIONSHIP between the European Court of Human Rights (ECtHR) and the national courts from the perspective of the UK Supreme Court, to my mind, raises two distinct but interrelated issues: first, the so-called dialogue between Strasbourg and the UK Supreme Court; and secondly, the effect of Strasbourg judgments in domestic law.

I. DIALOGUE

Judge Mahoney's chapter in this volume also addresses the issue of the dialogue between our two courts. I had initially intended my contribution on this topic to suggest that I did not think that these two courts were really engaged in anything like a dialogue. That remains my sense of things, but I acknowledge the irony of maintaining that position in what is essentially a conversation with Judge Mahoney.

I have spoken about this topic before,[2] and in that lecture I took account of the position in various Member States of the Council of Europe. I shall therefore confine my remarks here to the relationship between Strasbourg and the UK courts—in particular the UK Supreme Court.

While related to the effect of Strasbourg judgments in domestic law, which I shall turn to presently, there is in my view an important difference between these two

---

[1] The talk on which this chapter is based was delivered in May 2014. Since that time, there have been further cases of relevance to the issues discussed here which could not be worked into the fabric of the chapter anymore, in particular: *Moohan v Lord Advocate* [2014] UKSC 67 (and, in particular, Lord Wilson's dissenting judgment on the so-called Ullah principle); *Surrey County Council v P* [2014] UKSC 19; *R(Kaiyam) v Secretary of State for Justice* [2015] 2 WLR 76; *Lord Carlile of Berriew v SSHD* [2014] UKSC 60; and *Gaughran v Chief Constable of PSNI* [2015] UKSC 29.

[2] Lord Kerr, 'The Need for Dialogue between National Courts and the European Court of Human Rights' in S Flogaitis, T Zwart and J Fraser (eds), *The European Court of Human Rights and its Discontents: Turning Criticism into Strength* (Cheltenham, Edward Elgar, 2013) 104.

aspects of the relationship. The effect of judgments in domestic law is a question of purely domestic law, determining what the import of Strasbourg judgments is, whatever the outcome of any prior dialogue. But that prior dialogue is itself worthy of separate consideration, as it can shape the judgments to which we are—by and large—bound to give effect.

I am conscious that the Grand Chamber directly took on board in *Al-Khawaja and Tahery*[3] what the House of Lords had said in *Horncastle*.[4] But instances like those are relatively rare. By and large, Strasbourg must decide each case *despite* what the national courts have said. That is inevitable, and entirely proper: Strasbourg is a supranational court of review tasked with the enforcement and, indeed, development of a Europe-wide body of human rights law. It can take national courts' judgments about the situation in a particular country entirely at face value and in good faith, yet still arrive at the opposite result because its unique, pan-European view points towards it. In other words, as a matter of principle Strasbourg and the national courts cannot be engaged in much of a dialogue, because they are necessarily having different conversations. The main exception is where national courts are able, by design or otherwise, to point to factors that would indicate the application of a certain margin of appreciation by the Strasbourg Court.

The corollary of this privilege of Strasbourg's, of finding a violation of the Convention despite a national court's assessment of the conditions prevailing in a particular Member State of the Council of Europe, is of course that the Strasbourg Court must be assiduous not to step beyond the extent to which any European consensus on a point really exists. That is assuming that the other conditions are also present that would justify the Strasbourg Court in reaching its conclusion as a matter of the Convention's interpretation in light of the Vienna Convention on the Law of Treaties and the relevant principles of customary international law.

When Strasbourg carries out this function according to these principles, we in the national courts are bound simply to treat its decisions as to the obligations contained in the Convention as being the last word on the subject.

II. THE EFFECT OF STRASBOURG JUDGMENTS IN DOMESTIC LAW

The above discussion covers the position as a matter of the United Kingdom's international obligations, and in particular what is required of it by the European Convention on Human Rights (ECHR). But the Human Rights Act 1998 (HRA), to which I now turn my focus, is not the Convention. As trite as that sounds, failure to recognise it is the foundation of the House of Lords' and Supreme Court's jurisprudence on the Human Rights Act, tracing back to what Lord Bingham said in *Ullah*:[5] 'The duty of national courts is to keep pace with the Strasbourg jurisprudence as it evolves over time: no more, but certainly no less.' As often as this '*Ullah* principle' is

---

[3] *Al-Khawaja and Tahery v UK* (2012) 54 EHRR 23.
[4] *R v Horncastle* [2009] UKSC 14.
[5] *R (Ullah) v Special Adjudicator* [2004] UKHL 26, para 20.

cited to us, and by us, much more important is what Lord Bingham said immediately before it, which shows the misapprehension on which the *dictum* is founded:

> It is of course open to Member States to provide for rights more generous than those guaranteed by the Convention, but such provision should not be the product of interpretation of the Convention by national courts, since the meaning of the Convention should be uniform throughout the states party to it.[6]

Does it affect the meaning of the ECHR if the rights under the HRA are interpreted differently from how Strasbourg interprets the Convention? Not a whit. Of course the Human Rights Act copies the language of the ECHR; and of course the HRA was intended to transpose much of the ECHR into the legal systems of the United Kingdom. But transposition is just that: a process of copying that leaves the original unaffected. How could it affect the meaning of the Convention if our domestic Act is interpreted differently? It has no effect on the meaning of the Convention that other European countries have nothing like it in their own domestic legal orders. So it can even less sensibly be said to be affected if we follow it only without doing so slavishly.

Because the rights are domestic, they must be given effect according to the correct interpretation of the domestic statute. As Lord Hoffmann said in *Re G*: '[The courts'] first duty is to give effect to the domestic statute according to what they consider to be its proper meaning, even if its provisions are in the same language as the international instrument which is interpreted in Strasbourg.'[7]

Secondly, section 2 of the Human Rights Act is cast deliberately in terms which do not require strict adherence to Strasbourg jurisprudence. There are, of course, sound practical and policy reasons why our national courts should follow decisions of the ECtHR. The most important of these was touched on by Lord Hoffmann in *Re G*:

> The best reason is the old rule of construction that when legislation is based upon an international treaty, the courts will try to construe the legislation in a way which does not put the United Kingdom in breach of its international obligations. If Strasbourg has decided that the international Convention confers a right, it would be unusual for a United Kingdom court to come to the conclusion that domestic Convention rights did not. Unless the Strasbourg court could be persuaded that it had been wrong (which has occasionally happened) the effect would be to result in a finding that the United Kingdom would be in breach of the Convention. Thus section 2(1) of the 1998 Act allows for the possibility of a dialogue between Strasbourg and the courts of the United Kingdom over the meaning of an article of the Convention but makes this likely to be a rare occurrence.[8]

Lord Hoffmann was referring to what Lord Bingham had said in the earlier case of *Ullah*. In his speech in that case Lord Bingham had uttered the fateful sentence that has become the source of much judicial controversy: 'The duty of national courts is to keep pace with the Strasbourg jurisprudence as it evolves over time: no more but certainly no less.'[9] This gave life to the so-called mirror principle whereby

---

[6] ibid.
[7] *Re G* [2008] UKHL 38, para 34 (also known as *Re P*).
[8] ibid, para 34.
[9] *Ullah* (n 5) para 20.

the content and character of rights in the UK national sphere should precisely match Strasbourg pronouncements. The sentence is much quoted, as is what has been described as the characteristically stylish twist put on it by Lord Brown in *R (Al-Skeini) v Secretary of State for Defence* when he said that the sentence 'could as well have ended: "no less, but certainly no more"'.[10]

But, as I have already noted, although it is often overlooked in the citation of *Ullah*, what Lord Bingham said in the passage immediately preceding that notable sentence is, in some senses, far more important. He said:

> It is of course open to Member States to provide for rights more generous than those guaranteed by the Convention, but such provision should not be the product of interpretation of the Convention by national courts, since the meaning of the Convention should be uniform throughout the states party to it.[11]

Lord Bingham was careful to refer to the interpretation of the Convention (as opposed to the interpretation of the HRA) in this passage, but his judgment in *Ullah* has been used in a number of subsequent cases in support of the proposition that the content of the domestic rights under the HRA should not, as a matter of principle, differ from those pronounced by Strasbourg. Indeed, his judgment has been construed as indicating that unless the ECtHR has given clear guidance on the nature and content of a particular Convention right, the national courts of the UK should refrain from recognising the substance of a claimed entitlement under the ECHR. In my view, the courts that have espoused this approach have taken a fundamentally wrong turn.

I firmly believe that the essential message that Lord Bingham sought to convey in *Ullah* was that courts in this country should generally follow the jurisprudence of Strasbourg. With that I have no quarrel. He said that while the case law of the ECtHR was not strictly binding, our courts should follow 'any clear and constant jurisprudence' of that court. That particular rubric, 'clear and constant jurisprudence', seems to have made its first appearance in *Alconbury*,[12] where Lord Slynn employed the phrase as an encouragement to our courts to follow Strasbourg decisions. And, indeed, that is also the sense and purpose of Lord Bingham's speech in *Ullah*.

But what has come to be known as the *Ullah* or mirror principle depends on the use of the expression 'clear and constant jurisprudence' for a distinctly different purpose. In a succession of cases, the suggestion has been made that unless there is a clear and constant line of authority from Strasbourg, our courts should be slow to recognise a claimed Convention right. Thus in *Al-Skeini* Lord Brown suggested that where the ECtHR has not spoken, our courts should hold back, explaining that if it proved that Convention rights had been denied by too narrow a construction, the aggrieved individual could have the decision corrected in Strasbourg. And in *R (Smith) v Ministry of Defence*[13] Lord Phillips followed a similar line.

---

[10] *R (Al-Skeini) v Secretary of State for Defence* [2007] UKHL 26, [2008] 1 AC 153, para 106.
[11] *Ullah* (n 5) para 20.
[12] *R (Alconbury Developments Ltd) v Secretary of State for the Environment, Transport and the Regions* [2001] UKHL 23, [2003] 2 AC 295.
[13] *R (Smith) v Ministry of Defence* [2010] UKSC 29.

The case in which this debate came most clearly to the fore was *Ambrose v Harris*,[14] where the majority held that no rule could clearly be found in Strasbourg jurisprudence that police questioning of a suspect who has not had access to legal advice is unfair unless he is in custody. At least partly on that account, the Supreme Court by a majority dismissed an appeal against the admission of evidence obtained as a result of questioning when the suspect did not have access to legal advice. Lord Hope said that 'if Strasbourg has not yet spoken clearly enough on this issue, the wiser course must surely be to wait until it has done so'.[15]

In the sole dissenting judgment I disagreed with this approach. I was of the view that it is the court's duty, when presented with a Convention claim, to adjudicate upon it irrespective of whether Strasbourg has spoken. I remain of that view, although I acknowledge that the debate on this issue is still to be completely resolved. It has been the subject of lively academic discussion in, for instance, articles by Andenas and Bjorge.[16]

In *Rabone v Pennine Care NHS Foundation Trust*[17] one can detect a retreat from the mirror principle. In that case it was held that there was a positive obligation to protect the life of a mentally ill young woman who had been admitted to hospital informally because of serious attempts to take her own life. This decision was reached notwithstanding the fact that there was no authority from the ECtHR to that effect. Lady Hale referred to *Rabone* in the 2013 Warwick Law Lecture, pointing out that it went further than any Strasbourg decision had yet done and adding that Lord Brown, despite his earlier views in *Al-Skeini* and *Ambrose*, had said that it would be 'absurd' for us not to decide a question merely because Strasbourg had not done so. Why, asked Lady Hale, should we wait for something that might never come?[18] Why indeed?

Some echoes of the mirror principle can still be heard in recent judgments, however, such as *P v Cheshire West and P and Q v Surrey Council* of March 2014. In a joint dissenting judgment, Lords Carnwath and Hodge said, repeating words used by Lord Dyson in *Ambrose*,[19] that, short of a sufficiently clear indication in the Strasbourg jurisprudence of how the European court would resolve the question, the court 'should be cautious about extending a concept as sensitive as "deprivation of liberty" beyond the meaning which it would be regarded as having in ordinary usage'.[20] So, more ink may need to be spilled on this topic. My own view is that Lord Hoffmann's approach in *Re G* will prevail. What he said at para 33 of his judgment in that case encapsulates the point:

> As this House affirmed in *In re McKerr* [2004] UKHL 12, 'Convention rights' within the meaning of the 1998 Act are domestic and not international rights. They are applicable in

---

[14] *Ambrose v Harris (Procurator Fiscal)* [2011] 1 WLR 2435.

[15] ibid, para 15.

[16] M Andenas and E Bjorge, 'Ambrose: Is the *Ullah* Principle Wrong?' (2012) 128 *Law Quarterly Review* 319; M Andenas and E Bjorge, 'Leading from the Front: Human Rights and Tort Law in Rabone and Reynolds' (2012) 128 *Law Quarterly Review* 323.

[17] *Rabone v Pennine Care NHS Foundation Trust* [2012] UKSC 2, [2012] 2 AC 72.

[18] Baroness Hale, 'What's the Point of Human Rights?', Warwick Law Lecture, 28 November 2013, www.supremecourt.uk/docs/speech-131128.pdf (accessed April 2015) .

[19] *Ambrose* (n 14).

[20] *P v Cheshire West and Chester Council; P and Q v Surrey County Council* [2014] UKSC 19, para 93.

the domestic law of the United Kingdom and it is the duty of the courts to interpret them like any other statute. When section 6(1) says that it is unlawful for a public authority to act incompatibly with Convention rights, that means the domestic rights set out in the Schedule to the Act and reproducing the language of the international Convention.[21]

Moving away from the subject of the national courts' obligation to give effect to domestic rights, there are a number of other areas in which we may reach a decision that is not directly dependent on ECtHR jurisprudence.

The first such category of cases comprises those where Strasbourg has not given a judgment on all fours with that which we are invited to give, but it is clear enough that it would so hold if the instant case were to come before it. 'Keeping pace with Strasbourg' can involve keeping pace with a moving target, and there may be cases where it is both possible and legitimate to anticipate what Strasbourg would say, given the opportunity. Indeed, *Re G* is a case in point.

Then there are cases where we would find a violation of the Convention but Strasbourg has declined to do so bearing in mind the margin of appreciation. As Lord Hoffmann explained in *Re G*:

> It must be remembered that the Strasbourg court is an international court, deciding whether a Member State, as a state, has complied with its duty in international law to secure to everyone within its jurisdiction the rights and freedoms guaranteed by the Convention. Like all international tribunals, it is not concerned with the separation of powers within the Member State. When it says that a question is within the margin of appreciation of a Member State, it is not saying that the decision must be made by the legislature, the executive or the judiciary. That is a matter for the Member State.[22]

And at paragraph 37:

> The margin of appreciation is there for division between the three branches of government according to our principles of the separation of powers. There is no principle by which it is automatically appropriated by the legislative branch.[23]

The significance of this comes into sharp focus when dealing with claims by the State that interference with a qualified Convention right is justified. In *Pretty*[24] the ECtHR found that the blanket ban on assisted suicide did not breach Mrs Pretty's rights under Article 8 of the ECHR. That was because it was considered to be open to the UK to take the view that such a ban was required. We recently had to consider *Pretty* in the assisted suicide appeal case of *Nicklinson*, which was heard by the Supreme Court just before Christmas 2013.[25]

One of the issues we have had to deal with is the distinction to be drawn between, on the one hand, the approach of the supranational court in Strasbourg to the margin of appreciation and, on the other, the approach of the national court to the question of justification of interference with the Article 8 right. I suggest that

---

[21] *Re G* (n 7) para 33.
[22] ibid, para 32.
[23] ibid, para 37.
[24] *Pretty v UK* (2002) 35 EHRR 1.
[25] The judgment had not been delivered at the time of writing, but was since handed down: *A (Nicklinson) v Ministry of Justice and R (AM) v Director of Public Prosecutions* [2014] UKSC 38.

the difference can be stated in this way: Strasbourg conducts the examination at one remove and asks whether it is tenable that the interference is justified. The national court asks a different question—has the interference been shown to be justified in fact?

A second category comprises cases where we may choose to depart from Strasbourg altogether. *Horncastle*[26] was one, although not perhaps as exciting in terms of principle as it has been portrayed. We considered simply that Strasbourg had misunderstood the nature of England and Wales' rules on hearsay evidence and their role within that jurisdiction's wider framework of criminal evidence. We did not disagree about the standards against which those rules were to be measured. But it is widely agreed that the judgment of the Supreme Court in *Horncastle* was instrumental in bringing about a change of course in the Grand Chamber's decision in *Al-Khawaja*.[27]

What we have yet to come across, although there is room for one in theory, is a case in a possible third category where we disagree not on the application of the standard but on its content. Such a case may be rare to the point of being hypothetical. But sometimes extreme cases illuminate principle. The possibility of such a case derives from the very fact that the rights guaranteed by the HRA are domestic rights. This goes beyond the triviality that they have a different formal legal source. It reaches in fact to the heart of the matter: the rights guaranteed by the Act are enjoyed by virtue of belonging, however transitorily, to the United Kingdom's legal and political community, rather than that of the Council of Europe. Different political constituencies and institutions animate these polities. Different values may prevail.

These values will of course often overlap with those embodied by the Convention and the Council of Europe. Citizens of the United Kingdom are as much Europeans as anybody else and are entitled to cast a jealous eye at the rights their brethren in the rest of Europe enjoy by virtue of being European. And so United Kingdom judges should always interpret domestic rights with the importance of the United Kingdom's place in Europe firmly in mind.

[26] *Horncastle* (n 4).
[27] Al-Khawaja (n 2).

4

The UK and Strasbourg: A Strained Relationship—The Long View

ED BATES[*]

I. INTRODUCTION

T
HIS CHAPTER EXAMINES relations between the UK and the European Court of Human Rights (ECtHR), given the latter's capacity to set boundaries to what the former may do in the field of 'Convention rights'. It adopts a broad, long-term view. The introduction will undertake a brief examination of the current situation, acknowledging the risks of selectivity and generalisation.[1] Three illustrations of the strained relationship post-2009–10 will be provided, before some general reflections are offered.

The first example is the prisoner voting saga.[2] As is well known, British MPs (including some senior members of the government) have expressed deep-seated frustration at the fact that Strasbourg judges do not accept the politicians' collective view that all convicted prisoners in the UK should be disenfranchised while serving their sentence. This has led to some excited and confrontational reactions, magnified when Strasbourg refused to back down in 2012,[3] as some senior politicians and MPs see it. The offending law has not been amended,[4] and there has been talk of the need for a democratic override in respect of a Court that has abused its authority and aggrandised its jurisdiction, not only in respect of the relevant Convention provision (Article 3 of Protocol 1) but overall. MPs are adamant that the Court should show greater respect for what they say are reasonable policy choices made

---

[*] I would like to thank the editors of this volume, Professor Roger Masterman and Thomas Webber for their very helpful comments on an earlier draft. The usual disclaimer applies.

[1] For example, in this chapter it is convenient to refer to 'the UK', but this is not to suggest that there exists one single, national perspective on the matters addressed. A similar point may be made with respect to the references that follow to 'politicians', 'MPs' and 'senior members of the judiciary' etc.

[2] See E Bates, 'Analysing the Prisoner Voting Saga and the British Challenge to Strasbourg' (2014) 14 *Human Rights Law Review* 503; R Ziegler, 'Voting Eligibility: Strasbourg's Timidity' (ch 9), this volume.

[3] See *Scoppola v Italy No 3* (2013) 56 EHRR 19 (GC). *cf* earlier rulings, including *Hirst v UK (No 2)* (2006) 42 EHRR 41 (GC).

[4] The Committee of Ministers has been strongly critical of the UK; it has stated that it will return to the matter in September 2015. In December 2014 the British government announced that it 'will not be able to legislate for prisoner voting in this Parliament', ie before the May 2015 general election: Ministry of Justice, *Responding to Human Rights Judgments*, Report to the Joint Committee on Human Rights on the Government's Response to Human Rights judgment 2013–14 (December 2014) Cm 8962, 29.

at the national level, by affording Member States a greater margin of (national) appreciation—a view that has been echoed by some senior members of the judiciary speaking extra-judicially.[5]

A second example concerns restrictions on executive power in the field of deportation, and, in particular, regarding non-nationals suspected of terrorism.[6] The relevant Article 3 jurisprudence has been a sore point for the UK for over a decade,[7] but the matter flared up in 2012, Article 6(1) of the European Convention on Human Rights (ECHR) causing the main controversy. Senior politicians reacted strongly to a Strasbourg judgment[8] which held that that provision would potentially be violated were the UK to deport a suspected terrorist, Abu Qatada, to Jordan (at least on the facts as they then existed), given the risk that evidence obtained by torture would be used in his retrial. This was, in effect, Strasbourg's first detailed consideration of the relevant Article 6(1) point; it followed the approach taken by the Court of Appeal when it had considered the *Abu Qatada* case, not the House of Lords (as it then was), which had found no potential violation. The British Home Secretary accused the Court of 'mov[ing] the goalposts by establishing new, unprecedented legal grounds upon which [deportation was] blocked'.[9] More generally, the narrative, in fact going back some years, has been about Strasbourg failing to properly balance the needs of national security and human rights.[10] In 2013, the Home Secretary warned that if withdrawal from the Convention was necessary to 'fix' the UK's human rights laws, then this should be considered.[11] The Conservative Party has said that it will replace the Human Rights Act 1998 (HRA) with a British Bill of Rights;[12] here they foresee modified protection for Articles 3 and 8 in the context of immigration.

The UK judiciary's approach to section 2(1) HRA provides another aspect to this broad overview of the recent strained relationship. Section 2(1) requires British judges to 'take into account' Strasbourg case law in cases raising questions concerning 'Convention rights'. Nonetheless, in the post-2009 period suggestions were made that UK judges had become subservient to Strasbourg, and there emerged a type of supremacy question:[13] if necessary, would the UK courts be prepared *not*

---

[5]   See text accompanying n 142 and n 182 below.

[6]   The popular press and British politicians have also expressed great frustration at the barriers that Art 8 ECHR may present regarding the deportation of non-nationals who have committed serious criminal offences. This was the background to a reform of the relevant immigration legislation in 2014: see M Elliott, 'The Immigration Act 2014: A Sequel to the Prisoner-Voting Saga?' (*Public Law for Everyone*, 23 May 2014), publiclawforeveryone.com/2014/05/23/the-immigration-act-2014-a-sequel-to-the-prisoner-voting-saga.

[7]   See D Moeckli, '*Saadi v Italy*: The Rules of the Game Have Not Changed' (2008) 8 *Human Rights Law Review* 534.

[8]   *Othman (Abu Qatada) v UK* (2012) 55 EHRR 1.

[9]   HC Deb 8 July 2013, vol 566, col 23 (Theresa May MP).

[10]   For a recent perspective see David Cameron, 'Speech on the European Court of Human Rights' (25 January 2012), www.gov.uk/government/speeches/speech-on-the-european-court-of-human-rights.

[11]   See A Travis, 'Conservatives Promise to Scrap HRA After Next Election' *The Guardian* (London, 30 September 2013), www.theguardian.com/law/2013/sep/30/conservitives-scrap-human-rights-act.

[12]   See text following n 113 below.

[13]   See text following n 125 below.

to apply Strasbourg's clear and settled position on the meaning of a particular 'Convention right'? How this was resolved is discussed below in section V. For now it suffices to note that certain politicians insist that the HRA places the UK Supreme Court under Strasbourg's tutelage, and that supremacy now has to be wrestled back from Strasbourg. Those claims may be exaggerated; however, certain senior judges have indicated their considerable unease with Strasbourg's influence over UK law via the HRA, whilst an element of disdain for it, or so it seems, has been evident in certain extra-judicial speeches.[14]

With these three illustrations in mind, it is submitted that at the core of the strained relationship are concerns over national sovereignty, supremacy in the context of domestic law and, related to both, the legitimacy of Strasbourg's influence. The fear is that the UK's national authorities have become subservient to the ECtHR, supremacy on Convention rights issues resting with it, even if the UK national authorities adopt a different approach, taking the Convention into account. The legitimacy aspect questions why and how Strasbourg has the power that it has to (in effect) override what are generally seen to be reasonable British positions. It is often suggested that Strasbourg has pursued 'mission creep' in order to do so.

Adopting a 'long view', one aim of this chapter is to demonstrate that, if one looks at the history of UK–Strasbourg relations, British concerns over sovereignty go back to the very start of the Convention's life. Questions as to the legitimacy of the Court's influence over UK law have also been a recurring theme. Section II of this chapter seeks to demonstrate this via a brief analysis of British concerns during the Convention's drafting, and how the 'British' judge on the Court in the 1970s expressed strong legitimacy-related concerns (which certain modern-day critics of the Court echo). We shall also see, in section III, that national sovereignty concerns—and related questions concerning the legitimacy of Strasbourg's growing influence—were prevalent throughout the 1980s and up to the late 1990s, shaping the then Conservative administrations' policy toward the Convention, and so right up to the passage of the HRA under the Labour government of 1997.

Section IV jumps ahead to 2009–10, setting out how the growing dissatisfaction with the UK's human rights arrangements culminated in proposals that the HRA should be replaced by a UK/British bill of rights. For some that opens up the 'unfinished business' question of (what they see as) Strasbourg's domination of UK law, and, potentially, the UK's continuing membership of the Convention. Against that backdrop, section V suggests that, far from placating or resolving the concerns about the ECtHR that existed prior to the HRA, the UK's experience of that Act may have intensified them—for some at least. As already suggested, strains in the relationship have reached unprecedented levels since 2009–10 as questions over, firstly, supremacy in national law, and, secondly, the legitimacy of the ECtHR's

---

[14] See text accompanying nn 18 and 142 below. However, there have been a succession of speeches delivered by members of the judiciary which have been more positive about the Convention and the Court: see E Bates, 'The Senior Judiciary on "Strasbourg"—More Supportive Than Some Would Have You Believe' (UK Const L Blog, 28 May 2015), http://ukconstitutionallaw.org/2015/05/28/ed-bates-the-senior-judiciary-on-strasbourg-more-supportive-than-some-would-have-you-believe/.

international role have come under a bright spotlight. However, it is also suggested (in section V) that these issues, and the criticism of Strasbourg that they have entailed, have been very largely overtaken by important developments in *both* UK and ECtHR case law since 2010. It is argued that that case law indicates that the legal relationship between the UK and the ECtHR is reaching a new equilibrium—one which questions whether there really is a genuine need to radically reshape UK–Strasbourg relations as some politicians advocate.

II. 1950–79: THE DRAFTING AND SUBSEQUENT EVOLUTION OF THE ECHR

The British contribution to the Convention's drafting[15] is emphasised today by those who plead that the UK should not turn its back on a system it helped to establish, pointing to the input of figures such as Winston Churchill and Sir David Maxwell-Fyfe. Indeed, these individuals (especially the latter) did make a significant contribution to the Convention's genesis; however, right at the outset the real concern of the British (Labour, Atlee) government was with the potential loss of national sovereignty entailed by participation in an international system for the protection of human rights. This was one reason why, in 1950, there was a less-than-enthusiastic approach toward the Convention from the British government, which, amongst other things, opposed the establishment of a European Court of Human Rights.

This author has argued elsewhere[16] that, when it was opened for signature on 4 November 1950, the Convention amounted to a compromise between those who mainly saw it as an interstate pact to serve as an alarm bell for Europe to prevent a re-emergence of totalitarianism, and others who saw it as a potential European bill of rights for a 'new', post-war Europe. The British strongly opposed the latter, but ratified the Convention in 1951, reassured that both the right of individual petition (in fact, to the European Commission of Human Rights) and acceptance of the jurisdiction of the ECtHR were subject to optional clauses (which they did not intend to accept). Indeed, although the Convention contained articles on a Court, in the early 1950s it was not at all clear that such an institution would actually come into existence.[17]

So, concerns over sovereignty were sufficiently allayed in the course of 1950–51 for the UK to ratify the Convention, and it is fair to say, as Lord Hoffmann[18] has, that the UK undertook that step primarily to set an example for others, and not with the expectation that it would be found in violation itself, at least not regularly. And it is also valid to suggest, as Jack Straw (then MP) did in 2012, that a reason why

---

[15] There is a considerable literature on this, the most comprehensive being B Simpson, *Human Rights and the End of Empire* (Oxford, Oxford University Press, 2004).

[16] E Bates, *The Evolution of the European Convention on Human Rights* (Oxford, Oxford University Press, 2010) chs 3–5.

[17] Eight States had to accept the Court's optional jurisdiction for it to be instituted; in 1950 only a minority of States supported its creation: see ibid, 90 and 124.

[18] L Hoffmann, 'Human Rights and the House of Lords' (1999) 62 *Modern Law Review* 159, 166; see also L Hoffmann, 'The Universality of Human Rights' (2009) 125 *Law Quarterly Review* 416.

the States formulated the Court's powers in the broad terms expressed under what is today Article 46(1) ECHR—that is, without a 'democratic override' or something similar—may have been that the States 'never anticipated the vastly expanded role of the Court'.[19] However, two further, general observations are now required.

First, it was understood in 1950 that the Convention established international legal obligations which could achieve ascendancy over any aspect of domestic law, including legislation (to the extent that a feature of the legislation could be impugned in a case reaching the Court and found incompatible with the Convention) in cases where the UK was a respondent State. It was also understood in 1950 that the Convention system could develop into a type of European bill of rights.[20]

Secondly, 1950 was just the beginning of the story. What was originally more of a collective pact against totalitarianism evolved into more of a European bill of rights.[21] In 1960 the ECtHR came into being and, over the years, the States chose to accept its jurisdiction and the right of individuals to access the Strasbourg system, just as the UK did in 1966,[22] when it was aware of the Convention's potential to evolve. From the late 1970s onwards, the Court's jurisprudence started to flourish. Amending protocols to the Convention were drafted by the States, which necessarily require their input and their consent for their ratification. In this connection, acceptance of the Convention and continued participation in an evolving scheme of human rights supervision required the active consent of the relevant UK governments at key moments. The UK consistently renewed the optional clauses, and ratified relevant reforming protocols, most notably Protocol 11[23] in the 1990s, aware of the developments that had already occurred.

A. The Fledgling European Bill of Rights of the 1970s

The points made above may have some relevance to a recurring debate in the UK as to whether the ECtHR has illegitimately aggrandised its jurisdiction. Many of those who insist that it has done so draw comparisons between the origins of the Convention in 1950 and the modern role of the Court, as if the Convention's development into a form of European bill of rights is a recent phenomenon—but it is not. It was in the 1970s, a generation ago, that the aforementioned identity of the Convention really started to become apparent, and it was not uncontroversial then, as we now observe.

Space does not permit a detailed examination of the 1970s and early 1980s jurisprudence here; however, the approach adopted toward the Convention by the

---

[19] J Straw, *Aspects of Law Reform: An Insider's Perspective* (Cambridge, Cambridge University Press, 2013) 26.

[20] See E Bates, 'British Sovereignty and the European Court of Human Rights' (2012) 128 *Law Quarterly Review* 382, 384–89.

[21] Bates (n 16).

[22] A Lester, 'UK Acceptance of the Strasbourg Jurisdiction: What Really Went on in Whitehall in 1965' [1998] *Public Law* 237.

[23] See text following n 52 below.

'British' judge on the Court in the 1970s, Sir Gerald Fitzmaurice, will be discussed given its relevance to contemporary debates about aggrandisement. His Separate and Dissenting Opinions during his time on the bench at Strasbourg (1974–80) have a resonance with comments often made in the UK today by those who insist that the Court should go back to basics, adopt a more restrictive approach to the Convention's interpretation, and so, it is said, operate more as its drafters intended.[24]

Sir Gerald's dissent in *Marckx v Belgium*[25] exemplified his approach. The case concerned Belgian laws which, amongst other things, permitted differences in treatment between so-called 'legitimate' and 'illegitimate' children with respect to family affiliation, civil status and inheritance rights. The Court examined the case under Articles 8(1) (respect for family life), 14 (non-discrimination) and Article 1 Protocol 1 (right to possessions), finding various violations in a complex case. A flavour of Fitzmaurice's views, and how he saw the Strasbourg institutions as acting inappropriately, is provided by his insistence that, as conceived in 1950, Article 8(1) was concerned only with very severe intrusions into family life[26]—a world away from *Marckx*.

Sir Gerald's approach was guided by his view of the Convention, in particular its post-war origins and status as an international treaty, and his view that 'Convention rights' should not be equated with domestic, constitutional rights. That misconstrued the ECtHR's role, for it had 'never [been] instituted to act as a sort of general law-reformer'; rather its purpose was to protect 'genuine human rights'.[27] The latter were those associated with 'a deep seated and persistent feeling that [they were] so fundamental, so founded in nature and la condition humaine, as to constitute a different order of right' from those 'ordinary everyday … rights deriving from man-made laws'.[28] In Sir Gerald's eyes, then, in cases like *Marckx* his fellow judges had viewed the substantive text of the Convention as a 'good opportunity for plausibly imparting to the Convention a scope which it is virtually certain its originators never even thought of, much less intended'.[29] It was also verging on 'an abuse of the powers given to the Court' for it to in effect condemn the Belgian national law impugned in *Marckx*, which was not in itself 'unreasonable or manifestly unjust'.[30] Breaches

---

[24] See eg Chris Grayling MP (then Minister of Justice), 'Bill of Rights: Let us Concentrate on Real Human Rights' *Daily Telegraph* (London, 17 December 2012), www.telegraph.co.uk/news/uknews/law-and-order/9750518/Bill-of-Rights-Let-us-concentrate-on-real-human-rights.html; and as quoted in the *Daily Telegraph*, 'Chris Grayling: Senior Judges Back Me over Human Rights Reforms' (26 March 2014), www.telegraph.co.uk/news/politics/conservative/10724404/Chris-Grayling-Senior-judges-back-me-over-human-rights-reforms.html. See also the text accompanying nn 99 and 113 below.

[25] *Marckx v Belgium* (1979–80) 2 EHRR 330.

[26] '… the "domiciliary protection" of the individual', to prevent domestic intrusions such as 'the four o'clock in the morning rat-a-tat on the door': dissenting judgment of Sir Gerald Fitzmaurice in *Marckx v Belgium*, ibid, para 7.

[27] G Fitzmaurice, 'Some Reflections on the ECHR—and on Human Rights' in R Bernhardt (ed), *Völkerrecht als Rechtsordnung Internationale Gerichtsbarkeit Menschenrechte: Festschrift für Herman Molser* (Berlin, Springer Verlag, 1983) 202, 213.

[28] ibid, 209.

[29] ibid, 214.

[30] *Marckx v Belgium* (n 25) para 31.

of the Convention should only be found, the 'British' judge insisted, when they were clear-cut: 'No Government or authority [could] be expected to operate from within a strait-jacket of [the] sort [fashioned in *Marckx*] and without the benefit of a faculty of discretion functioning within defensible limits.'[31]

Strasbourg's contemporary critics may find Fitzmaurice's views appealing, and they might argue that the ECtHR has devalued the currency of 'human rights'. But, looking back, can that criticism really be made of cases such as *Marckx*, or for that matter those of *Tyrer v UK*,[32] *Golder v UK*,[33] *Airey v Ireland*[34] and other important cases of Fitzmaurice's era? The issues at stake in those cases may have been far removed from those that had inspired the Convention's drafters. But did the Court's handling of them not demonstrate the value of its role as a mechanism which could gently keep the laws of the Member States within reasonable bounds, the boundaries or parameters being set to reflect a minimum, common European standard, one which Belgium had not adhered to in *Marckx* (the Court identifying fault in a domestic legal regime which permitted discrimination against illegitimate children in issues such as family affiliation and inheritance rights)?

B. The UK and Europe

Obviously, Fitzmaurice's views did not amount to an official 'British' perspective on the Convention, although it is conceivable that they may have reflected a view at Whitehall in the 1970s that the Court had aggrandised its jurisdiction.[35] However, the argument that Convention rights could not be equated with constitutional rights never gained any traction in the Court's case law (or in international human rights jurisprudence generally). Moreover, even after the Convention's identity as a type of European bill of rights became apparent, there was a conscious political decision on the UK's part to remain committed to it, and to a point, of course, when the constitutional rights status of 'Convention rights' was acknowledged via the passage of the HRA.

This is not to deny that, rather than actively promoting the Convention's evolution, the UK may have been carried along (via political pressure at the European level) with it somewhat reluctantly.[36] What might account for such reluctance, and did Fitzmaurice's arguments reflect a rather British perspective on, firstly, the appropriate role of 'Europe' in this field, and secondly, a rather British understanding of what 'human rights' were, or ought to be?

As to the first point, the current President of the UK Supreme Court, Lord Neuberger, has pondered whether the very cautious and sometimes reluctant approach that characterises the UK in 'Europe' (including the European Union)

---

[31] ibid.
[32] *Tyrer v UK* (1979–80) 2 EHRR 1.
[33] *Golder v UK* (1979–80) 1 EHRR 524.
[34] *Airey v Ireland* (1979–80) 2 EHRR 305.
[35] See Bates (n 20) 394–95, 398–99.
[36] See text following n 52 below.

reflects a national resistance to being told what to do by European bodies. This may be less prevalent on the continent,[37] where history, attitudes to pooling sovereignty in the context of European integration, and approaches to constitutional law, particularly regarding the judicial enforcement of human rights, can differ significantly.

As to the second point, could it be that Fitzmaurice's perspective on 'human rights' was also rather British given the absence of a bill of rights, or an equivalent, in UK law prior to HRA?[38] That reflected the UK's attachment to the 'Westminster model', two aspects of which are particularly relevant to us: (i) parliamentary sovereignty is the bedrock principle, democratically elected politicians being seen as the primary, legitimate decision-makers, at least in relation to matters of policy; (ii) liberty was 'residual' to this, with common law rights[39] subservient to express legislation, rather than being positively protected as higher, constitutional rights. Adherence to that model has meant that in the UK it is seen as 'little short of offensive to notions of constitutional propriety'[40] that a court, let alone an international one, could overrule a decision of Parliament, or, in effect, require it to legislate, as may be the substantial effect of an ECtHR ruling. To the extent that this is not how matters are seen on the continent,[41] we may have a further explanation as to why there have been (and remain) greater anxieties about Convention membership in London compared to other European capitals.

C. 1985: 'Political Pressures will Demand a Fundamental Reassessment'

It is precisely because the model just described failed to sufficiently guarantee constitutional rights of the order the Convention protected that the campaign for incorporation of the ECHR goes at least as far back as the 1970s,[42] and that British lawyers increasingly resorted to the ECtHR from then onwards, it becoming 'in effect a supreme constitutional court of the UK'.[43] The disturbing effect that had on the Westminster model is summarised by comments made in 1985 by Terence Shaw, the *Daily Telegraph's* legal correspondent. He reported that

> whereas initially [Strasbourg's] decisions … tended to be regarded as minor irritants or useful checks on governmental power or failings, there appears now to be *growing resent-*

---

[37] Lord Neuberger, 'The British and Europe', 12 February 2014, para 10 and *passim*, www.supremecourt.uk/docs/speech-140212.pdf.

[38] This may also be of relevance to aggrandisement arguments: see Grayling (n 24); as to the enduring suggestion that there is a difference in order or class of rights to be protected at the international level, as opposed to domestically, see eg Hoffmann, 'The Universality of Human Rights' (n 18); J Laws, *The Common Law Constitution* (Cambridge, Cambridge University Press, 2013) 83.

[39] On which (including their recent revival) see R Clayton, 'The Empire Strikes Back' [2015] *Public Law* 2; B Dickson, 'Repeal the HRA and Rely on the Common Law?' (ch 7), this volume and M Elliott, 'Beyond the European Convention: Human Rights and the Common Law' (2015) 68 *Current Legal Problems* (forthcoming). See also text accompanying n 180 below.

[40] Neuberger (n 37) para 28.

[41] ibid; *cf* comments made by Laws LJ (n 38) 82–83.

[42] A Lester in A Lester, D Pannick and J Herberg (eds), *Human Rights Law and Practice* (London, LexisNexis, 2009) 12–13.

[43] ibid.

ment that groups of mainly foreign judges or jurists are increasingly replacing parliament and the domestic court as defenders of rights and liberties in the UK. Despite the margin of appreciation allowed to governments under many of the more sensitive of the Convention's provisions, one fears that the Court and the Commission, while carefully restricting their decisions to the facts and circumstances before them, are of necessity being *drawn into making political judgments seen by many as the province of democratically elected parliament.*[44]

Shaw added: 'Events in Britain appear to be moving fast to the point where political pressures will demand a fundamental reassessment of the relationship between the UK law and that of the Strasbourg institutions'.[45] Shaw's reference to 'political pressures' for a 'fundamental reassessment' provides a snapshot of how things were seen 30 years ago; however, the broader point he made offers a perspective upon what has followed, including the current era, as successive British governments worked out what to do about 'Strasbourg'. In the remaining parts of this chapter we examine how this matter was largely avoided from the 1970s onwards until tensions surfaced in the mid-1990s, which were followed by the passage of the HRA (Section III below). But it is argued in Sections IV and V that the UK's experiences of the domestic application of 'Convention rights' have led to a renewed focus on the points Shaw made three decades ago.

III. 1980–98: KEEPING THE EUROPEAN BILL OF RIGHTS IN STRASBOURG AND THEN BRINGING IT 'HOME'

The Thatcher (1979–90) and Major (1990–97) administrations remained steadfast to the British Westminster model, stressing the pedigree of the common law and Parliament at protecting the rights of the individual. These governments opposed the adoption of a domestic bill of rights, which 'risk[ed] transferring power away from parliament to legal courts [thereby] undermining the democratic supremacy of parliament as representatives of the people'.[46] Opposition to incorporation of the Convention naturally followed.

A. The Conservatives Live with, and then Attempt to Tame, the Court

Thus, over the 1980s and 1990s, the UK was in a curious position. Despite the 'growing resentment' identified by Shaw, manifested by reactions to certain Strasbourg judgments,[47] the UK was found in violation of its Convention obligations on more

---

[44] T Shaw, 'The Impact of the Case-Law of the Organs of the ECHR on Public Opinion' in Council of Europe, *Proceedings of the Sixth International Colloquy about the ECHR* (Martinus Nijhoff, 1988) 758, 770–72 (emphasis added), noting that it had become 'firmly entrenched in the public's mind ... that decisions of the British courts, Acts of Parliament, subordinate legislation and administrative decisions may be open to challenge and review in Strasbourg' (at 760).

[45] ibid (emphasis added).

[46] Conservative Party Manifesto 1997. See also N Lyell, 'Whither Strasbourg?' (1997) 2 *European Human Rights Law Review* 18 (Sir Nicholas Lyell was the Conservative government's Attorney-General in 1996).

[47] In 1995 the Court delivered its judgment in *McCann v UK* (1996) 21 EHRR 97, the so-called 'IRA-Gibraltar shootings' case, which was met with a strong euro-phobic reaction in the tabloid press and a

and more occasions. Yet there was no concerted response to the effect that the ECtHR's judgments should not be implemented, and no cases where the UK failed to act in response to a Strasbourg ruling. Withdrawal from the ECHR seemed out of the question.[48] So, in spite of the growing number of adverse judgments through the 1980s and 1990s, the Convention's role as a type of external bill of rights was tolerated. Why?

Perhaps the 'external' nature of Strasbourg review was important. It meant that the ECtHR and its influence could be kept at arm's length: sometimes the minimum necessary was done to secure compliance with its judgments, and after considerable delay. The absence of a domestic bill of rights or an equivalent must have been important too, for it meant that any suggestion of withdrawal from the ECHR would have been hotly opposed by campaigners who could point to the constitutional vacuum filled by the ECtHR. Related to this, and despite popular antipathy toward Strasbourg as noted by Shaw, the Court's legitimacy 'stock', so to speak, was high,[49] and was confirmed, it seems, by various extra-judicial speeches backing incorporation of the Convention into domestic law.[50]

Perhaps it was significant too that before 1998 the right of individual petition and acceptance of the jurisdiction of the ECtHR remained subject to optional clauses. Even though their non-renewal may have been a remote prospect, given the negative political reaction associated with non-renewal,[51] the possibility of such a step may not have been without influence. The stance adopted by the UK government during the negotiation of Protocol 11 to the Convention in 1994 suggested as much. The UK strongly opposed the proposal that the right of individual petition should become mandatory, as was being proposed.[52] The argument that it should remain subject to the individual State's periodic decision to continue to permit this was based on the view that this feature of the Convention was vital to maintaining 'the balance between the authority of the Court, and that of the elected government of Member States'.[53] It was necessary as, unlike the governments of the Convention States, the Court was 'accountable to no one', even though it could 'make binding decisions on domestic matters, which may oblige Parliaments to legislate'.[54] It was

venting of anti-Strasbourg sentiment from senior politicians; see S Kentridge, 'Parliamentary Supremacy: Some Lessons from the Commonwealth' [1997] *Public Law* 96, 101.

[48] As far as the author is aware, no senior politician advocated this publicly in the 1980s and 1990s.

[49] The preface to D Harris, M O'Boyle and C Warbrick, *Law of the ECHR*, 1st edn (London, Butterworths, 1995) pondered whether it was 'an exaggeration to suggest that the system has developed to the point that no European State could seriously contemplate resiling from the Convention' (vii). The Strasbourg institutions had 'rightfully earned the confidence of contracting parties by carrying out their tasks with the objectivity of judicial bodies and have earned a world-wide reputation for fairness, balance and intellectual rigour' (ibid).

[50] See T Bingham, 'The ECHR: Time to Incorporate' (1993) 109 *Law Quarterly Review* 390; H Woolf, 'Droit Public—English Style' [1995] *Public Law* 57.

[51] No Convention State which accepted the optional clauses ever failed to renew them.

[52] See A Drzemczewski, 'A Major Overhaul of the ECHR Control Mechanism: Protocol No 11' in Academy of European Law (ed), *Collected Courses of the Academy of European Law*, vol VI bk 2 (Leiden, Martinus Nijhoff, 1997) 121, 174 at fn 81.

[53] ibid.

[54] ibid.

submitted that this was an 'enormous responsibility' for the ECtHR to have, such that it was appropriate that the Member States should be able to continue to 'review [its] performance periodically, and make a conscious decision to renew the right of individual petition'.[55]

The UK government therefore fought to retain what it saw as a 'democratic safe-guard', one that it argued was 'absolutely essential'[56] to avoid the Court becoming an institution that, the government contended, was insufficiently accountable to the Member States. However, the initiative was unsuccessful. It lacked support across the negotiating table, and Protocol 11 made the right of individual petition manda-tory. When it entered into force in 1998 it also established a new, permanent Court (whose jurisdiction was also mandatory).

The UK ratified the Protocol in late 1994, but anxieties over the Convention at Whitehall appeared to be growing. The very next year saw a British initiative to bring political pressure to bear on the Court to curb its influence, in the form of a 1995 Foreign Office initiative which involved the circulation of a memorandum to other Convention States. It had a number of features,[57] the most important for us being that it called for the ECtHR to afford the States more margin of appreciation, 'to allow for diversity, particularly on those moral and social issues where the view of what is right may legitimately vary'.[58] It was proposed that the Committee of Ministers pass a resolution drawing the Court's attention to certain principles:

(a)   account should be taken of the fact that democratic institutions and tribunals in Member States are the best placed to determine moral and social issues in accordance with regional and national perceptions;
(b)   full regard should be paid to decisions by democratic legislatures and to differ-ing legal traditions;
(c)   long-standing laws and practices should be respected, except where these are manifestly contrary to the Convention.[59]

As far as the author is aware, this 1995 Foreign Office memorandum did not result in any specific response from the Committee of Ministers. We can only speculate as to whether that meant that the other States rejected the British government's implied criticism of the ECtHR, which frequently stressed the subsidiary nature of the Convention, and the margin of appreciation doctrine in its jurisprudence.[60]

---

[55]   ibid.
[56]   ibid.
[57]   For full details see 'Reform of the Court: The Foreign Office Position Paper' (editorial) (1996) 3 *European Human Rights Law Review* 229, 229–32.
[58]   para 7 of the British document, as quoted ibid, 230.
[59]   ibid, 231.
[60]   In a 1995 lecture the Court's President stated: 'The Convention is not intended to destroy the rich-ness of the cultural and other variety found in Europe by imposing rigid, uniform solutions in the vast field it covers', for the Court recognised 'the right of free societies, within limits, to choose for themselves the human rights policies that best suit them': R Ryssdal, 'The Coming of Age of the European Conven-tion on Human Rights' (1997) 2 *European Human Rights Law Review* 18, 25.

The mid-1990s was not a propitious time for these UK initiatives,[61] and one wonders if matters would have culminated in a 'fundamental reassessment' (Shaw) in defence of the Westminster model had the Conservatives retained power in 1997. As we know, they did not, the reassessment coming in a different form. The new Labour government of 1997 recognised that the UK was virtually alone in Europe, having neither incorporated the Convention nor adopted equivalent protection under a bill of rights or written constitution.[62] Rather than attempt to directly control Strasbourg as an external force on UK law, the new approach was for the UK to modify its own domestic arrangements for protecting human rights. And if so, would that not entail that the actual problem Shaw identified—'growing resentment that groups of mainly foreign judges' are replacing UK national authorities—would be alleviated?

B. The HRA 1998

The Labour Party committed itself to incorporation in 1993,[63] a step that was foreseen as 'cut[ting] costs, sav[ing] time and *giv[ing] power back to British courts'*.[64] According to Tony Blair, repatriating 'British rights to British courts' would also help transform attitudes *toward the Convention*; it would make it clear that 'protection afforded by [it] was *not some foreign import* but that it had been accepted by successive British governments and that it should apply throughout the UK'.[65] What then of arguments that incorporation would unsettle the UK constitutional model? Blair argued, 'we are already signatories to the Convention'—so, incorporation would simply mean 'allowing *British judges rather than European judges* to pass judgment'.[66]

The HRA sought to establish a human rights culture, with 'Convention rights'[67] as its focal point.[68] The 1997 White Paper, *Rights Brought Home: The Human Rights Bill*,[69] displayed a sense of superiority about the seriousness with which the

---

[61] *cf* Ryssdal's lecture, ibid.

[62] Although Lyell (n 46) 139 observed that, like the UK, States such as Italy, France and Austria, which had incorporated, had been found in violation of the Convention many times. *cf* J Straw and P Boateng, 'Bringing Rights Home: Labour's Plans to Incorporate the ECHR' (1997) 1 *European Human Rights Law Review* 71, 74, arguing that the UK was 'mark[ed] out' given the 'serious nature of the cases' and the absence of effective domestic remedies. At the time of writing Straw was Shadow Home Secretary and Boateng Shadow Minister for the Lord Chancellor's Department.

[63] This was originally part of a two-stage plan, part two being the adoption of a domestic bill of rights. By 1996 the commitment was reduced to that of incorporating the ECHR into UK law: see F Klug, 'The HRA: Origins and Intentions' in N Kang-Riou et al (eds), *Confronting the Human Rights Act* (Oxford, Routledge, 2012) 31, 35.

[64] Straw and Boateng (n 62) 71 (emphasis added).

[65] T Blair, 'John Smith Memorial Lecture' (February 1996), cited in F Klug, *Values for a Godless Age* (Harmondsworth, Penguin, 2000) 62 (emphasis added).

[66] ibid (emphasis added).

[67] See especially ss 1, 2(1), 3(1), 4, 6(1) and (2)(b), 7(1)(b), 10(1)(a) and 19 HRA.

[68] See especially s 6(1).

[69] 'Rights Brought Home: The Human Rights Bill', October 1997, CM 3782.

new government approached human rights protection compared to the old.[70] The line adopted was that the Convention was highly regarded,[71] that Strasbourg had proven itself as a trusted external auditor of human rights protection, and that it was high time that British courts should be allowed to apply 'Convention rights', and the Strasbourg jurisprudence, albeit under a scheme that, on its face, would not fundamentally disturb parliamentary sovereignty.[72]

Placing 'Convention rights' centre-stage in this way amounted to a remarkable vote of confidence in the Strasbourg system, and recognition of the constitutional-like nature of the rights protection it afforded. Incorporation would overcome the 'inordinate delay and cost'[73] of having to take a case to Strasbourg to vindicate 'Convention rights'.[74] It would also enable an interchange of views on 'Convention rights' between the UK and Strasbourg judiciaries, with each gently influencing the other.[75] But what was the real aim of the HRA? Was it narrow, to ensure that the ECHR would be complied with domestically, it making little sense for Strasbourg to keep correcting faults in UK law when British judges could do that? Or was it more ambitious, the idea being that the HRA should become a type of UK/British bill of rights? The Labour government was very ambivalent on these points when the Act was passed.[76]

The White Paper and the relevant parliamentary debates do, however, leave the impression that the path ahead for UK–Strasbourg relations was assumed to be a positive one and, although we have the advantage of hindsight, we might ask whether such optimism was misplaced. After all, before 1998 Strasbourg was popularly regarded as a foreign court, 'simply not respected' in the public's eyes, and viewed with 'resentment and suspicion'.[77] This was why Sir Sidney Kentridge, reflecting on his experiences of South Africa, argued that the best way to secure public confidence in a new constitutional system of human rights protection was to have a home-grown bill of rights,[78] *not* an instrument whose focus was primarily on an international treaty.

Perhaps in 1997–98 there was optimism and an expectation that the application of 'Convention rights' by British judges would be sufficient to infuse human rights protection in the UK with a newfound respect as far as the public were concerned.[79]

---

[70] ibid, para 1.17.

[71] The Convention was 'one of the premier agreements defining standards of behaviour across Europe': ibid, para 1.3. Strasbourg was 'well tried and tested'; the rights and freedoms in issue were 'ones with which the people of this country were plainly comfortable', so 'Convention rights' afforded 'an excellent basis' for the protections to be provided by the HRA. Moreover the Strasbourg system was in good standing elsewhere in Europe as evidenced by the fact that 'almost all' States Parties had incorporated it into their domestic law.

[72] ibid, and see s 4 HRA.

[73] *Rights Brought Home* (n 69) para 1.14.

[74] ibid, para 1.16 and 1.19.

[75] ibid para 1.16.

[76] Klug (n 63) 35–36.

[77] Kentridge (n 47) 101, commenting on British hostility toward Strasbourg.

[78] S Kentridge, 'Bill of Rights: The South African Experiment' (1996) 112 *Law Quarterly Review* 237, 258.

[79] *cf* Kentridge's optimism that '[the] enforcement of the Convention by a [British] judiciary which commands widespread even if not invariable respect will do more to entrench a culture of rights than any number of [Strasbourg] decisions': Kentridge (n 47) 102.

After all, foreign judges would no longer be, in effect, the first instance court for the positive enforcement of UK human (Convention) rights issues. Under the 'bringing rights home' agenda, the government emphasised the 'Britishness' of the Convention, given the important role played by the UK in its drafting. The rationale was that most breaches of 'Convention rights' would be resolved domestically, by 'home-grown' judges. Moreover, for cases that went to the ECtHR, European judges would now benefit from British judges' detailed views on the application of the Convention to the British context,[80] which would surely help to influence outcomes.

In summary, then, we may tentatively suggest that the view in 1998 may have been that the increased role that UK judges would have under the HRA would entail a commensurately decreased role—and, presumably, profile—for Strasbourg as a 'foreign' court.[81] Explaining how, in practice, matters seem to have culminated in unprecedented strains in UK–Strasbourg relations is the concern of the remaining parts of this chapter.

In Section V it is argued that the post 2009–10 period has seen a paradox unfold: the scheme and operation of the Act foreseen as heralding in a new, positive era in UK–Strasbourg relations may have had a part in elevating the UK's longstanding concerns about membership of the ECHR. Before that, in Section IV, we examine the debate that has developed recently about the HRA's future.

IV. 2009–15 (OVERVIEW): 'UNFINISHED BUSINESS'?

We now depart from our chronological approach and jump to 2009–10. It is argued that those years marked the beginning of the current era of strained relationship, one that has culminated in serious talk of repeal of the HRA, a Commission calling for a UK bill of rights—and talk of possible withdrawal from the ECHR. Let us now map out what has happened by reference to the 2012 recommendation of the Commission on a UK bill of rights ('the Commission')[82] that a 'fresh beginning' is required for the UK's domestic human rights arrangements.

A. Why a 'Fresh Beginning'?

In some respects the Commission's existence reflected the desire of the 2010 coalition government to avoid difficult questions about sovereignty and Strasbourg's influence that had arisen since the HRA entered into force. Crucially, its terms

---

[80] This point was made by eminent figures such as Anthony Lester (as he then was) and Lord Bingham: A Lester, 'Fundamental Rights: The UK Isolated?' [1984] *Public Law* 46, 66; Bingham (n 50).

[81] *cf* Moses LJ, 'Hitting the Balls Out of Court: Are Judges Stepping Over the Line?' (26 February 2014), 10, www.judiciary.gov.uk/wp-content/uploads/JCO/Documents/Speeches/moses-lj-speech-creaney-lecture-2014.pdf.

[82] Commission on a Bill of Rights, *A UK Bill of Rights: The Choice Before Us* (December 2012); see M Elliott, 'A Damp Squib in the Long Grass: The Report of the Commission on a Bill of Rights' (2013) 2 *European Human Rights Law Review* 137.

of reference,[83] formulated in May 2010, in the first weeks of the new coalition government, assumed the UK's continued membership of the ECHR, and that any bill of rights would build on the obligations it established. This favoured the pro-ECHR/pro-HRA Liberal Democrats, but was acceptable, at the time at least, to the Conservatives, whose 2010 manifesto spoke of replacing the HRA with a British bill of rights (a policy dating back to 2006). At the risk of oversimplifying matters, the latter reflected the unpopularity of the HRA over its first decade. Amongst the general public the view appeared to be that the Act protected the rights of the 'undeserving' at the expense of the majority, making the fight against terrorism and crime harder.[84] The highly influential tabloid press encouraged such views, campaigning against the Act[85] in what at times appeared to reflect hostility towards any European influence on UK law. Exaggeration, misinformation, myths and misreporting became associated with the Act, as well as Strasbourg's enduring role as an international court.[86] Lord Lester, a member of the Commission, had in mind the influence of an anti-Strasbourg tabloid press[87] and politicians, fuelling public resentment toward an Act regarded as European, not British, when he suggested that rather than 'bringing rights home', the HRA had had 'an alienating effect especially among those for whom "Europe" is a dirty word'.[88] Here we recall the backdrop of the UK's suspicion of and uneasy relationship with 'Europe',[89] and note how the domestic courts—and, vicariously, Strasbourg—came under an intense media spotlight in the 2000s, not least in the post-9/11 context.

It seems, then, that, up to 2011, the HRA's 'difficult and embattled life'[90] owed much to factors other than the pressures placed on the Westminster model. Indeed, there was little criticism of the constitutional mechanisms and regime established by the HRA in the Commission's Report.[91] Its conclusion that 'on balance, there [was] a strong argument in favour of the UK Bill of Rights',[92] and the need for a 'fresh beginning'[93] was essentially based on the premise that human rights protection in

[83] Which were, amongst other things, to 'investigate the creation of a UK Bill of Rights that incorporates and builds on all our obligations under the [ECHR], ensures that these rights continue to be enshrined in UK law, and protects and extend our liberties'; see *A UK Bill of Rights* (n 82) para 12.7.

[84] See comments made by Lord Dyson, 'What is Wrong with Human Rights?' (3 November 2011), 5, www.supremecourt.uk/docs/speech_111103.pdf.

[85] See, for example, comments made by Lord Lester in the House of Commons Political and Constitutional Reform Committee, UK Bill of Rights Commission—Oral and Written Evidence, 16 June 2011, 19 July 2011, HC Paper 1049-ii of session 2010–12.

[86] For a good overview see Dyson (n 84).

[87] See D Mead, '"You Couldn't Make It Up": Some Narratives of the Media's Coverage of Human Rights' (ch 23) and L Gies, 'Human Rights, the British Press and the Deserving Claimant' (ch 24), this volume.

[88] Lord Lester, 'A Personal Explanatory Note', Individual Paper included within *A UK Bill of Rights: The Choice Before Us* (n 82) 231 at 233.

[89] See text accompanying n 37.

[90] Lord Dyson (n 84) 1.

[91] H Kennedy QC and P Sands QC, 'In Defence of Rights', Individual Paper included within *A UK Bill of Rights: The Choice Before Us* (n 82) 221 at 222, noting that the Commission had failed to 'identify or declare any shortcomings' of the HRA itself.

[92] *A UK Bill of Rights: The Choice Before Us* (n 82) para 78.

[93] ibid, para 84.

the UK was seen as 'European'. It observed that, unlike the UK, virtually all other Convention States had their own written constitutions or bills of rights, setting out human rights protection in their own terms.[94] That mattered given the absence of 'widespread public acceptance of the legitimacy of our current human rights structures, including the role of the Convention and [Strasbourg]'. As the Commission understood it, there was 'a lack of public understanding and "ownership"' of the HRA, and especially so as regards the Convention and Strasbourg, such that 'many people feel alienated from a system that they regard as more "European" rather than British'.[95]

B. ... 'Unfinished Business'?

Essentially, then, the Commission's main point (by majority) appeared to be that the HRA needed changing to enhance the feeling of national 'ownership' over human rights issues. Restricted by its terms of reference,[96] however, it abstained from any real comment on whether the 'European rather than British' criticism it had identified was merely a superficial matter, or whether, in fact, Strasbourg's influence on UK human rights law was open to criticism.[97] This was 'the elephant in the room', as was evident from the Commission's earlier work[98] and the intense public debate occurring in parallel to it, hence the issues such as prisoner voting, and the protection afforded by Articles 3 and 8 (amongst others) referred to in the introduction to this chapter.

We observe then that Separate Opinions attached to the Commission's Report of late 2012 revealed divisions along pro- and anti-ECHR lines. One jointly authored Opinion, entitled 'Unfinished Business',[99] identified membership of the Convention as the central issue, attacking the ECtHR for its over-expansive interpretations. A different jointly authored Opinion[100] argued that the case for a UK bill of rights had not been made out (suggesting that the argument as to lack of 'ownership' had not been established). These authors were concerned that the time was 'not ripe' for change, suggesting that the real agenda for some of the Commission's members was to support a UK bill of rights as a preliminary step towards achieving the real ambition of withdrawing from the ECHR.

---

[94] ibid, para 79 and para 12.7.

[95] ibid, para 80.

[96] See n 83.

[97] For criticism of the Commission's failure to address key issues of controversy regarding the HRA, and more generally, see Elliott (n 82).

[98] The Commission's interim advice on future reform of the ECHR included a minority view that the Court should be subject to some sort of democratic override: see Bates (n 2) fn 137. One member of the Commission resigned, arguing that it was refusing to address the real issue (as he saw it) of whether Parliament rather than Strasbourg should have the final say on human rights issues: see C Urquhart, 'Bill of Rights Commissioner Resigns over Bypass of Commons' *The Guardian* (London, 11 March 2012), www.theguardian.com/law/2012/mar/11/uk-bill-of-rights-kenneth-clarke.

[99] Lord Faulks QC and Jonathan Fisher QC, individual Paper included within *A UK Bill of Rights: The Choice Before Us* (n 82) 182.

[100] Kennedy and Sands (n 91) 221.

As to the broader public debate, this had been growing since 2009–10 with Strasbourg as the primary target, either directly, in the context of affairs such as prisoner voting and that concerning Abu Qatada, or indirectly, via criticism of over-reliance on Strasbourg law in the context of the judicial application of the HRA. Very importantly, however, the criticism also came from quarters hitherto regarded as favourable to the Court. This included the political 'midwives' to the HRA, Jack Straw (then MP) (2013)[101] and Lord Irvine (2011).[102] Straw led opposition to a change in the law on prisoner voting,[103] and spoke directly in terms of Strasbourg, rather than the HRA itself, being the real problem.[104] This chimed with the strident and direct attacks on the Court made by a small number of senior judges,[105] speaking extra-judicially in the post-2009–10 period.

C. Keeping British Rights at Home?

The bright spotlight under which the ECtHR was put by these respected figures who would be expected to be championing Strasbourg's cause, not undermining it, lent credibility to the more vociferous opposition coming from the constituencies traditionally hostile to Strasbourg, including aspects of the media and many Conservative politicians. For the latter, frustration with Strasbourg rose to a critical point over the life of the 2010–15 Parliament, reflecting the view, it seems, that it was high time to push back what was seen as the overwhelming tide of Strasbourg's influence and reassert the Westminster model.[106] There were echoes then of the Conservatives' initiatives of the mid-1990s,[107] although now the perceived need was to address the ECtHR's influence not just in the international context (that is, as a court which retained jurisdiction over the UK),[108] but also in the domestic setting (that is, under the HRA).

The latter was associated with Conservative arguments that the HRA needed amendment to make it clear that 'parliament is the ultimate source of legal authority, and that the Supreme Court [not Strasbourg] is indeed supreme in the interpretation

---

[101] See Straw (n 19). However, in May 2015 Straw delivered a lecture which, in view of the Court's recent jurisprudence, was more supportive of it, see O Bowcott, 'Strasbourg court has backed off over rights rulings, says Jack Straw' *The Guardian* (21 May 2015) www.theguardian.com/law/2015/may/21/strasbourg-court-backed-off-human-rights-jack-straw.

[102] Derry Irvine, 'A British Interpretation of Convention Rights' [2012] *Public Law* 237.

[103] HC Deb 10 Feb 2011, vol 523, col 498.

[104] See text accompanying n 167 below.

[105] See text accompanying n 18 above and n 142 below; but see also Bates (n 14) above.

[106] The announcement of the creation of the Commission was linked to the Prime Minister's description of a Supreme Court judgment holding that placement for life on the sex offenders register could be incompatible with Art 8 as 'offensive'. It was 'about time', he said, that 'we started making sure decisions are made in this Parliament rather than in the courts': HC Deb 16 February 2011, vol 523, col 955. The week before that, MPs had voted overwhelmingly not to change the law on prisoner voting, anti-Strasbourg sentiment being vented in the process: see D Nicol, 'Legitimacy of the Common Debate on Prisoner Voting' [2011] *Public Law* 681.

[107] See text accompanying nn 52–59 above.

[108] On the 'democratic override' debate see Bates (n 2) n 137.

of the law'.[109] In terms of Strasbourg's external role, there was the confrontation with it on the prisoner voting issue, whilst the British government's negotiating position in the lead-up to the Brighton Declaration of 2012 was also notable: it was widely reported that the government attempted to secure a Declaration that would pressurise the ECtHR to apply the margin of appreciation doctrine more generously.[110] With that initiative perceived to be unsuccessful—although, in fact, it is suggested below that it was indeed influential[111]—over 2013–14 the Conservative Party adopted an increasingly aggressive anti-Strasbourg position.[112] In October 2014 proposals for changing the UK's human rights laws[113] were published, including the introduction of a British Bill of Rights and Responsibilities, should the Conservatives be elected in May 2015.

The full details of that document cannot be examined here. It received considerable criticism for its inaccuracies, amongst other things, from academics and commentators, including the by then former (Conservative) Attorney-General.[114] The proposals on substantive human rights issues seemed to be addressed to ensuring that 'Convention rights' (notably those concerning Articles 3 and 8 in the context of immigration) were read in a British (in fact, Conservative) rather than Strasbourg way. The document stated that under a future Conservative government Parliament should have to approve Strasbourg judgments finding the UK in breach of the Convention, those judgments being treated as advisory only. In a vendetta-like way it asserted that the ECtHR had undermined public confidence in human rights and, with echoes of Fitzmaurice, reference was made to the Court's illegitimate 'mission creep' (the aggrandisement argument). The UK, it said, stood by 'the commitments made when we signed the Convention', so the Convention would not be renounced unilaterally given that it was *not* 'our principled commitment to fundamental rights that ha[d] changed'. Thus, under a Conservative government, the UK would 'engage' with the Council of Europe to 'seek recognition that our approach [for example as regards reinterpreting Article 3 and 8] is a legitimate way of applying the Convention'—but if that recognition was not forthcoming, 'the UK would be left with no alternative but to withdraw from the Convention' when the new, proposed British Bill of Rights and Responsibilities entered into force.

It transpired, however, that the commitments set out in the Conservative Party manifesto for the May 2015 election, which it won, were more reserved than the October 2014 document. There was no mention of withdrawal, for example,

---

[109] *Protecting Human Rights in the UK* (n 113) 5.

[110] See N O'Meara, 'Reforming the ECtHR: The Impact of Protocols 15 and 16 to the ECHR' (ch 5), this volume.

[111] See section V.B.

[112] Domestic politics may have been relevant, given the increased popularity of the UK Independence Party.

[113] Conservative Party, *Protecting Human Rights in the UK: The Conservatives' Proposals for Changing Britain's Human Rights Laws* (3 October 2014), www.conservatives.com/~/media/Files/Downloadable%20Files/HUMAN_RIGHTS.pdf.

[114] Dominic Grieve QC MP, 'Why Human Rights Should Matter to Conservatives', lecture delivered at UCL, 3 December 2014, www.ucl.ac.uk/constitution-unit/constitution-unit-news/031214a. Grieve was Attorney General under the Coalition Government, but his appointment by the Prime Minister was not renewed in July 2014, it being reported that Grieve was too favourable toward the ECHR.

although it was stated that the '[t]he next Conservative Government [would] scrap the Human Rights Act, and introduce a British Bill of Rights' (the 'Rights and Responsibilities' label being dropped). Such a Bill would 'break the formal link between British courts and the European Court of Human Rights, and make our own Supreme Court the ultimate arbiter of human rights matters in the UK'.[115] The Bill would 'restore common sense to the application of human rights in the UK'. It would remain 'faithful to the basic principles of human rights, which we signed up to in the original European Convention on Human Rights', but it would 'reverse the mission creep that has meant human rights law being used for more and more purposes, and often with little regard for the rights of wider society'.[116]

No draft Bill of Rights had been produced in time for the election, or has been published by the time of writing. In fact, soon after the election questions arose as to whether the new government, with a majority of just 12 MPs, would be able to obtain the necessary support to repeal the HRA. It was also realised that the attempt to do so would be confronted by potential political obstacles and sensitivities arising in the context of the UK's devolution arrangements.[117] Against this backdrop, in late May 2015 the government's position was that it intended to fulfil its manifesto commitment to introduce a British Bill of Right, but would embark on a consultation process to do so. In these circumstances it would seem that, under the present government at least, the prospect of a UK withdrawal from the Convention has been significantly reduced.[118]

V. UK–STRASBOURG RELATIONS UNDER THE HRA: A NEW EQUILIBRIUM ALREADY REACHED?

Now that we have an overview of how the ECtHR's influence on UK law has become the focal point of intense criticism since 2009, we may stand back and reflect. In what follows it is argued that the particular experience of incorporating 'Convention rights' via the HRA may have served to aggravate, rather than placate,

---

[115] *The Conservative Party Manifesto 2015* at 60.

[116] ibid at 73. The document went on: '[a]mong other things the Bill will stop terrorists and other serious foreign criminals who pose a threat to our society from using spurious human rights arguments to prevent deportation'.

[117] See N Watt, 'Scotland bill may give Holyrood veto over Human Rights Act repeal' *The Guardian* (London, 28 May 2015), www.theguardian.com/politics/2015/may/28/scotland-bill-human-rights-act-repeal. See also M Elliott, 'Could the devolved nations block repeal of the Human Rights Act and the enactment of a new Bill of Rights?' (*Public Law for Everyone*, 12 May 2015), http://publiclawforeveryone.com/2015/05/12/could-the-devolved-nations-block-repeal-of-the-human-rights-act-and-the-enactment-of-a-new-bill-of-rights.

[118] See N Watt, 'Threat to exit human rights convention must be dropped, Tories tell Cameron' *The Guardian* (London, 27 May 2015), www.theguardian.com/law/2015/may/27/threat-exit-human-rights-act-convention-dropped-tories-cameron. However, in early June 2015 it was reported that the Prime Minister's position was that the possibility of withdrawal from the Convention should not be discounted, should this step ultimately be deemed necessary in the light of the plan identified for possible withdrawal set out in the Conservative's October 2014 document: see N Watt, 'David Cameron prepared to break with Europe on human rights' *The Guardian* (London, 2 June 2015), www.theguardian.com/politics/2015/jun/02/david-cameron-prepared-to-break-with-europe-on-human-rights.

the sensitivities that have historically characterised UK–Strasbourg relations and which have been a theme of this chapter, namely European sovereignty concerns and feelings of 'resentment' that foreign judges[119] control UK law. In this regard the print media have undoubtedly been most influential, fuelling popular perception that the Act significantly magnified the influence of what was seen as an 'alien jurisprudence'[120] on UK law, and, following that lead, it seems that the public's 'disconnect' from the Act, and the Convention, has been exacerbated by incautious remarks made by certain politicians.[121] Then again, we have just noted that figures who might have been expected to be the Court's traditional allies—the political midwives to the HRA, as well as some senior judges—have also been critical, adding a certain respectability to the anti-Strasbourg/anti-HRA agenda. So, what is at the root of their critiques?

It is submitted that two concerns dominate the debates. First, supremacy concerns came to be associated with the operation of the HRA, for the argument was made that, under it, the UK courts were subservient to Strasbourg's interpretation of 'Convention rights' (A, below). Related to this, secondly, concerns arose about Strasbourg's legitimacy—concerns which were also associated with its capacity to continue to find the UK in violation of 'Convention rights' in terms of its international obligations under the ECHR (B, below). With respect to both issues, it is argued below that, whether or not the concerns raised were valid, they have been considerably mitigated given recent case law from firstly, the UK courts (under the HRA) and, secondly, the ECtHR (given its subsidiary role).

A. Supremacy Concerns under the HRA—Still Valid?

The first issue grew out of a controversy that evolved over how the UK courts approached the application of Convention law when applying the HRA.[122] Over the first part of the HRA's life the judiciary adopted a narrow view of its purpose, reflecting more the notion that it was designed to facilitate the UK's domestic compliance with the Convention (and stop claimants having to go to Strasbourg to champion 'Convention rights') rather than establish a type of UK/British bill of rights.[123] At the risk of oversimplifying matters, the courts attempted to anticipate how Strasbourg would resolve the case before them. The 'mirror principle' set out

---

[119] See text accompanying n 44 (Shaw) and n 65 (Blair).

[120] See Dyson (n 84).

[121] *cf* comments noted in the context of the Wilton Park Conference on the future of the Court: '2020 Vision for the European Court of Human Rights' (17–19 November 2011), www.wiltonpark.org.uk/wp-content/uploads/wp1139-report.pdf, 5.

[122] See further Lord Kerr, 'The Relationship between the Strasbourg Court and the National Courts—As Seen from the UK Supreme Court' (ch 3) and R Clayton, 'Should the English Courts under the HRA the Strasbourg Case Law?' (ch 6), this volume.

[123] The intentions in 1998 were not clear: see text accompanying n 76 above. See also Clayton's discussion on the drafting history of s 2(1), ibid.

in the famous *Ullah* case[124] epitomised this approach and how, over the first decade or so of the HRA's life, Strasbourg's clear and consistent interpretation of the meaning of 'Convention rights' risked being treated as an authoritative exposition of the same for the purpose of assessing the human rights compatibility of domestic law under the HRA. This was the backdrop to Lord Rodger's famous statement in *AF*, '*Argentoratum locutum, iudicium finitum*'—'Strasbourg has spoken, the case is closed',[125] which apparently reflected unease at what had occurred in that case. In it the Laws Lords treated a recent authoritative Grand Chamber ruling[126] on Article 6(1) as practically closing down legal argument on the key issue before them, given that the Strasbourg case mirrored the precise fair trial issue that the House of Lords was considering. If Lord Rodger's latinised dictum was cynical, this may have been because some Law Lords regarded Strasbourg's position as questionable, some saying explicitly that it was wrong,[127] and as it was feared that its application (in *AF*) would have drastic consequences for a highly sensitive and important aspect of domestic law.[128]

However, *AF* (2009) seems to have marked the high-water mark of the *Ullah* approach, with subsequent case law exposing the increasing inaccuracy of the mirror metaphor.[129] It is 'now generally recognised that in the early years after the HRA the courts went too far in regarding themselves as virtually bound to follow every Strasbourg decision'.[130] It is accepted too that there may have been a tendency for UK courts initially to approach ECHR case law on the binding

---

[124] *R (Ullah) v Special Adjudicator* [2004] UKHL 26. See Clayton (n 122). See also R Masterman, 'Deconstructing the Mirror Principle', ch 5 in R Masterman and I Leigh, *The UK's Statutory Bill of Rights: Constitutional and Comparative Perspectives* (Oxford University Press, 2013), also providing a comprehensive account of the shift away from this principle. The mirror principle is also relevant to the question of whether domestic courts can go further than the level of protection afforded by the Convention, or resolve issues the ECtHR has not yet fully considered. This is not examined here; however see Clayton (n 122), and Masterman ibid.

[125] *Secretary of State for the Home Department (Respondent) v AF (Appellant)* [2009] UKHL 28, para 98. See Lady Hale, '*Argentoratum Locutum*: Is Strasbourg or the Supreme Court Supreme?' (2012) 12 *Human Rights Law Review* 65.

[126] *A v UK* (2009) 49 EHRR 29 (GC) (the Art 5(4) issue addressed in this case mirrored the precise Art 6(1) in issue in *AF*).

[127] Lord Hoffmann in *AF* (n 125) para 70; *cf* his criticism of the Court generally: see n 18.

[128] *AF* concerned the (Art 6(1)) fairness of procedures employed in (what were then) anti-terrorism control order hearings. There was foreboding among the Law Lords that the modifications required by Strasbourg law might affect the very viability of the control order regime (a central feature of the government's anti-terrorism agenda). In fact, this did not prove to be the case. As the Independent Reviewer of Terrorism Legislation reflected some years later, the 'upshot' was 'an improvement in the fairness of ... proceedings, with only a very limited loss of capacity to impose control orders': D Anderson, 'Shielding the Compass: How to Fight Terrorism without Defeating the Law' [2013] 3 *European Human Rights Law Review* 233, 246.

[129] See Masterman (n 124) 129–36, and especially the critique at 136 suggesting that aspects of the debate on a bill of rights have proceeded on a 'false premise'.

[130] Lord Toulsen, 'International Influence on the Common Law' (11 November 2014), para 36 and see para 37, www.supremecourt.uk/docs/speech-141111.pdf. For comment on the evolution of the UK court's approach, see the statements made by Lord Neuberger and Baroness Hale, *House of Lords Select Committee on the Constitution (Annual Oral Evidence from the President and Deputy President of the UK Supreme Court)*, 25 June 2014, 20–22.

precedent-setting basis common lawyers are familiar with, but that they are now far more circumspect, especially regarding Chamber judgments, and ready to depart from, or question, the ECtHR when they deem it appropriate.[131] The new direction was especially evident in *Horncastle*[132] (2009) and *Pinnock*[133] (2010), when the Supreme Court (instituted in October 2009) undertook a reappraisal of Lord Rodger's dictum in *AF*. As a result, the UK courts now look more generally at the ECtHR's law, expecting to follow it when (i) there is 'a clear and constant line of decisions', (ii) 'whose reasoning does not appear [from the UK perspective] to overlook or misunderstand some argument or point of principle', and (iii) 'whose effect' is 'not inconsistent with some fundamental substantive or procedural aspect of *our* law' (emphasis added). These '*Pinnock* criteria'[134] envisage criterion (iii) as a constitutional redline[135] when, contrary to Lord Rodger's suggestion, the Supreme Court ultimately reserves the right *not* to follow even a Strasbourg Grand Chamber.[136]

In spite of this reappraisal, however, the dominant narrative has been one of the UK courts' inappropriate subservience to Strasbourg under the mirror approach.[137] Lord Irvine (2011)[138] and Jack Straw (then MP) (2013)[139] have strongly argued that under *Ullah* the UK judiciary had been far too willing to regard Strasbourg views as determinative, thereby emboldening the ECtHR as a type of Supreme Court for the UK. Both were adamant that that certainly had not been intended when the 1998 Act was passed. Supremacy anxieties were also revived in *Chester*[140] in late 2013, when the Supreme Court, applying the *Pinnock* criteria, followed the ECtHR's unequivocal position that blanket bans on convicted prisoners voting

---

[131] *cf* comments made by Lord Neuberger, 'The Role of Judges in Human Rights Jurisprudence: A Comparison of the Australian and UK Experience' (8 August 2014), paras 29 and 32–38, www.supremecourt.uk/docs/speech-140808.pdf.

[132] *R v Horncastle* [2009] UKSC 14, paras 10–11, and 108 (Lord Phillips), 116–21 (Lord Brown). See Masterman (n 124) 130.

[133] *Manchester City Council v Pinnock* [2010] UKSC 45, para 48 (Lord Neuberger).

[134] ibid.

[135] In *Pinnock* (n 133), Lord Neuberger stated that Strasbourg law should not '[cut] across our domestic substantive or procedural law in some fundamental way': para 49. See also *R (on the application of Chester) v Secretary of State for Justice* [2013] UKSC 63, Lord Mance, paras 27 and 35 and Lord Sumption, para 137 ('fundamental feature of the law of the UK'); *R (on the applications of Haney, Kaiyam, and Massey) v Secretary of State for Justice* [2014] UKSC 66, paras 18–21 (Lords Mance and Hughes: relevant tests developed in *Pinnock* and *Chester* offer 'general guidelines' which are context specific: para 21). A tentative comparison may also be made with respect to the limits of the reception of EU law into UK law: see *R (HS2 Action Alliance Ltd) v Secretary of State for Transport* [2014] UKSC 3.

[136] *Pinnock* (n 129) para 48 (Lord Neuberger: UK courts are not bound by Strasbourg 'or (in theory, at least) to follow a decision of the Grand Chamber'). However, for earlier expressions of disagreement between the then Lord Chief Justice (Lord Judge) and the President of the Supreme Court (Lord Phillips) as to whether Strasbourg would prevail over the UK courts, see Hale (n 125) 67.

[137] *cf* the points also made by Masterman (n 124) 136.

[138] Irvine (n 102) *cf* M Wolfe-Robinson and O Bowcott, 'Lord Irvine: Human Rights Law Developed on False Premise' *The Guardian* (London, 14 December 2011), www.theguardian.com/law/2011/dec/14/lord-irvine-human-rights-law; see also P Sales, 'Strasbourg Jurisprudence and the Human Rights Act: A Response to Lord Irvine' [2012] *Public Law* 253.

[139] Straw (n 19).

[140] *Chester* (n 135).

whilst in detention were incompatible with the Convention.[141] This was met by comments in a small number of lectures from senior judicial figures critical of the ECtHR and its influence.[142] Lord Judge, the former Lord Chief Justice, argued that the HRA should be amended to make it clear that 'in this jurisdiction the Supreme Court is, at the very least, a court of equal standing with the Strasbourg Court'.[143] Media reporting of these and other speeches has played on British anxieties about Europe, the tone being that British judges are imploring their colleagues not to make themselves supine to Strasbourg. A measure of legal credibility was therefore given to sweeping arguments from the then Minister for Justice, Chris Grayling, that supremacy must be wrestled back from Strasbourg via repeal of the HRA.[144]

The matter is far more subtle than this, of course, for it is inaccurate to say that the Supreme Court is no longer supreme, whilst the actual need, based on restoration of supremacy grounds, to amend the HRA is very debatable.[145] On the one hand, there has been no case to date in which the Supreme Court has felt it necessary to invoke the constitutional redline envisaged by *Pinnock* criterion (iii), and we may note that the criteria themselves may yet become more robust.[146] On the other hand, some would suggest that, as things stand, the constitutional redline is drawn inappropriately, their point being, it seems, that it potentially constrains the domestic courts into accepting the ECtHR's final and unequivocal view (not the domestic judge's own preferred one) on a particular human rights matter that may

---

[141] Strasbourg's position was beyond doubt, as two Grand Chamber judgments (of 2005: *Hirst* (n 3); and 2012: *Scoppola* (n 3)) had concluded so; hence the Supreme Court regarded the matter as not susceptible to further dialogue. Furthermore, the constitutional redline (*Pinnock* criterion (iii)) was not in issue. According to Lord Mance, there could be reasonable differences of opinion on the prisoner disenfranchisement issue, but it would 'exaggerate their legal and social importance to regard them as going to "some fundamental substantive or procedural aspect of our law"'. Given the diverse approaches to the prisoner voting issue in Europe it was 'difficult to see prisoner disenfranchisement as fundamental to a stable democracy and legal system such as the United Kingdom enjoys': *Chester* (n 135) para 35. See also Lord Sumption at para 137, although he implied that Strasbourg's absolute stance on prisoner voting bans amounted to undue activism on its part. A declaration of incompatibility (s 4 HRA) had already been made in a previous case, so the Supreme Court in *Chester* declined to make a further declaration.

[142] Lord Sumption (member of the Supreme Court, who had sat in *Chester*), 'The Limits of Law' (20 November 2013), www.supremecourt.uk/docs/speech-131120.pdf (*cf* O Bowcott, 'Senior Judge: European Court of Human Rights Undermining Democratic Process' *The Guardian* (London, 28 November 2014), www.theguardian.com/law/2013/nov/28/european-court-of-human-rights); Laws LJ, 'The Common Law and Europe' (27 November 2013), www.judiciary.gov.uk/wp-content/uploads/JCO/Documents/Speeches/laws-lj-speech-hamlyn-lecture-2013.pdf (*cf* O Bowcott, 'Stop Deferring to Human Rights Court, Says Senior Judge' *The Guardian* (London, 27 November 2013), www.theguardian.com/law/2013/nov/27/stop-deferring-human-rights-court); Lord Judge (former Lord Chief Justice), 'Constitutional Change—Unfinished Business' (3 December 2013), www.ucl.ac.uk/constitution-unit/constitution-unit-news/constitution-unit/research/judicial-independence/lordjudgelecture041213 (*cf* O Bowcott, 'European Court is Not Superior to UK Supreme Court, Says Lord Judge' *The Guardian* (London, 4 December 2013), www.theguardian.com/law/2013/dec/04/european-court-uk-supreme-lord-judge). As to subsequent judicial lectures, more favorable to the Court, see Bates (n 14).

[143] Lord Judge, ibid, para 46.

[144] See 'Chris Grayling: Senior Judges Back Me over Human Rights Reforms' *Daily Telegraph* (London, 26 March 2014), www.telegraph.co.uk/news/politics/conservative/10724404/Chris-Grayling-Senior-judges-back-me-over-human-rights-reforms; see also n 109 above.

[145] In July 2014 Lord Neuberger suggested that 'an amendment would send a legislative message to the courts. However, I rather doubt whether it is strictly necessary': n 130, 21.

[146] Lord Neuberger (n 131) para 33.

still be of national interest and importance (eg prisoner voting) even though it falls short of being a 'fundamental substantive or procedural aspect' of UK law.[147] Put another way, the argument is that the criteria still leave UK law too vulnerable to Strasbourg's influence, potentially at least.

Of course, the HRA could be amended (or new legislation put in place) to make it clear that, even if there is a 'clear and constant' line of authoritative Strasbourg rulings, precisely on point, it may be ignored in any circumstances at all. But would this merely communicate a reassuring message about supremacy being retained? Section 2(1) HRA already makes it clear that the domestic courts are not bound by the ECtHR. Furthermore, in the context of concerns about supremacy two additional points may be made about the post-2010 adjustment in UK–Strasbourg legal relations.

First, *Pinnock* criteria (i) and (ii) will usually (albeit not in *Chester*)[148] offer a broad basis for the domestic courts to demonstrate their respect for Strasbourg but decline to follow it in a given case on the basis that the domestic court seeks a constructive and respectful dialogue with Strasbourg on whether one of its judgments is correct, or on the meaning of 'Convention rights'.[149] The outcome of this may be that the ECtHR adjusts its position in the light of the concerns communicated to it by the domestic court. Indeed, this has happened in cases concerning both the UK and other States.[150] Here we note that Strasbourg positively welcomes this dialogue approach,[151] which has been endorsed by the Brighton Declaration.[152] It is one that envisages fruitful interactions between the domestic courts and Strasbourg under a model which is at odds with sweeping suggestions that the latter acts as a type of infallible Supreme Court, disrespectful of national positions and unwilling to change course.

This brings us to the second point to be addressed in this section, which concerns the new equilibrium reached between Strasbourg and the UK courts in recent years.

---

[147] This would seem to be the view of Lord Judge (n 142) and Laws LJ (n 142). Lord Irvine would seem to agree: see (n 102) 242–45.

[148] See nn 135 and 140 above.

[149] *Horncastle* (n 132) para 11; *Pinnock* (n 133) para 48; *Chester* (n 135) para 27. On dialogue, see M Amos, 'From Monologue to Dialogue' in Masterman and Leigh (n 124) ch 6.

[150] Amos, ibid, 148. On fruitful dialogue between the ECtHR and the German Bundesverfassungsgericht see further J Rackow, 'From Conflict to Cooperation: The Relationship between Karlsruhe and Strasbourg' (ch 19), this volume.

[151] *cf* Judge Bratza's Separate Opinion in *Al-Khawaja v UK* (2012) 54 EHRR 23 (GC) (in this judgment the ECtHR adjusted its position on a specific aspect of the Art 6(1) jurisprudence, in direct response to the Supreme Court judgment in *Horncastle* (n 128)). There is now a large literature on 'dialogue' between the ECtHR and domestic courts including Amos (n 149); N Bratza, 'The Relationship between the UK Courts and Strasbourg' (2011) 5 *European Human Rights Law Review* 505; J-P Costa, 'The Relationship between the European Court of Human Rights and National Constitutional Courts' (2013) 3 *European Human Rights Law Review* 264 (Costa was one-time President of the Court, as was Bratza); P Mahoney, 'The Relationship between the Strasbourg Court and the National Courts' (2014) 130 *Law Quarterly Review* 568 and 'The Relationship between the Strasbourg Court and the National Courts—As Seen from Strasbourg' (ch 2), this volume (Mahoney is the current 'British' judge at the Court).

[152] Brighton Declaration (Declaration adopted by the Committee of Ministers of the Council of Europe on 20 April 2012 at the High Level Conference on the Future of the European Court of Human Rights, in Brighton), para 12(c) and (d).

To the extent that the supremacy concern is derived from the fear of an all-powerful and unaccountable Strasbourg judiciary ignoring matters of national interest and importance, account must be taken of what the ECtHR does in practice. The need for self-restraint on Strasbourg's part and sensitivity toward the national context is of great relevance here, and, as we shall see under the next heading, this is a matter that has been a central issue in recent years, there being a new emphasis on the subsidiarity principle. We turn then to Strasbourg's external review role.

B. Strasbourg's Role as an International Court

To explore this aspect of the strained relationship, perhaps a useful point of departure is to consider how the HRA may have shifted British expectations about the 'foreign' court that the ECtHR was seen as. For example, with 'Convention' 'rights brought home' by the HRA, it was understandable that questions would arise such as why, or upon what basis, their application by British judges should be subject to further review by Strasbourg.[153]

This was central to Lord Hoffmann's attack upon the Strasbourg Court in 2009,[154] when he expressed fundamental doubts as to the legitimacy of its role at international law. Meanwhile, and in connection with the reform process instituted by the Swiss government at Interlaken in 2010 and followed up at Izmir and Brighton, the UK government placed great emphasis on the principle of subsidiarity. The argument that primary responsibility for protecting rights should rest at the national level, with the ECtHR occupying a residual role only, is of course a very valid one, although the debate lies in how residual Strasbourg's role should be.[155]

It is submitted that, aside from the very occasional decision, the subsidiarity message is one that was thoroughly recognised in the Strasbourg jurisprudence before the reform process initiated at Interlaken got underway. Nonetheless, the respective declarations from Interlaken, Izmir and Brighton placed great emphasis on the subsidiarity principle and the margin of appreciation. As is well known, Protocol 15 to the ECHR envisages the insertion of a new paragraph into the Convention's Preamble referring to both.[156]

Reflecting on these and other developments, the Joint (Parliamentary) Committee on Human Rights (JCHR) has suggested that Protocol 15 'signifies a new era in the

---

[153] Lord Hoffmann posed this question *before* the HRA entered into force, when he was highly critical of Strasbourg, and expressed doubts over the case for the UK's continued adherence to the ECHR: see L Hoffmann, 'Human Rights and the House of Lords' (n 18).

[154] Hoffmann, 'The Universality of Human Rights' (n 18), and see ibid (the later article is the text of a lecture delivered soon after the *AF* case had been heard).

[155] The Brighton Declaration para 15(d) states: '[A]n application should be regarded as manifestly ill-founded within the meaning of Article 35(3)(a), inter alia, to the extent that the Court considers that the application raises a complaint that has been duly considered by a domestic court applying the rights guaranteed by the Convention in light of well-established case law of the Court including on the margin of appreciation as appropriate, unless the Court finds that the application raises a serious question affecting the interpretation or application of the Convention.'

[156] See O'Meara, this volume.

life of the Convention, an age of subsidiarity, in which the emphasis is on States' primary responsibility to secure the rights and freedoms set out in the Convention'.[157] The same Committee has observed that recent Strasbourg jurisprudence has verified this point, and the Court's willingness to extend a margin of appreciation in cases when the national authorities have already diligently applied the Convention.[158] According to the JCHR:

> In recent case-law, the Court has been increasingly explicit that … deference will be applied by the Court to Parliament's careful consideration of Convention compatibility. In a significant and growing number of recent cases against the UK, for example, the Court has demonstrated its willingness to defer to the reasoned and thoughtful assessment by national authorities (including Parliament) of their Convention obligations, resulting in legislation being upheld as being within the UK's margin of appreciation. Statutes prohibiting paid political advertising,[159] restricting the right of British citizens resident overseas to vote in parliamentary elections,[160] and prohibiting secondary strike action[161] have all been upheld by the Strasbourg Court, in part because of the extensive and detailed examination by Parliament of the Convention compatibility of the law, in which Parliament has taken into account the principles and case-law of the Convention.[162]

Yet there has been no real recognition of such points in criticisms of the Convention from high-profile figures, many continuing in the vein of Lord Hoffmann from 2009. Lord Judge has spoken of a 'democratic deficit' arising from Strasbourg's jurisdiction vis-a-vis national authorities on matters such as prisoner voting, stating that parliamentary sovereignty on such matters should not be exported to a 'foreign court'.[163] Other senior judges[164] have argued that Strasbourg undermines the democratic process,[165] and that the application of 'Convention rights' trespasses into political fields, contrary to what 'the respective roles of government and judiciary'[166] should be under the British constitutional set-up, with its emphasis on political constitutionalism. In his 2013 Hamlyn Lecture, Jack Straw stated, in sweeping terms, that, '[s]ince the passage of the Act, it has not been judgments of

---

[157] Joint Committee of Human Rights, 'Protocol 15 to the ECHR' HL Paper 71/ HC 837, para 3.17. See also R Spano, 'Universality or Diversity of Human Rights? Strasbourg in the Age of Subsidiarity' (2014) 14 *Human Rights Law Review* 487 (R Spano is a judge at the Court); see, by the current President of the Court, D Spielmann, 'Allowing the Right Margin: The European Court of Human Rights and the National Margin of Appreciation Doctrine—Waiver or Subsidiarity of European Review?' (13 December 2013), www.echr.coe.int/Documents/Speech_20140113_Heidelberg_ENG.pdf, and 'Whither the Margin of Appreciation?' (20 March 2014), www.echr.coe.int/Documents/Speech_20140320_London_ENG.pdf.

[158] In which connection, see *Von Hannover v Germany (No 2)* (2012) 55 EHRR 15 (GC).

[159] *Animal Defenders International v UK* (2013) 57 EHRR 21 (GC), para 107.

[160] *Shindler v UK* (2014) 58 EHRR 5.

[161] *National Union of Rail, Maritime and Transport Workers v UK* (2015) 60 EHRR 10.

[162] Joint Committee of Human Rights (n 157) para 3.15. See also A Donald, 'The Implementation of ECtHR Judgments against the UK: Unravelling the Paradox' (ch 8), this volume.

[163] Lord Judge (n 142) para 48; see also Lord Judge, 'The View From London', *Counsel* magazine (October 2014), www.counselmagazine.co.uk/articles/view-london.

[164] Laws LJ (Court of Appeal judge) (n 142).

[165] Lord Sumption (n 142) (and, before this, 'Judicial and Political Decision Making: The Uncertain Boundary' (9 November 2011), www.legalweek.com/digital_assets/3704/MANNLECTURE_final.pdf).

[166] Laws (n 38) 82.

the UK courts on Convention interpretations that have caused real difficulty ... but those of Strasbourg'.[167] He complained that '[o]ne of the aims of the HRA was to ensure that the [UK] was able to enjoy a much greater margin of appreciation from Strasbourg than pre-incorporation because our courts would now themselves be adjudicating on issues before they went to Europe'.[168] In fact, there is good evidence that this *has* occurred—and Straw himself conceded as much ('To some extent, this aim has been met')[169]—whilst the 'age of subsidiarity' to which the JCHR refers is precisely in keeping with this.

In summary, even if there may have been doubts in the past, the Court's recent jurisprudence evidences that it is very alert to being accused of not respecting its subsidiary position,[170] and very anxious to be seen to respect the democratic legitimacy of national authorities. This deference point may offer no guarantees, but it is of great relevance to the validity of concerns about Strasbourg's purported illegitimate domination of UK law when issues of national interest are at stake.

This brings us to *Hirst*[171] and the prisoner voting issue. When delivered 10 years ago, the judgment did not seem to attract much controversy. The ECtHR's case law does not require the enfranchisement of all convicted prisoners, and there is good reason to suggest that the ECtHR has become more lenient on this issue in response to UK pressure. Moreover, the parliamentary committee tasked with examining the case for reform, in the light of the ECtHR's rulings, supports an amendment to the existing law.[172] However, since the enforcement of *Hirst* became an issue from late 2010 onwards, for many MPs the case has become emblematic of the current strained relationship. Many regard it as exemplifying how, even after the passage of the HRA, the ECtHR continues to aggrandise its jurisdiction (by inappropriately reading a right to vote into Article 3 Protocol 1, they argue), and defies Parliament's express view on a matter that MPs do not see as raising a fundamental human rights issue. The saga has demonstrated that MPs can express Parliament's undoubted sovereign right *not* to amend British law in the light of a relevant ECtHR judgment, but that doing so could come at a significant political price—the reputational cost suffered by the UK if it is seen to defy the Court.[173] *Hirst* therefore cuts very deep, for it demonstrates the enduring relevance of the issues identified 30 years ago by Shaw, namely the pressure that Convention membership can place on the 'Westminster model' and parliamentary sovereignty, and the potential for the Convention to act like a European bill of rights, occasionally overriding the will of British MPs. It would seem that it is this 'constitutional' question that generates much of the controversy associated with *Hirst*. If so, then it is important that that question is viewed in the broader context noted above, and as pointed out by the JCHR, which suggests that the loss of sovereignty—parliamentary and national—occurring via Convention membership is far more apparent than real.

---

[167] Straw (n 19) 30.
[168] ibid, 44.
[169] ibid. See also the report of the lecture delivered by Straw in May 2015, Straw (n 101) above.
[170] *cf* n 157 above (Spano).
[171] See n 3.
[172] On these points, see Bates (n 2).
[173] ibid, 24.

VI. CONCLUSIONS

The depth and extent of the anti-Strasbourg agenda as it has evolved recently in the UK does seem peculiar to that country.[174] Why? Perhaps some insight into the answer emerges from our long view of UK-Strasbourg relations, and what it reveals about how the Convention has been viewed in the UK compared to other countries.

Lord Neuberger,[175] for example, has pointed to Germany, noting that its written Constitution (dating back to the immediate post-war period) 'generally grants parallel or even greater rights to citizens that they are accorded by the Convention'. Therefore, he suggests, unlike in the UK:

> (i) Germans are used to their courts challenging statutes and (ii) judgments of German courts, involving issues on which UK courts' decisions would be based on the Convention, are based on constitutional rights and either involve no consideration of the Convention or include a throw away paragraph,[176] sometimes a cross-check, on the Convention.

Lord Neuberger opines that 'the Convention [therefore] seems far more revolutionary in the UK than in other European countries', where there is also far less likelihood of the 'public suspicion of judicial aggrandisement ... [and] particularly in the light of their history which gives rise to rather less confidence in the democratic process than that of the UK'.[177]

By contrast, and as we have seen (Sections II and III), unease with the Convention in the UK dates at least as far back as the 1970s, when its 'revolutionary' (Lord Neuberger) influence started to be felt, with Terence Shaw suggesting in 1985 that the pressure Strasbourg was placing on the Westminster model would soon require a 'fundamental reassessment' of UK-Strasbourg relations. But this did not occur in the 1980s or 1990s (Section III); rather at the end of the 1990s *the Convention* itself was taken as the inspiration for the UK's new human rights regime, under the banner of rights being 'brought home'. Then, over the first decade or so of the HRA's life, the Convention (and the Court's jurisprudence, in particular) tended to be treated as the focal point for domestic human rights protection, the perception of its 'revolutionary' influence being magnified accordingly. It seems that this helped fuel the old supremacy and sovereignty anxieties Shaw had identified, to a point when, from 2010 onwards, the pressure for the predicted 'fundamental reassessment' reached a head.

---

[174] See, generally, J Gerrards and J Fleuren (eds), *Implementation of the ECHR and of the Judgments of the ECtHR in National Case-Law* (Antwerp, Intersentia, 2013) ch 9.

[175] See Neuberger (n 37) para 17. See also Lord Reed referring to the 'striking contrast between the approach taken to human rights law in France and Germany and the approach often taken in this country': Lord Reed, 'The Common Law and the ECHR' (11 November 2013), www.innertemple.org.uk/downloads/members/lectures_2013/lecture_reed_2013.pdf.

[176] *cf* observations that UK cases have been dominated by citation of, and reliance upon, Strasbourg jurisprudence: Lord Reed, ibid.

[177] In this connection see the concluding comments of Rackow (ch 19), this volume, also commenting on the generally harmonious relationship between the ECtHR and the German Bundesverfassungsgericht. See also comments made in *A UK Bill of Rights: The Choice Before Us* (n 82) para 36 (suggesting that populations are 'less antagonistic' towards the Convention in countries where human rights cases are usually decided by reference to domestic law human rights guarantees).

To sum up, for a country already highly suspicious of European influences on domestic law, and jealous of its national and parliamentary sovereignty, a European treaty, rather than domestic law, increasingly came to be seen as *the* primary reference point for judicial, 'constitutional' protection of human rights. As Lord Lester has put it: the 'weakness' of the HRA is that it depends upon the Convention 'to define our rights and freedoms', rather than 'asking whether our constitutional rights have been infringed'. That is 'not the way it works in the rest of Europe and the common law world where written constitutions protect the universal civil and political rights anchored in international treaties'.[178]

Lord Lester's point and those made by Lord Neuberger may go to the suggestion that reliance on Convention rights and Convention jurisprudence in the context of the HRA may have increased the desire (for some) for a backlash against Strasbourg, even though, had a UK/British Bill of Rights been established in 1998, it would probably have led to very similar jurisprudence to that under the HRA in the vast majority of instances. And at the time of writing change, and a backlash, certainly seems a real possibility, although no details have been provided by the new Conservative government of the form that a new, proposed UK/British Bill of Rights might take. It is clear, however, that one of the key drivers for the introduction of such a Bill is to reduce Strasbourg's influence on UK law. As noted, the Conservative manifesto says that the Bill will 'break the formal link between British courts and the European Court of Human Rights, and make our own Supreme Court the ultimate arbiter of human rights matters in the UK'.[179]

It remains to be seen what this means. But is the radical change that is suggested by this statement really required? And what dangers may lie ahead on the path to a UK/British Bill of Rights?

On the first question, looking back some might have criticised the HRA over its first ten years on the basis that not just Convention rights but *the ECHR jurisprudence* itself became too much part of domestic law. But we have noted (Section V) that over the last five years in particular there has been the start of what may be viewed as a new phase in the HRA's life. There has been a reappraisal whereby the domestic judiciary have become more circumspect about the ECtHR, and far more willing to question its case law in the context of the domestic protection of human rights. Also, that (domestic) case law[180] has started to place a renewed emphasis on and confidence in a home-grown dimension of rights protection, with the role of the common law at its forefront, not 'Convention rights', the narrative being that the latter supports 'the continuing development' of the former, without 'supplanting' it.[181] This may amount to some recognition of Lord Lester's comments, viz the

---

[178] Lord Lester, 'A Personal Explanatory Note' (n 88) 233.
[179] *The Conservative Party Manifesto 2015* at 60.
[180] See, inter alia, *Osborn v Parole Board* [2013] UKSC 61 and *Kennedy v Information Commissioner* [2014] UKSC 20; for commentary see Clayton (n 39); Lord Toulsen (n 130); Lord Reed (n 175); Lady Hale, 'UK Constitutionalism on the March?' (12 July 2014), www.supremecourt.uk/docs/speech-140712.pdf; Dickson, this volume.
[181] Lord Reed (n 175) 16.

weakness of the HRA, and an attempt to learn lessons from the continent, as implied by Lord Neuberger's comments above, regarding Germany. It could signal the transition to a new approach under the HRA, a British model whereby human rights protection is seen as a more autonomous issue for the UK, but one which still respects Strasbourg's position, which is residual, based on subsidiarity. If so, should this emerging model not be allowed to flourish?

For the reasons just stated, it would seem that, as regards the role of the domestic courts, a fundamental reassessment of UK-Strasbourg relations hardly seems necessary. And as for Strasbourg, it is submitted that concerns over its external review role should also be allayed in the light of the approaches noted in Section V, as it progresses into what has been termed a 'new age of subsidiarity'.

Yet the fear must be that the subtleties of the situation as it has evolved over the last five years will be totally ignored by politicians intent on showing that they are putting Strasbourg in its place (as they see it) via a UK/British Bill of Rights that is *seen* to deliver on an unnecessary manifesto promise of breaking the link with Strasbourg and restoring supremacy to UK courts. The concern is that there will be a damaging anti-Strasbourg response which is out of all proportion to the sovereignty and supremacy issues that are said to be in issue. This is especially so if the Conservative Party agenda remains, in the final analysis, to withdraw from the Convention if the Council of Europe does not accept that the ECtHR's judgments become merely advisory for the UK. It is almost certain that the Council of Europe would find such a proposal to be totally unacceptable.

We shall have to wait to see what unfolds. However, reflecting on the long view of UK-Strasbourg relations, as this chapter has sought to, and looking ahead, there may be an enduring issue underlying the future of the regime for human rights protection in the UK, whether that is under the HRA or a future UK/British Bill of Rights. Could it prove to be the case that the strains that have existed in UK-Strasbourg relations reflect not only British attitudes toward Europe and the role of a Court regarded as 'foreign', but also a traditional British view as to what the constitutionally appropriate role for the courts should be when it comes to resolving certain human rights issues? Some senior UK judges, for example, have argued that Strasbourg law risks challenging the democratic process, arguing for an approach that is more reliant on the common law, and so more suited, they say, to the 'British' way.[182] This view may not be widely shared, and the points made above about the ECtHR in a new 'age of subsidiarity' offer a response to it. Then again, and looking ahead, for steadfast adherents to political constitutionalism and a Westminster model that envisages Parliament as always having the 'last

---

[182] Lord Hoffmann (n 18); Lord Reed (n 175) 9; Lord Sumption (n 142) and (n 165) (also his judgment in *Chester* (n 141) para 137); Lord Judge (n 142) para 48; and see especially Laws LJ (n 38) 82–83 ('By our Constitution, there is an important difference between the protection of fundamental values and the formulation of State policy: broadly the former is the business of the courts and the latter the business of elected government. The greatest challenge of our human rights law [as influenced by Strasbourg] is that it appears to merge these two ideas'). It is important to note that these were the opinions of the speakers, some of whom appeared to be opposed to the influence of the Convention. For other judicial lectures delivered on this, see Bates (n 14) above.

word', it seems inevitable that there will be more occasions when membership of the Convention proves controversial for the UK, even if Strasbourg's influence is diminished in the context of the domestic regime of human rights protection. It is submitted that the responsible approach to any reform of the UK's domestic human rights arrangements must be to reduce the potential for such conflict. In this regard the new equilibrium existing between the UK courts and Strasbourg in recent years (Section V) is something that any future UK/British Bill of Rights must facilitate. It must continue to allow UK judges to take Strasbourg case law into account, for only then can Strasbourg continue to fulfil its essentially subsidiary role.

5

Reforming the European Court of Human Rights: The Impacts of Protocols 15 and 16 to the ECHR

NOREEN O'MEARA[*]

I. INTRODUCTION

REFORMS OF THE European Convention on Human Rights (ECHR) and to the European Court of Human Rights (ECtHR) are imprinted upon their respective histories. In recent years, the trend of steady, incremental reforms has given way to a near-constant cycle of reflections and reform initiatives, driven by the agendas of the High Level meetings at Interlaken (2010), Izmir (2011) and Brighton (2012). Whereas the reform agenda leading up to Brighton concentrated primarily on immediate adjudicatory challenges facing the ECtHR, it is already shifting to a focus on proposals to secure the ECtHR's longer-term future.[1]

That reform has become a constant reality for the Court is due in no small part to its own success. As is well known, the expansion of the Convention's geographical reach in recent decades inevitably had a significant impact on the Court's docket. In this context, the challenge of balancing the Court's mission to protect fundamental rights, with its keystone principle of the right to individual petition, whilst at the same time delivering justice in a timely manner, appeared to be becoming an overwhelming burden. In parallel with the Court's rising docket, increased uneasiness at the Court's approaches to the principles of subsidiarity and margin of appreciation among certain Contracting Parties fuelled political tensions, which, in the UK, have been further amplified by the press. It was against this thematic background of backlog and backlash that reforms were agreed at the Brighton Conference, held in April 2012. Key drivers for the reform agenda at the Brighton Conference included

[*] I would like to thank Loveday Hodson, Elizabeth Wicks and Katja Ziegler for inviting me to present at the MLR Workshop which led to this collection, and for their editorial comments on this contribution. I would also like to thank David Thór Bjørgvinsson for fruitful discussions and for sharing his comments on a draft version of this paper. Any errors are my sole responsibility. I completed this work whilst on research leave as a Visiting Fellow at iCourts (Danish National Research Foundation's Center of Excellence on International Courts), Faculty of Law, University of Copenhagen, and I gratefully acknowledge the funding and support provided.

[1] See eg *Proceedings, Conference on the Long-Term Future of the European Court of Human Rights*, Oslo, 7–8 April 2014 (Council of Europe, 2014).

the then urgent need to tackle the Court's unsustainable backlog, the desirability of enhancing the quality of the Court's work, and the need to enhance the consistency of its case law.[2] These issues were intertwined with a fundamental concern underpinning the work of the Court—how should the ECtHR address allegations that it lacks sufficient legitimacy, and enhance its relationships with the courts of Contracting Parties?

This chapter traces recent developments in the reform agenda of the ECtHR which sought to address these issues, focusing on the impacts of specific reforms agreed during the Brighton process, to be implemented via Protocols 15 and 16 to the ECHR.[3] Section II of this chapter examines the adoption of the Brighton Declaration, in the light of the intensifying backlash against the Convention system. Sections III and IV examine the impacts of Protocols 15 and 16 to the ECHR, which have resulted from the Brighton reform process, and which are currently open for signature. Analysis of these developments illustrates that the Court itself has been demonstrably willing to engage in the contested public and political arenas, and has proven receptive to political signals for reform, even prior to Protocols 15 and 16 entering into force. In section V, the chapter concludes with reflections on the success of these reform initiatives and on future reform directions.

It is ironic that the reform proposals discussed in this chapter were agreed as a particularly strong anti-Convention narrative emerged in the UK, with Conservative policies favouring a repeal of the Human Rights Act 1998 and showing apparent ambivalence to the UK's future as a Contracting Party to the Convention.[4] These domestic political developments also point to a stark disconnect between the objectives of the Council of Europe/ECtHR in driving the reform process (to reduce the Court's voluminous backlog, and to place it on a more sustainable footing) and the UK's objectives during its Chairmanship of the Council of Europe (driven by rhetoric seeking to prevent the ECtHR from functioning as a 'court of fourth instance').[5] Whilst the hostile political leverage exercised at Brighton succeeded in getting agreement on the amendment to the Convention Preamble,[6] a step which arguably sought

---

[2] Judge Spano, 'The European Court of Human Rights: Anti-Democratic or Guardian of Fundamental Values?' speech delivered at Chatham House, 13 October 2014, 4, www.chathamhouse.org/sites/files/chathamhouse/field/field_document/20141013EuropeanCourtHumanRightsJudgeSpano.pdf.

[3] Analysis of specific post-Brighton reforms considered by Steering Committee for Human Rights (CDDH) Drafting Groups C, D, E and G on the Reform of the Court does not form part of this chapter. These proposals concern(ed): interim measures (Rule 39) and proposals on a 'representative application procedure' (GT-GDR-C); best practice in relation to domestic remedies, state obligations in respect of the ECHR and the resolution of high volumes of applications arising from systemic issues (GT-GDR-D); the election of judges (GT-GDR-E); the Rules of Court, and the possible 'upgrading' to the Convention of certain provisions of the Rules of Court (GT-GDR-G). Relevant working documents and reports are accessible online at www.coe.int/t/dghl/standardsetting/cddh/reformechr.

[4] Conservative Party, *Protecting Human Rights in the UK: The Conservatives' Proposals for Changing Britain's Human Rights Laws* (3 October 2014), www.conservatives.com/~/media/Files/Downloadable%20Files/HUMAN_RIGHTS.pdf, 5–6. For a trenchant critique, note in particular D Grieve, 'Why Human Rights Should Matter to Conservatives', lecture delivered at UCL, 3 December 2014, www.ucl.ac.uk/constitution-unit/research/judicial-independence/cu_jip_dominic_grieve_speech_3_dec.pdf.

[5] D Cameron, 'The European Court of Human Rights', speech delivered at the Parliamentary Assembly of the Council of Europe, 25 January 2012, assembly.coe.int/nw/xml/News/News-View-en.asp?newsid=3800&lang=2.

[6] On the reform provided by Article 1, Protocol 15, which will incorporate the principles of subsidiarity and margin of appreciation in the Preamble to the Convention, see Section III E, below.

to shrink the ECtHR's role, the UK Government has been misguided in crediting the reforms agreed at Brighton as being exclusively responsible for '[r]efocusing the role of the Court' in a way which enables it to deal with a lower number of serious violations in a swifter way.[7] It is argued that the impacts of Protocols 15 and 16 will be more varied and more modest than the rhetoric of the UK Government suggests. The changes that will be introduced by Protocols 15 and 16, however, will soon be built upon further as the Council of Europe continues its reform agenda to secure the longer-term future of the Convention system and of the ECtHR.

II. THE BRIGHTON DECLARATION: NEGOTIATING REFORM IN A TENSE CLIMATE

Whilst the issue of reform of the ECtHR has recently become a prominent and ongoing project, reform has been a hallmark of the Convention system since its earliest days. Shortly after the Convention opened for signature in November 1950, work began on the drafting of its first Protocol to protect additional specific rights (to education, free elections and protecting property). Since then, successive reforms have focused on integrating additional substantive human rights protections, facilitating structural changes to the architecture and operation of the Convention system, and providing for procedural adjustments.

Various factors have highlighted the need for reform of the ECtHR over the past six decades. The dramatic expansion of the Convention system's geographical reach has been a primary factor. With 19 new Contracting Parties ratifying the Convention during the 1990s, membership of the Convention system rose from 22 to 41 in a short period of time. This rise in membership (which now stands at 47 Contracting Parties) held great promise for the future embeddedness of Convention norms in national legal orders across Europe, but also inevitably led to a considerable rise in the Court's substantive caseload.[8] With the advent of the 'new' Court following the entry into force of Protocol 11 to the ECHR in 1998, it immediately became clear that the Court's rising caseload would place a serious strain on its ability to handle applications in a timely manner.[9]

The urgent need to equip the ECtHR to keep pace with the rise in applications from Contracting Parties was addressed through various avenues. These ranged from the advisory roles of the so-called Wise Persons' Report[10] and Woolf

[7] S Hughes (Minister of State for Justice and Civil Liberties), Written Ministerial Statement, 'Protocols 15 and 16 to the Convention on the Protection of Human Rights and Fundamental Freedoms', Ministry of Justice, 28 October 2014, 1, www.parliament.uk/documents/commons-vote-office/2014-october/28th%20october/5.justice-protocols.pdf.

[8] The Russian Federation (16.8%), Ukraine (13.3%), Serbia (11.3%) and Romania (11.0%), which ratified the Convention between 1994 and 2004, generate the highest number of applications to the ECtHR: *The European Court of Human Rights in Facts and Figures 2013* (Council of Europe, 2013) 3.

[9] E Myjer, 'Why Much of the Criticism of the European Court of Human Rights is Unfounded' in S Flogaitis, T Zwart and J Fraser (eds), *The European Court of Human Rights and its Discontents: Turning Criticism into Strength* (Cheltenham, Edward Elgar, 2013) 42.

[10] Undertaken pursuant to the Warsaw Declaration (CM(2005)79 final) on the invitation of the Committee of Ministers. See *Report of the Group of Wise Persons to the Committee of Ministers* (CM(2006)203), 15 November 2006.

Review[11] to the High Level Conferences at Interlaken (2010), Izmir (2011) and Brighton (2012), convened in an effort to agree practical steps to secure the future of the ECtHR.[12] Aside from these inter-governmental initiatives, the ECtHR itself also made concerted efforts to inject greater efficiency into its proceedings, in ways that could be accommodated by its own Rules of Court. The 'priority policy', for example, initiated following the amendment of Rule 41 in June 2009, aimed to accelerate the processing of high-priority cases via a sevenfold categorisation of new applications.

In an effort to counteract the impact of the Russian Federation's delayed ratification of Protocol 14 to the ECHR, Jean-Paul Costa (then ECtHR President) supported calls for remedial measures.[13] The resulting 'Madrid Agreement' and Protocol 14*bis* allowed Contracting Parties to accept two of the reforms envisaged by Protocol 14: single-judge formations and three-judge committees. None of these steps, however, ultimately succeeded in addressing the scale of the Court's rising backlog, which peaked at approximately 160,200 pending cases in September 2011.[14] The key contributing factors to this rise were not of the Court's own making: the long delay prior to the entry into force of Protocol 14 in 2010 was to some extent responsible for the continued escalation of the backlog. Its pragmatic reforms needed time to bed down. Of these delayed Protocol 14 initiatives, the role of the single judge at the admissibility stage[15] would prove to be the primary factor enabling the ECtHR to reduce its backlog so rapidly,[16] by almost 100,000 applications in little over three years. The sheer scale of the disposal of applications by single judges, however, raises unresolved questions concerning its bluntness as an efficiency tool, and of the associated power of the Court's Registry in the mission to tackle the backlog.[17] Notwithstanding this context, when the Brighton Conference took place in April 2012, as the impacts of these reforms were just beginning to be felt, it was regarded as politically imperative to agree further reforms to place the ECtHR on a more sustainable footing.

In 2012, this appetite for reform coincided with a climate of increased political tensions concerning the relationships between Contracting Parties and the ECHR

---

[11] The Woolf Review was undertaken at the invitation of the Secretary General of the Council of Europe, and of the President of the Court. See The Right Honourable The Lord Woolf et al, *Review of the Working Methods of the European Court of Human Rights* (December 2005), www.echr.coe.int/Documents/2005_Lord_Woolf_working_methods_ENG.pdf.

[12] For a comprehensive insider view of the recent history of the reform process, see D Milner, 'Protocols No 15 and 16 to the European Convention on Human Rights in the Context of the Perennial Process of Reform: A Long and Winding Road' [2014] *Zeitschrift für Europarechtliche Studien* 20.

[13] See Steering Committee for Human Rights (CDDH), 'Preliminary Opinion on Putting into Practice Certain Procedures Envisaged to Increase the Court's Case-Processing Efficiency', CDDH(2008)014 Addendum I, para 6; Explanatory Report to Protocol No 14*bis*, section I, para 3.

[14] Following the entry into force of Protocol 14 ECHR, the ECtHR's backlog peaked at 160,200 pending cases in September 2011, before gradually falling in subsequent years: 'Reform of the Court: Filtering of Cases Successful in Reducing Backlog', Council of Europe press release ECHR 312 (2013), 24 October 2013. By 31 December 2014, the docket of pending cases stood at 69,900, with 56,250 cases allocated to a judicial formation in 2014: ECtHR Annual Report 2014 (Strasbourg: Council of Europe, 2015), 165.

[15] Pursuant to Protocol 14, Art 26(1) ECHR enables single judges gained the competence to strike out applications and declare applications inadmissible.

[16] DT Bjørgvinsson, 'The Role of Judges of the ECtHR as Guardians of Fundamental Rights of the Individual' (2015) iCourts Working Paper Series No 23 2015, 16–17.

[17] For a critical analysis of the role of the Registry, see: A Tickell, 'More "efficient" justice at the European Court of Human Rights: but at whose expense?' [2015] *Public Law* 206. See further, Bjørgvinsson, ibid, 17–18.

system.[18] In the UK context in particular, these have contributed to the apparent strain on the relationship between the UK and Convention system in a manner that has been remarkably sustained. In the immediate lead-up to the Brighton Conference, during the early months of 2012, criticism of the ECtHR and of the Convention system in general was being directed from the heart of the government.[19] Galvanised by political dismay at ECtHR judgments in the *Hirst* (prisoner voting)[20] and *Othman* (extradition) litigation,[21] it is unsurprising that the increasingly mainstream anti-Convention rhetoric meant that the Brighton Conference attracted considerable press attention.

Leaked draft versions of the Brighton Declaration[22] included a number of highly restrictive reform provisions,[23] which caused concern.[24] However, the fragmented nature of information that appeared in the public domain, and the acknowledgement that such material was a draft for the purposes of advancing negotiations, make public discussion of the negotiation process challenging.[25] Yet, it is striking that the ECtHR was highly engaged in the political and wider public domain in the lead-up to the Brighton Conference. Whilst proposals to extend the ECtHR's advisory jurisdiction had been mooted on several occasions, pre-Brighton drafts indicated that the idea had finally gained traction as concrete future reform. The ECtHR indirectly contributed to the pre-Brighton negotiations via its Reflection Paper on Advisory Jurisdiction, published in early March 2012.[26] The timing of the Reflection Paper provided an opportunity to present a (not necessarily consensus) view[27] on the draft proposals, highlighting how workable certain features of the reform would be in practice. This institutional engagement thus served to inform

---

[18] See Myjer (n 9) 41.

[19] See eg Cameron (n 5).

[20] *Hirst v UK (No 2)* (2006) 42 EHRR 41 (GC); see, further, *Greens and M T v UK* (2011) 53 EHRR 21.

[21] *Othman (Abu Qatada) v UK* (2012) 55 EHRR 1.

[22] Draft Brighton Declaration (23 February 2012), www.theguardian.com/law/interactive/2012/feb/28/echr-reform-uk-draft?fb=native; Draft Brighton Declaration (12 April 2012), s3.documentcloud.org/documents/336711/revised-draft-brighton-declaration.pdf.

[23] For example, draft provisions in the draft Brighton Declaration (23 February 2012), ibid, indicate that a reduction in the time limit to apply to the ECtHR to either two, three or four months was being considered (para 23a). A reduction to four months was agreed in the final version of the Brighton Declaration and will be introduced by Protocol 15 ECHR. Further, the 23 February 2012 version proposed an amendment to Art 35 ECHR barring applications unless 'the national court clearly erred in its interpretation or application' of Convention rights (para 23(c)(i)). This provision was dropped during the drafting process.

[24] Contemporaneous critical reaction to draft versions of the Brighton Declaration included E Bates, 'Who Should Have the Final Word on Human Rights?' UK Human Rights Blog (6 March 2012), ukhumanrightsblog.com/2012/03/06/who-should-have-the-final-word-on-human-rights-dr-ed-bates; N O'Meara, 'Reforming or Redefining the European Court of Human Rights?' UK Human Rights Blog (8 March 2012), ukhumanrightsblog.com/2012/03/08/reforming-or-redefining-the-european-court-of-human-rights-noreen-omeara; M Elliott, 'Law, Politics and the Brighton Declaration' UK Human Rights Blog (9 March 2012), ukhumanrightsblog.com/2012/03/09/law-politics-and-the-draft-brighton-declaration-dr-mark-elliot.

[25] Milner (n 12) 31.

[26] See *Preliminary Opinion in Preparation for the Brighton Conference* (20 February 2012), www.coe.int/t/dgi/brighton-conference/Documents/Court-Preliminary-opinion_en.pdf; *Reflection Paper on the Proposal to Extend the Court's Advisory Jurisdiction* (9 March 2012), www.coe.int/t/dgi/brighton-conference/documents/Court-Advisory-opinions_en.pdf.

[27] *Reflection Paper*, ibid.

and influence the negotiators. At an individual level, ECtHR judges also proved ready to step directly into the political and media arenas, pre-Brighton. Sir Nicolas Bratza's acceptance of an invitation to give evidence before the UK Parliament's Joint Committee of Human Rights (JCHR),[28] the first ECtHR judge to do so, and his (limited) media engagement prior to the Brighton Conference,[29] offered highly public opportunities to defend the Court's role and to explain the challenges facing it. Such engagement may not have defused existing political tensions, but it clearly demonstrated the seriousness with which the Court took the criticism facing it and its readiness to engage with solutions.

The resulting Declaration[30] affirmed Contracting Parties' 'deep and abiding commitment' to the Convention,[31] and their attachment to the 'cornerstone' right of individual petition to the Court.[32] Acknowledgement of the shared responsibility of the Court and Contracting Parties for effective implementation of the Convention,[33] and for ensuring the viability of the Convention system itself,[34] also featured prominently.

Focusing on two core themes, the substance of the Declaration sent clear signals from the Contracting Parties to the Court, which effectively invited the Court to refine its relationship with national legal orders, and to make further efforts to address its backlog. In relation to the first of these signals, in respect of subsidiarity and the margin of appreciation, the Brighton Declaration welcomed the Court's developing jurisprudence, whilst encouraging the Court to 'give great prominence' to and 'consistently' apply them in its case law.[35] Further, the Declaration called on the Committee of Ministers to adopt an instrument providing for the inclusion of explicit references to subsidiarity and the margin of appreciation in the Preamble to the Convention.[36] This provision is one of various reforms included in Protocol 15, discussed in greater detail in section III below. In respect of the second signal, based on Contracting Parties' concern for the ECtHR's ability to address its backlog and sustainably manage its working methods, the Brighton Declaration proposed a series of changes relating to admissibility, the relinquishment of jurisdiction to the Grand Chamber, judicial appointment and retirement ages, and the Court's advisory jurisdiction.

In sum, these reforms aimed to place the ECtHR on a more sustainable footing in terms of handling its caseload, whilst at the same time addressing perceived short-comings in respect of the Court's legitimacy. To that end, the Declaration invited the Committee of Ministers to draft the necessary instruments to give effect to its proposals. The key instruments adopted by the Committee of Ministers, Protocol 15 and (optional) Protocol 16, are discussed in the following sections of this chapter.

---

[28] Oral Evidence, Joint Committee of Human Rights, 13 March 2012 (HC 873-iii).

[29] J Rozenberg, 'Bratza Bemused by UK's Disdain for Strasbourg' *The Guardian* (31 January 2012).

[30] Brighton Declaration (Declaration adopted by the Committee of Ministers of the Council of Europe on 20 April 2012 at the High Level Conference on the Future of the European Court of Human Rights, in Brighton), wcd.coe.int/ViewDoc.jsp?id=1934031.

[31] ibid, para 1.

[32] ibid, para 2.

[33] ibid, para 3.

[34] ibid, para 4.

[35] ibid, para 12a.

[36] ibid, para 12b.

III. PROTOCOL 15: TOWARDS AN 'AGE OF SUBSIDIARITY'?[37]

Following the adoption of the Declaration, the Committee of Ministers charged the Steering Committee for Human Rights (CDDH) with overseeing the drafting process for legal instruments post-Brighton. The CDDH instructed the Drafting Committee responsible for drafting Protocol 15 to 'stay within the consensus of the Brighton Declaration, respect the balance of the existing preamble and be comprehensible to the general public'.[38] This aimed to ensure that the resulting Protocol would remain faithful to the core objectives of the Convention whilst accommodating the political agreements made during the Brighton Conference.[39] Protocol 15 was duly adopted by the Committee of Ministers on 16 May 2013 and opened for signature on 24 June 2013. Nineteen Contracting Parties have ratified Protocol 15 thus far, with a further 22 signatories.[40] In the Brighton Declaration, the Conference had called for a 'swift and successful' completion of its work.[41] Whilst Protocol 15 was adopted in little over a year post-Brighton, its ratification by all Contracting Parties and its subsequent entry into force may yet be some years away. The Parliamentary Assembly has called on legislative bodies to ensure Protocol 15's 'rapid signature and ratification'.[42]

Protocol 15 provides for the implementation of a collection of reform proposals agreed at Brighton. This section of the chapter first assesses key specific procedural reforms proposed by Protocol 15, before addressing a provision to insert a new recital on the principles of subsidiarity and margin of appreciation into the Preamble to the Convention.

A. Admissibility: Reducing the Time Limit to Apply to the ECtHR

The Protocol 15 reform most likely to curb the flow of applications reaching the ECtHR in the short term is the reduction of the time limit to make an application. As such, Article 4 of Protocol 15 provides for the alteration of Article 35(1) ECHR with the effect of reducing the time limit from six months to four months. Pursuant to Article 8(3) of Protocol 15, this reform would be effective from six months after the date on which Protocol 15 enters into force. Moreover, Article 4 of Protocol 15 will not apply to any applications in which remedies were exhausted within the meaning of Article 35(1) ECHR before the entry into force of that provision. As the Strasbourg Court has observed, these transitional arrangements provide safeguards

---

[37] R Spano, 'Universality or Diversity of Human Rights? Strasbourg in the Age of Subsidiarity' (2014) 14 *Human Rights Law Review* 487.

[38] CDDH Report, 75th Meeting, CDDH(2012)R75, para 6.i.

[39] Milner (n 12) 32.

[40] Status as of 22 July 2015. To date, seven states—Bosnia and Herzegovina, Croatia, Greece, Hungary, Latvia, Malta and Russia—have not signed Protocol 15. See Chart of Signatures and Ratifications, www.conventions.coe.int/Treaty/Commun/ChercheSig.asp?NT=213&CM=8&DF=&CL=ENG.

[41] Brighton Declaration (n 30) para 37.

[42] Opinion No 283 (2013) adopted by the Parliamentary Assembly of the Council of Europe on 26 April 2013, para 3.

in terms of legal certainty for litigants, and it will be particularly important that the public are kept informed about this reform and its impact on the procedure for applying to the Court. [43]

Whilst reaching political agreement was a smooth process, non-governmental organisations (NGOs) raised concerns regarding the shortening of the application time limit. The prospect of making it harder for the most vulnerable victims of human rights violations to access the ECtHR was deemed unacceptable, given the objective that the Brighton reforms should further strengthen, rather than dilute, the rights protection offered by the Strasbourg Court and enhance, rather than reduce, the accountability of states.[44] The limited time taken to reflect on the impact of this reform 'on applicants, on the substantive quality of applications and on the Court's effectiveness' was heavily criticised during and following the Brighton Conference.[45] As Tickell has argued, this reform, when taken in combination with updates to the Rules of Court made independently of the Protocol 15 drafting process, places a heavy additional burden on the most vulnerable (potential) applicants.[46]

However, the relative ease with which agreement was reached on this initiative was partly due to the ECtHR's own view, stated publicly, that the time was ripe to reform the deadline for applications. In the Court's Preliminary Opinion, delivered prior to the Brighton Conference, the Court noted that while a six-month time limit may have been 'entirely reasonable 50 years ago', both the impact of new technology on the litigation process and the shortening of limitation periods in Contracting Parties made it possible to justify a considerable reduction to the application time limit.[47] This first reduction in the time limit to apply to the ECtHR also appeared to be a logical next step, in light of the ongoing embeddedness of the Protocol 14 (and other) reforms aimed at targeting the Court's voluminous backlog. With hindsight, and considering the reform purely as a streamlining measure, it is questionable whether the reduced time limit was urgently needed, given the dramatic fall in the Court's backlog that had started to take effect prior to the Brighton Conference. This reform does mean, however, that when Protocol 15 enters into force, the Court's significantly reduced backlog and incoming applications will stand a greater chance of being managed efficiently and in a timely manner.

---

[43] Opinion of the Court on Draft Protocol No 15 to the European Convention on Human Rights, 6 February 2013, para 12.

[44] *Proceedings—High Level Conference on the Future of the European Court of Human Rights*, Brighton, 18–20 April 2012 (Council of Europe, 2013); Statement on behalf of NGOs—N Mole (AIRE Centre), 105–6.

[45] 'Joint Preliminary Comments on the Drafting of Protocols 15 and 16 to the European Convention for the Protection of Human Rights and Fundamental Freedoms' (Joint NGO Statement), DH-GDR(2012)008, 29 August 2012, section 2, coe.int/t/dghl/standardsetting/cddh/reformechr/DH_GDR/DH-GDR%282012%29008_Joint%20preliminary%20comments%20on%20the%20drafting%20of%20 Protocols%2015%20and%2016.pdf; Joint NGO Statement, 'Protocol 15 to the European Convention on Human Rights Must Not Result in a Weakening of Human Rights Protection', 24 June 2013, section B, opensocietyfoundations.org/publications/joint-ngo-statement-protocol-15-european-convention-human-rights-must-not-result.

[46] Tickell (n 19).

[47] *Preliminary Opinion* (n 26) para 37.

B. Admissibility: Adjusting the 'Significant Disadvantage' Test

A further key issue for NGOs during the Brighton process concerned an amendment to the 'significant disadvantage' admissibility criterion, originally introduced via Article 12 of Protocol 14 to the ECHR. Article 35(3)(b) ECHR provides that the Court may declare an individual application inadmissible where

> the applicant has not suffered a significant disadvantage, unless respect for human rights as defined in the Convention and the Protocols thereto requires an examination of the application on the merits and provided that no case may be rejected on this ground which has not been duly considered by a domestic tribunal.

When Protocol 14 was drafted, the imprecision of the text led a number of Contracting Parties to reject it initially.[48] It was clear that the ECtHR would play a decisive role in determining the impact of this reform, through its interpretation of 'significant disadvantage' in its case law.[49] By requiring a minimum level of severity in respect of the human rights violation(s) raised in applications, the introduction of this criterion aimed to free the ECtHR from the burden of arguably less meritorious applications,[50] in the interests of focusing its resources more efficiently. However, the delayed entry into force of Protocol 14 in 2010 meant that in the first two years this criterion was in place, it was applied in only 26 applications.[51] Its impact was expected to increase once Single Judges gained the power to apply it from 1 June 2012.[52] Whilst the ECtHR has taken opportunities to substantively develop the meaning of 'significant disadvantage',[53] and to discuss the role of this criterion in the light of the other admissibility criteria in the Convention,[54] the cases to which the criterion applied still represented a tiny proportion of the Court's docket.

In an effort to increase the impact of this criterion, the Brighton Declaration aimed to rectify an apparent anomaly in its construction. The existing criterion prevents the ECtHR from rejecting an application on the basis that no significant disadvantage has been suffered by an applicant where the case has not been considered by a domestic tribunal—the underlying rationales being to avoid a denial of justice to litigants and to promote the right of access to courts. The ECtHR addressed this latter safeguard for the first time on the date Protocol 14 entered into force, rejecting *Adrian Mihai Ioanescu v Romania* under Article 35(3)(b).[55] The Court's

---

[48] Namely, Austria, Belgium, Finland and Hungary: L Caflisch, 'The Reform of the European Court of Human Rights: Protocol No 14 and Beyond' (2006) 6 *Human Rights Law Review* 403, 410.

[49] Explanatory Report to Protocol 14 ECHR (CETS No 194), 13 May 2004, para 80. For a detailed analysis of relevant case law, see A Buyse, 'Significantly Insignificant? The Life in the Margins of the Admissibility Criterion in Article 35(3)(b) ECHR' in Y Haeck, B McGonigle Leyh, C Burbano Herrera and D Contreras Gurdano (eds), *The Realization of Human Rights: When Theory Meets Practice. Studies in Honour of Leo Zwaak* (Antwerp, Intersentia, 2014) 107.

[50] Explanatory Report to Protocol 14 ECHR, ibid, paras 39, 77.

[51] Research Report—*The New Admissibility Criterion under Article 35(3)(b) of the Convention: Case-Law Principles Two Years On* (Council of Europe, 2013) 10.

[52] *Preliminary Opinion* (n 26) para 10.

[53] *Adrian Mihai Ionescu v Romania* App no 36659/04, ECHR 1 June 2010.

[54] See eg *Shefer v Russia* App no 45175/04, ECHR 13 March 2012; *The New Admissibility Criterion* (n 51) 4.

[55] *Adrian Mihai Ioanescu v Romania* (n 53).

promptness in explaining its approach to the new admissibility criterion highlighted its inherently contradictory nature. Article 35(3)(b) ECHR was designed, in principle, to tighten admissibility and streamline the Court's docket, yet it included a safeguard effectively requiring it to accept applications which had not been given a judicial ruling at national level, regardless of the degree of disadvantage suffered. As such, pursuant to the Brighton Declaration, Article 5 of Protocol 15 provides for the deletion of the words 'and provided that no case may be rejected on this ground which has not been duly considered by a domestic tribunal' from Article 35(3)(b) ECHR.

This adjustment clearly serves to widen the ECtHR's scope to reject applications. However, its impact as a docket control measure is likely to be marginal at best. That the Court has only rejected applications based on this element of Article 35(3)(b) ECHR in a limited number of cases adds support to Buyse's view that its removal will be 'symbolic' rather than substantively significant.[56] The removal of the safeguard from Article 35(3)(b) ECHR, however, may well lead to outcomes—albeit in a small category of applications—which sit uneasily with the principles underpinning the rule of law, such as access to justice, which the ECtHR serves to promote.

C. Objecting to Relinquishment of Jurisdiction to the Grand Chamber

The Brighton Declaration's call to curb parties' power to object to the relinquishment of jurisdiction to the Grand Chamber was made in recognition of the Grand Chamber's key role in achieving consistency in the Court's case law.[57] The obligation to take account of parties' objections when Chambers decide to relinquish jurisdiction was introduced via Protocol 11 to the ECHR. Pursuant to Article 30 ECHR, where a case pending before a Chamber raises a 'serious question' affecting the interpretation of the Convention or its Protocols, or where the resolution of a question in proceedings before a Chamber may lead to a ruling which is inconsistent with existing jurisprudence, a Chamber 'may, at any time before it has rendered its judgment, relinquish jurisdiction in favour of the Grand Chamber, unless one of the parties to the case objects'.[58] Article 3 of Protocol 15 removes this right to object, deleting 'unless one of the parties to the case objects' from the text of Article 30 ECHR. Article 8(2) of Protocol 15 further provides that this reform shall not apply to any pending case in which a party has objected to relinquishment before the entry into force of Protocol 15. This reform will therefore effectively make decisions to relinquish jurisdiction automatic, speeding up the progress of certain cases to the Grand Chamber.

Curbing the right of a party to object to relinquishment, a reform proposed by the Court itself, was welcomed by NGOs. In its Preliminary Opinion, prior to the

---

[56] As Buyse observes, by the end of 2012, Art 35(3)(b) ECHR had been considered in some 50 cases, applied in around 30 cases and led to the rejection of 20: Buyse (n 49) 124. See, further, *The New Admissibility Criterion* (n 51).

[57] Brighton Declaration (n 30) para 25d.

[58] Art 30 ECHR.

Brighton Conference, the ECtHR was mindful of the need to preserve consistency in its jurisprudence when it favoured giving compulsory effect to the possibility of relinquishment where a Chamber envisages departing from settled case law.[59] The Court later shared NGOs' view suggesting that removing this procedural step would be beneficial in terms of expediting some of the most serious applications to the Grand Chamber.[60] Prior to the entry into force of Protocol 15, the Court has already tightened Rule 72 of the Rules of Court: whereas Chambers retain discretion to relinquish where a serious question on the interpretation of the Convention or its Protocols arises (unless a party objects),[61] Chambers are now required to relinquish where there is a possibility of departing from the Court's settled case law.[62] In both situations, prior to the entry into force of Protocol 15, parties retain the right to object to relinquishment. The current President of the ECtHR, Dean Spielmann, has emphasised that this full and exclusive rule-making power is entrusted to the Plenary Court with good reason: the power has enabled the Court to flexibly adapt its internal rules to inject efficiency into procedures.[63] This flexibility is particularly useful given the time delays associated with waiting for protocols to enter into force.

This reform is a welcome streamlining measure. In an effort to accelerate its proposed impact, the Brighton Declaration encourages Contracting Parties to refrain from raising objections to any proposal to relinquish jurisdiction, pending the entry into force of Protocol 15.[64] Both the ECtHR's steps taken to tighten Rule 72 in anticipation of the reform and the reform itself will eradicate the need for the ECtHR to consider parties' arguments on relinquishment where objections arise. The reform should serve to steer the most significant, sensitive cases directly to the Grand Chamber, avoiding extended proceedings which may have involved an appeal from the Chamber to Grand Chamber in the absence of relinquishment. This reform, however, will place an additional burden on the docket of the Grand Chamber, which tends to deliver no more than two dozen judgments each year. It may limit the extensiveness of judicial discussion in highly charged, sensitive cases, which would often otherwise involve an appeal from a Chamber judgment regardless of the outcome. In such cases, the benefit of an initial Chamber judgment can render a subsequent Grand Chamber judgment more robust—whether or not an earlier Chamber judgment is overturned.

D. Judicial Appointment and Retirement

In a reform which should reduce the turnover of judges at the ECtHR, Article 2(1) of Protocol 15 provides for an amendment to Article 23(2) ECHR, stipulating that

[59] Preliminary Opinion (n 26) paras 16, 38.
[60] ECtHR Opinion on Draft Protocol 15 (n 43) para 7; Joint NGO Statement (29 August 2012) (n 45) section A3; Joint NGO Statement (24 June 2013) (n 45) section D.
[61] Rules of Court (July 2014), Rule 72(1).
[62] ibid, Rule 72(2).
[63] D Spielmann, 'The European Court of Human Rights: Master of the Law but Not of the Facts?', speech delivered at the British Institute of International and Comparative Law, 6 November 2014, 3, echr.coe.int/Documents/Speech_20141106_Spielmann_BIICL.pdf.
[64] Brighton Declaration (n 30) para 25d.

'Candidates shall be less than 65 years of age at the date by which the list of three candidates has been requested by the Parliamentary Assembly'. This amendment will apply to lists submitted to the Parliamentary Assembly after the entry into force of Protocol 15.[65] As judges of the ECtHR are elected to a non-renewable nine-year term,[66] this uncontroversial reform effectively raises the maximum retirement age from 70 to 74 years.

The profile of judges at the ECtHR is notable for its broad range of age and experience, five of the current members having been appointed in their 30s.[67] This modest rise may—if Protocol 15 enters into force relatively soon—enable existing ECtHR judges who are close to the current retirement age to remain at the Court longer. It may also attract future judicial candidates from more senior levels in their home judiciaries, who may be close to reaching lower compulsory retirement ages at national levels. There is a high degree of variability of judicial retirement ages among Contracting Parties and in international courts,[68] with the trend of rising retirement ages sometimes controversially bucked.[69] In the UK, the statutory retirement age varies depending on one's date of judicial appointment.[70] At the highest levels in particular, this can increase the turnover of judicial talent. This reform to raise the ECtHR retirement age may therefore provide food for thought in any Contracting Parties reviewing statutory retirement ages for national judges.

E. Reinforcing the Principles of Subsidiarity and Margin of Appreciation

The emphasis placed on the principles of subsidiarity and margin of appreciation in the Brighton Declaration was unsurprising in light of the tense domestic political attitude towards the Court at the time of the Brighton Conference. With an incumbent government then engaged in long-running litigation aiming to extradite

---

[65] Protocol 15 to the ECHR, Art 8(1).

[66] ECHR, Art 23(1).

[67] On allegations that there is a link between the youthfulness of appointees and the quality of judges, note Bjørgvinsson (n 16) 10. For an alternative view, note MR Madsen, 'The legitimization Strategies of International Judges: The Case of the European Court of Human Rights' (2015) iCourts Working Paper Series No 12 2004, 24–25.

[68] National retirement ages across Contracting Parties vary widely, whilst at the international level neither the Inter-American Court of Human Rights nor the International Court of Justice currently has compulsory judicial retirement ages.

[69] With the entry into force of a new Hungarian Constitution on 1 January 2012, Art 26, Basic Law and Act 162 of 2011 reduced the judicial retirement age (70 years) to match the general state retirement age (62 years), with a view to raising the retirement age in future. The sudden move generated serious concerns that it might undermine judicial independence and the rule of law. The Hungarian authorities later legislated for a reduction to 65 years, phased for a transitional period of 10 years. On the background, see further T Gyulavári and N Hős, 'Retirement of Hungarian Judges, Age Discrimination and Judicial Independence: A Tale of Two Courts' (2013) 42 *Industrial Law Journal* 289.

[70] The standard statutory retirement age is 70 for judges first appointed to judicial office after 31 March 1995 (subject to provisions which may authorise a judge to continue in office for one year at a time, up to the age of 75, if it is in the public interest to do so): see, Judicial Pensions and Retirement Act 1993, ss 25 and 26. Judges first appointed before 31 March 1995 may sit until the age of 75.

the suspected terrorist Abu Qatada, and clearly averse to implementing *Hirst No 2*,[71] the UK's Chairmanship of the Council of Europe came at a time when the UK was motivated to transform its relationship with the ECHR system. High-level speeches made by the Prime Minister and Attorney-General reinforced the view—which was not exclusive to the UK—that reform must have the desirable effect of reinforcing the principle of subsidiarity and 're-balancing' the relationship between the ECtHR and national systems.[72] A perception remained that the ECtHR could go further in applying the margin of appreciation doctrine, a view which was shared by other Contracting Parties.[73] This perception remained strong despite Judge Spielmann's extra-judicial acknowledgement of the long-standing trend of 'judicial self-restraint' evident in ECtHR case law,[74] and his emphasis on the responsibilities contingent on both domestic authorities and the ECtHR to 'engage in a process of appreciation, or assessment, of the rights and interests at stake'.[75]

As is well known, the principles of subsidiarity and margin of appreciation lie at the heart of the Convention system, fostering not just a delineation of roles in human rights protection but also a sense of shared responsibility for guaranteeing it. As such, the ECtHR has developed these doctrines over the past four decades, notably in the early touchstone *Belgian Linguistic*[76] and *Handyside*[77] cases. Recent accusations that the margin of appreciation has 'shrunk'[78] provided an impetus for the Brighton Conference's proposal to reinforce the principle of subsidiarity in the Convention itself. In the UK Prime Minister's view, against the background of the *Othman* litigation which loomed (disproportionately) large as a political issue at the time,[79] the Court had become 'too ready to substitute its judgment for that of reasonable national processes' to the extent that it was acting more akin to an 'immigration tribunal' than an international court.[80] Whilst the Conference focused primarily on practical reforms to alleviate the Court's backlog, agreement was also reached on a measure aiming to reinforce the principle of subsidiarity.

[71] *Hirst (No 2)* (n 20).
[72] On the development of this narrative in other Contracting Parties, note A Donald, 'The Implementation of Judgments of the European Court of Human Rights against the UK: Unravelling the Paradox' (ch 8), this volume.
[73] Lord Phillips, 'European Human Rights: A Force for Good or a Threat to Democracy?', Centre of European Law Lecture, The Dickson Poon School of Law, King's College London, 17 June 2014, 7, kcl.ac.uk/law/newsevents/newsrecords/2013–14/assets/Lord-Phillips-European-Human-Rights--A-Force-for-Good-or-a-Theat-to-Democracy-17-June-2014.pdf. See further Myjer (n 9).
[74] D Spielmann (Judge, ECtHR), 'Allowing the Right Margin: The European Court of Human Rights and the National Margin of Appreciation Doctrine: Waiver or Subsidiarity of European Review?', Centre for European Legal Studies (CELS) Working Paper, University of Cambridge, February 2012, 23.
[75] D Spielmann (President, ECtHR), 'Allowing the Right Margin: The European Court of Human Rights and the National Margin of Appreciation Doctrine: Waiver or Subsidiarity of European Review?', speech delivered at the Max Planck Institute for Comparative Public Law and International Law, Heidelberg, 13 December 2013, 4, www.echr.coe.int/Documents/Speech_20140113_Heidelberg_ENG.pdf.
[76] *Belgian Linguistic case* (1968) 1 EHRR 252, para 10.
[77] *Handyside v UK* (1976) 1 EHRR 737.
[78] Cameron (n 5).
[79] *Othman (Abu Qatada) v UK* (n 21).
[80] A view which fails to reflect the tenor of the Izmir Declaration, to which PM Cameron was referring: Cameron (n 5).

To that end, Article 1 of Protocol 15 echoes the Brighton Declaration's requirement that references to the principles of subsidiarity and margin of appreciation are added to the Convention.[81] Article 1 of Protocol 15 provides for the insertion of a new recital at the end of the Preamble to the Convention, which will read as follows:

> Affirming that the High Contracting Parties, in accordance with the principle of subsidiarity, have the primary responsibility to secure the rights and freedoms defined in this Convention and the Protocols thereto, and that in doing so they enjoy a margin of appreciation, subject to the supervisory jurisdiction of the European Court of Human Rights established by this Convention …

The insertion of this recital will formally introduce a direct reference to the principles of subsidiarity and margin of appreciation to the Convention for the first time. The Brighton Declaration stressed that this insertion was necessary 'for reasons of transparency and accessibility', while acknowledging the development of both principles in the Court's case law.[82] When the Brighton Declaration was published, my initial view on its potential future impact was ambivalent: while the new recital could clearly serve as a further point of reference for the Court, I doubted whether this alone would prove pivotal in changing the Court's application of these principles in practice. After all, the ECtHR's long-standing development of the principles of subsidiarity and margin of appreciation as guiding principles in its own jurisprudence, in the absence of any such political reminder regarding their value, did not point to a sudden change of direction on the part of the ECtHR.[83] Sir Nicolas Bratza, President of the ECtHR at the time of the Brighton Conference, had questioned the necessity of taking this step:

> [W]e [the ECtHR] have difficulty in seeing the need for, or the wisdom of, attempting to legislate for it in the Convention, any more than for the many other tools of interpretation which have been developed by the Court in carrying out the judicial role entrusted to it.[84]

Since the Brighton Conference, however, the ECtHR has been keen to emphasise its receptiveness to the 'powerful political message'[85] conveyed by this particular Brighton reform. Both national and ECtHR judges have acknowledged that there have been times when a more refined approach to the ECtHR's application of the margin of appreciation may have been desirable. In this respect, Judge Spano of the ECtHR has suggested that criticisms of the Court's at times activist approach were 'not, in any sense, to be considered as wholly without foundation',[86] a view with which Lord Phillips, former President of the UK Supreme Court, has concurred.[87] Lord Phillips' view that on 'a growing number of occasions' the Strasbourg Court 'intervened to prefer its own views to that of courts of Member States that have not

---

[81] On the range of views expressed during the drafting process, see further Milner (n 12) 32–34.

[82] Brighton Declaration (n 30) para 12d.

[83] See further Spielmann (n 75) 8.

[84] Brighton Conference Proceedings (n 44), opening address delivered by Sir Nicolas Bratza, 19 April 2012, 74.

[85] A Patrick, 'Building on Brighton: A Foundation for the Future of the European Court of Human Rights?' (2012) 9 *Justice Journal* 32, 40.

[86] Spano (n 37) 489.

[87] Lord Phillips (n 73) 7.

erred in the principles that they have applied, but only, in the view of the Court, in the result of their application'[88] led him to call on the Strasbourg Court to 'pay regard' to the proposed new recital in the Convention's Preamble.[89]

In Judge Spano's view, the ECtHR has listened to this political signal and has been incentivised in its development of a 'qualitative, democracy-enhancing approach' to the principle of subsidiarity;[90] an approach which serves to bolster the Court's own legitimacy. As the ECtHR enters its 'age of subsidiarity'[91]—an era which demands a robust, nuanced and coherent approach to this principle—the post-Brighton cases against the UK which Judge Spano draws upon do illustrate sensitivity when assessing domestic decision-making. In *Animal Defenders International*,[92] for example, the Grand Chamber was finely split 9:8 against finding a violation of Article 10 ECHR in respect of a ban on paid political advertising in the UK under section 321(2) of the Communications Act 2003. The disagreement among the members of the Grand Chamber on the necessity of the restriction was apparent. However, the detailed exposition of the Court's approach to its consideration of the margin of appreciation provided by the majority opinion, and by Judge Bratza's Concurring Opinion, leaves one in no doubt about the broad spectrum of factors weighed by the Court in reaching its conclusions. The Court's exhaustive treatment of the margin of appreciation clearly showed its acknowledgement of the depth of prior consideration given by the UK Parliament when formulating the contested legislative provisions.

In *Shindler*, a case in which the ECtHR unanimously found no violation of Article 3 of Protocol 1 to the ECHR in respect of UK restrictions on the right of expatriates to vote in UK elections, divergent views on the margin of appreciation were laid bare.[93] Whilst the majority opinions in both *Shindler* and *Animal Defenders International* provide extensive discussions on the applicability of the margin of appreciation, Judge Kalaydjieva's Concurring Opinion in *Shindler* objected to recourse to the principle. In doing so, Judge Kalaydjieva echoed the Dissenting Opinion of Judge Rozakis in *Odièvre v France*,[94] which emphasised the 'subsidiary role' of the margin of appreciation in certain circumstances.[95] The presentation of polarised views on the margin of appreciation shows that there is often no settled view on this issue in specific cases, a factor which could undermine the ECtHR's articulation of a robust, coherent approach to the margin of appreciation doctrine. At the same time, it illustrates Judge Spano's acknowledgement that the Court is in the process of 'reformulating the substantive and procedural criteria that regulate the appropriate level of deference to be afforded to Member States so as to implement a more robust and coherent concept of subsidiarity'.[96] It is a process which involves tough judicial choices, though arguably one which could be facilitated by

---

[88] ibid.
[89] ibid.
[90] Spano (n 37) 491.
[91] ibid.
[92] *Animal Defenders International v UK* (2013) 57 EHRR 607 (GC).
[93] *Shindler v UK* (2013) 58 EHRR 148.
[94] *Odièvre v France* (2004) 38 EHRR 43 (GC).
[95] ibid, Concurring Opinion of Judge Rozakis, para 2.
[96] Spano (n 37) 498.

maximising the transparency, rigour and consistency with which the compatibility of national (draft) legislation and policy is examined by national authorities.[97] The forcefulness of both the majority and dissenting opinions in both *Animal Defenders International* and *Shindler* should—if nothing else—reinforce the view that the ECtHR is not taking its approaches to the margin of appreciation lightly.[98]

As van Zyl Smit *et al* have observed in relation to *Vinter*,[99] however, mere 'recitation' of the margin of appreciation in ECtHR judgments is not going to 'placate critics of the overall outcome' in controversial cases.[100] This was certainly the case in *Vinter*, perhaps the most controversial post-Brighton case involving the UK, in which the Grand Chamber found a violation of Article 3 ECHR in respect of the absence of a review mechanism for prisoners sentenced to whole-life terms in the UK.[101] Judge Mahoney's Concurring Opinion elaborates on the majority's reasoning in relation to relevant domestic case law in particular, and reinforces findings on the scope of the UK government's freedom in choosing how to comply with the judgment.[102] The Concurring Opinions in *Animal Defenders International*, *Shindler* and (in particular) *Vinter* have supported the ECtHR's objective of seeking a more nuanced approach to subsidiarity. While the explicitness of the Court's approach may placate neither the government nor the press, it plays a role in cultivating the kind of 'mutually respectful' dialogue[103] with national systems that both domestic courts and the Strasbourg court should strive to foster.

IV. PROTOCOL 16: THE 'PROTOCOL OF DIALOGUE'?[104]

A further reform that gained traction in the lead-up to the Brighton Conference was the proposal to reform the ECtHR's advisory jurisdiction.[105] Following a number

---

[97] On the Parliamentary Assembly's call for the enhancement of parliamentary scrutiny at national level to maximise Convention compliance of national legislation, note 'National Parliaments: Guarantors of Human Rights in EUROPE', PACE Resolution 1823 (2011), adopted 23 June 2011.

[98] On the recent approach of the Grand Chamber, note in particular *SAS v France* (2015) 60 EHRR 11 (GC), and *Fernández Martínez v Spain* (2015) 60 EHRR 3 (GC).

[99] *Vinter v UK* (2013) 55 EHRR 34 (GC).

[100] D van Zyl Smit, P Weatherby and S Creighton, 'Whole Life Sentences and the Tide of European Human Rights Jurisprudence: What Is to Be Done?' (2014) 14 *Human Rights Law Review* 59, 72.

[101] *Vinter v UK* (n 99).

[102] ibid, Concurring Opinion of Judge Mahoney, which addresses aspects of timing, reducibility and compliance in greater detail, and focuses on the UK context by reference in particular to national case law and the UK government's arguments.

[103] See further Lord Neuberger (President, UK Supreme Court), 'The Supreme Court and the Rule of Law', Conkerton Lecture 2014, Liverpool Law Society, para 19, www.supremecourt.uk/docs/speech-141009-lord-neuberger.pdf.

[104] President Spielmann has characterised Protocol 16 to the ECHR as '*le protocol du dialogue*': D Spielmann, speech delivered to the 123rd Session of the Committee of Ministers, 16 May 2013, 2, www.echr.coe.int/Documents/Speech_20130516_Spielmann_CM_FRA.pdf.

[105] While reforms to the Court's advisory jurisdiction had been mooted in recent years, notably in the Wise Persons' Report (2006) and in the Izmir Declaration (2011), discussions during the drafting process for Protocol 2 to the ECHR had considered an extended advisory opinion mechanism and preliminary ruling-style mechanism for the Convention system: A Robertson, *Human Rights in Europe*, 2nd edn (Manchester, Manchester University Press, 1977) 226–27.

of iterations in the leaked draft declarations, the final version of the Brighton Declaration called for

> the introduction into the Convention of a further power of the Court, which States Parties could optionally accept, to deliver advisory opinions upon request on the interpretation of the Convention in the context of a specific case at domestic level, without prejudice to the non-binding character of the opinions for the other States Parties.[106]

Whilst the Brighton Declaration justified this proposal on the basis that it would strengthen the relationship between the ECtHR and national authorities, this reform was also included as part of the broader range of measures aimed at reducing the ECtHR's caseload in the longer term. Following the drafting process overseen by the CDDH, Protocol 16 to the ECHR was opened for signature on 2 October 2013. To date, Protocol 16 has been ratified by San Marino, Slovenia, Georgia and Albania, and signed by 12 further Contracting Parties.[107] It will enter into force once the threshold 10 states have ratified it. President Spielmann, an enthusiastic proponent of Protocol 16, has indicated that the Court hopes the signatures will be followed by ratifications 'without too much delay'.[108]

The following section first outlines the essential features of Protocol 16, examining how it extends the scope of the ECtHR's advisory jurisdiction and the possible benefits of the Protocol. Subsequently, the section goes on to question the extent to which Protocol 16's objectives are likely to be achieved.[109]

A. Reforming Advisory Jurisdiction

The restrictiveness of the ECtHR's existing scope to deliver advisory opinions has meant that its advisory jurisdiction has had a marginal influence on the Convention system to date. The ECtHR has been empowered to deliver advisory opinions since the entry into force of Protocol 2, in 1970. Article 47(1) ECHR provides that the ECtHR may give advisory opinions on legal questions concerning the interpretation of the Convention and its Protocols. Such opinions may be requested by the Committee of Ministers,[110] and must not concern the interpretation of the content or scope of Convention rights.[111] As such, advisory opinions must avoid

[106] Brighton Declaration (n 30) para 12d.
[107] Status as of 22 July 2015. See Chart of Signatures and Ratifications, http://conventions.coe.int/Treaty/Commun/ChercheSig.asp?NT=214&CM=8&DF=18/05/2015&CL=ENG.
[108] Spielmann (n 63) 4.
[109] For extended analysis of the future role of Protocol 16 to the ECHR, see K Dzehtsiarou and N O'Meara, 'Advisory Jurisdiction and the European Court of Human Rights: A Magic Bullet for Dialogue and Docket-Control?' (2014) 34 *Legal Studies* 444. On the potential of Protocol 16 in the light of the preliminary reference procedure in EU law, note further: P Gragl, '(Judicial) Love is Not a One-Way Street: The EU Preliminary Reference Procedure as a Model for ECtHR Advisory Opinions under Draft Protocol No. 16' (2013) 38 *European Law Rev* 229; J Gerards, 'Advisory Opinions, Preliminary Rulings and the New Protocol No. 16 to the European Convention of Human Rights—A Comparative and Critical Appraisal' (2014) 21 *Maastricht Journal* 4.
[110] ECHR, Art 47(3).
[111] ibid, Art 47(2).

overlap with the ECtHR's contentious jurisdiction. Given this restrictiveness, it is unsurprising that the ECtHR has received only three requests for advisory opinions under Article 47 ECHR, and delivered just two advisory opinions on discrete procedural questions concerning the election of judges.[112]

Protocol 16 ECHR has the potential to transform the scope of the ECtHR's advisory jurisdiction. The impact of Protocol 16 ECHR will be tempered, however, both by its optional status and by the non-binding nature of advisory opinions—features agreed at Brighton and strongly supported by the ECtHR. From the perspective of requesting courts, the Protocol will allow 'highest national courts and tribunals' to request non-binding advisory opinions on 'questions of principle relating to the interpretation or application of the rights and freedoms defined in the Convention or the Protocols thereto' (Article 1(1)). Requesting courts or tribunals are required to 'give reasons' for their requests for advisory opinions, and to 'provide the relevant legal and factual background of the pending case'.[113] Notably, Protocol 16 does not oblige requesting courts to indicate their own views on how questions may be addressed by the ECtHR, though the Explanatory Memorandum encourages this practice.[114] This is arguably a missed opportunity to foster dialogue with highest courts, enabling the ECtHR to routinely and explicitly take requesting courts' views into account in this procedure.[115]

Requests for advisory opinions should arise in response to concrete cases, avoiding abstract review (Article 1(2)). There is no role for reviewing facts under Protocol 16's reformed advisory opinion procedure.[116] As President Spielmann has observed, the emphasis is squarely on interpretation and the provision of authoritative guidance, which reinforces the 'logical division of labour' between the referring court and the Strasbourg Court.[117] The highest national courts and tribunals competent to request advisory opinions under the Protocol 16 regime will be nominated by Contracting Parties, with the flexible gloss that such nominations may be changed 'at any later date' (Article 10).

From the ECtHR's perspective, the Grand Chamber will bear exclusive responsibility for deciding upon the admissibility of requests and the delivery of advisory opinions. Admissibility decisions will be delivered by a five-judge panel.[118] The final adopted version of Protocol 16 includes an obligation on the Court to provide reasons when rejecting requests for advisory opinions, an obligation which did not

---

[112] The first request was rejected by the ECtHR (*Decision on the competence of the Court to give an advisory opinion*, 2 June 2004 (GC), ECHR 2004-VI). The ECtHR's first two advisory opinions were delivered in 2008 and 2010: *Advisory Opinion on certain legal questions concerning the lists of candidates submitted with a view to the election of judges to the European Court of Human Rights (No 1)* (2009) 49 EHRR 33 (GC); *Advisory Opinion on certain legal questions concerning the lists of candidates submitted with a view to the election of judges to the European Court of Human Rights (No 2)* (2010) 50 EHRR SE10 (GC).

[113] Protocol 16, Art 1(3).

[114] Explanatory Report to Protocol 16, para 12.

[115] Dzehtsiarou and O'Meara (n 109) 464.

[116] See especially the Opinion of the Court on Draft Protocol No 16 to the Convention extending its competence to give advisory opinions on the interpretation of the Convention, 6 May 2013, para 8. See further *Reflection Paper* (n 26) para 33.

[117] Spielmann (n 63) 3.

[118] Protocol 16, Art 2.

appear in earlier draft versions.[119] This obligation is welcome: it would have been contradictory for a Protocol aimed at enhancing dialogue between courts not to require the ECtHR to provide reasons, however brief, for rejecting such requests. At the point of delivering an advisory opinion, 'any judge' is permitted to deliver a separate opinion if the advisory opinion 'does not represent, in whole or in part, the unanimous opinion of the judges'.[120] Although the Court has highlighted its past endeavours 'to speak with one voice' when delivering advisory opinions,[121] this scope for delivering separate opinions could contribute to uncertainty regarding the guidance delivered, potentially generating further litigation.

B. Achieving Docket Control and Dialogue?

As noted above, two objectives in expanding the Court's advisory role were high-lighted in the course of the Brighton process: enhancing dialogue and reducing the Court's caseload in the longer term. In view of the ECtHR's own success at tackling its backlog through the changes introduced under Protocol 14 and other efficiency measures, the docket-control objective has been undermined as a rationale for reforming the ECtHR's advisory jurisdiction via Protocol 16. Whilst Protocol 16 offers scope to reduce incoming applications in the medium- to long-term future, the extent to which this is possible will hinge on the nature of requests and the impact of advisory opinions delivered. Leaving this hypothetical issue aside, this section focuses on the dialogue-enhancing potential of Protocol 16, whilst highlighting a number of practical risks inherent in its construction which risk undermining the Court's efforts in respect of both docket control and the enhancement of dialogue with highest national courts.

Protocol 16 will enter into force once it has been ratified by 10 Contracting Parties.[122] The willingness of highest courts to exercise their right to request advisory opinions, and their choices of subject-matter, may offer genuine scope for the ECtHR to deliver substantively valuable advisory opinions and highlight perceived problems at national levels. Notwithstanding their non-binding status, advisory opinions delivered under Protocol 16 would be likely to influence judicial decision-making in Strasbourg and at national levels—enhancing the quality of national adjudication in relation to the Convention, and supporting the implemen-tation of ECtHR judgments.[123] However, despite shepherding the advisory opinions proposal through the Brighton process, the UK Government remains 'unconvinced' about the value of extending the Court's advisory jurisdiction, opting to 'observe' the impact of Protocol 16 in terms of the opinions generated, and any consequential

---

[119] Notwithstanding some apparent initial disagreement on this issue within the Court (ECtHR, Reflection Paper (n 22) para 21) and on the part of Drafting Group B on the Reform of the Court (GT-GDR-B), Protocol 16 provides that when the Court declines any request for an advisory opinion, reasons for refusal shall be provided (Art 2(1)).

[120] Protocol 16, Art 4(2).

[121] Opinion of the Court on Draft Protocol No 16 (n 116) para 11.

[122] Protocol 16, Art 8(1).

[123] Oslo Conference Proceedings (n 1), speech delivered by Judge Laffranque (ECtHR), 74.

impact on the ECtHR's caseload.[124] With other Contracting Parties likely to take a similar watch-and-wait approach, the early experiences with this procedure could inspire or dissuade Contacting Parties in their decision on ratification, and impact on nominated courts' preparedness to engage with Protocol 16.

In principle, the prospect of a new platform for dialogue which reinforces relationships with the highest national courts, and which facilitates the sound interpretation and application of Convention rights at national level, is attractive. Protocol 16's potential to support the emerging (if too often implicit) 'constructive dialogue' with national Supreme Courts appealed to the ECtHR.[125] In the UK context, in relation to the statutory duty to take 'account' of Strasbourg jurisprudence contained in section 3 of the Human Rights Act 1998, the UK Supreme Court's recent preparedness to question whether the ECtHR has taken due account of national law[126] offered scope for 'constructive' deliberative dialogue to develop between the UK Supreme Court and ECtHR. The dialogue evident between the courts in the cases of *Horncastle*[127] and *Al Khawaja*[128] provided a striking example of an open invitation from the UK Supreme Court to the ECtHR to engage in judicial dialogue[129]—an invitation that was explicitly accepted by the ECtHR.[130]

The benefits of such dialogue have been widely recognised by UK and ECtHR judges. Lord Neuberger, for example, has noted that such exchanges are ultimately 'of value to the development of the Convention law'.[131] Though acknowledging the important but limited nature of dialogue in this specific context (that of a Supreme Court opting not to adhere to Strasbourg jurisprudence in certain circumstances), Amos has suggested that this form of 'constructive dialogue' is but one of a variety of 'dialogues' that are apparent to varying degrees between the ECtHR and national (Supreme) courts.[132] In the absence of any plan for the UK to ratify Protocol 16 in the short- or mid-term future,[133] and in view of other Contracting Parties' caution towards Protocol 16 on subsidiarity grounds,[134] the continued fostering of such 'constructive' dialogue, judicially and extra-judicially, will continue to shape the UK–ECtHR relationship and the ECtHR's evolving relations with the highest courts of the other Contracting Parties.

Turning to specific risks in the construction of the Protocol 16 system, the consideration of requests and delivery of advisory opinions will add to the adjudicatory burden on the Grand Chamber. The scale of the impact is hard to predict in

---

[124] Written Ministerial Statement (n 7) 2.

[125] *Manchester City Council v Pinnock* [2010] UKSC 45, para 48; *Reflection Paper* (n 22) para 4.

[126] See *R v Horncastle* [2009] UKSC 14, [2010] 2 All ER 359; *Al-Khawaja and Tahery v UK* (2009) 49 EHRR 1.

[127] *R v Horncastle*, ibid.

[128] *Al Khawaja and Tahery v UK* (2012) 54 EHRR 23 (GC).

[129] C Murphy, 'Human Rights Law and the Challenges of Explicit Judicial Dialogue', Jean Monnet Working Paper No 10/12, 20. For further discussion see Dzehtsiarou and O'Meara (n 109) 454–55.

[130] See *Al Khawaja and Tahery v UK* (n 126) Concurring Opinion of Judge Bratza, para 2, and the Joint Partly Dissenting and Partly Concurring Opinion of Judges Sajó and Karakaş, para 1.

[131] *Pinnock* (n 125) para 48.

[132] Dzehtsiarou and O'Meara (n 109) 455.

[133] Written Ministerial Statement (n 7) 2.

[134] Oslo Conference Proceedings (n 1), speech delivered by Judge Paulus (German Federal Constitutional Court), 63.

advance, as much will depend on the enthusiasm with which highest courts engage with Protocol 16. Contracting Parties' nominations of highest courts competent to request advisory opinions will play a decisive role in shaping trends of judicial engagement with Protocol 16.[135] However, though offering clear potential to enhance the Grand Chamber's constitutionalist function,[136] any influx of requests for advisory opinions could impact on the Grand Chamber's already modest output of substantive judgments.[137] There is an associated risk that any delays to the Grand Chamber's delivery of advisory opinions could deter national courts from making requests, and as such could contribute to a chilling effect on dialogue between the ECtHR and national courts.[138]

The non-binding character of advisory opinions is a more complex factor that carries both benefits and risks associated with the reinforcement of dialogue between national courts and tribunals and the ECtHR. Noting that Protocol 16 is designed to operate 'in the context of the judicial dialogue between the Court and domestic courts and tribunals',[139] the Explanatory Report to Protocol 16 echoes the Court's own view that the nature of this dialogue means it should be for 'the requesting court to decide on the effects of the advisory opinion in the domestic proceedings'.[140] Though forming part of the Court's case law, the lack of binding status for advisory opinions frames judicial engagement with Protocol 16 as a consultative and collaborative process in which highest courts and tribunals are welcome to request advisory opinions, and are free to decide how such opinions will guide them when adjudicating on the national case. As such, complete reliance is placed on the good faith of the national court to adjudicate in accordance with the guidance provided. While it would seem unlikely that a requesting court would deliberately choose not to follow an advisory opinion, the possibility of this occurring—or of a national court misinterpreting the guidance in an advisory opinion—cannot be ruled out. The chances of this happening could partly depend on how prescriptive the ECtHR will be when delivering advisory opinions. Both possibilities would risk undermining the legitimacy of the procedure, and could lead to advisory opinions themselves generating further applications to the ECtHR.

In a situation where an advisory opinion is delivered during the course of national proceedings, and those proceedings eventually lead to an application being made to the ECtHR, the ruling delivered by the national court following its request for an advisory opinion would then come under the spotlight. As the Explanatory Memorandum to Protocol 16 states, where 'an advisory opinion has *effectively been*

---

[135] Romania's Declaration nominating 17 national courts (including 15 Courts of Appeal) took a broad approach to the 'highest courts and tribunals' criterion in Art 1, Protocol 16; Declaration contained in a Note Verbale from the Permanent Representation of Romania and handed over at the time of the signature of Protocol 16, 14 October 2014.

[136] K Dzehtsiarou and A Greene, 'Restructuring the European Court of Human Rights: Preserving the Right of Individual Petition and Promoting Constitutionalism' [2013] *Public Law* 710, 718.

[137] The Grand Chamber has delivered fewer than 30 judgments per year since 2006, and its output stands at 17.5 judgments per year on average (2007–14 inclusive).

[138] Dzehtsiarou and O'Meara (n 109) 466.

[139] Explanatory Report (n 114) para 25.

[140] Opinion of the Court on Draft Protocol No 16 (n 116) para 12. Note that the non-binding status of advisory opinions was a majority view within the Court.

followed' in the national court's ruling, aspects of a future application relating to the advisory opinion 'would be declared inadmissible or struck out.'[141] Subjecting the national court's engagement with Protocol 16 to scrutiny at the admissibility stage of any subsequent proceedings before the ECtHR would—in certain cases—put a contentious gloss on national courts' experience with an otherwise co-operative procedure.

These concerns associated with Protocol 16 therefore risk negatively impacting the Court's caseload, whilst offering the ECtHR further opportunities to clarify or reinforce its guidance in contentious case law. They constitute risks of varying likelihoods which the Grand Chamber will want to mitigate, as a priority, in its handling of requests under Protocol 16.

V. CONCLUDING REMARKS

The strength of the political signals transmitted to the ECtHR during the Brighton process, and the Court's receptivity to these signals, are equally important. Criticisms directed from political elites, amplified by the press, have resonated—at least to some extent—with public opinion.[142] This contributed to a perceived loss of legitimacy for the ECtHR, which, at the time of the Brighton Conference, was too damaging to ignore. Throughout and beyond this stage of the reform process, the ECtHR has been proactive in demonstrating how seriously these signals have been taken. Its receptivity to them has been evident in several key ways, independently of the reforms envisaged at Brighton and in anticipation of the entry into force of Protocols 15 and 16.

In respect of two issues on which the political spotlight was focused at Brighton, namely the Court's infamous backlog and its approach(es) to the principle of subsidiarity, notable progress has been made. The ECtHR's backlog was cut by almost 100,000 applications between 2011–14,[143] largely thanks to the delayed impacts of Protocol 14's initiatives, which are finally embedding in the system. While there is still significant room for further reductions to the Court's docket, this progress is already enabling the Court to respond more flexibly to the high volume of applications it continues to receive, particularly in relation to repetitive and non-priority cases. If the ECtHR has indeed embarked on what Judge Spano describes as its 'age of subsidiarity', this stage of its development should also lead to a more robust, nuanced and coherent articulation and application of the principles of subsidiarity and margin of appreciation.[144] The explicitness of recent judicial pronouncements on these principles—notably in *Animal Defenders International*[145]—points in this

---

[141] Explanatory Report (n 114), para 26 (emphasis added).
[142] T Zwart, 'More Human Rights than Court: Why the Legitimacy of the European Court of Human Rights is in Need of Repair and How it Can be Done' in Flogaitis, Zwart and Fraser (n 9) 71.
[143] See, 'Reform of the Court: Filtering of Cases Successful in Reducing Backlog' (n 13); ECtHR Annual Report 2014 (n 14) 165.
[144] Spano (n 37) 491, 497–99.
[145] *Animal Defenders International v UK* (n 92).

direction, demonstrating the ECtHR's renewed efforts to engage more sensitively with Contracting Parties.

Regarding the future impact of Protocol 16, the objectives of the Protocol are laudable: aiming to ultimately reduce the Court's incoming caseload, to offer a platform for reinforcing dialogue with national courts,[146] and to further embed the Convention through influencing the adjudication of contentious cases in Strasbourg and at national level. It is clear, however, that Protocol 16—particularly given its optional status—offers no real prospect of reducing the flow of applications to the ECtHR in the short or medium terms. In this respect, a significant fall in pending cases at the Court is already being achieved thanks to the delayed embeddedness of the Protocol 14 ECHR reforms and the ECtHR's own efficiency measures. It is possible, however, that a long-term impact on its caseload could materialise as a result of Protocol 16, which will depend on the number of Contracting Parties that ratify the Protocol, the highest courts and tribunals nominated, the number of advisory opinions sought, the nature of the questions received by the Court, and, above all, the approaches of the Grand Chamber and highest national courts to the advisory opinions delivered. However, as noted above, there are a number of practical risks which the Grand Chamber—under increased adjudicatory pressure—must mitigate if it is to make the Protocol 16 system a success.

In respect of Protocol 16's aim of enhancing dialogue, this reform does offer scope for the ECtHR to engage more intensively with (certain) highest national courts and to clarify substantive issues. In relation to promoting dialogue, however, the ECtHR has not rested on its laurels prior to the entry into force of Protocol 16. The Court appears increasingly keen to highlight evidence of 'dialogue' in its judgments. Its extra-judicial involvement, both in the ongoing reform processes and via extra-judicial speeches, has evidenced the Court's proactive engagement with Contracting Parties. The negative political climate vis-a-vis the Convention system (not exclusively in the UK)[147] also appears to have encouraged members of the ECtHR to publicly advance their views on a more regular basis, defending and celebrating the relationships between the ECtHR and national courts, and highlighting the successes of the Convention system itself. Dialogue, therefore, is already being achieved through multi-faceted means. The possible risks of chilling effects on dialogue which could materialise under Protocol 16 have also been highlighted in this contribution. The Grand Chamber will play a vital role in managing risks involved in the extension of its advisory jurisdiction, such as avoiding delays in the delivery of its substantive judgments and advisory opinions, and ensuring that advisory opinions are sufficiently clear so as not to generate further requests or applications.

Looking ahead, the Council of Europe's focus on reform has shifted to the longer-term future of the ECtHR and of the Convention system. Despite the potential offered by Protocols 15 and 16, it is acknowledged at the highest levels within the Council of Europe that the Convention system remains under 'strain'.[148] Following

---

[146] Dzehtsiarou and O'Meara (n 109) 457.

[147] See Myjer (n 9) 41.

[148] Oslo Conference Proceedings (n 1) opening address delivered by P Boillat (Director General, Directorate General of Human Rights and the Rule of Law, Council of Europe), 16.

an open consultation which yielded over 100 responses proposing further reforms, the CDDH is facilitating meetings on reform proposals with a view to presenting its final report by 31 December 2015.[149] Its task is far from straightforward. The challenges facing the ECtHR are diverse, and any future reforms undertaken may yet impact on the essential nature of the ECtHR itself.[150]

At the same time, the argument that the Convention system may be at risk of being over-problematised by the continuous reform agenda has resonance.[151] While keeping the performance of the ECtHR under constant review is a responsible attitude, there is a risk that this constant process fails to allow sufficient time for agreed reforms to fully bed down before reaching for new solutions. As illustrated in relation to Protocols 15 and 16, this trend risks undermining the justifications provided for those new solutions, which—with the Court's docket now apparently falling daily—may appear less urgent than they once were. Over-problematisation also overshadows the real successes of the ECtHR and its many positive impacts. Above all, in cultivating an impression that the shortcomings of the Convention system emanate from the door of the Court, this approach fails to reveal the full picture. Any agenda which aims to secure the longer-term future of the Convention system must prioritise efforts to reinforce implementation of the Convention and the execution of judgments at national level.[152] The nature and impact of this forthcoming 'third wave' of reforms to secure the long-term future of the Convention system will remain open questions for some time. However, if it succeeds in enhancing rights protection further at both the ECtHR and closer to home, it will be an agenda worth pursuing.

[149] The work on the long-term future of the ECtHR is led by Drafting Group F on the Reform of the Court (GT-GDR-F), which operates under the supervision of DH-GDR (Committee of Experts on the Reform of the Court), which in turn operates under the CDDH. See *Road-Map: Progress towards the Draft CDDH Report*, GT-GDR-F(2014)020, 26 September 2014.

[150] J Christoffersen and MR Madsen, 'Postscript: Understanding the Past, Present, and Future of the European Court of Human Rights' in J Christoffersen and MR Madsen (eds), *The European Court of Human Rights between Law and Politics* (Oxford, Oxford University Press, 2013) 242. On the challenges and proposed solutions, see generally A Føllesdal, B Peters and G Ulfstein (eds), *Constituting Europe: The European Court of Human Rights in a National, European and Global Context* (Cambridge, Cambridge University Press, 2013); Flogaitis, Zwart and Fraser (n 9); Oslo Conference Proceedings (n 1).

[151] Oslo Conference Proceedings (n 1) speech delivered by M Kuijer (Ministry of Security and Justice of the Netherlands), 35.

[152] On the desirability of a clear vision to achieve these goals, see LR Glas 'Changes in the Procedural Practice of the European Court of Human Rights: Consequences for the Convention System and Lessons to be Drawn' (2014) 14 *Human Rights Law Review* 671, 698–99.

6

Should the English Courts under the HRA Mirror the Strasbourg Case Law?

RICHARD CLAYTON

I. INTRODUCTION

A S A JOBBING practitioner who dabbles in the academic world, it is rare to write on a controversial topic[1] and then argue a Supreme Court case which raises that very issue. But in the recent case of *Kennedy v Charity Commission* I did so.[2] The Supreme Court's approach to the case law of the European Court of Human Rights (ECtHR) was striking—and is central to this paper.

In *Kennedy*, a *Times* journalist had concerns about how George Galloway MP ran his controversial Iraq charity, the Miriam Appeal. He alleged that public donations were used to fund visits by Mr Galloway to Iraq and to support political campaigns against UN sanctions and against Israel. Mr Kennedy complained to the Charity Commission. The Commission held three inquiries under the Charities Act 2006, which dismissed the complaint in very brief terms. Mr Kennedy then made requests under the Freedom of Information Act (FOIA) for information to explain the tribunal's conclusion—which were rejected by the first-tier tribunal, by the High Court, and in two hearings before the Court of Appeal.

Mr Kennedy appealed to the Supreme Court, which had to decide whether an absolute exemption from disclosure under the FOIA came to an end once the Commission's inquiry concluded, either as a matter of ordinary construction or under the extended meaning permitted by section 3 of the Human Rights Act 1998 (HRA). The Supreme Court dismissed the appeal, in the course of which it declined to apply seven Strasbourg decisions to the effect that the right to freedom of expression under Article 10 conferred a right of access to information.[3]

---

[1] See R Clayton, 'Smoke and Mirrors: The Human Rights Act and the Impact of Strasbourg Case Law' [2012] *Public Law* 639, written as part of a debate published in *Public Law* in response to Lord Irvine, 'A British Interpretation of Convention Rights' [2012] *Public Law* 237 and Sir Philip Sales, 'Strasbourg Jurisprudence and the Human Rights Act: A Response to Lord Irvine' [2012] *Public Law* 253.

[2] *Kennedy v Charity Commission* [2014] 2 WLR 808.

[3] *Matky v Czech Republic* App no 19101/03 (10 July 2006); *Tarsasag v Hungary* (2011) 53 EHRR 3; *Kenedi v Hungary* (2009) 27 BHRC 335; *Gillberg v Sweden* (2012) 34 BHRC 247; *Shapovalov v*

The *Kennedy* case raised in very stark terms the question of whether the English courts under the HRA should be seeking to mirror the Strasbourg case law.[4] In reality, as I shall demonstrate, there are very few arguments of principle which justify the mirror principle. The current position now seems to be that, unless a Grand Chamber decision dictates a particular result, it is open to the domestic court to take a different view; and where the Strasbourg case law is not relevant, it may be open to the domestic courts to go beyond Strasbourg. It therefore seems that the mirror principle has now been significantly dented.

II. THE OBLIGATION TO APPLY STRASBOURG CASE LAW UNDER THE HRA AND ITS LEGISLATIVE HISTORY

The obligation to apply the case law of the ECtHR is of course to be found in section 2(1) of the HRA:

A court or tribunal determining a question which has arisen in connection with a Convention right must take into account any—

(a)   judgment, decision, declaration or advisory opinion of the European Court of Human Rights,
(b)   opinion of the Commission given in a report adopted under Article 31 of the Convention,
(c)   decision of the Commission in connection with Article 26 or 27(2) of the Convention, or
(d)   decision of the Committee of Ministers taken under Article 46 of the Convention,

whenever made or given, so far as, in the opinion of the court or tribunal, it is relevant to the proceedings in which that question has arisen.

Section 2(1) therefore requires that a court or tribunal 'take account' of the various decisions made by the ECtHR. As a matter of ordinary language, the meaning of section 2(1) is plain. Had Parliament intended to make Strasbourg case law binding, it could easily have done so. However, Parliament did not take that line. The starting point to construing section 2 must, therefore, be that the weight to be given to the Strasbourg jurisprudence was a matter to be decided by the domestic courts; and that there was no statutory bar on the English judiciary departing from decisions of the ECtHR. The same approach is supported by the HRA's pre-legislative history.

The pre-legislative history emphasised that English judges should develop their own distinctive approach to human rights case law so as to contribute to the Strasbourg jurisprudence generally, rather than to treat the ECtHR case law as being determinative in HRA cases. When the Labour government introduced the Human Rights Bill in October 1997, it also published a White Paper, *Rights Brought Home: The Human Rights Bill*, which explained its purpose.[5] The White Paper has taken

---

Ukraine App no 45835/05 (31 July 2012); *Youth Initiative for Human Rights v Serbia* App no 48135/06 (25 June 2013); *Österreichische Vereinigung v Austria* App no 39534/07 (28 November 2013).

[4] The 'mirror principle' was a phrase coined in J Lewis, 'The European Ceiling on Human Rights' [2007] *Public Law* 720.
[5] Cm 3782.

on an iconic character in the subsequent HRA cases, and is a central plank in Lord Bingham's rationalisation of the mirror principle. It is therefore instructive to re-examine the case for incorporation that the government actually made in *Rights Brought Home*:

> The effect of non-incorporation on the British people is a very practical one. The rights, originally developed with major help from the United Kingdom Government, are no longer actually seen as British rights. And enforcing them takes too long and costs too much. It takes on average five years to get an action into the European Court of Human Rights once all domestic remedies have been exhausted; and it costs an average of £30,000. Bringing these rights home will mean that the British people will be able to argue for their rights in the British courts—without this inordinate delay and cost. It will also mean that the rights will be brought much more fully into the jurisprudence of the courts throughout the United Kingdom, and their interpretation will thus be far more subtly and powerfully woven into our law. And there will be another distinct benefit. British judges will be enabled to make a distinctively British contribution to the development of the jurisprudence of human rights in Europe.[6]

In other words, the government described its purpose in enacting the HRA in wider terms than the intention to secure the same rights and remedies for Convention breaches in the domestic courts as those which would be awarded by the ECtHR. Statements in a White Paper are highly relevant to the construction of section 2(1). Enacting history may always be used to ascertain the mischief Parliament intended to remedy by an enactment, although it is of persuasive authority only, with its weight depending on its nature and the surrounding circumstances.[7]

Furthermore, the idea that the English courts had a role in developing Convention jurisprudence was stressed when the Bill was promoted by the government spokesmen at its second reading, no doubt with an eye on *Pepper v Hart* principles.[8] At the beginning of his speech, Lord Irvine gave the issue particular prominence:

> I chair many Cabinet committees, but none that has given me greater satisfaction than the committee whose labours have brought this Bill forward in the first legislative Session. It occupies a central position in our integrated programme for constitutional change. It will allow British judges for the first time to make their own distinctive contribution to the development of human rights in Europe.[9]

The then Home Secretary, Jack Straw, made the same point when opening the debate in the Commons for the second reading. After highlighting the practical reasons for incorporating the Convention, he said:

> There will be another benefit: British judges will be enabled to make a distinctively British contribution to the development of the jurisprudence of human rights across Europe.[10]

It is worth emphasising that in the House of Lords debates, the Conservative Party proposed an amendment to section 2, stating that domestic courts must be bound

---

[6] ibid, paras 1.14–1.15.
[7] See generally FAR Bennion, *Statutory Interpretation*, 5th edn (London, Butterworths, 2007) paras 227–30.
[8] *Pepper v Hart* [1993] AC 593.
[9] HL Deb 3 November 1997, vol 582, col 1227.
[10] HC Deb 16 February 1998, vol 307, col 769.

by the Strasbourg case law. Lord Irvine robustly rejected the proposal.[11] He pointed out that the word 'binding' was inappropriate for a number of reasons. First, the Convention itself is the ultimate source of Convention law, not the ECtHR judgments. Secondly, the United Kingdom is not bound in international law to follow ECtHR judgments in cases to which the United Kingdom had not been a party. Thirdly, such a requirement would impose a 'straightjacket' on the domestic courts, and Lord Irvine stressed that 'our courts must be free to try to give a lead to Europe as well as to be led'.[12] During the parliamentary debates, Lord Bingham expressed similar views:

> [I]t seems to me highly desirable that we in the United Kingdom should help to mould the law by which we are governed in this area … British judges have a significant contribution to make in the development of the law of human rights. It is a contribution which so far we have not been permitted to make.[13]

The pre-legislative history therefore shows that the government intended from the outset that the domestic courts should take their own independent approach to Convention rights, and should develop a distinctive indigenous human rights jurisprudence. But once the HRA came into force, the courts emphatically rejected that perspective. Instead, Lord Bingham decided to champion the view that the English courts should strive to apply the case law of the ECtHR and, in effect, 'mirror' the reasoning of Strasbourg decisions.

III. THE FORMULATION OF A MIRROR PRINCIPLE

The effect of section 2(1) was first discussed by the House of Lords in *R (Alconbury Developments Ltd) v Environment Secretary*, where Lord Slynn observed that:

> Although the Human Rights Act 1998 does not provide that a national court is bound by these decisions it is obliged to take account of them so far as they are relevant. In the absence of some special circumstances it seems to me that the court should follow any clear and constant jurisprudence of the European Court of Human Rights. If it does not do so, there is at least a possibility that the case will go to that court, which is likely in the ordinary case to follow its own constant jurisprudence.[14]

However, the domestic courts have not found it easy to follow clear and constant Strasbourg jurisprudence, not least because of the difference between the style of ECtHR reasoning and the more discursive reasoning of the common law tradition. For example, in *Re McCaughey* Lord Hope held that a Grand Chamber decision prevailed over an earlier decision of the House of Lords, but commented that only the most starry-eyed admirer of the Strasbourg Court could describe the guidance

---

[11] HL Deb 18 November 1998, vol 594, cols 514–15.
[12] ibid.
[13] HL Deb 3 November 1997, vol 582, col 1245.
[14] *R (Alconbury Developments Ltd) v Environment Secretary* [2003] 2 AC 295, para 26.

the Grand Chamber offered as clear;[15] Baroness Hale said the relevant part of the Grand Chamber judgment was difficult to understand,[16] and Lord Dyson described it as extremely obscure.[17] Similarly, in *Gale v Serious Organised Crime Agency*[18] Lord Phillips[19] and Lord Brown said that it was highly desirable that the issues the appeal raised be considered by the Grand Chamber in order to clarify and rationalise what Lord Brown called 'this whole confusing area of the Court's jurisprudence'.[20]

In *R (Ullah) v Secretary of State for the Home Department*, Lord Bingham radically departed from the wording of section 2(1) itself and introduced a requirement that the domestic courts must faithfully apply the jurisprudence of the ECtHR when deciding HRA cases

> by [using] section 2(1) of the Human Rights Act 1998 to take into account any relevant Strasbourg case law. While such case law is not strictly binding, it has been held that courts should, in the absence of some special circumstances, follow any clear and constant jurisprudence of the Strasbourg court: *R (Alconbury Developments Ltd) v Secretary of State for the Environment*. This reflects the fact that the Convention is an international instrument, the correct interpretation of which can be authoritatively expounded only by the Strasbourg court. From this it follows that a national court subject to a duty such as that imposed by section 2 should not without strong reason dilute or weaken the effect of the Strasbourg case law ... It is of course open to Member States to provide for rights more generous than those guaranteed by the Convention, but such provision should not be the product of interpretation of the Convention by national courts, since the meaning of the Convention should be uniform throughout the states party to it. The duty of national courts is to keep pace with the Strasbourg jurisprudence as it evolves over time: no more, but certainly no less.[21]

The rationale for this mirror principle was spelled out by Lord Bingham in *Kay v Lambeth LBC*:

> [I]t is ordinarily the clear duty of our domestic courts, save where and so far as constrained by primary domestic legislation, to give practical recognition to the principles laid down by the Strasbourg court as governing the Convention rights specified in section 1(1) of the 1998 Act. That court is the highest judicial authority on the interpretation of those rights, and the effectiveness of the Convention as an international instrument depends on the loyal acceptance by Member States of the principles it lays down.[22]

Lord Bingham elaborated his reasoning to justify the obligation to mirror the Strasbourg case law in *R (SB) v Denbigh High School*:

> [T]he purpose of the Human Rights Act 1998 was not to enlarge the rights or remedies of those in the United Kingdom whose Convention rights have been violated but to enable those rights and remedies to be asserted and enforced by the domestic courts of this

---

[15] *Re McCaughey* [2011] 2 WLR 1279, para 73.
[16] ibid, para 89.
[17] ibid, para 130.
[18] *Gale v Serious Organised Crime Agency* [2011] UKSC 49.
[19] ibid, para 60.
[20] ibid, para 117.
[21] *R (Ullah) v Secretary of State for the Home Department* [2004] 2 AC 323, para 20.
[22] *Kay v Lambeth LBC* [2006] 2 AC 465, para 28.

country and not only by recourse to Strasbourg. This is clearly established by authorities such as *Aston Cantlow v Wallbank*;[23] *R (Greenfield) v Secretary of State for the Home Department*;[24] and *R (Quark Fishing Ltd) v Secretary of State for Foreign Affairs*.[25,26]

But the *Ullah* principle, in fact, rests on uncertain foundations. In *Ullah* itself, the House of Lords did not actually apply the mirror principle when deciding the case before it. *Ullah* concerned two asylum seekers who had entered the United Kingdom and claimed asylum, alleging that they feared religious persecution if returned to their own countries in breach of Article 9. The Court of Appeal held that the only Convention article preventing the removal of an individual from the United Kingdom was the substantial risk of a breach of Article 3, the prohibition against inhuman treatment. The Court of Appeal acknowledged that the ECtHR had contemplated applying this principle to other Convention articles but 'it ha[d] not yet taken it'.[27] Even though Lord Bingham famously stated that 'the duty of national courts is to keep pace with the Strasbourg jurisprudence as it evolves over time: no more, but certainly no less', the House of Lords actually extended the existing Strasbourg case law substantially, by relying on underlying principle to find that Article 9 prevented the removal of the asylum seekers.[28]

Nevertheless, there are pragmatic reasons which justify the domestic courts, at a bare minimum, mirroring Strasbourg decisions, as in *Secretary of State for the*

---

[23] *Aston Cantlow v Wallbank* [2004] 1 AC 546, paras 6–7, 44.

[24] *R (Greenfield) v Secretary of State for the Home Department* [2005] 1 WLR 673, paras 18–19.

[25] *R (Quark Fishing Ltd) v Secretary of State for Foreign Affairs* [2006] 1 AC 529, paras 25, 33, 34, 88, 92.

[26] *R (SB) v Denbigh High School* [2007] 1 AC 100, para 29; see also the rationale given by Lord Hoffmann in *Re G* [2009] 1 AC 174, paras 35–36.

[27] [2003] 1 WLR 770, para 47.

[28] Lord Bingham stated at para 21: 'Seeking to perform that duty, I consider that the only possible answer to the question posed at the outset of this opinion is Yes. I have accepted the *possibility* of relying on article 2 in para 15 above. I have questioned in para 16 whether a claim based on article 4 alone might *not* succeed. The authority cited in para 17 shows that the court has not *excluded* the possibility of relying on article 6, and even article 5, while fully recognising the great difficulty of doing so and the exceptional nature of such cases. I do not think, on authority briefly cited in para 18 and more fully discussed in *R (Razgar) v Secretary of State for the Home Department* [2004] 2 AC 368, that reliance on article 8 can be ruled *out* in principle. I find it *hard* to think that a person could successfully resist expulsion in reliance on article 9 without being entitled either to asylum on the ground of a well-founded fear of being persecuted for reasons of religion or personal opinion or to resist expulsion in reliance on article 3. But I would not rule out such a *possibility* in principle *unless* the Strasbourg court has *clearly* done so, and I am not *sure* it has. It is unnecessary for present purposes to consider other articles of the Convention. I would be inclined to accept, as the Court of Appeal decided in *R (Holub) v Secretary of State for the Home Department* [2001] 1 WLR 1359 and as Mr Blake conceded, that reliance could not in this context be placed on the right to education protected by article 2 of the First Protocol to the Convention, but this conclusion was resisted by Mr Rabinder Singh and it is unnecessary to decide the point.' Similarly, Lord Steyn rejected the Court of Appeal's approach at para 35, stating: 'I understand this to be a view that even where the European Court of Human Rights ruled that other articles are engaged or may become engaged this does not amount to an authoritative precedent in the absence of a finding of a violation in the particular case. In my view this is too narrow an approach to the evolving jurisprudence of the European Court. Where it concludes that there was no breach of a convention right, the European Court may nevertheless rule on the reach of the right.' Lord Carswell at para 67 said: 'The Court of Appeal concluded its review of the Strasbourg jurisprudence by stating at p 785, para 47 of its judgment that: "To date, with the possible exception of *Bensaid v UK*, the application of this extension has been restricted to article 3 cases." It was correct to state that the only actual decisions applying the extension were *Soering v UK and Chahal v UK*, both article 3 cases. But there is a strong current of authority contained in statements made by the

Home Department v AF (No 3),[29] where the Supreme Court applied the Grand Chamber decision in *A v UK*[30] and departed from its own earlier reasoning in *Secretary of State for the Home Department v MB*.[31] Lord Rodger remarked that, although the House of Lords was dealing with rights under a United Kingdom statute, in reality it had no choice: '*Argentoratum locutum, iudicium finitum*— Strasbourg has spoken, the case is closed.'[32] The inherent difficulties of persuading a domestic court to decline to follow authoritative Strasbourg case law was again demonstrated by *R (Chester) v Secretary of State of Justice*,[33] where the Attorney-General unsuccessfully argued that the Supreme Court should decline to follow two Grand Chamber decisions in the prisoner vote cases, *Hirst v UK (No 2)*[34] and *Scoppola v Italy (No 3)*.[35]

However, in *R (Al-Skeini) v Secretary of State for Defence*, Lord Brown took the mirror principle a step further:

> There seems to me, indeed, a greater danger in the national court construing the Convention too generously in favour of an applicant than in construing it too narrowly. In the former event the mistake will necessarily stand: the Member State cannot itself go to Strasbourg to have it corrected; in the latter event, however, where Convention rights have been denied by too narrow a construction, the aggrieved individual can have the decision corrected in Strasbourg.[36]

Lord Brown's point applies equally to all Member States of the Council of Europe, and it is striking that it has not been articulated elsewhere. Complex issues can

European Court to the effect that other articles *could* be engaged. Lord Bingham of Cornhill has set out in his Opinion the roll-call of Strasbourg cases in which this possibility has been accepted by the court, and I gratefully adopt this without repeating it. Both Lord Bingham and Lord Steyn have set out reasons why in *principle* articles 2, 4, 5, 7 and 8 could be engaged in appropriate cases, and I respectfully agree with their reasons and conclusions. I am myself satisfied that a fair reading of the Strasbourg cases requires a national court to accept that these articles could *possibly* be engaged and that the exception to the territoriality principle is not confined to article 3. There does not appear to be any *conceptual* reason why article 9 should not be capable in principle of engagement, although I find it difficult to envisage a case, bearing in mind the flagrancy principle to which I am about to refer, in which there could be a sufficient interference with the article 9 rights which does not also come within the article 3 exception.' (Emphasis added.)

[29] *Secretary of State for the Home Department v AF (No 3)* [2010] 2 AC 269.
[30] *A v UK* (2009) 49 EHRR 625.
[31] *Secretary of State for the Home Department v MB* [2008] AC 440.
[32] *Secretary of State for the Home Department v AF (No 3)* (n 29) para 98; see also Lord Hoffmann at para 70: '*A v United Kingdom* requires these appeals to be allowed. I do so with very considerable regret, because I think that the decision of the ECHR was wrong and that it may well destroy the system of control orders which is a significant part of this country's defences against terrorism. Nevertheless, I think that your Lordships have no choice but to submit. It is true that section 2(1)(a) of the Human Rights Act 1998 requires us only to "take into account" decisions of the ECHR. As a matter of our domestic law, we could take the decision in *A v United Kingdom* into account but nevertheless prefer our own view. But the United Kingdom is bound by the Convention, as a matter of international law, to accept the decisions of the ECHR on its interpretation. To reject such a decision would almost certainly put this country in breach of the international obligation which it accepted when it acceded to the Convention. I can see no advantage in your Lordships doing so.'
[33] *R (Chester) v Secretary of State of Justice* [2014] AC 271; see in particular the judgment of Lord Sumption.
[34] *Hirst v UK (No 2)* (2005) 42 EHRR 849.
[35] *Scoppola v Italy (No 3)* (2012) 56 EHRR 663.
[36] *R (Al-Skeini) v Secretary of State for Defence* [2008] 1 AC 153, para 106.

of course arise, depending on whether the Member State takes a monist or dualist approach to public international law and depending on the domestic status of treaties in that country's constitutional order and the fact that national rights instruments may be the primary reference point for courts.[37] But the UK is the only country in the Council of Europe which regards itself as having to mirror Strasbourg jurisprudence. Member States frequently have difficulties applying ECtHR cases where they conflict with well- established domestic law and practices. Nevertheless, it is worth pointing out that in France, for example, the Conseil d'Etat in the *Boussouar* and *Planchenault* cases judicially reviewed administrative decisions for alleged violations of prisoners' rights because 'to refuse to overturn the impugned decisions would be tantamount to agreeing to close your eyes until Strasbourg opens them for you'.[38]

In any event, as Lady Hale has observed, the reasoning behind the *Ullah* principle— that the interpretation of the Convention should be kept uniform throughout the Member States—does not make much sense. We cannot commit other Member States or the ECtHR to our interpretation of the rights, so why should they mind what we do, as long as we do at least keep pace with the rights as they develop over time?[39]

Leaving these arguments to one side, it must be recognised that Lord Brown's obiter remarks in *Al-Skeini* were not intended to be a general statement of principle, but were specifically addressed to Article 1 of the Convention—the provision that the Convention applies to 'everyone'. Lord Phillips appreciated the limited effect of Lord Brown's observations in *R (Smith) v Oxfordshire Assistant Deputy Coroner*,[40] and Lord Brown himself also acknowledged this in *Secretary of State v JJ*.[41] It should also be noted that Article 1 is not a Convention right enumerated in

---

[37] See generally H Keller and A Stone Sweet (eds), *A Europe of Rights: The Impact of the European Court of Human Rights on National Legal Systems* (Oxford, Oxford University Press, 2008) 108; see also Oxford University's Pro Bono Publico Submission to the Commission on a Bill of Rights, *Reconciling Domestic Superior Courts with the ECHR and ECtHR: A Comparative Perspective* (24 November 2011).

[38] *Boussouar*, No 290730, Conseil d'Etat, 14 December 2007; *Planchenault*, No 290420, Conseil d'Etat, 14 December 2007.

[39] See Lady Hale's lecture to the Salford Human Rights Conference on 4 June 2010, and B Hale, 'Argentoratum Locutum: Is Strasbourg or the Supreme Court Supreme?' (2012) 12 *Human Rights Law Review* 65.

[40] *R (Smith) v Oxfordshire Assistant Deputy Coroner* [2011] 1 AC 1, para 60: 'In *Al-Skeini* [2008] AC 153, para 107 Lord Brown expressed the view that the House should not construe article 1 as reaching any further than the existing Strasbourg jurisprudence clearly shows it to reach. I endorse that comment. We are here dealing with the scope of the Convention and exploring principles that apply to all contracting states.'

[41] *Secretary of State v JJ* [2008] 1 AC 385, para 106: 'I have given anxious thought to what Lord Bingham of Cornhill said in *R (Ullah) v Special Adjudicator* [2004] 2 AC 323, 350, para 20 about not construing the Convention as conferring greater rights than the Strasbourg jurisprudence itself establishes— something upon which, indeed, I myself commented in *R (Al-Skeini) v Secretary of State for Defence* [2008] 1 AC 153, paras 105–106. But whereas the issue in *Al-Skeini* was as to the reach of article 1 itself—an issue to which the European Court of Human Rights in *Bankovic v Belgium* (2001) 11 BHRC 435, paras 64 and 65, had made plain that the "living instrument" approach does not apply—here by contrast the court recognised in *Guzzardi*, at para 95 in the passage already quoted in para 94 above, that developing legal standards and attitudes will further increase the variety of forms of deprivation of liberty.'

HRA Schedule 1, that Article 1 therefore does not have direct effect in the domestic courts, and that its application and effect raise very different questions from those concerning whether the scope of statutory rights created by the HRA should be limited or defined by the Strasbourg case law.

IV. THE MIRROR PRINCIPLE IN PRACTICE

In practice, however, the House of Lords has been much more flexible than a strict commitment to the mirror principle might imply, and has departed from the Strasbourg case law where it has felt it appropriate to do so. This is equally true in terms of the House of Lords' failure to meet Strasbourg standards (as interpreted by the ECtHR), as well as exceeding the protection afforded by the ECHR. But this approach has become widely accepted as achieving a constructive dialogue between domestic courts and the ECtHR.

Thus, in *R v Horncastle* Lord Phillips held that there will be rare occasions when concerns arise as to whether an ECtHR decision sufficiently appreciates or accommodates particular aspects of the UK's domestic process, with the result that it is open to the domestic court to decline to follow the Strasbourg decision, giving reasons for adopting this course.[42] In *Horncastle* itself, the trial judge admitted hearsay evidence given by the victim of an assault to the police detailing the circumstances of the attack; the victim's witness statement was admitted in evidence because he died before trial, for reasons unconnected with that assault. At trial the judge admitted the statement in evidence under section 116 of the Criminal Justice Act 2003, even though the witness statement was the sole evidence against the defendants. On appeal, the defendants relied on *Al-Khawaja v UK*,[43] where the ECtHR decided that Article 6 is breached if a conviction is based solely (or decisively) on evidence from a person whom the accused has had no opportunity to cross-examine. However, the Supreme Court declined to apply the Strasbourg case law, concluding that the 2003 Act represented a crafted code enacted by Parliament to regulate the admission of hearsay evidence in the interests of justice and contained specific safeguards which rendered the ECtHR's 'sole or decisive' rule unnecessary. They took the view that the 2003 Act therefore struck the correct balance between ensuring the fairness of the defendant's trial and protecting the interests of the victim in particular and society in general, so that a guilty person should not be immune from conviction where a witness who had given critical and apparently reliable evidence in a statement was unavailable through death or some other reason to be called at trial. The Supreme Court's approach was subsequently vindicated[44] by the Grand Chamber in *Al-Khawaja*, which decided that the admitting hearsay evidence where it was the

---

[42] *R v Horncastle* [2010] 2 AC 373.
[43] *Al-Khawaja v UK* (2009) 49 EHRR 1.
[44] For an analysis of the interaction between the Supreme Court and the ECtHR, see H Fenwick, 'Enhanced Subsidiarity and a Dialogic Approach—or Appeasement in Recent Cases on Criminal Justice, Public Order and Counter-Terrorism at Strasbourg against the UK?' (ch 10), this volume.

sole or decisive evidence against a defendant would not automatically result in a breach of Article 6(1).[45]

The same result—that is, the UK courts declining to follow an existing Strasbourg ruling (and a subsequent interaction with the ECtHR)—obtained in *R (Animal Defenders International) v Secretary of State for Culture*.[46] The claimant, a non-profit-making company whose aims included suppressing animal cruelty, was prevented from placing an advertisement about the threat to the survival of primates on the ground that this would breach the ban on political advertising in section 321(2) of the Communications Act 2003.[47] Although the claimant then complained that Article 10 ECHR had been breached, and relied strongly on the ECtHR decision of *VgT Verein gegen Tierfabriken v Switzerland*,[48] the House of Lords disagreed.[49] The Grand Chamber also declined to apply *VgT Verein gegen Tierfabriken* and found that Article 10 had not been breached, preferring the principles set out in the House of Lords.[50]

But, equally, there are several House of Lords and Supreme Court cases which go well beyond the Strasbourg decisions.[51] This appears to be the position in respect of *Ullah* itself.[52] Furthermore, as Sir Nicholas Bratza, former President of the ECtHR, has pointed out,[53] under the HRA the domestic courts have leapt ahead of the Strasbourg case law in its analysis of the treatment of asylum seekers in *R (Limbuela) v Secretary of State for the Home Department*,[54] in finding that there was discrimination prohibiting unmarried parents from adopting children in *Re G (Adoption: Unmarried Couple)*[55] and in relation to the impact of Article 8 on the rights of a mother and child facing expulsion in *EM (Lebanon) v Secretary of*

[45] *Al-Khawaja* (n 43).

[46] *R (Animal Defenders International) v Secretary of State for Culture* [2008] 1 AC 1312, [2008] UKHL 15.

[47] s 321(2) prohibits 'political advertising if it is—(a) an advertisement which is inserted by or on behalf of a body whose objects are wholly or mainly of a political nature; (b) an advertisement which is directed towards a political end ...'

[48] *VgT Verein gegen Tierfabriken v Switzerland* (2001) 34 EHRR 159. In *VgT* a body campaigning against animal experiments wished to broadcast a commercial criticising pig farming and asking viewers to eat less meat. The Swiss broadcasting authority declined to broadcast the commercial because of its clear political message. However, the ECtHR held that the refusal to broadcast the commercial breached Art 10. The *VgT* case had a particular significance when the 2003 Act was enacted—the Secretary of State felt unable to make a statement of compatibility under s 19(1)(a) HRA. He instead made a statement under s 19(1)(b), stating that the government believed and had been advised that the ban on political advertising contained in clauses 319 and 321 of the Bill were compatible with Art 10, but because of *VgT* it could not be sure.

[49] *R (Animal Defenders International) v Secretary of State for Culture* (n 46).

[50] *Animal Defenders International v UK* (2013) 57 EHRR 21 (extracts).

[51] But contrast the approach in *Ambrose v Harris* [2011] 1 WLR 2435, where the Supreme Court declined to hold that a suspect is entitled to access to a lawyer before he is placed in detention, and held that the Strasbourg case law did not require such a conclusion, expressing the view that an impending Strasbourg application dealing with the very point made it wise to wait for the judgment. The pending application of *Abdurahman v UK* (App 41351/09) is discussed by Lord Hope at paras 47–49.

[52] See n 28 above.

[53] N Bratza, 'The Relationship between the UK Courts and Strasbourg' [2011] *European Human Rights Law Review* 505, 511.

[54] *R (Limbuela) v Secretary of State for the Home Department* [2006] 1 AC 396.

[55] *Re G (Adoption: Unmarried Couple)* [2009] AC 173.

State for the Home Department.[56] What is less easy to explain or justify (in terms of adhering to an obligation to apply the mirror principle) is that the House of Lords and Supreme Court have chosen to go beyond Strasbourg in at least three cases (*Limbuela, EM (Lebanon)* and *Rabone v Pennine Care NHS Trust*)[57] without expressly analysing the *Ullah* principle and the impact of *Ullah* upon their reasoning.

The developments I have just described foreshadow a fundamental difference in approach which the Supreme Court has now decided to take towards the Strasbourg case law. The inconsistencies in applying the mirror principle have now been explicitly superseded by a much more sceptical attitude towards the ECtHR's reasoning when deciding HRA cases.

V. THE TRANSFORMATION OF THE MIRROR PRINCIPLE

In 2011, the Supreme Court heavily qualified the mirror principle. In *Manchester City Council v Pinnock* Lord Neuberger stated that the Supreme Court

> is not bound to follow every decision of the European court. Not only would it be impractical to do so: it would sometimes be inappropriate, as it would destroy the ability of the court to engage in the constructive dialogue with the European court which is of value to the development of Convention law: see eg *R v Horncastle*. Of course, we should usually follow a clear and constant line of decisions by the European court: *R (Ullah) v Special Adjudicator*. But we are not actually bound to do so or (in theory, at least) to follow a decision of the Grand Chamber. As Lord Mance pointed out in *Doherty v Birmingham City Council*, section 2 of the 1998 Act requires our courts to 'take into account' European court decisions, not necessarily to follow them. Where there is a clear and constant line of decisions whose effect is not inconsistent with some fundamental substantive or procedural aspect of our law, and whose reasoning does not appear to overlook or misunderstand some argument or point of principle, we consider that it would be wrong for this court not to follow that line.[58]

The courts have also developed their approach regarding the principles to be applied where there is no clear and constant ECtHR jurisprudence. Frequently, public authorities try to argue that because no ECtHR case has expressly decided a point, a claim under the HRA must inevitably fail, since the mirror principle debars the domestic courts from going beyond Strasbourg. However, as Lord Brown observed in *Rabone*:

> Nobody has ever suggested that, merely because a particular question which arises under the Convention has not yet been specifically resolved by the Strasbourg jurisprudence, domestic courts cannot determine it—in other words that it is necessary to await an authoritative decision of the ECtHR more or less directly in point before finding a Convention violation. That would be absurd. Rather what the *Ullah* principle importantly establishes is that the domestic court should not feel driven on Convention grounds unwillingly to decide a case

---

[56] *EM (Lebanon) v Secretary of State for the Home Department* [2009] AC 1198.
[57] *Rabone v Pennine Care NHS Trust* [2012] 2 AC 72.
[58] [2011] 2 AC 104, para 48 (footnotes omitted).

against a public authority (which could not then seek a corrective judgment in Strasbourg) unless the existing Strasbourg case law clearly compels this … If, however, the domestic court is content (perhaps even ready and willing) to decide a Convention challenge against a public authority and believes such a conclusion to flow naturally from existing Strasbourg case law (albeit that it could be regarded as carrying the case law a step further), then in my judgment it should take that further step.[59]

The somewhat broad-brush merits-based approach described by Lord Brown makes it difficult to identify any principled justification or bright line distinction to be applied by the domestic courts. The correct approach, it is respectfully submitted, is that suggested by Lord Mance in *R (Smith) v Oxfordshire Assistant Deputy Coroner*:

[I]t is our duty to give effect to the domestically enacted Convention rights, while taking account of Strasbourg jurisprudence, although caution is particularly apposite where Strasbourg has decided a case directly in point or, perhaps, where there are mixed messages in the existing Strasbourg case law and, as a result, a real judicial choice to be made there about the scope or application of the Convention.[60]

The position was taken a stage further by Lord Neuberger in the recent assisted suicide case of *R (Nicklinson) v Ministry of Justice*, where he held that if the *Ullah* principle was not relevant, then the national courts must decide the issue for themselves, with relatively unconstraining guidance from the Strasbourg Court, albeit bearing in mind the constitutional proprieties and such guidance from the Strasbourg jurisprudence, and indeed our own jurisprudence, as seems appropriate.[61]

The current formulation of *Ullah* means that the Supreme Court has moved away from views articulated in earlier House of Lords cases. For example, Lord Hope has sometimes voiced a principled objection to the principle that it is open to domestic courts to extend Convention rights beyond the Strasbourg case law.[62] As he put it in *Ambrose v Harris*:

Lord Bingham's point [in *Ullah*], with which I respectfully agree, was that Parliament never intended to give the courts of this country the power to give a more generous scope to those rights than that which was to be found in the jurisprudence of the Strasbourg court. To do so would have the effect of changing them from Convention rights, based on the treaty obligation, into free-standing rights of the court's own creation … It is not for this court to expand the scope of the Convention right further than the jurisprudence of the Strasbourg court justifies.[63]

---

[59] *Rabone* (n 57) para 112.

[60] *R (Smith) v Oxfordshire Assistant Deputy Coroner* [2011] 1 AC 1, para 199, approved by Lord Dyson in *Ambrose v Harris* [2011] 1 WLR 2435, para 103.

[61] *R (Nicklinson) v Ministry of Justice* [2014] 3 WLR 200, para 70.

[62] See eg *N v Secretary of State for the Home Department* [2005] 2 AC 296, para 14: 'It is not for us to search for a solution to [the appellant's] problem which is not to be found in the Strasbourg case law. It is for the Strasbourg court, not for us, to decide whether its case law is out of touch with modern conditions and to determine what extensions, if any, are needed to the rights guaranteed by the Convention. We must take its case law as we find it, not as we would like it to be.'

[63] *Ambrose v Harris* (n 60) paras 19–20.

The idea that the domestic courts may in some circumstances go beyond the Strasbourg case law is no longer regarded as unacceptable, and there are a number of reasons why a different attitude is now appropriate. First, it is now widely recognised that both section 2 and the pre-legislative history indicate that the English courts were intended to have a role in developing the Strasbourg jurisprudence. Secondly, the idea that the domestic courts have a role in developing Convention jurisprudence can be justified on the ground that the courts should give effect to the principle that the HRA is a constitutional statute—because the courts have repeatedly stressed that the Convention is effectively our bill of rights.[64] Thirdly, and in any event, the idea that only Strasbourg can define Convention rights is circular and its force depends on whether it is to be assumed that it is illegitimate for domestic courts to expand Convention rights beyond the ECtHR's case law.

This idea that the domestic courts are entitled to go beyond Strasbourg also sidesteps another potential limitation on the interpretive powers of the English courts which arises by virtue of the fact that the UK (unlike other signatories to the Convention) has chosen to adopt the Convention as its constitutional template. Both Article 53 ECHR[65] and section 11 HRA[66] permit domestic courts to go beyond the Convention when deciding human rights cases by reference to 'any other laws', so that the Convention provides a floor, but not a ceiling, in human rights cases. But the effect of applying a mirror principle to HRA cases may lead to the surprising result that the UK has debarred itself from developing a more generous approach than Strasbourg—which defeats the purpose of Article 53 and section 11.

Furthermore, when the Supreme Court is making a real choice about defining the proper scope of Convention rights, it has shown a new readiness to draw on the rich menu offered by international human rights jurisprudence. Before the HRA was enacted, the House of Lords regularly examined a wide range of international cases to develop the common law—epitomised by *Derbyshire County Council v Times Newspapers Ltd*.[67] In that case the House of Lords decided that it was of the greatest public importance that a democratically elected governmental body should be open to uninhibited public criticism. Since the threat of civil actions for defamation would place an undesirable fetter on the freedom to express criticism, it would be contrary to the public interest for central or local government to have any common law right to bring a damages action for defamation. The House of Lords

[64] See, for example, the dicta of Lord Bingham in *Brown v Stott* [2003] 1 AC 681 at para 703 and of Lord Steyn at para 708, those of Lord Woolf CJ in *R v Offen* [2001] 1 WLR 253, 275, and the views of Laws LJ in *Thoburn v Sunderland City Council* [2003] QB 151. Similarly, in *McCartan v Times Newspapers* [2001] 2 AC 277, Lord Steyn stated at para 296 that the HRA was a constitutional measure designed to buttress freedom of expression, fulfilling the function of a Bill of Rights in our legal system. In *R (Laporte) v Chief Constable of Gloucestershire Constabulary* [2007] 2 AC 105, para 34, Lord Bingham described the HRA in giving effect to Arts 10 and 11 as representing a 'constitutional shift'.

[65] 'Nothing in this Convention shall be construed as limiting or derogating from any of the human rights and fundamental freedoms which may be ensured under the laws of any High Contracting Party or under any other agreement to which it is a Party.'

[66] 'A person's reliance on a Convention right does not restrict—(a) any other right or freedom conferred on him by or under any law having effect in any part of the United Kingdom; or (b) his right to make any claim or bring any proceedings which he could make or bring apart from sections 7 to 9.'

[67] *Derbyshire County Council v Times Newspapers Ltd* [1993] AC 534.

reached its conclusion by relying on decisions of the American Supreme Court[68] and the Supreme Court of South Africa,[69] as well as the Privy Council.[70] The use of international human rights jurisprudence has been, however, thwarted by the mirror principle. As Lord Bingham pointed out in *DPP v Sheldrake*:

> On a number of occasions the House has gained valuable insights from the reasoning of Commonwealth judges deciding issues under different human rights instruments ... Some caution is in any event called for in considering different enactments decided under different constitutional arrangements. But, even more important, the United Kingdom courts must take their lead from Strasbourg.[71]

By contrast, the Supreme Court has recently shown a great willingness to consider international jurisprudence in HRA cases by examining decisions of the Inter-American Court of Human Rights[72] and the United Nations Human Rights Committee[73] where they are relevant. Nevertheless, even applying the heavily modified mirror principle (as framed by Lord Neuberger in *Pinnock*),[74] the approach taken by the Supreme Court in *Kennedy* is striking.

VI. THE DECISION IN *KENNEDY* AND THE INTERPRETATION OF ARTICLE 10 ECHR

As indicated earlier, *Kennedy* concerned a journalist seeking disclosure by the Charity Commission of documents under the FOIA to explain its conclusions about a complaint concerning George Galloway MP and his Iraq charity. Mr Kennedy accepted that some of the information requested might attract absolute exemption from disclosure under FOIA (such as confidential information under section 41) and that other parts came within the scope of qualified exemptions under the FOIA, which required the Commission to weigh up rival public interests under section 2(2).

However, the Commission stated that all the documents were subject to an absolute exemption under section 32, on the basis that section 32 exempts the Commission from any duty to disclose documents held by a court or persons conducting an inquiry or arbitration. Mr Kennedy responded by arguing that the absolute exemption under section 32(2) fell away once the inquiry concluded, either as a matter of ordinary statutory construction or by interpreting section 32 in accordance with section 3 of the HRA. The Supreme Court had little difficulty in deciding against Mr Kennedy on the ordinary construction issue. The principal battleground therefore focused on the scope of Article 10 ECHR.[75]

---

[68] *New York Times Co v Sullivan*, 376 US 254 (1964).
[69] *Die Spoorbond v South African Railways*, 1946 AD 999.
[70] *Hector v Attorney-General of Antigua and Barbuda* [1990] 2 AC 312.
[71] *DPP v Sheldrake* [2005] 1 AC 264, para 33.
[72] *Kennedy v Charity Commission* [2014] 2 WLR 808.
[73] *Moohan v Lord Advocate* [2015] 2 WLR 141.
[74] See n 58.
[75] See my note on the general implications of the *Kennedy* case: 'The Curious Case of *Kennedy v Charity Commission*' UK Constitutional Law Blog (18 April 2004), ukconstitutionallaw.org/2014/04/18/

Unfortunately, the Strasbourg jurisprudence on whether freedom of expression entails a right of access to information is not entirely straightforward. In the older cases (which include Grand Chamber decisions), *Leander v Sweden*,[76] *Gaskin v UK*,[77] *Guerra v Italy*[78] and *Roche v UK*,[79] the ECtHR denied that a right of access to information fell within the scope of Article 10. However, a series of later cases, *Matky v Czech Republic*,[80] *Tarsasag v Hungary*[81] and *Kenedi v Hungary*,[82] say that Article 10 confers a right of access to information, at any rate for those who exercise the functions of a social watchdog, like the press.

Lord Judge CJ in *Independent News and Media* observed that the Strasbourg jurisprudence appears to have developed since *Leander* so that Article 10 seems to have a somewhat wider scope.[83] But when the point was argued before the Supreme Court in *Sugar v BBC*,[84] Lord Brown disagreed, holding in trenchant terms[85] that Article 10 creates no general right to freedom of information. Lords Mance and Wilson agreed with his analysis.[86] Since *Sugar* there have been four more ECtHR cases indicating that Article 10 confers a right of access to information: the Grand Chamber decision in *Gillberg v Sweden*,[87] *Shapovalov v Ukraine*,[88] *Youth Initiative for Human Rights v Serbia*[89] and *Österreichische Vereinigung v Austria*, which was, in fact, given after the oral argument in *Kennedy*.[90]

Mr Kennedy asked the Supreme Court to overrule *Sugar* before a seven-judge court. Lord Mance, giving the leading judgment (with which Lords Neuberger, Clarke and Sumption agreed), scrutinised the ECtHR decisions, including the four new decisions.[91] He concluded, on the unsatisfactory state of the case law, that Article 10 did not confer a positive right of access to information.[92] He also said that it was unfortunate that the ECtHR chambers did not refer cases to the Grand

---

richard-clayton-the-curious-case-of-kennedy-v-charity-commission. Having rejected the appellant's case on statutory construction and under s 3 HRA, the Supreme Court held obiter that it would have been open to Mr Kennedy to bring his case as an ordinary judicial review application, based on the common law right of open justice as developed by *R (Guardian Newspapers) v City of Westminster Magistrates' Court* [2013] QB 618, where the Court of Appeal held that the magistrates acted unlawfully in refusing to disclose the skeleton arguments, witness statements and other documents; and that he should have pursued that option. However, the applicant has declined to pursue a judicial review case, and Times Newspapers has made an application to the ECtHR. The question as to whether Article 10 includes a right of access to information was referred to the Grand Chamber in May 2015 in *Magyar Helsinki Bizottság v Hungary* (Application no 18030/11).

[76] *Leander v Sweden* (1987) 9 EHRR 433.
[77] *Gaskin v UK* (1989) 12 EHRR 36.
[78] *Guerra v Italy* (1998) 26 EHRR 357.
[79] *Roche v UK* (2005) 42 EHRR 30.
[80] *Matky v Czech Republic* (n 3).
[81] *Tarsasag v Hungary* (n 3).
[82] *Kenedi v Hungary* (n 3).
[83] *A v Independent News and Media* [2010] 1 WLR 2262, para 41.
[84] *Sugar v BBC* [2012] 1 WLR 439.
[85] ibid, paras 88–96.
[86] ibid, para 59 per Lord Wilson and para 113 per Lord Mance.
[87] *Gillberg v Sweden* (n 3).
[88] *Shapovalov v Ukraine* (n 3).
[89] *Youth Initiative for Human Rights v Serbia* (n 3).
[90] *Österreichische Vereinigung v Austria* (n 3).
[91] *Kennedy* (n 2) paras 76–96.
[92] ibid, para 94.

Chamber where they disagreed with older Grand Chamber judgments.[93] Lord Mance's approach is open to question on several grounds. His views appears to be out of line with current Strasbourg practice concerning referrals to the Grand Chamber, fails to acknowledge the dynamic interpretive techniques the ECtHR uses when considering the scope of Convention rights (which Lord Wilson stressed in his dissenting judgment),[94] and seems to imply that Strasbourg applies a system of precedent—which it does not.

One critical question the Supreme Court had to consider was how the ECtHR would itself decide the Article 10 issue. The reality is that the direction of travel is all one way—every recent ECtHR decision has stated that Article 10 confers a right of access to information. Lord Wilson in his dissent stated that the Supreme Court could 'confidently conclude' that Article 10 required an unwilling public authority to disclose information,[95] whereas Lord Carnwath held in his dissenting judgment that the general direction of travel (unless the Grand Chamber ruled otherwise) was clear.[96] In *R (Gentle) v Prime Minister*, Lady Hale indicated that when she considered the Strasbourg jurisprudence, she would be guided by what she could reasonably foresee the ECtHR would decide;[97] and in *Ambrose v Harris* Lord Dyson looked for a 'sufficient indication' of how the ECtHR would decide the case.[98] It is respectfully submitted that the conclusion of the majority on the scope of Article 10 is, therefore, unconvincing.

In contrast, the Supreme Court had no reservations about giving consideration to whether international jurisprudence supported Mr Kennedy's interpretation of Article 10. The Court examined Article 19 of the Universal Declaration of Human Rights 1948,[99] Article 13(1) of the Inter-American Convention on Human Rights[100] and the important decision of the Inter-American Court of Human Rights in *Claude-Reyes v Chile*[101] (followed in *Lund v Brazil*)[102] where it held: '[B]y expressly stipulating the right to "seek" and "receive" "information", article 13 of the Convention protects the right of all individuals to request access to state-held information, with the exceptions permitted by the restrictions established in the Convention.'[103] However, Lord Mance did not find that the international jurisprudence helped to define the scope of Article 10.[104]

---

[93] ibid, para 59.
[94] ibid, para 188.
[95] ibid, para 189.
[96] ibid, para 217.
[97] *R (Gentle) v Prime Minister* [2008] 1 AC 1356, paras 56–57.
[98] *Ambrose v Harris* (n 60) para 95.
[99] Art 19: 'Everyone has the right to freedom of opinion and expression; this right includes freedom to hold opinions without interference and to seek, receive and impart information and ideas through any media and regardless of frontiers.'
[100] Art 13(1) states: 'Everyone has the right of freedom of thought and expression. This right includes freedom to seek, receive, and impart information and ideas of all kinds, regardless of frontiers, either orally, in writing, in print, in the form of art, or through any other medium of one's choice.'
[101] *Claude-Reyes v Chile* (unreported), 19 September 2006, IACtHR.
[102] *Lund v Brazil* (unreported), 24 November 2010, IACtHR.
[103] ibid, para 77.
[104] *Kennedy* (n 2) paras 97–99.

VII. THE CURRENT APPROACH TO THE MIRROR PRINCIPLE

The Supreme Court decision in *Kennedy* shows that the domestic courts are consciously moving away from the *Ullah* principle.[105] As Lord Neuberger recently remarked in *R (Kaiyam) v Secretary of State for Justice*:

> The Convention rights are those set out in Schedule 1 to the Act. It follows from the wording of the Act that domestic courts in interpreting and applying such rights are not bound by the jurisprudence of the European court, but are bound to take it into account. Usually, domestic and Strasbourg jurisprudence march hand in hand, as contemplated by the 'mirror' principle 'no more, but certainly no less' (as put by Lord Bingham in *R (Ullah) v Special Adjudicator*) or 'no less, but certainly no more' (as put by Lord Brown of Eaton-under-Heywood in *R (Al-Skeini) v Secretary of State*). But increasingly it has been realised that situations are not always so simple. The domestic court may have to decide for itself what the Convention rights mean, in a context which the European court has not yet addressed: see eg *Rabone v Pennine Care NHS Foundation Trust*. More radically, the domestic court may conclude that such Strasbourg authority as exists cannot be supported, and may decline to follow it in the hope that it may be reconsidered: *R v Horncastle*.[106]

More recently, in *R (Chester) v Secretary of State for Justice*, Lord Mance said:

> In relation to authority consisting of one or more simple Chamber decisions, dialogue with Strasbourg by national courts, including the Supreme Court, has proved valuable in recent years. The process enables national courts to express their concerns and, in an appropriate case such as *R v Horncastle*, to refuse to follow Strasbourg case law in the confidence that the reasoned expression of a diverging national viewpoint will lead to a serious review of the position in Strasbourg. But there are limits to this process, particularly where the matter has been already to a Grand Chamber once or, even more so, as in this case, twice. It would have then to involve some truly fundamental principle of our law or some most egregious oversight or misunderstanding before it could be appropriate for this court to contemplate an outright refusal to follow Strasbourg authority at the Grand Chamber level.[107]

The degree of constraint imposed or freedom allowed by the phrase 'must take into account' is context specific, and it would be unwise to treat Lord Neuberger MR's reference to decisions 'whose reasoning does not appear to overlook or misunderstand some argument or point of principle' (in *Pinnock*) or Lord Mance's reference to 'some egregious oversight or misunderstanding' as more than attempts at general guidelines, or to attach too much weight to his choice of the word 'egregious', compared with Lord Neuberger MR's omission of such a qualification.

This more flexible approach reflects a number of developments. The HRA has now come of age and there are no self-evident reasons for prohibiting the domestic courts from taking their own direction when deciding Convention cases. The Supreme Court has no inhibitions about criticising the inadequacies in judgments of

---

[105] See Lord Neuberger, 'The Role of Judges in Human Rights Jurisprudence: A Comparison of the Australian and UK Experience' (8 August 2014), www.supremecourt.uk/docs/speech-140808.pdf.
[106] *R (Kaiyam) v Secretary of State for Justice* [2015] 2 WLR 76, paras 18–22.
[107] *R (Chester) v Secretary of State for Justice* [2010] EWCA Civ 1439, [2014] 1 AC 271, para 27.

the ECtHR or the Court of Justice of the European Union, as it perceives them.[108] This approach may also reflect broader political events, including the irun up to the 2015 general election. The Labour Party shadow Secretary of State, Sadiq Khan, wrote in June 2014 that

> too often, rather than 'taking into account' Strasbourg rulings and by implication, finding their own way, our courts have acted as if these rulings were binding on their decisions. As a result, the sovereignty of our courts and the will of Parliament have both been called into question.[109]

Similarly, in October 2014 the Conservative Party published *Protecting Human Rights in the UK*, arguing that the HRA should be abolished, partly because it is said that section 2 undermines the role of UK courts by applying problematic Strasbourg case law and because the ECtHR proportionality principle questions legislative and public authority decision-making through an essentially political evaluation of different policy considerations.[110] Thus, the new Conservative Government proposes to repeal the HRA and replace it with a Bill of Rights Act as political priority.

VIII. CONCLUSION

The *Ullah* principle has changed significantly since Lord Bingham's original formulation. For a myriad of reasons, the Supreme Court no longer regards the ECtHR cases as defining the limits of Convention rights under the HRA; and the mirror principle is no longer a concept which accurately encapsulates the Supreme Court's current approach. Of course, the growing self-confidence of the domestic courts carries a price, since, as in *Kennedy*, a disinclination to apply ECtHR case law may mean that a disappointed litigant must embark on the long road to Strasbourg. However, there are now compelling reasons for developing an indigenous human rights jurisprudence if the Convention rights are to be regarded as domestic rights and if the HRA is to be treated as a constitutional statute.

When analysing the roots of the *Ullah* principle, it is important to remember the difficulties the judiciary faced in identifying the proper approach to interpreting the HRA, following its enactment. Unlike the Canadian Charter of Rights and Freedoms or the South African Constitution Act, the HRA did not emerge as a result of a broadly based popular movement for fundamental constitutional reform. The HRA was, instead, a top-down commitment and important element in New Labour's constitutional programme. The HRA gave no particular steer to judges on how to tackle potentially difficult and controversial human rights claims,

---

[108] See eg *R (Buckinghamshire County Council) v Secretary of State for Transport* [2014] 1 WLR 324, judgments of Lord Neuberger and Sumption, para 196.

[109] S Khan, 'Labour will Shift Power Back to British Courts' *The Telegraph* (London, 3 June 2014), www.telegraph.co.uk/news/uknews/law-and-order/10870113/Labour-will-shift-power-back-to-British-courts.html.

[110] 'Conservatives Plan to Scrap Human Rights Act' *The Guardian* (London, 3 October 2014), www.theguardian.com/politics/interactive/2014/oct/03/conservatives-human-rights-act-full-document.

which confront more merits-based and policy questions than those envisaged by traditional *Wednesbury* principles.

Lord Bingham observed in October 2000 that the implementation of the HRA was 'something of the character of a religious event: an event eagerly sought and long awaited but arousing feelings of apprehension as well as expectation, the uncertainty that accompanies any new and untested experience'.[111] But the attacks on the World Trade Center in New York on 11 September 2001 fundamentally changed attitudes. The government committed itself to the 'War on Terror', the Prime Minister, Tony Blair, announced that 'the rules of the game are changing',[112] and the Labour government shifted away from its earlier support for the HRA.[113] These political events created immense practical difficulties for the judiciary when deciding cases which attracted government criticism, and probably inspired the unstated premise for the mirror principle—that under the HRA the domestic courts had no alternative but to apply the Strasbourg cases. Thus, Hugh Tomlinson and I have argued that the *Ullah* principle was developed to seek democratic legitimacy by means of a self-denying ordinance encapsulated in the mirror principle,[114] which had the effect of severely restricting the domestic courts' ability to be 'an international standard-bearer of liberty and justice', as originally envisaged by Lord Bingham in 1993 when he first argued the case for incorporating the Convention.[115]

In the final analysis, the underlying justification for the mirror principle is difficult to defend. The domestic courts should mirror the Strasbourg case law, but only up to a point. The development of a mature domestic human rights jurisprudence will, inevitably, require the courts to depart from Strasbourg cases, as and when it is appropriate to do so, and this new, more flexible approach has the further benefit of applying section 2 in a way which properly reflects the language of the provision.

---

[111] R Clayton and H Tomlinson, *The Law of Human Rights* (Oxford, Oxford University Press, 2000), preface.

[112] 'Blair Vows Hard Line on Fanatics' BBC News (5 August 2005), news.bbc.co.uk/1/hi/uk_politics/4747573.stm.

[113] See eg N Temko and J Doward, 'Revealed: Blair Attack on Human Rights Law' *The Guardian* (London, 14 May 2006), www.theguardian.com/politics/2006/may/14/humanrights.ukcrime.

[114] R Clayton and H Tomlinson, 'Lord Bingham and the Human Rights Act 1998: The Search for Democratic Legitimacy During the "War on Terror"' in M Andenas and D Fairgrieve (eds), *Tom Bingham and the Transformation of the Law: A Liber Amicorum* (Oxford, Oxford University Press, 2009).

[115] T Bingham, 'The European Convention on Human Rights: Time to Incorporate' in T Bingham, *The Business of Judging: Selected Essays and Speeches: 1985–1999* (Oxford, Oxford University Press, 2000).

7

Repeal the HRA and Rely on the Common Law?

BRICE DICKSON*

I. CONTEMPLATING REPEAL OF THE HUMAN RIGHTS ACT

IN THE IMMEDIATE aftermath of the UK's general election in May 2015 it became abundantly clear that in this year of the 800th anniversary of Magna Carta there was a distinct possibility that the days of the United Kingdom's Human Rights Act 1998 (HRA) were numbered. Its survival had depended on Labour winning enough seats to form a government on its own or on the Conservatives winning enough seats to form a government only with the support of the Liberal Democrats. In the end the Conservative's working majority in the House of Commons turned out to be 15, which rises to 35 if the votes of 10 unionist MPs from Northern Ireland are added. That makes it almost inevitable that a replacement for the 1998 Act will be passed in that House. Moreover, given the so-called Salisbury convention whereby the House of Lords will not vote down Bills which were promised in the government's election manifesto,[1] which this one was,[2] it is unlikely that the Bill will be halted in that forum. The manifesto commitment was presaged by a document published in October 2014, *Protecting Human Rights in the United Kingdom*,[3] where a promise was made to 'shortly

---

* This article is a revised version of papers given at the Oxford University Public Law Discussion Forum in November 2013 and the conference on the UK and European Human Rights at the University of Leicester in May 2014. I am grateful to participants in those events and to Professors Gordon Anthony, Philip Leach and Rory O'Connell for their comments on previous drafts of this piece, but responsibility for what is published remains entirely mine alone.

[1] See the House of Lords library note on this convention (2006), available at: www.parliament.uk/documents/lords-library/hllsalisburydoctrine.pdf.

[2] The manifesto said that the new Bill 'will break the formal link between British courts and the European Court of Human Rights, and make our own Supreme Court the ultimate arbiter of human rights matters in the UK' and it added that the Bill 'will restore common sense to the application of human rights in the UK'. While it 'will remain faithful to the basic principles of human rights, which we signed up to in the original European Convention on Human Rights … it will reverse the mission creep that has meant human rights law being used for more and more purposes, and often with little regard for the rights of wider society. Among other things the Bill will stop terrorists and other serious foreign criminals who pose a threat to our society from using spurious human rights arguments to prevent deportation': *The Conservative Party Manifesto* (2015), pp 60 and 73.

[3] Subtitled *The Conservatives' Proposals for Changing Britain's Human Rights Laws*, available at www.conservatives.com/~/media/Files/Downloadable%20Files/HUMAN_RIGHTS.pdf.

publish a draft British Bill of Rights and Responsibilities for consultation', but no such draft had appeared by the time of the election six months later. This earlier document added that the new Bill would create 'a better balance between rights and responsibilities', remove the requirement in section 2(1)(a) of the Human Rights Act 1998 that British judges 'take into account' any relevant decisions of the European Court of Human Rights (ECtHR), set a threshold to ensure that UK courts strike out trivial cases, and prevent human rights obligations from applying to British soldiers serving overseas.

In the run-up to the 2015 election the Lord Chancellor and Secretary of State for Justice, Chris Grayling, made very clear his personal opposition to the Human Rights Act, which he believed was fundamentally incompatible with Britain's way of life.[4] He made both general criticisms, such as that judges in Strasbourg and at home have taken the ECHR to places which its authors would never have imagined, as well as criticisms of specific decisions by the ECtHR in applications brought against the United Kingdom (for example on the right of prisoners to vote, in *Hirst v UK (No 2)*,[5] and on the right of life-sentenced prisoners to have at least the possibility of release before they die, in *Vinter v UK*).[6] On more than one occasion Mr Grayling indicated that he wanted to see the Supreme Court of the United Kingdom being in the United Kingdom and not in Strasbourg.[7] The new Lord Chancellor and Secretary of State for Justice, Michael Gove, who like his predecessor is not a lawyer, seems to hold very similar views. When he was still a humble think-tank employee, back in 2000, he wrote a tract which severely criticised the peace process in Northern Ireland and was particularly antagonistic to the then newly formed Northern Ireland Human Rights Commission:

> The NIHRC's creation, existence and growth is not a triumph for those who fought terrorism, it is a clear strategic gain for those who dislike the British way of doing things and wish to fundamentally reconstruct the social order and erode traditional liberties.[8]

However, it is not only senior politicians who have contemplated the demise of the HRA. At a press conference marking the end of the first year of the new UK Supreme Court in August 2010, the then Deputy President of the Court, Lord Hope, expressed the view that repealing the Human Rights Act would, by itself, make very little difference to the way such rights are enforced in our courts.[9] He pointed out that the most significant change to the UK's relationship with the ECHR came in 1966, when the government first notified the Committee of Ministers of the Council of Europe that it was allowing individuals to lodge applications in Strasbourg against the UK government and recognising the jurisdiction of the ECtHR to

---

[4] Interview with the *Daily Telegraph*: S Swinford, 'Grayling's Manifesto to Rescue Justice from Europe' *The Telegraph* (London, 2 November 2013), www.telegraph.co.uk/news/politics/conservative/10423032/Graylings-manifesto-to-rescue-justice-from-Europe.html.

[5] *Hirst v UK (No 2)* (2006) 42 EHRR 41 (GC).

[6] *Vinter v UK* (2012) 55 EHRR 34 (GC).

[7] J Forsyth, 'Chris Grayling: "I Want to See our Supreme Court Supreme Again"', interview with *The Spectator* (London, 28 September 2013), www.spectator.co.uk/features/9033091/the-echr-is-unacceptable.

[8] M Gove, *The Price of Peace: An analysis of British Policy in Northern Ireland*, London, Centre for Policy Studies, 53.

[9] www.lawgazette.co.uk/56501.article.

consider those application. Lord Hope claimed that that announcement prompted UK judges to feel obliged to take the Convention into account more frequently than before and to assume that Parliament always intended its legislation to be compatible with UK treaty obligations under the Convention. He conceded that lawyers had not fully got to grips with how those obligations could be developed,[10] but that the picture changed once the 1998 Act came along:

> [I]f you were to take away the Human Rights Act now ... all that jurisprudence is there ... So it's very difficult to see how simply wiping out the Human Rights Act is really going to change anything until we withdraw from the Convention—which, personally, I don't think is conceivable.[11]

From 1996 Lord Hope served on the Appellate Committee of the House of Lords alongside Lord Hoffmann, who retired just before the Committee was replaced by the UK Supreme Court in 2009. One of Lord Hoffmann's final extra-judicial forays into human rights law was his lecture delivered to the Judicial Studies Board, now the Judicial College, where he denounced the ECtHR for unduly extending its powers and, in effect, teaching domestic courts to suck eggs.[12] He was adamant that UK judges were able to strike justifiable balances between individuals' rights and society's interests, and in his own judgments in the House of Lords he was insistent, together with Lord Steyn, that UK courts were able to control high-handedness on the part of UK public authorities by applying 'the principle of legality'. Although neither of these judges was ever explicit as to what precisely that principle means, both suggested that it could even justify declaring an Act of Parliament to be unlawful (or unconstitutional). This was most evident in Lord Steyn's judgment in *R (Jackson) v Attorney-General*,[13] which concerned the power of the House of Commons to make laws without the consent of the House of Lords, but it also permeates his judgments in *Leech*[14] (when he was still a Lord Justice of Appeal), *Pierson*[15] and *Simms*[16]—all cases involving the rights of prisoners. Lord Hoffmann also sat in *Simms*, where he stressed that the significance of the House's decision was that it demonstrated that the principle of legality applies as much to subordinate

---

[10] This is something of an understatement, since judicial use of the ECHR prior to the Human Rights Act was meagre; see P Gardner and C Wickremasinghe, 'England and Wales and the European Convention' in B Dickson (ed), *Human Rights and the European Convention* (London, Sweet & Maxwell, 1997) ch 3, esp 95–109; also Murray Hunt, *Using Human Rights Law in English Courts* (Oxford, Hart Publishing, 1997). See too the pre- and post-1998 lectures delivered by Lord Irvine, a former Lord Chancellor, collected in *Human Rights, Constitutional Law and the Development of the English Legal System* (Oxford, Hart Publishing, 2003).

[11] Yet at the Conservative Party annual conference in 2013 the Home Secretary, Theresa May, told the audience: 'The Conservative position is clear—if leaving the European Convention is what it takes to fix our human rights laws, that is what we should do.' See A Travis, 'Conservatives Promise to Scrap Human Rights Act after Next Election' *The Guardian* (London, 30 September 2013), www.theguardian.com/law/2013/sep/30/conservitives-scrap-human-rights-act.

[12] Lord Hoffmann, 'The Universality of Human Rights' (2009) 125 *Law Quarterly Review* 416.

[13] *R (Jackson) v Attorney-General* [2005] UKHL 56, [2006] 1 AC 262, para 102. He was supported in this stance by Lord Hope (at paras 104–108) and by Lady Hale (para 159).

[14] *R v Secretary of State for the Home Department, ex parte Leech* [1994] QB 198.

[15] *Pierson v Secretary of State for the Home Department* [1998] AC 539.

[16] *R v Secretary of State for the Home Department, ex parte Simms* [2000] 2 AC 115.

legislation as it does to Acts of Parliament. He penned a couple of sentences which have been much cited since:

> In the absence of express language or necessary implication to the contrary, the courts therefore presume that even the most general words [of Parliament] were intended to be subject to the basic rights of the individual. In this way the courts of the United Kingdom, though acknowledging the sovereignty of Parliament, apply principles of constitutionality little different from those which exist in countries where the power of the legislature is expressly limited by a constitutional document.[17]

Lord Hoffmann added that the Human Rights Act 1998, which at that time was not yet in force, would supplement 'the principles of fundamental human rights which exist at common law'. Further evidence of Lord Hoffmann's firm belief in the ability of the common law to curtail the excesses of government can be found in his judgment in what is known as the first Belmarsh case,[18] where, alone amongst the nine Law Lords who heard the appeal, he held that a British court was perfectly entitled to rule that the government had no legal justification for asserting that there was a public emergency threatening the life of the nation.[19] Lords Steyn and Hoffmann clearly believed that the common law could not only adequately protect human rights but that it could do so even when Parliament (other than expressly) passed laws which had the effect of violating basic rights.

Which of the current Supreme Court justices are the firmest supporters of the ability of the common law to do the work of the Human Rights Act is a matter of some speculation. The most likely candidates, it is submitted, are Lady Hale DP, Lord Kerr and Lord Reed.[20] The President of the Supreme Court, Lord Neuberger, is a firm supporter of human rights, but he is not sympathetic to the idea that judges can challenge the legality of an Act of Parliament. He made this clear in a lecture he delivered just before taking up his current role,[21] although in a more recent lecture he conceded that 'in extreme circumstances which are most unlikely to occur' Parliament is not supreme.[22] Lady Hale DP, Lord Kerr and Lord Reed appear to be of the view that the common law *could* protect human rights to the same extent that the Human Rights Act has done but that at present it is not in a fit

---

[17] ibid, 131F.

[18] *A v Secretary of State for the Home Department* [2004] UKHL 56, [2005] 2 AC 68.

[19] When aspects of the first Belmarsh case were reconsidered in Strasbourg, the European Court was content to accept that the UK government's determination that a public emergency existed was justifiable: *A v UK* (2009) 49 EHRR 29 (GC), paras 173–81.

[20] Contrast the views of Lord Sumption, as expressed in a lecture he delivered just before assuming the role of Justice of the Supreme Court: 'Judicial and Political Decision-Making: The Uncertain Boundary', The FA Mann Lecture 2012, www.pem.cam.ac.uk/wp-content/uploads/2012/07/1C-Sumption-article. pdf. See too Lord Sumption's 27th Sultan Azlan Shah Lecture, 'The Limits of Law', 20 November 2013, www.supremecourt.uk/docs/speech-131120.pdf.

[21] Lord Neuberger, 'Who are the Masters Now?', The Second Lord Alexander of Weedon Lecture, 8 April 2011. See too the interesting contribution by John McGarry, 'The Principle of Parliamentary Sovereignty' (2012) 32 *Legal Studies* 577.

[22] Lord Neuberger, 'Judges and Policy: A Delicate Balance', lecture delivered at the Institute for Government, 18 June 2012, www.supremecourt.uk/docs/speech-130618.pdf.

state to play that role. In her Warwick Law Lecture delivered in November 2013,[23] Lady Hale noted that the Home Secretary had stated at the Conservative Party conference earlier that year that the UK should withdraw from the ECHR if that was what was required in order to 'fix our human rights laws', and she then remarked that such withdrawal 'would raise all sorts of interesting questions about the effect of the decisions which have been made during the period while the Act was in force and whether the common law would now embrace many of the rights which were established during that time'.

What Lady Hale sought to do in that lecture was to illustrate how and why there are fundamental rights referred to in the Act which were not given reasonable protection in domestic law before the HRA came into force. That is why she thought the HRA should not be repealed. Unfortunately Lady Hale did not directly address the intriguing question of whether judges could legitimately seek to develop the common law on human rights even though, by repealing the HRA, Parliament would have sent a clear signal that it did not wish human rights to be protected in the ways that had occurred prior to the repeal. Would a judicial attempt to use the common law to plug gaps left by repeal of the Human Rights Act leave the judges open to the charge that they were seeking to circumvent the will of Parliament? The answer to that question very much depends on the specific wording of the legislation which is enacted to replace the HRA: to put an end to judicial creativity in this field a so-called 'British Bill of Rights' would have to be explicit in limiting the discretion of the judges to mine the common law for principles that mirror those already adopted by the European Court of Human Rights.

Lady Hale was in part prompted to consider repeal of the Act because of a contribution made to the debate by a retired judge of the High Court of Australia, Dyson Heydon. In 2013 he gave a lecture entitled 'Are Bills of Rights Necessary in Common Law Systems?'[24] in which he criticised Bills of Rights as being costly, of dubious legitimacy, productive of uncertainty, and responsible for undermining national sovereignty. But his most serious complaint was that Bills of Rights allow judges to interpret 'amorphous and vaguely defined rights' based on their own assumptions 'about the way life is or should be', a process which he thought undermined the rule of law. Heydon's position, reflecting very closely that of Lords Hoffmann and Steyn, is that Bills of Rights should be replaced with the principle of legality. He observed:

> The principle of legality, though more limited than section 3(1) [of the Human Rights Act], can achieve a similar purpose without entailing the drawback of involving the courts in creating new legislative rules.[25]

---

[23] Lady Hale, 'What's the Point of Human Rights?', lecture delivered at the University of Warwick, 28 November 2013, www.supremecourt.uk/docs/speech-131128.pdf.

[24] The lecture was delivered at the Universities of Cambridge and Oxford, but also at the Inner Temple in London. See www.innertemple.org.uk/downloads/members/lectures_2013/lecture_heydon_2013.pdf. It was later published at (2014) 130 *Law Quarterly Review* 392.

[25] ibid, 408–09.

Heydon also observed that the specificity of common law and statutory rules are preferable to abstract rights since they are adapted to the resolution of particular problems and are generally coherent with each other and with the wider legal system. As a legislative example he cited the Police and Criminal Evidence Act 1984 and as a common law example he cited tort law and the rules of evidential inadmissibility. At the basis of Heydon's stance is the conviction that it is not the job of judges to make law to the extent that they have been doing when applying the HRA.[26] He neglects to point out that, as far as common law rules on rights are concerned, they can be every bit as 'amorphous and vaguely defined' as the so-called abstract rights in the ECHR. He also fails to acknowledge the value in setting down underlying principles as guides to future development of the law.

In a typically thought-provoking contribution to the debate, Mark Elliott has argued that of late there has been a 'common law resurgence' and that there is a grain of truth in the suggestion that the Human Rights Act is simply doing what the common law could have been doing all along.[27] This seems to me to be an overly optimistic view. There is evidence that the common law has not yet developed the theories, principles and objectives which a committed approach to the protection of human rights demands. While courts may therefore be able to match the Human Rights Act in some respects, it will not be able to do so in many others.

II. HUMAN RIGHTS AT COMMON LAW PRIOR TO THE HUMAN RIGHTS ACT

When the HRA was enacted in 1998, the common law did already protect many fundamental rights, but in a haphazard, unsystematic fashion. It did not call them 'human' rights and it did not spell out when they could justifiably be limited. There were no legal textbooks on human rights law, the subject being covered either in books on international human rights law (leaving the reader to calculate the chances of such standards being applied in UK courts) or in books on constitutional law under the rubric 'civil liberties'. Textbooks on criminal law, criminal justice, police law, tort law, medical law and property law made little or no reference to human rights claims. The principle prevailed that everyone had the right to do anything unless there was a law prohibiting it, a notion largely derived from Sir William Blackstone's *Commentaries on the Law of England*, published in the mid-eighteenth century.[28] It was Blackstone's exposition of rights that led Jeremy Bentham to

---

[26] It is worth noting that Heydon J himself, in the case of *Momciolovic v R* [2011] HCA 30, would have struck down as unconstitutional the Charter of Human Rights and Responsibilities Act 2006 of the Australian state of Victoria because it gave the Supreme Court of Victoria a role which in his opinion was incompatible with its constitutional role under the federal Constitution. He was in the minority in that case.

[27] Mark Elliott, 'Beyond the European Convention: Human Rights and the Common Law', available at http://papers.ssrn.com/sol3/papers.cfm?abstract_id=2598071 and soon to be published in [2015] *Current Legal Problems*.

[28] Sir William Blackstone, *Commentaries on the Laws of England* (1765–69), lonang.com/library/reference/blackstone-commentaries-law-england/bla-110. In vol 1 Blackstone famously stated that 'the principal aim of society is to protect individuals in the enjoyment of those absolute rights, which were

declare a hundred years later that rights are 'nonsense', and that human rights are 'nonsense on stilts'.[29]

Had anyone thought of asking why human rights law was not a category of law until the late twentieth century, he or she would surely have concluded that it was because the common law did not recognise the idea that individuals could have rights enforceable against the State.[30] The State, it was said, could not be sued—a rule which found expression in the common law's 'act of state' doctrine and also in various Crown Proceedings Acts. In certain circumstances prerogative writs were available to force the State to behave in particular ways (and the writ of habeas corpus was obviously crucial in protecting people's right to freedom from arbitrary loss of liberty), but even when the courts began to develop the modern remedy of judicial review of administrative action they insisted that they were not challenging the substance, or merits, of administrative decisions but only the procedures used in arriving at those decisions.

Various branches of the common law *indirectly* protected human rights, most notably tort law to the extent that it provided remedies to people who had been assaulted or falsely imprisoned, or whose property had been damaged or stolen, but the courts never directly justified those tortious remedies on the basis that they were vindicating the victim's right to life, security, liberty, freedom from ill-treatment or property. The fact that, at that time, human rights theory had not yet accepted that human rights are values which need to be protected per se, rather than only when State action is involved, is another reason why no one seems to have seriously argued for the delineation of a branch of law called human rights law. On the rare occasions that the courts did grapple with issues such as freedom of expression and assembly, they rarely enunciated grand principles to justify those freedoms or specific conditions for permitting limitations to those freedoms. This is one of the reasons why, before the enactment of the Human Rights Act, the European Commission and Court of Human Rights were asked to decide on 70 separate occasions whether the highest UK court—the Appellate Committee of the House of Lords—had decided a case in a way that was compatible with the ECHR and why, on 17 of those occasions, the Commission or Court found that the House of Lords had failed to identify a violation of at least one provision in the ECHR.[31] In many

---

vested in them by the immutable laws of nature, but which could not be preserved in peace without that mutual assistance and intercourse which is gained by the institution of friendly and social communities'.

[29] Jeremy Bentham, 'Anarchical Fallacies' in Ross Harrison (ed), *Jeremy Bentham: Selected Writings on Utilitarianism* (Wordsworth, 2000) 405.

[30] *cf* Lady Hale (n 23): 'Thus it was [after the UK recognized the right of individual petition in 1966] that we discovered that United Kingdom law did not always conform to the rights which had been spelled out in the Convention ... The idea that the citizen might have rights which he could assert against the state was unknown to us' (3–4).

[31] See Part A of Appendix 3 in B Dickson, *Human Rights and the United Kingdom Supreme Court* (Oxford, Oxford University Press, 2013); the figure of 17 includes three cases where the Commission promoted a friendly settlement between the applicant and the UK government—in effect a recognition by the latter that its chances of winning the case on the merits were slim. For further details see B Dickson, 'The Record of the House of Lords in Strasbourg' (2012) 128 *Law Quarterly Review* 354.

of these 17 cases the House of Lords had simply avoided the use of human rights language altogether.

The notion that the common law recognised a category of rights designated as 'constitutional rights' was just gaining support when the HRA came along, but in 2006 it was definitively squashed by the House of Lords in *Watkins v Secretary of State for the Home Department*.[32] It was almost as if the advent of the HRA had blinded their Lordships to any other source of human rights in English law.[33]

III. WHAT WOULD BE LOST IF THE HRA WERE REPEALED?

Repeal *simpliciter* of the Human Rights Act would immediately mean that the status of the ECHR in UK law would return to what it was before the coming into force of the Act.[34] The ECHR could thenceforth be used only as a guide to the development of UK law in situations where the meaning of that law was unclear and it would, as a result, have a greater role in the interpretation of legislation than in the development of the common law because the latter is not really 'interpreted' so much as constantly re-invented. Presumably provisions in other Acts using the term 'Convention rights' and defining it in the same way as the HRA would be impliedly, if not expressly, repealed too.[35] Provisions in Acts which devolve law-making powers to legislatures in Edinburgh, Cardiff and Belfast, and prohibit them and the ministers in the devolved governments from making legislation that is incompatible with Convention rights,[36] would fall into this impliedly repealed category, although as human rights are a devolved matter in Scotland and Northern Ireland such repeal would require the consent of the Scottish Parliament and Northern Ireland Assembly in line with the so-called Sewel convention.[37] Of course, as noted by Lord Hope in 2010,[38] unless the UK were to denounce the ECHR, which is allowable under Article 58 of the ECHR itself, it would remain possible for disappointed litigants to lodge an application in Strasbourg after exhausting their domestic remedies within the UK court system.[39]

A repeal of the HRA would also mean that the specific innovations contained in that Act would no longer apply.[40] In particular, the duty to 'take account' of

---

[32] *Watkins v Secretary of State for the Home Department* [2006] UKHL 17, [2006] 2 AC 395.

[33] Dickson (n 31) esp 20–39.

[34] For the pre-1998 position see n 9 above.

[35] eg the Extradition Act 2003, ss 21 and 87; UK Borders Act 2007, s 33(2)(a).

[36] Scotland Act 1998, ss 29(2)(d) and 57(2); Government of Wales Act 2006, ss 81(1) and 94(6)(c); Northern Ireland Act 1998, ss 6(2)(c) and 24(1)(a).

[37] See Paul Bowers, *The Sewel Convention*, House of Commons Library, Standard Note SN/PC/2084 (2005).

[38] See text at n 8 above.

[39] In its proposals for a British Bill of Rights and Responsibilities (see n 3), the Conservative Party has said (at p 8) that if it is unable to reach an agreement with the Council of Europe that its approach to the application of the ECHR is legitimate, 'the UK would be left with no alternative but to withdraw from the European Convention on Human Rights, at the point at which our Bill comes into effect'.

[40] For a detailed analysis of these innovations, see eg R Masterman and I Leigh, *The United Kingdom's Statutory Bill of Rights: Constitutional and Comparative Perspectives* (Oxford, Oxford University Press, 2013); M Amos, *Human Rights Law*, 2nd edn (Oxford, Hart Publishing, 2014).

Strasbourg jurisprudence imposed by section 2 would disappear, as would the duty under section 3 to interpret all legislation in a way which is compatible with Convention rights 'so far as it is possible to do so'. The removal of section 2 might not make too much difference, because a duty to 'take account' does not necessarily mean that domestic judges must follow what Strasbourg has said. In the absence of any replacement legislation specifically requiring UK courts not to tie themselves to Strasbourg decisions, domestic courts would be entitled to apply the approach which the Supreme Court has itself adopted, namely that decisions of the ECtHR should be followed if they represent a settled line of case law. As Lord Neuberger put it in *Manchester City Council v Pinnock*:

> Where, however, there is a clear and consistent line of decisions whose effect is not inconsistent with some fundamental substantive or procedural aspect of our law, and whose reasoning does not appear to overlook or misunderstand some argument or point of principle, we consider that it would be wrong for this court not to follow that line.[41]

As regards the repeal of section 3, this would have the effect of precluding UK courts from interpreting legislation in a Convention-compatible way if the legislation is unambiguous. To date the courts have been prepared to apply section 3 even to unambiguous legislation,[42] presumably because of the requirement to adopt a Convention-compliant interpretation 'so far as ... is possible'. In the absence of section 3, it is submitted, it would be *impossible* to do so when legislation is unambiguous. That, at any rate, is what the doctrine of parliamentary sovereignty entails, though as we shall see in the concluding section below there would remain an exception where an Act is implementing EU law.

At first sight, one of the most startling aspects of the Human Rights Act is the power conferred on senior judges by section 4 to declare legislation to be incompatible with Convention rights. But over time, judges and other commentators have come to realise that this power is not a particularly significant one. Under section 4(6) the impact of a declaration of incompatibility is rendered minimal, since it 'does not affect the validity, continuing operation or enforcement' of the legislative provision in question and the declaration 'is not binding on the parties to the proceedings in which it is made'. The only consequence flowing from a declaration is that it permits (not requires) a remedial order to be issued by the government under section 10 of the Act. To date the government has been willing to issue such remedial orders in instances where UK courts have issued a declaration of incompatibility and no further appeal is pending;[43] it has been slower to do so in situations where the ECtHR has found UK legislation to be in violation of a Convention right,[44] the best example of its reluctance being the failure to respond

---

[41] *Manchester City Council v Pinnock* [2010] UKSC 45, [2011] 2 AC 104, para 48. See too *R (Chester) v Parole Board* [2013] UKSC 63, [2013] 3 WLR 1076, paras 25–35 per Lord Mance and paras 136–38 per Lord Sumption.

[42] *R v A (No 2) (Rape Shield)* [2001] UKHL 25, [2002] 1 AC 45.

[43] Only three such orders have been issued to date: Mental Health Act 1983 (Remedial) Order 2001; Asylum and Immigration (Treatment of Claimants, etc) Act 2004 (Remedial) Order 2011; Sexual Offences Act 2003 (Remedial) Order 2012.

[44] One instance is the Terrorism Act 2000 (Remedial) Order 2011.

to the ECtHR's decision on the voting rights of prisoners in *Hirst v UK (No 2)*.[45] If section 4 were to be repealed, it is submitted that UK courts could still express the view that domestic UK legislation is not compatible with the ECHR, without issuing a formal declaration to that effect.[46] This could not result in any remedial order under section 10, since that would have been repealed too, but it would be an implied invitation to the losing litigant to lodge an application in Strasbourg. At times, that in itself might be sufficient to prompt the UK government to put matters right by amending the relevant legislation.

Possibly the most important consequence of the repeal of the Human Rights Act would be the loss of section 7, which confers on people who think that their Convention rights have been violated by a public authority the right to sue that authority. In effect the HRA creates a tort of breach of statutory duty, albeit one which is hedged around with limitations concerning the remedies that can flow from a finding of breach. To an extent, section 7 represents the way in which the UK attempts to comply with Article 13 of the ECHR (the right to an effective remedy), even though the definition of Convention rights within the HRA specifically excludes Article 13.[47] The problem is that, while UK courts have willingly upheld many claims brought under section 7, they have not reinforced that willingness by developing comparable common law rights of action for breaches of human rights. Even when some judges in the Court of Appeal and House of Lords were toying with the idea of creating a category of 'constitutional rights', they were still reluctant to provide meaningful remedies for violations of those rights.[48]

In cases brought under the Human Rights Act in which claims have also been based on the common law, the courts have not been prepared to develop existing common law principles to reflect the growing concern about human rights. A powerful example is provided by the conjoined appeals in *Van Colle v Chief Constable of Hertfordshire Police* and *Smith v Chief Constable of Sussex Police*.[49] In the former, where the claim was based solely on the Human Rights Act, the House of Lords held that there was no breach of the police's duty to avoid a real and immediate risk to the life of the claimants' son (who was to be a chief witness for the prosecution in a trial for armed robbery but had been murdered by the person accused of that robbery before the trial could start). In the latter, where the claim was based solely on the common law of negligence, the House of Lords held that it was not possible for a victim of or a witness to a crime to sue the police for their alleged negligence because that would divert the police from their main responsibility, which is to prevent and detect crime. Despite Lord Bingham's valiant attempt in *Smith* to create a

---

[45] *Hirst v UK (No 2)* (2006) 42 EHRR 41 (GC).

[46] Ben Boult has suggested that some other institution, such as the Parliamentary Joint Committee on Human Rights, be given the power to declare legislation, or perhaps just draft legislation, incompatible with the ECHR. See his 'How to Make a British Bill of Rights Work for Everyone' (3 November 2013), www.conservativehome.com/platform/2013/11/from-b_boult-how-to-make-a-british-bill-of-rights-work-for-everyone.html.

[47] Human Rights Act 1998, s 1(1)(a).

[48] See eg *Cullen v Chief Constable of the RUC* [2003] UKHL 39, [2003] 1 WLR 1763.

[49] *Van Colle v Chief Constable of Hertfordshire Police* [2008] UKHL 50, [2009] 1 AC 225; *Smith v Chief Constable of Sussex Police* [2008] UKHL 50, [2009] 1 AC 225.

'liability principle' at common law,[50] which would largely have matched the duty impliedly imposed by Article 2 ECHR, his fellow judges were having none of it.[51] A further example of the reluctance of UK judges to develop the common law in line with the ECtHR's jurisprudence is their refusal to accept outright that there is a right to privacy in English law. This was made apparent not only in the *Wainwright* litigation, where a mother and son who had been strip-searched when visiting a family member in prison lost their claim in the House of Lords[52] but won it in the ECtHR,[53] but also in the *Naomi Campbell*[54] and *Michael Douglas* cases,[55] where UK courts effectively provided relief to victims of breaches of privacy but felt compelled to wrap it up in the more traditional language of breach of confidentiality.

IV. THE SIDELINING OF THE COMMON LAW'S APPROACH TO HUMAN RIGHTS

A consequence of the failure of judges to establish a category of common law based around human rights has meant that, since the coming into force of the HRA, UK judges have allowed the Act to almost completely dominate their approach to the protection of human rights. It is laudable that they have applied the Act so enthusiastically (even if in some respects their decisions have been disappointing—on the applicability of the 'primary legislation defence' provided by section 6(2),[56] on the definition of 'public authority' provided by section 6(3) and 6(5),[57] and on the extent of judicial remedies available under section 8),[58] but in the process of embracing the Act they have neglected the development of the common law. Their approach is epitomised in the 'mirror' or *Ullah* principle—that domestic courts should protect Convention rights to no lesser extent, but also no greater, than the ECtHR is prepared to do.[59] Although it is arguable that when he first referred to this approach Lord Bingham did not intend that it should apply to cases which related to facts occurring entirely within the UK (in *Ullah* itself the question was the degree to which a UK court should take into account the likelihood of Convention rights being violated in a foreign country, outside of Europe), his dictum has been elevated to the status of a general rule. Lord Hoffmann convinced his colleagues that it should not be applied in situations where the ECtHR expressly

---

[50] ibid, paras 44–60.
[51] Lord Hope, para 77f, Lord Phillips, para 100f, Lord Carswell, para 109, Lord Brown, paras 127–40.
[52] *Wainwright v Home Office* [2003] UKHL 53, [2004] 2 AC 406. The decision was taken on facts that occurred before the Human Rights Act came into force.
[53] *Wainwright v UK* (2007) 44 EHRR 809.
[54] *Campbell v MGN Ltd* [2004] UKHL 22, [2004] 2 AC 457.
[55] *Douglas v Hello!* [2007] UKHL 21, [2008] 1 AC 1.
[56] *R (Hooper) v Secretary of State for Work and Pensions* [2005] UKHL 29, [2005] 1 WLR 1681.
[57] *YL v Birmingham City Council* [2007] UKHL 27, [2008] AC 95, which led to the insertion of s 145 into the Health and Social Care Act 2008.
[58] *R (Greenfield) v Secretary of State for the Home Department* [2005] UKHL 14, [2005] 1 WLR 673.
[59] *R (Ullah) v Special Adjudicator* [2004] UKHL 26, [2004] 2 AC 323.

allowed Member States a margin of appreciation, as when deciding who should be allowed to adopt children,[60] and valiant extra-judicial efforts have been made by Lord Kerr[61] and Lady Hale[62] to explain that the principle is not one that should be retained in its present form, but to date the Supreme Court has not presented an agreed alternative.[63] UK courts have also bought into a 'dialogic' approach, whereby they tailor their judgments to bring them into line with Strasbourg jurisprudence. The *Horncastle/Al-Khawaja* dialogue over hearsay evidence in criminal cases,[64] the *Pinnock/Kay* dialogue over eviction of tenants from social housing[65] and the *M'Loughlin Hutchinson* dialogue over whole life sentences[66] are the most outstanding instances of this phenomenon. On the first two occasions, no matter how the Supreme Court may try to present matters, the voice that won the day in these dialogues was that of the Strasbourg Court.[67] Only on the third occasion did the UK judicial view (as expounded by the Court of Appeal) prevail.

Domestic judicial fixation with the idea that the HRA can operate only against state bodies (ie vertically) is a further demonstration of an undue focus on an international approach to human rights. Hence, domestic courts have regularly refused

---

[60] See *Re G (Adoption: Unmarried Couple)* [2008] UKHL 38, [2009] 1 AC 173, where the issue was whether it was lawful to prevent unmarried couples from applying to adopt a child in Northern Ireland. The courts in Northern Ireland had upheld the compatibility of the relevant statutory provision (art 14 of the Adoption (NI) Order 1987) on the basis that it reflected the deliberate choice of the legislature at the time, given the conservative views of the people of Northern Ireland regarding unmarried heterosexual couples living together and homosexual couples bringing up children. Lord Hoffmann said that it was irrelevant that the ECtHR had not yet declared that States must allow unmarried couples to adopt children, because under the Human Rights Act 1998 UK courts had to uphold Convention rights in a way which *they* thought was appropriate. In his opinion, to draw a distinction in this context between married and unmarried couples was irrational because it applied a blanket rule in situations where the best interests of the child might lead to the conclusion that an unmarried couple should be permitted to adopt. He therefore concluded that under Art 14 of the ECHR the statutory provision was unjustifiably discriminatory. As the provision was a piece of secondary legislation, the House of Lords had the power to invalidate it. Delivered just nine months before his Judicial Studies Board lecture referred to earlier (see n 11 above), Lord Hoffmann's judgment is a clear indication that he was in favour of UK judges being the final arbiter as to what is or is not a human right in this country.

[61] See eg Lord Kerr, 'The UK Supreme Court: The Modest Underworker of Strasbourg' The Clifford Chance Lecture, 25 January 2012, www.supremecourt.uk/docs/speech_120125.pdf. See too Lord Kerr's dissenting judgments in *Ambrose v Harris* [2011] UKSC 43, [2011] 1 WLR 2435 (on a detainee's right of access to a solicitor) and in *Moohan v Lord Advocate* [2014] UKSC 67 (on the right of prisoners to vote in the Scottish referendum, where Lord Wilson also dissented).

[62] Lady Hale, '*Argentoratum Locutum*: Is Strasbourg or the Supreme Court Supreme?' [2012] *European Human Rights Law Review* 534; 'What's the Point of Human Rights?' (n 23). Lady Hale rightly points out, at 10–11, that in *Rabone v Pennine Care NHS Foundation Trust* [2012] UKSC 2, [2012] 2 AC 72 the Supreme Court went beyond the ECtHR's interpretation of the duty to protect life implied in Art 2 of the ECHR. She adds that the European Court later approved of *Rabone* in *Reynolds v UK* (2012) 55 EHRR 35.

[63] See also J Lewis, 'The European Ceiling on Human Rights' [2007] *Public Law* 720; R Singh, 'Interpreting Bills of Rights' (2008) 29 *Statute Law Review* 82.

[64] *R v Horncastle* [2009] UKSC 14, [2010] 2 AC 373; *Al-Khawaja and Tahery v UK* (2012) 54 EHRR 23 (GC); see generally Dickson (n 30) 212–16.

[65] *Manchester City Council v Pinnock* [2010] UKSC 45, [2011] 2 AC 104; *Kay v UK* (2012) 54 EHRR 30; Dickson (n 31) 246–56.

[66] *R v M'Loughlin* [2014] EWCA Crim 188, [2014] 1 WLR 3964; *Hutchinson v UK* App no 57592/08 judgment of 3 February 2015 (pending before the Grand Chamber).

[67] By way of contrast, it is arguable that the voice of the House of Lords prevailed over that of the ECtHR in the context of a public authority's tortious liability for failing to protect a person from assault: see *Barrett v Enfield London Borough Council* [2001] 2 AC 550; *Z v UK* (2002) 34 EHRR 3; *Van Colle v Chief Constable of Hertfordshire Police* (n 48); *Van Colle v UK* (2013) 56 EHRR 23.

to apply Convention rights horizontally, between private entities.[68] In addition, they have expressly adopted an 'outcome, not process' approach when considering whether public authorities have complied with their human rights obligations: contrary to how they normally deal with applications for judicial review, they are content in human rights cases to discover that the decision made by the public authority did not in the end violate rights even if during the process of reaching that decision the authority had little or no regard for those rights.[69] The judges have also tended to be deferential to decision-makers whom they have deemed to have greater constitutional competence in particular fields, as in *Huang v Secretary of State for the Home Department*,[70] where the Appellate Committee collectively supported the view that what might appear to be deference on the part of judges is in fact 'performance of the ordinary judicial task of weighing up competing considerations on each side and according appropriate weight to the judgment of a person with responsibility for a given subject matter and access to special sources of knowledge and advice'.[71] The top UK judges have tended to defer to devolved legislatures too, as in *AXA General Insurance Ltd v Lord Advocate*[72] and *Assembly Commission for Wales v Attorney-General*,[73] although the Supreme Court's more recent decisions in *Salvesen v Riddell*[74] and *In re Recovery of Medical Costs for Asbestos Diseases (Wales) Bill*[75] might be early signs of a more interventionist approach.

More generally, and more importantly, UK courts have consistently failed to enunciate clear common law principles in favour of human rights values such as liberty, freedom from ill-treatment, freedom of expression, equality and the franchise.[76] We can see this in relation to freedom of expression, for example, when we examine the history of decisions by the House of Lords being overturned in Strasbourg: *Sunday Times v UK* (1979),[77] *Harman v UK* (1984),[78] *Observer and Guardian v UK* (1991),[79] and *Goodwin v UK* (1996).[80] Eventually, in *Animal*

---

[68] See the decisions in *Campbell* (n 54) and *Douglas* (n 55).

[69] *R (Shabina Begum) v Governors of Denbigh High School* [2006] UKHL 15, [2007] 1 AC 100; *Belfast City Council v Miss Behavin' Ltd* [2007] UKHL 19, [2007] 1 WLR 1420.

[70] *Huang v Secretary of State for the Home Department* [2007] UKHL 11, [2007] 2 AC 167.

[71] ibid, para 16. This was the sole opinion of the whole Committee, comprising Lords Bingham, Hoffmann, Carswell and Brown, and Lady Hale.

[72] *AXA General Insurance Ltd v Lord Advocate* [2011] UKSC 46, [2012] 1 AC 868.

[73] *Assembly Commission for Wales v Attorney-General* [2012] UKSC 53, [2012] 3 WLR 1294. See too *Re Agricultural Sector (Wales) Bill* [2014] UKSC 43, [2014] 1 WLR 2622.

[74] *Salvesen v Riddell* [2013] UKSC 22. Here the Supreme Court (Lords Hope, Kerr, Wilson, Reed and Toulson) unanimously held that Mr Salvesen's right to peaceful enjoyment of his possessions as the landlord of a farm, under Art 1 of Protocol 1 to the ECHR, had been violated by s 72(10) Agricultural Holdings (Scotland) Act 2003 Act, which was therefore outside the competence of the Scottish Parliament to make. For the first time, the top UK court made an order (under s 102(2)(b) Scotland Act 1998) suspending the effect of its finding until the defect was corrected.

[75] [2015] UKSC 3, [2015] 2 WLR 481.

[76] On this last right see the recent decision of the UK Supreme Court (5:2) in *Moohan v Lord Advocate* [2014] UKSC 67.

[77] *Sunday Times v UK* (1979–80) 2 EHRR 245.

[78] *Harman v UK* (1984) 38 DR 53.

[79] *Observer and Guardian v UK* (1992) 14 EHRR 153.

[80] *Goodwin v UK* (1996) 22 EHRR 123. For a deeper analysis of the 'dialogue' between the House of Lords and the European Court in these cases on the right to freedom of expression, see Dickson (n 30) 281–91, 294–300.

Defenders International v UK (2013)[81] the ECtHR did hold (by the narrowest of majorities, 9:8) that the House of Lords had struck an appropriate balance between the rights of campaigners for policy change and the interest of society in regulating broadcasting, but this conclusion may say more about the conservatism of the current ECtHR than about the commitment of UK courts to a common law of human rights. In the recent case of *Kennedy v Charity Commission*, two of the seven Supreme Court justices who heard the appeal felt that the common law's protection of the right to information was not as extensive as that permitted by Article 10 ECHR.[82] But in two further recent decisions, and without any recourse to the ECHR, the Supreme Court has strongly upheld the rights of access to information and to freedom of expression: *R (Evans) v Attorney General*[83] and *O (A Child) v Rhodes*.[84]

V. THE OCCASIONAL RE-EMERGENCE OF THE COMMON LAW'S APPROACH TO HUMAN RIGHTS

Since the enactment of the HRA there have been a few occasions on which UK judges have fallen back on the common law in order to protect human rights, but they are the exceptions which prove the rule. They have mostly been instances where the judges have not been able to find strong support in the ECtHR's case law for propositions which are already well established at common law, so they have been content to rely on the latter alone. The cases often involve the right of access to justice or to a fair trial—the realm of Article 6 ECHR.

Thus, in *R (Roberts) v Parole Board*[85] two of the five Law Lords (albeit dissenting) held that, while it might not be a violation of Article 5 ECHR for the Parole Board to refuse to disclose to a prisoner's legal representatives material that was relevant to his parole review and to disclose it instead to specially appointed advocates who could ask questions on the prisoner's behalf at a closed hearing before the Board but without consulting with him directly, this *would* constitute unfairness under the common law. Having noted that 'the course proposed and so far adopted in the conduct of the appellant's parole review involves a substantial departure from the standards of procedural fairness which would ordinarily be observed in conducting a review of this kind', and having cited the words of Lord Hoffmann in *Simms* which I have quoted above, Lord Bingham added:

---

[81] *Animal Defenders International v UK* (2013) 57 EHRR 1.
[82] *Kennedy v Charity Commission* [2014] UKSC 20, [2014] 2 WLR 808.
[83] [2015] UKSC 21, [2015] 2 WLR 813. Here the Supreme Court found that the Attorney General had wrongly tried to prevent the publication of private correspondence between the Prince of Wales and government departments.
[84] [2015] UKSC 32; [2015] 2 WLR 1373. Here the Supreme Court allowed the publication of the appellant's personal memoir even though the way he described the abuse he had suffered as a child might cause psychological harm to his own son. Lady Hale and Lord Toulson said (at para 77): 'Freedom to report the truth is a basic right to which the law gives a very high level of protection'.
[85] *R (Roberts) v Parole Board* [2005] UKHL 45, [2005] 2 AC 738.

It would in my opinion violate the principle of legality, strongly relied on in argument by Mr Owen, and undermine the rule of law itself, if such a departure were to be justified as incidental or conducive to the discharge of the Board's functions.[86]

The learned judge supported his view by referring to several other situations in which the ordinary rules of procedural fairness were departed from, but in all of them the changes were expressly authorised by Parliament. He concluded that it is 'contrary to legal principle and good democratic practice to read such a power into a statute which contains no hint whatever that Parliament intended or even contemplated such a departure'.[87]

Lord Steyn also cited Lord Hoffmann's words in *Simms*, and he himself added:

The special advocate procedure strikes at the root of the prisoner's fundamental right to a basically fair procedure. If such departures are to be introduced it must be done by Parliament. It would be quite wrong to make an assumption that, if Parliament had been faced with the question whether it should authorise, in this particular field, the special advocate procedure, it would have sanctioned it. After all, in our system the working assumption is that Parliament legislates for a European liberal democracy which respects fundamental rights. Even before the Human Rights Act 1998 came into force, and a fortiori since then, the courts have been entitled to assume that Parliament does not lightly override fundamental rights.[88]

The majority in the House, however, were not persuaded by this view. Lords Woolf, Rodger and Carswell all held that there were ample express and implied powers for the Parole Board to proceed as it had done in this case. It did not require any more specific authorisation.

Later in 2005, in *A v Secretary of State for the Home Department (No 2)*,[89] the so-called second Belmarsh case, Lord Bingham was more successful in persuading six fellow Law Lords that there was a common law principle—even a constitutional principle—forbidding the admission in evidence of information obtained as a result of the torture of a third party. Discovering and applying this principle was crucial to the case because at that time there was no definitive ruling by the ECtHR to the same effect. The decision is therefore an excellent example of how UK judges have occasionally clarified and developed the common law on human rights even though the HRA is also applicable to the facts. Sadly, however, the seven judges then divided 4:3 over whether the prosecution or the defence should bear the burden of proving that information may indeed have been obtained by torture. The majority placed the burden on the defence,[90] even though Lord Nicholls thought that this

---

[86] ibid, para 25. This was said in light of the fact that para 1(2)(b) of Sched 5 to the Criminal Justice Act 1991 conferred on the Parole Board the capacity 'to do such things and enter into such transactions as are incidental to or conducive to the discharge of' some of its functions. As a statutory body and not a court, the Parole Board had no *inherent* powers.

[87] ibid, para 30.

[88] ibid, para 93. See too the Atkin Memorial Lecture delivered by Dinah Rose QC in 2011, 'Beef and Liberty: Fundamental Rights and the Common Law'.

[89] *A v Secretary of State for the Home Department (No 2)* [2005] UKHL 71, [2006] 2 AC 221.

[90] Lords Hope, Rodger, Carswell and Brown. The minority comprised Lords Bingham, Nicholls and Hoffmann.

would 'largely nullify' the admissibility principle and Lord Hoffmann said it would be 'absurd'. When the issue was taken to Strasbourg in a subsequent UK case, the ECtHR unanimously agreed with the minority view expressed in the Lords.[91] This further demonstrates the benefits of having two complementary systems to protect human rights: the common law system and the Convention system.

The common law was again invoked, once more in an Article 6 context, in *Ahmed v Her Majesty's Treasury*.[92] As in the minority judgments in *Roberts*, the principle that motivated the reasoning was that of legality. Because the legislation in question had been passed in furtherance of a UN Security Council resolution, which the House of Lords had previously confirmed was hierarchically superior even to the ECHR,[93] the judges did not consider the applicability of the HRA. Instead they simply ruled that the Orders in Council in question were ultra vires because the parent Act—the United Nations Act 1946—could not be assumed to have conferred a power to deprive someone of his or her assets merely because there was a reasonable suspicion that that person 'may be' participating in the financing of terrorism. Such a power would breach not just the fundamental right of unimpeded access to a court but also that of peaceful enjoyment of one's property. The Supreme Court again cited the words of Lord Hoffmann in *Simms*.

In relation to Article 8 ECHR, the right to a private and family life, the common law was called in aid in *R (Purdy) v DPP*,[94] which was the last decision ever issued by the Appellate Committee of the House of Lords (and expressly chosen for that honour). The judgments address the question of whether it is always a crime to assist another person to commit suicide. In answering it the Law Lords took account of the reprimand that had been issued by the Grand Chamber of the ECtHR a few years earlier in *Pretty v UK*,[95] where all 17 judges made it clear that the claim to have an assisted suicide did at least engage the right to a private life, contrary to what the majority of Law Lords had intimated when the *Pretty* case was before them.[96] As if to indicate that on this occasion the domestic court could go one better that the Strasbourg Court, the Law Lords in *Purdy* ruled that the Director of Public Prosecutions should issue guidelines on the factors he would take into account when deciding whether to consent to the prosecution of someone who had assisted a suicide. While not amounting to a new substantive approach to Article 8, the ruling does at least illustrate how much more room domestic courts have, especially in a common law system, for developing novel remedies in human rights cases. But in *R (Nicklinson) v Ministry of Justice* only a bare majority of the nine Supreme Court

---

[91] *A v UK* (2009) 49 EHRR 29.

[92] *Ahmed v Her Majesty's Treasury* [2010] UKSC 2, [2010] 2 UKSC 534.

[93] In *R (Al-Jedda) v Secretary of State for Defence* [2007] UKHL 58, [2008] AC 332 the House relied on Art 103 of the UN Charter, which reads: 'In the event of a conflict between the obligations of the Members of the United Nations under the present Charter and their obligations under any other international agreement, their obligations under the present Charter shall prevail.' However, when this case reached the ECtHR, the judges unanimously reversed the House of Lords' ruling and held that Art 103 did not have such an automatically overriding effect: *Al-Jedda v UK* (2011) 53 EHRR 23.

[94] *R (Purdy) v DPP* [2009] UKHL 45, [2010] 1 AC 345.

[95] *Pretty v UK* (2002) 35 EHRR 1.

[96] *R (Pretty) v DPP* [2001] UKHL 61, [2002] 1 AC 800.

justices were of the view that they had the constitutional authority to declare the general prohibition on assisted suicide imposed by section 2 of the Suicide Act 1961 incompatible with Article 8, and only two of the five justices in the majority (Lady Hale DP and Lord Kerr) were prepared to support such a declaration.[97]

Perhaps the most significant of the instances where the UK's senior judges have emphasised the survival of the common law on human rights is the Supreme Court case of *R (Osborn) v Parole Board*,[98] where a long judgment on three conjoined appeals was given by Lord Reed, with whom his four colleagues, including the President and Deputy President, concurred. As in *Roberts*, the case concerned oral hearings before the Parole Board. One of the appellants was a determinate sentence prisoner who had been released on licence but then recalled to custody, while the other two were indeterminate sentence prisoners who had already served their minimum terms. In setting out the factors that needed to be taken into account when deciding whether the Board should hold an oral hearing, Lord Reed peppered his judgment with reminders that in UK law human rights are protected not just by the Human Rights Act 1998 but also by the common law. He stated, for instance, that the HRA

> does not supersede the protection of human rights under common law or statute, or create a discrete body of law based on the judgments of the European Court. Human rights continue to be protected by our domestic law, interpreted and developed in accordance with the Act when appropriate.[99]

To some extent Lord Reed's emphasis on the common law in this context is understandable, because the wording of Article 5 ECHR makes it clear that Member States must protect the right to liberty not just in accordance with the minimum standards laid down in the Convention but also in accordance with the requirements of domestic law if those standards are higher. It was therefore necessary to stipulate what those domestic standards are. But it seems that Lord Reed was anxious to send out a parallel message—one that reasserts the commitment of the common law to the protection of human rights and provides an implicit reassurance that if for some reason the Human Rights Act were no longer available to protect human rights then UK judges could do so using the common law.

Laudable though this attempt at reassurance may be, there are still reasons to doubt whether the common law would be an adequate replacement for the Act. This is not just because, as discussed earlier, there is at least one major feature of the Act which will not be replicated by the common law (namely, its conferral of a right of action against public authorities which have allegedly contravened Convention rights). It is also because, taken together, the five examples which Lord Reed provides of the common law coming to the rescue of human rights[100] are not totally

---

[97] *R (Nicklinson) v Ministry of Justice* [2014] UKSC 38, [2014] 3 WLR 200.

[98] *R (Osborn) v Parole Board* [2013] UKSC 61, [2013] 3 WLR 1020.

[99] ibid, para 57. See too paras 55 and 56, in the latter of which Lord Reed writes: 'the Convention cannot therefore be treated as if it were Moses and the prophets.'

[100] ibid, paras 58–62. The cases are *R (Daly) v Secretary of State for the Home Dept* [2001] UKHL 26, [2001] 2 AC 532; *R (West) v Parole Board* [2005] UKHL 1, [2005] 1 WLR 350; the second Belmarsh

convincing proof of its capacity to plug all the gaps that would be left by the Act's repeal.

VI. CONCLUSION

If the HRA is repealed, it is likely that it will be replaced by some other statutory system for protecting human rights. But that system, almost by definition, will not be as protective as the HRA has been. This makes it all the more important that our senior judges make greater use of the common law's approach to human rights. They need to reaffirm that human rights are fundamental to the way in which the common law views the freedoms of individuals and the limits to the powers of the State. They also need to specify which of the principles associated with the ECtHR's approach to human rights they want to insert into the common law. It would be particularly helpful if, for example, they ruled that the legitimacy, necessity and proportionality tests which the ECtHR applies when assessing whether interferences with rights are justified[101] are ones which the common law applies as well. It may even be appropriate for the top courts to revive the concept of constitutional rights, which the House of Lords killed off in *Watkins v Secretary of State for the Home Department*.[102] That would accord human rights a constitutional status and could mean, for example, that legislation could not interfere with the essence of those rights unless Parliament expressly stated that that was its intention.

In fields in which the UK is implementing EU law, the courts may be able to turn instead—or as well—to the EU Charter of Fundamental Rights, the content of which overlaps greatly with the ECHR. It has been in force within the UK since 1 December 2009, when the Treaty of Lisbon took effect, but only when the UK is implementing EU law and subject to ongoing uncertainty regarding the effect of the so-called 'opt-out' which the UK government claims it negotiated under Protocol 30 to the Treaty of Lisbon.[103] The realisation that the EU Charter may lead to the entry of additional rights into UK law through the back door prompted Chris Grayling, the former Minister of Justice whose views on the Human Rights Act were summarised at the start of this chapter, to say that he is looking for a test case to check whether the Charter applies in the way that the Court of Justice of the European Union (CJEU) believes it does.[104] An example of what reliance on the EU Charter

case (see text at n 87 above); *R (Guardian News and Media Ltd) v City of Westminster Magistrates' Court* [2012] EWCA Civ 420, [2013] QB 618; *R (Sturnham) v Parole Board* [2013] UKSC 23, [2013] 2 WLR 1157.

[101] See generally DJ Harris, M O'Boyle, EP Bates and CM Buckley, *Harris, O'Boyle and Warbrick: Law of the European Convention on Human Rights*, 3rd edn (Oxford, Oxford University Press, 2014) 505–20.

[102] *Watkins v Secretary of State for the Home Department* [2006] UKHL 17, [2006] 2 AC 395.

[103] On this see Richard Clayton and Cian Murphy, 'The Emergence of the EU Charter of Fundamental Rights in United Kingdom Law' [2014] *European Human Rights Law Review* 469.

[104] He was reacting to the views expressed by Mostyn J in *R (AB) v Secretary of State for the Home Dept* [2013] EWHC 3453 (Admin), which concerned a claim that, as a result of UK authorities inserting

can achieve is provided by *Benkharbouche v Embassy of the Republic of Sudan (Jurisdictional Points: State Immunity)*, a decision of the Court of Appeal.[105] The case involved a claim by the government of Sudan that it could not be sued in a UK court by a disaffected employee of Moroccan nationality because it enjoyed state immunity under both UK law and international law. The Court of Appeal confirmed the view of the Employment Appeal Tribunal and held that it was not possible to interpret the State Immunity Act 1978 in a way which is compatible with the position of the ECtHR on Article 6,[106] or indeed Article 14, and that therefore the relevant provisions of the 1978 Act should be declared incompatible with Convention rights. But it also accepted the argument that the relevant provisions of the 1978 Act should be *disapplied* because they violated the rights to an effective remedy and to a fair trial conferred by Article 47 of the EU's Charter of Fundamental Rights.[107] That EU law can come to the rescue of human rights in a case such as *Benkharbouche* is likely to raise the ire of Conservative politicians even more than the HRA. In turn, that makes the potential role of the common law in this field more crucial than ever.

certain documents into his luggage prior to his deportation, the claimant was arrested and tortured in the country to which he was returned. The judge found the claim to be based on a pack of lies but, obiter, he expressed a view on the claimant's argument that as well as his right to a private life under Art 8 ECHR having been violated, so had his right to privacy under Art 7 EU Charter. Citing the decision of the CJEU in Joined Cases C-441/10 and C-493/10 *NS v Secretary of State for the Home Dept* [2012] 2 CMLR 9, Mostyn J posited that 'it can be seen that even if the Human Rights Act were to be repealed, with the result that Article 8 of the European Convention on Human Rights was no longer directly incorporated into domestic law, an identical right would continue to exist under the Charter of Fundamental Rights of the European Union, and this right is, according to the Court in Luxembourg, enforceable domestically'. See too Rosalind English, 'Watch that Charter' UK Human Rights Blog (8 November 2013), ukhumanrightsblog.com/2013/11/08/watch-that-charter.

[105] *Benkharbouche v Embassy of the Republic of Sudan* [2015] EWCA Civ 33.
[106] In particular s 16 of the 1978 Act, which runs counter to the view of the Grand Chamber of the European Court expressed in *Sabah El Leil v France* App no 34869/05 (29 June 2011). See too, in the context of a civil claim concerning torture, *Jones v UK* (2014) 59 EHRR 1.
[107] On the right to a fair trial under EU law see too Case C-402/05 P *Kadi v Council*, judgment of 3 September 2008 (*Kadi I*) and Case C-584 10 P *Commission v Kadi*, judgment of 18 July 2013 (*Kadi II*).

8

The Implementation of European Court of Human Rights Judgments Against the UK: Unravelling the Paradox

ALICE DONALD

I. INTRODUCTION

IN RECENT YEARS, the need for more effective national implementation of the European Convention on Human Rights (ECHR or 'the Convention'), including judgments of the European Court of Human Rights (ECtHR or 'the Court'), has become the overriding priority of the Council of Europe. It has been repeatedly stated both by the inter-governmental arm of the Council of Europe (the Committee of Ministers)[1] and its Parliamentary Assembly[2] that timelier and more systematic implementation of Convention standards and ECtHR judgments is critical to reducing the backlog of applications to the Court. The accumulation of pending applications peaked at 160,000 in September 2011, causing existential fears for the future of the Convention system. Since then, the Court has achieved a remarkable reduction in its caseload, due largely to changes introduced under Protocol 14 to the Convention to increase the efficiency of judicial decision-making. As of 31 March 2015, there were 64,850 pending applications, a large proportion of which were repetitive cases arising from structural or systemic violations of the Convention in a few States (notably, Ukraine, Russia, Turkey and Italy).[3] Having more than halved its docket in three years, the ECtHR has adopted a strategy to dispose of the remaining backlog.[4] Nevertheless, more

---

[1] See especially High-level Conference on the Implementation of the European Convention on Human Rights, our shared responsibility, Brussels Declaration, 27 March 2015.
[2] Parliamentary Assembly of the Council of Europe Resolution 1823 (2011), 'National Parliaments: Guarantors of Human Rights in Europe', 23 June 2011.
[3] European Court of Human Rights, Applications Allocated to a Judicial Formation, 31 March 2015.
[4] Steering Committee for Human Rights, Drafting Group 'F' on Reform of the Court (GT-GDR-F), Presentation to the 3rd meeting by the Registrar of the European Court of Human Rights, GT-GDR-F(2014)021, 24 September 2014, 9–10. See also A Donald, 'The Remarkable Shrinking Backlog at the European Court of Human Rights' UK Human Rights blog (1 October 2014), ukhumanrightsblog.com/2014/10/01/the-remarkable-shrinking-backlog-at-the-european-court-of-human-rights/.

effective domestic implementation of the Convention is required in order to stem the annual influx of 60,000–70,000 fresh applications to the Court.[5]

Better implementation is also crucial to reducing the backlog of non-executed judgments facing the Committee of Ministers, the body tasked (under Article 46(2) ECHR) with the formal process of supervision. As at 31 December 2014, 10,904 cases awaited execution, of which 1,513 were 'leading' cases; that is, cases revealing a structural or systemic violation and thus requiring the adoption of general measures (legislative, administrative, regulatory or policy changes) to prevent repetition.[6] Of the leading cases awaiting execution, 604 had been pending for more than five years.[7]

Within the European Convention system, executives are the principal domestic interlocutors of both the ECtHR and the Committee of Ministers. Yet the obligation under Article 1 ECHR to secure the rights and freedoms enshrined in the Convention is shared between all branches of the State—the executive, legislature and judiciary. Somewhat belatedly, in the Brussels Declaration of 2015, governments for the first time specified in a high-level declaration the steps that executive bodies should take to facilitate *parliamentary* engagement in the implementation of Convention standards and Court judgments.[8] The Committee on Legal Affairs and Human Rights ('Legal Affairs Committee') of the Parliamentary Assembly of the Council of Europe (PACE) has gone so far as to say that unless parliaments assume a more dynamic role in the implementation of judgments, 'the key role of the Convention, its supervisory mechanism and the Council of Europe as a whole, in guaranteeing the effective protection of human rights in Europe, is likely to be put in jeopardy'.[9] Since 2000, the Legal Affairs Committee has appointed a rapporteur on the implementation of Court judgments and has made this function of national parliaments the subject of numerous reports and resolutions.[10] In cases of executive or judicial negligence, delay or (rarely) refusal to implement a judgment, or where legislative reform is required to remedy a violation, the role of parliaments is indispensable. However, many parliaments in Council of Europe States still do not have adequate (or any) mechanisms for fulfilling this function.[11]

Against this backdrop, the UK presents an interesting case study with both positive and negative aspects. This chapter proceeds as follows. Section II examines the paradox presented by, on the one hand, the contentiousness of the Court and its judgments in the UK, and, on the other, the UK's relatively strong compliance record. Section III examines the institutional mechanisms for the implementation of

---

[5] Presentation to the 3rd meeting by the Registrar (n 4) 3.

[6] Committee of Ministers, *Supervision of the Execution of Judgments and Decisions of the European Court of Human Rights: 8th Annual Report of the Committee of Ministers 2014* (2015) 27, 29.

[7] ibid, 48.

[8] Brussels Declaration (n 1) paras B.1.b; B.2.a; B.2.f; B.2.h; and B.2.j.

[9] Parliamentary Assembly of the Council of Europe, Committee on Legal Affairs and Human Rights, *Implementation of Judgments of the European Court of Human Rights*, 7th report, AS/Jur (2010) 36, 9 November 2010, 1.

[10] See especially Resolution 1823 (n 2).

[11] Steering Committee for Human Rights, Drafting Group 'F' on Reform of the Court (GT-GDR-F), Presentation to the 3rd meeting by Dr Alice Donald, GT-GDR-F(2014)023, 24 September 2014.

ECtHR judgments against the UK. It focuses on the parliamentary Joint Committee on Human Rights (JCHR), widely viewed as an exemplar within the Council of Europe, and the role played by the Ministry of Justice. Section IV analyses the JCHR's role with respect to selected ECtHR judgments that required general measures and that exemplify the political nature of the implementation process. Section V examines the way in which the ECtHR takes into account the quality of democratic deliberation and decision-making when assessing state conduct for compliance with the Convention and how far this judicial assessment of parliamentary conduct might incentivise parliamentarians to take human rights obligations into account during the legislative process. Section VI assesses the impact of the JCHR with respect to the Council of Europe's priorities identified above and reflects on future risks to the UK's hitherto strong compliance record.

II. THE PARADOX OF THE UK'S RELATIONSHIP WITH THE ECtHR

In recent years, the possibility of withdrawal from the Convention has become normalised within political discourse in the UK. In October 2014, the Conservative Party issued a document proposing fundamental reform of UK human rights law,[12] including making judgments of the ECtHR merely advisory in respect of the UK[13] and breaking the formal link between domestic courts and the ECtHR created by the Human Rights Act 1998 (HRA).[14] The document states that should it be unable to secure the Council of Europe's agreement for these unilateral reforms, 'the UK would be left with no alternative but to withdraw' from the Convention.[15] The Conservative Party manifesto for the May 2015 general election omitted any reference to withdrawal from the Convention, but did, however, pledge to 'curtail the role of the European Court of Human Rights'.[16] At the time of writing, it remains to be seen what the Conservative government will include in the 'British Bill of Rights and Responsibilities' with which it proposes to replace the HRA.

The UK debate has been distinctive in its insistence on the primacy of Parliament vis-a-vis the Strasbourg Court; some politicians from both the Conservative and Labour parties have called for 'democratic override' of ECtHR judgments to which a majority in Parliament is opposed.[17] The former Justice Secretary, Chris Grayling, argued that the binding nature of ECtHR judgments under Article 46(1) ECHR has created a 'crisis of democratic legitimacy' and is 'wrong in principle'.[18] Opprobrium

---

[12] Conservative Party, *Protecting Human Rights in the UK: The Conservatives' Proposals for Changing Britain's Human Rights Laws* (2014).

[13] Under Art 46(1) ECHR, States undertake to abide by the final judgment of the ECtHR in any case to which they are a party.

[14] Under s 2 HRA, domestic courts are required to 'take into account' judgments, decisions, declarations and advisory opinions of the ECtHR.

[15] Conservative Party (n 12) 8.

[16] Conservative Party, *The Conservative Party Manifesto 2015*, 58.

[17] Jack Straw MP, HC Deb 11 February 2011, vol 523, col 503. See also J Straw, *Aspects of Law Reform: An Insider's Perspective* (Cambridge, Cambridge University Press, 2013) ch 2.

[18] Joint Committee on Human Rights (JCHR), Uncorrected Transcript of Oral Evidence on the Government's Human Rights Policy, 18 December 2013, Q8.

towards the ECtHR has been based on various grounds, relating to its alleged judicial activism,[19] the supposedly poor quality of its personnel and procedures,[20] its perceived intent to impose uniform standards on Member States,[21] and its purported cost to the UK.[22] Public opinion polling suggests that antipathy within the UK towards the Court (a Council of Europe institution) is fuelled by, and commonly confused with, scepticism about the European Union.[23] In this sense, criticism of the Court may be viewed as an extension of, or a proxy for, the concurrent controversy over the broader project of European integration.[24] It should be noted, however, that controversy about human rights law is principally a Westminster phenomenon, which should not be permitted to mask higher levels of political support for the HRA and the ECtHR in the devolved nations.[25]

Criticisms of the Court and its judgments have not been confined to the UK. Politicians in the Nordic States have expressed concern about the effects of 'European judicial review' of domestic legislative acts, including both review conducted by the ECtHR and (in respect of European Union law) by the European Court of Justice.[26] In March 2013, the right-wing Swiss People's Party made a parliamentary submission raising the possibility of withdrawal from the Convention, a move strongly rejected by the Swiss Federal Council.[27] A recent study examining the reception of the ECHR in Belgium, France, Germany, the Netherlands, Sweden and the UK concluded that '[in] Belgium, France, Germany and Sweden, the overall legitimacy of the Court and its judgments is hardly subject to debate'.[28] Controversy about the Court and its influence with respect to the Netherlands gained momentum in 2011 and 2012, but later subsided, due largely

[19] Lord Sumption, 'The Limits of Law', 27th Sultan Azlan Shah Lecture, Kuala Lumpur, 20 November 2013, www.supremecourt.uk/docs/speech-131120.pdf.
[20] For example, the incorrect assertion that judges of the ECtHR are unelected (eg 'Unelected Euro Judges are Bringing Terror to the Streets of Britain' *Daily Mail* (London, 18 January 2012), www.dailymail.co.uk/debate/article-2087831/Abu-Qatada-human-rights-Unelected-euro-judges-bringing-terror-streets-Britain.html) and mocking portrayals of judges of the Court (eg 'Europe's Court Jesters' *The Times* (London, 19 April 2012), 1).
[21] Lord Hoffmann, 'The Universality of Human Rights' Judicial Studies Board Annual Lecture, 19 March 2009, www.brandeis.edu/ethics/pdfs/internationaljustice/biij/BIIJ2013/hoffmann.pdf.
[22] L Rotherham, *Britain and the ECHR* (London, Taxpayers' Alliance, 2010).
[23] Equality and Diversity Forum, Public Attitudes to Human Rights: A Summary of Research Commissioned by the Equality and Diversity Forum (2012), 6.
[24] JK Schaffer, A Føllesdal and G Ulfstein, 'International Human Rights and the Challenge of Legitimacy' in A Føllesdal, JK Schaffer and G Ulfstein (eds), *The Legitimacy of International Human Rights Regimes: Legal, Political and Philosophical Perspectives* (Cambridge, Cambridge University Press, 2013) 11.
[25] For example, the Commission on a Bill of Rights, formed in 2011 to explore the creation of a new bill of rights to replace the HRA, acknowledged that there is 'little or no call' for such reform in Scotland, Wales and Northern Ireland. Commission on a Bill of Rights, *A UK Bill of Rights? The Choice Before Us*, vol 1 (2012), 15.
[26] A Føllesdal and M Wind, 'Introduction: Nordic Reluctance towards Judicial Review under Siege' (2009) 27 *Nordic Journal of Human Rights* 131, 132.
[27] Interpellation 13.3237—Dénonciation de la Convention de sauvegarde des droits de l'homme et des libertés fondamentales, presented by Toni Brunner in the National Council, 22 March 2013.
[28] J Gerards and J Fleuren (eds), *Implementation of the European Convention on Human Rights and of the Judgments of the ECtHR in National Case Law: A Comparative Analysis* (Antwerp, Intersentia, 2014) 369.

to an effective pro-Strasbourg counter-mobilisation in the Senate.[29] Only in the UK has discussion about withdrawal become a feature of *mainstream* political debate; to this extent, the anti-Strasbourg discourse in the UK may be viewed as an aberration within the Council of Europe.

There is a twofold paradox at the heart of the strife surrounding the UK's relationship with Strasbourg. First, the statistics do not bear out the assertion (whether explicit or implicit) that the ECtHR is increasingly prone to overrule decisions taken by UK authorities.[30] The UK's 'rate of defeat' in Strasbourg is extremely low. Between 1999 and 2010, of the nearly 12,000 applications brought against the UK, less than 2 per cent eventually resulted in an adverse judgment. This figure reflects the Court's strict admissibility criteria,[31] which mean that only a few applications of substantial merit proceed to a judgment. This low rate of defeat equated to an average of about 18 adverse judgments per year between 1999 and 2010.[32] In 2013, there were eight judgments against the UK;[33] and in 2014, only four.[34] To be sure, compared to the small numbers of judgments in 1970s and 1980s, the frequency of judgments against the UK increased markedly after the entry into force of Protocol 11 in 1998, after which individuals had the right of direct petition to the Court without having to apply initially to the (former) European Commission of Human Rights (ECommHR).[35] However, heightened hostility towards the ECtHR in recent years cannot be explained by any increasing tendency on the part of the Court to find violations in UK cases; nor has there been an increase in either the number of applications lodged against the UK or the proportion of applications declared admissible by the Court.[36] Further, there is no evidence that the UK fares worse at the ECtHR than other Council of Europe States in respect of, for example, the proportion of applications against it that are deemed admissible or the proportion of all judgments that find at least one violation.[37] Indeed, greater controversy about the UK's relationship with Strasbourg might have been expected in previous decades when, despite the lower numbers overall, the UK, having accepted the right of individual petition comparatively early, accounted for a significantly higher proportion of applications and judgments than other States. As a snapshot, in 1983, the UK accounted for a third of all applications registered by the ECommHR;[38] a little over three decades later, in the context of a greatly enlarged Council of Europe (up from

---

[29] Motion on the continued commitment to human rights in accordance with the obligations arising from the ECHR, tabled by Marie-Louise Bemelmans-Videc (CDA/Christian Democrat) on 10 May 2011: EK 32.500 V / 32.502 B.

[30] A Donald, J Gordon and P Leach, *The UK and the European Court of Human Rights*, Research Report 83 (Equality and Human Rights Commission, 2012), 30–36.

[31] European Court of Human Rights, Practical Guide on Admissibility Criteria (2011).

[32] Donald, Gordon and Leach (n 30) 32.

[33] European Court of Human Rights, *Annual Report 2013* (2014), 201.

[34] European Court of Human Rights, *Annual Report 2014* (2015), 175.

[35] House of Commons Library, *UK Cases at the European Court of Human Rights since 1975*, SN/IA/5611, 30 April 2013.

[36] Donald, Gordon and Leach (n 30) 36.

[37] European Court of Human Rights, *Statistics on Judgments by State* (2011).

[38] European Commission of Human Rights, *Stock-Taking on the European Convention on Human Rights: The First Thirty Years, 1954–1984* (1984), 325.

21 Member States in 1983 to 47 now), it accounts for just 1.8 per cent of pending applications.[39]

The second contradiction about the controversy is that the UK has a relatively strong record in implementing ECtHR judgments. Bates observes that from the 1970s onwards, despite the fact that the Convention was an irritant to British politicians, at least a minimal attempt was made to give effect to adverse judgments of the Court in every case.[40] Notable judgments from the early decades concerned the right of British passport holders of Asian descent in East Africa to enter or settle in the UK,[41] the use of interrogation techniques in Northern Ireland,[42] judicial corporal punishment,[43] the criminalisation of homosexuality,[44] and the interception of communications by law enforcement and intelligence agencies.[45] Even judgments which initially provoked defiance from the UK government were ultimately implemented.[46] Socially sensitive judgments concerning, for example, corporal punishment in schools[47] and in the family[48] also led to far-reaching, if belated, legislative reform.

The Ministry of Justice ventures that the UK's implementation of judgments has historically been 'timely and effective'.[49] On 31 December 2014, the UK was responsible for 26 pending cases before the Committee of Ministers, a mere 0.3 per cent of the total.[50] In March 2015, the JCHR commended the government for its 'generally very good record' on implementing Court judgments, in particular its swift implementation of several recent judgments and its success in resolving some older cases which had been under supervision by the Committee of Ministers for many years.[51] However, it noted that there were several cases in which there had been unacceptable delays in implementation, notably the *Hirst* and *Greens* judgments concerning prisoner voting rights.[52]

The Parliamentary Assembly has identified the UK as having 'significant implementation problems' stemming from its protracted delay in implementing the judgments on prisoner voting.[53] As a consequence, the leaders of the UK delegation to

---

[39] European Court of Human Rights, *Pending Applications Allocated to a Judicial Formation*, 31 December 2014, 2.

[40] E Bates, *The Evolution of the European Convention on Human Rights: From its Inception to the Creation of a Permanent Court of Human Rights* (Oxford, Oxford University Press, 2010) 317.

[41] *East African Asians v UK* (1973) 3 EHRR 76.

[42] *Ireland v UK* (1978) 2 EHRR 25.

[43] *Tyrer v UK* (1978) 2 EHRR 1.

[44] *Dudgeon v UK* (1981) 4 EHRR 149.

[45] *Malone v UK* (1984) 7 EHRR 14.

[46] eg *McCann v UK* (1995) 21 EHRR 97 (GC).

[47] *Campbell and Cosans v UK* (1982) 4 EHRR 293.

[48] *A v UK* (1999) 27 EHRR 611.

[49] Ministry of Justice, *Responding to Human Rights Judgments: Report to the Joint Committee on Human Rights on the Government Response to Human Rights Judgments 2011–12*, CM 8432 (2012), 15.

[50] Committee of Ministers (n 6) 37.

[51] JCHR, Seventh Report of Session 2014–15, *Human Rights Judgments*, HL Paper 130, HC 1088 (2015), para 2.12.

[52] ibid, para 3.15–3.26, referring to *Hirst v UK (No 2)* (2006) 42 EHRR 41 (GC) and *Greens and MT v UK* (2010) 53 EHRR 710.

[53] Parliamentary Assembly of the Council of Europe, Committee on Legal Affairs and Human Rights, *Implementation of Judgments of the European Court of Human Rights*, Doc 12455, 20 December 2010 (Rapporteur: Christos Pourgourides).

PACE were called before the Assembly's Legal Affairs Committee in January 2013 to account for the UK's failure to comply with its obligations, finding themselves in the ignominious position of being subject to the same heightened scrutiny as delegations from States such as the Russian Federation, Turkey, Ukraine and Moldova.[54] Yet despite the high-profile brinkmanship with the Court over prisoners' voting rights,[55] the UK's underlying record of compliance with judgments is one of the best in the Council of Europe. A recent empirical study of States' compliance with the Court's judgments found that the UK's overall compliance rate was 71 per cent, behind only Ireland and the Netherlands.[56]

One explanation for these apparent contradictions may lie in the contingent nature of the UK debate about the Court. Its frequently populist or intemperate tone, and the extent to which it appears at times wilfully misinformed,[57] suggest that characterisations of the Court as incompetent or illegitimate are driven as much by political opportunism as by principled reservations about the constitutional propriety of review by a supranational human rights court. The inconsistent nature of the anti-Strasbourg discourse is explored in section IV in respect of specific judgments. Here, it is submitted that a politically driven negative discourse about the Court has taken hold at the same time as, away from the public gaze, institutional arrangements for implementing ECtHR judgments have in fact become *more* robust and systematic. It is to these institutional arrangements that I now turn.

III. MECHANISMS FOR IMPLEMENTING EUROPEAN COURT OF HUMAN RIGHTS JUDGMENTS IN THE UK

A. The Joint Committee on Human Rights

Parliaments within the Council of Europe adopt different models for conducting their human rights work. These can be characterised as 'specialised', 'mainstreamed' and 'hybrid'.[58] The Parliamentary Assembly has declined to endorse any

---

[54] Parliamentary Assembly of the Council of Europe, Committee on Legal Affairs and Human Rights, Implementation of Judgments of the European Court of Human Rights—extracts from the minutes of hearings, organised by the Committee, held in Strasbourg in April 2012, in June 2012, in October 2012 and in January 2013, AS/Jur (2013) 13, 28 March 2013 at 10–11.

[55] E Bates, 'Analysing the Prisoner Voting Saga and the British Challenge to Strasbourg' (2014) 14 *Human Rights Law Review* 503.

[56] C Hillebrecht, *Domestic Politics and International Human Rights Tribunals: The Problem of Compliance* (Cambridge, Cambridge University Press, 2014) 48. Hillebrecht employs a disaggregated methodology to measure States' compliance with the discrete obligations contained within each judgment up to May 2009, thus permitting a more fine-grained assessment of States' full, partial or non-compliance with judgments than is permitted by the Committee of Ministers' binary approach of classifying cases as either closed or pending.

[57] For example, it has been erroneously stated that the ECtHR banned the imposition of whole-life tariffs even for the gravest crimes as being incompatible with Art 3 ECHR (see above, n 12 at 3). In fact, in *Vinter v UK* (2012) 55 EHRR 34, the Court stated (at para 119) that, to be compatible with Art 3, whole-life tariffs must be subject to review after a suggested period of no more than 25 years.

[58] Parliamentary Assembly of the Council of Europe, Parliamentary Project Support Division, *The Role of Parliaments in Implementing ECHR Standards: Overview of Existing Structures and Mechanisms: Background Memorandum*, PPSD (2014) 22, 13 October 2014.

single model, recognising that different approaches will be appropriate in different national contexts. The Assembly's Legal Affairs Committee has urged parliaments to create 'dedicated human rights committees *or appropriate analogous structures,* whose remits shall be clearly defined and enshrined in law'.[59]

The JCHR exemplifies the specialised model of a single standing parliamentary committee (or, in some parliaments, sub-committee) with a remit which is mainly or exclusively concerned with human rights. The Dutch Parliament typifies the mainstreamed approach, in which no single committee or sub-committee has a remit covering human rights matters, which are instead dealt with by different parliamentary committees as they arise within their respective mandates. In other parliaments a hybrid approach is taken, in which more than one parliamentary committee or sub-committee has human rights within its mandate; for example, in the German Bundestag, the Committee on Legal Affairs leads on all matters relating to the Ministry of Justice, including legislative reform necessitated by judgments of the ECtHR, while the Committee on Human Rights and Humanitarian Aid discusses human rights issues from a broad perspective, both on an international basis and in relation to Germany.

The JCHR's remit is broad, covering 'matters relating to human rights' in the UK, excluding individual cases.[60] Since its inception in 2000, the Committee has interpreted its mandate expansively, embracing pre-legislative scrutiny, thematic inquiries, and scrutiny of the government's compliance with all the UK's international human rights obligations.[61] In addition, the Committee conducts scrutiny of government responses to adverse judgments of the ECtHR and declarations of incompatibility by domestic courts under the HRA.[62]

In the early 2000s, whenever ECtHR judgments required general measures, the JCHR wrote to the relevant minister to request information about the proposed response.[63] In 2006, it published its first progress report on the implementation of Strasbourg judgments.[64] Following a review of its working practices in 2006, the Committee decided to integrate its monitoring of Strasbourg judgments, whether or not they might potentially give rise to remedial orders,[65] with enhanced scrutiny of declarations of incompatibility, leading to its first integrated report in 2007.[66]

---

[59] Resolution 1823 (n 2) para 1 (emphasis added).

[60] www.parliament.uk/business/committees/committees-a-z/joint-select/human-rights-committee/.

[61] For detailed accounts of the JCHR's work, see D Feldman, 'Can and Should Parliament Protect Human Rights?' (2004) 10 *European Public Law* 635; M Hunt, 'The Impact of the Human Rights Act on the Legislature: A Diminution of Democracy or a New Voice for Parliament?' (2010) 6 *European Human Rights Law Review* 601.

[62] Under s 4 HRA, a higher court may make a declaration of incompatibility if it determines that a provision of primary legislation is incompatible with a Convention right.

[63] JCHR, Nineteenth Report of Session 2004–05, *The Work of the Committee in the 2001–2005 Parliament,* HL Paper 112, HC 552 (2005).

[64] JCHR, Thirteenth Report of Session 2005–06, *Implementation of Strasbourg Judgments: First Progress Report,* HL Paper 133, HC 954 (2006).

[65] Remedial orders are a form of delegated legislation (provided for under s 2 and Sched 10 HRA) by which a minister may choose to amend primary legislation following a declaration by a UK court that it is incompatible with the ECHR or a Strasbourg judgment in a case concerning the UK.

[66] JCHR, Sixteenth Report of Session 2006–07, *Monitoring the Government's Response to Court Judgments Finding Breaches of Human Rights,* HL Paper 128, HC 728 (2007).

This report also recommended improvements to the way in which the UK government responded to judgments, including a coordinating role for the Ministry of Justice.[67] In addition, the JCHR committed itself to a more coherent approach to its own scrutiny work in this area.[68] In its 2008 report, the JCHR lamented the government's failure to provide a substantive response to the Committee's recommendations, which were reiterated and expanded to include, among other steps, an annual report by the executive on the implementation of human rights judgments.[69]

In its monitoring report published in 2010, the JCHR recommended further improvements in order to facilitate parliamentary scrutiny.[70] The Committee also produced guidance, including the stipulation of deadlines, for government responses to human rights judgments, given what it viewed as inconsistent and opaque practice across departments.[71] At the beginning of the 2010–15 Parliament, the Committee reaffirmed these requirements and announced that it would continue its predecessor's practice of scrutinising the government's responses to human rights judgments and periodically reporting to Parliament on their adequacy.[72] Between 2011 and 2014, the JCHR produced no further periodic reports; rather, it sought to integrate its work on human rights judgments into other aspects of its work, mainly by scrutinising the government's response to certain judgments in the context of its legislative scrutiny.[73] This approach indicated a shift to a more selective approach to this area of work, and the vulnerability of parliamentary oversight mechanisms both to changes in priorities between parliamentary terms and to fluctuations in the number of legal advisers attached to the Committee (which fell from three to one for much of the 2010–15 Parliament). In March 2015, the Committee produced its first report on human rights judgments in the 2010–15 Parliament.[74] Among other things, the JCHR observed that the relatively strong institutional mechanisms and practices that have been developed in the UK place it in a good position to provide strong leadership on this question within the Committee of Ministers, and urged the government to become a 'champion of increasing parliamentary involvement in the ECHR system'.[75]

---

[67] ibid, paras 151–63.

[68] ibid, para 162.

[69] JCHR, Thirty-First Report of Session 2007–08, *Monitoring the Government's Response to Human Rights Judgments: Annual Report 2008*, HL Paper 173, HC 1078 (2008).

[70] JCHR, Fifteenth Report of Session 2009–10, *Enhancing Parliament's Role in Relation to Human Rights Judgments*, HL Paper 85, HC 455 (2010), ch 4.

[71] ibid, 69–76 ('Annex: Guidance for Departments on Responding to Court Judgments on Human Rights').

[72] JCHR Press Notice, 'JCHR to Review Government's Response to Judgments Identifying Breaches of Human Rights in the UK', 10 September 2010.

[73] For example, the Committee's report on the Protection of Freedoms Bill scrutinised the Government's response in England and Wales to the ECtHR's judgment in *Marper v UK* (2009) 48 EHRR 50 on the legal framework for the retention of biometric data; Eighteenth Report of Session 2010–12, *Legislative Scrutiny: Protection of Freedoms Bill*, HL Paper 195, HC 1490 (2011), paras 6–87.

[74] JCHR (n 51).

[75] ibid, para 5.5.

(i) The JCHR and Other Actors

The JCHR collaborates with other institutional human rights actors in its monitoring of human rights judgments. A case in point is the liaison between the JCHR and the Independent Reviewer of Terrorism Legislation in their scrutiny of the government's response to *Gillan and Quinton v UK*,[76] which concerned the exercise of stop and search powers under section 44 of the Terrorism Act 2000 in relation to two individuals near an armaments fair. The ECtHR had found that the law was too broadly defined and contained insufficient safeguards to act as a curb on the wide powers afforded to the executive, amounting to a violation of the right to respect for private life under Article 8 ECHR. The government's response was to issue an urgent remedial order to repeal and replace the offending provisions with new, more circumscribed powers.[77] Both the JCHR[78] and the Independent Reviewer[79] reported to Parliament, welcoming the government's willingness to change the law but recommending amendments to the remedial order and accompanying Code of Practice, since the discretion conferred on officers remained too broad to remove the risk of arbitrariness. The government initially rejected the amendments as unnecessary.[80] However, following public consultation in 2012 on the revised draft Code of Practice, changes were made to satisfy some of the concerns raised by the JCHR and the Independent Reviewer.[81]

Across all strands of its work, the Committee invites civil society actors and legal experts to submit evidence and legal opinion on the continued effect of judicially impugned laws or the potential effect of proposed legislation. Such submissions are frequently cited as authoritative sources in JCHR reports. For example, the JCHR's consultation on the Gender Recognition Bill, prompted in part by the judgment in *Christine Goodwin v UK*,[82] drew submissions from transsexual people, organisations working with or representing transsexual people, and professionals with expertise in the medical and legal issues involved, as well as opponents of any recognition of gender reassignment. The Committee's recommendations for revision of the Bill were grounded in part on the weight of these various submissions.[83]

---

[76] *Gillan and Quinton v UK* (2010) 50 EHRR 45.

[77] Ministry of Justice, *Responding to Human Rights Judgments: Report to the Joint Committee on Human Rights on the Government's Response to Human Rights Judgments 2010–11*, CM 1862 (2011), 15–17.

[78] JCHR, Fourteenth Report of Session 2010–12, *The Terrorism Act 2000 (Remedial) Order 2011: Stop and Search without Reasonable Suspicion*, HL Paper 155, HC 1141 (2011); Seventeenth Report of Session 2010–12, *The Terrorism Act 2000 (Remedial) Order 2011: Stop and Search without Reasonable Suspicion (second Report)*, HL Paper 192, HC 1483 (2011).

[79] D Anderson (Independent Reviewer of Terrorism Legislation), *Report on the Operation in 2010 of the Terrorism Act 2000 and of Part 1 of the Terrorism Act 2006* (2011).

[80] *Gillan & Quinton v UK* App no 4158/05: Updated Information Submitted by the United Kingdom Government on 10 October 2011, DH—DD(2011)851E.

[81] D Anderson, *The Terrorism Acts in 2011: Report of the Independent Reviewer on the Operation of the Terrorism Act 2000 and Part 1 of the Terrorism Act 2006* (2012) para 8.19.

[82] *Christine Goodwin v UK* (2002) 35 EHRR 18 (GC).

[83] For example, the JCHR's recommendation that the Bill should have retrospective effect was informed by submissions which argued that it would be demeaning to require existing 'married' couples to undergo a gender recognition process and a further wedding ceremony: JCHR, Nineteenth Report of

(ii) 'Mainstreaming' Human Rights in Parliament

The JCHR is the natural focal point of Parliament's human rights work. It is also one of the few committees that is serviced by its own permanent legal advisers (as noted above, since 2000, the number has fluctuated between one and three). The provision of dedicated human rights legal advice is widely acknowledged to be critical to both the productivity and the credibility of the Committee. Nevertheless, there are limits to what a small, specialised committee can achieve. Murray Hunt, legal adviser to the JCHR since 2004, advocates a programmatic and anticipatory approach to human rights among legal advisers to committees other than the JCHR.[84] Such an approach, he suggests, would require lawyers in Parliament working in collaboration with both clerks from the two Houses and research and information services to bring to the attention of other committees any relevant human rights standards or rule of law considerations, including treaty obligations, court judgments and recommendations by UN treaty bodies. Hunt adds that 'mainstreaming' of this kind would also confer a 'legitimation advantage' by countering the tendency for politicians to view human rights as 'standards articulated and imposed on Parliament and government by outside actors, judges and lawyers in particular, who lack democratic legitimacy'.[85]

It is unusual for a judgment of the ECtHR to be debated on the floor of the House of Commons, even if it requires changes to legislation. Judgments appear to become politically salient when a group of MPs has a compelling interest in the issue at stake and/or an expectation of political gain to be made by pursuing it, often reinforced by a high-profile lobby outside Parliament and sustained media coverage. One such instance was the backbench debate in the House of Commons in February 2011 on a motion concerning the *Hirst* judgment on prisoner voting rights. However, the JCHR faces an uphill struggle in extending parliamentary interest beyond such exceptions. In respect of ECtHR decisions against the UK, debate in both Houses has rarely cited JCHR reports or recommendations on specific judgments.[86]

B. The Ministry of Justice

In 2010, the Ministry of Justice assumed coordination of the executive response to ECtHR judgments, as recommended by the JCHR. The role had previously been held by the deputy head of the UK mission to the Council of Europe, who was ill-placed to liaise with Whitehall departments. The Ministry introduced more systematic arrangements for implementation. The first stage is for the Foreign and

---

Session 2002–03, *Draft Gender Recognition Bill*, HL Paper 188-I, HC 1276-I (2003), para 36 and recommendations 3–5, 34–35.

[84] M Hunt, 'The Joint Committee on Human Rights' in A Horne, G Drewry and D Oliver (eds), *Parliament and the Law* (Oxford, Hart Publishing, 2013) 223, 247–48.

[85] ibid, 247.

[86] JCHR reports or recommendations relating to five judgments (including *Hirst*) were referred to between 2000 and 2010: M Hunt, H Hooper and P Yowell, *Parliaments and Human Rights: Redressing the Democratic Deficit* (Arts and Humanities Research Council Public Policy Series No 5, 2012), 39.

Commonwealth Office to alert the government department(s) responsible for the violation(s) to the judgment and to provide advice on, for example, the possibility of referring a Chamber judgment to the Grand Chamber of the ECtHR. Coordination of the executive response then passes to the Ministry of Justice, which sends the lead policy team(s) within the department(s) concerned a standardised form to elicit within a set timeframe what action they intend to take in response to the judgment.[87] The Ministry also acts as the conduit for information to the secretariat of the Committee of Ministers and the UK deputy head of mission in Strasbourg. The department responsible for the violation(s) acts as the lead in the event of questions or debate in Parliament about the government's proposed response.

Depending on the nature of the violation, coordination across government departments may be necessary, and this may significantly affect the speed of implementation. Two cases reported on by the JCHR in its early years illustrate this effect: *Christine Goodwin v UK*, concerning the legal recognition of transsexuals, and *Grieves v UK*,[88] concerning the independence and impartiality of naval courts martial. *Christine Goodwin* entailed considerable administrative complexity, as well as extensive review and debate in both Houses, and it was two years before the Gender Recognition Act 2004 made provision for the legal recognition of gender reassignment. In contrast, *Grieves*, which concerned the Ministry of Defence alone, was implemented within one month by means of an urgent remedial order.[89]

(i) Action Plans

Information obtained via the standardised process described above forms the basis of the government's 'action plan' in response to an adverse judgment of the ECtHR. The Committee of Ministers requires States to submit action plans (or action reports) within six months of a judgment becoming final, setting out the measures the respondent State intends to take (or has taken) to implement the judgment.[90] These are generally the first public and reasoned explanation of the government's intentions and have become the main focus of the Committee of Ministers' system of supervision. As a consequence, the JCHR has attached importance to regular scrutiny at the earliest possible stage of action plans and has secured a commitment from the Ministry of Justice to send it action plans at the same time as they are submitted to the Committee of Ministers.[91] The JCHR has occasionally corresponded with the executive *before* an action plan is published, suggesting options for remedy.[92]

---

[87] Ministry of Justice (n 77) 27.

[88] *Grieves v UK* (2004) 39 EHRR 51.

[89] Naval Discipline Act 1957 (Remedial) Order 2004.

[90] Recommendation CM/Rec(2008)2 of the Committee of Ministers to Member States on efficient domestic capacity for rapid execution of judgments of the European Court of Human Rights, para 6.

[91] Although action plans are published on the Committee of Ministers' website, this does not always happen as soon as they are received—a delay which might sometimes impede effective parliamentary scrutiny of the government's response.

[92] As happened, for example, within five days of the judgment in *Marper v UK* (n 73). See JCHR, Twenty-Seventh Report of Session 2008–09, *Retention, Use and Destruction of Biometric Data: Correspondence with Government*, HL Paper 182, HC 1113 (2009).

In addition, the JCHR has argued for domestic parliamentary and other scrutiny of government responses to be reported routinely within action plans in accordance with the principle of subsidiarity. Following *Gillan*, the JCHR deplored the fact that the government's action plan, as submitted to the Committee of Ministers, made no mention of the scrutiny undertaken by the JCHR and the Independent Reviewer of Terrorism Legislation.[93] A revised action plan later rectified this omission.

(ii) Annual Reports

In 2011, the government initiated the production of an annual report on its response to human rights judgments, as had been requested by the JCHR since 2008 (emulating practice in the Netherlands and Germany).[94] This proactive provision of information replaced the previous government practice of responding to the JCHR's own monitoring reports on human rights judgments. The reports have not been debated in Parliament and are secondary to action plans in informing the JCHR's 'real-time' scrutiny of the executive response to judgments. However, annual reports provide a valuable public record of the government's compliance performance. It may also be expected that the requirement to report annually, and the anticipation of public scrutiny of executive action or inaction, has a catalysing effect on government departments as they formulate their response to adverse human rights judgments.

IV. THE POLITICAL DIMENSION OF IMPLEMENTATION

The JCHR has argued that, given the discretion inherent in the Convention's supervision mechanism, the process of implementing a Strasbourg judgment is an 'unavoidably political process', albeit one constrained by the UK's legal obligations under the Convention. Parliamentary involvement, the JCHR argues,

> raises the political visibility of the issues at stake and provides an opportunity for public scrutiny of the justifications offered by the Government for its proposed response to the judgment or for its delay in bringing such a response forward.[95]

The Committee adds:

> In so doing it helps both to ensure a genuine democratic input into legal changes following Court judgments and to address the perception that changes in law or policy as a result of Court judgments lack democratic legitimacy.[96]

I have already alluded to the politicisation of debate about human rights in the UK since the early 2000s. Since its inception, then, the JCHR has operated against

---

[93] Seventeenth Report of Session 2010–12 (n 78) para 10.
[94] For the latest, see Ministry of Justice, *Responding to Human Rights Judgments: Report to the Joint Committee on Human Rights on the Government Response to Human Rights Judgments 2013–14*, CM 8962 (20143).
[95] JCHR (n 70) para 17.
[96] ibid.

the backdrop of dissensus concerning fundamental questions on human rights protection. This section examines how Parliament, and especially the JCHR, has managed these constraints. It focuses on contrasting political responses to ECtHR judgments concerning two issues: the right of convicted prisoners to vote, and the retention, use and destruction of biometric data.

A. Prisoners' Voting Rights[97]

The matter of prisoners' voting rights has become, according to former Justice Secretary Chris Grayling, 'totemic' for those who assert the primacy of Parliament over the Court or who argue that the UK should decouple itself from the Convention.[98] Referring to the intensification of the prisoner voting debate under the Conservative-led coalition, the former Deputy Registrar of the Court, Michael O'Boyle, argues that

> [t]he Court has never, in its 50-year history, been subject to such a barrage of hostile criticism as that which occurred in the United Kingdom in 2011 ... The issue of prisoners' voting rights was transformed into a national interrogation in the UK about the legitimacy of the ECtHR.[99]

The Grand Chamber ruled in the case of *Hirst* in 2005 that the automatic and indiscriminate ban on the right of convicted prisoners to vote breached Article 3 of Protocol 1 ECHR on the right to free elections.[100] Notably, the Grand Chamber found 'no evidence that Parliament had ever sought to weigh the competing interests or to assess the proportionality of a blanket ban on the right of a convicted prisoner to vote'.[101] In November 2010, the Court issued a 'pilot' judgment in the case of *Greens and MT*, which stipulated an obligation of parliamentary involvement by requiring that the UK government must, within six months of the judgment becoming final, 'bring forward ... legislative proposals' to render the law Convention-compliant.[102] Subsequently, the UK was granted an extension of this deadline, to take account of the referral of *Scoppola v Italy (No 3)* (a case similar to *Greens*) to the Grand Chamber and the UK's intervention in that case.[103] The Court granted an extension of six months from the date of the *Scoppola* judgment, which was handed down on 22 May 2012. On 22 November 2012, the government published the Voting Eligibility (Prisoners) Draft Bill, which was sent for pre-legislative scrutiny by a Joint Committee of both Houses.[104] In October 2013, some 2,500 clone cases

---

[97] For a detailed account of the prisoner voting saga, see Bates (n 55). See also R Ziegler, 'Voting Eligibility: Strasbourg's Timidity' (ch 9), this volume.

[98] Joint Committee on the Draft Voting Eligibility (Prisoners) Bill, Uncorrected Transcript of Oral Evidence, Session II, 20 November 2013 (QQ 206–40), Q223.

[99] M O'Boyle, 'The Future of the European Court of Human Rights' (2011) 12 *German Law Journal* 1862, 1862.

[100] *Hirst v UK* (n 52).

[101] ibid, para 79.

[102] *Greens and MT v UK* (n 52), operative para 6(a).

[103] *Scoppola v Italy (No 3)* (2012) 56 EHRR 34.

[104] Voting Eligibility (Prisoners) Draft Bill, Cm 8499, November 2012.

before the ECtHR, which had been frozen since *Greens*, were reinstated due to the failure to repeal the blanket prohibition.

From 2006, the JCHR issued several reports and engaged in protracted correspondence with ministers on the prisoner voting issue.[105] The JCHR repeatedly deplored executive inaction on the matter and, from 2006, characterised the need for a solution, by means of either a remedial order or amendments to other Bills, as urgent. It reiterated that the continued failure to remove the blanket ban was unlawful, tarnished the UK's reputation, and burdened the ECtHR with repetitive applications.

The JCHR has at no point proposed a specific remedy or options for remedying the violation identified in *Hirst*. The closest it came to expressing a view on the adequacy of any particular remedy was in 2010, when it argued that the Labour government was taking a 'very limited' approach to the judgment by consulting on a proposal to disenfranchise all prisoners sentenced to four years' imprisonment or more in any circumstances. The JCHR was not persuaded that automatic disenfranchisement based upon a set period of custodial sentence provided the discernible link between the conduct and circumstances of the individual and necessity for the removal of the right to vote required by the Grand Chamber.[106] Nevertheless, the Committee's 'overriding disappointment' was the government's failure to introduce *any* remedial measures.[107]

In February 2011, the House of Commons Political and Constitutional Reform Committee issued a summary report of evidence it had heard as to whether extending the right to vote to convicted prisoners in certain circumstances would be justifiable.[108] The Committee concluded that 'however morally justifiable it might be, this current situation is illegal under international law founded on the UK's treaty obligations'.[109] The Committee addressed its report to MPs preparing to take part in a backbench debate on a parliamentary motion on prisoner voting tabled by two MPs, Conservative member David Davis and Labour's Jack Straw.[110] The motion

---

[105] JCHR, Eleventh Report of Session 2005–06, *Legislative Scrutiny: Fifth Progress Report*, HL Paper 115, HC 899 (2006), paras 1.40–1.42; Thirteenth Report of Session 2005–06 (n 64) paras 51–53; Sixteenth Report of Session 2006–07 (n 66) paras 67–79; Thirty-First Report of Session 2007–08 (n 69) paras 47–63; Fourth Report of Session 2008–09, *Legislative Scrutiny: Political Parties and Elections Bill*, HL Paper 23, HC 204 (2009), paras 1.10–1.19; Seventeenth Report of Session 2008–09, *Government Replies to the Second, Fourth, Eighth, Ninth and Twelfth Reports of Session 2008–09*, HL Paper 104, HC 592 (2009), 36; Fifteenth Report of Session 2009–10 (n 70) paras 99–119; Sixth Report of Session 2010–11, *Legislative Scrutiny: (1) Superannuation Bill; (2) Parliamentary Voting System and Constituencies Bill*, HL Paper 64, HC 640 (2010), paras 2.7–2.15; Uncorrected Transcript of Oral Evidence, Minutes of Evidence taken before the Joint Committee on Human Rights: The Government's Human Rights Policy—Rt Hon Chris Grayling MP, 12 February 2013, Q13; Uncorrected Transcript of Oral Evidence, Minutes of Evidence taken before the Joint Committee on Human Rights: The Government's Human Rights Policy—Rt Hon Chris Grayling MP and Rosemary Davies, 18 December 2013.

[106] JCHR (n 70) para 107.

[107] ibid, para 108.

[108] House of Commons Political and Constitutional Reform Committee, Fifth Report of Session 2010–11, *Voting by Convicted Prisoners: Summary of Evidence*, HC 776 (2011).

[109] ibid, para 22.

[110] HC Deb 10 February 2011, vol 523, cols 493–584.

noted the ECtHR's view that there had been no substantive debate in Parliament on the continued justification for the general restriction on the right of convicted prisoners to vote and acknowledged the treaty obligations of the UK. It expressed support for the status quo with respect to the indiscriminate ban and asserted that 'legislative decisions should be a matter for democratically-elected lawmakers'.[111] Neither the government nor opposition front benches voted on the motion, which carried by 234 votes to 22.[112]

One regrettable feature of the backbench debate which has largely escaped comment is the role played by the UK's delegates to the Parliamentary Assembly of the Council of Europe.[113] Their conduct in the debate suggests that members of the PACE delegation do not view it as their responsibility to advocate for the UK to fulfil its obligations under the Convention. Only two out of the 12 MPs who were at the time full members of the UK's PACE delegation spoke in the Davis–Straw debate; both (including the leader of the delegation, Conservative MP Robert Walter) opined that the ECtHR had erred in *Hirst* and that it should not be implemented.[114]

As noted above, in November 2012 the government introduced the Voting Eligibility (Prisoners) Draft Bill, which proposed three options: a ban for prisoners sentenced to less than four years; a ban for prisoners sentenced to less than six months; and a restatement of the existing indiscriminate ban, an option which would leave the UK in outright breach of *Hirst*.[115] In December 2013, the Joint Committee formed to scrutinise the Bill recommended that the government bring forward a bill at the start of the 2014–15 parliamentary session giving the vote to all prisoners serving sentences of 12 months or less and those who are within six months of their scheduled release date.[116] The Committee stated that the UK was under a binding international law obligation to comply with *Hirst* and it would be unprecedented for any State that has ratified the Convention to enact legislation in defiance of a binding judgment of the ECtHR.[117] While the UK remains part of the Convention system, the Committee argued, it has obligations that cannot be the subject of 'cherry picking'.[118] The report, published almost a decade after the original *Hirst* judgment, is the first by a parliamentary body advancing a reasoned argument for a specific remedy. In its latest monitoring report published shortly before the May 2015 election, the JCHR recommended that the new government

---

[111] ibid, col 493.

[112] For contrasting appraisals of this debate, see Danny Nicol, 'Legitimacy of the Commons Debate on Prisoner Voting' [2011] *Public Law* 681; Janet Hiebert, 'The Human Rights Act: Ambiguity about Parliamentary Sovereignty' (2013) 14 *German Law Journal* 2253.

[113] Eighteen MPs and Lords are appointed by the Prime Minister to the UK delegation to PACE.

[114] HC Deb 10 February 2011, vol 523, cols 527–28 (Robert Walter MP) and 567–68 (Brian Binley MP). Walter added, however, that for the UK to withdraw from the Convention because of the judgment would be 'counter-productive, if not dishonourable'.

[115] Voting Eligibility (Prisoners) Draft Bill, Cm 8499, November 2012.

[116] Joint Committee on the Draft Voting Eligibility (Prisoners) Bill, Session 2013–14, *Draft Voting Eligibility (Prisoners) Bill: Report*, HL Paper 103, HC 924 (2013), para 25.

[117] ibid, para 229.

[118] ibid, para 112.

introduce legislation (whether primary legislation or a remedial order) at the earliest opportunity in the new Parliament to give effect to the recommendation of the Joint Committee on the Draft Voting Eligibility (Prisoners) Bill, given the near inevitability of further repetitive applications in Strasbourg against which the UK will have no defence.[119]

B. The Retention, Use and Destruction of Biometric Data

In political terms, a startling contrast to the prisoner voting controversy is presented by the case of *S and Marper*, which concerned the UK's policy (in place since 2003) of retaining indefinitely DNA profiles and samples of everyone arrested for a recordable offence.[120] The UK's National DNA Database contained around five million profiles, making it the largest in the world, both per capita and in absolute terms.[121] Around one million of these profiles belonged to people who had never been charged with or convicted of a criminal offence. The applicants in *S and Marper*, a child and an adult, fell into this category. In 2008, the Grand Chamber of the ECtHR unanimously held that the 'blanket and indiscriminate nature' of powers of retention of biometric data of persons suspected but not convicted of offences failed to strike a fair balance between competing public and private interests.[122] The retention of such information was held to constitute a disproportionate interference with the applicants' right to respect for private life under Article 8 ECHR.

In response, in the final days of the Labour government, the Crime and Security Act 2010 was passed (but not enacted) to restrict the retention of innocent people's DNA to six years for adults and three years, in most cases, for children. This response was considered inadequate by the Committee of Ministers,[123] as well as by the Home Affairs Committee[124] and the JCHR.[125] The JCHR criticised the government's 'very narrow approach' to the judgment, which was deliberately 'pushing the boundaries' of the Court's decision in order to maintain the thrust of its original policy on DNA retention. In the Committee's view, the blanket six-year

---

[119] JCHR (n 51) paras 3.21, 3.26.

[120] *S and Marper v UK* (n 73).

[121] Eric Metcalfe, *Freedom from Suspicion: Surveillance Reform for a Digital Age* (London, JUSTICE, 2011) 9.

[122] *S and Marper* (n 73) para 125.

[123] 1072nd (DH) meeting, 1–3 December 2009, Decisions adopted at the meeting, CM/Del/Dec(2009)1072, 7 December 2009; 1078th meeting (DH), 2–4 March 2010, Decisions adopted at the meeting, CM/Del/Dec(2010)1078, 8 March 2010.

[124] The Committee recommended a three-year retention period for adults: House of Commons Home Affairs Committee, Eighth Report of Session 2009–10, *The National DNA Database*, HC-222-I (2010), para 9 (Conclusions and recommendations) at 20.

[125] JCHR, Tenth Report of Session 2008–09, *Legislative Scrutiny: Policing and Crime Bill*, HL Paper 68, HC 395 (2009), paras 1.111–1.119; Twenty-Seventh Report of Session 2008–09, *Retention, Use and Destruction of Biometric Data: Correspondence with the Government*, HL 182, HC 1113 (2009); Twelfth Report of Session 2009–10, *Legislative Scrutiny: Crime and Security Bill etc*, HL 67, HC 402 (2010), paras 1.4–1.76; Fifteenth Report of Session 2009–10 (n 70) paras 41–58.

retention period remained disproportionate and potentially arbitrary and carried a significant risk of further litigation.

In the case of *Marper*, the JCHR was able to be unusually specific in its proposed remedy since an alternative regime for DNA retention already existed: the model used in Scotland, which the Grand Chamber had identified as achieving a more proportionate balance between, on the one hand, public protection through the investigation and prevention and crime, and, on the other, respect for a person's private life.[126] The incoming coalition government introduced the Scottish model to England and Wales as part of the Protection of Freedoms Act 2012. Unlike *Hirst*, the *Marper* judgment was 'widely applauded in British political and legal circles'.[127]

Perhaps motivated by the opportunity to develop a pro-civil liberties narrative in opposition to the Labour government, the Conservatives in opposition had pressed for its speedy implementation and were 'gratified' that the ECtHR had obliged the Labour government to revise its position.[128] Speaking less than a year after the judgment, the (then) shadow Security Minister, Dame Pauline Neville-Jones, complained that 'the UK, in the face of great criticism of the legislation in this country, is taking an excessive time to amend its legislation to conform to a judgment of the European court'.[129] The (then) shadow Home Secretary, Chris Grayling, also referred to the urgency of remedial measures.[130] In a parliamentary debate initiated by a Labour backbencher in 2009, while some members backed Labour's minimalist approach to implementation, none questioned the authority or legitimacy of the ECtHR's decision.[131] Press reporting, too, was largely favourable, even among newspapers generally hostile to the Court.[132]

The respect accorded to the judgment in *Marper* is all the more remarkable given that the Grand Chamber resoundingly rejected (17:0) the position of both the UK government and the Law Lords.[133] Moreover, the judgment implicitly rejected the position of Parliament, which had introduced the offending provision (via amendments to section 64(1A) of the Police and Criminal Evidence Act 1984) following public disquiet about cases in which, for example, DNA evidence linking one suspect to a rape and another to a murder had not been able to be used because the law as it stood had required that their samples be destroyed and disregarded.[134]

---

[126] Twelfth Report of Session 2009–10 (ibid), paras 1.64–1.74.

[127] N Bratza, 'Britain Should be Defending European Justice, Not Attacking It' *The Independent* (London, 24 January 2012), www.independent.co.uk/voices/commentators/nicolas-bratza-britain-should-be-defending-european-justice-not-attacking-it-6293689.html.

[128] HC Deb 20 October 2009, col 666.

[129] ibid, col 668.

[130] 'Conservatives Drop Opposition to DNA Proposals Following Alan Johnson Ultimatum' *The Guardian* (London, 7 April 2010), www.theguardian.com/politics/2010/apr/07/dna-database-reform-alan-johnson.

[131] HC Deb 9 December 2009, cols 104WH–127WH.

[132] See eg 'One Million Innocent People Could Have their Profiles Wiped from Britain's "Orwellian" DNA Database after Court Ruling' *Daily Mail* (London, 5 December 2008), www.dailymail.co.uk/news/article-1091880/One-million-innocent-people-profiles-wiped-Britains-DNA-database-court-ruling.html.

[133] *R (S) v Chief Constable of South Yorkshire Police and R (Marper) v Chief Constable of South Yorkshire Police* [2004] UKHL 3.

[134] *S and Marper* (n 73) para 15.

Yet, despite these considerations, *Marper* excited nothing like the opprobrium directed at *Hirst*. This disjuncture suggests that calls for the UK to consider taking the drastic step of withdrawal from the Convention on the basis of *particular* judgments which frustrate the will of Parliament are insufficiently grounded and disproportionate.

C. The JCHR and the Politics of Implementation

The dissonance between the responses to *Marper* and *Hirst* illustrate that, as the JCHR observes, the implementation of ECtHR decisions is not only a legal and technical process, but also an intensely *political* one. How may we characterise the approach of Parliament, and especially the JCHR, to managing these political constraints?

A recurrent feature of the JCHR's monitoring reports has been to insist that the government adopt an expansive rather than minimal approach to implementation.[135] A minimal approach, the JCHR argues, exacerbates the problem of repetitive cases because it leads to future litigation which can culminate in foreseeable findings of violation. The Committee identified such an approach in the Labour government's response to *Marper*. It made similar criticisms of ministers' 'narrow' response to the decision in *A v UK* concerning the unfairness caused by the use of secret evidence and special advocates in the context of legislation which authorised the detention of foreign nationals suspected of terrorism,[136] and of the government's 'passive and minimalist' approach following judgments in the domestic courts and the ECtHR concerning control orders, which permitted the Home Secretary to impose a wide range of restrictions on any person suspected of involvement in terrorism.[137] Conversely, the JCHR commended the government for its implementation of *B and L v UK*, concerning the prohibition on a parent-in-law from marrying their child-in-law unless their respective spouses had died, in violation of Article 12 ECHR.[138] The Marriage Act 1949 (Remedial Order) 2006 went further than removing the incompatibility found by the ECtHR in the particular case, and removed an age restriction on the right of a parent- and child-in-law to marry which, though not at issue in the case itself, would in the government's view inevitably have been found to be incompatible with Article 12 as a result of the Court's reasoning.

While the JCHR has consistently advocated a timely and comprehensive approach to implementation, it has generally avoided being either definitive in identifying potential breaches of the Convention or prescriptive in its proposed remedies. Rather, it has tended to direct open-ended questions to ministers about proposed responses to judgments and their justification, framing its conclusions in terms of the *risk* that a provision will be found incompatible with the Convention

---

[135] JCHR (n 70) paras 168–70.
[136] ibid, para 40, referring to *A v UK* (2009) 49 EHRR 29 (GC).
[137] JCHR, Ninth Report of Session 2009–10, *Counter–Terrorism Policy and Human Rights (Sixteenth Report): Annual Renewal of Control Orders Legislation 2010*, HL 64, HC 395 (2010), para 53.
[138] JCHR (n 70) para 169; *B and L v UK* (2006) 42 EHRR 11.

by a domestic court or the ECtHR. This risk-assessment approach reflects the Committee's reluctance, as a matter of constitutional propriety, to assume ultimate interpretive authority. Pragmatic considerations also favour such a strategy: a prescriptive approach might make it harder to achieve cross-party consensus. Moreover, a definitive pronouncement by the Committee that a legislative provision breaches the Convention runs the risk of being contradicted by a subsequent judicial finding, to the detriment of the Committee's credibility. A non-prescriptive approach also preserves flexibility for the Committee to advocate particular options that may rely on arguments *other* than strict legal compliance.[139] In summary, the Committee's role has been to promote informed deliberation of the alternative options in responding to human rights judgments and their respective merits, while consistently arguing that judicial decisions are to be treated as providing a minimum requirement for the protection of human rights.

Hunt observes that the Committee has always contained a wide range of intellectual conceptions of human rights, stretching from libertarianism to a strong adherence to positive rights.[140] Notwithstanding this diversity of views, the JCHR has almost invariably sought to work by consensus and to produce unanimous and non-partisan reports.[141] This has occasionally led the Committee to avoid inquiring into, or (as in the case of *Hirst*) issuing recommendations about, a particular issue on which agreement is likely to be elusive. Nevertheless, Hunt suggests, 'the capacity for human rights discourse to transcend political partisanship never ceases to surprise'.[142]

V. PARLIAMENT AND THE EUROPEAN COURT OF HUMAN RIGHTS

It was noted in section II that criticism of the ECtHR for its perceived democratic illegitimacy has gathered force in the UK, to the extent that there have been calls—unprecedented in a democratic State—for withdrawal from the Convention system. It was submitted that such proposals, and the associated populist rhetoric, are at least partly opportunistic, Strasbourg being a convenient proxy for Brussels in a climate of heightened euroscepticism. Yet the democratic critique of the Court in the UK (and its paler imitations elsewhere) cannot lightly be ignored. Increasingly, attention is being paid to the ways in which the Court might facilitate and incentivise domestic democratic oversight of human rights. Article 1 of Protocol 15 to the ECHR, which upon its entry into force will enshrine the principle of subsidiarity and the doctrine of the margin of appreciation in the Preamble to the Convention,

---

[139] For example, in its reviews of the introduction and continuation in force of the legislation that brought about control orders, the JCHR went beyond the application of judicial standards and made demands that were more exacting and expansive than those made by the courts: see A Sathanapally, *Beyond Disagreement: Open Remedies in Human Rights Adjudication* (Oxford, Oxford University Press, 2012) 208–09.

[140] Hunt (n 84) 243.

[141] D Oliver, 'Constitutional Scrutiny of Executive Bills' (2004) 33 *Macquarie Law Journal* 33, 48.

[142] Hunt (n 84) 243.

provides an opportunity for the Court to make such engagement more transparent and systematic. An important facet of this discussion is the way in which the Court takes into account the quality of democratic debate and decision-making when assessing state conduct for compliance with the ECHR and how far this judicial assessment of parliamentary conduct might motivate legislators to 'take rights seriously'.[143]

The appropriate degree of judicial deference to the elected branches of government is a matter of continuing debate, with some authors elaborating a doctrine of judicial restraint structured around certain explicit principles.[144] Notably, Kavanagh distinguishes between 'minimal' and 'substantial' judicial deference.[145] Minimal deference is always due and simply requires that judges 'cannot make light of, or be sceptical about, attempts by Parliament to solve a social problem in legislation'. Substantial deference has to be 'earned' by the elected branches and is justified only where a court considers that it suffers from particular institutional shortcomings with regard to a particular matter. These are cases where a court judges Parliament or the executive to have more institutional competence, more expertise and/or greater legitimacy to assess a particular issue.[146] Underpinning the conception of 'earned' deference is a vision of a modern, democratic constitutionalism, which eschews doctrines of either legislative or judicial supremacy in favour of a dialogic model in which all branches of the State—the executive, Parliament and the courts—share responsibility for protecting and promoting human rights.[147] Lazarus and Simonsen note that such an approach 'calls on the one hand to strengthen democratic oversight of human rights and on the other hand to find creative ways for courts to complement these participatory processes'.[148]

While the debate about deference has commonly focused onconstitutional arrangements within a State, it is also highly relevant to the ECtHR. The extent to which there has been well-informed and conscientious parliamentary scrutiny of the Convention-compliance of legislation may be an important factor in the Court's adjudications and, consequently, the success or otherwise with which States may invoke the margin of appreciation. The Court itself has frequently reiterated that,

> by reason of their direct and continuous contact with the vital forces in the society, national authorities—*and particularly national legislatures*—are in principle better placed than an

---

[143] A Kavanagh, 'Proportionality and Parliamentary Debates: Exploring Some Forbidden Territory' (2014) 34 *Oxford Journal of Legal Studies* 443, 479.

[144] See especially M Hunt, 'Sovereignty's Blight: Why Contemporary Public Law Needs the Concept of "Due Deference"' in N Bamforth and P Leyland (eds), *Public Law in a Multi-Layered Constitution* (Oxford, Hart Publishing, 2003); A Kavanagh, 'Defending Deference in Public Law and Constitutional Theory' (2010) 126 *Law Quarterly Review* 222; J King, *Judging Social Rights* (Cambridge, Cambridge University Press, 2012) pt II; A Young, 'In Defence of Due Deference' (2009) 72 *Modern Law Review* 554.

[145] A Kavanagh, 'Nature and Grounds of Judicial Deference' in A Kavanagh (ed), *Constitutional Review under the Human Rights Act* (Cambridge, Cambridge University Press, 2009) 181.

[146] ibid, 182.

[147] M Hunt, 'Reshaping Constitutionalism' in J Morison, K McEvoy and G Anthony (eds), *Judges, Transition and Human Rights* (Oxford, Oxford University Press, 2007) 467, 469.

[148] L Lazarus and N Simonsen, 'Judicial Review and Parliamentary Debate: Enriching the Doctrine of Due Deference' in M Hunt, H Hooper and P Yowell (eds), *Parliaments and Human Rights: Redressing the Democratic Deficit* (Oxford, Hart Publishing, 2015) 386.

international court to evaluate the local needs and conditions and to decide on the nature and scope of the measures necessary to meet those needs.[149]

Kavanagh highlights three common features of Strasbourg's approach to assessing the quality of democratic deliberation.[150] The first is the preponderance of 'positive-inference' cases (in which the Court has 'drawn a positive inference from (and given weight to) the fact that legislation was the product of meaningful parliamentary engagement with the rights issue') over 'negative-inference' cases (in which judges have drawn a negative inference from the absence of such parliamentary engagement).[151] The preeminent, but by no means only, example of the former is the case of *Animal Defenders International v UK*.[152] In this case, the Grand Chamber upheld by a narrow majority (9:8) the UK's ban on political advertising on television and radio as a necessary interference with the right to free expression.[153] The majority reaffirmed that,

> in order to determine the proportionality of a general measure, the Court must primarily assess the legislative choices underlying it ... The quality of the parliamentary and judicial review of the necessity of the measure is of particular importance in this respect, including to the operation of the relevant margin of appreciation.[154]

The Court found that the ban on political advertising in the broadcast media had been enacted by Parliament with cross-party support and without any dissenting vote: it was 'the culmination of an exceptional examination by parliamentary bodies of the cultural, political and legal aspects of the prohibition'.[155] It was this particular competence of Parliament—and the extensive pre-legislative consultation on the Convention compatibility of the prohibition—that explained the degree of deference shown by the domestic courts to Parliament's decision to adopt the ban.[156] For its part, the ECtHR attached 'considerable weight to these exacting and pertinent reviews, by both parliamentary and judicial bodies'.[157]

---

[149] *Animal Defenders International v UK* (2013) 57 EHRR 607, Concurring Opinion of Judge Bratza, para 12 (emphasis added).

[150] Kavanagh (n 145) 472–78. Kavanagh argues (at 477) that the ECtHR's approach to due deference is broadly similar to that of the UK courts, save for the more 'probing and exacting' standard it applied when assessing the degree of parliamentary engagement in relation to *Hirst*.

[151] ibid, 456–57 and 473–74.

[152] *Animal Defenders International* (n 149). See also *Hatton v UK* (2002) 34 EHRR 1, 129–29; *Murphy v Ireland* (2004) 38 EHRR 212, para 73; *Maurice v France* (2006) 42 EHRR 42, para 121; *Zdanoka v Latvia* (2005) 41 EHRR 659, para 134; *Evans v UK* (2007) 46 EHRR 34, para 86; *Friend v UK* and *Countryside Alliance v UK* (2010) 50 EHRR SE6, para 56; *A, B and C v Ireland* (2011) 53 EHRR 13, para 239; *SH v Austria* (2011) 52 EHRR 6, para 114; *Shindler v UK* (2014) 58 EHRR 5, para 117.

[153] The decision was a departure from previous case law in *VgT Verein gegen Tierfabrik v Switzerland* (2001) 34 EHRR 159, in which the Swiss authorities' refusal to broadcast a commercial concerning animal welfare was found to be a violation of Art 10.

[154] *Animal Defenders International* (n 149) para 108.

[155] ibid, para 114.

[156] ibid, para 115.

[157] ibid, para 116.

The most prominent example of a negative-inference case is *Hirst*, in which, as noted in section IV, the Grand Chamber highlighted the fact that there was no evidence that Parliament had ever sought to weigh the competing interests or to assess the proportionality of a blanket ban on the right of convicted prisoners to vote.[158]

It should be noted that in both *Animal Defenders International*[159] and *Hirst*[160] there were Separate Concurring or Dissenting Opinions which took a different position to that of the majority on the weight to be attached to the presence or absence of parliamentary engagement on the respective Convention issues. The lack of unanimity indicates that Strasbourg does not have a settled position on its approach to deference. Nevertheless, Judge Robert Spano has stated (extra-judicially) that the *Animal Defenders International* judgment and the line of similar cases

> demonstrate that the Strasbourg Court is currently in the process of reformulating the substantive and procedural criteria that regulate the appropriate level of deference to be afforded to Member States so as to implement a more robust and coherent concept of subsidiarity ...[161]

He continued that these judgments

> stand for the important proposition that when examining whether and to what extent the Court should grant a Member State a margin of appreciation, as to the latter's assessment of the necessity and proportionality of a restriction on human rights, the quality of decision-making, both at the legislative stage and before the courts, is crucial and may ultimately be decisive in borderline cases.[162]

Judge Spano's remarks highlight the second and third common features of Strasbourg case law identified in Kavanagh's analysis. The second is that the ECtHR 'tends to focus on the decision-making quality and its democratic pedigree, rather than assessing the merits of the individual arguments advanced in support of the policy'.[163] For example, the Court has variously deferred to parliamentary consideration that is 'careful and cautious',[164] 'comprehensive' in taking account of legal, ethical and social considerations,[165] or 'exceptionally detailed' and 'the fruit of much reflection, consultation and debate'.[166] In so doing, Kavanagh indicates, the Court has opted for a less exacting form of scrutiny of parliamentary conduct than would be involved in examining the detailed content of legislative proceedings and evaluating the sufficiency of the reasons and justifications for a rights-restricting

---

[158] *Hirst* (n 52). Other examples of negative-inference cases are *Christine Goodwin v UK* (2002) 35 EHRR 18 (GC), paras 92–93 and *Dickson v UK* (2008) 46 EHRR 41, para 83.

[159] *Animal Defenders International* (n 149). See especially Joint Dissenting Opinion of Judges Ziemele, Sajó, Kalaydjieva, Vučinić and de Gaetano, para 9.

[160] *Hirst* (n 52), Joint Concurring Opinion of Judges Tulkens and Zagrebelsky; Joint Dissenting Opinion of Judges Wildhaber, Costa, Lorenzen, Kovler and Jebens, para 7.

[161] R Spano, 'Universality or Diversity of Human Rights? Strasbourg in the Age of Subsidiarity' (2014) 14 *Human Rights Law Review* 487, 498.

[162] ibid, 498.

[163] Kavanagh (n 145) 476.

[164] *SH v Austria* (n 152) para 114.

[165] *Maurice v France* (n 152) para 121.

[166] *Evans v UK* (n 152) para 86.

measure.[167] The third feature is that, while the quality of debate and decision-making *may* (as Judge Spano notes) be decisive in some cases, this factor is not necessarily determinative, since 'there will be some issues where no amount of debate will save an otherwise rights-violating measure'.[168]

Lazarus and Simonsen welcome the Strasbourg Court's approach to evaluating the quality of parliamentary deliberation in *Animal Defenders International* but suggest that it is in 'urgent need of further substantiation'.[169] To this end, they propose various criteria which would structure judicial assessment of the degree of deference due to democratic deliberation about rights restrictions. For example, the criteria proposed include whether a parliament can demonstrate that, at the point of decision-making, all relevant interests were represented, especially of those who cannot vote (such as children, prisoners and asylum seekers) or who are otherwise excluded and marginalised, and whether that Parliament 'meaningfully engaged' with those interests.[170] Another criterion demands assessment of whether the Parliament heard evidence as to the necessity of a rights-restricting measure and considered alternatives to it.[171]

Lazarus and Simonsen acknowledge that such criteria might be resisted on grounds that they might increase the length or complexity of legal proceedings, or that they are insensitive to factors including the limited expertise of parliamentarians with respect tohuman rights and institutional constraints such as the crowded parliamentary agenda.[172] Fears might also be raised concerning the potential 'chilling' effect of judicial scrutiny on parliamentary speech.[173] At the European level, there is a risk that more systematic scrutiny of parliamentary conduct, especially in negative-inference cases, might engender resistance rather than providing a motivation for enhanced democratic deliberation. In this sense, the Court's developing approach to deference is not a risk-free enterprise.[174] Further, developing a consistent approach in respect of the deference paid to parliamentary deliberation poses particular challenges for a supranational court such as the ECtHR, which might potentially need to assess the quality of democratic engagement in any of 47 parliaments rooted in different political and legal systems across the Council of Europe. As Hooper observes, in any given case, in order to avoid making too superficial an assessment

---

[167] See, however, *Animal Defenders International v UK* (n 149), Dissenting Opinion of Judge Tulkens, joined by Judges Spielmann and Laffranque at paras 16–20.

[168] Kavanagh (n 145) 477. See eg *Shindler v UK* (n 152) para 117.

[169] Lazarus and Simonsen (n 148) 402.

[170] ibid, 394–97.

[171] ibid, 397–98.

[172] ibid, 392. See also Carolyn Evans and Simon Evans, 'Legislative Scrutiny Committees and Parliamentary Conceptions of Human Rights' [2006] *Public Law* 785, 786.

[173] HJ Hooper, 'The Use of Parliamentary Materials in Proportionality Judgments' in Hunt, Hooper and Yowell (n 148) 364–65.

[174] The author is grateful to Matthew Saul, Postdoctoral Fellow at the Centre for the Study of the Legitimate Roles of the Judiciary in the Global Order at the University of Oslo, for sharing his unpublished draft working paper on 'The Quality of Parliamentary Mobilisation for Human Rights: A Role for the International Human Rights Judiciary?', presented at Multirights, 18 March 2014, which discusses the risks associated with efforts by the international human rights judiciary to influence parliamentary engagement with human rights.

of parliamentary conduct, the Court may need to be apprised of different types of parliamentary material (such as ministerial statements to Parliament, plenary debates from different houses or chambers of Parliament, or the reports of committees or sub-committees); it may also need to understand the workings of the legislative agenda and the competing priorities facing Parliament as a whole and individual parliamentarians as part of their democratic mandate. Consequently,

> caution must be exercised by courts, especially supra-national courts from which there is no appeal, in their approach to judging the activities of parliaments for conformity with external standards on issues to which there can reasonably be a plurality of views.[175]

Equally, the Court must be alive to the risk that executives or parliaments may orchestrate proceedings to create the appearance of democratic deliberation in an attempt to 'earn' deference which is not, in fact, warranted.

These pragmatic considerations should guide the Court's developing approach, but they do not outweigh the larger goal of incentivising democratic dialogue. In the light of these concerns, the type of criteria proposed by Lazarus and Simonsen appear well-founded: they would prompt the Court to assess structural questions of representation and prevent it from giving undue weight to purely rhetorical or shallow 'rights talk'. Equally, they would permit the Court to recognise the presence of pertinent democratic debate on a matter of law or policy even when the language of rights is not explicitly used.[176] Such an approach accords with the parliamentary conception of rights envisaged by Evans and Evans which aims not to 'second guess judges or apply legal standards in a rote manner' but to bring political values and experience into play, moving away from legal notions when this best fits Parliament's conception of 'community understandings of rights'.[177] Overall, the proposed approach vindicates the Court's developing practice of attaching no *special* or *automatic* weight to legislative deliberation, but demonstrating transparently and consistently in its judgments when it has examined parliamentary proceedings and found cause to defer to the reasoned arguments advanced therein.

The wider question surrounding judicial deference by the ECtHR (or other domestic or supranational courts) to democratic institutions is whether, in practice, it acts as a 'catalyst for enhanced democratic deliberation'.[178] In theory, both positive- and negative-inference cases should provide an incentive for legislatures to take human rights standards and judgments into account and deliberate about them during the legislative process. In this way, domestic and international courts might have a 'democracy-forcing' effect.[179] Another effect of encouraging democratic institutions to earn deference from the ECtHR is that it may prompt *executives* to

---

[175] Hooper (n 173) 384. Hooper argues (at 383) that the ECtHR in its *Hirst* judgment 'based its consideration to refuse the benefit of the margin of appreciation on an extremely limited understanding of the legislative agenda, and in turn overlooked in many respects what Parliament does in a wider constitutional sense'.

[176] Lazarus and Simonsen (n 148) 398.

[177] Evans and Evans (n 172) 806.

[178] Kavanagh (n 145) 466.

[179] ibid.

assign greater importance to ensuring that legislative deliberation on human rights matters occurs, for example by inviting parliamentary scrutiny of legislation or draft legislation at an early stage or ensuring that parliaments are given timely and comprehensive information about the executive's proposed response to an adverse human rights judgment.[180] Indeed, given that executives are the main interlocutors of the Court, it may be within the executive that the signal sent by Strasbourg's scrutiny of the quality of democratic deliberation is heard first and loudest. The Court could encourage the institutionalisation of such behaviour by routinely requiring governments to provide it with all relevant evidence of parliamentary consideration of the human rights compatibility of laws which are the subject of applications, along with, for example, evidence of ECHR impact assessment in policy-making and reasoned statements of compatibility accompanying legislation.[181]

VI. CONCLUSION

Within the UK Parliament, the JCHR is the principal site of engagement with human rights judgments. The attention devoted by the JCHR to monitoring the executive's response to human rights judgments has varied over time, peaking between 2006 and 2010. How may we assess the effectiveness of this monitoring work in relation to the Council of Europe's imperative for full and rapid implementation of judgments?

In respect of the JCHR's legislative scrutiny, Hiebert points to the severe limitations on Parliament's ability to influence or constrain the executive: principally, government domination of Parliament and the centrality of disciplined political parties in the Westminster system.[182] These limitations apply equally to the post-judicial phase of the JCHR's monitoring work, which is further dependent on the timely provision of information by the executive in order that Parliament may seize the opportunity to influence the executive's response to judgments within the timeframe stipulated by the Committee of Ministers.

It is sometimes possible to identify the substantive influence of the JCHR in the sense of executive uptake of specific recommendations made by the Committee as to the means of remedying a violation (as in the case of *Gillan*). However, causality remains an open question, especially where other actors have made the same recommendations.[183] Similarly, it is difficult to say definitively that the JCHR's scrutiny

---

[180] The UK government showed itself to be aware of the benefits of ensuring parliamentary deliberation on human rights matters when in the course of its response to the ECtHR judgment on retention of biometric data (*S and Marper* (n 73)) it suggested that 'where a complex issue has been subjected to Parliamentary scrutiny, there is an argument that a wide margin of appreciation should be applied'. See Home Office Memorandum on the Protection of Freedoms Bill, February 2011, para 13.

[181] The author is grateful to Murray Hunt, Legal Adviser to the JCHR, for these practical suggestions, made in an unpublished submission to a Council of Europe consultation in November 2013 on the long-term future of the Convention and the Court.

[182] J Hiebert, 'Governing under the Human Rights Act: The Limitations of Wishful Thinking' [2012] *Public Law* 27.

[183] See Hunt, Hooper and Yowell (n 86) 43–44 for discussion of this methodological challenge in respect of the JCHR's legislative scrutiny.

has hastened implementation of judgments in particular instances. Multiple factors are likely to influence the timing of executive action, most obviously a change of government and a greater willingness on the part of incoming ministers to remedy violations that occurred under their predecessors (as in the cases of *Marper* and *Gillan*). Where a judgment requires legislative reform, and the JCHR (or another parliamentary committee) is able to scrutinise draft legislation and propose changes prior to the proposal's formal introduction into Parliament, its capacity to influence both parliamentary deliberation of the matter and the eventual outcome is likely to be greater than when this opportunity is lacking, as evidenced by the expansive approach of both the government and Parliament to implementing judgments on transgender rights.[184]

The JCHR's effectiveness in respect of its work in monitoring the implementation of judgments should be measured both in terms of executive uptake of recommendations relating to specific judgments and by the 'system-wide' improvements that its recommendations have helped to secure. The instigation of more systematic arrangements for co-coordinating the government's response to judgments, the timely and routine provision of information by the executive to Parliament, and improvements in the quality and timeliness of the UK government's action plans submitted to the Committee of Ministers may be regarded as a vindication of the JCHR's rigorous approach to monitoring up to 2010. In addition, the Committee's monitoring work has fostered the creation of an accessible public record of adverse ECtHR judgments (and declarations of incompatibility by domestic courts) and the government's responses to them, including the reasoning behind those responses. In this sense, the JCHR has ensured that ministers must justify their action or inaction, and has established that the requirement for justification extends to post-judicial as well as pre-legislative activity.

These improvements to the executive system of implementation, and its increased responsiveness to Parliament, have occurred at the same time as the anti-Strasbourg rhetoric has become more strident at Westminster and in sections of the press. Under changed political conditions, these contradictions, which have (with certain high-profile exceptions) permitted implementation of judgments to proceed smoothly and largely under the political radar, may become increasingly exposed. In this sense, the UK's institutional arrangements for responding to ECtHR judgments, which are among the most robust in the Council of Europe, may be vulnerable to future challenge and revision by a government intent on weakening the UK's ties to Strasbourg.

From one perspective, the *Hirst* saga appears to illustrate how exposing contentious issues to parliamentary debate can magnify or entrench political and philosophical differences concerning human rights, thereby limiting the scope for executive action and delaying implementation. Yet an alternative and, it is submitted, preferable reading of these events is the desirability of requiring Parliament *at the earliest possible stage* to engage with specific legislative proposals and justificatory arguments regarding the meaning and scope of the rights at stake.

---

[184] See Sathanapally (n 139) 166–72.

Maximising opportunities and incentives for such engagement is likely to increase parliamentarians' sense of responsibility for rights-based reform, along with their knowledge and awareness of the Convention system, and equip them to hold governments to account for their action, or inaction, in responding to human rights judgments. Moreover, such conduct may mean that laws and policies have a greater chance of surviving scrutiny by judges in Strasbourg, who are increasingly attuned to the relevance of domestic democratic deliberation to their own determinations.

Part II

Specific Issues of Conflict

9

Voting Eligibility: Strasbourg's Timidity

REUVEN (RUVI) ZIEGLER

I. INTRODUCTION

THIS CHAPTER APPRAISES recent jurisprudence of the European Court of Human Rights (ECtHR) concerning the undertaking in Article 3 of the First Protocol (A3P1)[1] to the European Convention on Human Rights (ECHR)[2] to hold 'free elections ... under conditions which will ensure the free expression of the opinion of the people in the choice of the legislature'. The Court famously held in its *Mathieu-Mohin*[3] judgment that A3P1 entails individual 'subjective' rights of participation, the 'right to vote' and the 'right to stand for elections to the legislature'.[4] It further held that, while the right to vote is not absolute, its exercise should not be curtailed to such an extent as to impair its 'very essence' and deprive it of its effectiveness.[5] It is submitted that questions of eligibility to vote, namely the determination whether a person is entitled to participate in a given electoral process, stand at the core of the right to vote, whereas questions concerning the conditions and procedural regulations which facilitate or hinder the exercise of a right to vote are at its penumbra.[6]

---

[1] Protocol to the Convention for the Protection of Human Rights and Fundamental Freedoms, 20 March 1952, 213 UNTS 262, ETS No 009 (entered in force 18 May 1954).

[2] Convention for the Protection of Human Rights and Fundamental Freedoms, 4 November 1950, 213 UNTS 222 (entered in force 3 September 1953).

[3] *Mathieu-Mohin and Clerfayt v Belgium* (1988) 10 EHRR 1.

[4] ibid, para 51. See also GS Goodwin-Gill, *Free and Fair Elections* (Geneva, Inter-Parliamentary Union, 2006) 103–04.

[5] ibid, para 52. *cf* Basic Law for the Federal Republic of Germany, Art 19, drawing a distinction between the essence of basic rights which 'in no case ... may be affected' in Art 19(2), and other aspects of rights in Art 19(1), which may be restricted pursuant to generally applicable laws. An English translation is available at www.gesetze-im-internet.de/englisch_gg/englisch_gg.html. See also Human Rights Committee, *General Comment No 27: Freedom of Movement (Art 12)*, 67th session (2 November 1999), para 13 ('in adopting laws providing for restrictions permitted by Article 12, paragraph 3, States should always be guided by the principle that the restrictions must not impair the essence of the right'), www1.umn.edu/humanrts/gencomm/hrcom27.htm.

[6] But see Kennedy LJ in *R (Pearson and Martinez) v Home Secretary* [2001] EWHC 239 (Admin), para 41 (maintaining that '[o]f course as far as an individual prisoner is concerned, disenfranchisement does impair the very essence of his right to vote, but that is too simplistic an approach, because what [A3P1] is really concerned with is the wider question of universal franchise, and the free expression of the opinion of the people in the choice of the legislature').

The main argument of this chapter is that Strasbourg jurisprudence has not clearly distinguished between the desirable level of scrutiny for questions relating to the choice of electoral systems ('first-past-the-post', the alternative vote, proportional representation, the single transferrable vote, etc) and the desirable level of scrutiny for questions relating to voting eligibility. It is contended that, even if Contracting States should enjoy a wide 'margin of appreciation' on grounds of democratic legitimacy regarding the choice of electoral system, such a margin is unwarranted when Strasbourg scrutinises legislation that affects individual access to the democratic process. It is submitted that, in its voting eligibility jurisprudence, Strasbourg has been timid rather than interventionist.

Part II analyses recent Strasbourg jurisprudence scrutinising electoral exclusion of convicts and non-residents. It demonstrates that, despite the Court's pronouncements in *Hirst (No 2)* that 'the presumption in a democratic state must be in favour of inclusion', and that 'any departure from the principle of universal suffrage risks undermining the democratic validity of the legislature thus elected and the laws it promulgates',[7] Strasbourg has adopted a cautious approach. Section A offers an overview of current and recent legal challenges to disenfranchisement legislation. Section B suggests that Strasbourg's timidity in this area manifests itself in three main ways: first, acceptance, with little scrutiny, of the legitimacy of legislative aims; secondly, acknowledgement in principle that deference to the legislature in matters concerning regulation of its franchise is warranted; and thirdly, extension of a wide margin of appreciation to Contracting States concerning exclusionary electoral measures.

Part III makes a normative case for Strasbourg adopting a more rigorous approach to scrutinising legislative measures regulating access to the democratic process. Section A argues that much of the critique of the ECtHR jurisprudence concerning regulation of the franchise emanates from a failure to recognise the intrinsic and instrumental significance of voting. Section B highlights the legitimating and facilitating roles performed by voting, thereby contributing to the maintenance of an 'effective political democracy'.[8] It is contended that, due to voting's invaluable roles, exclusionary measures merit rigorous judicial scrutiny, notwithstanding the sensitivities of matters concerning the election of a legislature.[9] Section C demonstrates how Strasbourg's restrictive interpretation of A3P1, which precludes its applicability to referendums, effectively delimits the contours of the right to vote in the UK. This is due to the combined effect of the prevalent reliance by UK courts on the 'mirror' principle[10] and to the absence of a codified constitutional right to vote in the UK constitutional order.

---

[7] *Hirst v UK (No 2)* (2006) 42 EHRR 41, para 59 (upholding (2004) EHRR 40).

[8] ECHR, Preamble.

[9] R O'Connell, 'Realising Political Equality: The European Court of Human Rights and Positive Obligations in a Democracy' (2010) 61 *Northern Ireland Legal Quarterly* 263, 265.

[10] For a critique of the reliance on the 'mirror' principle, see R Clayton, 'Should the English Courts under the HRA Mirror the Strasbourg Case Law?' (ch 6), this volume.

II. PRISONERS AND EXPATRIATES:
STRASBOURG AND THE UK

A. Context: Current and Recent Legal Challenges

This section surveys current and recent legal challenges to the blanket disenfranchisement of prisoners under UK legislation and to the electoral exclusion of its non-resident citizens who continuously reside outside its territory (appraisals of disenfranchisement practices of prisoners and expatriates as such are outside the remit of this chapter[11]). Unlike (some of) the challenges to disenfranchisement of convicts, legal challenges concerning electoral exclusion of non-resident citizens have been unsuccessful, and thus have largely passed under the public radar. However, in order to illustrate Strasbourg's cautious jurisprudential approach with regard to prisoner voting, it is useful to consider the two issues in tandem.

(i) Challenges to the Disenfranchisement of Convicts

In the UK, disenfranchisement of prisoners is sanctioned by section 3 of the Representation of the People Act (ROPA) 1983,[12] which stipulates that '[a] convicted person during the time that he is detained in a penal institution in pursuance of his sentence is legally incapable of voting at any parliamentary or local government election'. The High Court rejected a claim brought by three prisoners sentenced to life imprisonment challenging their disenfranchisement. Two of the claimants, Martinez and Hirst, were detained on preventative grounds.[13] Refused leave to appeal to the Court of Appeal in 2001,[14] Hirst brought a claim before the ECtHR. In March 2004, the Fourth Section Chamber held that section 3 of ROPA 1983 violates A3P1.[15] In October 2005, the Grand Chamber (by a majority

---

[11] For a broader analysis of prisoner voting, see R Ziegler, 'Legal Outlier, Again? US Felon Suffrage—Comparative and International Law Perspectives' (2011) 29(2) *Boston University International Law Journal* 197. For a discussion of out-of-country voting theory and practice, see R Ziegler, 'Out-of-County Voting: The Predicament of the Recognised Refugee' in J-P Gauci, M Giuffré and E Tsourdi (eds), *Exploring the Boundaries of Refugee Law: Current Protection Challenges* (Leiden, Brill, 2015) 298.

[12] Representation of the People Act 1983 (ROPA 1983) c 2, s 3, re-enacting the ban imposed by Representation of the People Act 1969, s 4 (and, indeed, the Forfeiture Act 1870 c 23, s 2). Disenfranchisement does not apply to those imprisoned for contempt of court or non-payment of fines. The Representation of the People Act 2000 c 2, s 3 re-enfranchised persons detained in mental hospitals. Section 1(1) of the Act sets the qualifications for voting in the UK general election: 'A person is entitled to vote as an elector at a parliamentary election in any constituency if on the date of the poll he (a) is registered in the register of parliamentary electors for that constituency; (b) is not subject to any legal incapacity to vote (age apart); (c) is either a Commonwealth citizen or a citizen of the republic of Ireland; and (d) is of voting age (that is, 18 years or over).' Section 2 defines the local government franchise as encompassing resident qualifying Commonwealth citizens, Irish citizens, and relevant citizens of the Union (such as a citizen who is not a Commonwealth citizen or a citizen of the Republic of Ireland: ibid, s 202(1)). The local government franchise also applies in elections *for the European Parliament*: see European Parliamentary Elections Act 2002 c 24, s 8.

[13] *Pearson* (n 6).

[14] Leave to appeal refused by the Court of Appeal [2001] EWCA Civ 927.

[15] *Hirst v UK (No 2)* (Chamber) (n 7). Certain elements of the reasoning will be discussed in Section B.

of twelve to five) upheld the decision.[16] In 2006, the then Labour government issued a Green Paper for public consultation.[17] The consultation was conducted in two phases, and the 2006 First Phase consultation paper included retention of the status quo as one of the options for consideration.[18] The 2009 Second Phase consultation paper, however, precluded both blanket disenfranchisement and full enfranchisement.[19] The government failed to introduce new legislation before the 6 May 2010 general election. Consequently, all serving prisoners were barred from voting in these elections. The Committee of Ministers of the Council of Europe reprimanded the UK for its failure to implement *Hirst (No 2)*.[20] It 'expressed profound regret that despite the repeated calls of the committee, the UK general election was held on 6 May 2010 with the blanket ban on the right of convicted prisoners in custody to vote still in place'.[21]

Meanwhile, UK courts adopted divergent approaches to the legal implications of *Hirst (No 2)*. In 2007, in *Smith v Scott*, the Registration Appeal Court of Scotland held that the refusal to register the applicant for the (then upcoming) elections to the Scottish Parliament pursuant to ROPA 1983 constituted a violation of A3P1.[22] It decided to issue a Declaration of Incompatibility under section 4 of the Human Rights Act 1998 (HRA).[23] In contrast, the (English) Court of Appeal refused to issue a similar declaration in *Chester*.[24]

Meanwhile, in Strasbourg, in 2010, the Fourth Section Chamber applied its 'pilot judgment procedure', finding the UK in violation of A3P1 in *Greens and MT*.[25] The Court ordered the UK to 'bring forward within six months of the date upon which the judgment became final legislative proposals intended to [amend the legislation in a] Convention-compliant [manner]', and to 'enact the required legislation within any such period as may be determined by the Committee of Ministers'.[26]

Responding to the judgment, Prime Minister David Cameron declared: 'I am very clear about this … no one should be in any doubt: prisoners are not getting the vote under this government.'[27] Despite this statement, on 17 December 2010 the Cabinet Office published a paper entitled *The Government's Approach to Prisoner Voting Rights*, according to which 'all offenders sentenced to four years or more will automatically be barred from registering to vote. Prisoners sentenced to less than

---

[16] *Hirst v UK (No 2)* (Grand Chamber) (n 7).

[17] Ministry of Justice, *Voting Rights of Convicted Prisoners Detained Within the UK*, CP 29/06 First Phase Consultation (2006), CP 6/09 Second Phase Consultation (2009), www.justice.gov.uk/consultations/prisoners-voting-rights.htm.

[18] First Phase Consultation, ibid, paras 57–58.

[19] Second Phase Consultation, ibid, 23–24.

[20] See eg summary of meetings held on 2–4 March 2010 and 15 September 2010, wcd.coe.int/ViewDoc.jsp?Ref=CM/Del/Dec%282010%291078&Language=lanEnglish&Ver=immediat&Site=CM&BackColorInternet=C3C3C3&BackColorIntranet=EDB021&BackColorLogged=F5D3.

[21] CM/Del/Dec (2010) 1086/18, 1086th meeting, 7 June 2010.

[22] *Smith v Scott* [2007] CSIH 9.

[23] c 42, s 4.

[24] *Chester v Secretary of State for Justice* [2010] EWCA Civ 1439.

[25] *Greens and MT v UK* (2011) 53 EHRR 21, para 6(a).

[26] Art 46(1) ECHR stipulates that '[t]he High Contracting Parties undertake to abide by the final judgment of the Court in any case to which they are parties'.

[27] HC Deb 24 October 2012, vol 551, col 923.

four years will retain the right to vote, unless the sentencing judge removes it.'[28] Interestingly, in its announcement, the coalition government indicated its intention to set the highest of the thresholds that had been proposed in the Labour government's consultation paper. The lack of clarity as to the government's position led to a special backbench parliamentary debate on 10 February 2011. The crossbench motion, which passed by a majority of 234 to 22, read:

> [This] House notes the ruling of the European Court of Human Rights in Hirst v. the UK in which it held that there had been no substantive debate by members of the legislature on the continued justification for maintaining a general restriction on the right of prisoners to vote; acknowledges the treaty obligations of the UK; is of the opinion that legislative decisions of this nature should be a matter for democratically-elected lawmakers; and supports the current situation in which no prisoner is able to vote except those imprisoned for contempt, default or on remand.[29]

Meanwhile, again in Strasbourg, the Grand Chamber was poised to hear the case of *Scoppola (No 3) v Italy*, where the Second Section Chamber found a violation of A3P1,[30] opting to apply the *Hirst (No 2)* principles as the First Section Chamber in *Frodl v Austria* interpreted them.[31] The applicant in *Scoppola (No 3)* challenged his disenfranchisement pursuant to the Italian legislation, according to which a person who has been sentenced to imprisonment for five years or more is permanently banned from public office and unable to vote for life, whereas a person who has been sentenced to imprisonment for three years or more is barred from public office for five years and unable to vote for that period. Under Italian law, disenfranchised persons could regain the vote if granted 'rehabilitation', which can be applied for three years after the main penalty has been completed and is conditional on 'consistent and genuine good conduct'.[32]

The UK intervened in the Grand Chamber hearings in *Scoppola (No 3)* by submitting written observations, and was consequently granted an extension to the *Greens and MT* deadline for compliance with the ratio of the *Hirst (No 2)* judgment: it now had to introduce legislation within six months after the Grand Chamber judgment in *Scoppola (No 3)*. On 23 May 2012, the Grand Chamber (by a majority of sixteen to one) reversed, upholding the impugned Italian legislation.[33] Nevertheless, it reiterated that the decision in *Hirst (No 2)* remains good law.

On 22 November 2012, the last day for compliance with the extended *Greens and MT* deadline, the UK government published the Voting Eligibility (Prisoners) Bill 2012.[34] The bill proposed rather unusually three options for legislative reform: barring

---

[28] www.cabinetoffice.gov.uk/news/government-approach-prisoner-voting-rights.
[29] HC Deb 10 February 2011, vol 523, col 493.
[30] *Scoppola v Italy (No 3)* [2011] ECHR 2417.
[31] *Frodl v Austria* (2011) 52 EHRR 5. The case involved a challenge to Austrian legislation which disenfranchised those serving a prison sentence exceeding one year for convictions for offences committed with intent. The Court held that 'the decision on disenfranchisement should be taken by a judge, taking into account the particular circumstances, and that there must be a link between the offence committed and issues relating to elections and democratic institutions'. Ibid, para 34.
[32] *Scoppola v Italy (No 3)* [2013] 56 EHRR 19 para 38 (citing Art 179 of the Italian Criminal Code, which concerns 'Conditions of rehabilitation').
[33] ibid.
[34] The bill and explanatory notes are available at www.justice.gov.uk/downloads/legislation/bills-acts/ voting-eligibility-prisoners/voting-eligibility-prisoners-command-paper.pdf.

prisoners sentenced to four years or more, barring prisoners sentenced to more than six months, or retaining the general ban on prisoner voting, but with a few minor changes. For the first time since the enactment of the HRA, the government proposed a legislative option which, according to the explanatory notes, '[t]he Government is ... unable to say [is ECHR] compatible'.[35] This is particularly noteworthy in view of the Declaration of Incompatibility issued in *Smith v Scott*.[36]

After the bill passed its second reading in the House of Commons, a Joint Committee on the Draft Voting Eligibility (Prisoners) Bill (the Joint Committee) was established. Prior to its reporting, a seven-judge panel of the UK Supreme Court declined to issue a declaration of incompatibility in two challenges brought by prisoners serving terms of life imprisonment against their disenfranchisement in UK general elections, European parliamentary elections and local government elections.[37] While the Supreme Court did not issue a declaration of incompatibility, it held that the *Hirst (No 2)* ratio as (re)interpreted in *Scoppola (No 3)* should be applied, thus rejecting the Attorney-General's view that the Supreme Court should accept the government's stance that the legislation is Convention-compatible.[38]

The Joint Committee reported on 16 December 2013.[39] Emphasising the UK's obligation to comply with *Hirst (No 2)* in light of Article 46 ECHR, the Committee asserted that, for Parliament to adhere to the rule of law, it 'should either enact legislation complying with the *Hirst* judgment or take steps to denounce the Convention'.[40] The Committee then recommended legislative reform that would enfranchise all prisoners serving sentences of 12 months or less in all UK parliamentary, local and European elections.[41]

---

[35] ibid, explanatory notes, para 88. See s 19 HRA.

[36] Above, n 22.

[37] *R (Chester) v Secretary of State for Justice and McGeoch v Lord President of the Council* [2013] UKSC 63. The appellants contended that their disenfranchisement in European parliamentary elections and in municipal elections violates their right to vote as EU citizens pursuant to the Charter of Fundamental Rights of the European Union (CFR) OJ C326/391(26 October 2012). Art 39(1) thereof stipulates that '[e]very citizen of the Union has the right to vote and to stand as a candidate at elections to the European Parliament in the Member State in which he or she resides, under the same conditions as nationals of that State'. Similarly, Art 40 stipulates that '[e]very citizen of the Union has the right to vote and to stand as a candidate at municipal elections in the Member State in which he or she resides under the same conditions as nationals of that State' (identical stipulations appear in Arts 20(2)(b) and 22(1), respectively, of the Treaty on the Functioning of the European Union [2008] OJ C115/47). It is contended that the principle of non-discrimination between EU citizens is premised on the assumption that EU Member States grant the respective rights to their own citizens, and so there was no need for its explicit assertion. A reference to the Court of Justice of the European Union (CJEU) would have facilitated the further development of EU citizens' rights jurisprudence, following Case C-34/09 *Zambrano v Office National de L'emploi* [2011] ECR I-1177 (prohibiting 'national measures which have the effect of depriving citizens of the Union of the genuine enjoyment of the substance of the rights conferred by virtue of their status as citizens of the Union'). However, the Supreme Court refused to make a reference to the CJEU.

[38] Lord Mance concluded, regarding the judgment in *Scoppola (No 3)*, that 'it can ... now be said with considerable confidence that the ban on Chester's voting is one which the UK Parliament can, consistently with the Convention right, and would maintain': *Chester and McGeoch* (n 37) para 40.

[39] Joint Committee on the Draft Voting Eligibility (Prisoners) Bill, *Report* (16 December 2013), www.publications.parliament.uk/pa/jt201314/jtselect/jtdraftvoting/103/103.pdf.

[40] ibid, para 229 (referring to Art 46(1) ECHR).

[41] ibid, para 239. If adopted, the Joint Committee proposal will rectify the (arguable) anomaly whereby those sentenced to less than one year of imprisonment can stand for elections pursuant to the Representation of the People Act 1981 c 34, s 1, but cannot vote, including for themselves.

In a letter to the Committee Chairman dated 25 February 2014, the then Justice Secretary Chris Grayling noted that

> the report makes a number of new observations and adds recommendations to the debate which require thorough consideration. I am committed to ensuring that those issues are fully thought through and wanted to assure you that the matter is under active consideration with government.[42]

The Voting Eligibility (Prisoners) Bill was notably absent from the Queen's Speech on 4 June 2014.[43] Consequently, the general election on 7 May 2015 was held on the basis of the current ECHR-incompatible franchise. On 25 September 2014, the Committee of Ministers 'recalled the number of years that have passed since the judgments *Hirst No 2* and *Greens and MT* became final, and the repeated calls of the Committee of Ministers to execute them',[44] and 'noted with profound concern and disappointment that the UK authorities did not introduce a bill to Parliament at the start of its 2014–2015 session as recommended by the competent parliamentary committee'.[45]

Elsewhere, the ECtHR has recently found Russia[46] and Turkey[47] to be in violation of A3P1 in cases concerning their blanket disenfranchisement legislation. On 12 August 2014, the Fourth Section Chamber found the UK in violation of A3P1 in *Firth v UK*, in respect of prisoners in Scottish prisons who were denied the right to vote in European parliamentary elections.[48] On 10 February 2015, the Fourth Section Chamber found the UK in violation of A3P1 in *McHugh v UK*, in respect of prisoners who were denied the right to vote in one or more of the following elections: elections to the European Parliament on 4 June 2009; the UK general election on 6 May 2010; and elections to the Scottish Parliament, Welsh Assembly, and/or Northern Irish Assembly on 5 May 2011, respectively.[49]

Almost 10 years have passed since *Hirst (No 2)* became final, yet the UK rather defiantly refuses to abide by the Grand Chamber judgment. The above overview exposes a totemic (and unprecedented) legal and political standoff between the ECtHR and the Committee of Ministers on the one hand, and Westminster and Whitehall on the other. In its cautious jurisprudence, Strasbourg (inadvertently) facilitates the continuation of this saga.

---

[42] The letter is available at www.parliament.uk/documents/joint-committees/Draft-Voting-Eligibility-Prisoners-Bill/Grayling-letter-to-Chair.pdf.

[43] https://www.gov.uk/government/speeches/queens-speech-2014.

[44] 1208th meeting, para 2, wcd.coe.int/ViewDoc.jsp?id=2237963&Site=CM.

[45] ibid, para 3.

[46] *Anchugov and Gladkov v Russia* [2013] ECHR 638 (the claimants were convicted of murder and other offences and sentenced to death; the sentence was commuted to 15 years' imprisonment. They were barred from voting in elections to the Duma and in presidential elections pursuant to Art 32(3) of the Russian Constitution).

[47] *Söyler v Turkey* [2013] ECHR 821 (the claimant was convicted for failing to honour his cheques; he was barred from voting in the 2007 Turkish general elections while incarcerated and in the 2011 elections upon conditional release); *Vural v Turkey* (2014) ECHR 1113 (the applicant was convicted under the law of offences against Ataturk and sentenced to 13 years' imprisonment; he was barred from voting in two sets of elections).

[48] *Firth v UK* [2014] ECHR 874.

[49] *McHugh v UK* [2015] ECHR 155.

(ii) Challenges to the Disenfranchisement of Non-Residents[50]

In recent years, the regulation of the UK franchise in relation to non-resident citizens has also been subject to ECtHR scrutiny. However, as noted above, these legal challenges have not been successful, and consequently, unlike in the prisoner voting saga, the Court has suffered no political or legal backlash. This section explores Strasbourg's non-interventionist approach to scrutinising disenfranchisement legislation in this area.

The Representation of the People Act (ROPA) 1985[51] enables non-resident UK citizens (but, notably, not non-resident Irish or Commonwealth citizens otherwise eligible to vote in a UK general election) to qualify as 'overseas voters' in the constituency in which they were last registered.[52] The initial entitlement was for five years of non-residence. ROPA 1989 extended the period of non-residence to 20 years;[53] the Political Parties, Elections and Referendums Act 2000 reduced it to 15 years.[54]

In 2007, the Fourth Section Chamber in *Doyle v UK* declared inadmissible a challenge brought by a UK citizen who had been residing in Belgium since 1983.[55] The Court noted its previous jurisprudence recognising a residence requirement to be, in principle, a non-arbitrary restriction on the right to vote.[56] The Court unanimously held the application to be 'manifestly ill-founded' as it did not 'perceive any effective disenfranchisement of the applicant or impairment of the very essence of the right to vote'.[57]

In 2011, the High Court in *Preston* rejected a claim that the legislation served as a deterrent for UK citizens qua EU nationals wishing to exercise their EU right to freedom of movement.[58] The High Court held that, while the claimant was aggrieved by the removal of the right to vote, the UK government could take the view that there is a legitimate objective which the rule is designed to achieve, namely to remove the right to vote from those whose links with the UK have diminished and who are not, for the most part at least, directly affected by the laws passed in the UK.[59]

In 2013, back in Strasbourg, the Fourth Section Chamber in *Shindler v UK* rejected a further challenge to ROPA 1985 (as amended).[60] The applicant, a Second

---

[50] cf *Sitaropoulos and Giakoumopoulos v Greece* (2013) 56 EHRR 9 (reversing the First Section Chamber judgment of 8 July 2010) (the claimants, Greek nationals residing in Strasbourg, were denied access to Out of Country Voting procedures, and required to return to Greece in order to vote. The Chamber, by a majority of five to two, found a violation of A3P1. The Grand Chamber unanimously reversed, holding that 'while traveling to Greece in order to exercise one's right to vote disrupts one's financial, family and professional lives, such disruption is not disproportionate to the point of impairing the very essence of the voting rights in question').

[51] C 50, s 1.

[52] Prior to the passage of the Act, non-resident UK citizens could not vote in a UK general election unless they were members of the armed forces or Crown servants.

[53] c 28, s 1.

[54] c 41, s 141.

[55] *Doyle v UK* [2007] ECHR 165.

[56] ibid.

[57] ibid.

[58] *Preston v Wandsworth Borough Council* [2011] EWHC 3174; upheld by the Court of Appeal in *R (on the application of Preston) v Lord President of the Council* [2012] EWCA Civ 1378.

[59] ibid, paras 39–42.

[60] *Shindler v UK* (2014) 58 EHRR 5.

World War veteran residing in Italy with his Italian wife, argued that the Court should revisit its earlier judgments in light of modern technology, which enables non-resident citizens to keep in contact with their State of origin.[61] He further contended that the fact that he is entitled to repatriate at any time indicates that his interests are directly affected, inter alia, by legislation concerning NHS reforms, pensions, banking regulations and taxation. Rejecting the case on the merits, the Court acknowledged that 'non-judicial bodies of the Council of Europe ... had demonstrated a growing awareness at European level of the problems posed by migration in terms of political participation in countries of origin and residence'.[62] Nonetheless, it concluded that 'the legislative trends are not sufficient to establish the existence of any common European approach concerning voting rights of non-residents'; hence, 'the margin of appreciation enjoyed by the State ... still remains a wide one'.[63]

It may be concluded from these decisions that the ECtHR refrains from offering generally applicable guidelines as to the circumstances in which the disenfranchisement of non-residents is (or may be) justified.

B. Strasbourg's Timidity in Action

The previous section surveyed recent jurisprudence of the ECtHR concerning UK disenfranchisement practices of convicts and non-residents. It is contended that the timidity of Strasbourg's jurisprudence manifests itself in three ways: first, the acceptance of poorly defined policy aims as legitimate, despite the fact that A3P1 contains no list of aims and, indeed, no list of qualifications to the enjoyment of rights;[64] secondly, rhetorical deference to legislative debate and scrutiny in matters concerning the regulation of the composition of the legislature; and thirdly, consistent reference to a wide margin of appreciation that ought to be afforded to States.[65] Strasbourg's approach to scrutinising the electoral exclusion of expatriates is further contrasted with the European Commission's position, expressed in its recommendations concerning EU citizens' voting rights.

---

[61] ibid, pp 4–5, applicant's submission (draft with author).

[62] ibid, para 114.

[63] ibid, para 115.

[64] *cf* Arts 8–11 ECHR. See also P Mahoney, 'Marvellous Richness of Diversity or Invidious Cultural Relativism?' (1998) 19 *Human Rights Law Journal* 2 (suggesting that 'the language of qualified rights under the convention implies that there are legitimate public objectives that are not important enough to warrant limiting the enjoyment of rights').

[65] See eg P Sales, 'Law and Democracy in a Human Rights Framework' in D Feldman (ed), *Law in Politics, Politics in Law* (Oxford, Hart Publishing, 2013) 217 (noting that Strasbourg 'generally allows a wide margin of appreciation to a state in determining who should be treated as constituting part of the demos with a right of participation in democratic procedures'). *cf Kiss v Hungary* (2013) 56 EHRR 38 (holding that a provision in the Hungarian Constitution disenfranchising persons under the partial guardianship of another due to their mental incapacity is in contravention of A3P1). Notably, however, the basis for narrowing the margin of appreciation in *Kiss* was the Court's determination that the impugned provision disenfranchises 'a particularly vulnerable group in society' rather than recognising generally the desirability of rigorous scrutiny in cases concerning voting eligibility.

(i) Broad Acceptance of Legislative Aims

This section demonstrates that, while Strasbourg's jurisprudence acknowledged the fundamentality of the right to vote and considered disenfranchisement legislation a prima facie infringement thereof, the Court has shown a willingness to accept, with little scrutiny, the legislative aims presented by the UK State. Notably, rejection of these aims should have led the Court to consider the legislative arrangements Convention-incompatible without having to resort to a proportionality assessment.

A3P1 does not contain an internal limitation clause, nor does it include a list of legitimate aims. It could have followed that, in view of the fundamentality of the right to vote, Strasbourg would rigorously scrutinise the aims of restricting legislation. Rather, the Grand Chamber has held that, absent a closed list of aims, States enjoy greater freedom to articulate policy aims.

In *Hirst (No 2)*, the UK presented two legislative aims for blanket disenfranchisement of prisoners: enhancing civic responsibility and increasing respect for the rule of law. The Fourth Section Chamber held that 'there is no clear, logical link between the loss of vote and the imposition of a prison sentence, where no bar applies to a person guilty of crimes which may be equally anti-social or "uncitizen-like" but whose crime is not met by such a consequence'.[66] Nonetheless, the Chamber refrained from holding that the legislative aims were illegitimate.[67] In contradistinction, the Grand Chamber held that A3P1 does not include a 'closed list' of legitimate aims, and that the above aims cannot be considered 'untenable or *per se* incompatible'.[68]

In *Scoppola (No 3)*, the Grand Chamber accepted the Italian government's submission and considered the aim of 'ensuring the proper functioning and preservation of the democratic regime' to be legitimate.[69] Without further analysis, the judgment proceeded on the assumption that the *Hirst (No 2)* aims are legitimate and applicable here, too. The additional aim, can be directly linked to some of the offences that, according to the Italian legislation, generate disenfranchisement. By contrast, the relevance of the *Hirst (No 2)* aims to disenfranchisement seems questionable.[70]

The probing of 'legitimate aims' received even less scrutiny in the non-resident voting cases: *Doyle*, technically an admissibility case, did not directly engage the issue. In *Shindler*, the Court revealingly noted that 'neither the applicant nor the respondent government identified the legitimate aim of the restriction', and went on to hold that 'the Court is satisfied that it pursues the legitimate aim of confining the parliamentary franchise to those citizens with a close connection with the UK and

---

[66] *Hirst (No 2)* (Chamber) (n 7) paras 46–47.
[67] ibid.
[68] *Hirst (No 2)* (Grand Chamber) (n 7) paras 74–75.
[69] *Scoppola (No 3)* (n 32) (Grand Chamber) para 92.
[70] *cf* the critique of identical legislative objectives (enhancing civic responsibility and respect for the rule of law) offered by the Canadian Supreme Court in *Sauvé v Canada (Chief Electoral Officer) (No 2)* [2002] 3 SCR 519, para 22 (holding that 'vague and symbolic objectives make the justification analysis more difficult. Their terms carry many meanings, yet tell us little about why the limitation on the right is necessary, and what it is expected to achieve in concrete terms. The broader and more abstract the objective, the more susceptible it is to different meanings in different contexts, and hence to distortion and manipulation').

who would therefore be most directly affected by its laws'.[71] Thus, the legitimacy of this aim was accepted without assessment.

(ii) Deference to the Legislature

This section demonstrates the rhetorical prevalence of deference to the legislature in ECtHR voting eligibility jurisprudence. In turn, Part III will consider the desirability of deference in relation to regulation of the franchise. In *Hirst (No 2)*, the Grand Chamber refused to attach

> weight ... to the position adopted by the legislature [as] ... it cannot be said that there was any substantive debate by members of the legislature on the continued justification in light of modern-day penal policy and of current human rights standards for maintaining such a general restriction on the right of prisoners to vote.[72]

Lady Justice Arden criticised the judgment for failing to acknowledge the fact that the UK legislation was drafted to give effect to the recommendations of a report laid before Parliament by a working party on electoral reform, and that Parliament could have held a substantive debate should it have wished to do so.[73] Notwithstanding the controversy regarding the (in)accuracy of the description in *Hirst (No 2)*, it could be concluded from Strasbourg's inclination to explain why it had chosen *not* to accord weight to parliamentary scrutiny that, as a matter of course, it would accord such weight.

Strasbourg's case law concerning expatriates confirms this. In *Doyle*, the Court noted (distinguishing *Hirst (No 2)*) 'that the impugned measure has been the subject of parliamentary scrutiny. There was a debate on the time limit in both Houses of Parliament before the legislation was adopted'.[74] Similarly, in *Shindler*, the Court (again distinguishing *Hirst (No 2)*) suggested that '[t]here is ... extensive evidence ... to demonstrate that Parliament has sought to weigh the competing interests and to assess the proportionality of the fifteen-year rule ... [including that the issue] has been examined twice by the Home Affairs Select Committee'.[75] The Court clarified that

> [t]his is not to say that because the legislature debates, possibly even repeatedly, an issue and reaches a particular conclusion thereon, that conclusion is necessarily Convention-compliant. It ... means that that review is taken into consideration by the court for the purpose of deciding whether a fair balance has been struck.[76]

Strasbourg thus apparently takes the view that, in principle, a measure of deference to the legislature is warranted in matters concerning the regulation of its franchise,

---

[71] *Shindler* (n 60) para 107.

[72] *Hirst (No 2)* (Grand Chamber) (n 7) para 79.

[73] LJ Arden, 'An English Judge in Europe' (25 March 2014) para 71 (referring to *Report of the Working Party on Electoral Procedures*, chaired by the Parliamentary Under-Secretary of State for Northern Ireland, presented to Parliament on 19 October 1999, Deb 1999 WA 435), available at www.judiciary.gov.uk/wp-content/uploads/JCO/Documents/Speeches/lj-arden-an-english-judge-in-europe.pdf.

[74] *Doyle* (n 55).

[75] *Shindler* (n 60) para 117. See also A Kavanagh, 'Proportionality and Parliamentary Debates: Exploring Some Forbidden Territory' (2014) 34 *Oxford Journal of Legal Studies* 443, 467 (characterising ECtHR reference to proceedings in Parliament as a 'deference-increasing factor').

[76] *Shindler* (n 60) para 117.

provided that meaningful debate (or other parliamentary engagement) has occurred. This interpretive stance shall be critiqued in Part III.

(iii) The 'Margin of Appreciation' and the 'European Consensus'

This subsection demonstrates that the Strasbourg Court relies on a wide margin of appreciation in its jurisprudence on voting eligibility and that the Court attributes significance to the existence (or emergence) of a European consensus. It then contrasts Strasbourg's approach with that of the European Commission.

Strasbourg has been reluctant to scrutinise the effects on applicants of generally applicable voting eligibility legislation. *Doyle* cited approvingly[77] the judgment in *Hilbe v Liechtenstein*,[78] where the claimant challenged his exclusion from voting in a referendum based on a residence requirement. In *Hilbe*, the Chamber held that '[i]t is possible that the applicant has not severed ties with his country of origin and that some of the factors indicated above are therefore inapplicable to this case. However, the law cannot take account of every individual case but must lay down a general rule.'[79] The Court reiterated its position in *Shindler*, albeit with a qualification that it would 'never discount ... completely the possibility that in some circumstances the application of a general rule to an individual case could amount to a breach of the Convention'.[80]

Strasbourg has also considered the presumed effect of States' divergent histories and cultures to justify extending a margin of appreciation even in relation to eligibility. In *Doyle*, the Court noted that '[t]he rules on granting the right to vote, reflecting the need to ensure both citizen participation and knowledge of the particular situation of the region in question, vary according to the historical and political factors peculiar to each State'. *Sitaropoulos* helpfully illustrates the ECtHR's current position. The Chamber held that

> as regards the margin of appreciation to be afforded to the respondent State ... the Court is more demanding when assessing restrictions on voting rights, that is to say, the 'active' aspect of the rights secured by Article 3 of Protocol No 1 than when dealing with the right to stand for election, that is to say, the 'passive' aspect of the rights secured by Article 3 of Protocol No 1.[81]

However, the Grand Chamber (reversing) reiterated that '[a]s regards, in particular, the choice of electoral system ... the Contracting States enjoy a wide margin of appreciation in this sphere', maintaining that

> for the purposes of applying [A3P1], any electoral legislation must be assessed in the light of the political evolution of the country concerned, so that features that would be unacceptable in the context of one system may be justified in the context of another.[82]

---

[77] Above, n 55.
[78] *Hilbe v Liechtenstein* App no 31981/06, ECHR 1999-VI; see also the discussion regarding Strasbourg's approach to referendums in section III.C.
[79] ibid.
[80] *Shindler* (n 60) para 105.
[81] *Sitaropoulos* (Chamber) (n 50) para 46.
[82] *Sitaropoulos* (Grand Chamber) (n 50) paras 65–66.

It is submitted that the reference to 'any electoral legislation' suggests that the Court does not distinguish between scrutiny of electoral systems and of electoral eligibility.

The reference to divergent practices across the Council of Europe features in Strasbourg's jurisprudence regarding electoral exclusion of convicts and non-residents. In *Hirst (No 2)*, the ECtHR held that the absence of a European consensus would not '*in itself be determinative* of the issue', not least as blanket disenfranchisement of convicted prisoners was in the minority.[83] The Court then noted that although

> the margin of appreciation [in this area] is wide it is not all-embracing [and that] a general, automatic and indiscriminate restriction on a vitally important Convention right must be seen as falling outside any acceptable margin of appreciation, *however wide that margin might be.*[84]

Nevertheless, the Court emphasised that States Parties adopt 'different ways of addressing the issue' and that it was up to the UK legislature to decide on the means used to secure the right to vote.[85]

The dissenting judges would have wanted the judgment to go further in this regard, arguing that due to 'the lack of any precision in the wording of the provision and the sensitive political assessments' States Parties should be given a wide margin of appreciation and be permitted to adopt diverging voting eligibility criteria.[86] The dissenting judges posited that they 'are not able to accept that it is for the Court to impose on national legal systems an obligation either to abolish disenfranchisement for prisoners or to allow it only to a very limited extent'.[87]

Perhaps in response to this critique, the *Greens and MT* judgment emphasised that 'the Court does not consider it appropriate to specify what should be the content of future legislative proposals'.[88] Furthermore, in *Scoppola (No 3)*, the Grand Chamber held that

> within certain limits, such matters [such as voting eligibility] were for each state to determine in accordance with historical development, cultural diversity and political thought within Europe which it is for each Contracting State to mould into their own democratic vision.[89]

---

[83] *Hirst (No 2)* (Grand Chamber) (n 7) para 81 (emphasis added). The Court cited a UK government survey which suggested that 18 Member States of the Council of Europe enfranchised all convicts, in 12 Member States some convicts were disenfranchised, and in 13 other Member States, all incarcerated individuals were disenfranchised (ibid, para 33). See also K Dzehtsiarou, 'European Consensus and the European Court of Human Rights' Evolutive Interpretation' (2011) 12 *German Law Journal* 1730, 1733 (arguing that the Court has often used the existence of a European consensus as a rebuttable presumption in favour of the solution adopted by the majority of Contracting Parties).

[84] ibid, para 82 (emphasis added).

[85] ibid, para 84. See also Joint Concurring Opinion of Judges Tulkens and Zagrebelsky (defining this area as one 'in which two sources of legitimacy meet, the court on the one hand and the national Parliament on the other', and positing that '[t]his is difficult and slippery terrain for the Court in view of the nature of its role, especially when it accepts that a wide margin of appreciation must be given to the Contracting states').

[86] ibid, Wildhaber, Costa, Lorenzen, Kovler and Jebens JJ (Dissenting Opinion), para 5.

[87] ibid, paras 8–9.

[88] *Greens and MT* (n 25) para 115.

[89] *Scoppola (No 3)* (Grand Chamber) (n 32) para 102.

Revealingly, in *Scoppola (No 3)*, the Grand Chamber 'justified' why it chose not to revisit the *Hirst (No 2)* ratio, noting:

> it does not appear … that anything has occurred or changed at the European and Convention level since the *Hirst (No 2)* judgment that might lend support to the suggestion that the principle … should be re-examined. On the contrary, analysis of the relevant international and European documents … and comparative-law information … reveals the opposite trend … towards fewer restrictions on prisoners' voting rights.[90]

Nonetheless, as Judge Björgvinsson asserted in his dissent, the *Scoppola (No 3)* judgment represents a 'retreat from the main arguments advanced [in *Hirst (No 2)*]',[91] seeing that 'the Italian legislation is just as blunt … albeit for slightly different reasons in that it effects a permanent ban on those unsuccessful in seeking rehabilitation or ineligible to do so'.[92]

The ECtHR has also attributed weight to factors that lie beyond its judicial remit to rationalise tolerating the disenfranchisement of non-resident citizens. In *Doyle*, the Chamber held that '[i]t is also open to the applicant, whether or not he so wishes, to seek to obtain the vote in the country of residence, if necessary by applying for citizenship'[93] based on the assumption that, qua citizen resident, the applicant would then be entitled to vote in their new State of citizenship. However, this reasoning is tenuous: the Court is not competent to scrutinise—let alone harmonise—naturalisation legislation across the Council of Europe: the ECHR does not enunciate a right to nationality, and offers no redress for refusal of an application for naturalisation. Indeed, it can be argued that, if voting eligibility is citizenship-dependent and naturalisation policies *as such* are not subject to scrutiny, then the ECtHR ought to be even more vigilant in scrutinising voting eligibility legislation. Moreover, tolerating the current exclusion of a citizen from elections in their State of origin based on the speculation that they may, in future, be enfranchised in their State of residence is incompatible with the Court's longstanding position regarding ECHR rights, namely that the Convention guarantees not rights that are 'theoretical or illusory' but rights that are 'practical and effective'.[94]

Finally, in *Shindler*, the ECtHR held that 'the legislative trends are not sufficient to establish the existence of any common European approach concerning voting rights of non-residents … [T]he margin of appreciation enjoyed by the State in this area still remains a wide one.'[95] However, in this instance the right of individual Europeans to vote is seriously compromised *because* there is no 'common European

---

[90] ibid, para 95.

[91] ibid (Björgvinsson J) (dissenting).

[92] ibid. See also EC Lang, 'A Disproportionate Response: *Scoppola No 3 v Italy* and Criminal Disenfranchisement in the European Court of Human Rights' (2013) 28(3) *American University International Law Review* 835, 853 (critiquing the judgment for upholding the Italian legislation).

[93] *Doyle* (n 55).

[94] *Airey v Ireland* (1980) 2 EHRR 305, para 24.

[95] *Shindler* (n 60) para 115. Earlier in the judgment, the Court noted that only three Member States of the Council of Europe disenfranchise most of their expatriates, with limited exceptions for diplomats, servicemen and the like; nine Member States, including the UK, apply divergent tests to disqualify expatriates whose residence abroad is not deemed to be temporary; whereas in 35 Member States, all expatriates retain their voting rights regardless of the length of their period of absence: ibid, paras 73–75.

approach': the UK disenfranchises its citizens based on continuous residence abroad, whilst members of the Council of Europe where these UK citizens reside exclude them from their elections qua non-citizen residents. Reliance on disharmonious voting eligibility legislation as a margin-of-appreciation-enhancing factor cuts against Strasbourg's European supervisory role, properly construed to necessitate the effective realisation of individual Europeans' rights.

The 29 January 2014 recommendation to EU Member States issued by the European Commission offers an insightful comparison.[96] The Commission recommended that '[w]here Member States' policies limit the rights of nationals to vote in national elections based exclusively on a residence condition, Member States should enable their nationals who make use of their right to free movement and residence in the Union to demonstrate a continuing interest in the political life in the Member State of which they are nationals, including through an application to remain registered on the electoral roll, and by doing so, to retain their right to vote'.[97] The contrast between the European Commission's rights-based approach, focusing on the ramifications of national legislation for individual EU citizens (to whom its remit extends), and Strasbourg's cautious jurisprudence, which extends a margin of appreciation to generally applicable laws despite their harmful effects, is revealing.

(iv) Interim Observation

Part II demonstrated that, despite the prevailing view, the ECtHR has been timid in its voting eligibility jurisprudence, and refrained from delineating clear, general principles for (non)justifiable exclusionary measures throughout the Council of Europe. The extent to which Strasbourg's approach may be considered non-interventionist is evident when a comparison is drawn with the European Commission's approach.

III. IN DEFENCE OF RIGOROUS SCRUTINY OF VOTING ELIGIBILITY

A. Issue-Framing: Recognition of the Fundamentality of Voting

The controversy in the UK regarding the *Hirst (No 2)* judgment may be partly explained by an apparent disagreement as to the fundamentality of the right to vote, and a failure to recognise its instrumental and intrinsic value. A realisable and effective right to vote (whether or not the right-holder chooses to exercise it) manifests human agency, carrying an autonomy-enhancing effect. Voting is an expressive act: voters may express themselves for constitutive reasons, seeking to project aspects of their identity such as their values, ideas and experiences in order to exert their position in society. Eligibility to vote serves as societal recognition of human dignity, which may be most clearly observed in its breach, namely the public pronouncement

---

[96] European Commission, Recommendation 2014/53/EU of 29 January 2014 addressing the consequences of disenfranchisement of union citizens exercising their right to free movement [2014] OJ C2014/391.

[97] ibid, para 1(1).

that a person is not (or is no longer) entitled to participate in communal decision-making. At its core, the right to vote is an affirmation of political equality in a given community. While recognition of the fundamentality of voting *as such* may not resolve legal challenges pertaining to exclusions from the franchise, it is critical for ascertaining the proper role of courts in scrutinising its legislative regulation.

The ECtHR's consistent jurisprudence in cases involving voting eligibility considers at the outset the right to vote in a modern democracy, the extent to which it is infringed in the relevant circumstances, and the justification(s) for such infringement(s). Compare this stance with Lord Sumption's judgment in *Chester and McGeoch*, where he maintained that

> [f]rom a prisoner's point of view the loss of the right to vote is likely to be a very minor deprivation by comparison with the loss of liberty … I [decline] to regard [imprisonment on election day resulting in disenfranchisement] as any more significant than the fact that it may coincide with a special anniversary, a long anticipated holiday or the only period of fine weather all summer.[98]

Indeed, Lord Falconer, the (then) Lord Chancellor, in his foreword to the post-*Hirst (No 2)* government consultation paper, postulated (on behalf of the UK government) that 'in the UK, the right to vote is considered by many to be a privilege as well as an entitlement'.[99]

A casual approach to (dis)enfranchisement is not uncommon in the UK: Lord Sumption's position was echoed by Lord Justice Laws in his 2013 Hamlyn Lecture, opining (inter alia in relation to prisoner voting) that 'the historic role of the law of human rights is the protection of what are properly regarded as fundamental values. It is not to make marginal choices about issues upon which reasonable, humane and informed people may readily disagree.'[100] Even Lord Mance's main judgment in *Chester and McGeoch* considered (and rejected) the proposition that prisoner disenfranchisement is 'fundamental to a stable democracy and legal system such as the UK enjoys'.[101] The question was thus framed by Lord Mance not as whether the right to vote is fundamental and, if so, which restrictions on its exercise may be acceptable, but rather whether existing restrictions are too fundamental to be challenged.

---

[98] *Chester and McGeoch* (n 37) para 115. See also Lord Sumption, 'The Limits of Law', Sultan Azlan Shah Lecture, 20 November 2013, www.supremecourt.gov.uk/docs/speech-131120.pdf. See also R Ziegler, 'The Missing Right to Vote: The UK Supreme Court's Judgment in Chester and McGeoch' UK Constitutional Law Blog (24 October 2013), ukconstitutionallaw.org.

[99] Consistently with this approach, one of the options that the government included in the First Phase consultation paper was retaining the status quo: First Phase Consultation (n 17) paras 57–58.

[100] Sir John Laws, 'Lecture III: The Common Law and Europe' in *The Common Law Constitution* (Cambridge, Cambridge University Press, 2014) 57. See also N Philips, 'The Elastic Jurisdiction of the European Court of Human Rights' (12 February 2014) (copy on file with author), posing the following question: 'would it really be earth shaking to give some short term prisoners the right to vote, which most of them would not bother to exercise?'. For a critique, see R Ziegler, 'The Worrisome Casual Approach to (Dis)enfranchisement' Oxford Human Rights Hub Blog (24 February 2014), ohrh.law.ox.ac.uk/?p=4649.

[101] *Chester and McGeoch* (n 37) para 35.

Importantly, the Joint Committee on the Draft Voting Eligibility (Prisoners) Bill, after consideration, distanced itself from a casual approach to the right to vote in concluding that

> [i]n a democracy all citizens possess a presumptive right to vote, thereby having a say in the making of the laws that govern them. The existence of such a right is the necessary corollary of universal suffrage ... It follows that the vote is a right, not a privilege: it does not have to be earned, and its removal without good reason undermines democratic legitimacy.[102]

However, that in 2013 this proposition had to be explicitly articulated is remarkable.

B. The Legitimating and Facilitative Roles of Voting

Section A highlighted the intrinsic significance of the right to vote. The following section appraises its legitimating and facilitative roles. It is argued that ill-construed and poorly justified restrictions on the exercise of the right to vote undermine the legitimacy of representative bodies. Participation manifests (albeit symbolically) consent to be governed, and election results (aim to) reflect the opinion of the people. Thus, even if one supports judicial deference in other contexts, deference to the legislature in matters concerning regulation of its franchise, or margin of appreciation thereto on a supranational level, is unwarranted.[103]

(i) The Legitimating Role of Voting

In 2001, rejecting the petition in *Pearson*, Lord Justice Kennedy opined that 'it is Parliament's role to maintain and enhance the integrity of the electoral process. Such considerations are by definition political and therefore warrant deference.'[104] As was noted earlier, at the heart of the 2011 House of Commons motion concerning prisoner voting stood the proposition that 'legislative decisions of this nature should be a matter for democratically elected lawmakers'.[105] This was not a parliamentary critique of judicial scrutiny by the ECtHR qua supranational court: the motion opposes judicial scrutiny of the regulation of the franchise per se. In *Chester and McGeoch*, Lord Sumption opined that the question of prisoner voting is a 'classic matter for political and legislative judgment'.[106]

Kavanagh suggests that legislation shown to be the product of meaningful parliamentary engagement 'can itself become a "deference-increasing factor", both

---

[102] Joint Committee Report (n 39) paras 154–55.
[103] See also HJ Steiner, 'Two Sides of the Same Coin? Democracy and International Human Rights' (2008) 41 *Israel Law Review* 445, 463, referring to long-standing debates about the desirability, effects and legitimacy of judicial review concerning its applicability to legislation enacted by a democratically elected legislature; Steiner argues that 'human rights and democracy have become inextricably intertwined. Each, unaccompanied by the other, can realise only part of its potential and survives at its peril' (at 477).
[104] *Pearson* (n 6) para 33.
[105] Above, n 29.
[106] *Chester and McGeoch* (n 37) para 137.

for epistemic reasons and for reasons of democratic legitimacy'.[107] It is contended that, if deference to the elected legislature is premised (albeit partly) on its perceived legitimacy and accountability to the electorate, then it is unwarranted for a court to defer to the very body whose mode of composition is under challenge.[108] Indeed, this is why scrutiny of access to the electoral process finds favour even with judicial review sceptics.[109] As Lady Hale articulated in *Chester and McGeoch*, '[p]arliamentarians derive their authority and legitimacy from those who elected them, in other words from the current franchise, and it is to those electors that they are accountable. They have no such relationship with the disenfranchised.'[110]

In the Canadian case of *Sauvé (No 2)*, which concerned legislation disenfranchising prisoners sentenced to prison sentences of two years and above, the Chief Justice of the Canadian Supreme Court poignantly held:

> This case represents a conflict between the right of citizens to vote … and Parliament's denial of that right. Public debate on an issue does not transform it into a matter of 'social philosophy', shielding it from full judicial scrutiny. It is for the courts, unaffected by the shifting winds of public opinion and electoral interests, to safeguard the right to vote.[111]

She added:

> While a posture of judicial deference to legislative decisions about social policy may be appropriate in some cases … it is precisely when legislative choices threaten to undermine the foundations of the participatory democracy guaranteed by the Charter that courts must be vigilant.[112]

As illustrated in Part II, unlike the Canadian Supreme Court, Strasbourg has attributed certain weight (albeit limited) to parliamentary debates and scrutiny. However, as Kavanagh notes, since *Hirst (No 2)*'s central objection to ROPA 1983 was that

---

[107] Kavanagh (n 75) 470. See eg *Animal Defenders International v UK* (2013) 57 EHRR 21, para 108 ('in order to determine the proportionality of a general measure, the Court must primarily assess the legislative choices underlying it. The quality of the parliamentary and judicial review of the necessity of the measure is of particular importance in this respect, including to the operation of the relevant margin of appreciation').

[108] See also TRS Allan, 'Parliamentary Sovereignty: Law, Politics, and Revolution' (1997) 113 *Law Quarterly Review* 443, 449 (suggesting that it would be 'absurd' to allow Parliament, 'whose sovereign law-making power was justified on democratic grounds to exercise that power to destroy democracy, as by removing the vote from sections of society').

[109] See eg JH Ely, *Democracy and Distrust* (Cambridge, MA, Harvard University Press, 1980) 161 (suggesting that there is a case for strong form of judicial review when a discrete minority has been shut out of the representative system).

[110] *Chester and McGeoch* (n 37) para 89. See also B Hale, 'What's the Point of Human Rights?', Warwick Law Lecture, 28 November 2013, para 19, positing that '[i]t is not at all obvious that the franchise should be decided only by those elected under the present franchise', www.supremecourt.gov.uk/docs/speech-131128.pdf.

[111] *Sauvé (No 2)* (n 70) para 13.

[112] ibid, para 15. See also *Franck et al v Attorney General of Canada*, 2014 ONSC 907 (2 May 2014) (Ontario Supreme Court), para 118 (holding that 'while deference may be appropriate on a decision involving competing social and political policies, it is not appropriate on a decision to limit fundamental rights'). The US Supreme Court held that 'deference usually given to judgment of legislators does not extend to decisions concerning which resident citizens may participate in the election of legislators and other public officials'. cf *Kramer v Union Free School District No 15*, 395 US 621, 627–28 (1969). But see *Richardson v Ramirez*, 418 US 24, 55 (1974) (holding that 'the people of the state of California' should decide whether to retain ex-felons' disenfranchisement).

it contained a 'general, automatic and indiscriminate restriction on a vitally important Convention right', a blanket ban would likely have been held to violate the
Convention no matter how much democratic deliberation had taken place.[113]

It is submitted that, in future, Strasbourg should refrain from deferring to
national parliaments on questions of voting eligibility. Indeed, as the Chamber judgment in *Hirst (No 2)* held, 'the right to vote ... [is] the indispensable foundation
of a democratic system', and 'any devaluation or weakening of that right threatens
to undermine that [democratic] system'.[114] While the Grand Chamber reiterated
that '[a]ny departure from the principle of universal suffrage risks undermining the
democratic validity of the legislature thus elected and the laws it promulgates',[115]
it nonetheless defers to the legislature in cases concerning voting eligibility. It is
asserted that, even if (a degree of) institutional respect may be warranted in other
instances, the legislature's self-assessment of the propriety of electoral exclusion
should be rigorously scrutinised.

(ii) The Facilitative Role of Voting

In addition to its intrinsic significance and its legitimating effect, the right to vote
fulfils a facilitative role: voters partake in decision-making regarding the ways in
which their societies intend to achieve their common goals, including protection of
rights.[116] Voting may thus be considered a necessary, though not sufficient, condition
for guaranteeing other rights. Waldron famously described the right to vote as 'the
right of rights'.[117] Rather than emphasising its moral or substantive primacy, this
depiction connotes that when individuals vote, they partake in decision-making
processes that implicate the protection of other rights. Waldron suggests that reasonable right-bearers resolve their disagreements about respective (other) rights
through the political process.[118] Dworkin's seminal account described (some) rights
as 'trumps'[119] that are supposed to protect vulnerable minorities from the 'tyranny
of the majority'.[120] In contradistinction, it could be argued that, since the right
to vote facilitates the electoral process itself, support for inclusive electoral
processes can be based on divergent perceptions of individual and community life.[121]

---

[113] Kavanagh (n 75) 476.

[114] *Hirst (No 2)* (Chamber) (n 7) para 41.

[115] *Hirst (No 2)* (Grand Chamber) (n 7) para 62.

[116] *cf* S Issacharof, 'Fragile Democracies' (2006–07) 120 *Harvard Law Review* 1465, 1470 (noting
that 'a representative democracy is defined by the people's election of a government of their choice').

[117] J Waldron, *Law and Disagreement* (Oxford, Clarendon Press, 1999) 232.

[118] ibid, 282.

[119] R Dworkin, *Taking Rights Seriously* (London, Duckworth, 1978) 328. See also G Lestas, *A Theory
of the Interpretation of the European Convention on Human Rights* (Oxford, Oxford University Press,
2007) 74 ('the purpose of human rights treaties, unlike that of many other international treaties, is to
protect the autonomy of individuals against the majoritarian will of their state, rather than give effect to
that will').

[120] See eg R Dahl, *On Democracy* (New Haven, Yale University Press, 1998) 64 (arguing that
'[d]emocratic governments can also inflict harm on a minority of citizens who *possess* voting rights but
are outvoted by majorities- the tyranny of the majority').

[121] J Cohen, 'For a Democratic Society' in S Freeman (ed), *The Cambridge Companion to Rawls*
(Cambridge, Cambridge University Press, 2003) 86, 109–10.

This view has led McGinnis and Somin to assert that 'controversial substantive rights' are better left to domestic democratic processes, and that international law should instead establish global norms facilitating democracy in order to ensure that governments are periodically held accountable to their peoples.[122]

Now, if one object and purpose of the ECHR is facilitation of an effective political democracy alongside protection of fundamental rights, then a margin of appreciation based on legitimacy and diversity of practices *may* be justified on some occasions. It is not implausible to argue that the fact that choices of electoral systems across the Council of Europe reflect divergent cultural and historical contexts merits (a degree of) institutional respect. However, the determination of eligibility to take part in decision-making processes in such matters should not itself be left without rigorous scrutiny. It is submitted that, in *Zdanoka v Latvia*, the Court unhelpfully referred to voting eligibility as an aspect of 'organising and running' electoral systems.[123]After repeating the holding in *Hirst (No 2)* that 'a general, automatic and indiscriminate restriction on all detained convicts' right to vote fall[s] outside the acceptable margin of appreciation',[124] the judgment emphasised that

> [t]here are numerous ways of organising and running electoral systems and a wealth of differences, *inter alia*, in historical development, cultural diversity and political thought within Europe, which it is for each Contracting State to mould into its own democratic vision.[125]

The Dissenting Opinion in *Hirst (No 2)* went further, arguing that 'the lack of precision in the wording of the Article and the sensitive political assessment involved' as well as the absence of a European consensus necessitate a cautious approach.[126]

Now, regulation of the franchise is indeed politically sensitive, but in this instance, rather than a justification for deference, this is a reason for courts to be vigilant in scrutinising exclusionary policies. This chapter does not engage the general merits of the margin of appreciation doctrine and, in particular, the extent to which the absence of a European consensus should affect the ECtHR's interpretation.[127] Nevertheless, it is contended that, for those who advocate the ECtHR assuming a

---

[122] J McGinnis and I Somin, 'Democracy and International Human Rights Law' (2009) 84 *Notre Dame Law Review* 1739, 1742–47.

[123] *Zdanoka v Latvia* (2007) 45 EHRR 17 (Grand Chamber). See also *Scoppola (No 3)* (Grand Chamber) (n 32) per Judge Björgvinsson, dissenting (maintaining that, notwithstanding the wide margin of appreciation that States enjoy and ought to enjoy regarding the organisation of the electoral system and the electoral process, the Court should closely scrutinise voting eligibility).

[124] *Zdanoka v Latvia* (n 123) para 103.

[125] ibid, para 105.

[126] *Hirst (No 2)* (Grand Chamber) (n 7) Wildhaber, Costa, Lorenzen, Kovler and Jebens JJ (Dissenting Opinion), paras 5–6.

[127] See eg D Spielmann, 'Allowing the Right Margin: The European Court of Human Rights and the National Margin of Appreciation Doctrine: Waiver or Subsidiarity of European Review?', CELS Working Paper, University of Cambridge, February 2012, www.cels.law.cam.ac.uk/cels_lunchtime_seminars/ Spielmann%20-%20margin%20of%20appreciation%20cover.pdf (referring to the margin of appreciation as the 'room for manoeuvre' that the ECtHR is prepared to accord national authorities in fulfilling their obligations under the ECHR). Protocol 15 to the ECHR amends its preamble by adding a new recital, which reads: 'affirming that the High Contracting Parties, in accordance with the principle of subsidiarity, have the primary responsibility to secure the rights and freedoms defined in this Convention and the Protocols thereto, and that in doing so they enjoy a margin of appreciation, subject to the supervisory jurisdiction of the European Court of Human Rights established by this Convention'. Strasbourg, 24 June 2013, CETS 213 (not yet in force).

subsidiary supervisory role that pays due respect to divergent national practices, rigorous scrutiny of the franchise is essential in order to ensure that national policies represent the opinion of the people and are reached democratically.[128]

It is asserted that, even if one endorses the justifiability and utility of the margin of appreciation doctrine, the doctrine is premised on a functioning democracy as a valid rationale for an international court to give discretion.[129] As Benhabib postulated, 'without the right to self-government, which is exercised through proper legal and political channels, we cannot justify the range of variation in the content of basic human rights as being legitimate'.[130] It follows that the guarantee of 'an effective political democracy' is a precondition for the application of a margin of appreciation by the ECtHR in other cases.

Applying Strasbourg's characterisation of the margin of appreciation in *Handyside* to questions of voting eligibility arising in different Council of Europe States, national authorities are not 'in principle in a better position than the international judge' to determine whether and if a political democracy is still effective if part of the body-polity is disenfranchised.[131] Indeed, in *Handyside* the Court emphasised that its 'supervisory functions oblige it to pay the utmost attention to the principles characterising "democratic society"',[132] of which voting eligibility is fundamental.

C. The Scope of A3P1: Ramifications for the Right to Vote in the UK

The unsuccessful challenge in the UK courts to the exclusion of prisoners from participating in the 18 September 2014 Scottish Independence Referendum[133] serves as a testament to the constitutional significance in the UK of the (in)ability to mount

---

[128] See J Rivers, 'Proportionality and Variable Intensity of Review' (2006) 65(1) *Cambridge Law Journal* 174, 175 (asserting that an international court also has to take account of the cultural diversity of human rights conceptions among nations in a way inappropriate for courts of a single political community). For a qualified defence of the margin of appreciation doctrine see S Dothan, 'In Defence of Expansive Interpretation in the European Court of Human Rights' (2014) 3 *Cambridge Journal of International and Comparative Law* 508, 520 (arguing that Strasbourg should opt for expansive interpretations when citizens are not politically represented, or when cases concern non-citizens). For a critique, see A Lester, 'Universality versus Subsidiarity: A Reply' (1998) 1 *European Human Rights Law Review* 73, 78 (expressing concern about a 'variable' geometry of human rights eroding the *acquis* of existing jurisprudence and giving undue deference to local conditions, traditions and practices).

[129] J Krachtovil, 'The Inflation of the Margin of Appreciation by the European Court of Human Rights' (2011) 29 *Netherlands Quarterly of Human Rights* 324, 327.

[130] S Benhabib, 'The Future of Democratic Sovereignty and Transnational Law', Max Weber Lecture 2012, cadmus.eui.eu/bitstream/handle/1814/22565/MWP_LS_2012_04_Benhabib.pdf?sequence=1.

[131] *Handyside v UK* (1979–80) 1 EHRR 737, para 48. cf *Zdanoka v Latvia* (2005) 41 EHRR 31 (per Levits J, dissenting), paras 17–18 (maintaining that 'when examining applications under [A3P1], the Court always faces a certain dilemma … it is the Court's task to protect the electoral rights of individuals … but … it should not overstep the limits of its explicit and implicit legitimacy and try to rule instead of the people of the constitutional order which this people creates for itself').

[132] *Handyside*, ibid, para 49.

[133] For discussion of the franchise in independence referendums see R Ziegler, J Shaw and R Bauböck (eds), *Independence Referendums: Who Should Vote and Who Should be Offered Citizenship?* (Florence, Robert Schuman Centre for Advanced Studies, European University Institute Publishing, 2014), eudo-citizenship.eu/images/docs/RSCAS_2014_90.pdf.

A3P1-based challenges regarding participation in referendums and, more broadly, to the precarious legal status of the right to vote in the UK constitutional order.

The undertaking in A3P1 is to hold 'elections at reasonable intervals' to 'ensure the free expression of the opinion of the people in the choice of the legislature'. Strasbourg has thus far declined to define the scope of application of A3P1 more expansively so as to enable judicial scrutiny of exclusions from participation in referendums. *X v UK*[134] was concerned with the 1975 UK referendum on EEC membership. A prisoner who was excluded from voting in the referendum challenged the exclusion. As part of its reasoning, the Court noted that the referendum was consultative, and that it was not required by law. The ratio of this decision was followed in numerous subsequent admissibility decisions.[135]

Strasbourg's most recent judgment on the applicability of A3P1 to referendums concerned the exclusion of prisoners from participation in the 2013 referendum on the adoption of the Alternative Vote system in the UK. Declaring *McLean and Cole*'s A3P1-based claim inadmissible, the Court held that

> Article 3 … is limited to elections concerning the choice of the legislature and does not apply to referendums … There is nothing in the nature of the referendum *at issue in the present case* which would lead the Court to reach a different conclusion here. It follows that complaint concerning the alternative vote referendum is incompatible *ratione materiae* with the provisions of the Convention and its Protocols.[136]

The Court has not revisited the reasoning in *X v UK* in relation to the legislated and binding nature of the referendum on the Alternative Vote or, indeed, the direct effect that it has on voters qua voters. Furthermore, the Court has not drawn on the language of Article 25 of the International Covenant on Civil and Political Rights (ICCPR)[137]that all Council of Europe Member States have ratified[138] and which stipulates, inter alia, that '[e]very citizen shall have the right and the opportunity … (a) To take part in the conduct of public affairs, *directly* or through freely chosen representatives'.[139] (emphasis added)

In contrast, in a case concerning conscientious objection, the ECtHR drew on international law materials, 'reiterate[ing] … that the Convention is a living instrument which must be interpreted in the light of present-day conditions *and of the ideas prevailing in democratic States today*'.[140] The Court explained that

---

[134] *X v UK* App no 7096/75 (unreported, 3 October 1975).

[135] See *Bader v Austria* (1996) 22 EHRR CD 213; *Nurminen v Finland* App no 27881/95 (unreported, 26 February 1997); *Castelli v Italy* [1998] ECHR 114; *Hilbe* (n 78); *Borghi v Italy* App no 54767/00, ECHR 2002-V; *Santoro v Italy* (2006) 42 EHRR 38; *Comitato Promotore Referendum Maggioritario v Italy* App no 56507/00 (unreported, 8 July 2003); *Z v Latvia* [2008] ECHR 76; *Niedzwiedz v Poland* (2008) 47 EHRR SE2.

[136] *McLean and Cole v UK* (2013) 57 EHRR SE8, paras 32–33 (emphasis added).

[137] 16 December 1966, 999 UNTS 171 (entered in force 23 March 1976).

[138] The list of States Parties is available at www.ccprcentre.org/select-country/.

[139] Human Rights Committee, General Comment No 25, *The Right to Participate in Public Affairs, Voting Rights, and the Right of Equal Access to Public Service*, adopted by the Committee at its 1510th meeting (57th session) (12 July 1996), paras 6 and 19 (emphasis added), www1.umn.edu/humanrts/gencomm/hrcom25.htm.

[140] *Bayatyan v Armenia* (2012) 54 EHRR 15, para 102 (emphasis added). The term 'living instrument' was introduced by the ECtHR in *Tyrer v UK* (1978) 2 EHRR 1, where the practice of birching in juvenile delinquency cases on the Isle of Man was held to contravene the prohibition on inhuman and

'[t]he consensus emerging from specialised international instruments may constitute a relevant consideration for the Court when it interprets the provisions of the Convention in specific cases'.[141]

The fate of a judicial review (JR) claim brought by prisoners in Scotland against the blanket disenfranchisement of prisoners in the 18 September 2014 Scottish Independence Referendum which relied, inter alia, on the application of A3P1, has been decisively determined by the abovementioned Strasbourg jurisprudence. Section 3(1) of the Scottish Independence Referendum (Franchise) Act 2013 enunciates that '[a] convicted person is legally incapable of voting in an independence referendum for the period during which the person is detained in a penal institution in pursuance of the sentence imposed on the person'.[142] Conscious of the fact that, under the Scotland Act 1998, it is unlawful for the Scottish Parliament to legislate in contravention of the ECHR,[143] the Scottish government did not even attempt to offer a principled justification for this legislative choice.[144]

On 24 July 2014, the UK Supreme Court, sitting as a panel of seven, dismissed (by a majority of five to two) an appeal[145] against the judgments of the Outer and Inner Houses of the Court of Session in the JR claim.[146] Lord Glennie's judgment in the Outer House rejected six JR grounds (discussed below). The first JR ground concerned the applicability of A3P1 to referendums and the consequent breach of the right to vote. Lord Glennie's judgment relied, inter alia, on the ECtHR's judgment in *Mclean*.[147] He noted:

> It is … quite possible—I put it no higher or lower than that—that at some time in the future the Strasbourg court may revisit the ambit of A3P1 and hold that it protects the right to vote not only in elections to the legislature but also in referendums, or at least those which meet certain defined criteria. But it has not done so yet.[148]

---

degrading punishment set out in Art 3 of the Convention. See also J-P Costa, 'On the Legitimacy of the European Court of Human Rights' Judgments' (2011) 7(2) *European Constitutional Law Review* 173, 179 (observing that 'the preamble states that one of the means of pursuing the statutory aims of the council of Europe is the maintenance and further realisation of human rights and fundamental freedoms'). For a vociferous critique of Strasbourg's 'living instrument' doctrine, inter alia in the context of prisoner voting, see N Herbert, 'What is Wrong with Rights' Kingsland Memorial Lecture, 28 November 2012, www.policyexchange.org.uk/images/pdfs/whats%20gone%20wrong%20with%20rights%20-%20nick%20herbert%20speech%2027112012.pdf.

[141] *Bayatyan* (n 140) para 102. See also Vienna Convention on the Law of Treaties (VCLT), 1155 UNTS 331 (entered in force 27 January 1980), Art 31(3)(c) (requiring treaty interpreters to take into account 'together with the context … any relevant rules of international law applicable in the relations between the parties').

[142] 2013 Acts of the Scottish Parliament 13.

[143] Scotland Act 1998 c 46, s 29(2)(d).

[144] Policy Memorandum, Scottish Independence Referendum (Franchise) Bill, 11 March 2013, para 13 (noting that '[t]he ECHR ruling (and human rights case law) does not relate to referendums, and convicted prisoners will not be able to vote in the referendum irrespective of whether UK electoral law is amended to extend the vote to prisoners for parliamentary elections before the referendum in 2014'), www.scottish.parliament.uk/S4_Bills/Scottish%20Independence%20Referendum%20Franchise%20Bill/b24s4-introd-pm.pdf.

[145] *Moohan v Lord Advocate* [2014] UKSC 67.

[146] *Moohan, Gibson and Gillon v Lord Advocate* [2013] CSOH 199 and [2014] CSIH 56, respectively.

[147] *McLean and Cole v UK* (n 136).

[148] ibid, para 33.

In the Supreme Court, Lord Hodge, delivering the main judgment, held that the words of A3P1 on their ordinary meaning refer to an obligation to hold periodic elections to a democratically elected legislature, and that the requirement that they be held 'at reasonable intervals' suggests that the drafters did not have referendums in mind.[149] He emphasised the 'clear and consistent line of decisions' from Strasbourg delineating the scope of a Convention right.[150] Importantly, however, as Lord Glennie noted, the following facts were not disputed:

> [t]he importance of the referendum for the future of Scotland; the constitutional imperative for there to be a referendum on a subject as important as this; and the fact that agreement has been reached between the Scottish and UK Governments guaranteeing, in effect, that the result of the referendum will be binding, in practice if not in law.[151]

Indeed, an independence referendum is *the* political question: it involves an existential choice in the life of the nation whose life-long effects are arguably greater than those of a regular parliamentary election where a blanket ban would be considered contrary to A3P1.

Lord Kerr, dissenting from the Supreme Court's judgment, stressed the desirability of a 'living instrument' approach to the interpretation of A3P1 (contra Lord Hodge's reference to the intentions of the drafters).[152] He emphasised that a fundamental purpose of the Convention, namely to ensure an effective political democracy, would be 'frustrated by preventing the safeguards applicable to ordinary legislative elections from applying to this most fundamental of votes'.[153]

Lord Wilson, also dissenting, mounted a challenge to the apparent application of the 'mirror' principle. Presenting a trajectory of arguable retreats from adherence thereto,[154] he stipulated that 'where there is no directly relevant decision of the ECtHR with which it would be possible (even if appropriate) to keep pace, we can and must do more'.[155] Indeed, Strasbourg has never had the opportunity to consider the application of A3P1 to an independence referendum. It may be suggested that such a referendum concerns 'the choice of the legislature' in the sense of which Parliament (Holyrood or Westminster, in the case of the Scottish Independence Referendum) will have ultimate sovereign power in the territory.

Like the lower courts, the Supreme Court unanimously rejected five alternative grounds for JR: four grounds concerned an alleged breach of the right to freedom of expression enunciated in Article 10 of the ECHR as a free-standing basis for the right to vote;[156] an alleged breach of EU law in light of the effect of a referendum on EU citizens' rights;[157] an alleged breach of the UK's treaty obligations under Article 25

---

[149] *Moohan* (n 145) para 8.
[150] ibid, para 13.
[151] ibid, para 16.
[152] ibid, para 67.
[153] ibid, para 68.
[154] ibid, paras 103–04.
[155] ibid, para 105.
[156] ibid, para 19.
[157] ibid, paras 23–24, reiterating the ratio of *Chester and McGeoch* (n 37).

of the ICCPR;[158] and an alleged breach of the rule of law as a general principle of the UK constitutional order.[159]

The rejection of the fifth alternative ground of JR, namely that the disenfranchisement of prisoners breaches their 'common law' right to vote, is pertinent for this chapter's purposes. While Lord Hodge had 'no difficulty in recognising the right to vote as a basic or constitutional right',[160] he stressed that the right to vote has for centuries been derived from statute, and that it would be inappropriate for the courts 'to develop the common law in order to supplement or override the statutory rules which determine our democratic franchise'.[161] Lady Hale opined that 'it would be wonderful if the common law had recognised a right of universal suffrage' but 'it has never done so'.[162] Lord Kerr came closest to recognising a common law right to vote, noting that 'it is ... at least arguable that exclusion of all prisoners from the right to vote is incompatible with the common law'.[163] Crucially, however, he acknowledged that, if a common law right to vote conflicted with the expressed will of Parliament as manifested in ROPA 1983, the will of Parliament would prevail.[164]

Now, it could be argued that the ECHR protection ought to be a 'floor', not a 'ceiling'. States may (indeed, should) protect rights more generously than the Strasbourg jurisprudence requires them to. Hence, the right to vote ought to be protected in domestic constitutional order, independently of treaty-based commitments. However, at present, the combined effect of the UK Supreme Court judgment in *Chester and McGeoch*[165] and its dismissal of the appeal in *Moohan*[166] on the basis of Strasbourg jurisprudence is, therefore, that absent a codified constitution enunciating a constitutional right to vote, the legal basis for an individual right to vote in the UK is precarious: it is dependent on the continued incorporation of the ECHR rights into domestic law and its scope of application as interpreted by Strasbourg. While the dissenting judges in *Moohan* were willing to dismiss the 'mirror' principle and adopt a more expansive interpretation of A3P1 than Strasbourg's, the majority preferred to follow the ECtHR's consistent line of jurisprudence. Hence, when the ECtHR determines the scope of A3P1, it effectively sets the contours for challenges to voting eligibility in the UK.[167]

---

[158] ibid, paras 28–30, noting that the ICCPR (unlike the ECHR) has not been incorporated into UK domestic law.

[159] ibid, para 38.

[160] ibid, para 33. See also *Watkins v Secretary of State for the Home Department* [2006] 2 AC 395, Lord Bingham, para 25 (maintaining that 'now, of course, [we] regard the right to vote as basic, fundamental or constitutional'); Lord Rodger, para 61 (suggesting that the right to vote falls 'within everyone's notion of a "constitutional right"').

[161] ibid, para 30.

[162] ibid, para 56.

[163] ibid, para 87.

[164] ibid, para 88.

[165] *Chester and McGeoch* (n 37).

[166] *Moohan* (n 145).

[167] See in this context Art 53 ECHR, stipulating that 'nothing in this Convention shall be construed as limiting or derogating from any of the human rights and fundamental freedoms which may be ensured under the laws of any High Contracting Party or under any other agreement to which it is a party'. Notably, no provision is made for determining voting eligibility in referendums: Political Parties, Elections and Referendums Act 2000 c 41.

Against this background, it is noteworthy that the Political and Constitutional Reform Committee's (draft) Constitution, published in July 2014, enunciates a right to vote modelled after Article 25 ICCPR.[168] The draft provision explicitly stipulates an individual right to vote, and its scope of application includes direct electoral processes such as referendums. This is not an argument for (or against) constitutional codification in the UK; rather, it aptly illustrates the significant role of the Convention in protecting the right to vote, and the role that ECtHR jurisprudence can play by opting for purposive interpretations of the scope of the Convention and its protocols.

IV. CONCLUDING REMARKS

These are testing times for the ECtHR in the UK.[169] As Judge Spano has recently noted, 'the charges levelled against the court in the UK in the past two years have been unprecedented'.[170] This chapter has demonstrated that, despite prevailing views and perceptions to the contrary, the ECtHR has been very cautious in its jurisprudence regarding regulation of the franchise in relation to the disenfranchisement of convicted adult citizens, and to the electoral exclusion of some non-resident citizens. The ECtHR has accepted ill-defined legislative aims, deferred to parliamentary committee reports and debates on voting eligibility, and extended a wide margin of appreciation even when it was bound to have detrimental effects. Meanwhile, the UK's non-compliance with *Hirst (No 2)* persists despite the wide margin of appreciation that it was afforded to rectify the incompatibility of ROPA 1983 with A3P1.

Furthermore, Strasbourg has adopted a restrictive, literal approach regarding the scope of application of A3P1, by refusing to extend it beyond elections to legislatures even when the impugned legislation disenfranchised otherwise eligible voters based on identical criteria to those which the ECtHR found to be incompatible with A3P1 regarding parliamentary elections. In turn, the UK Supreme Court 'mirrors' Strasbourg's interpretation in its judgments; consequently, Strasbourg's

---

[168] House of Commons, Political and Constitutional Reform Committee, *A New Magna Carta?* (3 July 2014), www.publications.parliament.uk/pa/cm201415/cmselect/cmpolcon/463/463.pdf, Art 25 ('The Franchise') '(2) A British national [defined in Article 6 Citizenship and Nationality] who has attained the age of 18 years is entitled to vote in elections for, and stand for election to, Parliament, the European Parliament, the Assemblies and the other elected bodies established by this Constitution, subject to such disqualifications as Act of Parliament shall prescribe'. See also Art 36 ('Bill of Rights') s 14 (which mimics Art 25 ICCPR): 'Every adult citizen has the right and the opportunity, without unreasonable restrictions— (a) to take part in the conduct of public affairs directly or through freely chosen representatives; (b) to vote and to stand for election at genuine periodic elections, which shall be by universal and equal suffrage and shall be held by secret ballot, guaranteeing the free expression of the will of the people; (c) to participate, on general terms of equality, in public service.'

[169] See, for example, the Conservative Party's policy document entitled *Protecting Human Rights in the UK: The Conservatives' Proposals for Changing Britain's Human Rights Laws* (3 October 2014), www. conservatives.com/~/media/Files/Downloadable%20Files/HUMAN_RIGHTS.pdf.

[170] R Spano, 'Universality or Diversity of Human Rights' (2014) 14(3) *Human Rights Law Review* 487. See also M O'Boyle, The Future of the European Court of Human Rights (2011) 12 *German Law Journal* 1862 (asserting in 2011 that 'the court has never in its 50-year history been subject to such a barrage of hostile criticism as that which has occurred in the UK in February 2011').

jurisprudence has effectively, even if unintentionally, set a 'ceiling' for the protection of the right to vote in the UK.

The ECtHR should employ more rigorous scrutiny in relation to regulation of the franchise. Deference to the legislature is unwarranted due to the legitimating role of the right to vote. Moreover, due to the facilitating role of the right to vote in decision-making processes, applying a wide margin of appreciation may undercut the rationale for its application in other matters on the premise that eligible voters are represented: 'Embodied in the Convention is an express acknowledgment of certain common values that all Member States share as regards minimum guarantees of human dignity and protection.'[171] By ensuring an effective political democracy, the ECtHR can adjudicate other matters on the assumption that those political choices genuinely reflect the will of the respective people. Lastly, the Convention has recently been conspicuous in its absence: Strasbourg's hitherto refusal to extend the application of A3P1 to certain types of referendums has led to the dismissal of a JR claim against the blanket disenfranchisement of prisoners in the Scottish Independence Referendum.

It is beyond the remit of this chapter to explore whether Strasbourg's jurisprudence in other areas may be characterised as (too) expansive. But this is certainly not the case regarding the ECtHR's approach to scrutinising the regulation of the franchise. Strasbourg's decisions concerning voting eligibility reflect timidity, where a democracy-enhancing approach requires rigorous scrutiny.

[171] Spano (n 170) 493.

10

Enhanced Subsidiarity and a Dialogic Approach—Or Appeasement in Recent Cases on Criminal Justice, Public Order and Counter-Terrorism at Strasbourg Against the UK?

HELEN FENWICK

I. INTRODUCTION

THIS CHAPTER IS written against a backdrop of rising hostility to the European Convention on Human Rights (ECHR) in an increasingly nationalistic Britain which is currently confronting the threat represented by Russian action in Ukraine and the threat of ISIS expansion in Iraq and Syria. In that context, at present, the defence of British national sovereignty against encroaching European power so that government can take necessary measures to protect the public commends itself with particular force to much of the media, and parts of the population.[1] The Conservative Party recently announced plans to curb the power of the European Court of Human Rights (ECtHR) by passing legislation—a new British bill of rights (BoR)—to render its judgments 'advisory' only in the UK.[2] The intention of scrapping the Human Rights Act in the BoR

---

[1] YouGov polling for the *Sunday Times* (20 July 2014) on the ECHR found that the British public are divided on the question of whether the UK should stay in (38%) or withdraw from the Convention (41%): see www.yougov.co.uk/news/2014/07/20/scepticism-about-human-rights-well-echr. A YouGov poll on 26 August 2011 found that 75% of British people think that the Human Rights Act 'is used too widely to create rights that it was never intended to protect': see cdn.yougov.com/today_uk_import/yg-archives-pol-yougovitv-humanrights-240311.pdf.

[2] See Conservative Party, *Protecting Human Rights in the UK: The Conservatives' Proposals for Changing Britain's Human Rights Laws* (3 October 2014), 5, www.conservatives.com/~/media/Files/Downloadable%20Files/HUMAN_RIGHTS.pdf. This proposal had been foreshadowed for some time: see eg the *Daily Mail*'s (25 September 2014) report on Cameron's stance on the HRA in relation to ISIS fighters returning from Syria or Iraq: 'Foreign terrorists will be free to come to Britain safe in the knowledge that they will never be sent home unless the Human Rights Act is scrapped, David Cameron has warned … The Tory leader dismissed criticism of his plans to replace Labour's controversial legislation with a new Bill of Rights, the first in British law for more than 300 years. Mr Cameron said the Act was "practically an invitation for terrorists and would-be terrorists to come to Britain" … He also rejected calls to pull Britain out of the European Convention on Human Rights (ECHR) altogether … The best option,

and of breaking the formal link between British courts and the European Court of Human Rights featured in the 2015 Conservative Manifesto—albeit briefly.

This chapter considers the devices, including the principle of subsidiarity, and the notion of dialogue with domestic courts, which the European Court of Human Rights (ECtHR) is increasingly under pressure to employ in order to avoid head-on clashes with Britain in relation to especially sensitive issues. The discussion will be placed in the context of the Interlaken and Brighton Declarations leading to Protocols 15 and 16. It will consider whether, and how far, the notion of 'enhanced subsidiarity', which underpins those declarations, had an impact on some recent Court judgments, especially in the counter-terror context, as an example of an especially sensitive area of Strasbourg jurisprudence. It will also consider whether reliance on the dialogic approach is tending to lead to a curbing of the 'living instrument' interpretive approach of the Court to the Convention.[3]

The prisoners' voting rights saga, dealt with elsewhere in this book,[4] obviously provides a further currently highly significant example of the existence of strong tensions between the UK and the Strasbourg Court. It can be asked whether the decision in *Hirst v UK (No 2)*[5] represents a failure of the dialogic approach, bearing in mind that emphasis on both dialogue and enhanced subsidiarity was less apparent at the time of that decision. A similar stand-off might be avoided in future if both dialogue and subsidiarity are now receiving greater emphasis at Strasbourg and domestically. Such emphasis might perhaps have been anticipated in that context, given the exceptionally qualified nature of Protocol 1 Article 3, the broad exceptions to the right accepted by the Strasbourg Court, its relativistic approach to it, and the lack of consensus on this matter in the various Member States. The findings in *Scoppola*[6] and recently in *Firth*[7] arguably represent attempts at compromise and at repairing relations with the British government, which in this instance may be too late.[8]

---

he said, was for new British legislation clearly setting out people's rights while strengthening the hand of the authorities in the fight against crime and terrorism': www.dailymail.co.uk/news/article-392385/ Cameron-terror-warning-Human-Rights-Act.html#ixzz3EJo9kRZH. Cameron's speech—his strongest attack on the HRA to date—was delivered at the Centre for Policy Studies, a centre-right think tank. See also Cameron's attack on the HRA in relation to the August 2011 riots (speech to House of Commons, 11 August 2011; speech to his constituency, 15 August 2011). Theresa May had previously announced the Conservative Party's willingness to repeal the HRA and consider withdrawal from the ECHR over legal disputes connected with terrorism and prisoner voting; see A Travis, 'Conservatives Promise to Scrap the Human Rights Act After Next Election' *The Guardian* (London, 30 September 2013), www.theguardian. com/law/2013/sep/30/conservitives-scrap-human-rights-act.

   [3] Under that approach the Court has treated the Convention as a flexible instrument that can be subject to a dynamic interpretation, developing and creating a more expansive interpretation of the rights to meet changing circumstances. See eg G Letsas, *A Theory of Interpretation of the European Convention on Human Rights* (Oxford, Oxford University Press, 2007) 65 ff.
   [4] See R Ziegler, 'Voting Eligibility: Strasbourg's Timidity' (ch 9), this volume.
   [5] *Hirst v UK (No 2)* (2004) 38 EHRR 40.
   [6] *Scoppola v Italy (No 3)* (2013) 56 EHRR 19.
   [7] *Firth v UK* App nos 44784/09 etc (14 August 2014).
   [8] See further H Fenwick, 'Prisoners' Voting Rights, Subsidiarity, and Protocols 15 and 16: Re-Creating Dialogue with the Strasbourg Court?' UK Constitutional Law Blog (26 November 2013), http://ukconstitutionallaw.org/2013/11/.

A number of judges have recently expressed their preference for viewing the interaction between Strasbourg and the UK courts as a dialogue within which both parties seek to find an acceptable balance between the rights of the applicants and countervailing considerations (in particular Lord Neuberger,[9] Baroness Hale[10] and Sir Nicholas Bratza).[11] But if domestic courts are prepared to show deference to State arguments in the counter-terror context, might a dialogic approach at the international level, especially bearing the margin of appreciation doctrine in mind, result in according the State a double dose of deference?

This chapter will suggest that enhanced subsidiarity combined with a form of 'dialogic' approach has shown some potential to lead to introducing proportionality or contextually-based exceptions or diluting recalibrations into non-materially qualified or absolute rights, in particular Articles 5 and 3. The chapter will ask whether, especially in the light of the emphasis on giving greater prominence to the principle of subsidiarity in the Court's judgments, dialogue has at times given way to mere appeasement of the government. In other words, is the Court tending to revisit the 'true' scope of the ECHR in a more deferential spirit, especially in relation to the UK? If so, is that an almost inevitable and possibly welcome development at a time when the relationship between the UK government and the Court is in greater jeopardy[12] (in the view of this author) than at any time since the UK's acceptance of the right of individual petition?

In this chapter the term 'principle of subsidiarity' will be used to refer to the primacy of the role of the signatory States, in contrast to the secondary role of the Court, in ensuring that the rights under the Convention are protected. The role of the States is of course captured in Articles 1 and 13 ECHR. However, merely asserting that States have the primary role in securing the protection of the rights says very little about the operation of that role in practice and, more importantly, about the impact that the States' role should have on that of the Court. That impact could be taken to mean, at one end of a possible spectrum of subsidiarity, that the Court should not interfere in States' discharging of their role if the balancing of the protection to be offered to the right in question against various societal interests has been fully debated in the legislative body, possibly also taking account of judicial input into any relevant legislation via decided cases in the higher courts in the signatory State ('strong' or 'enhanced' subsidiarity). The democratic 'pedigree' of the legislation in question in relation to the ECHR would be relevant: it could be important to consider the extent to which the right in question had been fully debated, and how far evidence had been received as to the basis for taking a restrained approach to its scope. At the other end of the spectrum, adherence to the principle of subsidiarity

---

[9] O Bowcott, 'Senior Judge Warns over Deportation of Terror Suspects to Torture States' *The Guardian* (London, 5 March 2013), www.theguardian.com/law/2013/mar/05/lord-neuberger-deportation-terror-suspects.

[10] B Hale, '*Argentoratum Locutum*: Is Strasbourg or the Supreme Court Supreme?' (2012) 12(1) *Human Rights Law Review* 65.

[11] O Bowcott, 'Sir Nicholas Bratza Defends the European Court of Human Rights' *The Guardian* (London, 21 October 2012), www.theguardian.com/law/2012/oct/21/sir-nicolas-bratza-defends-echr.

[12] See n 2.

by the Court could merely be taken to mean that in certain especially sensitive, more subjective matters, where there is a lack of consensus in the Member States on an issue, a wide margin of appreciation (as a generally accepted aspect of the subsidiarity principle) should be accorded to the State. The Court has not of course accepted expressly that subsidiarity in the strong sense just referred to should be a determinative factor in its judgments, but this chapter will argue that there are signs that it is moving towards such an acceptance. So doing would not run counter to Article 46 ECHR (requiring States to abide by final judgments against themselves) since a judgment influenced by such acceptance would not oppose decisions arrived at by the State's legislative body.

This chapter will refer to a 'dialogic approach' at various points: in so doing it will mainly refer to dialogue between the higher courts of Member States and the ECtHR, but the term could also refer to dialogue between legislatures and the Court. Such an approach is obviously relevant to the operation of the principle of subsidiarity since the Court would need to be convinced as to the depth of the analysis of the right in question, and of the countervailing interests, in the courts in question before coming to the conclusion that the judgment arrived at in the Member State should not be disturbed.

II. REFORM OF THE STRASBOURG COURT VIA 'ENHANCED SUBSIDIARITY'

Recently, various reforms of the Court were considered at three High Level Council of Europe conferences on 'the Future of the European Court of Human Rights'—the Interlaken conference in 2010, the Izmir conference in 2011, and the Brighton conference in 2012. This chapter will not discuss these moves towards 'reform' of the ECtHR, which eventually resulted in Protocols 15 and 16, in any detail since they are discussed elsewhere in this book.[13] The idea that a greater emphasis on subsidiarity should form an aspect of reform of the Court system gained purchase within the Interlaken Declaration in 2010, which was focused on creating enhanced subsidiarity. That Declaration stated:

> The Conference, acknowledging the responsibility shared between the States Parties and the Court, invites the Court to ... take fully into account its subsidiary role in the interpretation and application of the Convention ... [and] invites the Court to ... avoid reconsidering questions of fact or national law that have been considered and decided by national authorities, in line with its case law according to which it is not a fourth instance court.[14]

The Interlaken follow-up focussed solely on the principle of subsidiarity, finding that the form of subsidiarity at issue—so-called 'complementary subsidiarity'—meant that: 'the

---

[13] See N O'Meara, 'Reforming the ECtHR: The Impact of Protocols 15 and 16 to the ECHR' (ch 5), this volume.

[14] High Level Conference (chaired by Switzerland) on the Future of the European Court of Human Rights, Interlaken Declaration of 19 February 2010, www.echr.coe.int/Pages/home.aspx?p=court/reform&c=#n1365510045079_pointer, Point 9. See also the High Level Conference (chaired by Turkey) at Izmir on the Future of the European Court of Human Rights, 27 April 2011.

Court's powers of intervention are confined to those cases where the domestic institutions are incapable of ensuring effective protection of the rights guaranteed by the Convention'.[15]

Britain's recent chairmanship of the Council of Europe[16] provided the Conservative leadership with an opportunity to present proposals at the Brighton High Level Conference intended to allow the current use of the margin of appreciation doctrine to be taken much further, creating greater subsidiarity.[17] The government's plans for reform of the Court were extensively trailed in the run-up to the Brighton conference in April 2012. In a similar vein, intervening in *Scoppola v Italy No 3*,[18] the (then) UK Attorney-General Dominic Grieve said that greater acknowledgment of the doctrine of the margin of appreciation would result in the EtCHR intervening only when 'the decision of the national authorities is manifestly without reasonable foundation'.[19]

David Cameron's speech to the Parliamentary Assembly of the Council of Europe in 2012[20] reiterated the theme of seeking enhanced subsidiarity as a key reform. He referenced counter-terrorism and prisoners' voting rights as examples of issues in which the Court should be very slow to intervene, once democratic debate on the issue and full scrutiny in national courts—taking the Convention into account—had occurred. Referencing the *Qatada*[21] case as illustrating the need for reform, he said: 'We have gone through all reasonable national processes ... yet we are still unable to deport [or detain] him.'[22]

A draft declaration for the Brighton conference was 'leaked',[23] which gave much greater prominence to the principle of subsidiarity than the eventual Brighton Declaration itself did.[24] The leaked proposals stated that the principle should be enhanced by its express inclusion in the Convention itself. The Declaration that was adopted at Brighton emphasised subsidiarity to an extent, but not as far as the Conservative leadership had wanted—as expressed in the leaked draft declaration. The final Declaration stated:

> The Conference (a) welcomes the development by the Court in its case law of principles such as subsidiarity and the margin of appreciation, and encourages the Court to give great

---

[15] Note by the Jurisconsult Principle of Subsidiarity—Interlaken Follow-Up, ibid.

[16] It began on 07 November 2011.

[17] According to parliamentary written answers and statements: M Harper, HC Deb 18 March 2011, vol 525, col 31WS: '[W]e will be pressing ... to reinforce the principle that states rather than the [Court] have the primary responsibility for protecting Convention rights.'

[18] *Scoppola v Italy (No 3)* (n 6).

[19] D Grieve, 'European Convention on Human Rights: Current Challenges' speech at Lincoln's Inn, 24 October 2011, www.gov.uk/government/speeches/european-convention-on-human-rights-current-challenges.

[20] David Cameron, 'The European Court of Human Rights' speech delivered 25 January 2012, www.gov.uk/government/speeches/speech-on-the-european-court-of-human-rights.

[21] *Othman v UK* (2012) 55 EHRR 1.

[22] Cameron (n 20).

[23] 'Draft Brighton Declaration on the Future of the European Court of Human Rights: A Leaked Draft of the UK's Proposals for the Reform of the Strasbourg Court' *The Guardian* (London, 28 February 2012), www.theguardian.com/law/interactive/2012/feb/28/echr-reform-uk-draft?fb=native.

[24] Point 23(b) of the leaked document on options for amending the admissibility criteria had proposed controversially that an application should be declared inadmissible if it was the same in substance as a matter that has already been determined by the national courts *unless* the Court considered that the national court 'clearly erred in its application or interpretation of the Convention rights'. But that proposal did not make its way into the final declaration.

prominence to and apply consistently these principles in its judgments … and (b) Concludes that … a reference to the principle of subsidiarity and the doctrine of the margin of appreciation as developed in the Court's case law should be included in the preamble to the Convention.[25]

That aspect of the Declaration was then captured in Protocol 15 Article 1. The Brighton Declaration also emphasised the need for the use of dialogue: it 'welcomes and encourages dialogue, particularly dialogues between the Court and the highest courts of the States Parties'.[26]

Subsidiarity is linked to a dialogic approach in the sense that if the Strasbourg Court perceives itself as providing a level of protection of rights that is subsidiary to that provided domestically, then it needs to pay close attention to national views as to the form of protection that the rights should receive nationally and to their context. That is especially the case where such views demonstrably take account of key Convention principles at stake in the particular instance, such as that of proportionality. Protocol 16, which makes provision for advisory opinions to be sought by courts in Member States, could appear to support such a dialogic approach.[27]

The discussion below suggests that the formal mechanisms introduced in June 2013 under new Protocols 15 and 16 ECHR (which are not yet in force) may in future play a role in enhancing subsidiarity or dialogic opportunities, although informal mechanisms already under development are also significant. There may be no necessary opposition between the two: formal and informal mechanisms may inter-react. The phrase 'informal mechanisms' is merely meant to refer to mechanisms that may exist under the banner of the tags of 'margin of appreciation' or 'the concept of subsidiarity' but which need further delineation and definition, relying on the Strasbourg jurisprudence. O'Meara has argued recently that these changes under the two new protocols will enhance dialogue.[28] It is suggested that that may well be the case, but it is also important to examine the existing factors that may impel the Court to listen to the domestic authorities.

While the provision in Protocol 15 is much less radical than the leaked proposals, it is possible that its effect, combined with the impact of the emphasis on subsidiarity from Interlaken and Izmir, has been to persuade the Court to rein itself in, to an extent not formally required under the provision itself. Express inclusion of the principles of subsidiarity and the margin of appreciation in the preamble, and urging the Court to give 'great prominence' to them, may appear to have a merely tokenistic or symbolic nature, but so doing sends a clear message to the Court about its role.[29] The emphasis on subsidiarity in all three Declarations and in Protocol 15

[25] High Level Conference on the Future of the European Court of Human Rights, Brighton Declaration of 19 April 2012, available at www.echr.coe.int, Point 12. In contrast, the leaked proposals stated that the principles should be *enhanced* by their express inclusion in the Convention itself.

[26] ibid, Point 12(c).

[27] See further N O'Meara, 'Advisory Jurisdiction and the European Court of Human Rights: A Magic Bullet for Dialogue and Docket-Control?' (2014) 34 *Legal Studies* 444.

[28] See N O'Meara, 'Reforming the European Court of Human Rights through Dialogue? Progress on Protocols 15 and 16 ECHR' UK Constitutional Law Blog (31 May 2013), www.ukconstitutionallaw.org.

[29] An echo of that message can arguably be found in the Joint Concurring Opinion of Judges Casadevall et al in the recent case of *Jaloud v The Netherlands* App no 47708 (20 November 2014) in the Grand Chamber. The case concerned a shooting at a checkpoint (in the belief that there was a need to act in

has arguably had an influence in the more recent cases in this context considered below, at times, however, arguably redolent more of an appeasement rather than a 'dialogic' approach. The growing emphasis on subsidiarity explains, it is contended, the less activist stance taken more recently by the Court. But the enterprise of 'reform' of the Strasbourg Court appeared to give way in autumn 2014, to contemplation of a wholesale abandonment or curtailment of the ECHR project by Britain, especially bearing in mind, from the perspective of the Conservative leadership, the failure to push through more radical proposals at Brighton.[30] The result of the general election in 2015 has obviously brought that possibility closer to realisation, although withdrawal from the ECHR did not appear in the Conservative manifesto.

III. THE SCOPE OF ARTICLE 5(1) ECHR: INTERACTIONS BETWEEN STRASBOURG, THE UK GOVERNMENT AND THE DOMESTIC COURTS

Having considered the general trend of recent reforms of the Strasbourg system, this section turns to considering their impact on specific groups of cases. Some very significant decisions against the UK have considered inter alia the scope that should be accorded to Article 5(1) ECHR. The discussion is seeking to show that a change of stance is apparent when decisions from 2010 are compared with later ones, bearing in mind the growing emphasis on enhanced subsidiarity combined with a dialogic approach discussed above.

In *A v UK*[31] the government argued, contrary to the conclusions of the House of Lords in the 'Belmarsh' case (*A v Secretary of State for the Home Department*)[32] concerning indefinite detention without trial of non-national suspects of terrorism, that the derogation from Article 15 should be upheld, and in the alternative that the detention had not led to a breach of Article 5.

In cases concerning derogation under Article 15 ECHR, the Strasbourg Court has usually accorded a wide margin of appreciation to the national authorities, and has therefore upheld the derogation, normally relating to the use of executive detention, as in this instance.[33] But in finding under Article 15 that the measures taken (detention without trial for suspect non-nationals) were not strictly required by

---

self-defence, subsequently found to be mistaken) under the jurisdiction of the Netherlands during action in Iraq in a volatile situation, where the checkpoint had just been attacked, which resulted in the death of the applicant's father. The Grand Chamber found procedural failings in the resulting investigation by the Netherlands into the death; thus it found a breach of Art 2 ECHR, on procedural grounds. The Concurring Opinion found: 'we respectfully regret that the Grand Chamber also found it appropriate to scrutinise the investigations in Iraq in such a painstaking way that eyebrows may be raised about the role and competence of our Court' (para 5).

[30] See n 2 and n 12. The removal of Dominic Grieve as Attorney-General in 2014 appeared to indicate that David Cameron wished to create flexibility as to repeal of the HRA and as to the relationship between the UK and the Court after the 2015 election. See A Travis, 'Grieve, Clarke and Green were Last Protectors of our Human Rights Laws' *The Guardian* (London, 15 July 2014), www.theguardian.com/law/2014/jul/15/grieve-clarke-green-human-rights-conservatives-europe.

[31] *A v UK* (2009) 49 EHRR 29.

[32] *A v Secretary of State for the Home Department* [2004] UKHL 56, [2005] 2 AC 68.

[33] See eg *Brannigan and McBride v UK* (1994) 17 EHRR 539.

the exigencies of the situation, the Grand Chamber in *A v UK* relied on the Lords' judgment in *A*, finding that the domestic courts are part of the 'national authorities' to which the Court affords a wide margin of appreciation under Article 15:

> [T]he Court considers that it would be justified in reaching a contrary conclusion only if satisfied that the national court had misinterpreted or misapplied Article 15 or the Court's jurisprudence under that Article or reached a conclusion which was manifestly unreasonable.[34]

In other words, the Grand Chamber could have upheld the derogation if the House of Lords had done so, so long as the decision had been fully reasoned in reliance on the ECHR. The Court proceeded to agree with the House of Lords on both the public emergency and proportionality issues under Article 15.

As regards Article 5, the UK government argued that the principle of fair balance underlies the whole Convention. It reasoned therefore that sub-paragraph (f) of Article 5(1), the arguably applicable exception, allowing for detention pending deportation, had to be interpreted so as to strike a balance between the interests of the individual and the interests of the State in protecting its population from malevolent aliens. Detention, it was argued, struck that balance by advancing the legitimate aim of the State to secure the protection of the population without sacrificing the predominant interest of the alien to avoid being returned to a place where he faced torture or death.[35]

In seeking to broaden the exception, the government sought to rely on a version of the argument that had been put on behalf of the Secretary of State in a number of the domestic control order cases.[36] The argument was to the effect that the purpose of a measure in ensuring national security, should be taken into account in finding that it satisfied the demands of proportionality, and, therefore, on that basis it would fall outside the scope of Article 5. Thus, the national security risk posed by an applicant should enable the scope of Article 5 to be narrowed so that measures taken against the applicant commensurate with the risk he posed fell outside it. This was an argument that the Eminent Panel of Jurists[37] in 2009 found that a number of governments have been seeking to use in the counter-terror context. The argument was that rights should be reinterpreted and recalibrated rather than derogating from them, adopting a purposive approach. In other words, the purpose of the measure in the national security context should affect the scope of the right. However, narrowing the scope of Article 5(1) in *A v UK* would have run contrary to the approach of the ECtHR, in particular in the *Guzzardi* case.[38] The Court's approach has been an activist (or dynamic) as opposed to an originalist one, to the effect that the scope of Article 5(1) should be extended so as cover (marked) non-paradigm interferences with liberty.

---

[34] *A v UK* (n 31) para 174.

[35] ibid, para 148.

[36] In particular, *SSHD v JJ* [2007] UKHL 45. See H Fenwick, 'Recalibrating ECHR Rights' (2010) 63 *Current Legal Problems* 153.

[37] Report of the Eminent Jurists Panel on Terrorism, Counter-Terrorism and Human Rights, *Assessing Damage, Urging Action* (Geneva, International Commission of Jurists, 2009).

[38] *Guzzardi v Italy* (1981) 3 EHRR 333.

Rejecting the government's argument, the Court found that the Article 5 exceptions are exhaustive and to be narrowly interpreted:

> [I]f detention does not fit within the confines of the [exceptions] as interpreted by the Court, it cannot be made to fit by an appeal to the need to balance the interests of the state against those of the detainee.[39]

Thus, the purpose of the detention—to counter terrorism—was not allowed to limit the ambit of Article 5 via the introduction of a new exception.

Similar arguments were also rejected in *Gillan v UK*[40] in relation to Article 5. In the domestic decision in *R (Gillan) v Commissioner of Police for the Metropolis*,[41] on suspicion-less stop and search under section 44 of the Terrorism Act 2000 (TA), Lord Bingham defended the wide scope of section 44 on the basis of its purpose: it ensured 'that a constable is not deterred from stopping and searching a person whom he does suspect as a potential terrorist by the fear that he could not show reasonable grounds for his suspicion'.[42] So the interference with the applicants' liberty was found to fall outside the scope of Article 5, failing to amount to a deprivation of liberty. The Strasbourg Court found in contrast that suspicion-less stop and search under section 44 TA had all the hallmarks of a deprivation of liberty, although it did *not* find a breach of Article 5, rejecting the government's argument that the purpose of the search should allow it to fall outside the scope of the Article.[43]

The Court then was again resistant in *Gillan* to executive arguments as to the need to maintain a narrow scope of Article 5(1) ECHR in the terrorism context, and contemplated a higher standard as to the liberty of the subject than the House of Lords had done.[44] The refusal to find the breach under the non-materially qualified Article, however, maintains some leeway for States to introduce and maintain non-paradigmatic (and non-trial-based) coercive measures interfering with liberty.[45] But *A v UK* and *Gillan v UK* did indicate that Strasbourg was unreceptive to the conversion in effect of Article 5 into a right qualified further than by the list of express exceptions in Article 5(1) to a much more widely qualified right similar to the model of Articles 8–11 ECHR. In the counter-terror context, then, there has been reluctance to accept the argument that the scope of Article 5 can be narrowed because the purpose of a restriction should take it outside that scope so long as the demands of proportionality are met. It may however be noted that in neither case were those specific arguments accepted at domestic level, since they were not put forward in the domestic litigation in *A* and were not examined in detail in *Gillan*. However, outside the counter-terror context, and at a point when the pressure to show greater

---

[39] *A v UK* (n 31) para 171.

[40] *Gillan v UK* (2010) 50 EHRR 45.

[41] *R (Gillan) v Commissioner of Police for the Metropolis* [2006] UKHL 12, [2006] 2 WLR 537.

[42] *Gillan* (n 41) para 35.

[43] *Gillan v UK* (n 40) paras 55, 57.

[44] ibid, para 87. A breach of Art 8 ECHR was found on that basis. Section 44 was repealed under s 59 of the Protection of Freedoms Act 2012.

[45] The specific replacement for s 44 in s 61 of the Protection of Freedoms Act 2012, inserting s 47A into the TA, is itself probably compliant with Art 5 under Art 5(1)(b): *R (Gillan) v Commissioner of Police for the Metropolis* (n 41) para 26, per Lord Bingham.

acceptance of subsidiarity was higher, the argument later received acceptance in the House of Lords. This acceptance was then echoed at Strasbourg.

The decision in the House of Lords in *Austin v Commissioner of Police of the Metropolis*[46] found that 'kettling' peaceful protesters and bystanders for seven hours did not create a deprivation of liberty. Lord Hope in *Austin* considered that in making a determination as to the scope of Article 5(1), the purpose of the interference with liberty could be viewed as relevant; if so, he found, it must allow for a balance to be struck between what the restriction sought to achieve and the interests of the individual.[47] Having found that purpose was relevant to the scope of Article 5(1), Lord Hope found that the purpose must take account of the rights of the individual as well as the interests of the community, and therefore any measures taken must be proportionate to the situation that made the measures necessary. If so, such measures would fall outside of Article 5(1).

When this decision was challenged at Strasbourg in *Austin v UK*,[48] the Grand Chamber took a stance towards the question of deprivation of liberty which in effect followed that of the House of Lords, finding:

> [T]he context in which action is taken is an important factor to be taken into account, since situations commonly occur in modern society where the public may be called on to endure restrictions on freedom of movement or liberty in the interests of the common good ... If necessary to avert a real risk of serious injury or damage, and action is kept to the minimum required for that purpose, such action should not be described as 'deprivations of liberty'.[49]

Affirming that 'subsidiarity is at the very basis of the Convention, stemming as it does from a joint reading of Articles 1 and 19',[50] the Court found that, relying on the context of the imposition of the measure (the 'kettle'), the purpose of its imposition must be taken into account. Although the Court did not refer expressly to proportionality, it clearly adverted to that concept in finding that the measure taken appeared to be the 'least intrusive and most effective means to be applied'.[51] On that basis no deprivation of liberty was found; essentially the Grand Chamber's judgment in *Austin v UK* did not differ from that of the House of Lords despite the fact that it ran counter to the findings of the ECtHR in *A v UK* on the interpretation of Article 5.

A strong Joint Dissenting Opinion trenchantly criticised the findings of the majority as creating a new and objectionable proposition. It was found to be objectionable because States could circumvent Article 5 for various reasons going beyond the express exceptions if in the public order context liberty-depriving measures were deemed to lie outside the scope of Article 5 if claimed to be necessary for any legitimate/public-interest purpose.[52]

---

[46] *Austin v Commissioner of Police of the Metropolis* [2009] UKHL 5, [2009] 2 WLR 372.
[47] ibid, para 27.
[48] *Austin v UK* (2012) 55 EHRR 14.
[49] ibid, para 59.
[50] ibid, para 61.
[51] ibid, para 66.
[52] para 6 Dissenting Opinion.

Austin in effect creates a new, very broad exception to Article 5, while purporting to avoid relating the public interest argument to the scope of the right. The Grand Chamber reiterated, on the basis of the principle of subsidiarity, that it should interfere in a domestic decision as to facts only on very cogent grounds. But impliedly it went further: it applied that principle not to the findings of fact only, but to the interpretation of Article 5(1). So the Grand Chamber's stance would be in accordance with an expansive approach to subsidiarity as manifested in the Interlaken and Brighton Declarations, and Protocol 15, not merely in relation to national law or fact-finding, but also in relation to the interpretation of the Convention.

Superficially speaking, this interaction between the UK government, domestic courts and the Strasbourg Court could be seen to fall within a domestic dialogic model of rights protection and, on an international level, a subsidiary model of such protection. The Strasbourg Court relied on the principle of subsidiarity to support the outcome of an interaction with the highest UK court and the UK government which resulted in restricting the scope of Article 5, based on proportionality arguments akin to those applicable under the materially qualified Articles, even in the face of the Strasbourg Court's own recent analogous decision. In reality the ideas of dialogue and of subsidiarity may be seen to be in tension, arguably veiling a capitulation to an appeasement approach in *Austin v UK*. *Austin* may create some leeway to allow this purposive principle to make its way into the counter-terror context in respect of non-paradigm interferences with liberty via non-trial-based civil restriction measures imposing periods of house arrest and restrictions on movement. At present these are relied on in the UK in the form of Terrorism Prevention and Investigation Measures (TPIM), which are about to be made more restrictive.[53] They are measures that can be imposed without a criminal trial to restrict the activities of terrorism suspects. They have succeeded control orders and could be accompanied in future by further measures under the Enhanced Terrorism Prevention and Investigation (ETPIM)[54] Bill. These measures already potentially tend to skirt or cross the boundaries of Article 5(1) tolerance.

There is a case for considering a new exception to Article 5 which could cover some non-paradigm interferences with liberty,[55] but this should be considered openly in the Council of Europe, in the context of public order, and possibly terrorism, rather than being imported into Article 5 by stealth. Or, in the current situation in the UK in which the threat level has recently been raised to severe,[56] a derogation

---

[53] See Cameron's speech on 1 September 2014, HC Deb 1 September 2014, vol 585, cols 24–26, in relation to the problem posed by returning fighters from Syria, and the recourse of relying on enhanced terrorist prevention and investigation measures. The Counter-Terrorism and Security Act 2015 goes further than the current Terrorism Prevention and Investigation Measures Act 2011 (TPIMA 2011), in particular by including a relocation requirement;; see further H Fenwick, 'Designing ETPIMs around ECHR Review or Normalisation of "Preventive" Non-Trial-Based Executive Measures?' (2013) 76 *Modern Law Review* 876.

[54] In the Enhanced Terrorism Prevention and Investigation Bill 2012, not yet in force. See Fenwick, ibid.

[55] See D Feldman, 'Containment, Deprivation of Liberty and Breach of the Peace' (2009) 68 *Cambridge Law Journal* 243.

[56] See MI5 press release, 'Threat Level to the UK from International Terrorism Raised to Severe' (29 August 2014), www.mi5.gov.uk/home/news/news-by-category/threat-level-updates/threat-level-to-the-uk-from-international-terrorism-raised-to-severe.html.

from Article 5 should again be considered to cover the use of measures on the control order model. The possibility of relying on Article 17 ECHR to create in effect a new exception to Article 5 against individuals or groups adhering to Salafism or Wahabism should also be considered, given that such groups are clearly of the type that Article 17 was designed to cover, given their extreme racist tendencies and intolerance of the exercise of a range of Convention rights, including religious freedom.[57]

IV. REINING IN ARTICLE 3?

Hints of a more relativistic or 'balancing' approach are visible in some cases concerning Article 3 ECHR. The UK government had argued, as intervener in *Saadi v Italy*,[58] that the risk of torture in the receiving country should be balanced against the risk to the community of the terrorist suspect's continued presence.[59] That argument was not accepted in that instance. However, the ECtHR's approach in *Ahmad v UK*[60] on Article 3 ECHR in the counter-terror context showed some parallels with the one accepted in *Austin*. The ECtHR accepted the UK's argument in *Ahmad* which had also been accepted domestically by the UK Supreme Court. Although the Court in *Ahmad* did not overtly accept the balancing argument, in relation to Article 3, it appeared to rely on the terrorist context.[61] It found that no breach of Article 3 would arise in extraditing the applicants to face the 'supermax' regime in the US, applied to high-profile terror suspects. It found that factors revealing a breach of Article 3 in a domestic context might not mean that a breach would arise in an expulsion context. That stance was somewhat redolent of the relativistic approach to Article 3 taken by the House of Lords in *Wellington*,[62] even though the Court purported to reject the *Wellington* stance.[63]

Post-9/11, the UK government has for some time viewed itself as confronted by a dilemma in respect of persons who are suspected of being international terrorists but who cannot be removed from Britain, because there are grounds to think that they would be subject to forms of ill-treatment in the receiving country which might violate certain Convention rights. This is particularly relevant in the case of

---

[57] See eg *Lesihideux v France* App no 24662/94 (23 September 1998); *Norwood v UK* (2005) 40 EHRR SE11; *Glimmerveen v The Netherlands* (1982) 4 EHRR 260. Such groups' intolerance of religious freedom obviously includes intolerance of Judaism, of Shia Muslims, Christianity and Atheism; see eg A Anthony, 'Anjem Choudary: The British Extremist who Backs the Caliphate' *The Observer* (London, 7 September 2014), www.theguardian.com/world/2014/sep/07/anjem-choudary-islamic-state-isis.

[58] *Saadi v Italy* (2009) 49 EHRR 30, paras 117–23.

[59] ibid, para 122: 'in cases concerning the threat created by international terrorism, the approach followed by the Court in *Chahal* ... had to be altered and clarified ... the threat presented by the person to be deported must be a factor to be assessed in relation to the possibility and the nature of the potential ill-treatment ... [making] it possible ... to weigh the rights secured to the applicant by Article 3 against those secured to all other members of the community by Article 2.'

[60] *Ahmad v UK* (2013) 56 EHRR 1.

[61] ibid, para 243.

[62] *R (on the Application of Wellington) (FC) (Appellant) v Secretary of State for the Home Department* [2008] UKHL 72, [2009] AC 335.

[63] *Al-Skeini v UK* (2011) 53 EHRR 18, para 141.

Article 3, following the principle stemming from *Chahal*.[64] The problem the *Chahal* case poses for the government has to an extent been alleviated by the decision of the Strasbourg Court in *Othman v UK*.[65] For some time prior to the decision in *Othman* the government had sought to gain acceptance domestically and at Strasbourg of a balancing argument under Article 3, similar to the one discussed under Article 5 in relation to legal challenges to the attempts to extradite or deport a certain group of suspects. The idea was to achieve modification of the *Chahal* principle at Strasbourg, by arguing for the creation of a restrained scope for Article 3.

As indicated, the UK government had intervened in order to argue for a more relativistic approach in *Saadi*.[66] There were two relevant aspects to this argument. The government argued not only that the risk of torture should be balanced against the risk represented by the suspect,[67] but also that where there is evidence that he represents a national security risk, that should affect the standard of proof he has to adduce as to the likelihood of his being tortured. He should have to prove that it is more likely than not: '[I]f the respondent State adduced evidence that there was a threat to national security, stronger evidence had to be adduced to prove that the applicant would be at risk of ill-treatment in the receiving country.'[68] Thus, the government appeared to be seeking to justify deporting persons at risk of Article 3 treatment abroad on the basis of implying a proportionality test into Article 3. The Court found in response[69] that the UK's first argument was incompatible with the absolute nature of Article 3, and that its second argument (for balancing the risk of harm if the person was sent back against the risk of harm to the community if not) was misconceived: '[T]hey are notions that can only be assessed independently of each other … Either the evidence that is adduced before the court reveals that there is a substantial risk if the person is sent back or it does not.'[70]

The rejection of the UK government's argument in *Saadi* meant that the issue that arose in the House of Lords in *RB, U, OO v SSHD*[71] was of special significance because the case had the potential to determine whether deportation of a particular group of suspects, and in particular of Abu Qatada, could occur. In the House of Lords the argument raised in *Saadi* was not re-raised; instead the case focused on the use of diplomatic assurances to reduce the risk of Article 3 treatment, and on the real risk of treatment of Qatada in flagrant breach of Article 6 in Jordan at his retrial there. The Special Immigration Appeals Commission (SIAC) had previously found that the assurances given by Jordan in relation to Qatada, to the effect that he would not be subjected to treatment contrary to Article 3, could be relied upon.

---

[64] *Chahal v UK* (1996) 23 EHRR 413, paras 130–31.
[65] *Othman v UK* (n 21).
[66] *Saadi v Italy* (n 58) paras 117–23.
[67] See n 59.
[68] *Othman v UK* (n 21) para 122.
[69] ibid, paras 137–49.
[70] ibid, para 139.
[71] *RB (Algeria) (FC) and another (Appellants) v SSHD, OO (Jordan) (Original Respondent and Cross-appellant) v SSHD (Original Appellant and Cross-respondent)* [2009] UKHL 10, [2010] 2 AC 110 (the 'Othman' case in the House of Lords); on appeal from: *MT (Algeria) v Secretary of State for the Home Department* [2007] EWCA Civ 808 and *Othman (Jordan) v Secretary of State for the Home Department* [2008] EWCA Civ 290.

The key issue raised in the appeal on behalf of Qatada was that assurances in relation to individuals cannot be relied upon where there is a pattern of human rights violations in the receiving State, coupled with a culture of impunity for state agents in the security service, and for the persons perpetrating such violations. Therefore, it was argued, SIAC's reliance on the diplomatic assurances that had been given against ill-treatment of Qatada in Jordan was irrational. In the House of Lords, Lord Phillips noted that in two claims against Russia[72] the Strasbourg Court had spoken of the need for assurances to 'ensure adequate protection against the risk of ill-treatment' contrary to Article 3.[73] Lord Phillips also noted that in *Mamatkulov v Turkey*[74] the assurances against ill-treatment were treated by the ECtHR as part of the matrix that had to be considered when deciding whether there were substantial grounds for believing in the existence of a real risk of inhuman treatment. He further found that the ECtHR had applied a similar approach in *Shamayev v Georgia and Russia*,[75] and so, he pointed out, had the United Nations Committee Against Torture (CAT) in *Hanan Attia v Sweden*.[76] The political realities in Jordan, the bilateral diplomatic relationship with the UK, and the fact that Othman (Qatada) would have a high public profile were, according to Lord Phillips, the most significant factors in SIAC's assessment of the Article 3 risk, which disclosed no irrationality.[77]

Lord Hope agreed, noting the UN position[78] to the effect that in a regime that systematically practises torture, the principle of *non-refoulement* must be strictly observed and diplomatic assurances should not be resorted to.[79] However, he viewed that position as indicating that the question of reliance would always be a matter of fact, dependent on particular circumstances relating to the individual in question. He relied on the finding in *Saadi*[80] to the effect that the burden was on the government to dispel any doubts as to the non-reliability of evidence showing substantial grounds for believing that he would be exposed to ill-treatment adduced by the applicant.[81] The Lords followed SIAC, which had concluded that those doubts had been dispelled due to the assurances, and SIAC's assessment was found to be rational.[82]

When the Lords' decision was challenged at Strasbourg in *Othman v UK*,[83] the Court's stance echoed that of the House of Lords as far as Article 3 was concerned. It considered that only in rare cases would the general situation in a country mean

[72] *Ismoilov v Russia* (2009) 49 EHRR 42, para 127; *Ryabikin v Russia* (2009) 48 EHRR 55, para 119.
[73] *RB (Algeria) v SSHD, OO (Jordan) v SSHD* (n 71) para 113.
[74] *Mamatkulov v Turkey* (2005) 41 EHRR 25. The ECtHR said that it was unable to conclude that substantial grounds existed for believing that the applicants faced a real risk of treatment proscribed by Art 3 (at para 77).
[75] *Shamayev v Georgia and Russia* App no 36378/02, ECHR 2005-III.
[76] *Hanan Attia v Sweden* CAT/C/31/D/199/2002, 17 November 2003, Communication No 199/2002.
[77] *RB (Algeria) v SSHD, OO (Jordan) v SSHD* (n 71) para 126.
[78] Cited in *Sing v Canada (Minister of Citizenship and Immigration)* 2007 FC 361, para 136, from UN Doc A/59/324.
[79] *RB (Algeria) v SSHD, OO (Jordan) v SSHD* (n 71) para 238.
[80] *Saadi v Italy* (n 58) para 129.
[81] *RB (Algeria) v SSHD, OO (Jordan) v SSHD* (n 71) para 239.
[82] ibid, para 241.
[83] *Othman v UK* (n 21).

that no weight at all would be given to assurances. It found that its only task was to examine whether the assurances obtained in a particular case were sufficient to remove any real risk of ill-treatment.[84] The ECtHR found that on the evidence the Jordanian criminal justice system lacked many of the standard, internationally recognised safeguards to prevent torture and punish its perpetrators.[85] Nevertheless it found that the assurances under the Memorandum of Understanding (MOU) between Jordan and the UK that the applicant would not be ill-treated upon his return to Jordan were superior to those that the Court had previously considered in both detail and formality. They were found to have been given in good faith by the Jordanian government, at the highest levels of that government, and therefore capable of binding the State. The MOU was also found to be unique in that it had withstood the extensive examination that had been carried out by SIAC, which had had the benefit of receiving evidence adduced by both parties, including expert witnesses. The Court concluded on that basis that the applicant's return to Jordan would not expose him to a real risk of ill-treatment, meaning that no violation of Article 3 was found.[86] Thus, the argument as to the assurances accepted in the House of Lords also guided the Strasbourg decision.

That decision partially eased relations between Strasbourg and the UK government since it provided the government with a way of addressing the dilemma posed by suspects such as Qatada as regards Article 3. The findings at Strasbourg were part of a dialogue with the domestic courts in the sense that the 'balancing approach' to Article 3 rejected in *Saadi* was not pursued domestically, and was replaced by the 'dispelling of doubts' approach that *Saadi* appeared to endorse, and which the House of Lords accepted. In turn the Court in *Othman* accepted that in principle that approach could be followed.

V. A 'BALANCING APPROACH' UNDER ARTICLE 6 ECHR?

In the context of Article 6 ECHR, *Al-Khawaja v UK*[87] is another instance where guidance from the domestic court was available. In this case the Grand Chamber allowed itself to be guided towards a position in harmony with that taken by the national court, even where that meant departing from its own previous judgment in the same case.[88] In *Al-Khawaja v UK*, as others have pointed out (for example Baroness Hale),[89] the Grand Chamber was guided by the findings of the Supreme Court in *R v Horncastle*[90] in reaching a decision on the scope of Article 6, which was contrary to its previous stance as to acceptance of hearsay evidence under Article 6 in the Chamber. The Supreme Court took a more pragmatic, less absolutist approach to Article 6 requirements than the ECtHR had previously done, and the

---

[84] ibid, para 186.
[85] ibid, para 191.
[86] ibid, para 205.
[87] *Al-Khawaja v UK* (2012) 54 EHRR 23 (GC).
[88] *Al-Khawaja v UK* App no 26766/05 (Fourth Section, 20 January 2009).
[89] Hale (n 10).
[90] *R v Horncastle* [2009] UKSC 14, [2010] 2 WLR 47.

Grand Chamber then accepted that approach. The question was whether hearsay evidence (evidence not derived from oral testimony before the court) could be relied on as the sole or decisive evidence in securing a conviction where the victim-witness, or other witness, had died or was too intimidated to give oral evidence. Consideration of Article 6 was fully embedded in the Supreme Court's judgment. Lord Philips stated as follows:

> I believe that those provisions strike the right balance between the imperative that a trial must be fair and the interests of victims in particular and society in general that a criminal should not be immune from conviction where a witness, who has given critical evidence in a statement that can be shown to be reliable, dies or cannot be called to give evidence for some other reason. In so concluding I have taken careful account of the Strasbourg jurisprudence. I hope that in due course the Strasbourg Court may also take account of the reasons that have led me not to apply the sole or decisive test in this case.[91]

This approach of the Supreme Court gave greater weight to the interests of victims of crime than had the Chamber. It was characterised by looking at the fairness of the proceedings as a whole in relation to defence as well as victim, under Article 6, rather than demanding an absolutist application of a particular rule of evidence, regardless of overall fairness—an approach that is typical of common law reasoning. The Grand Chamber stated:

> It would not be correct, when reviewing questions of fairness, to apply [the rule in question] in an inflexible manner ... To do so would transform the rule into a blunt and indiscriminate instrument that runs counter to the traditional way in which the Court approaches the issue of the overall fairness of the proceedings, namely to weigh in the balance the competing interests of the defence, the victim, and witnesses, and the public interest in the effective administration of justice.[92]

The Grand Chamber concluded:

> [V]iewing the fairness of the proceedings as a whole, the Court considers that, notwithstanding the difficulties caused to the defence by admitting the statement and the dangers of doing so, there were sufficient counterbalancing factors to conclude that the admission in evidence of ST's statement did not result in a breach of Article 6(1) read in conjunction with Article 6(3)(d) of the Convention.[93]

Very recently the Court applied the ruling in *Al-Khawaja v UK* to *Horncastle v UK*.[94] The applicants invited the Court to modify substantially the Grand Chamber's decision in *Al-Khawaja*. In *Horncastle v UK* the Court stated:

> [I]n the applicants' case the Supreme Court said that it declined to apply the so-called 'sole or decisive rule', as it was at that time understood following the judgment of the Chamber in *Al-Khawaja and Tahery*. However, this does not, of itself, lead to a violation of Article 6 of the Convention, since the Grand Chamber's subsequent judgment in that case made it clear that the admission of sole and decisive absent-witness evidence may be compatible with Article 6 if the appropriate counterbalancing measures are present.[95]

---

[91] ibid, para 108.
[92] *Al-Khawaja v UK* (n 87) para 146.
[93] ibid, para 158.
[94] *Horncastle v UK* App no 4184/10 (16 December 2014).
[95] ibid, para 139.

The Court proceeded to find that even where or if (in relation to the different applicants) the hearsay evidence had been taken as 'decisive' in terms of the outcome, it was satisfied that there were sufficient counterbalancing factors to compensate for any difficulties caused to the defence by the admission of the statement.[96] It therefore found no breach of Article 6. *Al-Khawaja v UK* and *Horncastle v UK* provide clear examples of dialogue between the Supreme Court and the ECtHR, and indicate that the ECtHR is prepared to depart from an absolutist stance as to Article 6 requirements in favour of a balancing approach.

The Grand Chamber's findings as to Article 6 in *Al-Khawaja v UK* can be contrasted with the Court's earlier judgment in *A v UK*[97] on minimum disclosure of material forming the grounds for suspicion against terror suspects in non-trial-based proceedings. Here the ECtHR held that the fairness of procedure required a minimum of disclosure, regardless of the possibility that the proceedings as a whole could be viewed as fair.

The previous House of Lords decision on the question of minimum disclosure of material in *MB*[98] had taken an approach that paid attention to the fairness of the proceedings as a whole. Baroness Hale held that with 'strenuous efforts from all', it should usually be possible to accord the controlled person 'a substantial measure of procedural justice'.[99] Thus she stopped short of ruling that where the detail lay in the closed case, and it remained wholly undisclosed, a fair hearing would be precluded. The Grand Chamber in *A v UK*, in contrast, found that regardless of the possibility that the proceedings as a whole could be viewed as fair, an absolute rule as to minimum disclosure must be upheld. It was clear that the Grand Chamber's stance differed from that of the Lords in *MB* in that the majority in the Lords had sought to ensure that a substantial measure of procedural justice could be ensured even where *all* the details of the case were in the closed material, whereas the Grand Chamber considered that even where full disclosure did not occur a degree of disclosure was essential.[100] The ECtHR found that although a balance could be struck between national security demands and fair process, the national security interest could not justify that *no* disclosure of the basis for suspicion need occur. The more pragmatic, overall balancing approach in *MB*, characteristic of common law reasoning, was rejected.[101] Arguably, however, that approach was apparent in *Mohammed, Omar, Ibrahim v UK*[102] in which it was found that although there had been a delay in allowing the accused access to a lawyer before police interviews, the trial overall was fair, due to the weight of evidence against the defendants.

---

[96] ibid, para 142.

[97] *A v UK* (n 31).

[98] *Secretary of State for the Home Department v MB* [2007] UKHL 46, [2008] 1 AC 440. This decision did not result in a Strasbourg challenge. It was a coincidence that *A v UK* arose after *MB* and dealt with a similar issue in relation to fairness of proceedings.

[99] ibid, para 66. Baroness Hale also said: 'I do not think that we can be confident that Strasbourg would hold that every control order hearing in which the special advocate procedure had been used, as contemplated by the 2005 Act and Part 76 of the Civil Procedure Rules, would be sufficient to comply with article 6.'

[100] *A v UK* (n 31) para 220.

[101] See further Fenwick (n 36).

[102] *Mohammed, Omar, Ibrahim v UK* App nos 50541/08 50571/08 50573/08 (15 December 2014).

The decision in *Othman v UK*[103] as regards Article 6 also stands in contrast to *Al-Khawaja v UK*. At the domestic level, SIAC had found that there was a real risk that confessions would be relied on in Othman's retrial in Jordan which had been obtained by treatment that breached Article 3; but their admission would be the consequence of a judicial decision, within a system at least on its face intended to exclude evidence which was not given voluntarily.[104] So SIAC had found no likelihood of a total denial of the right to a fair trial under Article 6. However, the Court of Appeal then went on to find that SIAC had erred in law:

> The use of evidence obtained by torture is prohibited in Convention law ... because of the connexion of the issue with article 3, a fundamental, unconditional and non-derogable prohibition ... SIAC was wrong not to recognise this crucial difference between breaches of article 6 based on this ground and breaches of article 6 based simply on defects in the trial process or ... composition of the court.[105]

In the House of Lords, Lord Phillips had not accepted the conclusion of the Court of Appeal[106] that it required a high degree of assurance that evidence obtained by torture would not be used in the proceedings in Jordan before it would be lawful to deport Othman to face those proceedings. He found that the principle at issue was that the State

> must stand firm against the conduct that has produced the evidence, but that that did not require a different state to retain to the detriment of national security a terrorist suspect absent a high degree of assurance that evidence obtained by torture would not be adduced in the receiving state.[107]

The Strasbourg Court in *Othman* agreed with the Court of Appeal rather than the House of Lords. The ECtHR found, applying its 'living instrument' approach, that the admission of torture-tainted evidence would be manifestly contrary not just to the provisions of Article 6, but also to the most basic international standards of a fair trial.[108] Having made that finding, the remaining two issues which the Court had to consider were: (i) whether showing a real risk of the admission of torture evidence would be sufficient; and (ii) if so, whether a flagrant denial of justice (a breach so fundamental as to amount to a nullification of the very essence of the right guaranteed by Article 6) would arise in this case.[109] The ECtHR found that on any retrial of the applicant in Jordan, it would undoubtedly be open to him to challenge the admissibility of statements made against him, alleged to have been obtained by torture. However, the difficulties he would face in trying to do so many years after the event, and before the very court that had already rejected a claim of

---

[103] *Othman v UK* (n 21).

[104] ibid, paras 44–47.

[105] *Othman (Jordan) v Secretary of State for the Home Department* [2008] EWCA Civ 290, paras 45, 49 (Court of Appeal judgment).

[106] *RB (Algeria) v SSHD, OO (Jordan) v SSHD* (n 71) para 154. See further M Garrod, 'Deportation of Suspected Terrorists with "Real Risk" of Torture: The House of Lords Decision in *Abu Qatada*' (2010) 73 *Modern Law Review* 631.

[107] *Othman v UK* (n 21) para 153.

[108] ibid, para 267.

[109] ibid, para 271.

inadmissibility of the evidence (and which routinely rejected all such claims), were very substantial indeed.[110]

The ECtHR therefore concluded that the applicant had discharged the burden that could be fairly imposed on him of establishing that the evidence that could be used against him was obtained by torture. So the Court, in agreement with the Court of Appeal, found that there was a real risk that the applicant's retrial would amount to a flagrant denial of justice, and therefore that his deportation to Jordan would create a breach of Article 6.[111] Thus, the decision on the Article 6 question took a strict stance,[112] rejecting an overall balancing approach to the question of fairness: the judgment held that the prospective use of evidence obtained by torture would automatically constitute a flagrant denial of justice in a foreign State, regardless of other safeguards or of its importance to the outcome of the trial.[113] That finding can be reconciled with its finding on the Article 3 issue. If assurances could be relied on to dispel concerns as to the use of torture in the receiving State, then the same would apply to an agreement capable of mitigating the risk that evidence obtained by torture might be relied on. Jordan did in fact agree that torture-tainted evidence used in Qatada's previous trial would not be used in the retrial, and it may be noted that Qatada was eventually acquitted in Jordan of the charges against him.[114] Thus safeguards available in the national legal system in the receiving country, or able to be agreed upon before a deportation, against admitting or relying on torture-tainted evidence, and the likelihood of their being determinative in the particular case, should be given weight. Thus, the deportation or extradition of terrorist suspects to countries such as Jordan that have used torture, and have allowed such evidence to be admitted in criminal trials, can be undertaken, so long as the relevant assurances are forthcoming.

The two strands of the decision in *Othman*—as to Article 3 and Article 6— indicate, it is contended, that the Court is not prepared to accept an overt balancing approach within the absolute or non-materially qualified rights in relation to the possible use of torture. This is the case even where such an approach has been accepted in the highest domestic court, which has also rehearsed the Convention arguments fully. Thus, insofar as the House of Lords' approach to the Article 6 issue relied on taking account of the risk to national security represented by the applicant, the Court was unreceptive to that approach. But outside the Article 3-linked context, the Court has shown itself to be prepared to be guided by the domestic courts towards a balancing approach under Article 6, as *Al-Khawaja* demonstrates.

---

[110] ibid, para 279.

[111] ibid, paras 280, 282.

[112] See on the Art 6 issue *Gäfgen v Germany* (2011) 52 EHRR 1 and *El-Haski v Belgium* (2013) 56 EHRR 31; in *Gäfgen* it was found that the risk of admission of such evidence was not viewed as *automatically* creating a flagrant denial of justice, but as raising serious issues as to the fairness of the proceedings.

[113] After the decision of the ECtHR, SIAC found in *Othman v SSHD* [2012] UKSIAC 15/2005_2 that the Secretary of State should not have declined to revoke the deportation order, because she had not satisfied the judges that, on a retrial in Jordan, there would be no real risk that the impugned statements apparently obtained by torture would be admitted.

[114] See S Malik and A Su, 'Abu Qatada Cleared of Terror Charges by Jordan Court and Released from Jail' *The Guardian* (London, 24 September 2014), www.theguardian.com/world/2014/sep/24/abu-qatada-cleared-terror-charges-jordan-court.

VI. CONCLUSIONS

This chapter has sought to suggest that a growing acceptance of a doctrine of enhanced subsidiarity is evident in certain of the recent Strasbourg judgments. A range of findings of the British domestic courts are arguably being given greater weight at Strasbourg in the context of the Izmir, Interlaken and Brighton Declarations and Protocol 15—*if* the Convention right has been considered fully by the domestic court. The UK courts have shown a degree of acceptance of a balancing approach, especially under Articles 5 and 3 ECHR, which it is argued has also found some purchase in the more recent Strasbourg judgments under the guise of paying attention to the 'context'. So long as the domestic courts fully rehearse the Convention arguments, as Lord Bingham failed to do in *Gillan*,[115] the Court is currently showing some reluctance to depart from their findings.

The conclusion of this piece is that the mechanisms for dialogue and subsidiarity are already present, but that the UK government and the Court need to learn to operate them more transparently, effectively and sensitively. Protocol 15 does not add very much, it is suggested, to that process in formal terms, but although it is not yet in force it may be helping to impel the Court to take a more cautious approach to sensitive issues of the type discussed, and to pay greater attention to consistency in its operation of the margin of appreciation doctrine (a sensitivity which was absent in *Hirst*).[116] The domestic courts appear to recognise that the UK's margin of appreciation is more likely to be triggered in respect of a particular decision if a full balancing analysis has occurred. Protocol 16 might be of some value in future in allowing the Court to talk to the Supreme Court at an earlier stage in potential conflicts, and so to furthering such an analysis.

The use of dialogue between the domestic courts and Strasbourg is of value in terms of avoiding derailment of the whole ECHR project. But this chapter argues that full awareness of the implications of such dialogue is necessary. It may be questioned whether a dialogic approach is fully consonant with maintaining subsidiarity. If, as discussed, domestic courts are more receptive to State arguments as to a balancing approach based on the purpose of a measure, as in *Austin*[117] and *Wellington*,[118] then those arguments may be able to gain some unacknowledged purchase at the international level. A Strasbourg approach that appears to accord an enhanced role to subsidiarity and the dialogic approach has at times obscured its appeasement effects. The line to be drawn between appeasement of a signatory State and a 'proper' reliance on the principle of subsidiarity is a fine one, especially as—as indicated at the outset—the principle has recently received greater emphasis. A desire to appease the UK, which has for some time argued for a more subsidiary role for the Court, and is currently threatening to withdraw from the Convention system altogether, may underlie a number of the decisions considered, albeit in an unacknowledged way.

---

[115] *R (Gillan) v Commissioner of Police for the Metropolis* (n 41).
[116] *Hirst v UK* (n 5).
[117] *Austin v Commissioner of Police of the Metropolis* (n 46).
[118] *R (Wellington) v SSHD* (n 62).

The consensus that marked the inception of the ECHR, and which has remained apparent until fairly recently as the Court has extended its influence, may be in danger of unravelling at the present time. But clearly, if in some of the instances explored above appeasement is occurring it has not yet gone far enough, in populist terms. The difficulty of satisfying the Conservative leadership and sections of the public, especially in England, that the Court is not encroaching too far on the autonomy of the Westminster Parliament is only likely to increase after the 2015 general election. After the 2015 election the new Justice Secretary, Michael Gove, indicated that Chris Grayling's 2014 plan would be implemented,[119] and that Britain would withdraw from the ECHR if the Council of Europe rejected the proposal that judgments against states should no longer bind them (as is currently the position under Article 46 ECHR).

It can hardly be doubted that the ECtHR has a role in providing a minimum level of non-negotiable protection of human rights at the international level. But its 'living instrument' approach has taken it some way beyond the text of the rights, so the question arises as to the nature of such minimum standards. For example, Article 6 has nothing to say about acceptable fair trial standards in a country receiving a deportee, but that did not stand in the way of the findings on that point in *Othman*. At the present time the 'living instrument' approach is coming under pressure, especially as States attempt to address violent manifestations of Wahabism or Salafism and seek to head off responses from the extreme right to such manifestations. With a view to its own future, and to the project of maintaining a *degree* of rights protection, especially in the counter-terror arena, the ECtHR may therefore be relying on an interpretation of subsidiarity and acceptance of a dialogic approach to seek to distance itself from the image it has acquired in the eyes of the Conservative leadership: that of a quasi-constitutional, highly over-activist institution, which is suffering from 'mission creep'. At the present time, that stance may represent a strategically sound one in terms of maintaining more harmonious relations with the UK. That could mean that maintaining a minimum level of protection of rights may come at the cost of resiling somewhat from the 'living instrument' approach, especially in relation to counter-terrorism. This chapter has pointed out the potential dangers in that approach. But the impact on the general acceptance of Convention standards as maintained by the Court in certain States, such as Russia, if the UK were to leave the Convention system or defy the Court openly, provides a basis for adoption of a flexible approach by the Court towards UK cases at the present time, especially where sound Convention-based reasoning in the Supreme Court is available as a guide.

[119] See n 2.

11

Article 8 ECHR, the UK and Strasbourg: Compliance, Cooperation or Clash? A Judicial Perspective

MARK OCKELTON

I. INTRODUCTION

THE TITLE I have been given for this contribution invites treatment of the set-piece disputes between issues of the right to private life and government policy, as determined by the European Court of Human Rights (ECtHR): where there is suspicion of terrorism, for example, or the more mundane but hardly less fraught issue of prisoners' rights to vote. But I cannot improve on the analyses offered by other contributors, and I could add little more than anecdote. I devote this chapter not to the few obviously difficult cases but to more routine ones that arise in their thousands. These are the cases in which a person's continued presence in the United Kingdom depends solely or largely on whether Article 8 of the European Convention on Human Rights (ECHR) prevents his removal. If the conclusion is that it does, there may well be criticism in the press of a decision said to inflate 'human rights' above the rights of victims or of common sense.

There is no clash between the courts in Strasbourg and the UK in relation to these cases. The tensions and their sources are much more subtle. One the one hand are the press, purportedly representing public opinion, and the government, purportedly representing the public interest and purportedly doing so in a balanced and informed way. On the other hand are the demands of individual determination of human rights by reference to all the relevant facts and the judges who have to make those determinations. The latter can be seen or represented as soft, fuddy-duddy, and out of touch with the real needs of society; they have the useful characteristic that they never reply to criticism or expand on their judgments. Extra stress may be applied by representing the issues as influenced by supranational, unelected judges at Strasbourg; and more or less ignorant comment added by those who think that the government is doing too much, or too little, or is simply always wrong. The tensions are then between the notion of the applicability of Article 8 and those who oppose its results. I want to argue that the real problem is that the present law has the unfortunate but inevitable consequence of providing material for the ill-disposed; but I regret that although a solution is available, it is unlikely to be applied. In short, the present situation is too valuable to those who want to maintain the tensions.

Even to those who have considerable experience in public law, immigration law is daunting: not only is it about those from abroad; it is itself a foreign country. I must start therefore by outlining the structure of immigration control and the role of the courts and tribunals (II). I will then go on to discuss the way in which the majority of Article 8 decisions are made (III) and then add some observations about how the government responds to cases it has 'lost' (IV).

II. THE STRUCTURE OF IMMIGRATION CONTROL AND THE ROLE OF THE JUDGE

In principle, States are permitted to control the entry and sojourn of non-nationals. In the United Kingdom that is the task of the Home Office, operating under statute, the immigration rules, numerous statutory instruments and published policies. It makes decisions in individual cases. Many adverse decisions carry a right of appeal. An adverse decision may be a refusal of something that was applied for—a visa, further leave as a student, protection as a refugee, or it may be a free-standing decision the person affected did not seek: removal, deportation, curtailment of leave. In the end, it is for most purposes the removal decisions of various sorts that count, for our purposes, because they potentially raise Article 8.

The right of appeal is to the first-tier tribunal, where a judge, normally sitting alone, will look at the matter afresh and determine whether the person did meet the requirements of the rules or whether his removal is illegal, or whatever. The judge is not concerned with process, but with substantive merit: this is appeal, not judicial review.

Following the coming into force of the Human Rights Act 1998 (HRA) on 2 October 2000, it was not immediately clear what the role of the judge was in cases where the resistance to the adverse decision was based on a protected Convention right that was not absolute, so that the legality of the interference with it involved an assessment and judgment of proportionality. The matter was settled for present purposes in the decision of the House of Lords in *Huang v Secretary of State for the Home Department*.[1]

In *Huang* the House of Lords set out the task of the appellate authorities in assessing an Article 8 claim against removal by a person who could not comply with the immigration rules. The House unambiguously rejected the notion, previously endorsed by the Court of Appeal,[2] that an immigration judge was confined to considering whether the government's decision was within the lawful range of responses to the facts. To limit the jurisdiction in that way would be to allow mere

---

[1] *Huang v Secretary of State for the Home Department* [2007] UKHL 11.
[2] *Edore v Secretary of State for the Home Department* [2003] EWCA Civ 716.

review and would fail to implement the clear intention of Parliament[3] that a person should have a right of appeal on the ground that the decision infringed Convention rights. The original decision, on the same or similar facts, 'is always relevant and may be decisive', but

> the appellate immigration authority, deciding an appeal ... is not reviewing the decision of another decision-maker. It is deciding whether or not it is unlawful to refuse leave to enter or remain, and it is doing so on the basis of up to date facts.[4]

The last phrase is relevant because

> [t]he first task of the appellate immigration authority is to establish the relevant facts. These may well have changed since the original decision was made. In any event, particularly where the applicant has not been interviewed, the authority will be much better placed to investigate the facts, test the evidence, assess the sincerity of the applicant's evidence and the genuineness of his or her concerns and evaluate the nature and strength of the family bond in the particular case. It is important that the facts are explored, and summarised in the decision, with care, since they will always be important and often decisive.[5]

The tribunal will 'consider and weigh all that tells in favour of the refusal', including the general need to maintain immigration control by rules that are rational, fair and cause like cases to be decided in like manner, and special factors such as those relating to serious criminals:

> The giving of weight to factors such as these is not, in our opinion, aptly described as deference: it is performance of the ordinary judicial task of weighing up the competing considerations on each side and according appropriate weight to the judgment of a person with responsibility for a given subject matter and access to special sources of knowledge and advice. That is how any rational judicial decision-maker is likely to proceed.[6]

On the other hand, the mere fact that a person did not succeed under the Immigration Rules[7] could not be regarded as the end of the matter.[8] The Strasbourg jurisprudence must be taken into account, as section 2 of the HRA 1998 itself requires. The cases indicate where the balance is to be struck in a variety of fact-situations, and illuminate the core social and family values that Article 8 exists to protect. Although individuals and families have no right to decide to live in a country of which they are not nationals, the individual facts of each case may show that the interference proposed is not proportionate.[9] In assessing proportionality, the *de Freitas*[10] questions remained relevant, but as the House had emphasised

---

[3] Then in s 65 Immigration and Asylum Act 1999 and paras 21–22 of its Sched 4; the legislation has subsequently been recast but without effect on the result. See now s 84(1)(c) and (g) Nationality, Immigration and Asylum Act 2002, in the course of being replaced again with new appeal rights and new wording by s 15 Immigration Act 2014.

[4] *Huang* (n 1) para 13.

[5] ibid, para 15.

[6] ibid, para 16.

[7] *Statement of Changes in Immigration Rules* (HC 395) 1994, as (frequently) amended.

[8] *Huang* (n 1), para 17.

[9] ibid, para 18.

[10] *De Freitas v Permanent Secretary of Ministry of Agriculture, Fisheries, Lands and Housing* [1999] 1 AC 69, 80 (PC).

in *R (Razgar) v Secretary of State for the Home Department*,[11] there was always a need to strike a fair balance between the interests of society and those of the individual. Thus:

> In an article 8 case where this question is reached, the ultimate question for the appellate immigration authority is whether the refusal of leave to enter or remain, in circumstances where the life of the family cannot reasonably be expected to be enjoyed elsewhere, taking full account of all considerations weighing in favour of the refusal, prejudices the family life of the applicant in a manner sufficiently serious to amount to a breach of the fundamental right protected by article 8. If the answer to this question is affirmative, the refusal is unlawful and the authority must so decide.[12]

In other words, the decision of the Secretary of State on the proportionality of interference in the individual case, made on the basis of the material available to the Secretary of State, may be wholly replaced by the decision of the judge, made on the basis of the material available to the judge.

The decision in *Huang* is, I think, widely regarded as a triumph of the rule of law over executive power. It asserts the supremacy of the courts and makes clear the role of the judiciary in protecting human rights from unlawful interference by the executive. Unfortunately, however, experience of those on the coal face, in tens of thousands of cases a year, in many of which human rights issues of one sort or another are raised, suggests the contrary. Lord Bingham's expectation, recorded in paragraph 20, that the number of claimants entitled to succeed under Article 8 despite not meeting the requirements of the Rules, would be a 'very small minority' may well not have been realised. What is clear, however, is that the hint at paragraph 14 of the judgment, that the tribunal's task 'might be difficult …, in practice, to perform', was no understatement. The decision in *Huang*, desirable as it might be in principle, is the route to decisions that are, and were always bound to be, less than fully informed, irrational, inconsistent, and uncontrollable.

III. THE CHALLENGES OF ARTICLE 8 DECISIONS IN JUDICIAL PRACTICE

Why then is the decision in *Huang* not without problems for the day-to-day decisions that immigration judges make? There are problems at different levels. Reasons relate to the fact that judges do not have the material on which *ordinary* decisions on proportionality can be made, and that the judicial role is not adapted to making such decisions. It might even be doubtful whether it is proper for judges to make such decisions.

This proposition clearly needs some expansion. But really it is quite obvious. Proportionality is a matter of balance. There is a balance to be struck between the Convention rights of an individual and wider public concerns, including 'maintaining immigration control'. That will be informed by a number of factors. Government

---

[11] *R (Razgar) v Secretary of State for the Home Department* [2004] UKHL 27, para 20.
[12] *Huang* (n 1) para 20.

policy is one; executive judgment and knowledge is another. The way in which similar cases have been treated is another. The way in which dissimilar cases—a little more or a little less apparently deserving—have been treated is another. And of course the true facts of the case, presented not in the parties' own way, but dispassionately, especially where the interests of people other than the appellant him- or herself are concerned, constitute another.

A judge may have some access to the last of these, but often does not. Even the most basic information is often desperately partial. Two types of case concerning children make this clear. In one of the leading cases the Supreme Court dealt in some detail with the need to take into account the British citizenship of children, without referring at all to their dual nationality.[13] And frequently a deportation appeal is supported by a claim that it is 'clearly' in the best interests of children to have access to their father—but suppose the father, threatened with deportation, is a convicted drug dealer who has taken little interest in them? Or at least little interest in them until he was threatened with deportation? And how does one decide, particularly if there is no professional assessment of the best interests of the children, but only assertions made by one or both of the parents in the context of the threatened deportation?

Of course the appeals process could be improved. Judges could be given access to better evidence; cases could be better prepared; court experts could be appointed. But even so, the other difficulties would remain.

The problem is that judges are judges. They judge individual cases. They take pride in not making decisions based on statistics. They may be well enough informed to know a lot about an individual case, but they know (or are deemed to know) little or nothing about any other case. Everything a judge does know has to be brought into the arena: only in this way can the individual case be the subject of a fair, open decision in which the parties can make submissions about matters that may influence the judge. The judge cannot, for example, decide a case on the basis that deportation seems to be more (or less) proportionate a response in the present case than in the previous one in the day's list. In making their own judgments assessing proportionality, judges cannot readily take into account the judgments of other judges in similar cases: matters of fact and assessment do not create precedent.[14] Each case falls to be decided in a void. There are getting on for five hundred full-time and part-time judges engaged in this exercise. Consistency appears to be impossible. And, supposing that a judge is aware of some similar decision by another judge, and is influenced by it in some way, that surely is worse still, because the judge's decision has become less than transparent.

---

[13] *ZH (Tanzania)* [2011] UKSC 4. I do not of course offer any criticism of the result; but the fact that the debate places weight on nationality only when it is British nationality might raise some post-colonial eyebrows.

[14] The task of assessing damages in personal injury cases might be thought to be similar, but the similarity is only superficial. There, the judge is concerned with a relatively closely constrained issue, and subject to a well-established legal principle of maintaining of consistency by appeals if necessary. There is always a sound basis of independent expert evidence and the contest is not between an individual's hopes and a largely inchoate 'public interest'. The Art 8 assessment contrasts on each of these points.

Not only is each case itself in a void, but the void itself is in a vacuum. The jurisprudence on Article 8 is about actual or potential breaches of the Convention, overwhelmingly in the context of immigration removals. There is almost no authoritative statement of the positive content of Article 8 when it is not under stress. Even more to the point, there is almost no treatment of the extent to which interference with the rights protected by Article 8 is permitted outside the context of immigration removals. Sending somebody to prison for a long time may separate him from his family more comprehensively than deporting him, because of the limits on electronic communication with prisoners: but we see no multitude of challenges to prison sentences on that ground. Denial of parental contact similarly separates family members: but there is no suggestion that judicial decisions in that sphere should be made on typological assumptions of the dynamics of family life rather than expert opinion focused on an individual case. It almost seems as though Article 8 in immigration cases is not the same Article 8 as found in the rest of the law.

There is more. Judges hear appeals: they only ever hear about the adverse decisions, because only adverse decisions can be appealed. The executive, however, does not make only adverse decisions. Judges can have no concept of the cases in which the original decision-maker has struck the balance in favour of the person affected. They cannot know whether allowing an appeal produces a decision which is now consistent with other positive decisions being made by the executive or is wildly out of line with them. They thus are required to assess proportionality without the basic material that might give a sense of proportion to their decisions.

Finally, judges are not policy-makers and can themselves make no decisions about, for example, the *relative* importance of maintaining immigration control against a long-term overstayer, a person convicted of a single offence of dealing class A drugs, a person convicted of a long series of house burglaries, a student, a doctor, an influential religious leader, an unemployed person, a person with kidney failure. The question of the variation of factors for and against each of these people is essentially a matter of executive analysis or judgment, probably made on the basis of public policy and on the basis of an appreciation of the numbers of individuals in each category (and hence the damage to 'immigration control' if individual circumstances are allowed to override the general law in each of these categories).

This is not to say that the process as a whole should not have judicial supervision. It is obviously right that judges should be entitled to say 'that is wholly disproportionate' and to examine the process of decision-making. But judges are not able satisfactorily to make decisions on the merits of the vast number of proportionality cases. Individual judges cannot make decisions in isolated cases in a way that is either properly informed or able to promote consistency.

But, like it or not, following *Huang*, that is what the judges do. And the result is, obviously, that occasionally (or more often) there are decisions that appear, particularly to somebody who is only partially informed about the facts, very generous to the individual concerned. These are, of course appeals which the government has lost. So the question is, what does the government do about them?

IV. GOVERNMENT RESPONSES TO 'ADVERSE' IMMIGRATION DECISIONS

There are various ways in which the government may 'respond' to immigration appeals it has lost. First, in individual cases it may appeal. But appeals having been restricted to a point of law only (to prevent a multiplicity of appeals by individuals), the government finds that its right of appeal, so restricted, does not help it in cases where the judgment of the first-tier tribunal, albeit at the most generous end of the scale, was not actually unlawful on the material presented. The government has made some progress in medical cases, and also in the interpretation of the Rules, but in general appeals against generous first-tier tribunal decisions do not succeed because a decision at the generous end of the scale is not an error of law.

Secondly, more generally, a government that is upset by losing appeals may respond by removing rights of appeal. If there is no right of appeal (as is increasingly the case in points-based cases),[15] *Huang* does not apply: the reasoning there was based on the distinction between appeals (where the tribunal's task is to substitute, if necessary, its own judgment on the merits) and review, where the tribunal's (or court's) task is to consider whether the decision is one that the decision-maker was entitled to reach. Even the more intense judicial review of *Daly*[16] does not typically involve the judge in the impossible task faced by those determining immigration *appeals*: the question on a judicial review is whether the decision-maker could lawfully reach the assessment that was reached.

Thirdly, it can try to set out how the balance is to be struck by decision-makers taking into account the public interest. This has been done most recently by Appendix FM to the Immigration Rules and associated amendments,[17] which attempt to replace individual assessment of the proportionality of an interference with Article 8 by a preordained set of rules. For the first time the Immigration Rules specifically attempt to deal with claims under Article 8 (which had previously been treated as necessarily outside the Rules) and, in so doing, avowedly express the government's view of the classes of case in which the public interest in maintaining immigration control may be outweighed by individual circumstances. This is far from completely useless. For example, if paragraph 276ADE says that a person seeking indefinite leave to remain on the basis of long (unlawful) residence is to be granted leave if and only if his residence is more than 20 years, that gives an indication, approved by Parliament, of the government's expression of the public interest in enforcing immigration control against overstayers or illegal entrants, by not allowing those to stay who have remained only for much shorter periods. To an extent, therefore, it helps to provide information on the cases, otherwise hidden

---

[15] The structure of appeal rights changed markedly in April 2015 on the coming into force of the provisions of Part 2 of the Immigration Act 2014. Most existing rights of appeal are removed; but one of the survivors is an appeal against the refusal of a 'human rights claim' on the ground that removal of the appellant from the United Kingdom would be unlawful as a breach of s 6 Human Rights Act 1998: s 15, substituting new wording for ss 82 and 84 Nationality, Immigration and Asylum Act 2002.

[16] *R v SSHD, ex parte Daly* [2001] UKHL 26.

[17] Inserted by *Statement of Changes in Immigration Rules*, HC 194, and mostly in force from 9 July 2014.

from judges, where the individual's application would be successful. But it does not give much help where the stay was 19-and-a-half years; or where the stay was very much shorter but the person has a serious medical condition; or his mother does. Or, far from unusual, where the person tested his status five years ago by an appeal, which he lost, but no steps were taken to remove him. What price the importance of maintaining immigration control then? If removal soon after the unsuccessful appeal was not necessary, why is it necessary or proportionate now?

Anyway, even with Appendix FM, with all its detailed rules, and the associated changes in the body of the Rules, it is clear that when an adverse decision is challenged the judgment of proportionality is still for the first-tier tribunal judge. The difference is that he now has at least something to see on the other side of the equation in the general case.[18] The problem is, of course, that the judge is looking at the specific case. That is recognised by the Rules themselves, which envisage the 'exceptional circumstances', subsequently changed to 'very compelling circumstances' where the public interest in the deportation of criminals may be outweighed by personal factors.[19] A judge needs to consider whether the case at issue is one in which the application of the Rules results in a disproportionate interference with the rights protected by Article 8,[20] and at this point it seems that the whole enterprise of routine consideration by reference to stated elements of the public interest vanishes, and the judge is left in the original position of ignorance as to any comparator. Guidance in the Rules, or statutory provisions as to what must be taken into account, may well fail in their purpose at precisely the point at which they are supposed to provide the answer.

Certainly judges are doing their very best in these extraordinary conditions to make good, fair, accurate decisions on proportionality, though they cannot be expected to make consistent ones. The obvious solution to the problems with the system would be to reverse *Huang*. Leave the judges to supervise the process, or reverse a decision that was off the scale; but allow the executive to reach its own judgements provided those judgements are lawful, that is, within the range of permissible responses to the facts. That such a regime is lawful and practicable is demonstrated by the existence of cases in which the only method of challenge is judicial review rather than appeal. Nothing more is required by the ECHR or the ECtHR. Provided that a decision does not interfere disproportionately with a Convention right, it does not matter who made it, as long as there was the possibility of judicial supervision; and in adjudicating the matter the Strasbourg Court will apply a margin of appreciation, recognising the interests of the individual State.

But I do not think that *Huang* will be reversed, because of the fourth type of reaction to generous decisions against the government. Governments like to be

---

[18] ss 117A–D Nationality, Immigration and Asylum Act 2002 (inserted by s 91 Immigration Act 2014) also make a number of assertions concerning the public interest and require that it be taken into account.

[19] para 398 as inserted by HC 194 and then as amended by HC 532 (28 July 2014); and see *MF (Nigeria) v SSHD* [2013] EWCA Civ 1192.

[20] *Gulshan (Article 8—new Rules—correct approach)* [2013] UKUT 640 (IAC), para 24(b). The decision in *MM*, to which reference is made in para 24 and elsewhere in the judgment, was reversed by the Court of Appeal at [2014] EWCA Civ 985, but the process set out in *Gulshan* remains the correct one.

able to blame others for decisions that are, or may be, unpopular. From numerous instances I choose two in order to avoid making any party-political point. A striking example, albeit on Article 3 ECHR rather than Article 8, is to be found in the evidence, recorded by Field J in *Youssef v The Home Office*,[21] relating to the removal of a person to Egypt as conducive to the public good. The government hoped to be able to obtain an undertaking that if removed he would not be ill-treated, and kept him (and three others) in detention pending deportation. He was pressing the High Court for his release. The Home Secretary eventually reached the conclusion that continued detention would be unlawful, and so advised the Prime Minister on 3 June 1999 as follows:

> As we have already ruled out the possibility of removing the men to anywhere other than Egypt this means that there is no longer a basis for detaining them under immigration powers. I will therefore have no option other than to agree to their very early release.[22]

The Prime Minister's response to this was:

> The Prime Minister is not content simply to accept that we have no option but to release the four individuals. He believes that we should use whatever assurances the Egyptians are willing to offer, to build a case to initiate the deportation procedure and to take our chance in the courts. If the courts rule that the assurances we have are inadequate, then at least it would be the courts, not the government, who would be responsible for releasing the four from detention.[23]

That 'at least' is revealing.

My second example has to be the 'case of the cat', castigated in a speech by a Home Secretary of a very different political persuasion. The Home Secretary said that the 'misinterpretation' of Article 8 by judges prevented the government deporting 'people who should not be here'; she then went on to explain that 'among the perverted interpretations of the Convention ... was the case of "the illegal immigrant who cannot be deported because—and I am not making this up—he had a pet cat"'.[24]

This is a particularly interesting reaction to, and description of, a case to which the Home Secretary was a party: she not only had all the knowledge of the facts that any party to a case does have, but she also had, as a party, the opportunity to challenge the decision if it was wrong in law by reason of 'misinterpretation' of the Convention. The preferred method of attack was ridicule, based on a misstatement of the facts in a case which the government had accepted it ought not to win.

The appeal in question concerned a person who, like thousands of others, had not been subject to any enforcement for years after he last had leave to remain. There was a longstanding policy endorsed by the government that a person who had been in a relationship akin to marriage for two years would not now normally

[21] *Youssef v Home Office* [2004] EWHC 1884 (QB).
[22] ibid, para 34.
[23] ibid, para 38.
[24] M Easton, 'Government v Judiciary on Article 8' BBC News (4 October 2011), www.bbc.co.uk/news/uk-15167619.

be subject to enforcement action. At first instance the judge had considered whether the relationship between the appellant and his partner was a genuine one. He looked at all the evidence, and noted amongst other things that the two of them had lived together, been on holiday together, and owned a cat together. The last fact, said the judge, reinforced his conclusion that the couple had a genuine relationship. He allowed the appeal. The Home Secretary appealed, but then *conceded* that the policy meant that because of the finding that the relationship was genuine and of more than two years' standing, there should have been no enforcement action and that the appeal therefore ought to have succeeded.[25] Given the actual facts it is not easy to see the ground for criticising the judicial decisions.

V. CONCLUSION

Giving an impossible and frequent task to judges, as required by *Huang*, satisfies both constitutional theory anxious to protect the rule of law on the one hand and a government struggling to devise a coherent, transparent and effective immigration policy, and unwilling also to accept the decisions of judges on the other. The great advantage of blaming the judges is that they never correct the facts[26] or answer back. From the point of view of both press and government, the vast bulk of decisions in this politically peculiarly sensitive area provides frequent material to orchestrate clashes of ethos between the public and Strasbourg; and it seems unlikely therefore that there will ever be pressure to remove that opportunity. It is striking that governments are unwilling to proclaim and celebrate the Convention as a protection of individual rights: instead, it is a focus for criticism of 'foreign' law.[27]

So there is no real clash in ordinary immigration cases between Strasbourg and the United Kingdom. The clash is that between constitutional theory and the practicalities of judicial decision making. And for the most part, immigration cases are not really an exemplification of stresses between the United Kingdom and Strasbourg; they are rather the ammunition in a quite different battle.

---

[25] The judgment on appeal, under file no IA/14578/2008, can be found at www.theguardian.com/law/2011/oct/04/theresa-may-wrong-cat-deportation.

[26] Some modest correction was provided by the Judicial Press Office in relation to the 'cat case'; but corrections are never as newsworthy as exaggerations.

[27] *cf* the Wilders case: *GW* (EEA reg 21: 'fundamental interests') Netherlands [2009] UKAIT 00050, paras 32–35.

12

Application of the ECHR during International Armed Conflicts

CLARE OVEY[1]

T HE PRINCIPLES RELATING to the application of the European Convention
on Human Rights (ECHR) during extraterritorial armed conflicts have, to a
very large extent, been expounded by the European Court of Human Rights
(ECtHR) in cases against the United Kingdom—particularly cases involving its
military activity in Iraq from 2003. This case law was the subject of lectures given
by two senior members of the English judiciary in 2014.[2] It also attracted negative
comment in the Conservative Party's paper outlining the reforms that it would
make to human rights legislation in the United Kingdom if elected by a majority
in May 2015,[3] and was the subject of a robust response by the former Attorney-
General, Dominic Grieve.[4]

This is a developing area of case law. In each successive Grand Chamber case on
the topic the ECtHR has been called upon to address a different factual scenario and
a different set of arguments, and the principles have therefore emerged in a rather
piecemeal way, although the underlying doctrinal framework is becoming increasingly apparent and coherent. The British courts have also contributed substantially
to the law in this area, with the clear analysis and critique of the Strasbourg case
law as it then stood contained in the House of Lords judgments in *Al-Skeini* and
Al-Jedda[5] and the recent judgment on the application of the ECHR to armed forces
serving overseas, *Smith v The Ministry of Defence*,[6] which broached a subject not
yet tackled in Strasbourg.

---

[1] The views expressed in this article are purely my own. I would like to thank Olga Chernishova and
Jack Meek for their assistance.
[2] Lord Dyson MR, 'The Extraterritorial Application of the European Convention on Human Rights:
Now on a Firmer Footing, but is it a Sound One?', speech delivered at the University of Essex, 30 January
2014; Lord Phillips of Worth Matravers, 'The Elastic Jurisdiction of the European Court of Human
Rights', speech delivered at the University of Oxford, 12 February 2014, both available at www.judiciary.
gov.uk.
[3] Conservative Party, *Protecting Human Rights in the UK: The Conservatives' Proposals for Changing
Britain's Human Rights Laws* (3 October 2014).
[4] D Grieve, 'Why it Matters that the Conservatives Should Support the European Convention on
Human Rights', speech delivered at University College London, 3 December 2014, www.ucl.ac.uk/
constitution-unit/constitution-unit-news/031214a.
[5] *Al-Skeini v Secretary of State for Defence* [2007] UKHL 26; *R (on the application of Al-Jedda) v
Secretary of State for Defence* [2007] UKHL 58.
[6] *Smith v Ministry of Defence* [2013] UKSC 41.

In the final case in the series concerning the British in Iraq, *Hassan v UK*,[7] the United Kingdom government asked the Grand Chamber of the ECtHR to hold that the State's obligation to secure the rights and freedoms set out in the ECHR did not apply in the active hostilities phase of an international armed conflict. The Court rejected this argument, holding that such a conclusion would be inconsistent with its own previous case law and with that of the International Court of Justice. In this chapter, I will explore how the Court has interpreted the notion of 'jurisdiction' in Article 1 ECHR so that it does, indeed, have an application in certain circumstances where a State is involved in armed conflict outside its national territory. I will also examine the extent to which, hand in hand with this development of the case law on jurisdiction, there has been recognition by the Court that the Convention rights should be interpreted and applied in a way which takes into account the legal and factual particularities of armed conflict.

I. EXTRATERRITORIAL JURISDICTION IN SITUATIONS OF INTERNATIONAL ARMED CONFLICT

Under Article 1 ECHR, the High Contracting Parties agree to secure the rights and freedoms contained in Section 1 of the Convention to 'everyone within their jurisdiction'. 'Jurisdiction' in Article 1 is an admissibility or threshold criterion: the Court cannot examine a claim under the Convention if the facts did not fall within the State's jurisdiction, just as it cannot examine a claim if the application was not lodged within the six-month time limit set by Article 35 ECHR.

The Court's first case law on jurisdiction in conflict (or post-conflict) areas related to the Turkish occupation of Northern Cyprus. In the *Loizidou* case, brought by a Cypriot national who complained that, since the Turkish invasion in 1974, she had been denied access to property she had owned in northern Cyprus, the Court made its finding on jurisdiction in two steps. In the first judgment, *Loizidou v Turkey* (preliminary objections), the Court held that 'although Article 1 sets limits on the reach of the Convention, the concept of "jurisdiction" under this provision is not restricted to the national territory of the High Contracting Parties'. It continued:

> Bearing in mind the object and purpose of the Convention, the responsibility of a Contracting Party may also arise when as a consequence of military action—whether lawful or unlawful—it exercises effective control of an area outside its national territory. The obligation to secure, in such an area, the rights and freedoms set out in the Convention derives from the fact of such control whether it be exercised directly, through its armed forces, or through a subordinate local administration.[8]

Since the Turkish government had acknowledged that the applicant's loss of control of her property stemmed from the occupation of the northern part of Cyprus by Turkish troops and the establishment there of the 'Turkish Republic of Northern

---

[7] *Hassan v UK* (2011) 53 EHRR 18 (GC), para 71.
[8] *Loizidou v Turkey* (Preliminary Objections) (1995) 20 EHRR 99, para 62.

Cyprus', it followed that the acts complained of were 'capable of falling within Turkish "jurisdiction" within the meaning of Article 1' of the Convention.[9]

The Court returned to the issue of jurisdiction in its judgment on the merits,[10] finding that it was obvious, in light of the fact that there were 30,000 Turkish troops stationed throughout northern Cyprus, that the Turkish army exercised effective overall control there. Having found such 'effective control', the Court did not consider it necessary to determine the extent to which Turkey exercised detailed management of the policies and actions of the authorities of the 'TRNC'. Turkey's 'effective control' entailed responsibility for the policies and actions of the 'TRNC' and those affected by them came within the 'jurisdiction' of Turkey for the purposes of Article 1 of the Convention.

The next key case concerning jurisdiction in situations of international armed conflict was *Banković v Belgium*.[11] In this case there was no question of any occupation or effective control of the territory in question by one or more Convention States. Instead, the applicants complained that their relatives had been killed when a radio and television broadcasting company's buildings were destroyed by a missile launched by a NATO forces aircraft on 23 April 1999, in the course of the Kosovo conflict. The applicants argued that their deceased relatives had been brought within the jurisdiction of the respondent States by the air strike; they asked the Court to apply the 'effective control' principle established in *Loizidou* in a manner proportionate to the degree of control exercised. In other words, in a case where, as in northern Cyprus, the respondent State enjoyed virtually complete military control by virtue of the occupation of the territory by its troops, the ECtHR should require the State to guarantee to those living in the occupied territory the full range of Convention rights and freedoms. In contrast, where, as in their case, the respondent States struck a target outside their territory, they should not be obliged to do the impossible, but should just be held accountable only for those Convention rights within their control in the situation in question.[12] The respondent governments strongly urged the Court to reject this approach. They argued that, if the Court were to find jurisdiction on such grounds, it would have serious consequences for international military collective action as it would render the Court competent to review the participation of Contracting States in military missions all over the world.[13]

In a unanimous decision, the Grand Chamber of the Court found in favour of the respondent States. It held that 'jurisdiction' under Article 1 ECHR was primarily limited to a State's territorial boundaries and that a State could exercise extraterritorial jurisdiction only in exceptional circumstances. Three examples were given, based on past cases, of 'exceptional circumstances' which would give rise to

---

[9]   ibid, paras 62–64.
[10]   *Loizidou v Turkey* (Merits) (1997) 23 EHRR 513.
[11]   *Banković v Belgium, the Czech Republic, Denmark, France, Germany, Greece, Hungary, Iceland, Italy, Luxembourg, the Netherlands, Norway, Poland, Portugal, Spain, Turkey and the United Kingdom* (2007) 44 EHRR SE5 (GC).
[12]   ibid, para 47.
[13]   ibid, para 43.

extraterritorial jurisdiction: first, effective military control of an area outside the State's national territory, as in the northern Cyprus cases; secondly, the exercise by the Convention State, on the territory of another State, and with that State's 'consent, invitation or acquiescence', of 'all or some of the public powers normally to be exercised by [the government of the territorial State]'; and thirdly, 'other recognised instances of the extra-territorial exercise of jurisdiction by a State', such as the acts of consular and diplomatic agents and acts on-board craft and vessels registered in, or flying the flag of, the State. The Court rejected the approach to jurisdiction that had been put forward by the applicants, stating that it considered this 'tantamount to arguing that anyone adversely affected by an act imputable to a Contracting State, wherever in the world that act may have been committed or its consequences felt, is thereby brought within the jurisdiction of that State for the purpose of Article 1 of the Convention'.[14] It found no support in the text of the Convention for the applicants' suggestion that the positive obligation under Article 1 to secure 'the rights and freedoms defined in Section I of this Convention' could be 'divided and tailored in accordance with the particular circumstances of the extra-territorial act in question'.[15] Finally, the Court, responding to the applicants' argument that if it did not find jurisdiction in this case there would be a lacuna in human rights protection, commented that

> the Convention is a multi-lateral treaty operating, subject to Article 56 of the Convention, in an essentially regional context and notably in the legal space (*espace juridique*) of the Contracting States. The FRY clearly does not fall within this legal space. The Convention was not designed to be applied throughout the world, even in respect of the conduct of Contracting States. Accordingly, the desirability of avoiding a gap or vacuum in human rights' protection has so far been relied on by the Court in favour of establishing jurisdiction only when the territory in question was one that, but for the specific circumstances, would normally be covered by the Convention.[16]

The Court returned to the question of Article 1 jurisdiction in the context of international military operations in *Al-Skeini v UK*.[17] The United Kingdom, as part of a military coalition led by the United States, invaded Iraq in March 2003. The United States and United Kingdom announced that major combat operations had been completed by 1 May 2003, and on 8 May 2003 representatives of the two countries sent a letter to the President of the United Nations Security Council in which they declared that they had created a Coalition Provisional Authority (CPA) to govern Iraq until elections could be held, and that until that time the United States and the United Kingdom, through the CPA, would inter alia provide for security in Iraq. The United Kingdom took particular responsibility for the maintenance of security in the south-east of the country, including Basra. This situation remained in place until 28 June 2004, when full authority was transferred from the CPA to the Iraqi interim government and the CPA ceased to exist.

---

[14] ibid, para 75.
[15] ibid, para 75.
[16] ibid, para 80.
[17] *Al-Skeini v UK* (2011) 53 EHRR 18 (GC).

The six applicants were relatives of Iraqi nationals killed in Basra between 8 May 2003 and 10 November 2003 in the course of security operations carried out by British troops. They complained that the deaths were not properly investigated, as required by Article 2 ECHR. The preliminary question of jurisdiction was joined to the merits and the Grand Chamber set out a number of general principles relating to its approach to Article 1. First, it referred to the principle expressed in *Banković* that a State's jurisdictional competence under Article 1 is primarily territorial and that acts of the Contracting States performed, or producing effects, outside their territories could constitute an exercise of jurisdiction only in exceptional cases. The Court identified two types of situation which could give rise to extraterritorial jurisdiction. The first was where, as in the northern Cyprus cases, as a consequence of lawful or unlawful military action, a Contracting State exercised effective control of an area outside that national territory. The second basis for extraterritorial jurisdiction arose where a State, through its agents, exercised authority and control over a person outside its national borders—so-called 'state agent authority' jurisdiction.

The Court in *Al-Skeini* referred to two examples of state agent authority jurisdiction which had already been set out in *Banković*: first, the exercise of authority and control by a diplomatic or consular agent and, secondly, the exercise of authority and control by a state agent acting extraterritorially pursuant to 'custom, treaty or other agreement' allowing the authorities of the Contracting State to 'carry out executive or judicial functions on the territory of another State'. In addition, the Court in *Al-Skeini* referred to a third instance of state agent authority which would be sufficient to engage jurisdiction under Article 1, namely the use of force by a State's agents operating outside its territory.[18] This basis of jurisdiction, which had in fact been accepted by the respondent States in *Banković*,[19] had been seen in previous cases where an individual had been taken into the custody of state agents abroad, for example the irregular extradition of Abdullah Öcalan, who was arrested by Turkish agents in Kenya,[20] and of Ilich Ramírez Sánchez ('Carlos the Jackal'), who was placed on a French military aircraft by French agents in Sudan,[21] or the detention of two Iraqi nationals in a British-run detention facility in Iraq.[22]

The Court further clarified that, contrary to the dicta in *Banković* referred to above, in relation to 'state agent authority' jurisdiction, the State was under an obligation to secure to the individual in question only the rights and freedoms under Section I of the Convention that were relevant to his or her situation; in this sense, therefore, the Convention rights could be 'divided and tailored'.[23] This must be correct; for example, in irregular extradition cases like *Öcalan* and *Sánchez Ramírez*, the basis of jurisdiction is the taking of the applicant into custody and the only Convention rights that the State is in a position to secure are those related to the applicant's situation as a detainee. The position must be contrasted with

---

[18] ibid, paras 134–36.
[19] *Banković* (n 11) paras 36–37.
[20] *Öcalan v Turkey* (2005) 41 EHRR 45 (GC).
[21] *Sánchez Ramírez v France* App no 28780/95, Commission Decision of 24 June 1996, D&R 86-B, 155.
[22] *Al-Saadoon and Mufdhi v UK* (2010) 51 EHRR 9.
[23] *Al-Skeini* (n 17) paras 133–37.

'effective control of an area' jurisdiction, where the State with effective control is responsible for securing all the Convention rights and freedoms to the population concerned. The Court further made it clear that the application of the ECHR was not limited to the European '*espace juridique*', again as had already been apparent from the above irregular extradition cases.

The Court found that the United Kingdom had exercised jurisdiction over the applicants' relatives at the moments they were killed, because this occurred in the course of British security operations and because of the United Kingdom's prior assumption of responsibility for the maintenance of security in south-east Iraq. In this way the case was closer to *Drozd and Janousek v France and Spain*,[24] where, in accordance with customary law, French judges exercised judicial authority in Andorran courts, or *X and Y v Switzerland*,[25] where pursuant to treaty the Swiss immigration authorities operated to control immigration in Liechtenstein, than to the earlier Cyprus cases concerning military occupation. In the event, the Court did not make any finding as to whether the United Kingdom had effective control in the region at the relevant time. Such a finding would have appeared to be in contradiction to the evidence led in the domestic proceedings in the UK as to the extreme state of violence and anarchy that prevailed in south-east Iraq during the period of British administration.

It can be seen, however, that *Al-Skeini*, while clarifying and elaborating on the principles set out in *Banković*, did not represent a break with this previous case law. The examples given of state agent authority and control had all either been expressly set out by the Court in the *Banković* decision or cited by the respondent governments as well-established grounds of jurisdiction. The Grand Chamber in *Al-Skeini* did not find that the infliction of violence by a state agent was in itself sufficient to establish jurisdiction; there had to be some prior exertion of authority and control, such as an arrest or detention. Nor did it endorse the reasoning of an earlier Chamber judgment, *Issa v Turkey*, where the Court had formulated a much wider test of state agent authority, as follows:

> Moreover, a State may also be held accountable for violation of the Convention rights and freedoms of persons who are in the territory of another State but who are found to be under the former State's authority and control through its agents operating—whether lawfully or unlawfully—in the latter State (see, *mutatis mutandis, M. v. Denmark*, application no. 17392/90, Commission decision of 14 October 1992, DR 73, p. 193; *Illich Sanchez Ramirez v. France*, application no. 28780/95, Commission decision of 24 June 1996, DR 86, p. 155; *Coard et al. v. the United States*, the Inter-American Commission of Human Rights decision of 29 September 1999, Report No. 109/99, case No. 10.951, §§ 37, 39, 41 and 43; and the views adopted by the Human Rights Committee on 29 July 1981 in the cases of *Lopez Burgos v. Uruguay* and *Celiberti de Casariego v. Uruguay*, nos. 52/1979 and 56/1979, at §§ 12.3 and 10.3 respectively). Accountability in such situations stems from the fact that Article 1 of the Convention cannot be interpreted so as to allow a state party to perpetrate violations of the Convention on the territory of another State, which it could not perpetrate on its own territory (ibid.).[26]

---

[24] *Drozd and Janousek v France and Spain* (1992) 14 EHRR 745.
[25] *X and Y v Switzerland* App nos 7289/75 and 7349/76, Commission Decision of 14 July 1977, DR 9, 57.
[26] *Issa v Turkey* (2005) 41 EHRR 27, para 71.

In an interesting Concurring Opinion annexed to the judgment, Judge Bonello criticised the Court's case law on jurisdiction as lacking coherence. Instead of developing the exceptions to the territorial principle on a case-by-case basis, he urged the Court to adopt a 'functional jurisdiction' test[27] which is, in essence, the 'cause and effect' model of jurisdiction rejected by the Court in *Banković*.

The final case in this series is *Jaloud v the Netherlands*,[28] which also concerned the killing of an Iraqi national during the period of the United States and United Kingdom occupation and the alleged failure properly to investigate it. Following the declaration of the end of hostilities in May 2003, the Netherlands government contributed troops to the Stabilisation Force in Iraq (SFIR) and these were stationed in the south-eastern area under the command of an officer of the armed forces of the United Kingdom. The applicant's son was shot at a vehicle checkpoint under Netherlands command on the night of 21 April 2004. Earlier that same night the checkpoint had come under fire and the Iraqi soldiers stationed there had returned fire, apparently without causing casualties on either side. Netherlands servicemen had been called to the checkpoint to investigate that incident. Very shortly after they arrived, the car in which Mr Jaloud was sitting in the passenger seat approached the checkpoint at speed. The driver later submitted that he had not even seen it and he did not stop. The car came under fire, first from the contingent of Iraqi soldiers and then from a Netherlands soldier ('Lieutenant A'), who claimed to have thought that the shots fired by the Iraqis had come from inside the car. The car came to a halt and it became clear that Mr Jaloud had been mortally wounded. It was not possible to tell in the course of the subsequent investigation whether it was an Iraqi soldier or Lieutenant A who had fired the lethal shots.

Both the Netherlands government and the government of the United Kingdom, which intervened as a third party, disputed that the Netherlands had jurisdiction in respect of the incident. They reasoned that the case was distinguishable from *Al-Skeini* since the Netherlands had never assumed any of the public powers normally to be exercised by a sovereign government and since there had been no assertion of physical authority and control over Mr Jaloud before he was shot. The respondent government also insisted that the killing could not be attributed to the Netherlands, since the Netherlands troops in Iraq were under the command of the United Kingdom and since, in any event, the checkpoint had been manned by Iraqi soldiers, with the Netherlands troops present only to observe and advise.

The Grand Chamber recited the principles on jurisdiction set out in *Al-Skeini*. It went on to find that the shooting was attributable to the Netherlands, since it retained full command over its military personnel in Iraq and, in particular, had authority over the rules of engagement they followed. In addition, while the checkpoint where the shooting happened was manned by Iraqi personnel, they were under the command and direct supervision of a Netherlands Royal Army officer. The Court continued:

> The checkpoint had been set up in the execution of the SFIR's mission, under United Nations Security Council Resolution 1483 ... to restore conditions of stability and security

---

[27] Concurring Opinion of Judge Bonello in *Al-Skeini* (n 17) paras 3 ff.
[28] *Jaloud v The Netherlands* App no 47708/08 (GC, 20 November 2014).

conducive to the creation of an effective administration in the country. The Court is satisfied that the respondent Party exercised its 'jurisdiction' within the limits of its SFIR mission and for the purpose of asserting authority and control over persons passing through the checkpoint. That being the case, the Court finds that the death of Mr Azhar Sabah Jaloud occurred within the 'jurisdiction' of the Netherlands, as that expression is to be construed within the meaning of Article 1 of the Convention.[29]

The Grand Chamber's finding on jurisdiction was explained further in the Joint Concurring Opinion of Judges Casadevall, Berro-Lefevre, Šikuta, Hirvelä, López Guerra, Sajó and Silvis, as follows:

> This judgment establishes that a Contracting State may have its own jurisdiction under the Convention in respect of military operations conducted abroad as part of a stabilisation force in cooperation with another State which enjoys full status as an Occupying Power. Like the United States of America, the United Kingdom was an occupying power in Iraq in 2004 within the meaning of United Nations Security Council Resolution 483, whereas the Netherlands military merely assisted the United Kingdom in this occupation. However, the Netherlands authorities remained in full command of their military in the Iraqi province of Al Muthanna, and they exercised full authority and responsibility for establishing security in that region. Thus, Iraqi citizens passing a vehicle checkpoint between Ar Rumaythah and Hamsa, run by ICDC (Iraqi military) personnel who were operating under exclusive Netherlands command, found themselves within the jurisdiction of the Netherlands, as it is defined by the Court's interpretation of Article 1 of the Convention. We agree with this part of the judgment, which is in line with and logically builds on the Court's earlier case-law on jurisdiction, most notably *Al-Skeini and Others v the United Kingdom*.

Given that prior to the shooting there was no physical contact with or restraint placed on the deceased (indeed, the driver of the car gave evidence to the investigation that he had not even been aware of the checkpoint until his car came under fire), the decision on jurisdiction in *Jaloud* could be seen as a significant extension of the 'state agent authority' basis of jurisdiction, coming very close to the 'cause and effect' jurisdiction rejected by the Court in *Banković*. However, as explained in the Joint Concurring Opinion of Judge Casadevall et al, it may be better to see the finding of jurisdiction as grounded in the particular circumstances of the occupation of Iraq.

II. THE INTERPRETATION OF CONVENTION RIGHTS TO TAKE ACCOUNT OF THE CONTEXT OF ARMED CONFLICT

It can be seen, therefore, that the notion of 'jurisdiction' in Article 1 has been interpreted and applied by the Court to cover certain extraterritorial acts of a Contracting State's agents in the course of international armed conflict and belligerent occupation. This development has, however, been accompanied by a degree of recognition by the Court that the other Articles of the Convention should be interpreted and applied in a way which takes into account this particular context.

---

[29] ibid, para 152.

A mechanism exists in Article 15 ECHR to permit a State, '[i]n time of war or other public emergency threatening the life of the nation', to take measures derogating from certain of its obligations under the Convention 'to the extent strictly required by the exigencies of the situation'. No derogation is permitted from Article 2, 'except in respect of deaths resulting from lawful acts of war', or from Articles 3, 4(1) and 7.

However, there is some doubt as to whether Article 15 could apply in the context of an international armed conflict, since it could be argued that the words 'threatening the life of the nation' qualify 'war' as well as 'other public emergency' and that conflicts in countries remote from the Contracting State do not threaten its national life. In any event, the Court has never been called upon to decide this point since, as demonstrated by the research set out in *Hassan*,[30] States have not, to date, filed derogations under Article 15 in respect of their activities in international armed conflicts. Leaving aside a number of declarations made by the United Kingdom between 1954 and 1966 in respect of powers put in place to quell uprisings in a number of its colonies, the derogations made by Contracting States under Article 15 of the Convention have all made reference to emergencies arising within the territory of the derogating State.

In the absence of any derogation, the Court has been prepared, to a certain extent, to interpret the Convention rights in a manner which takes account of the military context and also, in certain conditions, the principles of international humanitarian law, including both the powers available to States in times of war and the obligations on them to minimise suffering.

A. The Substantive Aspect of Article 2 ECHR

This approach was first to be seen in relation to complaints of breaches of the right to life, protected by Article 2 ECHR, in the context of two conflicts that might be described as non-international armed conflicts. In *Ergi v Turkey*[31] the applicant's sister was killed during a bombardment of her village in south-eastern Turkey by Turkish soldiers who had set up an ambush purportedly to capture members of the PKK. When it examined whether the planning and conduct of the operation had been compatible with the State's duties under Article 2, the Court described the relevant legal principle as follows:

> [T]he responsibility of the State is not confined to circumstances where there is significant evidence that misdirected fire from agents of the State has killed a civilian. It may also be engaged where they fail to take all feasible precautions in the choice of means and methods of a security operation mounted against an opposing group with a view to avoiding and, in any event, to minimising, incidental loss of civilian life.

---

[30] *Hassan* (n 7) paras 40–42.
[31] *Ergi v Turkey* (2001) 32 EHRR 18, para 79.

Commentators[32] have noted that this test is strongly reminiscent of Additional Protocol I to the Geneva Conventions (1977). Article 57(2)(a)(ii) of the Protocol provides:

> Those who plan or decide upon an attack shall take all feasible precautions in the choice of means and methods of attack with a view to avoiding and, in any event, to minimizing, incidental loss of civilian life, injury to civilians and damage to civilian objects.

A similar approach was followed in two cases that arose out of the second Chechen war of 1999–2000. In *Isayeva v Russia*,[33] the applicant's village (Katyr-Yurt) was bombed by Russian forces seeking to kill Chechen rebels who had gathered there. When the applicant and her family, along with other villagers, sought to flee in the belief that the military had granted civilians safe passage, they again came under aerial attack. The applicant's 23-year-old son and three young nieces were killed. She complained before the Court of breaches by Russia of its obligations under Article 2 to protect her and her family's lives and to investigate the deaths of her son and nieces.

With regard to the substantive obligation to safeguard life, although Russia had not lodged any derogation under Article 15, the Court 'accept[ed] that the situation that existed in Chechnya at the relevant time called for exceptional measures by the State in order to regain control over the Republic and to suppress the illegal armed insurgency'. It continued:

> Given the context of the conflict in Chechnya at the relevant time, those measures could presumably include the deployment of army units equipped with combat weapons, including military aviation and artillery. The presence of a very large group of armed fighters in Katyr-Yurt, and their active resistance to the law-enforcement bodies, which are not disputed by the parties, may have justified use of lethal force by the agents of the State, thus bringing the situation within paragraph 2 of Article 2.[34]

Article 2(2) ECHR provides that a deprivation of life will not amount to a breach of the right to life when it results from a use of force which is 'no more than absolutely necessary' to defend a person from unlawful violence, or to effect a lawful arrest, or 'in action lawfully taken for the purpose of quelling a riot or insurrection'. In the Court's first judgment on Article 2, *McCann v UK*,[35] the Court explained that the term 'absolutely necessary' in Article 2(2) required it to assess whether the force used was 'strictly proportionate' to the achievement of the aims set out in sub-paragraphs 2(a), (b) and (c).

[32] A Reidy, 'The Approach of the European Commission and Court of Human Rights to International Humanitarian Law' (1998) 80 *International Review of the Red Cross* 513; E Tamura, 'The Isayeva Cases of the European Court of Human Rights: The Application of International Humanitarian Law and Human Rights Law in Non-International Armed Conflicts' (2011) 10 *Chinese Journal of International Law* 129.

[33] *Isayeva v Russia* (2005) 41 EHRR 38.

[34] ibid, paras 180–81.

[35] *McCann v UK* (1996) 21 EHRR 97, para 149.

In *Isayeva* the Court examined the evidence and concluded that it had been fore-seen that Chechen fighters would occupy the village and that the Russian military response had been planned. It continued:

> The Court regards it as evident that when the military considered the deployment of aviation equipped with heavy combat weapons within the boundaries of a populated area, they also should have considered the dangers that such methods invariably entail. There is however no evidence to conclude that such considerations played a significant place in the planning ...

> The Court considers that using this kind of weapon in a populated area, outside wartime and without prior evacuation of the civilians, is impossible to reconcile with the degree of caution expected from a law-enforcement body in a democratic society. No martial law and no state of emergency has been declared in Chechnya, and no derogation has been made under Article 15 of the Convention ... The operation in question therefore has to be judged against a normal legal background. Even when faced with a situation where, as the Government submit, the population of the village had been held hostage by a large group of well-equipped and well-trained fighters, the primary aim of the operation should be to protect lives from unlawful violence. The massive use of indiscriminate weapons stands in flagrant contrast with this aim and cannot be considered compatible with the standard of care prerequisite to an operation of this kind involving the use of lethal force by state agents ...

> To sum up, accepting that the operation in Katyr-Yurt on 4–7 February 2000 was pursuing a legitimate aim, the Court does not accept that it was planned and executed with the requisite care for the lives of the civilian population.[36]

In another judgment delivered that same day and arising out of the same conflict, *Isayeva v Russia*,[37] the applicants were part of a civilian convoy that left Grozny in October 1999, shortly after the start of hostilities, again believing that they would be granted safe passage, but again coming under missile attack from Russian air-craft. When the Court came to assess whether the use of force had been absolutely necessary, it set out a test similar to that in *Isayeva*:

> The Court accepts that the situation that existed in Chechnya at the relevant time called for exceptional measures on behalf of the State in order to regain control over the Republic and to suppress the illegal armed insurgency. These measures could presumably include employment of military aviation equipped with heavy combat weapons. The Court is also prepared to accept that if the planes were attacked by illegal armed groups, that could have justified use of lethal force, thus falling within paragraph 2 of Article 2.[38]

Later, having assessed the evidence, the Court concluded:

> In the absence of corroborated evidence that any unlawful violence was threatened or likely, the Court retains certain doubts as to whether the aim can at all be said to be applicable. However, given the context of the conflict in Chechnya at the relevant time, the Court will assume in the following paragraphs that the military reasonably considered that there was an attack or a risk of attack from illegal insurgents, and that the air strike was a legitimate response to that attack.[39]

---

[36] *Isayeva* (n 33) paras 189–200.
[37] ibid.
[38] ibid, para 178.
[39] ibid, para 181.

The Court's reasoning in this judgment has been interpreted by one commentator[40] as an indication that, in the context of a non-international armed conflict, the Court was applying a lower standard of necessity for the use of force than that set out and applied in the peacetime context of *McCann*. Thus it has been argued that if the Court had really been applying the *McCann* test of absolute necessity it would not so easily have accepted that the military 'reasonably' considered the occurrence of an attack or even a 'risk' of attack and that in the *Isayeva* cases 'the Court seems to interpret "absolute" necessity so liberally as to amount to substantially applying "reasonable" necessity, i.e. the necessity principle of [international humanitarian law]'.[41] However, this suggestion, while intriguing, is not supported by the reasoning in the rest of the *Isayeva* judgment. In the passage just quoted, the Court was merely stating that it would assume that the force had a legitimate aim. In subsequent paragraphs it went on to assess whether the use of force was proportionate to that aim, applying the 'absolute necessity' test of proportionality. This was also its subsequent practice in cases arising out of the conflict in Chechnya, where it clearly employed the 'absolute necessity' test in respect of situations involving a high degree of violence.[42] Furthermore, the Court's failure in *Ergi* and the *Isayeva* cases to assess whether the force used against the PKK or Chechen insurgents was 'absolutely necessary' cannot be seen as a sign that it was applying international humanitarian law principles to hold that enemy personnel were legitimate targets of military force. Instead, this omission is probably best explained by the fact that the applications were brought by civilians, or the relatives of civilians who had come under attack, in contrast to, for example, the situation in *McCann* where the application was brought by the relatives of the IRA members killed by United Kingdom security forces in the belief that they were on the point of detonating a bomb.

The Court did not expressly refer to the interrelationship between Article 2 and international humanitarian law until *Varnava v Turkey* in 2009. In that judgment, the Court stated that

> Article 2 must be interpreted so far as possible in light of the general principles of international law, including the rules of international humanitarian law which play an indispensable and universally accepted role in mitigating the savagery and inhumanity of armed conflict.[43]

The principal complaint in the case concerned the failure of the Turkish authorities to conduct an effective investigation into the fate of nine men who disappeared during the 1974 invasion of Cyprus. Two of the men were known to have been taken into Turkish custody, and the other seven were last seen in an area which shortly afterwards fell under the control of Turkish troops. In deciding whether Turkey bore

---

[40] Tamura (n 32).
[41] ibid 138.
[42] *Khatsiyeva v Russia* App no 5108/02 (17 January 2008), para 138; *Kerimova v Russia* App nos 17170/04, 20792/04, 22448/04, 23360/04, 5681/05 and 5684/05 (3 May 2011), paras 247–48.
[43] *Varnava v Turkey* App nos 16064/90, 16065/90, 16066/90, 16068/90, 16069/90, 16070/90, 16071/90, 16072/90 and 16073/90 (ECHR 2009), para 185.

the burden of proving what had happened to them, the Court relied on principles of international humanitarian law, holding that

> in a zone of international conflict Contracting States are under obligation to protect the lives of those not, or no longer, engaged in hostilities. This would also extend to the provision of medical assistance to the wounded; where combatants have died, or succumbed to wounds, the need for accountability would necessitate proper disposal of remains and require the authorities to collect and provide information about the identity and fate of those concerned, or permit bodies such as the ICRC to do so.

Although this was a step in the Court's reasoning leading to a finding of a breach of the procedural obligation under Article 2, the principles expressed would also apply in respect of the substantive obligation to protect life in a war zone.

B. The Procedural Obligation Under Article 2 ECHR

In the *McCann* judgment mentioned above, the Court held that, in addition to the substantive requirements under Article 2 to protect life and to refrain from the use of lethal force unless absolutely necessary, there is a procedural obligation to review the lawfulness of the use of lethal force by State authorities.[44] In subsequent cases, the Court has expressed the view that, where the killing took place in the course of an armed conflict, the context should be taken into account when assessing whether the State authorities did all that was required of them in relation to this procedural obligation.

In the *Al-Skeini* case discussed above, the killings to be investigated occurred in Basra in the aftermath of the invasion, during a period when serious crime and violence were endemic. Although major combat operations were declared to have been completed by 1 May 2003, the Coalition Forces in south-eastern Iraq, including British soldiers and military police, were the target of over a thousand violent attacks in the subsequent 13 months. In tandem with the security problems, there were serious breakdowns in the civilian infrastructure, including the law enforcement and criminal justice systems. The United Kingdom government argued that procedural duty should not be interpreted in such a way as to place an impossible or disproportionate burden on a Contracting State. If it were to apply extraterritorially, it had to take into account the fact that the United Kingdom had neither full control over the territory nor legislative, administrative or judicial competence. In response, the Court emphasised the importance of the duty to investigate killings by state agents, since without such investigations there would be a risk of impunity for the arbitrary use of lethal force. In order to be effective, the investigation had to be capable of showing whether the force used was justified and who should be held responsible if it was not, and this procedural obligation continued to apply even in situations of armed conflict.

The Court accepted that where the death to be investigated occurred in circumstances of generalised violence, armed conflict or insurgency, obstacles might be

---

[44] *McCann* (n 35) para 161.

placed in the way of investigators and concrete constraints might compel the use of less effective measures of investigation or may cause an investigation to be delayed. Nonetheless, the obligation under Article 2 to safeguard life entailed that, even in difficult security conditions, all reasonable steps had to be taken to ensure that an effective, independent investigation was conducted into alleged breaches of the right to life.[45]

When examining whether the procedural obligation was complied with in the applicants' cases, the Court took

> as its starting-point the practical problems caused to the investigating authorities by the fact that the United Kingdom was an Occupying Power in a foreign and hostile region in the immediate aftermath of invasion and war. These practical problems included the breakdown in the civil infrastructure, leading, inter alia, to shortages of local pathologists and facilities for autopsies; the scope for linguistic and cultural misunderstandings between the occupiers and the local population; and the danger inherent in any activity in Iraq at that time. As stated above, the Court considers that in circumstances such as these the procedural duty under Article 2 must be applied realistically, to take account of specific problems faced by investigators.

> Nonetheless, the fact that the United Kingdom was in occupation also entailed that, if any investigation into acts allegedly committed by British soldiers was to be effective, it was particularly important that the investigating authority was, and was seen to be, operationally independent of the military chain of command.[46]

The Court found that the investigation into each death was not sufficiently independent since the Special Investigations Branch of the Royal Military Police, which conducted the investigations, was not at the time operationally independent of the military chain of command.

In the *Jaloud* case, discussed above, the Court also found a violation of the procedural obligation under Article 2. The shooting at the checkpoint was investigated by officers of the Royal Military Constabulary, who arrived at the scene a couple of hours later. The applicant's son's body was initially taken to a camp hospital, then to the local Iraqi hospital, where a post mortem was carried out by an Iraqi doctor in the absence of a police witness. Statements were taken from the eye-witnesses, including Lieutenant A (the Netherlands soldier who had fired at the car). Three bullet fragments were sent by the Iraqi police to be tested in Baghdad, but it was impossible to determine what type of gun had fired them. Subsequently the fragments were mislaid. The investigation was closed in June 2004 and it was decided that no action should be taken against Netherlands personnel, on the supposition that Mr Jaloud had been hit by a bullet fired by Iraqi personnel and that Lieutenant A had acted in self-defence. The applicant challenged the prosecutor's decision before the Netherlands courts. On 7 April 2008 the Court of Appeal of Arnhem upheld the prosecutor's decision, finding that Lieutenant A had acted within the military instructions on the use of force in self-defence.

In response to the applicant's complaint that the investigation did not meet the standards of Article 2, the Strasbourg Court stated that it was 'prepared to

---

[45] *Al-Skeini* (n 17) paras 161–67.
[46] ibid, paras 168–69.

make reasonable allowances for the relatively difficult conditions under which the Netherlands military and investigators had to work' and in particular the fact that 'they were engaged in a foreign country which had yet to be rebuilt in the aftermath of hostilities, whose language and culture were alien to them, and whose population ... clearly included armed hostile elements'.[47] Despite this, the Court found that the investigation fell short of the expected standard in a number of ways: first, the Court of Appeal had not been provided with the statements taken from the Iraqi personnel present at the checkpoint; secondly, no precautions had been taken to prevent Lieutenant A colluding with other witnesses prior to his interview with the investigating officers at around 11 o'clock on the morning following the shooting; thirdly, no attempt was made to carry out the autopsy 'under conditions befitting an investigation into the possible criminal responsibility of an agent of the State' and the resulting report was inadequate; and fourthly, the bullet fragments had been lost.[48]

The seven judges who joined in the Concurring Opinion mentioned above agreed with the majority of the Court as regards the failure to provide the domestic Court of Appeal with the full file of witness statements. However, they considered that the majority judgment entered too much and too critically into the fine detail of the investigation, without making due allowance for the obstacles caused by the conflict situation. For example, the concurring judges considered that the majority, in criticising the autopsy, failed to take into account that there was no legal basis on which the Netherlands authorities could have claimed control over Mr Jaloud's body once it had been transferred to an Iraqi civilian hospital or insisted on the presence of an officer of the Royal Military Constabulary during the autopsy. In addition,

> according to the Government, the situation was becoming very tense: wider escalation might have followed if a confrontation had been sought; the Netherlands personnel who were present in the hospital reported their fear of being taken hostage and left the premises for that reason. Is this not an example of concrete constraints which may compel the use of less effective measures of investigation?

The minority judges also disagreed with the majority as regards the finding that the investigation was flawed because of the failure to isolate Lieutenant A prior to his questioning:

> This raises questions. Is it really within the competence of our Court to set the standards for investigations at this detailed level in unstable situations such as these which prevailed in Iraq? That would be a very hazardous exercise. It seems obvious that concerns for security at a vehicle checkpoint continued to exist while the investigations were going on. The witnesses to the incident were also responsible for that security. Separating all the witnesses on the spot could have interfered with that duty. Equally, to separate persons in a command position from their military personnel abruptly and in such an unstable environment seems rather dangerous. There were obviously more dimensions to be taken into account than just the investigation, and it is not easy to imagine all of them.[49]

---

[47] *Jaloud* (n 28) para 226.
[48] ibid, para 227.
[49] *Jaloud*, Joint Concurring Opinion of Judges Casadevall, Berro-Lefevre, Šikuta, Hirvelä, López Guerra, Sajó and Silvis, paras 7–8.

C. Article 5 ECHR

As far back as its 1976 judgment in *Engel v the Netherlands*,[50] the Court recognised that, even within a State's territory, the right to liberty under Article 5 may sometimes have to be 'tailored' to fit the particular circumstances of military service. However, it is not straightforward to interpret Article 5(1) in the light of international humanitarian law because of the Article's structure, which includes an exhaustive list of the circumstances in which it is permissible for a State to arrest and detain someone.

This question was raised in two more cases concerning the military activities of the British in Iraq. The applicant in *Al-Jedda v UK*[51] was held in internment by British forces in Basra between October 2004 and December 2007. During this period, the United Kingdom was no longer in occupation of Iraq and British troops remained in the country as part of the Multi-National Force at the request of the Iraqi government and pursuant to United Nations Security Council Resolution 1546, adopted on 8 June 2004, which decided inter alia that

> the Multinational Force shall have the authority to take all necessary measures to contribute to the maintenance of security and stability in Iraq in accordance with the letters annexed to this Resolution expressing, *inter alia*, the Iraqi request for the continued presence of the Multinational Force and setting out its tasks, including by preventing and deterring terrorism, so that, *inter alia*, the United Nations can fulfil its role in assisting the Iraqi people as outlined in paragraph 7 above and the Iraqi people can implement freely and without intimidation the timetable and programme for the political process and benefit from reconstruction and rehabilitation activities.

The respondent government agreed that the applicant's detention did not fall within any of the categories listed in sub-paragraphs (a) to (f) of Article 5(1) which, as the Court held, did not include 'internment or preventive detention where there is no intention to bring criminal charges within a reasonable time'.[52] However, it argued that the above Security Council Resolution placed the United Kingdom under an obligation to keep the applicant in internment and that, because of Article 103 of the United Nations Charter,[53] this obligation had to take primacy over the United Kingdom's obligations under Article 5 of the Convention.

The Court did not address the issue of whether the State's obligations under the United Nations Charter had to prevail over those under the Convention, because it did not find that, in this case, there was a conflict between the two. Instead it found that, since the United Nations was created to promote respect for human rights and fundamental freedoms, amongst other things, and since the Security Council was required by the Charter to 'act in accordance with the Purposes and Principles of the United Nations', there had to be a presumption, when interpreting its resolutions,

---

[50] *Engel v The Netherlands* (1979-80) 1 EHRR 647, para 59.
[51] *Al-Jedda v UK* (2011) 53 EHRR 23 (GC).
[52] ibid, para 100.
[53] Which states: 'In the event of a conflict between the obligations of the members of the United Nations under the present Charter and their obligations under any other international agreement, their obligations under the present Charter shall prevail.'

that the Security Council did not intend to impose any obligation on Member States to breach fundamental principles of human rights. In the event of any ambiguity in the terms of a United Nations Security Council resolution, the Court had therefore to choose the interpretation which was most in harmony with the requirements of the Convention and which avoided any conflict of obligations.

> In the light of the United Nations' important role in promoting and encouraging respect for human rights, it [was] to be expected that clear and explicit language would be used were the Security Council to intend States to take particular measures which would conflict with their obligations under international human rights law.[54]

The Court then examined the text of Security Council Resolution 1546 and found that, although the States which made up the Multi-National Force were instructed 'to take all necessary measures to contribute to the maintenance of security and stability in Iraq', this did not indicate unambiguously that the Security Council intended to place Member States under an obligation to use measures of internment without charge. The Court concluded that,

> [i]n the absence of clear provision to the contrary, the presumption must be that the Security Council intended States within the Multinational Force to contribute towards the maintenance of security in Iraq while complying with their obligations under international human rights law.[55]

The final case brought before the Court concerning the activities of United Kingdom forces in Iraq also concerned detention, albeit for a much shorter period. The brother of the applicant in *Hassan*[56] was captured by British soldiers approximately one month after the invasion of Iraq. The applicant was a senior member of the local Ba'ath Party and a General in the Party's private army. His brother was found by the British forces at the applicant's house, armed with a machine gun, and was taken into custody with a view to determining whether he should be held as a prisoner of war or as a civilian posing a threat to security, pursuant to the Third and Fourth Geneva Conventions. He was detained for just over a week as a United Kingdom prisoner in a United States-run camp (Camp Bucca) and questioned by British and United States military interrogators, and was released once it had been established that he had no intelligence value, was not a combatant and did not constitute a threat.

As in *Al-Jedda*, the Court held that detention with no intention to bring criminal charges, including detention under the powers provided for in the Third and Fourth Geneva Conventions, did not fall within the permitted grounds listed in Article 5(1). The United Kingdom had not purported to derogate under Article 15 from any of its obligations under Article 5. Instead, for the first time in a case before the Court, the respondent government requested that the Court disapply its obligations under Article 5 or in some other way to interpret them in the light of powers of detention available to it under international humanitarian law.

---

[54] *Al-Jedda* (n 51) para 102.
[55] ibid, para 105.
[56] *Hassan* (n 7).

The starting point for the Court's examination was its constant practice of interpreting the Convention in the light of the rules set out in the 1969 Vienna Convention on the Law of Treaties. Article 31(3) of the Vienna Convention provided that

> there shall be taken into account, together with the context, (a) any subsequent agreement between the parties regarding the interpretation of the treaty or the application of its provisions; (b) any subsequent practice in the application of the treaty which establishes the agreement of the parties regarding its interpretation; and (c) any relevant rules of international law applicable in the relations between the parties.

In relation to (b), as mentioned above, the Court found that the practice of the High Contracting Parties was not to derogate from their obligations under Article 5 in order to detain persons on the basis of the Third and Fourth Geneva Conventions during international armed conflicts. In relation to (c) it found that the principle that the Convention had to be interpreted in harmony with other rules of international law, of which it forms part, applied no less to international humanitarian law:

> The four Geneva Conventions of 1949, intended to mitigate the horrors of war, were drafted in parallel to the European Convention on Human Rights and enjoy universal ratification. The provisions in the Third and Fourth Geneva Conventions relating to internment, at issue in the present application, were designed to protect captured combatants and civilians who pose a security threat.[57]

The Court observed that it had to endeavour to interpret and apply the Convention in a manner which was consistent with the framework under international law delineated by the International Court of Justice, which had held that the protection offered by human rights conventions and that offered by international humanitarian law coexist in situations of armed conflict.[58] In the light of the above considerations, the Court accepted the government's argument that the lack of a formal derogation under Article 15 did not prevent it from taking account of the context and the provisions of international humanitarian law when interpreting and applying Article 5 in this case, although it emphasised that in future cases the provisions of Article 5 would be interpreted and applied in the light of the relevant provisions of international humanitarian law only where this was specifically pleaded by the respondent State, since it was not for the Court to assume that a State intended to modify the commitments which it had undertaken by ratifying the Convention in the absence of a clear indication to that effect.

The Court explained its approach to the coexistence of international humanitarian law powers of detention and Article 5 rights as follows:

> Nonetheless, and consistently with the case law of the International Court of Justice, the Court considers that, even in situations of international armed conflict, the safeguards under the Convention continue to apply, albeit interpreted against the background of the

---

[57] ibid, para 102.
[58] *The Legality of the Threat or Use of Nuclear Weapons* (Advisory Opinion), ICJ Rep 1996; *The Legal Consequences of the Construction of a Wall in the Occupied Palestinian Territory* (Advisory Opinion), ICJ Rep 2004; *Armed Activities on the Territory of the Congo (Democratic Republic of Congo (DRC) v Uganda)*, ICJ Rep 2005.

provisions of international humanitarian law. By reason of the co-existence of the safeguards provided by international humanitarian law and by the Convention in time of armed conflict, the grounds of permitted deprivation of liberty set out in subparagraphs (a) to (f) of that provision should be accommodated, as far as possible, with the taking of prisoners of war and the detention of civilians who pose a risk to security under the Third and Fourth Geneva Conventions. The Court is mindful of the fact that internment in peacetime does not fall within the scheme of deprivation of liberty governed by Article 5 of the Convention without the exercise of the power of derogation under Article 15 … It can only be in cases of international armed conflict, where the taking of prisoners of war and the detention of civilians who pose a threat to security are accepted features of international humanitarian law, that Article 5 could be interpreted as permitting the exercise of such broad powers.

As with the grounds of permitted detention already set out in those subparagraphs, deprivation of liberty pursuant to powers under international humanitarian law must be 'lawful' to preclude a violation of Article 5 § 1. This means that the detention must comply with the rules of international humanitarian law and, most importantly, that it should be in keeping with the fundamental purpose of Article 5 § 1, which is to protect the individual from arbitrariness.[59]

In respect of the procedural guarantees under paragraphs 2 and 4 of Article 5, the Court held:

[I]n relation to detention taking place during an international armed conflict, Article 5 §§ 2 and 4 must also be interpreted in a manner which takes into account the context and the applicable rules of international humanitarian law. Articles 43 and 78 of the Fourth Geneva Convention provide that internment 'shall be subject to periodical review, if possible every six months, by a competent body'. Whilst it might not be practicable, in the course of an international armed conflict, for the legality of detention to be determined by an independent 'court' in the sense generally required by Article 5 § 4 … nonetheless, if the Contracting State is to comply with its obligations under Article 5 § 4 in this context, the 'competent body' should provide sufficient guarantees of impartiality and fair procedure to protect against arbitrariness. Moreover, the first review should take place shortly after the person is taken into detention, with subsequent reviews at frequent intervals, to ensure that any person who does not fall into one of the categories subject to internment under international humanitarian law is released without undue delay.[60]

The Court considered that the applicant's brother's capture and detention had been consistent with the powers available to the United Kingdom under the Third and Fourth Geneva Conventions, and had not been arbitrary. It had not, therefore, given rise to a violation of Article 5(1).

III. CONCLUSION

In his speech at Essex University in January 2014,[61] Lord Dyson expressed the view that '[a]ll courts make mistakes from time to time' and that the reasoning in

---

[59] *Hassan* (n 7) paras 104–05.
[60] ibid, para 106.
[61] Above, n 2.

Bankovič had been one of those mistakes, which 'put the jurisprudence off course for around ten years'. He concluded, however, that,

> since *Al-Skeini*, it has now returned to a position that many would regard as more principled and more acceptable. It is likely that, if it were faced with the facts of *Bankovič* today, the Court would reach the same conclusion as it did in 2001, but its analysis would now depend on the degree of authority and control the respondent State exercised over the applicants, not where they were located or whether their cases could be squeezed into one of the exceptional categories to territorial jurisdiction.[62]

I have much sympathy for this view. Even though the Court in its judgments on extraterritorial jurisdiction still cites *Bankovič* and repeats some of the language used in that decision, it is clearly moving towards the more principled 'functional' approach advocated by Judge Bonello in his Concurring Opinion annexed to the *Al-Skeini* judgment.[63] This is not to say that, contrary to the outcome in *Bankovič*, any extraterritorial use of force by the State will give rise to a finding of jurisdiction. In the case law to date, the Court has consistently required either effective control over an entire region or effective authority and control over a person, in the form of detention, assumption of responsibility over a person or assumption of responsibility for public functions in relation to that person. It is clear, nonetheless, that this approach is sufficient to bring many acts of Contracting States' armed forces within the scope of the ECHR.

In the light of this, it is important that the ECtHR continues to take the special context of extraterritorial armed conflict into account when it interprets and applies the ECHR in such cases. The Grand Chamber's judgment in *Hassan*[64] was a milestone in this connection. One commentator has written of that judgment that 'its importance for anyone interested in extraterritoriality, detention and the relationship between international humanitarian law and international human rights law cannot be overstated'.[65] This was the first time that any international court had set out a detailed model of the interaction between humanitarian law and human rights in the context of an international armed conflict and applied it in a concrete case. The Court's judgment can be seen as a pragmatic step towards reconciling the two coexisting bodies of treaty law. It recognises the realities of wartime practice, while ensuring that individuals are not deprived of all protection of their human rights.

There are still, clearly, many unanswered questions; the Court's task is to rule on the specific complaints brought before it, and it does not usually give guidance on issues not raised by them. The interstate case of *Georgia v Russia (II)* is currently pending before the ECtHR Grand Chamber. In its admissibility decision of 13 December 2011[66] the Fifth Section of the Court summarised the parties' arguments on this topic, and in particular the Russian government's submission that as 'the conflict between Georgia and the Russian Federation was an international

---

[62] Lord Dyson (n 2) 19.
[63] Above, n 27.
[64] *Hassan* (n 7).
[65] L Hill-Cawthorne, *EJIL: Talk!* (16 September 2014), www.ejiltalk.org.
[66] *Georgia v Russia (II)* (2012) 54 EHRR SE10.

one, the events relating to it and the acts allegedly committed during it should be examined under the rules of international humanitarian law and not the provisions of the Convention'.[67] The Court decided to join this preliminary objection to the merits of the case. The Grand Chamber's judgment in this case, which raises complaints, inter alia, of breaches of Russia's substantive obligations under Articles 2, 3, 5 and 8 ECHR and Article 1 of Protocol No 1, relating to the killing, ill-treatment and detention of civilians and the destruction and looting of property, will raise the challenge for the Court further to elaborate on the framework set out in *Hassan*.

---

[67] ibid, para 69.

Part III

The Interplay of Human Rights in Europe: ECHR, EU and National Human Rights

13

Fundamental Rights, Not Euroscepticism: Why the UK Should Embrace the EU Charter of Fundamental Rights

SIONAIDH DOUGLAS-SCOTT

I. INTRODUCTION

THE UK EVINCES a certain amount of scepticism towards both human rights and Europe. Lord Mance remarked in a recent speech that 'the European flag does not fly over Whitehall buildings (which happen to include our Supreme Court), as it does in other European capitals'.[1] Taken together, the combination of human rights and Europe can become toxic for certain sections of British society. There has been much publicity about the plans of a Conservative government to repeal the UK Human Rights Act 1998 (HRA),[2] since its victory in the 2015 General Election. Such a move would considerably change the human rights landscape in the UK, and possibly jeopardise the UK's membership of the Council of Europe, and as a result its EU membership as well.

However, should the HRA be repealed, another European human rights charter would still remain in force in the UK—the EU Charter of Fundamental Rights (EUCFR). Perhaps, unsurprisingly, this instrument has also come under attack. The Conservative government plans a referendum on the UK's continued EU membership, and a vote to leave the EU would lead to the repeal or drastic amendment of all EU law currently applicable in the UK, including the EU Charter.[3] Furthermore, the same document that threatens to repeal the HRA also states:

> [We] are clear that our relationship with the EU will be renegotiated in the next parliament, and if there is anything in that relationship which encroaches upon our new human

---

[1] Lord Mance, 'Destruction or Metamorphosis of the Legal Order?' paper given at the World Policy Conference, Monaco, 14 December 2013, www.supremecourt.uk/docs/speech131214.pdf.

[2] The report detailing these plans, *Protecting Human Rights in the UK*, may be accessed at https://s3.amazonaws.com/s3.documentcloud.org/documents/1308198/protecting-human-rights-in-the-uk.pdf.

[3] For further clarification on the constitutional implications of a UK exit from the EU, see S Douglas-Scott, 'Constitutional Implications of a UK Exit from the EU: Some Questions That Really Must Be Asked' UK Const L Blog (17th Apr 2015) (available at http://ukconstitutionallaw.org).

rights framework, then that is something it will be open for us to address as part of the renegotiation.[4]

A more direct attack was made on the Charter by the 2014 recommendation of the House of Commons European Scrutiny Committee that legislation be passed by the UK Parliament disapplying the Charter in the UK.[5] The adoption of such legislation would place the UK in breach of its obligations under EU law and render it open to financial penalties. However, in the absence of a UK withdrawal from the EU (which may also be sought in due course, although it could be a long drawn out process),[6] legislative disapplication of the EU Charter, and repeal of the HRA, may be embraced by those seeking to remove European influence from British human rights law.

In this chapter I consider the impact of the Charter in the UK, arguing that the European Scrutiny Committee is misguided in its call for its disapplication. Much of the argument in the Committee's report targets a lack of clarity in certain aspects of the Charter, including a fear that it could be used to extend EU competences. The report also expresses some frustration that the UK's so-called 'opt-out', in Protocol 30 to the Lisbon Treaty, is in fact incapable of operating as such, despite the great claims made for it by some politicians at the time of its drafting. However, I argue that, while there are some uncertainties in the Charter's application, these are no greater than those that exist in human rights law generally, and the case law of the Court of Justice of the European Union (CJEU) is in any event clarifying this law. In contrast, however, we should be clear that the alternative of disapplying the Charter in the UK would lead to far greater legal uncertainty and also expose the UK to infringement actions which may lead to large fines for breaching EU law (Article 260 Treaty on the Functioning of the European Union (TFEU)). But crucially, the Committee report also ignores the important protections and safeguards that the Charter offers against an overreaching EU—safeguards which have become visible in cases such as *Digital Rights Ireland*,[7] in which the CJEU invalidated an EU measure in its entirety for failing to comply with the Charter. These safeguards are particularly important in the absence of EU accession to the ECHR. Sections II to V of this chapter enlarge on these arguments, while the last section (VI) considers the Committee's recommendation as a part of a broader euroscepticsm about fundamental rights, both within the UK and in the EU more generally.

---

[4] ibid.

[5] House of Commons European Scrutiny Committee, 43rd report, *The Application of the EU Charter of Fundamental Rights in the UK: A State of Confusion* (HC 979).

[6] The procedure whereby a State may choose to leave the EU is set out in Art 50 Treaty on European Union (TEU), and is long and complex.

[7] Case C-293/12 *Digital Rights Ireland* [2014] ECR I-0000.

II. THE UK AND THE EU CHARTER: A TWISTED
AND TORMENTED RELATIONSHIP?

A. The Importance of the Charter

Why should there be animosity towards the EU Charter? The Charter became legally binding on 1 December 2009,[8] nine years after it was first declared by EU Institutions. It is undeniable that both the CJEU and national courts are now frequently confronted with arguments based on the Charter and have no choice but to work with fundamental rights aspects of EU law. Eurosceptics have woken up to the existence of the Charter. Indeed, in some ways, the Charter provides a stronger source of human rights than the HRA, and there are at least three reasons why the Charter may appear more threatening as a fundamental rights instrument than the HRA.

First, the Charter binds the EU itself, and provides an additional source of human rights law, as it importantly includes rights that are not in the European Convention on Human Rights (ECHR). Second, even where the Charter makes reference to rights similar or identical to the ECHR, under Article 52(3) EUCFR it may set higher standards than in the ECHR. Third, when the Charter applies, it can be directly enforced in national courts, which can set aside incompatible national law due to the supremacy of EU law; in contrast, under the HRA, which protects parliamentary sovereignty, UK courts may only issue a declaration of incompatibility, and may not set aside incompatible national law. For these reasons, the Charter provokes fear in the hearts of some. However, a resolution to pass legislation to disapply the Charter is an extreme measure, and further investigation is necessary to probe the motivations for such a move.

B. Background to the Charter

Fundamental rights were not a pressing concern in the early European Economic Community (EEC). The original EEC Treaty was an economic treaty of limited ambitions, which aimed to create a common market. There were no sections on fundamental rights because the EEC founders did not think this relevant to a treaty with mainly economic aspirations. The ECHR was also, of course, already in existence and probably thought sufficient to operate as a 'bill of rights' for Europe. Over time, however, the scope of the EU Treaties has come to extend far beyond purely economic matters. EU law today covers many fields capable of having a human rights dimension. Cases have been heard by the CJEU concerning eg equal treatment of transsexuals (*Grant*), economic sanctions on possible terrorist activities (*Kadi I* and *Kadi II*), and the issue of whether one has an online right to be forgotten

---

[8] ie, with the coming into force of the Lisbon Treaty.

(*Google Spain*).[9] The increased competences of the EU have ensured that a breach of fundamental rights by the Union is not merely a theoretical possibility. However, in spite of this, the EU only proclaimed its own Charter of Fundamental Rights in December 2000. Notably, the Union also continues to lack a general legislative competence in the field of human rights.[10]

The Charter was 'solemnly proclaimed' by the European Parliament, Commission and Council of Ministers at Nice in December 2000. The Cologne European Council in 1999 had set out the main objective for a Charter, which was that 'the fundamental rights applicable at Union level should be consolidated in a Charter and thereby made more evident'.[11] This was not such a bad objective, given that protection of fundamental rights for the first 40 years of European integration developed through the case law of the European Court of Justice in a somewhat ad hoc, and certainly complicated way; as a result it was uncertain which rights EU citizens possessed, and when they could enforce them—a fact which supported the case for the EU Charter. However, from the start, the British government's attitude to the EU Charter was hardly positive. In October 2000, Keith Vaz, then Minister of State for Europe, remarked of the Charter that: 'This is not a litigator's charter. Nobody can sue on the basis of it.' He famously claimed that it had no more legal effect than a copy of *The Beano*.[12] And in spite of the fact that the Charter was drafted from the outset 'as if' incorporated into the Treaties, the government made clear that it would veto any attempt to make it legally binding. Tony Blair, for example, stated in December 2000 that 'Our case is that it should not have legal status, and we do not intend it to'.[13] There was surely something ironic about this pronouncement: support being given by the UK government for the Charter only if it had no effect.

In any event, the Charter had no binding legal effect in EU law until the Lisbon Treaty came into force in 2009. It was six years before the Court of Justice itself, as opposed to its Advocates General, or the Court of First Instance (as it then was), even referred to the Charter at all—it first being mentioned in *Parliament v Council*.[14] However, thereafter the Court's references kept coming. Yet the UK government's attitude did not become more benign towards the Charter.

C. The UK and Polish Protocol

At a European Council meeting in June 2007, then Prime Minister Tony Blair claimed that he had secured a legally binding 'opt-out' from the EU Charter in

---

[9] Case C-249/96 *Grant v South West Trains* [1998] ECR I-621; Case C-402/05 *Kadi v Council and Commission* [2008] ECR I-6351; Case C-131/12 *Google Spain, Google v Agencia Espanola de Protection de Datos* [2014] ECR I-0000.

[10] Although Art 19 TFEU constitutes what is, in essence, a general competence for equality legislation.

[11] See European Council Decision on the drawing up of a Charter of Fundamental Rights of the European Union, europa.eu.int/council/off/conclu/june99/june99_en.htm.

[12] George Jones and Ambrose Evans-Pritchard, 'European Summit Charter on Rights "No More Binding than the Beano"' *The Telegraph* (London, 14 October 2000), www.telegraph.co.uk/news/worldnews/europe/1370340/European-summit-Charter-on-rights-no-more-binding-than-the-Beano.html.

[13] HC Deb 11 December 2000, vol 359, col 354.

[14] Case C-540/03 *Parliament v Council (Immigration Policy)* [2006] ECR I-5769, para 38.

the Lisbon Treaty, through a joint UK and Polish Protocol to the Treaties. 'It is absolutely clear,' stated Mr Blair in response to questions in Parliament, 'that we have an opt-out from … the charter.'[15] This document takes the form of Protocol 30 Treaty of Lisbon[16] and reads as follows:

Article 1

1. The Charter does not extend the ability of the Court of Justice of the European Union, or any court or tribunal of Poland or of the United Kingdom, to find that the laws, regulations or administrative provisions, practices or action of Poland or of the United Kingdom are inconsistent with the fundamental rights, freedoms and principles that it reaffirms.
2. In particular, and for the avoidance of doubt, nothing in Title IV of the Charter creates justiciable rights applicable to Poland or the United Kingdom except in so far as Poland or the United Kingdom has provided for such rights in its national law.

Article 2

To the extent that a provision of the Charter refers to national laws and practices, it shall only apply to Poland or the United Kingdom to the extent that the rights or principles that it contains are recognised in the law or practices of Poland or of the United Kingdom.

It has long been argued that the so-called 'opt-out' from the Charter is no such thing.[17] But it is only since the Lisbon Treaty entered into force on 1 December 2009 and the Charter became legally binding that the point has become more significant. Yet, as the European Scrutiny Committee stated in its 2014 report, there appears to be some confusion as to the exact status of the Charter in the UK. The Committee's inquiry and report was prompted by a sequence of events in November 2013 that in turn related to an earlier case, which will now be detailed.

D. The Charter in the UK Courts

Further back, in 2010, in the UK High Court case of *R (Saeedi) v Secretary of State for the Home Department*,[18] Cranston J held that, given the wording of the Polish and UK Protocol, the Charter 'cannot be directly relied on as against the United Kingdom, although it is an indirect influence as an aid to interpretation'. However, on appeal, the government no longer sought to support such a finding. The Home Secretary accepted that,

in principle … fundamental rights set out in the Charter can be relied upon against the United Kingdom, and submits that the Judge erred in holding otherwise … The purpose of

---

[15] HC Deb 25 June 2007, vol 462, cols 37 and 39.
[16] Protocol No 30 on the Application of the Charter of Fundamental Rights of the European Union to Poland and the United Kingdom [2010] OJ C83/313.
[17] See, for example, the evidence given to the House of Lords EU Select Committee, 10th Report of Session 2007–08, *The Treaty of Lisbon: An Impact Assessment*, vol I: Report, 13 March 2008 (HL Paper 62-I).
[18] *R (Saeedi) v Secretary of State for the Home Department* [2010] EWHC 705 (Admin).

the Charter Protocol is not to prevent the Charter from applying to the United Kingdom, but to explain its effect.[19]

This would appear to be an important concession that Protocol 30 did not function as an 'opt-out'. This interpretation was confirmed when *Saeedi* was referred to the CJEU (where it became the *NS* case). In *NS*, the CJEU held: 'Protocol (No 30) does not call into question the applicability of the Charter in the United Kingdom or in Poland, a position which is confirmed by the recitals in the preamble to that protocol.'[20] One might have thought that the matter was settled. However, in 2013, we find Mostyn J in some confusion in another UK High Court case, *R (AB) v Secretary of State for the Home Department*, in which he stated: 'I was sure that the British government had secured ... an opt-out from the incorporation of the Charter into EU law and thereby via operation of the European Communities Act 1972 directly into our domestic law.' However Mostyn J went on to state that, as a result of the judgment of the CJEU in *NS*, '[n]otwithstanding the endeavours of our political representatives at Lisbon it would seem that the much wider Charter of Rights is now part of our domestic law'.[21]

This particular statement helped to reignite the debate as to whether Protocol No 30 functions to exclude the application of the EU Charter within the UK. However, Mostyn J's comments were themselves surprising to those who never believed that the UK had secured an opt-out from the operation of the Charter. For example, the House of Commons European Scrutiny Committee itself, in its Third Report of 2007, stated:

> It is clear that the Government accepts that the Charter will be legally binding, and it has stated that the Protocol is not an opt-out. Since the Protocol is to operate subject to the UK's obligations under the Treaties, it still seems doubtful to us that the Protocol has the effect that the courts of this country will not be bound by interpretations of measures of Union law given by the [CJEU] and based on the Charter.[22]

In the 2012 case of *Rugby Football Union v Consolidated Information Services*, the UK Supreme Court confirmed that the Charter takes effect in national law, 'binding Member States when they are implementing EU law'.[23]

E. Contradiction and Confusion: European Scrutiny Committee 2014 Report

Notwithstanding its 2007 report, confusion about the Charter's status led the European Scrutiny Committee to comment on 'an urgent need for clarification' and to conduct its enquiry and publish its 2014 report. Contradictory statements from successive governments about whether Protocol 30 was an opt-out had contributed

---

[19] *R (Saeedi) v Secretary of State for the Home Department* [2010] EWCA Civ 990, paras 6 and 7.
[20] Joined Cases C-411/10 *NS v Secretary of State for the Home Department* and C-493/10 *ME* [2011] ECR I-13905, para 119.
[21] *R (AB) v Secretary of State for the Home Department* [2013] EWHC 3453, para 14.
[22] European Scrutiny Committee, Third Report of Session 2007–08, *EU Intergovernmental Conference: Follow-Up Report*, HC 16-iii, para 38.
[23] *Rugby Football Union v Consolidated Information Services* [2012] UKSC 55, paras 26–28.

to widespread confusion about its purpose. In addition, the coalition government did little to explain the effect of the Charter. Indeed, whilst the former Secretary of State for Justice, Chris Grayling, was correct to say in the debate in the House of Commons in November 2013 that Protocol 30 was not an opt-out, he continued:

Of course [the Charter] now does have legal force in European law. The issue is about whether that legal force extends to UK law. We regard that matter as being exceptionally important. If there were any question of that linkage being made, we would have to take steps on it ... I am absolutely clear that the Charter should not apply in UK law, and we would take serious action if there were any suggestion that it could do.[24]

Such a statement denies the supremacy of EU law and potentially places the UK in breach of it.

The European Scrutiny Committee's 2014 report was clear that the UK had not secured an opt-out, but did stress that many of the Charter's effects were unclear. It requested that the UK government set out its legal position as regards the correct interpretation of the Charter. While the UK government is apparently planning to intervene in cases concerning the Charter, in order to clarify its scope of application in particular, the Committee did not believe that this was likely to be successful. Therefore it concluded:

[I]n particular in relation to the field of application, and the certainty that the jurisdiction of the ECJ will range across an even wider field with increasingly unintended consequences, *we recommend that primary legislation is introduced by way of amendment to the European Communities Act 1972 to exclude, at the least, the applicability of the Charter in the UK.* This is what most people thought was the effect of Protocol 30. They were wrong. It is not an opt-out, but for the sake of clarity and for the avoidance of doubt we urge the Government to amend the European Communities Act 1972, as we propose.[25]

In summary, therefore: the European Scrutiny Committee recommended in its April 2014 report that the UK pass an Act of Parliament to disapply the EUCFR in the UK. Its main criticism was the state of confusion as to the effect of the Charter in UK law. In particular, it expressed concern as to the scope of the Charter's application, its distinction between rights and principles, its ability to go beyond the ECHR, and its capacity to have horizontal application. A continued concern of the Committee seems to be a suspicion of the CJEU's willingness to develop the Charter in an expansive manner. I gave evidence to the European Scrutiny Committee[26] in preparation for its 2014 report and I believe they are wrong in their conclusions, for reasons I will now discuss.

---

[24] HC Deb 19 November 2013, vol 570, col 1091.
[25] *The Application of the EU Charter* (n 5) 58, para 172 (emphasis added).
[26] When I gave my opinion on the feasibility of primary UK legislation disapplying the Charter, I was met with very short shrift: '*Professor Douglas-Scott:* (Why would you want to do this?) To disapply those very constraints that operate on the European Union, which are ways of lessening the competences of the EU and keeping a brake on it through the application of fundamental rights, strikes me as a rather curious thing to do. *Chair:* I will pass on to the next professor at that point.' Transcript of oral evidence, data. parliament.uk/writtenevidence/committeeevidence.svc/evidencedocument/european-scrutiny-committee/ the-application-of-the-eu-charter-of-fundamental-rights-in-the-uk/oral/5574.pdf.

There are three major problems with their suggestion.

1. Although the Committee rightly identifies confusion as to some aspects of the Charter's application in the UK, its recommendations would not remedy this. Indeed, the Committee's approach risks creating further confusion (section III below).
2. Its suggestion is particularly troubling, in that it recommends that the UK conspicuously breach EU law, ultimately risking large fines (section IV below).
3. Most importantly, human rights-based arguments militate against the disapplication of the Charter (section V below).

III. CONFUSION ABOUT THE CHARTER

Is the Charter a dangerously confusing document? I argue that it is not, and consider the contentions of the European Scrutiny Committee in turn.

A. Scope of Application of the Charter

Article 51(2) EUCFR provides:

> The Charter does not extend the field of application of Union law beyond the powers of the Union or establish any new power or task for the Union, or modify powers and tasks as defined in the Treaties.

Nonetheless, the Committee was particularly concerned that the Charter's potential scope was far too broad, thus risking interfering with national competences, and a good part of its investigation was concerned with this point. Yet the Charter is clearly not an instrument of limitless general review. Article 51(1) EUCFR specifies that it is 'addressed to the institutions ... of the Union ... and to the *Member States only when they are implementing Union law*'.[27] This, in turn, begs the question of what exactly is covered by Member States in the act of implementing EU law. In this context, we should note that the Charter's Official Explanations[28] potentially go further than Article 51(1), stating that the Charter is 'binding on Member States when they act *within the scope* of Union law',[29] citing previous case law of the CJEU to that effect, and the European Court of Justie (ECJ) has now confirmed the correctness of this approach in *Åkerberg Fransson*.

(i) *Åkerberg Fransson*[30]

But there is more than just the wording of Article 51(1), for CJEU case law now exists. The leading case on the interpretation of Article 51(1) is now *Åkerberg*

---

[27] Emphasis added.
[28] Official Explanations relating to the Charter of Fundamental Rights [2007] OJ C303/02.
[29] Emphasis added.
[30] Case C-617/10 *Åkerberg Fransson* [2013] ECR I-0000.

Fransson, in which the Swedish referring court asked the CJEU whether the principle of double jeopardy, in Article 50 EUCFR, could be used to set aside domestic law. Fransson had provided false information to the revenue authorities, and had already incurred an administrative penalty, but additionally faced criminal prosecution for the same misconduct. The Swedish court was uncertain whether the Charter applied, as it was unclear whether the Swedish dual system of tax penalties fell within the 'implementation of Union law'. However, EU law was clearly of some relevance in that Directive 2006/112 entitles States to 'impose other obligations which they deem necessary to ensure the correct collection of VAT and to prevent evasion'. Was this sufficient to bring the Swedish tax law within the scope of the Charter? The CJEU decided that it was. It highlighted that provisions of EU law require Member States to collect VAT and prevent VAT evasion, and noted that any shortcoming in the domestic collection of VAT affects the EU budget, and so, even if the Swedish legislation was not designed to transpose Directive 2006/112, its application penalised the infringement of that Directive and, as a result, the Charter applied.[31]

Åkerberg Fransson has been criticised by those who think it broadens the scope of application of the EU Charter. However, we should not necessarily jump to the conclusion that *Åkerberg Fransson* illustrates an expansive approach to EU competences. As Paul Craig has pointed out:

> The determinative issue is therefore not whether the Swedish law in issue in *Åkerberg Fransson* was itself enacted to implement the VAT directive, but whether *it was being used to implement* the obligations flowing from the directive, which it clearly was. The contrary conclusion entails the following untenable proposition: the Charter would be triggered if a Member State chose to implement the relevant obligations by, for example, enacting discrete legal provisions dealing with the enforcement obligation solely in relation to the EU VAT directive, but it would not be applicable if the Member State chose to meet the obligations through application of existing enforcement rules to EU VAT, even though the content of the rules is the same. Nor with respect do I agree with the view that the interaction between the national law and EU law was in some way merely incidental in *Åkerberg Fransson*. VAT is a primary source of EU revenue, and the penalty regime for evasion is therefore central to that revenue base.[32]

We may also note that the UK did not intervene in *Åkerberg Fransson*, an option open to it if it wished to contest the application of the Charter. The UK government has also accepted *Åkerberg Fransson* as a legitimate decision, in contrast to the European Scrutiny Committee's report, which states: 'We question the legitimacy of the ECJ's approach in *Åkerberg Fransson* and … and disagree with some of the expert evidence we took on this point.'[33]

In any event, in more recent case law, the CJEU has taken a more limited approach to the scope of the Charter. The *Siragusa* case,[34] subsequent to *Åkerberg*

---

[31] The Court held that Art 50 EUCFR (double jeopardy principle) did not in this case preclude Sweden from imposing a combination of administrative tax penalties and criminal penalties.

[32] Paul Craig, Submission of Evidence to European Scrutiny Committee January 2014 (second submission), para 6, http://data.parliament.uk/writtenevidence/committeeevidence.svc/evidencedocument/european-scrutiny-committee/the-application-of-the-eu-charter-of-fundamental-rights-in-the-uk/written/5176.html.

[33] *The Application of the EU Charter* (n 5) 57.

[34] Case C-206/13 *Siragusa* [2014] ECR I-0000.

Fransson, illustrates this. Mr Siragusa had built on a protected site without planning permission and was required to destroy his buildings. He argued that this violated his property rights, and a reference was made to ask the CJEU whether the national decision breached Article 17 EUCFR, the right to property. According to the CJEU, the Charter could not be invoked, as there were insufficient links to EU law. Siragusa relied on several different EU measures, but the Court ruled that none of these were sufficient to provide the required link with EU law, as none was 'intended to implement' EU law. None of the EU measures referred to by Siragusa imposed specific obligations to protect the landscape, even though landscape protection is referred to in several EU legal instruments.[35]

(ii) Lack of References to the Charter in the Context of the Eurozone Crisis

We may also find other evidence of the CJEU's cautious approach to the Charter's scope. For example, the CJEU has not referred to the Charter in the context of the Eurozone crisis. The scope and impact of the measures taken by the EU in its attempts to solve this crisis have been formidable, considering, for example, 'conditionality' clauses in bailout agreements. Many of these measures appear to bring the EU into conflict with both human rights and its own Treaties. For example, those clauses which impose restrictions on collective bargaining show little concern for freedom of association recognised in the ECHR and EU Charter of Fundamental Rights. Yet the CJEU has refused to rule on whether such austerity measures breach the Charter. This was notable in the *Pringle* case,[36] where the Court held that the Treaty Establishing the European Stability Mechanism did not breach the principle of effective judicial protection under Article 47 EUCFR because the Member States were not implementing Union law within the meaning of Article 51(1) of the Charter. As Barnard suggests,[37] however, ultimately, such an approach, with crisis-related measures in the slow lane, is not legally, politically or practically sustainable.

So the European Scrutiny Committee's assumption that the Court's jurisdiction regarding the Charter will apply to 'an ever wider field with increasingly unintended consequences' is not supported by the facts. It is further notable that in many other cases, arguments alleging the incompatibility of national measures with the Charter have been dismissed by the CJEU, often in summary fashion or by reasoned order,[38] and that such an approach may be criticised for being unduly restrained. It therefore cannot be argued that, contra Article 51(2), the Charter is being used to create new

---

[35] eg Directive 2011/92 on environmental impact assessment and Directive 2003/4 on environmental information.

[36] The *Pringle* case concerned the European Stability Mechanism (ESM) Treaty. However, many other of the Eurocrisis measures, such as the 2011 measures colloquially known as the 'Six-Pack', are measures of EU law. And yet challenges brought on the basis of the Charter have not been accepted.

[37] Catherine Barnard, 'The Charter, the Court—and the Crisis', University of Cambridge Faculty of Law Research Paper No 18/2013, http://papers.ssrn.com/sol3/papers.cfm?abstract_id=2306957.

[38] eg Case C-27/11 *Vinkov* [2012] ECR I-0000, para 59; see also orders in Case C-339/10 *Estov* [2010] ECR I-11465, para 14; Case C-457/09 *Chartry* [2011] ECR I-819, para 25; Case C-314/10 *Pagnoul*, [2011] ECR I-136, para 24.

competences for the EU. In conclusion, the prospect of an activist CJEU pushing for a broader competence for fundamental rights is rather slim.

B. Relationship Between the Charter and the ECHR

Another concern of the European Scrutiny Committee appears to be the Charter's ability to transcend the ECHR. The Charter does this by providing an additional source of human rights law: it includes rights which are not specifically mentioned in the ECHR, and can go beyond the protection afforded by the ECHR. Article 52(3) EUCFR clarifies explicitly that, even where the Charter's rights are similar in content to those of the ECHR, it can set higher standards than the ECHR. I argue, contrary to the European Scrutiny Committee's conclusions, that the Charter is to be welcomed in presenting a more contemporary, relevant catalogue of fundamental rights than the mid-twentieth-century ECHR.

Some of the new rights in the Charter are specifically introduced to deal with contemporary problems such as protection of personal data, given the proliferation of information about persons in the EU,[39] and new innovations in bioethics, such as cloning.[40] The Charter is also innovative in that it contains, in a single instrument, both economic and social rights along with the more traditional civil and political rights, which has never been done before in a European human rights instrument. In this way the Charter presents in sharpest relief the *indivisibility* of human rights.

Yet is the existence of a larger body of rights in the Charter a fact to be condemned? The ECHR reflects the time and circumstances of its drafting, and things have moved at a very rapid pace since then. Why should the efforts of the Charter to deal with pressing contemporary issues in biotechnology be regretted? Is the acknowledgement of social rights to be lamented, particularly when the Charter hedges them with the sop to eurosceptics of their limited protection (that is, only 'in accordance with national laws and practices') and the fact that they may well be protected only as 'principles' rather than 'rights'?[41]

Furthermore, although Article 52(3) EUCFR states that the Charter can set higher standards than the ECHR, it also specifies that, insofar as its rights correspond to those in the ECHR, the meaning and scope of those rights 'shall be the same as those laid down by the said convention'. In *Dereci*[42] and *J McB*,[43] the CJEU added

---

[39] Art 8 EUCFR states that 'Everyone has the right to the protection of personal data concerning him or her'. The Schengen Information System or Europol collect information on individuals.

[40] Art 3(2) EUCFR (right to the integrity of the person) states that, inter alia, the following must be respected: '(b) the prohibition of eugenic practices, in particular those aiming at the selection of persons; (c) the prohibition on making the human body and its parts as such a source of financial gain; (d) the prohibition of the reproductive cloning of human beings.'

[41] See eg Art 30 EUCFR (protection in the event of unjustified dismissal): 'Every worker has the right to protection against unjustified dismissal, in accordance with Union law and national laws and practices.' In this case, the acknowledgement of the right is heavily tempered with the obligation that it operate within the frame of national laws and practices. For more detail see C below.

[42] Case C-256/11 *Dereci* [2011] ECR I-11315, para 70.

[43] Case C-400/10 *J McB v LE* [2010] ECR I-8965, para 53.

the proviso that the meaning and scope of those rights should be the same as that interpreted by the case law of the European Court of Human Rights (ECtHR). This approach increases the coherence of European fundamental rights law. We might also add that, given that the EU will accede to the ECHR,[44] thereby exposing EU law to the full scrutiny of the ECtHR, it might be desirable for the CJEU to take full account of the ECHR, in order to diminish a future risk of having to accept a reversal of case law.

C. The Distinction Between Rights and Principles

The Committee argues that the Charter's distinction between rights and principles is unclear. This is true. Article 52(5) EUCFR provides that: 'The provisions of this Charter which contain principles may be implemented by legislative and executive acts ... They shall only be judicially cognizable in the interpretation of such acts and in the ruling on their legality.' In other words, rights which are 'principles' are deemed incapable of creating any directly enforceable rights.

Rather unhelpfully, Article 52(5) does not indicate which provisions are 'rights' and which are 'principles'. It is often suggested that 'principles' refer to economic, social and cultural rights,[45] although only three provisions in the Charter explicitly use the word 'principle'.[46] The Charter's accompanying explanations are of little help, especially as they note that some Articles may contain both rights and principles.[47] This leaves scope for the CJEU to resolve such questions in its case law. Although the distinction between rights and principles was an important argument in the *Association de Médiation Sociale (AMS)*[48] case, the Court did not in *AMS* follow the reasoning of AG Cruz Villalón, who considered whether Article 27 should be considered a 'right' or 'principle' (and concluded that it should be understood as a principle but that did not prevent the invocation of the Article). The CJEU, however, did not discuss the distinction between rights and principles at all. So the distinction remains obscure, and it represents a confusion the Committee rightly regrets.[49]

However, this confusion arises from the supranational nature of the EU and the differing perceptions of rights and consequences attached to principles among some members of the Charter's drafting team. Indeed, it seems that the distinction was a matter that the drafters of the Charter could not agree upon, and deliberately left to the Court to decide.[50]

---

[44] Art 6(2) TEU.

[45] See, further, S Douglas-Scott, 'The EU and Human Rights after the Treaty of Lisbon' (2011) 11 *Human Rights Law Review* 645, 652.

[46] Arts 23, 37 and 47.

[47] For instance, Arts 23, 33 and 34.

[48] Case C-176/12 *Association de Médiation Sociale* [2014] ECR I-0000.

[49] Also, in the earlier Case C-282/10 *Dominguez* [2012] ECR I-0000, AG Trstenjak interpreted Art 31(2) EUCFR on paid annual leave as a right rather than a principle, but the Court did not rule on the matter.

[50] C Ladenberger, *Protection of Fundamental Rights Post-Lisbon: The Interaction between the Charter of Fundamental Rights, the ECHR and National Constitutions*, Institutional Report XXV FIDE Congress, 30 May–2 June 2012, 32.

D. Horizontal Effect

The European Scrutiny Committee was also concerned about the Charter's potential horizontal effect, stating:

> [W]e are concerned, again, by the legal uncertainty that surrounds this principle. Private individuals and bodies (including employers and their employees) may as a consequence find it difficult to predict whether they may assert a legal right or be vulnerable to legal liability because of the Charter's application.[51]

Given that Article 51(1) limits the legal effect of Charter rights to EU institutions and bodies, and to Member States only when implementing Union law, it might be thought that the Charter could not bind private parties. However, some Charter Articles strongly suggest horizontal effect. For example, Article 23 requires equality to be ensured between men and women 'in *all* areas' and Article 24(2) covers actions relating to children 'whether taken by public authorities *or private institutions*'.[52] An argument can also be mounted that if the Charter is 'addressed to the institutions and bodies of the Union' this includes the Court of Justice itself, and the question of horizontal effect is thereby left to the Court to decide. Such an approach would follow that of the UK's HRA, which imposes obligations on public authorities but leaves room for the courts, which are themselves public authorities under section 6(3)(a) HRA, to decide whether and how to give horizontal effect.

In *Kücükdeveci*[53] the CJEU held that some general principles of EU law can have horizontal effect. However, there is no specific authority on the horizontal effects of the Charter. Again, the *AMS* case provided an opportunity that was not taken up by the CJEU. In *AMS*, AG Cruz Villalón found that the potential for horizontal effect differed from right to right. Given that the right at issue, Article 27 EUCFR, itself referred to the right being granted 'within the undertaking', this would imply at least some legal obligations for companies. He therefore concluded that it could be relied upon in principle between private parties. However, in its rather short judgment, the CJEU did not follow his reasoning and left the law on the horizontal effect of the Charter somewhat ambiguous.[54] However, in the 2015 national case of *Benkharbouche*,[55] EU Charter rights were found actionable by the Court of Appeal in a UK dispute between private parties. Therefore, both the EU and national case law have implications for the application of the EU fundamental rights, indicating that the Charter has the potential to operate between private parties.

The European Scrutiny Committee was clearly uneasy with horizontal effect of Charter rights and the burden they felt this could place on private individuals and business, concluding, however, 'We acknowledge that the uncertainty of horizontal application of human rights may be a common feature of human rights frameworks in general'.[56]

---

[51] *The Application of the EU Charter* (n 5) 56.
[52] Emphasis added in both cases.
[53] Case C-555-07 *Seda Kücükdeveci v Swedex GmbH* [2010] ECR I-365.
[54] ibid. See also Case C-356/12 *Wolfgang Glatzel v Freistaat Bayern* [2014] ECR I-0000.
[55] *Benkharbouche v Embassy of the Republic of Sudan* [2015] EWCA Civ 33.
[56] *The Application of the EU Charter* (n 5) 56.

To be sure, the notion of horizontal effect can be controversial when applied to fundamental rights. Rights are traditionally justified as individual protections against the State, but if applied instead as obligations on citizens, then they are liable to appear as intrusions into private liberty. However, against this, it may be argued that some private entities are just as capable as the State of wielding power in a way that affects the rights of citizens, and so horizontal effect of fundamental rights provides protection against this. The idea of indirect effect of human rights provisions is also accepted in some legal systems outside the EU. The South African Constitution of 1996 and its employment of the German concept of *mittelbare Drittwirkung* might be cited here, namely that human rights have an indirect impact on the development of all jurisprudence by means of a constitutional requirement that 'when developing the common law ... every court must promote the spirit, purport and objectives of the Bill of Rights'.[57] Also of relevance is the German Federal Constitutional Court's approach developed in the *Lüth* judgment,[58] in which it held that fundamental rights go beyond a defensive function (protecting the citizen against the State) to establish an objective order of values. Therefore, a horizontal effect of fundamental rights, binding on private parties, is clearly recognised in many constitutional orders, and indeed establishes an important protection against the abuse of power in a society.

E. Title IV of the Charter and the UK 'Opt-Out'

The UK's concerns regarding the Charter have been most acute in relation to rights of a social or economic nature. Title IV of the Charter concerns rights of solidarity and covers Articles 27–38 EUCFR. It contains, for example, Article 30: 'Protection in the event of unjustified dismissal', and Article 28 on the right to collective bargaining, 'including strike action'. These rights were of particular concern to the UK (as there is no explicit right to strike under UK domestic law) and have been perceived as a threat to the UK's flexible labour markets. This is where the UK's attempted 'opt-out' becomes especially pertinent. If any part of Protocol 30 is capable of functioning as an 'opt-out' then it would be Article 1(2), which specifically refers to Title IV and intends that 'for the avoidance of doubt' nothing in Title IV shall create justiciable rights in the UK. But can it function in this way?

To date, there is no clear authority on the status of Article 1(2) from the CJEU. In the *NS* case, the CJEU held that '[s]ince the rights referred to in the cases in the main proceedings do not form part of Title IV of the Charter, there is no need to rule on the interpretation of Article 1(2) of Protocol (No 30)'.[59] Many commentators on the Protocol have suggested that Article 1(2) merely confirms the distinction between

---

[57] Sidney Kentridge QC, 'Lessons from South Africa' in B Markesinis (ed), *The Impact of the Human Rights Bill on English Law* (Oxford, Oxford University Press, 1999).

[58] Entscheidungen des Bundesverfassungsgerichts (BVerfGE) 7, 198 I. Senate (1 BvR 400/51,) Lüth decision).

[59] Case C-411/10 *NS v Secretary of State for the Home Department* [2011] ECR I-13905.

rights and principles in Article 52(5) EUCFR. However, as we have seen, Article 52(5) does not clearly distinguish which provisions are to be interpreted as 'rights' and which as 'principles'. Therefore, it cannot be said with certainty that Title IV contains only principles, although it may be that those provisions in Title IV that are principles are not justiciable. But this would be the case anyway under the Charter and not require an opt-out.

However, an important question is whether Article 1(2) of Protocol 30 might reach beyond Article 52(5) EUCFR and succeed in establishing that even provisions of Title IV which are classified as *rights* are not justiciable unless the UK has provided for them in national law. For example, the Article 28 right of collective bargaining and strike action presents itself as a right not a principle, but it could be argued that the effect of Article 1(2) of the Protocol is to ensure that it is not justiciable. However, Article 28 EUCFR itself provides that workers have these rights 'in accordance with Union law and national laws and practices'. A provision such as Article 28 must already be the subject of national legislation in order to be justiciable. UK law only permits strikes under limited conditions, and there is no 'right to strike' as such. So it would appear that, even according to the provisions of the Charter itself, the right must be grounded in national law and practices, and thus Article 1(2) of Protocol 30 adds little in this case.

So the Protocol was not necessary to protect UK established practice. There are already enough 'safeguards' in the Charter, whose provisions are unable to override settled principles of UK labour law, social security and employment policy. In any case, further EU Treaty provisions also limit the potential of EU legislation in such matters as freedom of association, the right to strike, and with regard to Member States' social welfare systems.[60]

However, an approach that stresses the limited effect and efficacy of Title IV and of the Charter's socio-economic rights misses something important. Such rights are essential for a life of dignity, security and freedom, and are very much linked with other human rights—a fact recognised by the Charter's structure in that it houses them all within one document. For example, it is impossible for people who are homeless to vote, and very hard for those who are ill and without access to health-care to actively participate in society. Human rights thus comprise an integrated framework of the crucial elements for human flourishing. A human rights structure built on only a partial achievement of this framework will produce inadequate results and engender public disquiet.

F. Importance of General Principles of Law

The European Scrutiny Committee's conclusion ignores a crucial element of EU fundamental rights law: the existence of general principles of law independently of the

---

[60] Art 153(5) TFEU expressly precludes EU interference with pay, the right of association, the right to strike and the right to impose lock-outs. Art 153(4) provides that 'no social policy provision of the EU shall affect the right of a Member State to establish its own social welfare system or to affect the financing thereof'.

Charter. If the Charter were disapplied in the UK, general principles of law would continue to apply, and this would create a confusion far greater than anything existing under current arrangements.

Article 6(3) TEU states that fundamental rights as guaranteed by the ECHR and 'as they result from the constitutional traditions common to the Member States' constitute general principles of EU law. So, although the Charter was said to be necessary to make these pre-existing rights more visible, it does not replace them. This residual system of human rights in the EU should by no means be underestimated. Given the absence of any specific EU bill of rights until 2000, protection of fundamental rights for the first 40 years of European integration developed through the case law of the Court of Justice, which played a very important role, and there exists a developed body of binding jurisprudence which continues to apply. Although the Charter now seems to have become the first point of reference for fundamental rights in the EU, general principles are not obsolete. In the *Åkerberg Fransson* and *NS* judgments, the Court stated that the scope of the Charter and general principles is the same.[61]

The Committee recommends disapplication of the Charter but not of general principles in the UK. This would not remedy the uncertainties the Committee finds with the Charter. In fact, it was the scattered and ad hoc nature of general principles that made the case for a codified Charter so compelling.[62] All sorts of problems would arise from a disapplication of the Charter but not of general principles in the UK—not least the question of whether CJEU case law specifically focused on the Charter also applied to general principles.

To be sure, the Committee could have urged that the UK should disapply both the Charter and the general principles within the UK. But disentangling general principles from the operation of EU law at large would have been difficult in the extreme. In this way, EU law is curiously like the uncodified British Constitution, which Dicey vaunted as so much more efficacious than 'continental' declarations of rights because of its enduring nature. According to Dicey, suspension of the constitution (in itself almost impossible to achieve in the case of Britain's largely unwritten Victorian Constitution) could not remove the rights of the Englishman because they are so embedded in the common law, and upheld by remedies in the courts. For Dicey, nothing short of a complete social revolution would succeed in removing them:

> The matter to be noted is, that where the right to individual freedom is a result deduced from the principles of the constitution, the idea readily occurs that the right is capable of being suspended or taken away. Where, on the other hand, the right to individual freedom is part of the constitution because it is inherent in the ordinary law of the land, the right is one which can hardly be destroyed without a thorough revolution in the institutions and manners of the nation.[63]

---

[61] Case C-617/10 *Åkerberg Fransson* [2013] ECR I-0000; Case C-411/10 *NS v Secretary of State for the Home Department* [2011] ECR I-13905.

[62] See eg evidence of Lord Goldsmith to the European Scrutiny Committee 2014 investigation in *The Application of the EU Charter* (n 4) ch 2.

[63] AV Dicey, *Introduction to the Study of the Law of the Constitution* (London, Macmillan, 1902) 119–20.

The same might be said of the EU's uncodified general principles of law.

It is hard to imagine how general principles of law could be disapplied in the UK without disapplying most of EU law itself. Indeed, this may be why the Committee abandoned its earlier attempt to disapply both the Charter and EU principles and rights more generally.[64] As was pointed out to the Committee, such a broader attempt to disapply EU rights appeared to apply to all rights, freedoms and principles deriving from the EU Treaties and might even be intended as an opt-out from the entirety of European law. If so, then surely the honest thing would be to state this objective explicitly?

To conclude: the Committee's recommendation, of adopting legislation to disapply the Charter in the UK, whether or not such legislation includes general principles of law, would only create the greatest possible legal uncertainty, thus abnegating any aspiration of the Committee to reduce confusion.

IV. UK IN VIOLATION OF EU LAW

If the UK adopted legislation disapplying the Charter, it would be in straightforward violation of EU law. The UK cannot unilaterally alter EU law (although as a matter of purely UK constitutional law it might be able to adopt such legislation, if one takes a Diceyan, or orthodox, approach to the question of parliamentary sovereignty). The Charter imposes obligations on the UK as an EU Member State, and the only permissible derogations are those agreed unanimously with all other Member States in the formation or amendment of EU Treaties and secondary law. If the UK, or any other Member State, fails to apply binding EU law, the Commission may bring an infringement action against that State. It can seek a judgment in the CJEU and, in case of non-compliance with that judgment, ask the Court to impose fines upon the UK under Article 260 TFEU. To date, the UK has never received a fine from the Court of Justice, but if imposed, these fines operate on the basis of a daily penalty with interest, and could be very large indeed. In addition, there would also exist the separate potential, under the *Francovich* case law, for individuals to bring suits in UK courts for breach of EU law in case of failure to apply the Charter.[65] So the Committee's recommendation brings with it a very considerable cost risk for the UK.

Further, the UK would also risk an action being brought under Article 7 TEU, which allows the EU to suspend the membership rights of a Member State where that State is in serious and persistent breach, or there is a clear risk of such breach, of the EU's common values, which include fundamental rights. Article 7 has not been put into effect to date, and it would be a matter of grave regret if it were to

---

[64] The earlier draft read as follows: 'Notwithstanding any provision of the European Communities Act 1972, none of the rights, freedoms or principles referred to in Art 6(3) of the Treaty on European Union, or in the Charter of Fundamental Rights of the European Union, or deriving elsewhere from within the EU Treaties, or otherwise determined by the Court of Justice, shall form part of the law applicable in any part of the UK.' See *The Application of the EU Charter* (n 4) 38.

[65] Joined Cases C6/90 and C9/90 *Francovich and Bonifaci* [1991] ECR I-5357.

be applied in the case of the UK. Yet the disapplication of EU fundamental rights in the UK represents exactly such a serious and persistent breach of the EU's most fundamental values. In that case, there would also be some irony: the eurosceptics' longed for 'Brexit', or termination of EU law in the UK, would occur not through an 'in–out' referendum but through expulsion from the EU—a humiliating and shameful end to the UK's relationship with the EU.

V. EMBRACING THE CHARTER?

Moreover, there are further arguments of a less legalistic kind which provide a strong reason for the UK to embrace the Charter, rather than seek to expunge it from the UK.

First, and crucially, the Charter provides a bulwark against EU powers. As the scope of EU law has come to extend far beyond purely economic matters, it has become ever more important to have protection against the potentially overreaching powers of the EU. For example, in 1997, with the Treaty of Amsterdam, the EU created the Area of Freedom Security and Justice (AFSJ). Within the scope of the AFSJ, the EU adopts many measures not traditionally associated with EU action, including measures on terrorism, migration, visas and asylum, privacy and security, the fight against organised crime and criminal justice. These measures impact directly on human rights and civil liberties. The Charter however, is highly relevant, and able to provide protection for individuals from the EU institutions in these areas. To give just one example: in *Digital Rights Ireland*[66] the CJEU annulled an EU measure in its entirety for violating individual privacy rights. This legislation required telecoms companies to retain personal telephone and internet records, with the aim of ensuring that law enforcement authorities could use such records in future investigations. The European Court criticised the sweeping nature of the measure, and held that the directive 'entails an interference with the fundamental rights of practically the whole European population'.[67] Why should UK citizens lack the protection of the Charter in areas such as these? Furthermore, in the absence of EU accession to the ECHR (mandated by Article 6(2) TEU),[68] no body external to the EU controls the EU vis-a-vis its compliance with human rights. In the absence of such accession (and indeed, even in tandem with any future accession) the Charter provides a crucial means of control over the EU. If we survey other jurisdictions and historical periods, we may see that the need for a human rights document has been quickly appreciated as protection against ever more powerful authorities. There was no Bill of Rights in the original American Constitution, when it was thought that the federal government would be insufficiently powerful to require a bulwark against its powers in the form of guaranteed rights, but one was quickly added within a

---

[66] Joined Cases C-293/12 *Digital Rights Ireland* and C-594/12 *Kärntner Landesregierung* [2014] ECR I-0000.

[67] ibid, para 56.

[68] In *Opinion 2/13* [2014] ECR I-0000 the CJEU found the draft accession agreement on EU accession to the ECHR to be incompatible with EU law.

few years. Likewise, the necessity of a European Charter has been recognised, and its disapplication in Britain would only exclude British residents from an important bulwark against the misuse of power.

The second reason why the UK should embrace the Charter is that the Charter can function to improve the quality of EU legislation and policy. Not only are the courts able to use the Charter to set limits on EU action, but EU officials must work with the Charter in mind from the moment that they begin to formulate policy and legislation. Officials and MEPs have had to take care in drafting EU law to ensure that it complies with Charter rights, a duty clearly recognised in EU law. Therefore, the Charter has helped to improve the quality of EU legislation—in itself no small thing.

Third, the EU may perform a particularly important role in the UK. As Lord Mance has stated, there are few limits to the dominance of EU law in the UK:

> One is that there are other constitutional statutes, such as Magna Carta, the Bill of Rights 1989, the Act of Union 1707 and the Human Rights Act 1998, which (it might be argued) cannot themselves have been intended to be affected by the 1972 Act ... Even before the Human Rights Act, common law courts were in the process of developing a concept of fundamental common law right, to which some special preference might in this context also be given. But, *if and so far as these limitations exist, they are self-evidently less effective deterrents to European pro-activity than those which a country with a written constitution possesses.*[69]

UK law, because of the strength of parliamentary sovereignty, is less able to protect itself against the encroachment of EU law than countries such as Germany, which possess a written constitution. The German Constitutional Court, in its *Solange* jurisprudence, threatened not to uphold the primacy of EU law in the face of its encroachment on German constitutional rights. The most important challenge to UK law came in the *Factortame* case, in which the House of Lords accepted the supremacy of EU law over a parliamentary statute. Although parliamentary sovereignty may allow the UK ultimately to pass a statute repealing the European Communities Act 1972, there is little constitutional scope for a less drastic remedy of contesting the primacy of EU law without leaving the Union.[70] Thus the Charter provides a valuable protection against the encroachment of EU law in the UK. The UK should not be seeking protection from the Charter, but should rather view the Charter as protection against an overreaching EU.

Finally, one cannot ignore the value that human rights bring in and of themselves, and the Charter's role in upholding them within the scope of EU law. For many people, it is both essential and inevitable to turn first to human rights in the search for a moral element in law. It has become commonplace to describe them as a 'secular religion'[71] for our times. The EU and its Member States are required to assume

---

[69] Lord Mance (n 1) (emphasis added).

[70] Although *cf* certain comments made by the UK Supreme Court in *R (HS2 Action Alliance Ltd) v Secretary of State for Transport* [2014] UKSC 3.

[71] E Wiesel, 'A Tribute to Human Rights' in Y Danieli, E Stamatopoulou and C Dias (eds), *The Universal Declaration of Human Rights: Fifty Years and Beyond* (Amityville, Baywood, 1999).

respect for human rights. It has already been argued that the Charter provides an important bulwark against abuse by the EU of its powers. But it is to be hoped that the EU would not commit the very gravest human rights abuses, such as torture or inhuman and degrading treatment. However, many EU States are still regularly found in violation of even the core human rights such as Article 3 ECHR,[72] the prohibition on torture. Some States, such as Greece, have difficulties complying with human rights obligations to asylum-seekers. In *NS*, the CJEU was prepared to give precedence to fundamental rights over the obligations of Member States to comply with the provisions of the EU Dublin II Regulation, recognising that Member States must not return asylum seekers to other EU States when there would be a real risk of their being subjected to inhuman or degrading treatment within the meaning of Article 4 EUCFR.[73] In this way, the Charter provides very important protection to individuals against other Member States abusing fundamental rights. The further the EU goes down the road of requiring mutual recognition of other States' practices (whether it be of food standards, technical requirements or criminal justice systems), the more the Charter is needed to provide human rights-based exceptions to otherwise enforced recognition.

Therefore, in conclusion, rather than seeking to disapply the Charter in the UK, perhaps at the next general amendment of the EU Treaties, the UK should seek to repeal Protocol 30 entirely.

VI. FUNDAMENTAL RIGHTS AS A SOURCE OF EUROSCEPTICISM

Why should it be that fundamental rights, in particular, appear to give rise to a vehement euroscepticism? One of the notable, central elements of British euroscepticism is its opposition to an EU-wide fundamental rights doctrine. To date, much eurosceptic wrath has been directed towards the European Court of Human Rights, but senior Conservative ministers have made it clear that the EU is also a cause for concern. In April 2014, in response to (then) Commissioner Reding's comment that the Charter of Fundamental Rights was 'becoming a reality', UK former Lord Chancellor Chris Grayling responded that such comments revealed 'why we need a major re-think of our future relationship with the EU'.[74] He also attacked Labour for failing to veto the EU Charter during the Lisbon Treaty negotiations. Notably, the furore over the ECtHR ruling in *Hirst*[75] on prisoner voting rights has provided

---

[72] For a small sample of recent cases in which States have been found to breach the prohibition in Art 3 ECHR, see *RR v Poland* (2011) 53 EHRR 31; *Hellig v Germany* (2012) 55 EHRR 3; *VC v Slovakia* (2014) 59 EHRR 29; *Yoh-Ekale Mwange v Belgium* (2013) 56 EHRR 35; *El Shennawy v France* App no 51246/08 (20 January 2011).

[73] Art 4 EUCFR is identical to Art 3 ECHR and reads: 'No one shall be subjected to torture or to inhuman or degrading treatment or punishment.'

[74] B Waterfield, 'EU Bill of Rights Becoming a Reality, Says European Commission' *The Telegraph* (London, 15 April 2014), www.telegraph.co.uk/news/newstopics/eureferendum/10766412/EU-Bill-of-Rights-becoming-a-reality-says-European-Commission.html.

[75] *Hirst v UK (No 2)* [2005] ECHR 681; see also R Ziegler, 'Voting Eligibility: Strasbourg's Timidity' (ch 9), this volume.

fuel for eurosceptics to protest further EU integration in the criminal law field, particularly those regarding suspects' rights.

To be sure, it is not just the UK that witnesses such a rights-based euroscepticsm. As the powers of the EU have increased, they have been more likely to intrude into areas of traditional national sovereignty, including criminal law, social policy, and moral issues such as same sex marriage or abortion. This provokes a 'value-based euroscepticism', namely 'the perception that the EU, via its fundamental rights policy, unduly interferes in matters where value systems and core domestic preferences on ethical issues are at stake'.[76] For many, this is built on the belief that European integration, should it exist at all, should be a purely economic project, and has no business entering the domain of moral issues, where there is much disagreement among Member States. Even the ECtHR has allowed that, as there is often no European consensus on morals, so States should have a 'margin of appreciation'. The Treaty of Lisbon introduced a statement of values for the EU into the Treaties for the first time, in Article 2 TEU, suggesting a move towards a shared European conception of morals. Yet is this evidence of an imperialist colonisation by the EU that will eat away more and more at national competences? Why should fundamental rights be seen to pose a particular threat to national sovereignty rather than such other areas as economic management?

A. The Shape of Things to Come? A 'Federalising' EU Charter of Rights?

The answer to these questions depends partly on the extent to which the CJEU develops its fundamental rights mandate. Are we witnessing the onset of a new chapter of self-empowerment of the CJEU, in which fundamental rights are used as tools of European integration? I do not think so.

To be sure, sceptics have identified some cases as 'expansionist', including *Mangold, Carpenter* and *Test-Achats*.[77] While some of this criticism of the Court may be justified, this is not always the case on closer reading of the case law. For example, the *Test-Achats* ruling, which established that insurers may not charge different premiums to men and women because of their gender, has come under criticism because the CJEU disapplied a specific derogation permitting such differential treatment on the basis of Articles 21 and 32 EUCFR. Martin Howe QC argued that this was

> a violation of the sovereignty of Member States which had unanimously agreed to the derogation; an extension of the scope of EU law; an unwarranted transfer of power from the democratically-elected to the judiciary; and a warning that opt-outs and derogations from EU law which had been politically agreed could be undone by the ECJ.[78]

---

[76] C Leconte, 'The EU Fundamental Rights Policy as a Source of Euroscepticism' (2013) 15 *Human Rights Review* 83.

[77] Case C-144/04 *Werner Mangold v Rüdiger Helm* [2005] ECR I-9981; Case C-60/00 *Mary Carpenter* [2002] ECR I-6279; Case C-236/09 *Association Belge des Consommateurs Test-Achats ASBL v Conseil des ministres* [2011] ECR I-773.

[78] *The Application of the EU Charter* (n 5) views of expert witnesses, www.publications.parliament.uk/pa/cm201314/cmselect/cmeuleg/979/97907.htm.

Yet the Directive itself sets out a very clear principle of sex equality. One of the reasons the Court annulled the derogation was that it found a lack of coherence in a poorly drafted Directive that set out quite clearly the requirement of non-discrimination but then inserted an exemption clause with almost unlimited applicability. The fact that the Directive made references to the Charter in its preamble strengthened that point, because it showed the urge of the European institutions to respect the principle of equal treatment. In cases such as *Tests-Achats*, the generator for litigation has been a failure in the political domain, resulting in poorly drafted litigation and legal uncertainty that requires litigation for clarification. We should not blame the Court for political deficiencies and deficits.

Nonetheless, there is some fear that the CJEU will read the scope of EU fundamental rights widely in order to create a 'federal' standard, by which all national measures may be assessed. In the 2011 *Ruiz Zambrano* case,[79] one of the most far-reaching suggestions regarding the potential scope of EU fundamental rights law was made by AG Sharpston. The main issue for determination by the CJEU was whether Mr Ruiz Zambrano, a Colombian national, could claim a right of residence in Belgium under EU law following the birth of his children (who were EU citizens) in 2003 and 2005, notwithstanding that his EU citizen children had yet to exercise their right of free movement within the Union, which would normally be a requirement for triggering the application of EU law.

Although most of the discussion turned on EU citizenship, AG Sharpston, in her Opinion, considered the role of fundamental rights in EU law, arguing that they should protect the European citizen in all areas of EU competence, regardless of whether such competence has actually been exercised. She compared the present EU law on fundamental rights, with its uncertain scope of EU competence, to an ideal of consistent protection of fundamental rights.[80] AG Sharpston did, however, acknowledge that this was likely to be too bold a step for the Court to take unilaterally at present, but she nonetheless suggested that the Court should consider that the evolution of EU fundamental rights law in the context of the now binding nature of the Charter, and proposed EU accession to the ECHR, might require a more robust scrutiny of fundamental rights. The Court in *Ruiz Zambrano*, however, did not discuss this point. Interestingly, AG Sharpston also stated that:

> Simply put, a change of that kind would be analogous to that experienced in US constitutional law after the decision in *Gitlow v New York* ... [It] would alter, in legal and political terms, the very nature of fundamental rights under EU law. It therefore requires both an evolution in the case-law and an unequivocal political statement from the constituent powers of the EU (its Member States), pointing at a new role for fundamental rights in the EU.[81]

AG Sharpston's reference alerts us to the 'federalising' movement of the US Supreme Court, which, in the earlier twentieth century, incorporated the US federal Bill of Rights and applied it to the States through a very wide interpretation of the due

---

[79] Case C-34/09 *Ruiz Zambrano* [2011] ECR I-1177.
[80] Opinion of AG Sharpston in Case C-34/09 *Ruiz Zambrano* [2011] ECR I-1177, paras 164–70.
[81] ibid, paras 172–73.

process clause of the14th Amendment of the US Constitution. In the 1925 case of *Gitlow v New York*, the US Supreme Court held that the First Amendment of the US Bill of Rights could also apply to the States through the operation of the 14th Amendment (which specifically applies to the States). Since then, the US Supreme Court has applied the Bill of Rights to State laws even when the States are acting within their own sphere of competence. In this way, the US Supreme Court has created a unified constitutional order of fundamental rights.

It seems clear, however, that the EU Charter does not permit the CJEU to emulate the US Supreme Court and identify a 'federal' or EU standard of fundamental rights against which all national laws may be assessed and even invalidated. Nor is there any evidence that the CJEU itself (as opposed to AG Sharpston) would suggest that it should do so. Notably, in *Zambrano*, AG Sharpston recognised that extending the reach of EU fundamental rights would require an 'unequivocal' endorsement from the Member States, which is unlikely to be forthcoming at present. So there is little evidence that the CJEU is seeking unilaterally to extend the reach of EU fundamental rights law.

Therefore, however wide the scope of EU law, there will continue to be domestic situations in which it cannot be applied. For example, the Supreme Court in the *Chester* case[82] unanimously dismissed two prisoners' claims that the UK government's refusal to allow them to vote whilst in prison breached their EU rights, on the basis that the case did not fall within the scope of EU law.

B. Resistance from the National Courts?

In any case, evidence of use of the Charter by the CJEU to centralise rights protection at the EU level could be very unpopular with at least some national courts, which have traditionally seen themselves as the ultimate guardians of rights. For example, *Åkerberg Fransson* was subject to criticism by the German Federal Constitutional Court. In a 2013 judgment[83] concerning a national counter-terrorism database, the German Court insisted that the case before it was clearly outside the scope of the Charter, as it pursued national objectives with only a possible 'indirect' effect on the functioning of legal relationships under EU law. This looks like quite a clear warning to the CJEU. And of course, famously, in its 1974 *Solange I* ruling,[84] the German Constitutional Court had held that, in the case of conflict between EEC law and fundamental rights protected under the German Constitution, German constitutional rights would prevail over any conflicting norm of EEC law.

The British higher judiciary has also shown some propensity to reject European Courts as having the last word in rights matters. Instead they have sought to

---

[82] *R (Chester) v Secretary of State of for Justice; McGeoch (AP) v The Lord President of the Council* [2013] UKSC 63.

[83] 1 BvR 1215/07, judgment of 24 April 2013, www.bundesverfassungsgericht.de/SharedDocs/Entscheidungen/DE/2013/04/rs20130424_1bvr121507.html?nn=5399828.

[84] *Internationale Handelsgesellschaft v Einfuhr und Vorratsstelle für Getreide und Futtermittel* (BVerfGE 37, 271; [1974] 2 CMLR 540).

promote and resurrect the common law in the human rights field.[85] For example, in his Hamlyn lectures, Sir John Laws stated that national courts should follow their own interpretations of human rights issues. Sir John was particularly concerned that 'political controversies and resentments concerning Europe' might undermine the confidence people should have in the law's 'use of principles which were born or have flourished in Luxembourg and in Strasbourg'.[86] Further, in the 2013 case of *R (Osborn) v Parole Board*[87] the UK Supreme Court emphasised that the starting point in fundamental rights cases should be 'our own legal principles rather than the judgments of the international court'.[88] Yet does the unwritten common law have any great advantage over the codified ECHR and EU Charter? There are problems with looking to the common law as the source for our constitutional principles and fundamental rights in that it appears to leave too much room for judicial intuition and 'a feeling for the right or the good result'.[89] As Aidan O'Neill argues:

> These charters and the bodies of law which have built up around them should not be too readily abandoned, nor the mechanisms for their enforcement be too readily disparaged by our own courts, echoing political and popular sentiment. The architecture of enforcement involved international courts and bodies ... precisely to ensure the advantages of distance and, to an extent, a necessary isolation from the immediate national political fray. This was, and is, seen as necessary in order to ensure a degree of objectivity and protection for the individual.[90]

Interestingly, other national constitutional courts have not followed the direction of the German[91] or British courts in seeking a distinctively national focus on human rights. For example, in 2012 the Austrian Verfassungsgerichtshof took the landmark decision that the rights guaranteed by the Charter 'may also be invoked as constitutionally guaranteed rights' in proceedings before it.[92] In this way, the Charter, functioning as a contemporary catalogue of fundamental rights, may itself be used and come to be relied upon by national constitutional courts as a document of prime importance.[93]

---

[85] See further in this regard B Dickson, 'Repeal the Human Rights Act and Rely on the Common Law?' (ch 7), this volume.

[86] J Laws, *The Common Law Constitution*, Hamlyn Lectures(Cambridge, Cambridge University Press, 2014).

[87] [2013] UKSC 61, [2013] 3 WLR 1020.

[88] See Lord Reed's judgment, ibid, para 62.

[89] A O'Neill, 'Not Waving, but Drowning? European Law in the UK Courts' (22 July 2014), http://ukscblog.com/waving-drowning-european-law-uk-courts.

[90] ibid.

[91] For a recent softening of the approach of the German Federal Constitutional Court with regard to the ECHR see J Rackow, 'From Conflict to Cooperation: The Relationship between Karlsruhe and Strasbourg' (ch 19), this volume.

[92] Joined Cases U 466/11-18, U 1836.

[93] See further, with regard to Austria, A Müller, 'An Austrian *Ménage à Trois*: The Convention, the Charter and the Constitution' (ch 15), this volume.

C. The CJEU to Become a Fundamental Rights Court?

The important role played by the CJEU in the development of EU fundamental rights law is well known. This role is, however, ambivalent. The charge that the CJEU is most concerned with integration and with the autonomy of EU law, rather than fundamental rights per se, is an old criticism, dating back to its earliest case law on fundamental rights such as *Internationale Handelsgesellschaft*,[94] in which it asserted the EU's respect for fundamental rights in order to maintain the primacy of what was then EEC law. Alongside this charge has been the claim that EU fundamental rights protection too strongly reflects the specific form of the EU and its stress on the internal market. The Court's willingness to equate fundamental market freedoms such as the free movement of goods and services with fundamental rights has drawn fire,[95] and provoked the counterclaim that the free movement of goods and services are in no way equivalent to fundamental rights.

Even though the competences of the EU have moved beyond its economic origins and the internal market, the EU still maintains its focus on the economic, as cases such as *Viking* and *Laval* reveal, in which the European Court required the fundamental social right to strike to be exercised proportionately in order to comply with the free movement of services.[96] Although AG Maduro, in *Centro Europa 7*, interpreted the provisions for fundamental rights in Article 6 TEU as ensuring that 'the very existence of the European Union is predicated on respect for fundamental rights'[97] (a statement which was notably not adopted by the CJEU), fundamental rights were in fact not acknowledged in the original Treaty of Rome, and the EU still lacks a comprehensive fundamental rights competence.

The EU's current *design* reveals its limited capability as a human rights organisation. The Charter does not declare a freestanding fundamental rights competence for the EU but only applies to EU institutions and to the Member States in certain circumstances. The deliberate decision not to incorporate the Charter into the Treaties by the Lisbon Treaty amendments, while nonetheless according them the same legal status as the Treaties under Article 6(1) TEU, also suggests an ambivalence as to the constitutional nature of Charter rights. The EU's main concern has been with market building and regulation,[98] the very role to which the eurosceptic would wish to confine it. In this, it differs from traditional State constitutions and human rights regimes. Part of the problem is that most litigation brought by individuals comes to the CJEU by way of a preliminary reference from the national courts, in which the Court of Justice is only seized of certain aspects of a case,

---

[94] Case 11/70 Internationale Handelsgesellschaft [1970] ECR 1125.

[95] eg J Coppell and J O'Neill, 'The European Court of Justice: Taking Rights Seriously?' (1992) 29 *Common Market Law Review* 689.

[96] Case C-341/05 *Laval* [2007] ECR I-11767; Case C-438/05 *ITWF v Viking Line* [2007] ECR I-10779.

[97] AG Maduro in Case C-380/05 *Centro Europa 7* [2008] ECR I-349, para 19.

[98] See eg A von Bogdandy, 'The EU as a Human Rights Organization?' (2000) 37 *Common Market Law Review* 1307.

and fundamental rights are often pleaded in a collateral or tangential manner. This can be contrasted with approaches of human rights courts, such as the ECtHR, in which fundamental rights themselves are the basis for an application. Given this, it is likely that the CJEU will continue to determine issues of fundamental rights on a case-by-case basis, with a particular focus on the proportionality of any infringement of rights, rather than with an eye to the development of a coherent, substantive fundamental rights law.

In these circumstances, there does not seem to be much risk of the CJEU taking up an evangelising mission of pursuing human rights as a course of further integration or as a federal standard for Europe. If anything, it must be feared that the EU will not be activist enough in its human rights policy. The Commission was slow to act against abuses of human rights in Hungary,[99] which saw a direct governmental interference with the independence of the judiciary. The CJEU has been slow in the past to annul EU measures for breaches of human rights.

Although former Justice and Home Affairs Commissioner Viviane Reding enthusiastically opined that 'I could imagine that one day citizens in the Member States will be able to rely directly on the Charter—without the need for a clear link to EU law. The Charter should be Europe's very own Bill of Rights',[100] that day has certainly not yet come. Eurosceptics may rejoice in this conclusion. Those who value human rights may not.

[99] See eg 'EU Weighs Fines for Democratic Breaches after Hungary Tensions' *Financial Times* (London, 11 July 2013).
[100] 'Fundamental Rights: Importance of EU Charter Grows as Citizens Stand to Benefit', European Commission press release, 14 April 2014, http://ec.europa.eu/justice/newsroom/fundamental-rights/news/140414_en.htm.

14

Of Tangled and Truthful Hierarchies: EU Accession to the ECHR and its Possible Impact on the UK's Relationship with European Human Rights

PAUL GRAGL

I. INTRODUCTION

HAVING BEEN FIRST envisaged and discussed as early as 1979 in a European Commission Memorandum,[1] the European Union's (EU's)[2] accession to the European Convention on Human Rights (ECHR) seemed to be a never-ending story. In fact, accession appeared to be legally impossible after major setbacks such as Opinion 2/94, in which the Court of Justice of the EU (CJEU) held that, as Union law stood back then, the EU had no competence to accede to the Convention.[3] This deficit in competence was not remedied until 2010, after a lengthy struggle to bring into force both the Lisbon Treaty[4] and Protocol No 14 to the ECHR,[5] which granted the Union this very competence. This story came to a conclusion (albeit provisional) in April 2013, when a Final Report on accession was submitted to the Council of Europe's Human Rights Steering Committee (CDDH). This report included a Draft Revised Agreement on EU accession to the ECHR and a Draft Explanatory Report to the agreement.[6]

---

[1] Commission of the European Communities, 'Memorandum on the Accession of the European Communities to the Convention for the Protection of Human Rights and Fundamental Freedoms', Bulletin, Supplement 2/79, COM (79) 210 final, 20 May 1979.

[2] For the sake of legibility, only the European Union is referred to in this text, even if the terms 'European Economic Community' (EEC) and 'European Community' (EC) were legally and historically correct in lieu thereof.

[3] Opinion 2/94 *Accession by the Community to the ECHR* [1996] ECR I-1759, para 36.

[4] See especially Art 6(2) Treaty on European Union (TEU), both enabling and obliging the EU to accede to the Convention.

[5] See especially Art 17 of Protocol No 14, amending Art 59 ECHR, thus allowing for accession.

[6] Fifth Negotiation Meeting between the CDDH ad hoc Negotiation Group and the European Commission on the Accession of the European Union to the European Convention on Human Rights, Final Report to the CDDH, 10 June 2013, 47+1(2013)008rev2.

After this overwhelming success, December 2014 nonetheless saw another blow for the accession project, when the CJEU held in Opinion 2/13 that the accession agreement was not compatible with the Union Treaties. For the Court, this incompatibility mainly lies in the agreement's potential adverse effects on the specific characteristics and autonomy of EU law.[7] While a renegotiation of the 'problematic' parts of the accession agreement and further delay in finalising the accession procedure seem inevitable, the author is optimistic that Luxembourg's verdict does not frustrate accession after all: hopefully it will, in hindsight, be a mere bump on the road—albeit an irritating one—towards a unified system of European human rights protection.

Opinion 2/13 deals primarily with the incompatibilities of accession with the legal order of the EU itself, which is not the focus of this chapter (and which deserves an analysis in its own right). The chapter at hand examines the consequences of accession for the EU Member States in general and the United Kingdom in particular, and Opinion 2/13 will therefore only be taken into account where it is relevant to the situation of the Member States.

Given that the European Court of Human Right (ECtHR) currently lacks any jurisdiction *ratione personae* over the European Union,[8] the overall object and purpose of EU accession to the ECHR is to close gaps in the European system of fundamental rights protection. After the EU continued to acquire competences in fields which had previously been the exclusive *domaine réservé* of the Member States, these gaps in human rights protection became most evident in cases where an EU Member State was obliged to implement Union law in violation of the Convention. The legal status quo in such a case *prior to* accession leads not to a sanction being imposed on the actual 'perpetrator', namely the Union, but on the Member State implementing the legal act in question. This deficiency will, however, be redressed by the EU's future accession to the Convention[9] by formally binding the EU to the ECHR.

Furthermore, accession is also intended to bring about a more coherent protection system and confirm the EU's standing as a community based on the rule of law,[10] and as a legal order that is fully committed to respecting and promoting human rights. By acceding to the Convention, the EU will become subject to the external supervision of the Strasbourg Court,[11] which will then have the last say in human rights and ensure, in the event of normative conflicts, a coherent and uniform interpretation of these rights throughout Europe. This objective will be achieved by enabling individuals to submit individual complaints under Article 34 ECHR directly against the European Union in the case of an alleged violation of Convention rights[12]—with

---

[7] Opinion 2/13 *EU Accession to the ECHR* [2014] ECR I-0000, para 258.

[8] See *Bosphorus Hava Yollari Turizm ve Ticaret Anonim Şirketi v Ireland* (2006) 42 EHRR 1, para 155.

[9] P Gragl, *The Accession of the European Union to the European Convention of Human Rights* (Oxford, Hart Publishing, 2013) 5.

[10] HC Krüger, 'Reflections concerning Accession of the European Communities to the European Convention on Human Rights' (2002/03) 21 *Penn State International Law Review* 89, 93–94, 97.

[11] 47+1(2013)008rev2 (n 6) Preamble, recital 5.

[12] J-P Jacqué, 'The Accession of the European Union to the European Convention on Human Rights and Fundamental Freedoms' (2011) 48 *Common Market Law Review* 995, 1007; see also Art 1(b) of Protocol 8 to the EU Treaties.

the reservation, however, that the application of national standards of protection (through Article 53 ECHR) must not be used to compromise the level of protection provided for by the Charter or the supremacy, unity and effectiveness of EU law.[13]

But despite these apparent benefits for individuals and the overall development of human rights protection in general, British scepticism towards European human rights law may be further fuelled by this unprecedented step in the history of international law. Today, human rights in the UK are protected domestically by the Human Rights Act 1998 (HRA),[14] which has attracted enormous criticism for giving an expansive effect to both the Convention rights and ECtHR jurisprudence within UK law. This incorporation of an international human rights treaty into a domestic legal order has been criticised both because it shifts political power from the executive and legislative branches to the judiciary[15] and because it allegedly undermines parliamentary sovereignty.[16] ECtHR judgments such as the now (in-)famous *Prisoner Voting Rights* cases[17] have led to allegations of illegitimate judicial activism on the part of the Strasbourg Court by casting 'its shadow over the HRA'[18] through section 2(1) HRA, obliging the UK courts to 'take into account' any relevant Strasbourg jurisprudence on a particular Convention right. Scepticism vis-a-vis ECtHR case law, coupled with increasing criticism of European Union law (most prominently of the division of competences between the EU and the UK, particularly in the field of free movement of persons and so-called 'social tourism'), clearly illustrate why EU accession to the ECHR may not be a very popular step in the UK. From a critical point of view, accession could not only further add delays to litigation by introducing new mechanisms and procedures before the ECtHR[19] and entangle the UK legal order in a multi-layered labyrinth of European human rights,[20] but also lead to a creeping transformation of both the Convention and Strasbourg's jurisprudence into domestic law through the back door of the supremacy of EU law. In the eyes of the sceptics, EU accession to the ECHR could thus result in 'a tighter net forming around UK membership to the Convention creating a Gordian knot from which Britain would struggle to be freed'.[21]

In the light of this considerable criticism, this chapter will explore in part II the *negative* aspect of EU accession to the ECHR, or—in other words—what accession is *not* about: it is not about the Member States, but about the European Union itself

---

[13] Opinion 2/13 (n 7) para 188.

[14] Human Rights Act 1998 c 42.

[15] KD Ewing, 'The Human Rights Act and Parliamentary Democracy' (1999) 62 *Modern Law Review* 79, 79.

[16] S Besson, 'The Reception Process in Ireland and the United Kingdom' in H Keller and A Stone Sweet (eds), *A Europe of Rights: The Impact of the ECHR on National Legal Systems* (Oxford, Oxford University Press, 2008) 49–52.

[17] *Hirst v UK (No 2)* (2006) 42 EHRR 41; *Greens and MT v UK* (2011) 53 EHRR 21.

[18] R Bellamy, 'Political Constitutionalism and the Human Rights Act' (2011) 9 *International Journal of Constitutional Law* 86, 97.

[19] *In concreto*, the co-respondent mechanism and the prior involvement procedure, which will be discussed in detail below.

[20] HM Government, 'Review of the Balance of Competences between the United Kingdom and the European Union—Fundamental Rights', 22 July 2014, § 5.11.

[21] ibid, § 5.17.

and its subjection to the external scrutiny of the ECtHR. Moreover, it is crucial to note that the UK's membership of both the EU and the ECHR has already changed the concept of parliamentary sovereignty, and that accession will not further negatively impact on the UK constitutional system. Accordingly, the argument that the European human rights system now encompasses too many layers of protection, and would be further complicated by EU accession to the ECHR, will be rebutted.

Subsequently, part III will examine the *positive* aspects of accession and demonstrate that its advantages far outweigh the British fears. Particular attention will be paid to how the Member States might benefit from a (more or less) unified European human rights system in which only disputes between EU Member States might be exempt from Strasbourg's jurisdiction.[22] After accession, sceptics can expect not only a 'tamer' version of the EU, which will be subject to the external supervision of the ECtHR, but also a 'truthful' hierarchy through the 'unification' of the Member States' international obligations under EU and ECHR law: in contrast to cases such as *Bosphorus*,[23] EU accession to the ECHR will prevent any future normative conflicts between EU law and the ECHR for the Member States, as the final say will in any case rest with the ECtHR.

II. TANGLED HIERARCHIES? RISK ASSESSMENT IN LIGHT OF THE STATUS QUO

Before analysing what (negative) impact EU accession to the ECHR might have on the UK, it is necessary to illustrate the legal reasons for the existing British scepticism towards accession—namely, the doctrine of parliamentary sovereignty and the dualist approach of the UK towards international treaty law. This illustration of the legal status quo will help to explain how the doctrine of parliamentary sovereignty has already been modified by the UK's integration into both EU and ECHR law and by the European Communities Act 1972 (ECA)[24] and the HRA. We will then assess what risks accession might entail for the British constitution: whether accession will in fact add another layer of human rights protection and thus further complicate the already intricate three-dimensional web of fundamental rights regimes,[25] tangle the hierarchies of domestic and international law, and (allegedly) further erode the sovereignty of Parliament (for example by 'smuggling' the ECHR into domestic law as a Trojan horse of EU law by complicating the workings of domestic courts and by empowering the EU at the expense of the Member States); or whether the focus and

[22] Opinion 2/13 (n 7) paras 201–14; seeing that, upon accession, the ECHR will become an integral part of EU law, the CJEU claims to have exclusive jurisdiction in any dispute between EU Member States and between Member States and the EU regarding compliance with the ECHR on the basis of Art 344 TFEU.
[23] *Bosphorus v Ireland* (n 8).
[24] European Communities Act 1972 c 68.
[25] M Claes and Š Imamović, 'National Courts in the New European Fundamental Rights Architecture' in V Kosta, N Skoutaris and V Tzevelekos (eds), *The EU Accession to the ECHR* (Oxford, Hart Publishing, 2014) 160.

impact of accession is not on the Member States at all, but on the European Union itself, meaning that there is thus no imminent risk for the UK legal order.

A. British Exceptionalism: Parliamentary Sovereignty and Legal Dualism

One reason for the UK's protective approach towards certain constitutional fundamentals vis-a-vis international law lies in Dicey's 'orthodox' constitutional theory, according to which Parliament is supreme and sovereign, and which subsequently entails that it has the exclusive right to make or unmake any law or to override its legislation.[26] Furthermore, the United Kingdom is—at least when it comes to treaties[27]—living proof of a dualist system. This means that the rights and obligations created by international treaties have no automatic effect in domestic law and that the supreme power of Parliament remains intact[28]—a defensive attitude that is also directed against other international bodies of law, such as Union and Convention law.

If, however, as emphasised in the *Thoburn* case, the common law were to accept, inter alia, the HRA and the ECA as 'constitutional' statutes, making them immune to implied (but not express) repeal by Parliament,[29] a framework would already exist within which such superior constitutional norms could limit the authority of Parliament.[30] This approach could provide a firm and clear basis for construing statutes in a way which does not impinge upon constitutional rights protected by the common law. The courts may certainly not challenge the validity of legislation itself, but they could construe legislation in such a way as to effectively minimise any interference with fundamental rights.[31] Judicial review of primary legislation, however, remains—with two notable exceptions which will be discussed below—beyond the reach of the courts.

Conflicts between international and constitutional law could then be resolved by consistent interpretation in concrete cases, and not on the basis of a normative hierarchy.[32] Prima facie, the same is also true for the ECHR and the EU Treaties, on the basis of which Parliament enacted both the ECA and the HRA and thus gave effect to the law of the EU and the ECHR—nonetheless with certain problems for the doctrine of parliamentary sovereignty.

---

[26] AV Dicey, *Introduction to the Study of the Law of the Constitution* (London, Macmillan, 1902) 37–38.

[27] Customary international law is usually considered to form part of the common law: see eg *Ex parte Pinochet (No 1)* [2000] 1 AC 61, 98; *Ex parte Pinochet (No 3)* [2000] 1 AC 147, 276; *R v Jones* [2006] UKHL 16.

[28] A Aust, 'United Kingdom' in D Sloss (ed), *The Role of Domestic Courts in Treaty Enforcement: A Comparative Study* (Cambridge, Cambridge University Press, 2009) 476–77.

[29] *Thoburn v Sunderland City Council* [2003] QB 151, [62] and [68]–[69].

[30] M Elliott, 'Parliamentary Sovereignty and the New Constitutional Order: Legislative Freedom, Political Reality and Convention' (2002) 22 *Legal Studies* 340, 369.

[31] KA Armstrong, 'United Kingdom: Divided on Sovereignty?' in N Walker (ed), *Sovereignty in Transition* (Oxford, Hart Publishing, 2003) 337–38.

[32] A Peters and UK Preuss, 'International Relations and International Law' in M Tushnet, T Fleiner and C Saunders (eds), *Routledge Handbook of Constitutional Law* (London, Routledge, 2013) 42.

B. UK Membership of the EU

The ECA, which gave effect to EU law within the United Kingdom, is of particular interest to constitutional lawyers, as it raises the question of whether the principle of supremacy of Union law brought about the end of parliamentary sovereignty[33] and thus the end of the very 'Grundnorm' of British legislative power.[34] The view that the ECA was conceived as an ordinary statute which was not intended to limit parliamentary sovereignty[35] can no longer be seriously upheld. Proponents of the orthodox view may argue that section 2(1) ECA is the necessary constitutional turn of the tap which permits the flow of EU law into the UK legal order,[36] as it states that legal acts under the Treaties shall be given legal effect in the UK. However, Parliament cannot simply pass another statute and thereby constrain the domestic effects of EU law by impliedly repealing the ECA,[37] because this would conflict not only with the relevant CJEU case law on supremacy[38] but also with the UK courts' acceptance of that very supremacy[39] and the alleged 'constitutional' nature of the ECA.[40] Moreover, section 3(1) ECA expressly states that the meaning and effect of EU law are to be determined by the CJEU (which therefore has the last say on supremacy), while section 2(4) ECA practically obliges domestic courts to disapply primary legislation[41] which is inconsistent with Union law.[42] This means, in conclusion, that a partial distortion of the Hartian rule of recognition[43] or the Kelsenian 'Grundnorm' of the British constitutional system[44] has already taken place and that in the context of EU law Parliament's will may no longer be entirely sovereign.[45] In other words, on the basis of the ECA, EU law, in all its manifestations, may 'freely flow' into the UK legal order and prevail over the latter, as confirmed by section 18 of the European Union Act 2011.[46] Yet all of this has been done under parliamentary authority and continues to be correctly done under valid law, at least as long as Parliament chooses to refrain from express repeal of the ECA 1972.[47]

---

[33] FA Trindade, 'Parliamentary Sovereignty and the Primacy of European Community Law' (1972) 35 *Modern Law Review* 375, 375.

[34] M Martinez, *National Sovereignty and International Organizations* (The Hague, Kluwer, 1996) 152.

[35] *Felixstowe Dock v British Transport Docks Board* [1976] CMLR 655.

[36] Armstrong (n 31) 330.

[37] G Martinico and O Pollicino, *The Interaction between Europe's Legal Systems* (Cheltenham, Edward Elgar, 2012) 118.

[38] First clarified in Case 6/64 *Costa v ENEL* [1964] ECR 585.

[39] *R v Secretary of State for Transport, ex parte Factortame (No 2)* [1991] 1 AC 603.

[40] *Thoburn v Sunderland City Council* (n 29) para 69.

[41] J Jaconelli, 'Constitutional Review and Section 2(4) of the European Communities Act 1972' (1979) 28 *International and Comparative Law Quarterly* 65, 67–69.

[42] *R v Secretary of State for Transport, ex parte Factortame (No 1)* [1990] 2 AC 85; *R v Secretary of State for Employment, ex parte Equal Opportunities Commission* [1995] 1 AC 1.

[43] Sir W Wade, 'Sovereignty: Revolution or Evolution?' (1996) 112 *Law Quarterly Review* 568, 574.

[44] G Winterton, 'The British Grundnorm: Parliamentary Sovereignty Revisited' (1976) 92 *Law Quarterly Review* 591, 614–15.

[45] Sir W Wade, 'What Has Happened to the Sovereignty of Parliament?' (1991) 107 *Law Quarterly Review* 1, 2.

[46] European Union Act 2011 c 12.

[47] N MacCormick, 'Beyond the Sovereign State' (1993) 56 *Modern Law Review* 1, 3.

C. UK Membership of the ECHR

In contrast to the ECA, the HRA does not incorporate the international treaty in question—the Convention—into domestic law per se, but rather gives effect to certain ECHR provisions by giving a defined status to 'Convention rights' in the UK legal system.[48] By domesticating the ECHR through substantive incorporation of only particular Convention provisions, the HRA remains a domestic statute placing European human rights norms in a constitutional context[49] without binding the domestic courts directly to the ECtHR. Under section 2(1) HRA, domestic courts are merely required to 'take into account' Strasbourg case law. Accordingly it has been argued that the HRA does not conflict with parliamentary sovereignty.[50]

Nonetheless, there is considerable scepticism vis-a-vis the HRA and Strasbourg's jurisprudence which lies in section 3(1), providing that 'so far as it is possible to do so' legislation 'must be read and given effect in a way which is compatible with Convention rights'. The main difference between the ECA and the HRA is that Acts of Parliament in contravention of the HRA are merely subject to a 'declaration of incompatibility' (section 4 HRA) which does not affect the validity, application or enforcement of the law and accordingly respects parliamentary sovereignty. As a result, the ultimate decision as to whether to amend the law rests with Parliament, and not the courts.[51] However, the HRA's real power rests more in interpretive techniques of conflict avoidance under section 3(1) than in declarations of incompatibility.[52] Section 3(1) decrees a far-reaching interpretive obligation and thus may require the UK courts to depart from the textual meaning of legislation. In other words, it requires the courts to depart from Parliament's legislative intention[53]—a feature which does not sit easily with orthodox constitutional theory.[54] One could certainly argue that when a court approaches the outermost boundary of its interpretive leeway, a declaration of incompatibility must be issued, since the use of section 3(1) HRA in such a case would inevitably cross the constitutional divide between interpreting and legislating.[55] And although the introduction of the HRA certainly is an indication that a profound constitutional change has taken place,[56] the broad terms of the HRA necessarily require elaboration by the courts in order to be applied to the circumstances of new cases.[57] Lastly, this also means that if a

---

[48] KD Ewing, 'The Human Rights Act and Parliamentary Sovereignty' (1999) 62 *Modern Law Review* 79, 84.

[49] Armstrong (n 31) 332–33.

[50] *R v Secretary of State for the Home Department, ex parte Simms* [1999] QB 349.

[51] A Donald, J Gordon and P Leach, *The UK and the European Court of Human Rights*, Equality and Human Rights Commission Research Report 83 (London Metropolitan University, 2012) 23.

[52] Armstrong (n 31) 334.

[53] *Ghaidan v Mendoza* [2004] UKHL 30, [2004] 3 WLR 113, [30].

[54] A Kavanagh, *Constitutional Review under the UK Human Rights Act* (Cambridge, Cambridge University Press, 2009) 96.

[55] L Lazarus et al, 'Reconciling Domestic Superior Courts with the ECHR and the ECtHR: A Comparative Perspective', Submission to the Commission on a Bill of Rights (University of Oxford, 2011) 70.

[56] Armstrong (n 31) 343.

[57] A Kavanagh, 'The Elusive Divide between Interpretation and Legislation under the Human Rights Act 1998' (2004) 24 *Oxford Journal of Legal Studies* 259, 267.

court is issuing such a declaration, it is simply doing what Parliament has instructed it to do under section 4 HRA.[58]

D. EU Accession to the ECHR: Adding Layers and Tangling Hierarchies?

Seeing that both the ECA and the HRA have already considerably altered the UK's constitutional landscape, we must now ask what this means for accession. Does it really add new legal layers of human rights protection to the existing system of the domestic plane (informed by both the ECA and the HRA), the EU level (consisting of the 'general principles of law' developed by the CJEU and the EU Charter of Fundamental Rights (EUCFR)), and the 'Strasbourg regime' (comprising the Convention and the ECtHR)? Does accession in fact tangle the hierarchies of domestic, EU and ECHR law, and thus further encroach upon parliamentary sovereignty? The following sections will answer these questions not only by presenting and analysing the most persuasive arguments against accession, but also by showing that they can easily be rebutted. They will show that, in fact, not much will actually change on the domestic level, as accession is about binding and constraining the EU, and not its Member States, and that any concerns about further intrusions into the doctrine of parliamentary sovereignty are unfounded.

(i) 'Timeo Danaos et dona ferentes': *The ECHR as a Trojan Horse in EU Law*

There is considerable anxiety that the UK constitutional order will gradually lose full control of the 'domesticated' ECHR,[59] that is, the HRA and its domestic effects. It is feared that after EU accession the ECHR might assume features similar to those enjoyed by EU law, namely direct effect and supremacy.[60] The 'gift' of effective human rights protection under the ECHR is therefore—to borrow from Virgil[61]—often seen as a Trojan horse, enjoying supremacy over the UK constitution in the guise of EU law. It is true that, upon accession, the EU will be bound under international law by the Convention. Pursuant to the settled case law of the CJEU, the Convention will, as an international agreement entered into by the Union, also form an integral part of the EU legal order.[62] Given its clear and precise provisions, which are largely not subject to subsequent implementation measures,[63] the Convention will thus—in its manifestation as EU law—also have direct effect

---

[58] *R v Secretary of State for the Home Department, ex parte Anderson* [2002] UKHL 46, [63].

[59] G Martinico, 'Is the European Convention Going to be "Supreme"? A Comparative-Constitutional Overview of ECHR and EU Law before National Courts' (2012) 23 *European Journal of International Law* 401, 424.

[60] H Keller and A Stone Sweet, 'Assessing the Impact of the ECHR on National Legal Systems' in H Keller and A Stone Sweet (eds), *A Europe of Rights: The Impact of the ECHR on National Legal Systems* (Oxford, Oxford University Press, 2008) 681.

[61] Virgil *Aeneid*, bk II, 49.

[62] Case 181/73 *Haegeman v Belgian State* [1974] ECR 449, para 5; confirmed in Opinion 2/13 (n 7) para 180.

[63] Case 12/86 *Demirel* [1987] ECR 3719, para 14.

in and supremacy over domestic law.[64] Within the scope of application of EU law, all national courts will become 'human rights courts' under the EU obligation to review domestic law in the light of the ECHR and therefore be obliged to enforce the ECHR within the interpretive boundaries of EU law by, for instance, disapplying contravening national law.[65] Convention rights will thus not flow into the UK legal order through the interpretive filter mechanism of the HRA, but through the fully opened tap of the ECA. This also implies that under section 3(1) ECA, the last say on this issue will rest with the CJEU, which remains the ultimate guardian of Union law, including 'unionised international law'.[66] In the UK, this will extend the powers and responsibilities of the courts, which must, in cases of conflict with domestic law, set contravening law aside under the ECA, and not leave the review of compliance of primary legislation to Parliament.[67]

However, things are not as intrusive as they seem at first glance, as the ECHR is already indirectly binding via EU law. Whenever Member States are implementing EU law (Article 51(1) EUCFR) or are acting 'within the scope of EU law', that is, in all situations governed by EU law,[68] they are bound by the directly effective and supreme EU Charter of Fundamental Rights. And most importantly, under Article 52(3) EUCFR, the meaning and scope of those Charter rights which correspond to Convention rights shall be, at the minimum, the same as those laid down by the Convention (subject to a more extensive protection of fundamental rights by the EU). Furthermore, this same obligation to comply with EU fundamental rights which correspond to ECHR rights in the domestic application of Union law even existed before the Charter entered into force, namely through the general principles of EU law, which are informed by the ECHR[69] and are binding on both the Union and its Member States via Article 6(3) TEU.[70] This means that even prior to accession, the UK courts are, within the scope of EU law, already bound by the ECHR[71] and Strasbourg jurisprudence[72] through the EUCFR under the duty of consistent interpretation found in Article 52(3) EUCFR.[73]

However, the crucial caveat is that, even though the ECHR may have the same effects as EU law, it can only have these effects *qua* EU law. In accordance with

---

[64] Gragl (n 9) 98–99.

[65] Claes and Imamović (n 25) 167.

[66] eg Case C-280/93 *Germany v Council (Bananas—Common Organization of the Markets)* [1994] ECR I-4973, para 144; Case C-149/96 *Portugal v Council (Market Access in Textile Products)* [1999] ECR I-8395, paras 47 ff.

[67] Claes and Imamović (n 25) 167.

[68] Case C-617/10 *Åklagaren v Åkerberg Fransson* [2014] ECR I-0000, para 19.

[69] See eg Case C-260/89 *ERT* [1991] ECR I-2925, paras 41–45.

[70] Claes and Imamović (n 25) 167.

[71] Case C-400/10 PPU *McB* [2010] ECR I-8965, para 53; Joined Cases C-92/09 and C-93/09 *Schecke and Eifert* [2010] ECR I-11063, paras 51–52.

[72] Case C-279/09 *DEB* [2010] ECR I-13849, para 35.

[73] This finding is all the more important after the CJEU's judgment in Joined Cases C-411/10 *NS v Secretary of State for the Home Department* and C-493/10 *ME* [2011] ECR I-13905, paras 116–22, where the Court held that Protocol No 30 to the Treaties does not exempt the UK from the obligation to comply with the Charter; see also Steve Peers, 'The "Opt-Out" that Fell to Earth: The British and Polish Protocol concerning the EU Charter of Fundamental Rights' (2012) 12 *Human Rights Law Review* 375, 384.

its own judgment in *Melloni*,[74] the CJEU held in Opinion 2/13 that Article 53 ECHR must not be interpreted as granting Member States the power to guarantee a standard of protection that does not correspond to the Charter and a uniform interpretation and application of Union law.[75] Furthermore, Article 6(3) TEU 'does not require the national court, in case of conflict between a provision of national law and the ECHR, to apply the provisions of that Convention directly, disapplying the provision of national law incompatible with the Convention'.[76] Even if the CJEU changed its position and granted the ECHR supremacy and direct effect after accession,[77] this would still occur *qua* EU law and would not change the Member States' situation in comparison with the status quo under Article 6(3) TEU.[78]

The elephant in the room remains, nonetheless, a potential spillover effect from EU competence into areas of non-competence. In other words, the CJEU, may—as it has occasionally done, for example in *Åkerberg Fransson*—impose a fuller fundamental rights review over Member State action and move beyond the application of fundamental rights within the scope of EU law. Such competence creep is more likely in the area of fundamental rights than in other areas, because it is difficult to separate the different interlocking layers of European fundamental rights protection. On the other hand, the CJEU may be careful not to stretch its competence given the obvious opposition of the Member States. In fact, concerns regarding the creeping incorporation of the rights laid down in additional protocols to the ECHR which have not been ratified by the UK[79] turn out to be unfounded. Admittedly, the Explanations to the Charter expressly state that their 'reference to the ECHR covers both the Convention and the Protocols to it',[80] which enable the CJEU to take them into account as interpretive tools. However, although the CJEU referred to the relevant Strasbourg case law regarding the *ne bis in idem* principle and Protocol No 4 to the ECHR in cases such as *Åkerberg Fransson*[81] and *Bonda*,[82] the Court only used these two Convention rights and the ECtHR case law in order to resolve difficult interpretive issues in the context of Article 50 EUCFR,[83] which is binding on the Member States anyway. Accession will not change this status quo, as the EU will only accede to Protocol Nos 1 and 6 to the ECHR under Article 1 of the Accession Agreement, simply because only these two Protocols have already been

---

[74] Case C-399/11 *Melloni* [2013] ECR I-0000, paras 55–64.
[75] Opinion 2/13 (n 7) para 189.
[76] Case C-571/10 *Kamberaj v IPES* [2012] ECR I-0000, para 63.
[77] G Bianco and G Martinico, 'Dialogue or Disobedience? On the Domestic Effects of the ECHR in the Light of the *Kamberaj* Decision' (2014) 20 *European Public Law* 435, 449.
[78] Opinion 2/13 (n 7) para 180.
[79] The UK has not ratified Protocol No 4 (CETS No 46), Protocol No 7 (CETS No 117) or Protocol No 12 (CETS No 177) to the Convention.
[80] Explanations relating to the Charter of Fundamental Rights, OJ C303/17, 14 December 2007, Art 52, 33.
[81] Case C-617/10 *Åklagaren v Åkerberg Fransson* (n 68) paras 14–15.
[82] Case C-489/10 *Criminal Proceedings against Łukasz Marcin Bonda* [2012] ECR I-0000, paras 23 and 36.
[83] Steve Peers and Sacha Prechal, 'Article 52' in Steve Peers, Tamara Harvey, Jeff Kenner and Angela Ward (eds), *The EU Charter of Fundamental Rights: A Commentary* (Oxford, Hart Publishing, 2014) para 52.114.

ratified by all EU Member States. In the end, there is no need for concern at all in this regard, as most of the rights set forth in the additional protocols are also protected under the Charter (see, for example, Protocol No 12 on non-discrimination and Article 21 EUCFR, or Protocol No 13 on the abolition of the death penalty in times of peace and war and Article 2 EUCFR).[84] Thus in the context of additional protocols, no real legal issues arise for the UK.

The European Commission correctly emphasised in its application for Opinion 2/13 that the pre-accession situation of the Member States in relation to the Convention must be preserved, as indicated in Article 2 of Protocol No 8 to the Treaties, because some Member States have made reservations under Article 57 ECHR in respect of some provisions of the Convention or of one or more of the Protocols. Consequently, Article 1(3) of the Accession Agreement limits the scope of the Union's commitments *ratione personae* to the EU alone, and accordingly, accession does not create any new obligations under Union law which '[go] beyond the scope of the pre-existing individual legal situations of the Member States in relation to the Convention and its protocols'.[85]

In conclusion, the revolutionary change dreaded by UK sceptics will not happen upon accession; it already occurred long ago, when the UK became a Member State of the ECHR and the EU. For the Member States, accession therefore rather seems like old wine in new bottles.[86]

(ii) Complicating the Work of National Courts

Even prior to accession, national courts are often confronted with ambiguity of and departures from previous jurisprudence by the Luxembourg and Strasbourg Courts, which may be difficult to absorb into the domestic system. This is particularly the case where the CJEU or ECtHR has misunderstood the domestic law position.[87] As the lynchpins in enforcing both the law of the EU and the Convention, the Member State courts are, to an increasing extent, confronted with two extremely intricate bodies of law which must be implemented at the national level.[88] Besides this already-existing complexity, it is feared that accession will bring about new procedural relationships and issues, and hitherto unknown dynamics, which could prove detrimental to the effective work of the UK courts and thus the overall protection of human rights.[89] This tangling of hierarchies through such new procedural routes (for example by the prior involvement procedure, discussed below) may force individual litigants to incur enormous financial costs and procedural delays,

---

[84] Jacqué (n 12) 1003.
[85] European Commission, 'Request for an Opinion', SJ.F(2012) 2701339, 4 July 2013, paras 81–84.
[86] Claes and Imamović (n 25) 168.
[87] The Rt Hon Lady Justice Arden DBE, 'Peaceful or Problematic? The Relationship between National Supreme Courts and Supranational Courts in Europe' (2010) 29 *Yearbook of European Law* 3, 8–9.
[88] N O'Meara, '"A More Secure Europe of Rights?" The European Court of Human Rights, the Court of Justice of the European Union and EU Accession to the ECHR' (2011) 12 *German Law Journal* 1813, 1829.
[89] Claes and Imamović (n 25) 169.

which, at the end of the day, could prove more detrimental than beneficial to the cause of human rights protection. Moreover, whatever one might speculate in terms of the exact impact accession will have on national courts, it is noteworthy that the Accession Agreement fails to address this issue at all, in order to not interfere with the division of competences between the EU and the Member States and thus the autonomy of the Union legal order. This means that domestic judges will have to work these problems out for themselves.[90]

The main problem the Member States will face after accession is a scenario in which individuals allege that their fundamental rights have been violated, and where the courts must—if such a case is within the scope of EU law—decide whether or not to request a preliminary ruling from the CJEU. Member State courts of last resort are obliged under Article 267(3) of the Treaty on the Functioning of the European Union (TFEU) to request a preliminary ruling from Luxembourg when the interpretation of EU law in general or the validity of Union legislation is at issue,[91] but these rules are not watertight: a domestic court may, for instance, assume that the EU legislation in question was compatible with fundamental rights and consequently valid,[92] and thus not request a preliminary ruling. Because individual applicants do not have a right to request a preliminary reference, they might submit their case directly to the ECtHR. Strasbourg would then be required to adjudicate upon the conformity of an EU act with human rights, without the CJEU first having the opportunity to decide on the validity of a provision of secondary law or the interpretation of a provision of primary law.[93] However, the Accession Agreement foresees and addresses this scenario. In this event, the so-called 'prior involvement procedure' under Article 3(6) of the Accession Agreement will be triggered, under which Strasbourg has to afford the CJEU sufficient time to assess the compatibility of EU law with the Convention rights at issue, if it has not already done so before the ECtHR considers the case. This procedure will not only provide Luxembourg with the opportunity to interpret EU law before Strasbourg does so, but it will thus also comply with the requirement that local remedies be exhausted before the ECtHR accepts a case (Article 35(1) ECHR). Following Opinion 2/13, the prior involvement procedure must also ensure that it will not be the ECtHR deciding whether the CJEU has already given a ruling on the question at issue in that case, but the competent EU institution, and that the scope of the procedure will not be limited solely to questions of validity of secondary law, but to its interpretation as well.[94]

A major concern of the domestic courts is the lengthy litigation that would be caused by involving three court systems, and the cost of justice being delayed. The UK courts will of course have an interest in having such cases off their dockets as quickly as possible, and passing them on to either the ECtHR or the CJEU

---

[90] O'Meara (n 88) 1831.

[91] Case 314/85 *Firma Foto-Frost v Hauptzollamt Lübeck-Ost* [1987] ECR 4199, para 15.

[92] T Lock, 'End of an Epic? The Draft Agreement on the EU's Accession to the ECHR' (2012) 31 *Yearbook of European Law* 162, 181.

[93] 47+1(2013)008rev2 (n 6) 27, para 65.

[94] Opinion 2/13 (n 7) paras 236–41, 242–47.

(although the case will return from the latter court), and not to further increase their workload. Lastly, domestic courts will also struggle with the question of overlapping fundamental rights catalogues and the question of when to apply which body of law and the consequences that this will entail.[95]

However, none of these concerns is caused or further worsened by accession: first, the UK courts already are under an obligation to request a preliminary ruling in cases where Article 267(3) TFEU is applicable, which will prevent the triggering of the prior involvement procedure and hence not differ from the status quo. If, however, the prior involvement mechanism is initiated, the Explanatory Report to the Accession Agreement provides that the CJEU shall ensure that its rulings are delivered quickly in order not to unduly delay the proceedings in Strasbourg. Such accelerated procedures before the CJEU already exist, such as the expedited preliminary ruling procedure under Article 23(a) of the CJEU Statute and Article 105 of the CJEU Rules of Procedure, which allow the Luxembourg Court to give rulings within six to eight months.[96] In comparison with the overall length of proceedings, this rather short period of time appears to be a minimal price to pay for a more effective protection of human rights. Finally, sceptics must also accept that the combined application of overlapping fundamental rights catalogues is not a new phenomenon brought about by accession: even today, Member State courts are already confronted with minimally three spheres of human rights protection and must accordingly deal with an intricate system of multilevel human rights protection. So far, the UK courts have fared well in this respect, particularly by interpreting the relevant domestic piece of legislation (the ECA and the HRA) consistently with the EU Treaties and the Convention. Hence there is no reason why this should change for the worse after accession and the introduction of the prior involvement procedure.

(iii) EU Competence Creep, in Particular through Positive Obligations

One of the major reasons for British scepticism towards EU accession to the ECHR lies in the minefield that is the division of competences between the Union and the Member States. The first concern is the EU's potential gain of competences at the expense of the Member States in the course of accession. The second concern is that, subsequently, parliamentary sovereignty could be further undermined by EU law imposing positive obligations on the UK which would then be obliged to enact relevant legislation. Such an effect on Member State competences is above all seen in the thorny field of social rights[97]—especially because of the ECtHR's continuing reading of such obligations into the Convention.[98] Seeing that the Union in any

---

[95] Claes and Imamović (n 25) 169–70.

[96] 47+1(2013)008rev2 (n 6) 27, para 69.

[97] T Schilling, 'On Equal Footing: The Participation Rights Envisaged for the European Union after its Accession to the European Convention on Human Rights' (2014) 14 *Human Rights Law Review* 197, 217.

[98] D Harris, M O'Boyle, E Bates and C Buckley, *Law of the European Convention on Human Rights*, 3rd edn (Oxford, Oxford University Press, 2014) 22–24.

event has only little competence[99] in the area of fundamental rights protection,[100] the possible imposition of positive obligations on the EU (which would then be subsequently 'passed on' to the Member States) upon accession sits uncomfortably with the sceptics who consider this an excessive intrusion into national sovereignty.[101] And even though the CJEU declared that respect for fundamental rights cannot 'have the effect of extending the scope of the Treaty provisions beyond the competences of the [Union]',[102] these anxieties have persisted. As the EU will assume the same duties as its Member States under Article 1 ECHR to secure the Convention rights to everyone within its jurisdiction, the ECtHR can only be expected to apply consistent reasoning and thus claim that merely refraining from violations may be insufficient.[103]

In order to alleviate these anxieties, Article 6(2) TEU not only sets forth the competence and obligation of the EU to accede to the Convention, but also provides that accession 'shall not affect the Union's competences as defined in the Treaties'. This assurance is reiterated almost verbatim in Article 2 of Protocol No 8 to the Treaties, according to which the Accession Agreement 'shall ensure that accession ... shall not affect the competences of the Union or the powers of its institutions'. This requirement was duly taken into account by the drafters of the Accession Agreement and is now reflected in its Article 1(3), which states that '[n]othing in the Convention or the protocols thereto shall require the European Union to perform an act or adopt a measure for which it has no competence under European Union law'.

Nonetheless, sceptics might interject that all human rights, even those outside the Union's competences, could hypothetically be relevant for the EU and the Member States, as the example of Regulation 1236/2005/EC[104] demonstrates in the area of free movement of goods, since it prohibits the transfer of instruments which could be used for torturing.[105] Subsequently, the ECtHR could, after accession, determine that the Union has violated the Convention by *not* enacting a particular piece of legislation. And if this very piece of legislation were not to fall within EU competence, the competence in this field of law might implicitly shift to the Union at the expense of the Member States[106]—which may subsequently lead to an obligation under EU law for the UK to implement the relevant Union rules or adopt relevant legislation under the aegis of the EU.

---

[99] See eg Art 19 TFEU giving the Union the competence to take appropriate action in order to combat any form of discrimination.

[100] E Dubout, 'The Protection of Fundamental Rights and the Allocation of Competences in the EU: A Clash of Constitutional Logics' in L Azoulai (ed), *The Question of Competence in the European Union* (Oxford, Oxford University Press, 2014) 193.

[101] C Stubberfield, 'Lifting the Organisational Veil: Positive Obligations of the European Union following Accession to the European Convention on Human Rights' (2012) 19 *Australian International Law Journal* 117, 141.

[102] Case C-249/96 *Grant v South-West Trains Ltd* [1998] ECR I-621, para 45.

[103] Stubberfield (n 101) 133.

[104] Council Regulation (EC) 1236/05 concerning trade in certain goods which could be used for capital punishment, torture, or other cruel, inhuman or degrading treatment or punishment [2005] OJ L200/1.

[105] G Gaja, 'Accession to the ECHR' in A Biondi, P Eeckhout and S Ripley (eds), *EU Law after Lisbon* (Oxford, Oxford University Press, 2012) 183–84.

[106] Gragl (n 9) 195.

However, this is incorrect for a number of reasons. First of all, the Union is, in the exercise of its competences, very restricted due to the principle of conferral in Article 5(2) TEU which permits the EU only to act within the competences conferred upon it by the Member States in the Treaties. Any competences not conferred upon the EU in the Treaties remain with the Member States. This corresponds to Article 1(1) TEU, underscoring the position of the Member States as 'Masters of the Treaties' which have voluntarily conferred competences upon the EU. Thus, given the EU's lack of legislative *Kompetenz-Kompetenz* (that is, the competence to extend its own legislative powers without Member State consent), it is unlikely that an international court such as the ECtHR could interfere with the division of competences between Member States and the EU and unilaterally change this balance of powers. This would evoke severe criticism on part of Member States, in the light of the *Lissabon*[107] and *Honeywell*[108] decisions of the German *Bundesverfassungsgericht*, and the UK would definitely not stand alone in such an event. Moreover, the CJEU itself held in its Opinion 1/91 that it will not accept either any external interference with the Union-internal division of competences[109] or any hidden amendments to the Treaties in international agreements.[110]

Lastly, even if a question regarding any positive obligations of the Union outside its competences arose in Strasbourg, the Member State in question may subsequently join the EU as co-respondent under Article 3(3) of the Accession Agreement.[111] In this case, the ECtHR would then hold the Member State and the EU jointly responsible, pursuant to Article 3(7) of the Accession Agreement, without the further need to adjudicate on the allocation of powers. The respondents may then decide how to remedy the violation of the Convention on the basis of EU law, and Strasbourg would not 'clandestinely' afford the EU additional competences at the expense of the Member States.[112] In Opinion 2/13, the CJEU voiced concerns that Article 3(7) would not preclude a Member State from being held responsible for the violation of a provision of the ECHR to which that Member State may have made a reservation under Article 57 ECHR.[113] This, however, is logically impossible, given that the EU can only join proceedings as co-respondent where there is a Member State as respondent. This presupposes that the Member State is under an obligation under the Convention, and has—in other words—not made a reservation in the first place. This problem therefore seems to be pre-empted on the basis of the ECHR anyway.[114] This means, in conclusion, that accession will not have any effect of

---

[107] 2 BvE 2/08, 2 BvE 5/08, 2 BvR 1010/08, 2 BvR 1022/08, 2 BvR 1259/08, 2 BvR 182/09 *Lissabon—Entscheidungen des Bundesverfassungsgerichts* (BVerfGE) 123, 267.

[108] 2 BvR 2661/06 *Honeywell*—BVerfGE 126, 286.

[109] Opinion 1/91 *EEA I* [1991] ECR I-6079, paras 34–35.

[110] ibid, paras 58 and 61.

[111] The 'co-respondent mechanism' will be considered in detail in section III.B below.

[112] Gragl (n 9) 195.

[113] Opinion 2/13 (n 7) paras 226–28.

[114] T Lock, 'Oops! We Did It Again—The CJEU's Opinion on EU Accession to the ECHR' *Verfassungsblog*, 18 December 2014, www.verfassungsblog.de/en/oops-das-gutachten-des-eugh-zum-emrk-beitritt-der-eu/#.VJf3-AIAKY.

imposing obligations on the EU which are beyond the scope of its competences,[115] and that any anxieties regarding the further undermining of parliamentary sovereignty in the UK are unfounded.

III. TRUTHFUL HIERARCHIES: THE BENEFITS OF ACCESSION

Having applied some soothing balm to the sceptics' doubts regarding accession, in the present section we will now analyse its positive aspects and demonstrate that the advantages of accession will far outweigh any fears on the part of the Member States. Given the absence of a codified UK Constitution, it may be more difficult for the British than for representatives of Continental legal orders to accept that a constitutional debate can result in a single document[116] which unifies and hierarchises a multitude of legal bodies, such as the ECHR, the EU and the Member States. The status quo of these three bodies of law is shaped by a heterarchical plurality of legal systems, where there is no ultimate authority to decide which system would prevail in the case of conflict, and each system will ultimately resolve such clashes by confirming its own autonomy and supremacy.[117] The advantage of accession is, however, that it will unify the European human rights system and give Strasbourg the final say in matters of human rights, make the EU and its Member States equal partners in proceedings before the ECtHR (which would also prevent future normative conflicts between EU law and the ECHR), and establish clear legal hierarchies, which may ideally simplify the current pluralist status quo of European human rights law. The following subsections will demonstrate how the Member States, including the UK, will benefit from this unified and hierarchised system.

A. External Scrutiny and the Taming of the Shrew

It is evident that the EUCFR cannot compensate for the added value of impartial, objective and external scrutiny that an international court[118] such as the ECtHR brings. Moreover, accession would also remove the increasing contradiction between the human rights commitments required from future EU Member States and the Union's lack of accountability vis-a-vis the ECtHR.[119] Otherwise, it would remain highly hypocritical to make ratification of the Convention a condition for EU

---

[115] European Commission, 'Request for an Opinion' (n 85) para 76.

[116] I Pernice, 'Multilevel Constitutionalism in the European Union' (2002) 27 *European Law Review* 511, 514.

[117] P Eeckhout, 'Human Rights and the Autonomy of EU Law: Pluralism or Integration?' (2013) 66 *Current Legal Problems* 169, 173.

[118] R Alonso García, 'The General Provisions of the Charter of Fundamental Rights of the European Union' (2002) 8 *European Law Journal* 492, 500–01.

[119] Krüger (n 100) 94.

membership, when the Union itself is exempt from Strasbourg's scrutiny.[120] This is all the more important in situations where there is no Member State involvement, but only action by the EU. This reveals considerable gaps in the protection afforded by the ECtHR.[121] In the *Connolly* case, for example, Strasbourg found that the alleged violation was not attributable to any Member State, nor was the EU bound (yet) by the ECHR.[122] A similar gap can be seen in the *Biret* case, in which an importer attempted to claim damages from the Union for an embargo against the importation of US beef, and failed before the CJEU.[123] When the company subsequently claimed an infringement of its procedural rights under Articles 6 and 13 ECHR, because it did not have a chance to directly challenge the relevant EU directives before the CJEU, the ECtHR concluded that these violations related solely to deficits in the judicial protection offered by the European Union and were thus not attributable to the Member States. Due to this lack of jurisdiction *ratione personae* over the EU, the case was declared inadmissible.[124] Accession will eventually close this gap in the external scrutiny of the ECtHR, as the EU will subsequently be directly responsible in such cases.[125]

In this respect, sceptics might dread that the Member States will be subject to new constraints under EU law in relation to the Convention, and that due to the increasingly interwoven European human rights system after accession, it will solely be the CJEU that will take the role of the national courts in the international human rights discourse. Yet it remains incorrect to assume that the Luxembourg and Strasbourg Courts are the only two European courts, to the exclusion of national courts, as both will continue to depend on the support of the Member State courts.[126] After defining the scope of application of Union law in *Åkerberg Fransson*,[127] the CJEU aptly proved in a couple of more recent decisions that certain fundamental rights matters are better left with the relevant Member State authorities, provided they conform to the principle of proportionality,[128] respect EU fundamental rights as yardsticks when acting within the limits of their national procedural autonomy,[129] and where they act outside the scope of Union law.[130] These cases reveal that Luxembourg is

---

[120] P Alston and JHH Weiler, 'The European Union and Human Rights: Final Project Report on an Agenda for the Year 2000' in A Cassese (ed), *Leading by Example: A Human Rights Agenda for the European Union for the Year 2000* (Florence, European University Institute, 1998) 55.

[121] Lock (n 92) 164.

[122] *Connolly v 15 Member States of the European Union* App no 73274/01 (ECtHR, 9 December 2008).

[123] Case C-93/02 P *Biret International v Council* [2003] ECR I-10497.

[124] *Biret v 15 Member States of the European Union* App no 13762/04 (ECtHR, 9 December 2008).

[125] Lock (n 92) 164.

[126] C Eckes, 'EU Accession to the ECHR: Between Autonomy and Adaptation' (2013) 76 *Modern Law Review* 254, 284.

[127] D Sarmiento, 'Who's Afraid of the Charter? The Court of Justice, National Courts, and the New Framework of Fundamental Rights Protection in Europe' (2013) 50 *Common Market Law Review* 1267, 1277.

[128] Case C-234/12 *Sky Italia* [2013] ECR I-0000, para 26.

[129] Case C-418/11 *Texdata Software GmbH* [2013] ECR I-0000, para 85.

[130] Case C-206/13 *Siragusa v Regione Sicilia* [2014] paras 26–36.

not as intrusive as is often presented and that it does not unnecessarily intervene in questions of national law.[131] Accordingly, there is no reason to assume that this approach would change after accession.

In fact, accession could prove very beneficial for the UK in terms of a feared EU competence creep. Accession is expected to bring forth a 'tamer' version of the EU, because it is subjected to the external jurisdiction of the Strasbourg Court. Given this new scrutiny of EU legal acts by the ECtHR, it is doubtful whether the CJEU or any other Union institution would attempt to claim any new competences at the expense of the Member States. Even though new competences would primarily mean additional powers of legislation and adjudication, they would also include new responsibilities. These might, eventually, lead to an increased number of judgments against the European Union in Strasbourg. As a matter of fact, the *Bosphorus* case in itself should be a reason for the UK to support accession: if the EU did not accede to the Convention and the Member States were to implement future EU legislation in violation of the ECHR, there would be a risk of Member States being held accountable by the ECtHR for human rights violations of the EU. Currently this possibility is mitigated by the presumption that the Union protects fundamental rights in a manner equivalent to that of the Convention as a result of which the ECtHR restricts its review of Member States' responsibility for EU acts.[132] But there is no guarantee that the ECtHR will not depart from this presumption in the future, even in a non-accession scenario. In such an event, the UK, or any other Member State, would stand alone in Strasbourg, and would be required to take the entire blame for the implementation of EU law in contravention of the ECHR. After accession, however, both the Member State in question and the Union will have the right to defend their actions as equal partners before the ECtHR.

B. The Co-Respondent Mechanism: Equal Partners in Strasbourg

To the chagrin of many law students, the EU's specific legal status as a non-State entity of quasi-federal character is highly complicated, as the 'federation' (EU) legislates and the 'States' (Member States) implement such legislation,[133] and, conversely, the 'States' enact the 'federation's' constitution (the Treaties) and the latter implements it. After accession, when questions regarding the compatibility of national measures with the Convention arise, individual applicants will have to face the question of responsibility: is the Member State which enacted the measure responsible for the alleged human rights violation, or can the EU be held responsible for the underlying EU legal act which the Member State authorities had to

---

[131] Eeckhout (n 117) 186.

[132] *Bosphorus v Ireland* (n 8) paras 155–58.

[133] X Groussot, T Lock and L Pech, 'EU Accession to the European Convention on Human Rights: A Legal Assessment of the Draft Accession Agreement of 14th October 2011', Fondation Robert Schuman policy paper, European Issues No 218 (2011), 1, 13.

apply?[134] In order to ensure that individual applications will be correctly addressed to the Member States and/or the Union as appropriate (Article 1(b) of Protocol No 8 to the Treaties), Article 3 of the Accession Agreement introduces the so-called co-respondent mechanism. Under this new mechanism, Member States may join the EU as co-respondents in proceedings before the ECtHR if a primary EU law provision is allegedly in violation of the Convention (Article 3(3)); or the EU may join one or more Member States as co-respondent if a provision of primary or secondary EU law is allegedly infringing the ECHR, and this alleged infringement could only have been avoided by a Member State disregarding an obligation under Union law (for example, when an EU law provision leaves no discretion to a Member State as to its implementation at the national level) (Article 3(2)).[135]

It is particularly this latter scenario which is of specific interest to the Member States. In Opinion 2/13, the CJEU found that the ECtHR's power to decide on a request from the EU to intervene as co-respondent under Article 3(5) of the Accession Agreement was incompatible with EU law.[136] Luxembourg sees this incompatibility in the ECtHR's right to ask for reasons for the intervention from which it can subsequently deduce that the conditions for the EU's participation in the procedure are met. In carrying out such a review, the ECtHR would be prompted to interfere with the EU's legal autonomy when determining which entity is the correct respondent and how responsibility should be allocated between the EU and the Member States on the basis of their division of powers.[137] This, however, is not true. Article 3(5) constrains Strasbourg to merely assess such a request to the extent that it is *plausible* in the light of Articles 3(2) and (3). '*Plausible*' is not a very persuasive or powerful word, and would consequently not require the ECtHR to immerse itself in the internal division of competences between the EU and the Member States. This also means that no competence creep at the expense of the Member States may occur after accession, for example by the ECtHR deciding on the Union-internal division of competences.[138] More importantly, cases such as *Matthews*,[139] *Bosphorus*[140] and *Nederlandse Kokkelvisserij*[141] illustrate that this mechanism will be applied only in a limited number of cases.[142] Consequently, in the light of potential normative

---

[134] B de Witte, 'Beyond the Accession Agreement: Five Items for the European Union's Human Rights Agenda' in Kosta, Skoutaris and Tzevelekos (n 25) 351.

[135] 47+1(2013)008rev2 (n 6) 24, paras 48–49.

[136] Art 3(5) provides that any High Contracting Party may only become a co-respondent 'either by accepting an invitation from the Court or by decision of the Court upon the request of that High Contracting Party'.

[137] Opinion 2/13 (n 7) paras 222–24.

[138] Gragl (n 9) 156–57, 160.

[139] *Matthews v UK* (1999) 28 EHRR 361.

[140] *Bosphorus v Ireland* (n 8) para 147.

[141] *Cooperatieve Producentenorganisatie van de Nederlandse Kokkelvisserij v The Netherlands* (2009) 48 EHRR SE18.

[142] Eighth Working Meeting of the CDDH Informal Working Group on the Accession of the European Union to the European Convention on Human Rights (CDDH-UE) with the European Commission, Draft Legal Instruments on the Accession of the European Union to the European Convention on Human Rights, 19 July 2011, CDDH-UE(2011)16, 17, para 44, and fn 18.

conflicts where the Member States can only implement EU law by simultaneously violating the ECHR, it is in their own interest that this mechanism will enable the EU as the legislator of secondary law, and thus as the actual 'perpetrator', to join the proceedings and to share responsibility for the infringement of Convention rights.

Lastly, the sceptics might interject that the UK would not benefit from the co-respondent mechanism because the EU would be able to refuse to join the proceedings because of the mechanism's voluntary nature under Article 3(5) of the Accession Agreement. This must be criticised because of its sub-optimal results regarding the efficiency of individual human rights protection.[143] Yet, even though the co-respondent mechanism will be voluntary as a matter of international law,[144] this issue may look different from the perspective of EU law: the principle of sincere cooperation (Article 4(3) TEU) obliges both the Union and the Member States to assist each other in carrying out the tasks which flow from the Treaties. This was confirmed by the CJEU when it held that the Union has an interest in compliance by both the Union itself and its Member States with the commitments entered into under international agreements.[145] Hence it can easily be argued that the EU would also have an obligation under Union law to join the proceedings as co-respondent[146] in order to assist the Member State in question.

The main benefit of accession for the UK would therefore lie in its 'unifying' effect on Member States' international obligations under both EU and ECHR law: in contrast to cases such as *Bosphorus*, where the Member States were left no discretion, EU accession to the ECHR will prevent any future normative conflicts for Member States, as the last say will in any case rest with the ECtHR—which might also lead to a judgment against the European Union, the polity actually responsible for the alleged human rights violation.

C. Truthful Hierarchies Instead of Pluralist Enmeshments

The final argument in favour of accession presented here relates to establishing a genuine and truthful hierarchical system of European human rights protection. The current heterarchically informed pluralist structure of domestic, EU and international law is practically unable to account for fundamentally hierarchical concepts in non-domestic law.[147] With regard to EU law, it cannot explain hierarchy-building notions such as the direct effect and supremacy of EU law,[148]

---

[143] Lock (n 92) 173.

[144] Giving the co-respondent mechanism a compulsory nature might have been considered by the EU to encroach upon the EU's legal autonomy; see Opinion 1/91 *EEA I* (n 109).

[145] Case C-239/03 *Commission v France (Etang de Berre)* [2004] ECR I-9325, para 29.

[146] A Delgado Casteleiro, 'United We Stand: The EU and its Member States in the Strasbourg Court' in Kosta, Skoutaris and Tzevelekos (n 25) 118.

[147] Eeckhout (n 117) 190–91.

[148] B de Witte, 'Direct Effect, Primacy and the Nature of the Legal Order' in P Craig and G de Búrca (eds), *The Evolution of EU Law*, 2nd edn (Oxford, Oxford University Press, 2011) 358–62.

the obligation to disapply domestic law in contravention to Union law,[149] and Luxembourg's monopoly on declaring EU acts invalid.[150] With regard to the Convention, it disregards the ECHR's existence beyond the jurisdiction of the High Contracting Parties,[151] Strasbourg's (albeit limited) competence to exercise and supervise functions traditionally reserved to States,[152] and the ECtHR's power to adopt binding judgments, to award compensation, and, if appropriate, to require the respondent party to take general measures in its domestic legal order to put an end to the violation found by the Court and to redress the effects.[153]

The continuing use of the terms 'legal' or 'constitutional pluralism' and 'multilevel constitutionalism' to describe the status quo may seem very appealing in terms of a non-organised spirit of cooperation, judicial dialogue and avoidance of normative conflicts. In fact, however, these pluralist enmeshments of three legal orders without any clear-cut hierarchy are unable to solve normative conflicts,[154] continuously erode the rule of law and any legal certainty,[155] and merely provide a disaggregating legal patchwork quilt instead of a rational and intelligible unity of law.[156] Furthermore, the desire for legal pluralism on the part of some Member States cannot detract from the fact that national courts are nonetheless already bound by EU fundamental rights and Luxembourg's case law, and, therefore have to give them supremacy in their legal orders. In the case of normative conflicts, they cannot, as a matter of EU law, let their respective constitutional laws prevail without infringing their obligations under international or EU law.[157]

Upon accession, the CJEU will find itself in a position similar to that of any Constitutional or Supreme Court of the Member States vis-a-vis Strasbourg, and the EU—in its entirety—will be subordinate to the international legal system of the Convention.[158] In particular, the prior involvement procedure under Article 3(6) of the Accession Agreement introduces a quasi-federal element by giving the CJEU the opportunity to step in as the Union's 'supreme court' and to guarantee the uniform interpretation and application of EU law. This court-centric approach is

---

[149] Case C-106/77 *Amministrazione delle Finanze dello Stato v Simmenthal SpA* [1978] ECR 629, para 21.

[150] Case 314/85 *Foto-Frost v Hauptzollamt Lübeck-Ost* [1987] ECR 4199, para 11.

[151] See Art 34 ECHR and the individual right to submit applications to Strasbourg; *Mamatkulov and Askarov v Turkey* (2005) 41 EHRR 25, paras 100 and 122.

[152] See, on the margin of appreciation doctrine, *Handyside v UK* (1979–80) 1 EHRR 737, paras 48–49.

[153] See Art 46(1) ECHR; *Verein gegen Tierfabriken (VgT) v Switzerland (No 2)* (2011) 52 EHRR 8, paras 85–86.

[154] G Letsas, 'Harmonic Law: The Case against Pluralism' in J Dickson and P Eleftheriadis (eds), *Philosophical Foundations of European Union Law* (Oxford, Oxford University Press, 2012) 91.

[155] GR Woodman, 'Legal Pluralism and the Search for Justice' (1996) 40 *Journal of African Law* 152, 160.

[156] K Kress, 'Coherence' in D Patterson (ed), *A Companion to Philosophy of Law and Legal Theory*, 2nd edn (Oxford, Wiley-Blackwell, 2010) 523–24.

[157] Claes and Imamović (n 25) 173.

[158] O de Schutter, 'The Two Europes of Human Rights: The Emerging Division of Tasks between the Council of Europe and the European Union in Promoting Human Rights in Europe' (2008) 14 *Columbia Journal of European Law* 509, 560–61.

by no means pluralist, but it is undoubtedly constitutionalist,[159] and despite the negative outcome of Opinion 2/13, the entire endeavour of accession conveys the overwhelming impression that all judicial and political actors involved are willing to create formal links between the two European institutions rather than perpetuate the current status of informal coordination, non-binding dialogue and pluralist uncertainty. It is without doubt more desirable for the UK to establish an explicitly coherent fundamental rights order than to maintain a system of multiple conflicting orders. With the ECtHR at the apex of the future European human rights edifice, a clear-cut judicial hierarchy will not encroach upon either national or parliamentary sovereignty; rather it will bring more coherence and legal certainty to fundamental rights protection.[160] It seems that accession is a crucial tool in bringing to an end the deficiencies of legal pluralism. Legal pluralists might object that the structure of the post-accession order bears some resemblance to Neil MacCormick's pluralism under international law, according to which both the Member States and the European Union cohere within a common legal universe governed by international law and thus within a monistic framework.[161]

MacCormick admits, however, that this particular strand of pluralism is in fact just an instance of Kelsenian monism, with the notable exception that both Member State and EU legal orders enjoy equal ranking, juxtaposed with one another, subordinate only to international law.[162] EU accession to the ECHR should therefore rather be seen as crucial to realising Kelsen's monism of legal hierarchies, which regards international and domestic law as parts of a single, unified legal order.[163]

IV. CONCLUSIONS

There are two ways of viewing the European Union's accession to the Convention. One view would be to dread this step as a further encroachment upon Member States' sovereignty in general and the parliamentary sovereignty of the UK in particular. However, as Lady Justice Arden has correctly stated, we tend to react to certain controversial cases at the European level on an unreflective, ad hoc basis, instead of thinking in a long-term way about a thriving and beneficial relationship in its entirety.[164] One should therefore not jump to any conclusions and not forget another view: that the UK became part of the European system of human rights protection at its inception and that EU accession to the ECHR is not about further restricting Member State competences, but about closing the last gaps in the

---

[159] L Lixinski, 'Taming the Fragmentation Monster? International Constitutionalism, "Pluralism Lite" and the Common Territory of the Two European Legal Orders' in Kosta, Skoutaris and Tzevelekos (n 25) 232.

[160] L Zucca, 'Monism and Fundamental Rights' in Dickson and Eleftheriadis (n 154) 349 and 351.

[161] N MacCormick, *Questioning Sovereignty* (Oxford, Oxford University Press, 1999) 116–17.

[162] N MacCormick, 'Risking Constitutional Collision in Europe?' (1998) 18 *Oxford Journal of Legal Studies* 517, 530.

[163] Hans Kelsen, *Pure Theory of Law*, 2nd edn (Berkeley, University of California Press, 1967) 328–44.

[164] Arden (n 87) 4.

already close-meshed web of European human rights law. In fact, if sceptics fear the subversion of the British constitutional order by the EU and the ECHR, they should accept that this revolution already happened when the UK became a member of these two supranational systems.

As this chapter has shown, accession does not entail any significant risks for the British constitution: EU accession to the ECHR does not add another layer of human rights protection, nor does it further complicate the three-dimensional web of fundamental rights regimes. Moreover, it will not tangle the hierarchies of the dualist UK legal order, which can only give effect to the law of the EU and the ECHR via the enactment of domestic legislation (that is, the HRA and the ECA) and international law. Hence it does not erode further the sovereignty of Parliament. Accession is about 'taming' the EU and subjecting it to Strasbourg's external scrutiny, and not about further limiting Member State sovereignty. Therefore the Member States, including the United Kingdom, should welcome accession as a pivotal move in the right direction. Accession does not take away any powers from the Member States; on the contrary, it will remedy the shortcomings of a currently pluralist system by unifying and hierarchising the European human rights order, and thus strengthen the rule of law and legal certainty for everybody.

15

An Austrian Ménage à Trois: The Convention, the Charter and the Constitution

ANDREAS TH MÜLLER*

I. INTRODUCTION

WHY *MÉNAGE À trois*? In its literal sense, this phrase means 'household of three'. And indeed, since the entry into force of the EU Charter of Fundamental Rights ('the Charter')[1] in 2009 there has been cohabitation of three in terms of sources of protection of human rights in Austria:[2] the European Convention on Human Rights ('the Convention'),[3] the Charter, and fundamental rights as guaranteed by the Austrian Constitution.[4] Alas, this is a far cry from being extraordinary. The fact that all EU Member States are also States Parties to the Convention puts all of them in the identical situation of having to deal with a tripartite system of fundamental rights protection since the Charter's coming into effect—at least within the scope of application of Union law. This also holds true for the UK, where—in addition to domestic human rights and civil liberties— the HRA makes (relevant provisions of) the Convention applicable within the UK, as does the European Communities Act 1972[5] with regard to the Charter.

Yet, it is submitted in the following that in Austria the recent 'constitutionalisation'[6] of the Charter by the Constitutional Court has taken this cohabitation

* I would like to thank Dr Maria Bertel (University of Innsbruck), Associate Professor Dr Christoph Bezemek (WU Wien), Clara Rauchegger (University of Cambridge) and Assistant Professor Dr Sebastian Schmid (University of Innsbruck) for their valuable comments on earlier versions of this contribution.

[1] [2010] OJ C83/389.

[2] See eg T Öhlinger, 'Die europäische Grundrechtsordnung nach dem Vertrag von Lissabon und ihre Auswirkungen auf den Grundrechtsschutz in Österreich' in R Feik and R Winkler (eds), *Festschrift für Walter Berka* (Vienna, Jan Sramek, 2013) 142, 144ff ('Dreiebenensystem des Grundrechtsschutzes', ie 'three-level system of fundamental rights protection').

[3] Convention for the Protection of Human Rights and Protection of Fundamental Freedoms of 4 November 1950, 213 UNTS 222.

[4] See below, II.A.

[5] By virtue of s 2(1) European Communities Act 1972, as amended by European Union (Amendment) Act 2008 (ch 7), s 2.

[6] The term 'constitutionalisation' refers to the granting of constitutional status to statutory provisions. Such 'normative upgrade' is normally reserved to Parliament (see below, II.A), but was effectuated with regard to (relevant parts of) the Charter by virtue of a judgment of the Constitutional Court (see below, III).

considerably further than in most, if not all, EU countries. When we look up 'ménage à trois' in the dictionary, we find the definition: 'a relationship or domestic arrangement in which three people ... live together or are romantically or sexually involved'.[7] In Austria, the three mentioned sources of fundamental rights—the Convention, the Charter and national fundamental rights—are now indeed intimately related to each other as constitutionally guaranteed rights. In contrast to a relationship frequently identified and deplored as one of conflict when discussing the interplay of several sources of human rights elsewhere in Europe, their relationship in Austria rather resembles a love affair.

At first sight, therefore, Austria does not offer a useful comparison, let alone a role model, for the UK, where the impact of the Charter has been thought to be restricted, or at least tempered, by virtue of Protocol No 30 to the Treaty of Lisbon,[8] whatever legal effects may be ascribed to it.[9] At the same time, Austria and the UK are in the same boat inasmuch as in both countries the domestic fundamental rights regime relies heavily on the Convention so far, particularly because a fully fledged domestic fundamental rights catalogue, such as we find in the German Basic Law, is lacking.[10] The emergence of the Charter as a new, complementary and/or competing fundamental rights catalogue challenges familiar schemes and traditional solutions for dealing with the impact of European human rights on the domestic legal order. The Austrian case may provide a particularly intriguing example—and to some UK lawyers perhaps a cautionary tale—of the complex relationship and interplay between the three sources of fundamental rights protection: it demonstrates the enormous dynamic and reformatory potential arising from the Charter and the important role that 'activist' courts may assume when it comes to (re)arranging the relative balance of European and domestic human rights.

To this effect, it is necessary first to explain the status of the Convention and of EU law within the Austrian domestic legal system (II) in order to lay the ground for better understanding the gist and ramifications of the Charter Judgment of the

---

[7] Oxford English Dictionary, www.oed.com.

[8] Protocol (No 30) on the application of the Charter of Fundamental Rights of the European Union to Poland and to the United Kingdom, in particular its Art 1(1): 'The Charter does not extend the ability of the Court of Justice of the European Union, or any court or tribunal of ... the United Kingdom, to find that the laws, regulations or administrative provisions, practices or action of ... the United Kingdom are inconsistent with the fundamental rights, freedoms and principles that it reaffirms.'

[9] While some conceive of the Protocol in terms of an 'opt-out' excluding the application of the Charter to the UK, the prevailing view is that the Protocol has merely, if at all, minor legal effects. See in particular Joined Cases C-411/10 *NS v Secretary of State for the Home Department* and C-493/10 *ME*, para 120, according to which Art 1(1) of the Protocol 'explains Article 51 of the Charter with regard to the scope thereof and does not intend to exempt the ... United Kingdom from the obligation to comply with the provisions of the Charter or to prevent a court of one of those Member States from ensuring compliance with those provisions'; see also P Craig and G de Búrca, *EU Law: Text, Cases and Materials*, 5th edn (Oxford, Oxford University Press, 2011) 395; S Peers, 'The "Opt-Out" that Fell to Earth: The British and Polish Protocol concerning the EU Charter of Fundamental Rights' (2012) 12 *Human Rights Law Review* 375; House of Commons, European Scrutiny Committee, *The Application of the EU Charter of Fundamental Rights in the UK: A State of Confusion*, 43rd Report of Session 2013–14, 2 April 2014, www.publications.parliament.uk/pa/cm201314/cmselect/cmeuleg/979/979.pdf.

[10] As regards the case of Austria, such a catalogue is at least lacking in the constitutional charter itself; see below, II.A.

Austrian Constitutional Court of 14 March 2012, which effectively elevated the Charter to the rank of constitutional law (III). On this basis, different dimensions of the 'Europeanness' of the Constitutional Court's Charter Judgment will be assessed and evaluated (IV), thus enabling us to draw some conclusions as to its potential impact on other Member States and the European system of human rights protection more generally (V).

II. SETTING THE SCENE

A. The Austrian Constitution and the Convention: The Convention as Part of the Constitution

While the UK was a founding member of the Council of Europe and thus an original State Party to the 1950 Convention, Austria only acceded to the Council of Europe in 1956[11] after having regained its full sovereignty,[12] and subsequently ratified the Convention in 1958.[13] The first years of the Convention's application were burdened with the looming question of its legal status within the domestic legal order. In 1964, this dispute was eventually solved by fiat of the (constitutional) legislator, by elevating the Convention to the rank of constitutional law.[14]

This was possible due to the peculiar structure of Austria's Federal Constitution: it consists not only of a central constitutional charter—the so-called 'Bundes-Verfassungsgesetz' or 'B-VG' ('Federal Constitutional Law')—but also of a substantial number of additional laws and provisions which form part of 'the Constitution'. In order to join the 'bloc of constitutionality', these laws or provisions must meet the double requirement enshrined in Article 44(1) of the Federal Constitutional Law: first, certain quora and voting thresholds must be met when these laws or provisions are voted upon in Parliament; and secondly, they must be expressly specified as having a 'constitutional' character.[15] The Convention became part and parcel of the Austrian Constitution in that way in 1964. This puts Austria in a unique position vis-a-vis other Convention States, as has repeatedly been noted in the academic literature.[16]

---

[11] *Bundesgesetzblatt* 121/1956. The *Bundesgesetzblatt* (*BGBl*) is the (Austrian) Federal Law Gazette and can be accessed via www.ris.bka.gv.at/Bund.

[12] State Treaty for the Re-Establishment of an Independent and Democratic Austria of 15 May 1955, 217 UNTS 2949.

[13] *Bundesgesetzblatt* 210/1958.

[14] *Bundesgesetzblatt* 59/1964 (with retroactive effect from Austria's accession to the Convention in 1958).

[15] Art 44(1): 'Constitutional laws or constitutional provisions contained in simple laws can be passed by the National Council only in presence of at least half of the members and by a two thirds majority of the votes case; they shall be explicitly specified as such ("constitutional law", "constitutional provision").'

[16] See D Thurnherr, 'The Reception Process in Austria and Switzerland' in H Keller and A Stone Sweet (eds), *A Europe of Rights: The Impact of the ECHR on National Legal Systems* (Oxford, Oxford University Press, 2008) 311, 325: 'Austria was the first State to fully incorporate the Convention in its constitutional legal order'; C Grabenwarter and K Pabel, *Europäische Menschenrechtskonvention*, 5th edn (Munich, CH Beck, 2012) 16.

Moreover, the Convention is at the very core of fundamental rights protection in Austria, similar to its role in the UK since the adoption of the HRA. In contrast to many other European constitutions, the Federal Constitutional Law does not contain a fundamental rights catalogue.[17] After World War I, the major political parties could not agree on such a catalogue because of the ideological rift between them.[18] Instead, they decided to continue—presumably on a temporary basis—with the Basic Law of 1867 on the General Rights of Citizens, which contains a number of civil and political rights.[19] For better or worse, the 1867 Law is still alive and kicking today, in spite of the fact that circumstances have changed quite drastically over the past 150 years.

This first pillar of the Austrian system of fundamental rights protection was joined, complemented and modernised by the Convention in the wake of its 'constitutionalisation' in 1964. Since then, Austria has had two major sources of fundamental rights upon which individuals can draw. Both the 1867 Basic Law and the Convention serve as standards of review before the Verfassungsgerichtshof (VfGH), the Austrian Constitutional Court. A person claiming that his or her Convention or Basic Law rights have been violated by an Austrian law or the decision of an Austrian authority may file a constitutional complaint to the Constitutional Court with a view to having the respective law or decision annulled for violation of higher constitutional law.[20]

B. The Austrian Constitution and EU Law: EU Law as 'Ordinary' (but Higher Ranking) Law

In contrast, the Constitutional Court has consistently held since Austria's accession to the European Union in 1995 that EU law is generally not a standard for judicial review before that Court.[21] This does not mean, however, that the Constitutional Court does not feel itself bound by EU law. On the contrary, it insists that it has

---

[17] Apart from scattered provisions displaying a fundamental rights character, eg Art 7(1) (principle of equality before the law) or Art 83(2), Art 87(3) and Art 135(3) of the Federal Constitutional Law (B-VG) (right to the lawful judge); as regards the latter, see in particular S Schmid, 'Der EuGH und das Recht auf ein Verfahren vor dem geschäftsverteilungsmäßigen Spruchkörper' in W Obwexer and W Schroeder (eds), *Der Schutz der Grundrechte in der Europäischen Union nach Lissabon. Neuerungen im europäischen Grundrechtsschutz am Beispiel Österreich* (Vienna, Verlag Österreich, 2015).

[18] See T Öhlinger and H Eberhard, *Verfassungsrecht*, 10th edn (Vienna, facultas.wuv, 2014) 45, 297; Thurnherr (n 16) 312; H Tretter, 'Austria' in R Blackburn and J Polakiewicz (eds), *Fundamental Rights in Europe: The European Convention on Human Rights and its Member States, 1950–2000* (Oxford, Oxford University Press, 2001) 103.

[19] Staatsgrundgesetz über die allgemeinen Rechte der Staatsbürger, 21 December 1867, *Reichsgesetzblatt (RGBl)* 142/1867.

[20] In contrast to the UK Supreme Court, which is restricted to declarations of incompatibility in cases of breach of Convention rights under s 3(1) HRA.

[21] Verfassungssammlung—Ausgewählte Entscheidungen des Verfassungsgerichtshofes (VfSlg) (Constitutional Court Reports—Selected Decisions of the Constitutional Court) 14886/1997, 15753/2000, 15810/2000; see also Constitutional Court, U 466/11-18 and U 1836/11-13, Judgment of 14 March 2012, VfSlg 19632/2012 ('Charter Judgment'), para 24 with further references. The English text of the

[f]rom the outset ... concurred with the case law of the Court of Justice of the European Union ... according to which the primacy of directly applicable rules over domestic law results from the autonomous validity of Community [now: European Union] law.[22]

Thus, when the Constitutional Court states in its *jurisprudence constante* that EU law is generally not a standard of its judicial review, it refers to the division of responsibilities enacted by the Austrian Constitution amongst the three highest courts of the country (the Constitutional Court, the Supreme Court and the Supreme Administrative Court). Among these, the Constitutional Court is specifically responsible for the protection of the so-called 'constitutionally guaranteed rights' (*'verfassungsgesetzlich gewährleistete Rechte'*). These are individual rights entrenched in the Constitution[23] which are adopted respecting the required quora and voting thresholds and which are expressly designated as constitutional provisions. Such constitutionally guaranteed rights are partly found in the constitutional charter itself, that is, the Federal Constitutional Law[24], but mostly in the Basic Law of 1867 on the General Rights of Citizens and in the Convention.[25]

In contrast, the EU Treaties and the law emerging from them were never 'constitutionalised' like the Convention. EU law, therefore, is not deemed to have constitutional status. Even though it enjoys primacy over national law, including constitutional law, and even though this primacy is expressly recognised by the Constitutional Court,[26] EU law only constitutes 'ordinary' law: it is therefore not a standard of review of legislative or administrative acts in the Constitutional Court. Hence, as opposed to rights entrenched in the 1867 Basic Law or the Convention,[27] if a person sees his or her rights under EU law violated by an Austrian law or the decision of an Austrian authority, he or she must turn to the ordinary or administrative courts, and in the last resort to the Supreme Court[28] in civil and criminal matters or the Supreme Administrative Court in administrative affairs,[29] to have the law or decision set aside. Hence, the primacy of EU law does not as such modify the division of responsibilities among the three highest courts of the country. In this respect, the Constitutional Court is specifically responsible for safeguarding constitutionally guaranteed rights, which, from the point of view of the Austrian constitutional system, do not include the rights arising from EU law.

Charter Judgment is cited from the version published on the Constitutional Court's website: www.vfgh.gv.at/cms/vfgh-site/attachments/9/6/0/CH0006/CMS1353421369433/grundrechtecharta_english_u466-11.pdf.

[22] Charter Judgment, ibid, para 19.
[23] VfSlg 17507/2005.
[24] Above, n 17.
[25] Above, II.A.
[26] See citation above, n 22.
[27] See text accompanying n 20.
[28] See Art 92(1) Federal Constitutional Law: 'The Supreme Court is the court of final instance in civil and criminal suits.'
[29] See VfSlg 14886/1997: '[S]ince from the perspective of the Constitutional Court a violation of Community law would be tantamount to a violation of simple (i.e. not of constitutional status) domestic law, which would be for the Supreme Administrative Court to address.'

This logic would also exclude the Charter rights from having the status of constitutionally guaranteed rights. As has been said, EU law, including EU primary law, was never 'constitutionalised' in Austria in the sense of submitting it to the procedure of Article 44(1) of the Federal Constitutional Law. This also held true for the Charter, which, pursuant to Article 6(1) of the Treaty on European Union (TEU), forms part of primary EU law. The Constitutional Court confirmed this expressly in a judgment of 24 September 2011.[30] However, this is no longer the case following the 2012 Charter Judgment.

III. THE CHARTER JUDGMENT OF THE AUSTRIAN CONSTITUTIONAL COURT: GIVING CONSTITUTIONAL RANK TO THE EU CHARTER OF FUNDAMENTAL RIGHTS

In a landmark judgment of 14 March 2012,[31] the Austrian Constitutional Court, deviating from its previous case law, declared (relevant parts of) the Charter to have constitutional status and therefore to entrench constitutionally protected rights which, as a consequence, serve as a standard of review for the Constitutional Court.

A. Facts of the Case

The Constitutional Court had to decide complaints against decisions of the Federal Asylum Tribunal concerning two Chinese nationals who had applied for international protection (asylum) in Austria in 2010. In both cases, the Tribunal had rejected their applications for an oral hearing.[32] They argued that their constitutionally guaranteed right to an effective remedy and a fair trial pursuant to Article 47 of the Charter had been violated because they had been denied an oral hearing.

In the well-established logic of Austrian constitutional law, the two complainants would have had a promising case before the Constitutional Court if they could have relied on Article 6 of the Convention because it is a constitutionally guaranteed right by virtue of the 1964 'constitutionalisation' of the Convention. Alas, this Convention provision was of no avail in the cases at hand: according to the jurisprudence of the European Court of Human Rights, proceedings concerning asylum and the residence of aliens in the territory of a State do not concern civil rights and obligations or criminal charges within the meaning of Article 6 of the Convention and therefore do not fall within its scope of application.[33]

In contrast, the scope of Article 47 of the Charter is not restricted to the determination of civil rights and obligations or of criminal charges, and it also includes purely administrative procedures, thus being broader than Article 6 of the Convention.[34]

---

[30] VfSlg 19496/2011; see in this regard A Gamper, 'Wie viel Kosmopolitismus verträgt eine Verfassung?' (2012) 134 *Juristische Blätter* 763, 770.

[31] VfSlg 19632/2012; as already seen above at n 21.

[32] See Charter Judgment (n 21) paras 5, 12.

[33] *Maaouia v France* (2001) 33 EHRR 42, para 40.

[34] See in particular the explanation on Art 47 of the Charter (OJ 2007 C303/30): 'In Union law, the right to a fair hearing is not confined to disputes relating to civil law rights and obligations.'

Against this background, the only option the complainants, or rather their resourceful lawyers, saw was to argue on the basis of Article 47 of the Charter—against all odds, as EU law was at the time no standard of review in the Constitutional Court. The Constitutional Court now had to decide whether Article 47 of the Charter constituted a 'constitutionally guaranteed right' under the Austrian Constitution.[35] To more or less everyone's astonishment,[36] the Court responded in the affirmative, even though it eventually concluded that the rights of the complainants under Article 47 of the Charter were not violated *in casu*.[37]

B. Reasoning of the Court

To support its core holding, namely that the Charter in general and its Article 47 in particular constitute constitutionally guaranteed rights under the Austrian Constitution, the Constitutional Court could not rely on Article 44 of the Federal Constitutional Law. In contrast to the Convention, the Charter was never formally denoted as 'constitutional law' by the Austrian Parliament.[38]

Instead, the Court—somewhat surprisingly—resorted to the principle of equivalence of remedies in EU law,[39] according to which procedural rules governing actions for safeguarding rights which individuals derive from EU law must not be less favourable than those governing similar domestic actions.[40] On this basis, the Constitutional Court came to the conclusion that the principle of equivalence, in combination with the peculiar domestic legal situation in Austria, required it to concede the status of 'constitutionally guaranteed rights' also to rights enshrined in the Charter.[41] The Court's reasoning was as follows: First, it claimed that

> [t]he system of legal protection set out in the Federal Constitutional Act provides in general for a concentration of claims for violation of constitutionally guaranteed rights with one instance, i.e. the Constitutional Court, which also is the only instance to adjudicate on such violations through general norms, i.e. statutory acts and regulations, and the only instance that has competence to set aside such norms.[42]

---

[35] See Charter Judgment (n 21) para 17: 'First one must verify whether the alleged violation of the Charter of Fundamental Rights actually gives rise to the competence of the Constitutional Court and whether the Charter of Fundamental Rights is a standard of review ...'

[36] A member of the Constitutional Court had, not long before the Charter Judgment (n 21), anticipated a shift in the Court's take on the Charter, though in a different direction; see R Müller, 'Verfassungsgerichtsbarkeit und Europäische Grundrechtecharta' [2012] *Österreichische Juristen-Zeitung* 159, 167f.

[37] See Charter Judgment (n 21) para 65.

[38] See text accompanying n 26.

[39] See Charter Judgment (n 21) para 27. As to the equivalence principle see, for instance, Craig and de Búrca (n 9) 237ff; in the context of the Constitutional Court's judgment see also M Pöschl, 'Verfassungsgerichtsbarkeit nach Lissabon. Anmerkungen zum Charta-Erkenntnis des VfGH' (2012) 67 *Zeitschrift für öffentliches Recht* 587, 592ff.

[40] See eg Case C-326/96 *Levez* [1998] ECR I-7835, para 18; see most recently Case C-112/13 *A v B*, EU:C:2014:2195, para 45, with further references.

[41] See Charter Judgment (n 21) para 35: 'The Constitutional Court has thus concluded that, based on the domestic legal situation, it follows from the equivalence principle that the rights guaranteed by the Charter of Fundamental Rights may also be invoked as constitutionally guaranteed rights ... and that they constitute a standard of review in general judicial review proceedings in the scope of application of the Charter of Fundamental Rights.'

[42] ibid, para 33.

If this special venue of judicial protection is opened up for fundamental rights complaints exclusively based in the domestic legal order, it must, by virtue of the equivalence principle, also be open for rights guaranteed under the Charter. This is because the Charter

> has at any rate for the scope of application of Union law the same function in many of its provisions—the 'rights'—as the constitutionally guaranteed rights have for the (autonomous) area of Austrian law. Largely overlapping areas of protection emerge from this intended near-identity in substance and similarity in wording of the Charter of Fundamental Rights and the ECHR, whose rights are constitutionally guaranteed rights in Austria. It would counter the notion of a centralized constitutional jurisdiction provided for in the Austrian Federal Constitution if the Constitutional Court were not competent to adjudicate on largely congruent rights such as those contained in the Charter of Fundamental Rights.[43]

Yet, given the fact that 'some of the individual guarantees afforded by the Charter of Fundamental Rights totally differ in their normative structure, and some, such as e.g. Article 22 or Article 37, do not resemble constitutionally guaranteed rights, but "principles"',[44] this reasoning only holds true 'if the guarantee contained in the Charter of Fundamental Rights is similar in its wording and determinateness[45] to rights that are guaranteed by the Austrian Federal Constitution'.[46] In the Constitutional Court's opinion, this question must be decided on a case-by-case basis.[47]

The Constitutional Court's reasoning might be summarised, admittedly in a rather colloquial manner, in the saying: It looks like a duck, it sounds like a duck, it must be a duck. As from the point of view of the Court (certain) Charter rights appear to function similarly to constitutionally guaranteed rights in the domestic legal system, it feels compelled to treat them analogously and to include them under the umbrella of constitutionally guaranteed rights. Some might have asked themselves whether the phrase used by the Court[48] suggested an identical or (only) comparable treatment of the two.[49] The doctrinal hair-splitting that might have arisen from this question calls to mind the early-Christian theological controversy over whether the Son was *homoousian* (identical in substance) or *homoiousian* (similar in substance) to the Father. Fortunately, in light of a recent judgment,[50] the Constitutional Court seems to have decided this looming controversy—just as in the case of the Nicene

---

[43] ibid, para 34.
[44] ibid, para 36.
[45] The English translation provided by the Constitutional Court says 'purpose'; but see below, n 56.
[46] Charter Judgment (n 21) para 35.
[47] See ibid, para 36.
[48] See ibid, para 30: 'verbürgt ... Rechte, wie sie die österreichische Verfassungsordnung in gleicher Weise als verfassungsgesetzlich gewährleistete Rechte garantiert' ('enshrine[s] ... rights as they are guaranteed by the Constitution in a similar manner as constitutionally safeguarded rights').
[49] Öhlinger (n 2) 150 seems to lean towards the second interpretation; see also T Öhlinger, 'Verfassungsrecht: Vorlagepflicht bei Verstoß eines nationalen Gesetzes gegen Art. 47 GRCh' [2014] *Europäische Zeitschrift für Wirtschaftsrecht* 950, 956 ('*Quasi-Verfassungsrang*', ie 'quasi-constitutional status').
[50] Constitutional Court, B 166/2013-17, Judgment of 12 March 2014, para 19: '... dass auch die von der GRC garantierten Rechte vor dem Verfassungsgerichtshof als verfassungsgesetzlich gewährleistete Rechte gemäß Art. 144 B-VG geltend gemacht werden können' ('... that also the rights guaranteed by the Charter may be relied upon before the Constitutional Court as constitutionally guaranteed rights pursuant to Article 144 of the Federal Constitutional Law', translation by the author); see also ibid, para 20.

orthodoxy—in favour of treating Charter rights that pass the test of wording and determinateness identically, that is as fully-fledged, constitutionally guaranteed rights in the meaning of the Austrian domestic legal system.[51]

IV. ASSESSING THE 'EUROPEAN-NESS' OF THE CHARTER JUDGMENT

For the Austrian legal system, the Charter Judgment is certainly a landmark decision. It has led to manifold and intense reactions from Austrian legal academia, sometimes embracing the outcome of the case, but generally (and occasionally quite harshly) criticising the reasoning in which the bench engages.[52] However, the implications of the judgment clearly go beyond Austria's borders. This can be namely seen in the fact that no less a figure than the President of the Court of Justice of the European Union (CJEU), Vassilios Skouris, reacted to the Charter Judgment (also on behalf of his fellow judges in Luxembourg) by sending a congratulatory note to the President of the Austrian Constitutional Court, Gerhart Holzinger.[53] This notable document states, amongst other things:

> The fact that the oldest constitutional court in Europe takes such a Europe-friendly position at this very moment in time deserves respect. By doing so, you make a substantial contribution to transforming the Fundamental Rights Charter into a common good of Europe and to developing the cooperation between the European Court of Justice and the national constitutional courts to the benefit of fundamental rights protection in Europe. We owe you much praise for that.[54]

The judgment is a remarkable and, in several respects, even brave step. It certainly stands out, as President Skouris stresses, as a 'Europe-friendly' ruling. Yet, its Europe-friendliness is not free of ambiguities. By making the very choices it made, the Constitutional Court saw itself forced to accept certain argumentative weaknesses and shortcuts which it apparently deemed unavoidable in view of the task before it. Against that background, four issues in relation to the 'European-ness' of the Constitutional Court's judgment deserve to be elaborated further: the faithfulness of the Constitutional Court's take on the Charter to its place in EU law (A), the problem of legal certainty and the uniform interpretation of Charter rights (B),

---

[51] With the only reservation that Charter rights fulfil this function only within the scope of application of Union law in the meaning of Art 51 of the Charter; see Charter Judgment (n 21) para 30.

[52] See rather benevolently M Potacs, 'Glosse zu VfGH 14.3.2012, U 466/11, U 1836/11' (2012) 134 *Juristische Blätter* 503, 511 ('*nicht unvertretbar*', ie 'not an indefensible position'); B-C Funk, 'Neue Doktrin des VfGH zur Anwendung europäischen Unionsrechts' [2012] *ecolex* 827, 829; K Lachmayer, 'The Austrian Approach towards European Human Rights' (2013) 7 *Vienna Journal on International Constitutional Law* 105, 106 ('The re-interpretation of Austrian constitutional law in the light of the European constitutional network is comprehensible and consistent'). For a more critical evaluation see, eg, Pöschl (n 39); F Merli, 'Umleitung der Rechtsgeschichte' (2012) 20 *Journal für Rechtspolitik* 355, 359ff; and in particular R Winkler, 'Die Grundrechtecharta und das österreichische Verfassungsrecht' [2012] *Fremden- und asylrechtliche Blätter* 2, 14, 16 and 19f.

[53] Letter of 25 May 2012 (on file with the author); see also the reference by the then Vice-President of the European Commission, Viviane Reding, to the 'Austrian model of Charter incorporation', as mentioned in Öhlinger (n 49) 956.

[54] Letter of 25 May 2012 (n 53) (translation by the author).

the separation of powers between the political and the judicial branches (C), and the division of responsibilities among different courts (D).

A. Is the Constitutional Court's Take on the Charter Faithful to its Place in EU law?

First, the Constitutional Court has not given up on its original idea that EU law is generally not a standard of review for its decisions. The Charter is an exception in that regard, or, to put it more precisely: those guarantees in the Charter which are 'similar in [their] *wording and purpose* to rights that are guaranteed by the Austrian Federal Constitution'[55] benefit from the exceptional constitutional status. In the German original, this passage reads '*in ihrer Formulierung und Bestimmtheit*', which should better be translated as 'wording and determinateness'.[56]

The starting point and basis of the reasoning of the Constitutional Court is the assumption that the Charter is different and therefore distinguishable from the rest of EU law. This premise might make sense in the light of the argumentative needs from a domestic perspective, but it is problematic when placed in the bigger picture. To claim that 'the Charter is an area that is markedly distinct from the "Treaties"'[57] is not easily reconcilable with Article 6(1) TEU, which actually emphasises that the Charter has 'the same legal value' as the Treaties.

Even less convincing is the attempt to argue that there is a categorical difference between the Charter and the rest of EU (fundamental rights) law by referring to the former as 'a detailed catalogue of rights and duties ... [which] is not comparable to the derivation of legal provisions from general legal principles'.[58] The effort to separate the Charter prong of EU fundamental rights from its general principles prong is doomed to fail for a number of reasons.

First and foremost, the very existence and structure of Article 6 TEU indicates that there is *one* integrated concept of EU fundamental rights which has different manifestations,[59] as exemplified in the three paragraphs of this article. Article 6(1) is eager to underscore the identical legal status of the Charter with the Treaties. This is a far cry from reading the provision as indicating a gap (or as the Constitutional Court is forced to argue: a trench) between the Charter and the Treaties.[60] Second,

---

[55] Charter Judgment (n 21) para 35 (emphasis added).

[56] See C Bezemek, 'Wording and Determinateness—Indeterminately Worded. A Few Remarks on Questions to be Asked Again' (2013) 7 *Vienna Journal on International Constitutional Law* 95, 97f; see in this regard also Pöschl (n 39) 594.

[57] See Charter Judgment (n 21) para 25, referring to Art 6(1) TEU which speaks of 'the Charter of Fundamental Rights and the Treaties', thus treating them as different legal entities.

[58] ibid, para 38.

[59] For the UK context see eg the statement of Professor Douglas-Scott in House of Commons Report (n 9) 30.

[60] This point was made by several commentators; see eg Pöschl (n 39) 591; Merli (n 52) 356; Winkler (n 52) 15; S Mayr, 'Verfassungsgerichtlicher Prüfungsgegenstand und Prüfungsmaßstab im Spannungsfeld nationaler, konventions- und unionsrechtlicher Grundrechtsgewährleistungen' [2012] *Zeitschrift für Verwaltung* 401, 410; Bezemek (n 56) 96 fn 13.

very much in the same line of argument, the Charter itself underscores in its Preamble that its purpose is 'to strengthen the protection of fundamental rights ... by making those rights more visible in a Charter'. This appears to be the exact opposite of conceiving of the Charter as something distinct from the rest of EU law.[61] Third, there is no indication whatsoever in the case law of the CJEU since the entry into force of the Charter that would militate in favour of, or even indicate, a clear-cut distinction between written and unwritten fundamental rights. Finally, it is difficult to see how the Charter can credibly be conceived of as a source of guarantees categorically distinguishable from the Treaties, notably given the fact that a considerable number of the rights contained in the Charter are virtually identically enshrined in the Treaties,[62] such as the prohibition on discrimination, some fundamental freedoms and the rights of Union citizens.[63] If one adds to the picture the body of EU fundamental rights law as developed by the CJEU through its general principles jurisprudence (Article 6(3) TEU), hardly any Charter guarantee is left that could claim independence vis-a-vis the remaining body of written and unwritten primary law (particularly if one keeps in mind that for the Constitutional Court only those guarantees count that meet the 'wording and determinateness' threshold). Thus, there is simply too much overlap to allow for a neat dissection of the Charter from the rest of EU law as suggested in the judgment's reasoning.

In sum, the approach taken by the Constitutional Court represents an arguably calculated *relecture* (or should one say: misreading) of EU law and of the place of the Charter within it. The motivation to emancipate the Charter and to somewhat upgrade it vis-a-vis the rest of EU (primary) law seems to be predominately triggered by the domestic purposes pursued by the Court.[64]

B. Legal Certainty and Uniform Interpretation of Charter Rights

According to the Constitutional Court, the question of which elements of the Charter actually represent constitutionally guaranteed rights can only be decided on a case-by-case basis. This depends, as we have seen, on whether the Charter provisions are similar regarding their 'wording and determinateness' to rights guaranteed under the Austrian Constitution, notably Convention rights. After all, Article 52(3) of the Charter expressly envisages that it contains 'rights which correspond to rights guaranteed by the [Convention]'.

This approach might prove detrimental to legal certainty, because it is not clear which other Charter rights—apart from Article 47—will qualify as constitutionally

---

[61] See Merli (n 52) 356.

[62] Art 52(2) of the Charter explicitly takes note of such rights: 'Rights recognised by this Charter for which provision is made in the Treaties shall be exercised under the conditions and within the limits defined by those Treaties.'

[63] See, for instance, Arts 15, 16, 21 and 36 as well as 39–46 of the Charter. It is very telling in this regard that the Constitutional Court itself has in its case law following the Charter Judgment expressly acknowledged that Art 21(2) of the Charter and Art 18(1) TFEU correspond to each other as regards their content; see Constitutional Court, B 533/2013-18, Judgment of 5 March 2015, para 26.

[64] See in more detail below, IV.D.i.

guaranteed rights. Yet, and this is just another proof that the judgment is a well-calculated manoeuvre of the Constitutional Court, its docket is now filling with complaints seeking to clarify whether other provisions of the Charter constitute constitutionally guaranteed rights. For instance, Article 21(1) and (2) has meanwhile been accorded this status, while Articles 22 and 37 of the Charter have been struck off the list of candidates.[65]

From the perspective of EU law, the dynamics arising from the Charter Judgment that can be witnessed in Austria have the potential to challenge the uniform application of EU law. After all, we must never forget that it is the Charter of Fundamental Rights *of the European Union* that the Constitutional Court is expounding.[66] Everything depends on the Court's preparedness to turn to the CJEU for preliminary references. So far, the Constitutional Court has been remarkably open-minded in this regard,[67] in notable contrast to other European constitutional courts such as the German Bundesverfassungsgericht.[68] In addition, in the Charter Judgment the Court explicitly confirmed that it would request clarification from the Luxembourg Court regarding the interpretation of the Charter.[69] At the same time, the Constitutional Court failed to submit the very question of the reach of the equivalence principle even though the interpretation of that principle by the Constitutional Court was far from being an instance of *acte clair*.[70] In the same vein, as the Constitutional Court is increasingly involving itself in the 'Charter adjudication business', its record in terms of requests for preliminary references appears to be rather modest so far.[71]

---

[65] As regards Arts 22 and 37 see already Charter Judgment (n 21) para 36, and the reaffirmation in the judgment of 12 March 2014 (n 50) para 19; as regards the recognition of Art 21(1) of the Charter as a constitutionally guaranteed right see the latter judgment, para 20; see the judgment of 5 March 2015 (n 63), paras 19, 27, confirming Art 21(1) of the Charter and newly recognising Art 21(2) of the Charter as a constitutionally guaranteed right; see also Constitutional Court, G 47/2012-49 ua, Judgment of 27 June 2014, para 144 in relation to Art 7 and 8 of the Charter; Constitutional Court, G 95/2013-14, Judgment of 9 October 2014, para 101 and G 107/2013-11, Judgment of 3 March 2015, paras 54, 55 in relation to Art 15 and 16 of the Charter; as regards the pertinent case law see in particular A Orator, 'Rechtsprechungsübersicht: Verfassungsgerichtshof und Unionsgerichte. Administrativrechtlich relevante Judikatur im Jahr 2014 (Teil 1)' (2015) *Zeitschrift für Verwaltung* 75, 77. For further discussion see Öhlinger (n 2) 151, notably regarding Arts 1 (dignity) and 18 (right to asylum) of the Charter.

[66] Chief Justice Marshall famously wrote in 1819: 'we must never forget it is a constitution we are expounding': US Supreme Court, *McCulloch v Maryland*, 17 US (4 Wheaton) 316, 407 (1819).

[67] See notably V Trofaier-Leskovar, 'The Charter of Fundamental Rights of the European Union in the Austrian Constitutional Court's Case Law' (2013) 7 *Vienna Journal on International Constitutional Law* 71, fnn 1 and 2, with further references. See in particular the reference of the Austrian Constitutional Court in the data retention case: Joined Cases C-293/12 and C-594/12 *Digital Rights Ireland and Seitlinger*, EU:C:2014:238.

[68] The German Federal Constitutional Court (Bundesverfassungsgericht) has only recently, for the first time ever in its history, submitted a preliminary question to the CJEU (concerning the OMT Decision of the European Central Bank); see Decision of 14 January 2014, 2 BvR 2728/13 et al; see also Case C-62/14 *Gauweiler et al*, EU:C:2015:400.

[69] See Charter Judgment (n 21) para 40.

[70] See Winkler (n 52) 15.

[71] For instance, the case at the basis of the judgment of 12 March 2014 (n 50) should not have been decided without turning to Luxembourg for a preliminary reference. In the light of the alternative reasoning of the Court, it should have—the first alternative (see ibid, paras 22ff)—asked for clarification of the *Åkerberg Fransson* jurisprudence (Case C-617/10 *Åkerberg Fransson* [2013] ECR I-0000), in combination with the rights flowing from Union citizenship, given the fact that even the use of one's mother tongue in criminal or civil proceedings falls within the scope of Union law (Case C-274/96 *Bickel und Franz*

C. Separation of Powers Between the Political and Judicial Branches

Another aspect of the criticism levelled against the Constitutional Court's Charter Judgment relates to the question of separation of powers. The Austrian Constitution monopolises the right to amend the Constitution with the Federal Parliament. With its judgment, the Court has—by virtue of its own authority—effectively added new elements to the 'bloc of constitutionality', thus bypassing the requirements of the Federal Constitutional Law.

This fuels the long-standing criticism that there is an ongoing shift in the balance from the political to the judicial branch, thus raising fears of a *gouvernement des juges*. This is an accusation often made vis-a-vis the European courts.[72] However, it seems that several high domestic courts have developed a tendency of becoming more 'activist' themselves, under the impression, if not pressure, of the Europeanisation of the fundamental rights system and the dynamic jurisprudence of the Strasbourg and Luxembourg Courts.[73]

In this regard, it is well worth mentioning that the first calls for the constitutional legislator to ratify and thereby to seal the judicial 'constitutionalisation' of the Charter by formally elevating it to the rank of constitutional law were voiced not long after the Charter Judgment had been handed down.[74] Such as step would constitute a remarkable spillover: the judicial activism of the Constitutional Court might sooner or later prompt the real 'maker of the constitution', that is, Parliament, to simply follow suit and endorse the *fait accompli* (or rather *droit accompli*) set by the Constitutional Court. Of course, alternatively, the constitutional legislator could also impose its will on the Constitutional Court by formally 'de-constitutionalising' the Charter or confirming its non-constitutional character via authentic interpretation under the requirements of Article 44(1) of the Federal Constitutional Law. However, neither is it realistic that a two-thirds majority could be found within Parliament to correct the Constitutional Court's advance, nor does the mere possibility of returning to the previous status quo justify the self-arrogation of constitutionalising powers by the Constitutional Court. In addition, to the extent

---

[1998] ECR I-7637; Case C-322/13 *Rüffer*, EU:C:2014:189), let alone the question whether a homosexual couple should have access to national courts for the purpose of having their Dutch marriage repeated in Austria in order to clarify their status as a married couple in that country, as was the issue in the case at hand; see also A Wimmer, 'Die Anwendung der Grundrechte-Charta durch Verwaltungsbehörden und nicht-oberstinstanzliche Gerichte als Normenkontrollmaßstab' in W Obwexer and W Schroeder (eds), *Der Schutz der Grundrechte in der Europäischen Union nach Lissabon. Neuerungen im europäischen Grundrechtsschutz am Beispiel Österreich* (Vienna, Verlag Österreich, 2015; in print) in this regard. In the second alternative (see ibid, paras 26 ff), the Constitutional Court should have turned to the CJEU to offer it an opportunity to pronounce itself on the relation of Art 21(1) of the Charter and Art 14 of the Convention; see also below, n 106.

[72] See among many others H Rasmussen, *On Law and Policy in the European Court of Justice: A Comparative Study in Judicial Policymaking* (Dordrecht, Martinus Nijhoff, 1986).

[73] See, for instance, Merli (n 52) 359, who aptly describes the phenomenon of 'Europeanization of law, in particular of fundamental rights law' where national fundamental rights are increasingly being 'pushed way, substituted or superseded' by European fundamental rights.

[74] See in particular C Grabenwarter, 'Europäische Grundrechte in der Rechtsprechung des Verfassungsgerichtshofes' (2012) 20 *Journal für Rechtspolitik* 298, 304.

that one is prepared to embrace the Constitutional Court's (albeit far from cogent) reasoning which is after all based on the EU law principle of equivalence of remedies, the primacy of EU law might be opposed to a such move.

D. Division of Responsibilities among Courts

The Charter Judgment of the Constitutional Court is also telling in terms of the interplay between different judicial actors, both at the domestic level and in a European context.

(i) The Domestic Level: Promoting the Rivalry or Even a Battle of Courts?

The key conclusions of the Charter Judgment are immediately preceded, and prepared, by the Court's dicta on the structure of the domestic system of fundamental rights protection under the Austrian Constitution.[75] There the Constitutional Court refers to the 'concentration of claims for violation of constitutionally guaranteed rights with one instance, i.e. the Constitutional Court' and to a 'centralized constitutional jurisdiction'. The Court thus accords itself a privileged role in the domestic adjudication of the Charter, or at least of those elements in it that are 'similar in wording and determinateness' to Convention rights (qua domestic fundamental rights).

This claim has been strongly criticised both in academia and from within other superior courts in Austria, namely the Supreme Court and the Supreme Administrative Court, which conceive of themselves as equally qualified 'fundamental rights courts'.[76] It is well worth pointing out once more that the original jurisprudence of the Constitutional Court would have kept it entirely out of the 'Charter adjudication business'.[77] By virtue of its 2012 landmark decision, the Court not only stripped off this self-imposed restriction, it even went as far as seeking, if not a monopoly, then at least a *primus inter pares* role for itself in the adjudication of the Charter,[78] to the detriment of its sister courts.[79]

---

[75] See Charter Judgment (n 21) paras 33 and 34; as to the Constitutional Court's position in the Austrian legal system see A Gamper and F Palermo, 'The Constitutional Court of Austria: Modern Profiles of an Archetype of Constitutional Review' (2008) 3 *Journal of Comparative Law* 64, 67ff; C Bezemek, 'A Kelsenian Model of Constitutional Adjudication' (2012) 67 *Zeitschrift für öffentliches Recht* 115, 119f.

[76] As to the Supreme Court, see below, n 82; as regards the Supreme Administrative Court, see Judgment of 23 January 2013, 2010/15/0196, 2.3. See further Pöschl (n 39) 595f; Merli (n 52) 358; Potacs (n 52) 509; Bezemek (n 56) 96, all with further references; see also the 'stock-taking' on the part of (former) President of the Supreme Administrative Court C Jabloner, 'Das Verhältnis zwischen europäischer Gerichtsbarkeit und Verwaltungsgerichtshof' in C Grabenwarter and E Vranes (eds), *Kooperation der Gerichte im europäischen Verfassungsverbund* (Vienna, Manz, 2013) 171, 174ff.

[77] See the 2011 judgment of the Constitutional Court (n 30).

[78] See the judgment of 12 March 2014 (n 50) para 22 which speaks of the '*Leitfunktion*' ('leading role') of the Constitutional Court concerning 'the interpretation of constitutionally protected rights of the Austrian Federal Constitution' and refers, in this regard, to its judgment in VfSlg 19730/2012: '*Leitfunktion für die einheitliche Auslegung und Anwendung des Verfassungsrechts*' ('leading role for the uniform interpretation and application of constitutional law').

[79] See Potacs (n 52) 511; Merli (n 52) 359; Mayr (n 60) 409, 416.

On the one hand, pursuant to Article 133(5) of the Federal Constitutional Law, legal matters pertaining to the competence of the Constitutional Court are excluded from the competence of the Supreme Administrative Court. Thus, claims of Charter violations which hitherto were treated as violations of 'ordinary' law falling within the Supreme Administrative Court's competence now fall into the realm of constitutional questions for which the Constitutional Court is responsible. On the other hand, according to Article 89(2) of the Federal Constitutional Law, 'should a court of justice have concerns ... regarding a law on the ground of its being unconstitutional ..., the court shall file an application with the Constitutional Court to repeal that piece of legislation'.[80] In the light of the 'constitutionalisation' of Charter questions, the Supreme Court and the Supreme Administrative Court understandably feared being compelled to turn to a Constitutional Court which would function as a domestic 'doorkeeper', seeking to monopolise the Charter interpretation or at least to control access to the CJEU as final interpreter of the Charter.[81]

This might cast a different light on the preliminary reference of the Supreme Court in the case of *A v B*.[82] On its surface, it deals with a rather technical question of civil procedure law relating to the *Brussels I* Regulation. In essence, however, it arguably embodies a tactical move by the Supreme Court to outplay the Constitutional Court via the Luxembourg Court. In its reference decision, the Supreme Court indicates that the Charter Judgment might imply that where Austrian law violates the Charter, it may not be sufficient that the Supreme Court simply disapplies Austrian law because of the primacy of EU law. According to the Supreme Court, it might be obligated under Article 89(2) of the Federal Constitutional Law to first turn to the Constitutional Court for formal annulment of that law because, by virtue of the Charter Judgment, it violates constitutionally guaranteed rights.[83]

By formulating the preliminary question in the way it did,[84] the Supreme Court raised not only the issue of the proper distribution of competences among the Austrian highest courts (that is, in the domestic realm), but also that of the distribution of competences between national constitutional courts and the CJEU (that is, in a vertical perspective). In fact, the Supreme Court suggested to the CJEU that the Charter Judgment was a 'Europe-friendly' judgment only on its face; it might actually undermine the supremacy of EU law.

---

[80] In conjunction with Article 135(4) of the Federal Constitutional Law as regards the administrative courts as well as the Supreme Administrative Court. As to the reach of this provision see, for instance, A Wimmer, 'Wann muss ein Gericht die Aufhebung eines Gesetzes beim VfGH beantragen?' (2013) 68 *Zeitschrift für öffentliches Recht* 417, with further references. As regards the recent changes in relation to Art 89(2) of the Federal Constitutional Law see *BGBl* I 114/2013 as well as M Bertel, 'Der Parteiantrag auf Normenkontrolle' (2013) 21 *Journal für Rechtspolitik* 269, 273; L Khakzadeh-Leiler, 'Der Parteienantrag auf Normenkontrolle' [2015] *Österreichische Juristen-Zeitung* 543.

[81] As to this aspect, see below, IV.D.ii.

[82] Supreme Court, Decision of 17 December 2012, 9 Ob 15/12i. The underlying case deals with tort claims following the alleged abduction of Kazakh nationals by the late Kazakh ambassador in Austria, Rakhat Aliyev.

[83] Case C-112/13 *A v B*, EU:C:2014:2195, para 25.

[84] ibid, para 27, in particular first sub-question.

(ii) European Level: The Question of the 'Last Say'

The CJEU has, as is commonly known, always reacted reluctantly, if not with hostility, to attempts by national constitutional (or highest) courts to establish or promote special procedures that might undermine the willingness or ability of domestic courts to make preliminary references to the Luxembourg Court and thereby weaken the effectiveness of EU law.[85] In its preliminary reference mentioned above, the Supreme Court sought to present the Constitutional Court as doing precisely that.[86] Advocate-General Bot seemed to follow this reasoning when he stated in his Opinion that the use of the equivalence principle by the Constitutional Court (as presented by the Supreme Court) might lead to the paradoxical result of weakening the primacy of EU law.[87] The Advocate-General emphasised, however, that a national special procedure before the Constitutional Court is not per se incompatible with EU law if it neither eliminates nor suspends, impairs or defers each court's ability to make a preliminary reference to the CJEU.[88]

The CJEU, for its part, has clearly identified the reasoning of the Constitutional Court and the ensuing preliminary reference of the Supreme Court as touching upon 'the' core question of the relationship between EU law and domestic law: no less an issue than the primacy of EU law is at stake here.[89] At the same time, the Luxembourg Court seemed to generally accept the Constitutional Court as an 'honest broker' in reconciling the needs of (Austrian) constitutional law and the requirements of EU law.[90] At least it expressly, and benevolently, took note of the Constitutional Court's profession of loyalty to the *Melki and Abdeli* jurisprudence.[91] Hence, while the Luxembourg Court responded to the Supreme Court's request in the affirmative, it required the Supreme Court judges to ascertain whether national provisions, such as Article 89(2) of the Federal Constitutional Law, can be construed in such a way as to comply with EU law.[92] According to *Melki and Abdeli*, national legislation providing for an interlocutory procedure for the review of the constitutionality of national law is permitted

---

[85] See already Case 106/77 *Simmenthal* [1978] ECR 629; Joined Cases C-188/10 and C-189/10 *Melki and Abdeli* [2010] ECR I-5667.

[86] See Case C-112/13 *A v B*, EU:C:2014:2195, para 26. This appears as a quite biased reading of the Constitutional Court's Charter Judgment (n 21) which expressly acknowledges the *Melki and Abdeli* case law of the CJEU; see Charter Judgment (n 21) para 42.

[87] Opinion of Advocate-General Bot in Case C-112/13 *A v B*, EU:C:2014:207, paras 68f.

[88] See ibid, para 70.

[89] Case C-112/13 *A v B*, EU:C:2014:2195, para 29.

[90] A member of the Austrian Constitutional Court has characterised the Charter Judgment as 'a very European and integration-friendly offer for a European fundamental rights community': see M Holoubek, 'Das Verhältnis zwischen europäischer Gerichtsbarkeit und Verfassungsgerichtshof' in C Grabenwarter and E Vranes (eds), *Kooperation der Gerichte im europäischen Verfassungsverbund* (Vienna, Manz, 2013) 157, 165ff.

[91] Case C-112/13 *A v B*, EU:C:2014:2195, para 32. In Case C-188/10 *Melki and Abdeli* [2010] ECR I-5667, para 57, the CJEU held that EU law 'precludes Member State legislation which establishes an interlocutory procedure for the review of the constitutionality of national laws, in so far as the priority nature of that procedure prevents all the other national courts or tribunals from exercising their right or fulfilling their obligation to refer questions to the Court of Justice for a preliminary ruling'.

[92] Case C-112/13 *A v B*, EU:C:2014:2195, para 46.

in so far as the other national courts ... remain free, to refer to the Court of Justice for a preliminary ruling, at whatever stage of the proceedings they consider appropriate ... any question which they consider necessary, to adopt any measure necessary to ensure provisional judicial protection of the rights conferred under the European Union legal order, and to disapply, at the end of such an interlocutory procedure, the national legislative provision at issue if they consider it to be contrary to EU law.[93]

There can be hardly any doubt that such harmonious interpretation of Article 89(2) of the Federal Constitutional Law is both possible and plausible.[94] Therefore, the attack by the Supreme Court on the Constitutional Court was doomed to fail.

Yet, there remains a problem with regard to the Constitutional Court's purported role as 'honest broker' between the needs of constitutional law and EU law. The Luxembourg Court acknowledges that the repeal of a national law due to its unconstitutionality may in many contexts[95] also promote the effectiveness of EU law. Even though Article 267 TFEU makes all domestic courts part and parcel of the 'system of cooperation'[96] between the courts at the Union and national levels, in recent times the CJEU appears to have leant more strongly towards certain judicial key actors in the Member States, amongst them first and foremost the national constitutional courts[97] inasmuch as they are amenable to active cooperation with the Luxembourg Court. The Austrian Constitutional Court would seem to be a model actor in this regard[98] and may thus rightly hope to obtain a certain measure of support from the Luxembourg Court for its 'doorkeeper' ambitions. It thus comes as no surprise that the Constitutional Court got the benefit of doubt,[99] to the detriment of the Supreme Court which, by conveying its preoccupation regarding the respect of the primacy of EU law to the CJEU, sought to recommend itself as an exemplary partner in Luxembourg.

Alas, the approach of relying on privileged partners stands and falls with their preparedness to actually make use of the preliminary reference procedure under Article 267 TFEU. The Constitutional Court has, in the Charter Judgment, rearticulated its preparedness to refer every Charter-related issue to Luxembourg where this is required by EU law.[100] However, its approach appears to be strangely selective. As a general rule, the Court will request a preliminary ruling from the CJEU if it has doubts about the interpretation of the Charter. At the same time, it

---

[93] Case C-188/10 *Melki and Abdeli* [2010] ECR I-5667, para 57. The CJEU expressly confirmed this jurisprudence in Case C-112/13 *A v B*, EU:C:2014:2195, para 46.

[94] This is also the view articulated by the Constitutional Court; see Charter Judgment (n 21) para 42.

[95] But not in all; see Case C-112/13 *A v B*, EU:C:2014:2195, paras 42f.

[96] See ibid, para 39; see recently Opinion 2/13 of 18 December 2014, para 176 ('dialogue between one court and another').

[97] For an analogy (admittedly a remote one), see the new Protocol No 16 to the Convention (not yet in force) according to which 'highest courts and tribunals of a High Contracting State ... may request the Court to give advisory opinions on questions of principle relating to the interpretation and application of [the Convention]'.

[98] Above, n 67.

[99] See in this regard the aforementioned Letter of 25 May 2012 (n 53) in which President Skouris, on behalf of the CJEU, expressly compliments the Constitutional Court on the Charter Judgment reasoning 'because it places particularly strong emphasis on the cooperation between [the two courts]'.

[100] Charter Judgment (n 21) para 40.

has announced that it would not to do so in case of an interpretive question relating to the Convention per se, the Convention not forming part of the body of EU law.[101] However, the Constitutional Court seems to include in this latter category constellations where the interpretation of the Convention might indirectly affect the interpretation of EU law:

> If [doubts about the interpretation of a provision of Union law] do not arise, in particular in light of the ECHR and pertaining case law of the European Court of Human Rights and other supreme courts, the Constitutional Court will decide without seeking a preliminary ruling.[102]

This referral policy could arguably violate EU law. In a case of implementation of EU law within the meaning of Article 51(1) of the Charter, the Charter is applicable, and the Constitutional Court as a court of last resort is in principle obliged, under Article 267(3) TFEU, to request a preliminary ruling when questions of interpretation of the Charter arise. However, the Constitutional Court reasons that a request for a preliminary ruling is not required 'if the issue is not relevant for the decision' and if 'the answer, whatever it is, can have no impact on the decision of the case'.[103] In doing so, it seems to misconceive of the very function of the preliminary ruling procedure. Whether 'a constitutionally guaranteed right, especially a right of the ECHR, has the same scope of application as a right of the Charter of Fundamental Rights'[104] can only be known *after* consulting the Luxembourg Court, notably for its assessment of the impact of Article 52(3) of the Charter to the question at hand.[105] It is not, and cannot be, decisive that the Constitutional Court considers the scope of application to be coextensive 'in light of the ECHR and pertaining case law of the European Court of Human Rights and other supreme courts'.[106]

This standard appears to be a relaxed and attenuated version of an *acte clair* doctrine, not properly reflecting the rather strict *CILFIT* criteria laid down by the CJEU.[107] Furthermore, the *Melloni* jurisprudence of the CJEU suggests that Article 53 of the Charter only allows deviating national human rights standards to apply 'provided that the level of protection provided for by the Charter, *as interpreted by the Court*, and the primacy, unity and effectiveness of EU law are not thereby compromised'.[108] Hence, it is not so much the result of Article 89(2) of the Federal Constitutional Law, as suggested by the Supreme Court, but rather the Constitutional Court's announcement that in such cases it 'will base its decision on

---

[101] ibid.

[102] ibid.

[103] ibid, para 44.

[104] ibid.

[105] See also Pöschl (n 39) 598; C Brenn, 'VfGH versus Unionsrecht. Unionsrechtliche Würdigung des Grundrechteerkenntnisses' [2012] *Österreichische Juristen-Zeitung* 1062.

[106] The problematic nature of this approach has already become apparent in the judgment of 12 March 2014 (n 50). In the second part of its alternative reasoning, the Constitutional Court, without making a preliminary reference to the CJEU, relied on its own understanding of Art 52(3) of the Charter to reach the conclusion that Art 21(1) of the Charter, like Art 14 of the Convention, leaves the Member States a significant margin of appreciation; see n 71 above.

[107] See Case 283/81 *CILFIT* [1982] ECR 3415, para 21.

[108] Case C-399/11 *Melloni* [2013] ECR I-0000, para 60 (emphasis added).

the Austrian Constitution without there being a need for reference for a preliminary ruling under the terms of Article 267 TFEU'[109] that puts the Constitutional Court in jeopardy of violating EU law.

The 'constitutionalisation', and in that sense the upgrade, of the Charter within the Austrian legal order is therefore not an automatic guarantee that the Charter will be strengthened in its European aspirations. The ramifications of the Charter Judgment are much more complex. Such a move might also result in a domestic high court seeking to incorporate the Charter into its own vision of fundamental rights protection, which tends to be dominated by the needs of the domestic constitutional order. Even though the Constitutional Court stresses in its judgment the need for a 'coherent' or harmonising interpretation of the various sources of fundamental rights in Europe,[110] such an approach might endanger the uniform interpretation and application of those rights across Europe. In addition, it gives rise to the equally crucial question of who will eventually decide on how this coherence is to be brought about and who has the final say in these matters.

V. CONCLUDING REMARKS: THE SUBSTANTIVE *MÉNAGE À TROIS* AND THE INSTITUTIONAL *MÉNAGE À TROIS* (QUATRE)

The Charter Judgment of the Austrian Constitutional Court furthers the openness and 'Europe-friendliness' of the Austrian legal system, which has been one of its characteristic traits,[111] not only since accession to the EU in 1995, but already (at least) since the 1964 elevation of the Convention to the rank of constitutional law. Without being able to delve into this question in more detail, this phenomenon is certainly linked to the 'non-monolithic' character of the Austrian Constitution, not so unlike the UK's constitutional order in this regard, and its evolution and enrichment over time by components of very different pedigree and character.[112]

In addition, it has correctly been noted that the peculiar Austrian 'enthusiasm towards European integration through human rights protection', in contrast to the German Constitutional Court's position, is also due to the fact that 'the Austrian constitutional identity has never been similarly interweaved with a "constitutional patriotism" regarding human rights'.[113] On the one hand, whereas the *Grundgesetz* has long been considered to constitute an 'objective system of values' ('*objektive*

---

[109] Charter Judgment (n 21) para 44.

[110] See ibid, para 46. According to Gamper (n 30) 880, the Court applies 'a conglomerate standard which nourishes itself from most different sources—constitutional law, international law and European law'. Bezemek (n 56) 95 acknowledges the Constitutional Court's objective of 'aiming for a more coherent fundamental rights jurisprudence within the Austrian judiciary'.

[111] See Gamper (n 30) 880, praising the Court's jurisprudence as 'open, cooperative and dialogue-oriented' (see also the references ibid, 880 note 58); see also T Öhlinger, 'Die Offenheit der österreichischen Bundesverfassung gegenüber dem Völkerrecht und dem Europarecht' in T Giegerich (ed), *Der 'offene Verfassungsstaat' des Grundgesetzes nach 60 Jahren* (Berlin, Duncker & Humblot, 2010) 367.

[112] Above, II.A and II.B.

[113] C Fuchs, 'An Austrian Enthusiasm towards European Human Rights Protection' (2013) 7 *Vienna Journal on International Constitutional Law* 108.

Wertordnung'),[114] the Austrian approach towards constitutional law in general and fundamental rights in particular has traditionally been more sober and pragmatic. This is often said to be due to, amongst other things, the heritage of legal positivism, which still plays a major role in the self-perception of Austrian constitutional law scholars. At the same time, the prevailing methodological approach has substantially (some would say drastically) changed over the past decades, the predominant theory of constitutional interpretation, at least in the field of fundamental rights, having first been subject to a process of 'Germanisation' and now 'Europeanisation'. The Charter Judgment itself is a telling example of this development as its style of reasoning is indeed a far cry from the interpretive orthodoxy of the days of *Hans Kelsen*.

On the other hand, it should be kept in mind that in Austria the three highest courts—the Constitutional Court, the Supreme Court and the Supreme Administrative Court—are generally in a relationship of equals.[115] In particular, as opposed to the approach taken by the *Grundgesetz*, a judgment of the Supreme Court or the Supreme Administrative Court cannot be 'appealed' to the Constitutional Court on the grounds that it violates a constitutionally guaranteed right. Thus, the Constitutional Court cannot impose its understanding of the Austrian Constitution upon its sister courts in the same manner as the Bundesverfassungsgericht can in Germany. It comes as no surprise, therefore, that the Supreme Court and the Supreme Administrative Court also conceive of themselves as interlocutors in their own right with both the Strasbourg and the Luxembourg Courts where fundamental rights questions are concerned. This institutional set-up lowers the chances of successfully pursuing a distinctive national approach in terms of fundamental rights, as the Bundesverfassungsgericht did (or has at least aspired to do) in a number of areas, and makes it more attractive to enter into the European judicial dialogue. This may help to explain, inter alia, why the three highest courts in Austria have generally opted to embrace the jurisprudence of the European courts and to constructively integrate it into their own case law rather than oppose it as unwarranted external interference.

Moreover, apart from the courts (but arguably under their influence), other key actors in Austria—the legislators, government officials and the media—generally do not have a dismissive, let alone hostile, attitude to the Austrian fundamental rights protection system being substantially influenced and shaped by European standards and by a European judiciary. In particular, unlike in the UK, it has not been common for the Austrian media to campaign against rulings from the Strasbourg Court even

---

[114] See notably *BVerfGE* 7, 198 (205)—*Lüth*.

[115] There are special procedural contexts, however, where the Constitutional Court finds itself in a superior position vis-a-vis the Supreme Court and the Supreme Administrative Court, notably regarding the Constitutional Court's exclusive competence on rescinding general norms by declaring laws unconstitutional and ordinances contrary to law (Arts 139 and 140 of the Federal Constitutional Law); on deciding conflicts of competence between the highest courts, including the Constitutional Court itself (Art 138 of the Federal Constitutional Law); and on deciding on State liability claims in regard to decisions of the highest courts, including the Constitutional Court itself (Art 137 of the Federal Constitutional Law; VfSlg 17019/2003, 17095/2003).

though there have been some quite controversial judgments against Austria as well (for example regarding the rights of homosexual persons).

The Charter Judgment fits well in this broader picture of actively contributing towards an integrated European fundamental rights protection system. In this respect, it certainly constitutes a courageous step forward inasmuch as it raises the visibility and importance of the EU Charter of Fundamental Rights within the Austrian legal system, and in that sense serves the promotion of European law.[116] However, the 'constitutionalisation' of the Charter by judicial fiat of the Constitutional Court proves ambiguous. In spite of President Skouris' congratulatory note expressly commending the Constitutional Court's judgment, and in spite of the Luxembourg Court's judgment in *A v B*, which, by and large, whitewashed the Constitutional Court's approach, one should not underestimate the risk of such a move turning out to be a 'Greek gift' to EU law and the European system of fundamental rights protection more generally.[117] There can be no doubt that the Constitutional Court's ruling was about *defending rights*, but we may, and indeed must, ask whose rights the judgment actually sought to defend: was it really about strengthening the legal protection of individuals, as suggested by relying on the equivalence principle, or was it rather about the self-assertion of a Constitutional Court, fearing a loss of power and relevance in the process of Europeanisation of fundamental rights protection?[118]

Hence, we face a very peculiar *ménage à trois* in terms of fundamental rights protection in Austria. There are now three sources of fundamental rights in the sense of constitutionally guaranteed rights: the time-honoured rights arising from the Austrian Constitution domestically (notably the 1867 Basic Law), the Convention, and the Charter. The really interesting question, however, as has emerged from the above discussion, is who is in charge of running this household. The substantive *ménage à trois* is therefore complemented and superseded by an institutional one: the *dramatis personae* are the Constitutional Court and the other Austrian (high) courts as well as the Luxembourg Court. If one adds the Strasbourg Court,[119] this would make it an institutional *ménage à quatre*.[120]

In that regard, by orchestrating the recent 'constitutionalisation' of the Charter, the Constitutional Court has quite boldly, and successfully, brought itself into the game as a player, albeit at the price of rendering a decision that is rather

---

[116] Notwithstanding the Charter Judgment's ambiguous implications, it is worth re-emphasising that the decisive legal argument for constitutionalising the Charter is the equivalence principle, ie a principle of EU law.

[117] See also, in this regard, Jabloner (n 76) 178, who acknowledges that the Constitutional Court's Charter Judgment was benevolently received by the European Union institutions, but questions whether they were foreseeing all relevant implications of that decision.

[118] See Merli (n 52) 358; Pöschl (n 39) 597; Mayr (n 60) 409, 416; Öhlinger (n 49) 956; see also the references above at n 79.

[119] Even though the EU's accession to the Convention, which is mandated by Art 6(2) TEU, is blocked for the foreseeable future by Opinion 2/13 of 18 December 2014, the Luxembourg and Strasbourg Courts are continuously engaged in a judicial dialogue on the interplay between the Convention and EU fundamental rights (notably the Charter).

[120] See House of Commons Report (n 9) 29.

questionable from the methodological point of view.[121] The outlook is unclear: from the substantive perspective, it is very likely that the Constitutional Court's leadership in this question (or judicial activism, as others may put it) will significantly contribute to an even more intimate relationship between the different sources of fundamental protection and in particular to a coherent reading of the Convention and the Charter. At the same time, one may doubt whether from an institutional perspective this will occur without friction. The one or other judicial skirmish, both horizontally (with the Supreme Administrative Court and the Supreme Court) and vertically (with the Luxembourg Court) may well be expected. But no one has ever claimed that even a good relationship is always without conflict, let alone a *ménage à trois*.

---

[121] See, however, Öhlinger (n 49) 956, who is rather doubtful about the prospects of success of the Constitutional Court's move in the Charter Judgment.

Part IV

Perspectives from Other Jurisdictions: Contrasts and Comparisons with the UK Experience

16

Compliance with Strasbourg Court Rulings: A General Overview

LUIS LÓPEZ GUERRA

I. THE EVOLUTION OF THE COURT'S 'DECLARATORY' APPROACH

THE EUROPEAN COURT of Human Rights (ECtHR) has repeatedly stated that the European Convention on Human Rights (ECHR) intends to offer real and effective protection for the rights it proclaims.[1] This implies that its rulings must be effectively implemented by national authorities in order to have any practical consequences. In the words of the Council of Europe's Committee of Ministers, the 'speedy and efficient execution [of judgments] is essential for the credibility and efficiency of the European Convention on Human Rights as a constitutional instrument of European public order on which the democratic stability of the continent depends'.[2] Ensuring compliance with the ECtHR's rulings is a process that involves a high degree of interaction between international and domestic human rights protection systems[3] and, as such, the process of execution of the ECtHR judgments plays a key role in the overall protection of human rights.

The Convention is short on mandates concerning the execution of ECtHR rulings. The main substantive provisions on the matter are contained in Articles 41 and 46 ECHR. Due to the scarcity of such provisions, the way in which ECtHR rulings are implemented is largely a result of the Court's interpretation of those mandates, as well as the interpretation offered by the Council of Europe's Committee of Ministers as the agency in charge of supervising Convention countries' execution of the Court's judgments and, last but not least, the interpretation made by Convention countries themselves.

---

[1] *Airey v Ireland* (1979) 2 EHRR 205, para 24: 'The Convention is intended to guarantee not rights that are theoretical or illusory but rights that are practical and effective.'

[2] Reply to Parliamentary Assembly Recommendation 1576 (2002), adopted by the Committee of Ministers on 26 March 2003 at the 833rd meeting of the Ministers' Deputies (CM/AS(2003) Rec 1576 final). For wider comments on this matter, see *Background Paper 2014: Implementation of the Judgments of the European Court of Human Rights: A Shared Judicial Responsibility?*, www.echr.coe.int/Pages/home.aspx?p=echrpublications/seminar.

[3] See M Lobov, '*Restitutio in Integrum* in the System of the European Convention on Human Rights' in O Chernishova and M Lobov (eds), *Russia and the European Court of Human Rights: A Decade of Change. Studies in Honor of Anatoly Kovler* (Oisterwijk, Wolf Legal Publishers, 2013).

The ECtHR traditionally assumed that its judgments were 'declaratory' in nature.[4] According to this view, the Court's role formally ended with its 'declaration' of a Convention right violation. According to Article 41 ECHR, the only exception was the possibility of providing just satisfaction to the injured party as a substitute measure. Specific enforcement of Court rulings was the task of State authorities, under the supervision of the Committee of Ministers. Following this traditional principle, the Court's case law consistently maintained that

> The Contracting States that are parties to a case are in principle free to choose the means whereby they will comply with a judgment in which the Court has found a breach. This discretion as to the manner of execution of a judgment reflects the freedom of choice attaching to the primary obligation of the Contracting States under the Convention to secure the rights and freedoms guaranteed.[5]

But today this traditional approach is not entirely valid. The changes to the Convention introduced by Protocol 14 provided the ECtHR with additional powers of enforcement. Indeed, the Protocol added two elements to the process, making it possible for the Committee of Ministers to seek interpretive assistance from the ECtHR as well as to institute proceedings before it to determine whether the respondent State had complied with a judgment. But, even disregarding this reform (which to date has not been put into practice), the ECtHR has progressively abandoned (or at least radically modified) its declaratory approach. Both in its reasoning and in the operative part of its judgments the Court now often includes instructions to States concerning enforcement that extend beyond merely declaring the breach of a Convention right. And, in practice, both the Committee of Ministers and State authorities have taken those instructions into account, adjusting their compliance procedures accordingly.

In that regard it should be noted that the ECtHR has interpreted Article 46 as including a variety of obligations for the States Parties, both individual and general. The comments in that respect in the 2012 judgment in *Konstantin Markin v Russia* are revealing, since they reflect an evolution in the Court's case law:

> Although the primary purpose of the Convention system is to provide individual relief, its mission is also to determine issues on public-policy grounds in the common interest, thereby raising the general standards of protection of human rights and extending human rights jurisprudence throughout the community of the Convention status.[6]

From this point of view, Article 46(1) ('The High Contracting Parties undertake to abide by the final judgment of the Court in any case to which they are parties') has been interpreted as including a series of obligations on States, not only concerning

---

[4] For instance, *Marckx v Belgium* (1979) 2 EHRR 230, para 58: 'the Court's judgment is essentially declaratory and leaves to the State the choice of the means to be utilised in its domestic legal system for performance of its obligation under Article 53.'

[5] *Papamichalopoulos v Greece* (Article 50) (1995) 16 EHRR 440, para 34. This formula appears in many judgments. For another example see *Iatridis v Greece* (Just Satisfaction) App No 31107/96 ECHR 2000-XI 97 (GC), para 33.

[6] *Konstantin Markin v Russia* (2012) 56 EHRR 8 (GC), para 89.

the specific judgment to be executed, but also extending to other similar situations, both present and future.

Thus it is possible to distinguish between the individual and general effects of the ECtHR's rulings and, as a consequence, between different types of obligations, both individual and general, derived from those judgments. In both respects, the Court's role has progressively become more proactive, indicating to and sometimes imposing on States measures that they must adopt in order to comply with its judgments. And on quite a number of occasions, these changes have been prompted by the Council of Europe's Committee of Ministers.

II. SPECIFIC EFFECTS OF THE COURT'S JUDGMENTS IN INDIVIDUAL CASES

Concerning the individual effects of ECtHR rulings, a State's duty to comply with the Court's final judgments includes two types of obligations: negative and positive. Negative obligations require the State in question to immediately cease any declared violation. As stated, for instance, in *Iatridis*, 'the Court reiterates that a judgment in which it finds a breach imposes on the respondent State a legal obligation to put an end to the breach'.[7] But the ECtHR's case law has consistently considered that obligations derived from the declaration of a Convention violation also include positive obligations to redress the violation of that right. In *Iatridis*, immediately after the previously quoted affirmation the Court added the requirement that the State 'make reparation for its consequences in such a way as to restore as far as possible the situation existing before the breach'.[8]

The positive obligation to provide redress would appear to be a logical consequence of a declared Convention violation, but it is also confirmed *a contrario* in Article 41 ECHR, which stipulates that the ECtHR can provide just satisfaction if the State's legal order 'allows only partial reparation to be made'. Reparation therefore appears as the primary obligation of the respondent State, while the ECtHR will provide compensation in those cases in which the State can only provide partial reparation. As to the definition of reparation, since its ruling in *Piersack v Belgium*[9] the ECtHR has interpreted it as implying a return to the status quo ante. Reflecting previous consistent case law, *Iatridis* also provided that 'if the nature of the breach allows for *restitutio in integrum*, it is for the respondent State to effect it, the Court having neither the power nor the possibility of doing so itself'.[10] Thus the most adequate reparation for a Convention violation is a return to the status quo ante to be provided by the States.

---

[7] *Iatridis* (n 5) para 32.
[8] ibid.
[9] *Piersack v Belgium* (Article 50) (1984) 5 EHRR 169, para 12: 'Like the Delegate of the Commission, the Court will proceed from the principle that the applicant should as far as possible be put in the position he would have been in had the requirements of Article 6 not been disregarded.'
[10] *Iatridis* (n 5) para 33.

III. INDIVIDUAL EFFECTS ON NATIONAL COURTS

Experience has shown that the States' *restitutio in integrum* obligations resulting from the ECtHR's findings of individual Convention violations may have relevant effects on previous and subsequent rulings issued by national courts. These result from the principle of subsidiarity reflected in Article 35(1) ECHR, which establishes as a requirement for the admissibility of individual requests that 'all domestic remedies have been exhausted according to generally recognized rules of international law'. Domestic remedies usually include judicial proceedings and, as a result, when an individual files an application at the ECtHR, his case has already been decided by domestic judicial rulings, in many cases by the highest courts. In most instances, the finding of a Convention violation derives either from the substance of a judicial ruling or from the failure to observe essential procedural requirements prior to a ruling. Consequently, in those cases a return to the status quo ante would require reversing those rulings or, at least, re-opening the proceedings in which they were rendered.

Although this re-opening of the proceedings seems to contravene the *res judicata* principle as an expression of the principle of legal certainty (which precludes re-opening a proceeding once a final judgment has been issued, except in exceptional cases established by law), in many cases this re-opening might be the only way to obtain a true redress of the violation of a Convention right. This is the position of the Council of Europe's Committee of Ministers, as the body in charge of supervising the execution of Court judgments. In its Recommendation 2(2000), based on a draft submitted by the Council of Europe Steering Committee on Human Rights (CDDH),[11] the Committee of Ministers affirmed that 'in exceptional circumstances the re-examination of a case or a re-opening of proceedings has proved the most efficient, if not the only, means of achieving *restitutio in integrum*'.

Despite the declaratory nature of its rulings, since the 2003 judgment in *Gençel v Turkey*[12] the ECtHR has consistently underscored that at times re-opening a case is the most appropriate way for national authorities to execute the Court's judgments. This was the conclusion, for instance in *Salduz v Turkey*,[13] among many others. When deciding on the application of Article 41 ECHR to the case, the ECtHR cited abundant prior case law and explicitly stated that

> The Court reiterates that the most appropriate form of redress for a violation of Article 6 § 1 would be to ensure that the applicant, as far as possible, is put in the position in which he would have been had this provision not been disregarded ... The Court finds that this principle applies in the present case as well. Consequently, it considers that the most appropriate form of redress would be the retrial of the applicant in accordance with the requirements of Article 6 § 1 of the Convention, should the applicant so request.[14]

---

[11] Steering Committee on Human Rights (CDDH) Draft Recommendation CM(99)173.
[12] *Gençel v Turkey* App no 53431/99 (23 October 2003), para 7.
[13] *Salduz v Turkey* (2008) 49 EHRR 19 (GC).
[14] ibid, para 72. *cf Sejdovic v Italy* (2006) 42 EHRR 17 (GC), paras 126–27: 'The Court accordingly considers that, where, as in the instant case, an individual has been convicted following proceedings that have entailed breaches of the requirements of Article 6 of the Convention, a retrial or the re-opening of the case, if requested, represents in principle an appropriate way of redressing the violation ... However,

As we shall see below, the Court specifically insisted on this aspect in *Laska and Lika v Albania*.[15]

It should be noted that in those cases in which there is a procedural violation of Article 6 ECHR, as a general rule the ECtHR considers that it is not entitled to speculate on what the final judgment would have been if that violation had not occurred.[16] Only a re-opening of the proceedings is able to show what the result of the proceedings would have been had there been no Convention violation.

In that regard, Convention countries have found different ways of complying with *restitutio in integrum* obligations derived from ECtHR judgments. In some cases the domestic courts have reinterpreted national laws to enable proceedings to be re-opened to comply with a ECtHR judgment, without altering existing law. This new interpretation not only provides an individual remedy for the case in question, but also enables proceedings to be re-opened in future similar cases. That was the method initially adopted by the Belgian court in its execution of *Piersack v Belgium* and by the Austrian court in its enforcement of *Unterpertinger v Austria*.[17] Particularly significant was the Italian Constitutional Court's judgment in *Dorigo*.[18] In that case, which involved the execution in Italy of a resolution of the Council of Europe's Committee of Ministers,[19] the Italian Constitutional Court, ruling on a question of unconstitutionality (*questione de constitutitonalità*), declared unconstitutional those provisions of the Italian Criminal Procedure Code that prevented its criminal courts from re-opening prior proceedings as a result of a judgment of the ECtHR.

It should be noted that the re-opening of judicial proceedings by domestic authorities may be a consequence not only of the ECtHR's finding of a violation of the Convention's due process guarantees, but also of a violation of substantive Convention rights. Such was the case, for instance, in *Welch v UK*[20] in which the Court's finding of a violation of Convention Article 7 led a UK court to quash a previous court's sentence. As another example, in *Jersild v Denmark*[21] the Court found that the applicant's rights to freedom of expression had been violated by a sentence to pay a fine (and, in case of non payment, to five days imprisonment) for having broadcasted an interview containing racist comments from persons interviewed. As a result of the Court judgment, criminal proceedings against the applicant were

---

the specific remedial measures, if any, required of a respondent State in order for it to discharge its obligations under the Convention must depend on the particular circumstances of the individual case and be determined in the light of the Court's judgment in that case, and with due regard to the Court's case-law ... In particular, it is not for the Court to indicate how any new trial is to proceed and what form it is to take. The respondent State remains free, subject to monitoring by the Committee of Ministers, to choose the means by which it will discharge its obligation to put the applicant, as far as possible, in the position he would have been in had the requirements of the Convention not been disregarded ... provided that such means are compatible with the conclusions set out in the Court's judgment and with the rights of the defence.'

[15] *Laska and Lika v Albania* App nos 12315/04 and 17605/04 (20 April 2010).
[16] *Martinie v France* (2006) 45 EHRR 433 (GC), para 59.
[17] *Unterpertinger v Austria* (1986) 13 EHRR 175.
[18] Judgment of the Corte Costituzionale 113/2011, 4 April 2011.
[19] Interim Resolution DH (99) 258 of 15 April 1999.
[20] *Welch v UK* (1995) 20 EHRR 247.
[21] *Jersild v Denmark* (1994) 19 EHRR 1.

re-opened in Denmark, applying Article 441 of the Code of Civil Procedure. The applicant was finally acquitted.[22]

However, in some cases domestic laws do not provide (or provide very restrictively) for the review of final criminal or civil judgments as a consequence of ECtHR rulings. For example, this type of review is not provided for under Spanish procedural law, and, as a consequence the possibility of the Constitutional Court's re-opening a case in such circumstances is very limited. In the ordinary courts, until recently, it was practically non-existent. With respect to the Constitutional Court, it is extremely unlikely that it will agree to hear an *amparo* complaint based on a ECtHR judgment finding a violation of an applicant's Convention rights. With respect to *Barberà, Messegue and Jabardo*[23] and *Ruiz Mateos*,[24] among others the Constitutional Court established that re-opening a constitutional proceeding by way of a *recurso de amparo* is only possible when the violation found by the ECtHR implies the actual and present existence of a violation of a constitutional right at the moment the *amparo* appeal is filed. However, with respect to the ordinary courts, and more specifically the Supreme Court, there has been a recent development. Formerly, the Supreme Court had consistently maintained that a ECtHR judgment did not constitute a 'new fact' that would justify re-opening a case for review (*revisión*).[25] But in October, 2014 the Plenary Assembly of the Criminal Chamber of the Supreme Court ruled that until the Spanish legal order expressly provides a means for implementing the judgments of the ECtHR, the Supreme Court will apply by analogy the general legislation concerning judicial review, and will agree to re-open closed cases if the ECtHR declares a violation of a Convention Right.[26]

In view of the difficulty, or even impossibility, that courts are faced with when reinterpreting procedural legislation, many Convention countries (some of them even prior to the Committee's Recommendation) have already reformed their procedural laws (mainly criminal procedure codes) to provide for re-opening proceedings. This is the case, for instance, in Austria where the Criminal Procedure Code was reformed to enable the re-opening of proceedings as a result of the ECtHR's judgments in *Oberschlick v Austria*[27] and *Kremzow v Austria*.[28] A similar reform was introduced in 2000 in the French Criminal Procedure Code (Arts. 626-1, 626-7). In fact, according to data from 2006, no fewer than 38 countries have amended their

---

[22] See Resolution DH(1995)212 of the Committee of Ministers, concerning execution.

[23] *Barberá, Messegue and Jabardo v Spain* (1988) 11 EHRR 360.

[24] *Ruiz-Mateos v Spain* (1993) 16 EHRR 505. On the Spanish case, see M Candela Soriano, 'The Reception Process in Spain and Italy' in H Keller and A Stone Sweet (eds), *A Europe of Rights: The Impact of the ECHR on National Legal Systems* (Oxford, Oxford University Press, 2008) 393–450.

[25] For an account of the Spanish case law on the matter, see F Irurzun Montoro, 'La ejecución de las sentencias del Tribunal Europeo de Derechos Humanos: una aproximación a la práctica española' in A Queralt (ed), *El Tribunal de Estrasburgo en el espacio jurídico europeo* (Cizur Menor, Aranzadi, 2013) 131. I make reference to this matter in 'Coincidencias y divergencias: el diálogo entre el Tribunal europeo y los tribunales nacionales' (2013) 32 *Teoría y Realidad Constitucional* 139.

[26] Resolution ('acuerdo') of the Plenary of the Criminal Chamber of the Supreme Court of 21 October 2014. The Chamber has already applied this decision to several cases (Decisions of 27 October 2014, *Almenara*, and 5 November 2014, *Llop*).

[27] *Oberschlick v Austria (No 1)* (1991) 19 EHRR 389. See D Thurnherr, 'The Reception Process in Austria and Switzerland' in Keller and Stone Sweet (n 24) 311, 371.

[28] *Kremzow v Austria* (1993) 17 EHRR 322.

legislation to provide for the re-opening of proceedings, as an exception to the *res judicata* principle.[29] In Spain two consecutive drafts of a new Criminal Procedure Code (*Ley de Enjuiciamiento Criminal*) have introduced the possibility of reviewing final judgments as a consequence of ECtHR rulings, but to-date no legal provision has been approved in that regard.

This re-opening of proceedings seems to be an adequate tool with respect to criminal procedure, but the question is more complex where civil cases are concerned. Nevertheless, in 2006 a total of 23 countries had already reformed their civil procedure laws to enable proceedings to be re-opened as a result of ECtHR rulings.[30] In any case, an academic analysis of the Committee of Ministers' reports[31] seems to indicate that even when the domestic legislations provide for that possibility, the re-opening of the internal proceedings is infrequently requested at the domestic courts by those applicants who have obtained a favorable judgment form the Court, based on a finding of procedural or substantive Convention violations. On the contrary, with respect to execution, applicants are mainly interested in receiving the economic compensation awarded by the ECtHR. This may be explained by the additional costs and inconvenience of starting new internal proceedings, as well the uncertainty of their outcome.[32]

IV. OTHER INDIVIDUAL MEASURES

The re-opening of prior (criminal or civil) proceedings and awards of just compensation are not the only means of returning an applicant to his *statu quo ante* prior to a Convention violation. Many other measures are possible. In some cases, such measures have been taken at the initiative of the States themselves. This may include administrative measures or other actions that do not involve reviewing prior judicial proceedings. For instance, the State administration may provide compensation for expropriated property or the competent authorities may pardon an applicant subject to a penalty (*Neumeister v Austria*).[33] In addition, the authorities may clear the applicant's criminal record, or a person serving a sentence may be released (*Van Mechelen v The Netherlands*).[34] Such measures are usually taken by the States and then notified to the Committee of Ministers. But very frequently the ECtHR makes direct reference to how its judgments should be executed: providing economic compensation; suggesting a possible alternative to that compensation; proposing the most appropriate way to execute its ruling; or, finally, ordering the State to immediately execute its judgment in the terms stated in the ruling. In all of these cases it is clear that the Court's decisions are not merely 'declaratory'.

---

[29] CDDH (2006) 008, Addenda I, II and III.

[30] ibid.

[31] See E Lambert Abdelgawad, 'L'exécution des arrêts de la Cour Européenne des Droits de l'Homme' (2012) 92 *Revue Trimestrielle des Droits de l'Homme* 861, 867.

[32] ibid.

[33] *Neumeister v Austria* (Article 50) (1974) 1 EHRR 91.

[34] *Van Mechelen v The Netherlands* (Article 50) App nos 21363/93, 21364/93, 21427/93 and 22056/93, *Reports of Judgments and Decisions* 1997-VII.

V. INDIVIDUAL MEASURES AND JUST SATISFACTION

Concerning economic compensation or 'just satisfaction', experience has shown that in many instances there is no judicial or administrative measure in the domestic legal system that would afford *restitutio in integrum*. As indicated previously, Article 41 ECHR envisions such cases when it states that if the internal law of a Convention State allows only partial reparation to be made, the ECtHR shall, if necessary, provide just satisfaction to the injured party. In such cases the Court's judgments cease to be merely declaratory, since they order the payment of economic compensation. However, the Court's case law has also consistently underscored that ordering just compensation does not release States from complying with other obligations derived from the finding of a Convention violation.

The ECtHR initially issued separate judgments to address the merits of a case and any possible compensation due to the applicant. Later, it became common practice to deal with both matters in same judgment. But it is important to note that first the Committee of Ministers (in *Hakkar v France*)[35] and later the ECtHR underscored that payment of monetary compensation is compatible with other obligations imposed on States in order to provide sufficient remedies for Convention violations. For instance, in *Scozzari and Giunta v Italy*[36] the Court explicitly stated:

> It follows, inter alia, that a judgment in which the Court finds a breach imposes on the respondent State a legal obligation not just to pay those concerned the sums awarded by way of just satisfaction, but also to choose, subject to supervision by the Committee of Ministers, the general and/or if appropriate, individual measures to be adopted in their domestic legal order to put an end to the violation found by the Court.[37]

It concluded that

> Accordingly, under art. 41 of the Convention the purpose of awarding sums by way of just satisfaction is to provide reparation solely for damage suffered by those concerned to the extent that such events constitute a consequence of the violation which cannot otherwise be remedied.[38]

Since then, it has become frequent practice for ECtHR rulings to provide (either in their reasoning or in the operative part of the judgments) for other measures to be taken by the respondent State, in addition to any compensation awarded. In some cases, the Court may offer the State the possibility of complying with its obligations either by paying compensation or by performing some other measure. The proposed measure thus provides a (non-binding) alternative to the payment of monetary compensation. For instance, in *Katz v Romania*[39] the Court offered such an alternative

---

[35] The case was brought to the European Commission of Human Rights (*Hakkar v France* (Report) App no 19033/91 (27 June 1995)). On this matter the Committee of Ministers issued its Interim Resolution DH (97) 475 and its Final Resolution DH (2001) 4. See Lobov (n 3) 91–93.

[36] *Scozzari and Giunta v Italy* (2000) 35 EHRR 12 (GC).

[37] ibid, para 249.

[38] ibid, para 250.

[39] *Katz v Romania* App no 29739/03 (20 January 2009). The Court held: 'Par ces motifs, la Cour, à l'unanimité, 1. Déclare la requête recevable quant au grief tiré de l'article 1 du Protocole no 1 et irrecevable pour le surplus; 2. Dit qu'il y a eu violation de l'article 1 du Protocole no 1 à la Convention; Dit que

to the State, providing in the operative part of the judgment the possibility of either restoring a property to its owner or, if such restitution was not made within three months, paying the estimated price of the property in question.

VI. SPECIFYING INDIVIDUAL MEASURES

In certain cases the ECtHR dispenses with this alternative formula and in its judgment indicates specific measures that must be adopted in the execution of its rulings, underscoring that they are mandatory. Since its 2004 judgment in *Assanidze v Georgia*,[40] many of the Court's judgments have become more executive in nature. In this regard, in several cases the court has included direct mandates to State authorities in the operative part of its judgments, reinforcing its imperative style. In *Assanidze* the Court unanimously held that the respondent State must secure the applicant's release at the earliest possible date.[41] Similar direct orders to States appear in many other subsequent judgments, such as *Ilaşcu v Moldova and Russia*,[42] *Gladysheva v Russia*,[43] *Oleksander Volkov v Ukraine*[44] and *Gluhaković v Croatia*.[45]

In the latter judgment, when invoking Article 46 the ECtHR indicated the specific measure to be taken in this family law case:

> Having regard to the particular circumstances of the case and the urgent need to put an end to the violation of Article 8 of the Convention, the Court considers that to discharge its obligation under Article 46 of the Convention, the respondent State shall secure effective contact between the applicant and his daughter at a time which is compatible with the applicant's work schedule and on suitable premises, on the basis of the judgment by the Rijeka Municipal Court of 8 March 2010.[46]

l'État défendeur doit restituer au requérant le bien litigieux dans les trois mois à compter du jour où l'arrêt sera devenu définitif conformément à l'article 44 § 2 de la Convention; b) qu'à défaut d'une telle restitution, l'État défendeur doit verser au requérant, dans le même délai de trois mois 50 000 EUR (cinquante mille euros) pour dommage matériel, plus tout montant pouvant être dû à titre d'impôt.'

[40] *Assanidze v Georgia* (2004) 39 EHRR 32 (GC).

[41] The terms employed by the Court in paras 202 and 203 of its reasoning are of interest: '202. As regards the measures which the Georgian State must take (see paragraph 198 above), subject to supervision by the Committee of Ministers, in order to put an end to the violation that has been found, the Court reiterates that its judgments are essentially declaratory in nature and that, in general, it is primarily for the State concerned to choose the means to be used in its domestic legal order in order to discharge its legal obligation under Article 46 of the Convention, provided that such means are compatible with the conclusions set out in the Court's judgment … However, by its very nature, the violation found in the instant case does not leave any real choice as to the measures required to remedy it. 203. In these conditions, having regard to the particular circumstances of the case and the urgent need to put an end to the violation of Article 5 § 1 and Article 6 § 1 of the Convention (see paragraphs 176 and 184 above), the Court considers that the respondent State must secure the applicant's release at the earliest possible date.'

[42] *Ilaşcu v Moldova and Russia* (2004) 40 EHRR 46 (GC).

[43] *Gladysheva v Russia* App no 7097/10 (6 December 2011).

[44] *Oleksandr Volkov v Ukraine* (2013) 51 EHRR 1.

[45] *Gluhaković v Croatia* App no 21188/09 (12 April 2011).

[46] ibid, para 89.

This reasoning was applied in the operative part of the judgment.[47] In a similar way and using a similar formula, in *MSS v Belgium and Greece* (2011)[48] the ECtHR ordered the Greek government to refrain from deporting the applicant while his asylum request was being examined.[49]

In the judgment in *Del Rio Prada v Spain*,[50] the Court amply justified its order to release the applicant by stating:

> It is true that in principle the respondent State remains free to choose the means by which it will discharge its legal obligation under Article 46 of the Convention, provided that such means are compatible with the conclusions set out in the Court's judgment ... However, in certain particular situations, with a view to assisting the respondent State in fulfilling its obligations under Article 46, the Court may seek to indicate the type of individual and/or general measures that might be taken in order to put an end to the situation that gave rise to the finding of a violation ... In other exceptional cases, the nature of the violation found may be such as to leave no real choice as to the measures required to remedy it and the Court may decide to indicate only one such measure.[51]

The Court ended its reasoning by stating:

> Having regard to the particular circumstances of the case and to the urgent need to put an end to the violations of the Convention it has found, it considers it incumbent on the respondent State to ensure that the applicant is released at the earliest possible date.

It should be noted that the Spanish judicial authorities immediately complied. The judgment was issued on 21 October 2013. On the following day the applicant was released by virtue of a unanimous decision of the full bench of the National Court's Criminal Division. In its meeting on 5 December, the Council of Europe's Committee of Ministers 'noted that the applicant was released on 22 October 2013 following a decision given by the Audiencia Nacional and welcomed the response given to the urgent individual measure indicated by the European Court [of Human Rights]'.[52]

VII. GENERAL MEASURES

A traditional topic of discussion in the literature on the ECtHR is whether its judgments have only *inter partes* effects, or whether they also produce general effects, as

---

[47] ibid, operative part, para 3: 'The Court ... (3) Holds that the respondent State shall secure effective contact between the applicant and his daughter at a time which is compatible with the applicant's work schedule and on suitable premises, on the basis of the judgment by the Rijeka Municipal Court of 8 March 2010.'

[48] *MSS v Belgium and Greece* (2011) 53 EHRR 2 (GC).

[49] § 402: 'Having regard to the particular circumstances of the case and the urgent need to put a stop to these violations of Articles 13 and 3 of the Convention, the Court considers it incumbent on Greece, without delay, to proceed with an examination of the merits of the applicant's asylum request that meets the requirements of the Convention and, pending the outcome of that examination, to refrain from deporting the applicant.'

[50] *Del Rio Prada v Spain* (2013) 58 EHRR 37 (GC).

[51] ibid, para 138.

[52] Decision of the Committee of Ministers, 1186th meeting, 5 December 2013: 'The Deputies ... welcomed the response given to the urgent individual measure indicated by the European Court.' The decision can be found at CM/Del/OJ/DH(2013)1186/19.

they introduce principles derived from the interpretation of the Convention which must be applied in cases similar to the one decided in a particular judgment, extending their consequences further than the specific case they resolve.[53] In that respect, experience has shown that the Court's judgments have broad general effects on the legal order of Convention countries, due not only to the Court's pronouncements on the matter, but also to the Committee of Ministers' interpretation of those judgments as well as, remarkably, to the practice of the Convention countries themselves, as they proceed to apply in a general way the principles contained in those judgments.

As underscored previously, in the light of ECtHR case law and Member State practice, the States' obligation to comply with Court judgments finding a Convention violation also includes the obligation to prevent similar future violations. Pursuant to the Article 32 principle of *res interpretata*, ECtHR rulings not only resolve a specific case, but also establish patterns for interpreting Convention mandates to be applied by national authorities in future cases. This has consequences for Member States' legal systems, either affecting their domestic courts' interpretation of existing law or possibly resulting in amendments to the laws presently in force. The comments in that regard in the 2012 judgment in *Konstantin Markin v Russia* mentioned above[54] are revealing, since they reflect the evolution of the ECtHR's case law.

But prior to any pronouncement on the part of the ECtHR, many States had already taken the initiative when extending the effects of Court judgments generally. Reference has already been made to the changes made by national courts in the interpretation of existing laws to bring them in line with ECtHR case law, such as the case in Austria and Belgium after the judgments in *Unterpertinger* and *Piersack*. Spain also provides good examples of ECHR cases with such general effects.

As a first example, the Court's 1998 *Valenzuela Contreras v Spain* judgment[55] found a violation of Article 10 of the Convention with respect to telephone tapping, due to the imprecise wording of Article 579 of the Criminal Procedure Law, which afforded judges a wide discretion in such matters. In the following years, the Law was never amended to satisfy the ECtHR's requirements. Nevertheless, both the Constitutional Court and the Supreme Court proceeded to reinterpret the ECtHR's mandates in a way that remedied the defects found in its judgment. As a consequence, based on its decision in *Coban v Spain*,[56] the ECtHR has declared subsequent applications on the matter inadmissible, stating that the Spanish legal order, including the Spanish courts' case law, now provides the necessary legal certainty concerning telephone tapping.[57]

---

[53] See eg G Ress, 'The Effects of Judgments and Decisions in Domestic Law' in R St J Macdonald et al (eds), *The European System for the Protection of Human Rights* (Dordrecht, Martinus Nijhoff, 1993) 801; E Lambert, *Les effets des arrêts de la Cour européenne des droits de l'homme* (Brussels, Bruylant, 1999) 321–31.

[54] See above, n 6.

[55] *Valenzuela Contreras v Spain* (1998) 28 EHRR 37. On this judgment and its effects, see I Sanchez Yllera, '*Valenzuela Contreras contra España* (STEDH de 30 de julio de 1998): la deficiente calidad de las normas que habilitan la intervención de las comunicaciones telefónicas' in R Alcacer Guirao, M Beladiez Rojo and JM Sanchez Tomas (eds), *Conflicto y diálogo con Europa: las condenas a España del Tribunal Europeo de Derechos Humanos* (Madrid, Civitas, 2013) 140–470.

[56] *Coban v Spain* App no 17060/02 (25 September 2006).

[57] For instance, the decision of inadmissibility in *Fernandez Saavedra v Spain* App no 47646/06 (7 September 2010).

The abovementioned case of *Del Rio Prada v Spain*[58] provides another interesting example of the general effects of Strasbourg judgments. In *Del Rio* the ECtHR found that the Spanish courts' interpretation of a criminal procedure rule for determining the duration of custodial sentences (the so-called *Parot* doctrine) violated Articles 5 and 7 ECHR.[59] The operative part of this judgment concerned only this specific case and, as indicated previously, ordered the immediate release of the applicant from incarceration. But the Spanish courts' response to the judgment extended far beyond this case. The applicant in question was immediately released, but the Spanish courts likewise immediately applied the *Del Rio* judgment to other prisoners affected by the *Parot* doctrine. In successive decisions over the course of three months the National Court and provincial criminal courts released over 60 additional prisoners in decisions confirmed indirectly by the Spanish Supreme Court and the Constitutional Court.[60]

In addition to the general effects that Member State courts have derived from ECtHR judgments, the Court itself has more recently begun to indicate general measures (usually of a legislative nature) that States must adopt in order to comply with its rulings, doing so in two ways. First, in what may be considered a 'soft approach', the Court issues a sort of admonition urging the States to put these general measures into practice. A more 'hard-core' approach can be found in the so-called 'pilot judgments'.

Concerning the 'soft approach', a frequent method is to simply underscore in the reasoning of a judgment that the State needs to adopt general measures to remedy a Convention breach. In some cases this advice is stated in very broad terms. For instance, in *Laska and Lika v Albania*,[61] with respect to the re-opening of proceedings to redress a Convention violation, the Court proposed reforms of a more general nature, leaving the State a margin of discretion:

> The Court notes that the respondent State's criminal legal system does not provide for the possibility of re-examining cases, including reopening of domestic proceedings in the event of this Court's finding of a serious violation of an applicant's right to a fair trial ... Moreover, the Contracting States are under a duty to organize their judicial systems in such a way that their courts can meet the requirements of the Convention. This principle also applies to the reopening of proceedings and the re-examination of the applicants' case.[62]

In other cases, the ECtHR's terms have been more precise. For instance, invoking Convention Article 46 in its 2010 judgment in *Gözel and Öser v Turkey*,[63] the Court found a violation of freedom of expression and in its reasoning made express reference to Article 2 of Turkish Law 3673: 'the violation in the case of

---

[58] See above, n 52.

[59] *Del Rio Prada v Spain* (2013) 58 EHRR 37 (GC).

[60] On the application of the *Del Rio Prada* judgment, see Y Cacho Sanchez, 'Fundamento de las críticas al Tribunal Europeo de Derechos Humanos en el asunto *Del Río Prada c. España*' (2014) 48 *Revista de Derecho Comunitario Europeo* 491.

[61] See above, n 15.

[62] *Laska and Lika v Albania* App nos 12315/04 and 17605/04 (20 April 2010), para 76.

[63] *Gözel and Özer v Turkey* App nos 43453/04 and 31098/05 (6 July 2010).

the applicants of the right recognized by Art. 10 of the Convention derives from a problem concerning the redaction and interpretation of this mandate.'[64] As a result, the ECtHR considered that 'putting in agreement the domestic law with the cited article of the Convention would represent an adequate form of reparation which would put an end to the found violation'.[65]

Thus, in this case the ECtHR proposed amending the text of a specific law as a means of providing adequate redress in respect of a Convention breach. In other cases the Court has proposed broader reforms. For instance, in *Klaus et al v Georgia*,[66] the Court considered that the violation of Article 1 of Protocol 1 was the result of deficiencies in the Georgian legal order. In its reasoning, the Court stated that in order to execute its ruling, a series of measures was necessary at the domestic level and that legislative, administrative and financial measures should be urgently adopted in order to enable the applicants to effectively exercise their Convention rights.[67] But, in addition, in the operative part of the judgment the Court indicated that if those measures were not adopted, the defendant State should pay the applicants compensation.

This approach is becoming very common in the ECtHR's case law. When the Court's general mandates are included in the operative part of judgments, they appear to be similar to pilot judgments. An initial example can be found in *Lukenda v Slovenia*,[68] where the operative part stated that the violations of Convention Articles 6(2) and 13 found in the judgment originated in the malfunctioning of domestic legislation and practice, and that the respondent State should secure the right to trial within a reasonable time through the appropriate legal measures and administrative practices.

VIII. PILOT JUDGMENTS

From this perspective, the use of pilot judgments is not an extraordinary occurrence in the ECtHR's case law, but rather an effective means of establishing general effects for its rulings when the number of repetitive cases brought before the Court suggests that there is a systemic defect in the State's legal order. After *Broniowski*,[69] pilot judgments generally include instructions to the defendant State concerning changes to be made to its legal order to bring it in line with ECtHR principles. With a variable degree of precision, these instructions are included in the operative part of the judgment and a time limit for complying with the ECtHR's proposals is clearly stated. The time may vary from six (*Olaru et alii v Moldova*)[70] to 18 months (*Maria*

---

[64] ibid, para 76.
[65] ibid.
[66] *Klaus and Iouri Kiladzé v Georgia* App no 7975/06 (2 February 2010).
[67] ibid, para 85.
[68] *Lukenda v Slovenia* (2005) 47 EHRR 32.
[69] *Broniowski v Poland* (2004) 40 EHRR 21 (GC).
[70] *Olaru v Moldova* (Just Satisfaction) App no 476/07 (12 October 2010).

Atanasiu v Romania).[71] In *Greens and MT v UK*,[72] the Court's judgment indicated that the defendant State should

> (a) bring forward, within six months of the date upon which the present judgment becomes final, legislative proposals intended to amend the 1983 Act and, if appropriate, the 2002 Act in a manner which is Convention-compliant; and (b) enact the required legislation within any such period as may be determined by the Committee of Ministers.[73]

In any case, it is not uncommon for the ECtHR to extend time limits imposed on defendant States. But the *general* effect of these judgments is certainly of an indirect nature. If the State in question introduces the proposed changes, any pending applications before the Court will be declared inadmissible, since a means of remedying the alleged violations now exists in the domestic legal order. If not, the Court will have to address a number of violations of one or more Convention rights in a series of repetitive cases. In summary, the introduction of the pilot judgment formula represents a step forward in the evolution of the ECtHR's case law that departs further from the 'classical' concept of purely declaratory rulings.[74]

IX. THE COURT'S 'PROACTIVE' ROLE AND THE EFFECTIVE PROTECTION OF CONVENTION RIGHTS

As previously underscored, the ECtHR has increasingly taken a proactive role in the execution of its judgments—a fact that has been not only well received, but also supported by the bodies in charge of judgment enforcement.[75] This progressive participation in the execution process has influenced the way in which States implement the ECtHR's judgments, and the way in which the Committee of Ministers supervises their execution.

A relevant aspect concerns changes introduced in the Committee of Ministers' procedures for monitoring the execution of judgments, which are closely linked to the evolution of the ECtHR's case law in that regard. Commencing in 2011, the Committee established two separate execution-monitoring procedures based on the content and individual circumstances of judgments: a standard procedure and an enhanced one.[76]

---

[71] *Maria Atanasiu v Romania* App nos 30767/05 and 33800/06 (12 October 2010).

[72] *Greens and MT v UK* (2010) 53 EHRR 20.

[73] ibid, operative part, para 6.

[74] Art 61 of the Rules of Court outlines the procedures to be followed by these judgments. On this matter see P Leach et al, *Responding to Systemic Human Rights Violations: An Analysis of 'Pilot Judgments' of the European Court of Human Rights and their Impact at National Level* (Antwerp, Intersentia, 2010).

[75] As stated in *Supervision of the Execution of Judgments of the European Court of Human Rights. 7th Annual Report of the Committee of Ministers* (Strasbourg, Council of Europe, 2014) 11: 'Also the Court has continued to deploy special efforts to assist execution by including in certain judgments, with reference to Article 46, different indications of relevance for the solution of structural problems. This immediate support, from the Court already in the judgment, has been well received both by the States concerned and the Committee of Ministers when supervising execution of the Court's judgments, even if it is evident that many choices and problems appear only once the execution process has been engaged.'

[76] A commentary on the development and effects of these proceedings may be found in *Supervision of the Execution of Judgments*, ibid.

The standard monitoring procedure is applied in cases involving specific individual measures ordered by the Court, usually the payment of compensation. The Committee of Ministers' data for this category is useful for evaluating the practical effects of the ECtHR's judgments. In that regard, in 2012 compensation awarded by the ECtHR amounted to 176 million euros. In 2013 the sum was somewhat less, amounting to 135 million. In 2014, in the interstate case of *Cyprus v Turkey*,[77] 90 million euros were awarded, including moral and material damages. 2014 also saw the highest compensation awarded in the Court's history to date in the case of *Oao Neftyanaya Kompaniya Yukos v Russia*[78] (awarding 1,886 million euros for material damages, plus 300,000 euros for court costs). With respect to this type of individual measure, the main enforcement problems involve delays in payment on the part of the Member States, but the Committee of Ministers' statistics show an improvement in that aspect.[79]

The enhanced procedure involving closer supervision of execution is applied to so-called 'leading cases'. Amongst others, this category includes cases in which urgent individual measures are ordered, pilot judgments, and judgments addressing significant structural problems in defendant States.

Concerning judgments classified as 'leading cases' and involving the adoption of general measures, the Committee of Ministers' statistics on the enhanced monitoring procedure provide some revealing data concerning Convention State compliance. The number of this type of cases has remained fairly constant (252 cases in 2011; 251 in 2012; 228 in 2013; and fewer cases, 211, in 2014).[80] But as a result of the increased difficulty in ensuring compliance with the ECtHR's proposed measures, the number of cases still pending final execution is on the rise (1,337 in 2011; 1,431 in 2012; 1,497 in 2013 and 1,513 in 2014).[81] Nevertheless, the fact that the ECtHR specifies the measures to be adopted facilitates the States' execution of Court judgments. For instance, concerning pilot judgments, in its 2013 *Activity Report* the Council of Ministers indicated that 'From this perspective, it has been most encouraging to note the commitment demonstrated, both by States and by the Committee of Ministers, to ensure the execution of pilot judgments. Indeed, as matters stand today no pilot judgment is unexecuted.'[82] This affirmation appears to be confirmed by other data. According to the Committee of Ministers' procedures, the Committee's interim resolutions provide a means of imposing a certain type of (mostly symbolic) sanction in the event of non-compliance or excessive delays in the

---

[77] *Cyprus v Turkey* (Just Satisfaction) App no 25781/94, ECHR 2014 (GC).

[78] *OAO Neftyanaya Kompaniya Yukos v Russia* (Article 50) App no 14902/04 (31 July 2014).

[79] Supervision of the Execution of Judgments (n 75) 55.

[80] The data from 2011 and 2012 are from Supervision of the Execution of Judgments (n 75) 37. The data for 2013 and 2014 are from Supervision of the Execution of Judgments of the European Court of Human Rights. 8th Annual Report of the Committee of Ministers (Strasbourg, Council of Europe, 2015) 30–31.

[81] ibid. With respect to 2013, the Director General of Human Rights of the Council of Europe stated that, 'The number of pending leading cases has thus continued to increase as a result of the fact that the number of new leading cases continued to be higher than the number of closed cases. It is, however, noteworthy that the increase was less important than in 2012 and that the Court produced less such cases this year than earlier years'. *Supervision of the Execution of Judgments* (n 75) 10.

[82] ibid, 11.

execution of judgments, publicly criticising the State in question.[83] However, it is revealing that, in spite of the considerable number of leading cases pending execution, the number of interim resolutions issued is quite low. In 2011 there were only four resolutions of this type, affecting Russia, Moldova and Ukraine. In 2013 the Committee of Ministers issued five interim resolutions concerning Albania, Russia, Bosnia and Turkey. In comparison with the number of cases in execution, these are modest figures. In any case, the Committee of Ministers also issues less severe communications to the States to demonstrate its concern for lengthy delays in executing ECtHR judgments.[84]

X. CONCLUSION

The purpose of this chapter was to explore the evolution of ECtHR case law from a predominantly 'declarative' approach to a more 'proactive' one. But it is worth noting that this development does not seem to derive from a mere desire of the Court to assume additional jurisdiction. There are factors resulting from the nature of the Convention system itself that explain this development not only as logical but also as necessary.

One factor accounting for the Court's increasing role in implementing its judgments is the complexity of the implementation process, which involves several different instances: the Court itself, the domestic authorities (legislative, executive, judicial), and the Council of Europe's Committee of Ministers. This complex process has in many cases required certain guiding principles to be put in place in order to avoid confusion, uncertainty or even contradictions between the different instances involved in the implementation of the ECtHR judgments. On several occasions the Court has endeavoured to fulfil this task by issuing directives concerning both the individual and general effects of its judgments to the executing and supervising authorities in order to guarantee adequate redress for declared Convention violations.

The need for directives concerning the individual effects of the Court's judgments may derive from the particular nature of the declared violation and its remedy, in order to assure effective and not 'merely theoretical or illusory' protection of the

---

[83] Rule 16 of the *Rules of the Committee of Ministers for the Supervision of the Execution of Judgments and of Terms of Friendly Settlements*: 'In the course of its supervision of the execution of a judgment or of the terms of a friendly settlement, the Committee of Ministers may adopt interim resolutions, notably in order to provide information on the state of progress of the execution or, where appropriate, to express concern and/or to make suggestions with respect to the execution.'

[84] For instance, Decision of the Committee of Ministers DH-DD(2013)1261E, 19 November 2013, 1186 DH meeting (3–5 December 2013) with respect to execution in the cases of *Hirst* and *Greens*: 'The Deputies welcomed that the Secretary General of the Council of Europe had attended to give evidence before the competent parliamentary committee on 6 November 2013, but expressed its serious concern about the on-going delay in the adoption of legislation to comply with the Convention. It noted with concern that the Court has therefore found it necessary to decide not to further adjourn the proceedings in all similar applications pending before it, and urged the United Kingdom authorities to rapidly comply with the judgment by adopting legislation to ensure that future elections are held in compliance with the Convention, thus avoiding new repetitive applications before the European Court.'

Convention right. In some cases this may require restricting or even eliminating domestic authorities' margin of discretion when executing Court judgments. In such cases the Court has assumed an active role, either pointing out the acceptable existing remedies (as in *Katz v Romania*) or recommending the most adequate one (as in *Salduz v Turkey*) or, finally, by establishing certain execution measures as mandatory and binding on the State in question (as in *Assanidze v Georgia*, or *Del Rio Prada v Spain*).

The Court's active role in providing positive guidance to Member State authorities (and to the Committee of Ministers) concerning the implementation of its judgments is even clearer with respect to the general effects of those rulings, particularly when the Court resorts to the use of the pilot judgment procedure. In that regard, when the Court finds that the violation of a Convention right in a given case (which is actually one out of hundreds or even thousands of similar 'repetitive' cases before the Court) is the result of a 'systemic' failure in the State's legal order, the directives issued to correct the failure detected and remedy present and any probable future violations represents an (indirect) mandate to the State in question that is far removed from any 'declaratory' approach.

A final question still remains unanswered: How will the reform of Article 46 ECHR introduced in Protocol 14 affect the process of implementing Court judgments? This reform expressly grants the Court an active role in the execution of its rulings, since it provides for the possibility that the Committee of Ministers may request an interpretation of the Court's judgment or a pronouncement as to whether the State in question has actually complied with the Court's ruling. This provision certainly implies a radical change in the letter of the Convention concerning the Court's role in execution proceedings. But, in any case, and whatever use the Committee of Ministers may eventually make of this provision, existing case law already shows that ECtHR judgments can hardly be described as being 'purely declaratory' in nature.

17

The ECHR in French Law: Status, Implementation and Debates

CONSTANCE GREWE

I. INTRODUCTION

THE FRENCH LEGAL system of today would be quite different without European law: European Union (EU) law and the European Convention on Human Rights (ECHR) form a substantial part of the body of norms applied on a daily basis. Whilst being one of the founding States, France ratified the ECHR only in 1974 and accepted the individual application procedure in 1981.

The focus of this contribution is the judicial protection of human or fundamental rights in France. In fact, it is impossible to separate constitutional protection from protection through the Convention, although courts of different jurisdictions are competent for each: on the one hand, the Conseil Constitutionnel (the French constitutional court) is responsible for reviewing constitutional aspects; on the other, the ordinary courts, composed of the judicial branch with the Cour de Cassation at its top and the administrative branch supervised by the Conseil d'Etat, are responsible for reviewing aspects relating to the Convention. Both forms of rights protections have evolved considerably, and they are linked by a complex and shifting relationship. In order to analyse these modifications and to try to specify the relations between these two sorts of protection, I will focus first on the period between the 1970s and 2009, which is the stage of emergence and development of human rights protection (section II). This period is characterised at the same time by the progressive development of constitutional review with respect to fundamental rights by the Conseil Constitutionnel and the emergence of so-called 'conventional' review by the ordinary courts.

In 2008, a very important constitutional amendment[1] was adopted which introduced a new constitutional review procedure to the French legal system: the 'priority preliminary ruling on the issue of constitutionality',[2] which entered into force

---

[1] Constitutional amendment No 2008-724, 23 July 2008, *Journal Officiel de la République Française* (*JORF*) 0171, 24 July 2008, 1189 on modernisation of the institutions of the Vth Republic.
[2] In French: *question prioritaire de constitutionnalité* (QPC).

in 2010.[3] Thus I will concentrate in the section dedicated to the period 2010–14 (section III) on the possible impact of this constitutional reform on the protection and implementation of the ECHR by the French courts. In this section it will be shown how ambiguous the case law of the Conseil Constitutionnel is with respect to ECHR rights, how deeply the Cour de Cassation and Conseil d'Etat are involved in constitutional review, and how they are permanently improving their conventional review. As a result, both of these courts may perhaps appear as the winners of the constitutional reform. In some brief concluding remarks (section IV) I will recapitulate the arguments presented and reflect on the role of the French Parliament in this context.

II. EMERGENCE AND DEVELOPMENT OF THE JUDICIAL PROTECTION OF FUNDAMENTAL RIGHTS (1971–2009)

In the history of the Convention's implementation in France, the Conseil Constitutionnel has increasingly played an important role, not only because it is competent to review the constitutionality of statutes (A), but also because of its case law regarding the distribution of competences between constitutional judges and ordinary judges in the field of international law (B). The latter has been completed by the case law of the Cour de Cassation and Conseil d'Etat, thus allowing for the development of conventional review (C).

A. The Conseil Constitutionnel and the Protection of Constitutional Rights

Since the French Revolution, statute law has been considered 'sacred', being an 'expression of the general will'.[4] Not surprisingly, the constitutional systems of the Third (1875–1940) and Fourth Republics (1946–58) highlighted the role of statutory law while playing down constitutional supremacy.[5] The Fifth Republic put an end to this kind of parliamentary sovereignty and created the Conseil Constitutionnel as a sort of watchdog against Parliament. In fact, far from being instituted as a guardian of the Constitution, the Conseil Constitutionnel saw its

---

[3] The constitutional amendment was completed by organic law (*loi organique*) No 2009-1523 of 10 December 2009 on the application of Article 61-1 of the Constitution, *JORF* 11 December 2009, 21379, @no1; the organic law has been subject to an obligatory review of the Conseil Constitutionnel: CC No 2009-595 DC, 3 December 2009 and implemented by the Decree No 2010-148 of 16 February 2010, *JORF* 18 February 2010, No 7.

[4] Article 6 of the 1789 Declaration of the Rights of Man and of the Citizen: 'The Law is the expression of the general will. All citizens have the right to take part, personally or through their representatives, in its making. It must be the same for all, whether it protects or punishes. All citizens, being equal in its eyes, shall be equally eligible to all high offices, public positions and employments, according to their ability, and without other distinction than that of their virtues and talents.' (Translation available on the website of the Conseil Constitutionnel: www.conseil-constitutionnel.fr.)

[5] For a general view, see M Troper and F Hamon, *Droit constitutionnel*, 35th edn (Paris, LGDJ, 2014), 359 ff and 388 ff. For further analysis by one of the classic authors see R Carré de Malberg, *La loi, expression de la volonté générale. Etude sur le concept de la loi dans la Constitution de 1875* (Paris, Sirey, 1931).

primary function as being the supervision of Parliament in order to prevent any interference in the new executive competences.

Therefore, at the beginning of this era, the constitutional review of laws was conceived in a quite limited manner. In order to safeguard the traditional authority of statutory law, the Conseil Constitutionnel was authorised to review laws and treaties only before their entry into force or ratification. In addition, only a few officials[6] could challenge a law or treaty before the Council. The standard of review of the Conseil Constitutionnel was limited to the provisions contained in the text of the Constitution, and thus review primarily concerned compliance with legislative procedure. The Council was not able to examine the consistency of statutory laws with fundamental rights because fundamental rights are not included in the corpus of the 1958 Constitution. The latter are included both in the 1789 Declaration of the Rights of Man and of the Citizen and also in the Preamble to the 1946 Constitution. As for the Preamble to the 1958 Constitution, this declares:

> The French people solemnly proclaim their attachment to the Rights of Man and the principles of national sovereignty as defined by the Declaration of 1789, confirmed and complemented by the Preamble to the Constitution of 1946, and to the rights and duties as defined in the Charter for the Environment of 2004.[7]

In 1971, the Conseil Constitutionnel revised its initial restrained approach in respect of constitutional review and fundamental rights. When legislation concerning freedom of association was referred to it, it used the opportunity to rule that henceforth the Preamble would be included as a standard of the Council's constitutionality review.[8] In doing so, it extended the review of laws in respect of their consistency with fundamental rights. The Preamble thus acquired constitutional status, forming—together with the numbered articles of the Constitution—the so-called 'block of constitutionality', serving as the benchmark for its review.[9]

In 1974, this extension of review was consolidated by a constitutional amendment opening up referral before the Conseil Constitutionnel to a group of 60 deputies or senators.[10] From that moment on, the political opposition was able to bring cases before constitutional judges. In the period that followed, referrals before the Conseil Constitutionnel increased significantly and when the political majority changed in 1981, the Council played an important role by facilitating the handover of political power.[11]

Nevertheless, compared with other European constitutional courts, the power of the Conseil Constitutionnel appeared to be limited because its review consisted

---

[6] The President of the Republic, the Prime Minister and the Presidents of the two Chambers of the Parliament.

[7] Translation: website of the Conseil Constitutionnel, www.conseil-constitutionnel.fr.

[8] CC decision No 71-44 DC, 16 July 1971, *Liberté d'association*; all the decisions of the Conseil Constitutionnel and very often an English translation are available on its website: www.conseil-constitutionnel.fr.

[9] '*Bloc de constitutionnalite*'. For more detail in English, see M-C Ponthoreau and F Hourquebie, 'The French Conseil Constitutionnel: An Evolving Form of Constitutional Justice' in A Harding and P Leyland (eds), *Constitutional Courts: A Comparative Study* (London, Wildy, Simmons & Hill, 2009) 81–83.

[10] Loi constitutionnelle no 74-904 of 29 October 1974, amending Article 61 of the Constitution, *JORF* 30 October 1974, 11035.

[11] See especially L Favoreu, La politique saisie par le droit: alternances, cohabitation et Conseil Constitutionnel (Paris, Economica, 1988).

only of a preliminary, abstract review and authorised no assessment of the concrete implementation of the law in question. Therefore, after 1990 several drafts were produced in order to bolster the existing review process with a more concrete procedure.[12] Finally, the proposals of the so-called 'Balladur Committee'[13] led to a constitutional amendment adopted in 2008, which entered into force in 2010.[14]

B. The Case Law concerning the Legal Status of International and European Law

Pursuant to Article 55 of the French Constitution,

> Treaties or agreements duly ratified or approved shall, upon publication, prevail over Acts of Parliament, subject, with respect to each agreement or treaty, to its application by the other party.

As is apparent, the French Constitution takes a monist approach to international treaties, as they do not need incorporation by means of a statute. However, this formulation raises several questions: what is the value of international conventional norms with respect to the Constitution, and what are the consequences in terms of judicial review of the legal status thus defined?

While the first question has not received a precise answer, the second one was answered by the Conseil Constitutionnel in an important decision of 1975 relating to the termination of pregnancy,[15] and thus the right to life, which is recognised by Article 2 ECHR but is not recognised by the French Constitution. In this decision, the Conseil Constitutionnel established a radical separation between constitutional and conventional review.[16] Referring to the hierarchy of norms, *constitutional* review operates to affirm constitutional supremacy and expresses a judgment on the validity of statutory laws with respect to the Constitution. Therefore any unconstitutional law is invalid and must be quashed. *Conventional* review, by contrast, addresses the relationship between domestic and international law. Yet, according to the Conseil Constitutionnel,

> while these provisions [Article 55] confer upon treaties, in accordance with their terms, an authority superior to that of statutes, they neither *require* nor *imply* that this principle must be honoured within the framework of constitutional review as provided by Article 61.[17]

---

[12] A draft law to this end had been submitted to the French National Assembly on 30 March 1990: Projet de loi constitutionnelle No 1203 portant révision des articles 61, 62 et 63 de la Constitution et instituant un contrôle de la constitutionnalité des lois. Later on, another draft was submitted to the French Senate on 11 March 1993: Projet de loi constitutionnelle no 231 portant révision de la Constitution du 4 octobre 1958 et modifiant ses titres VII, VIII, IX et X. See generally V Bernaud and M Fatin-Rouge Stefanini, 'La réforme du contrôle de constitutionnalité une nouvelle fois en question? Réflexions autour des articles 61-1 et 62 de la Constitution proposés par le Comité Balladur' [2008] *Revue française de droit constitutionnel* 169.

[13] On the work and the conclusions of this committee, see www.comite-Constitutionnel.fr.

[14] See above, nn 1 and 3.

[15] CC decision No 74-54 DC, 15 January 1975.

[16] See C Grewe, 'Contrôle de constitutionnalité et contrôle de conventionalité: à la recherche d'une frontière introuvable' [2014] *Revue française de droit constitutionnel* 961.

[17] Point 3, CC decision No 74-54 DC, 15 January 1975 (emphasis added).

As a result, Article 55 has to be interpreted by the competent authorities as a conflict of laws rule[18] giving simple priority to the application of international law. Similar to the way constitutional review is practised in the USA, the offending law should only be set aside in the particular case; it should not be declared invalid.

The radical separation between constitutional and conventional review not only implied a new distribution of judicial competences, but also resulted in a more or less dualistic orientation of the constitutional system. In fact, the question of the value of conventional norms appeared less important from the moment international and European law were in a way excluded from the domestic vertical hierarchy and set aside within a conflict of laws system. So it is not surprising that this question was resolved only later by the three highest courts and in favour of constitutional supremacy in the domestic order.[19]

Thus the main substance of the abortion decision was to deny the competence of the constitutional judge and to underline that conventional review was not a form of constitutional review. In this context, it is important to recall the traditional hostility in France towards review of statutory laws, which is translated into the fear of 'government by judges'.[20] Nevertheless, the Cour de Cassation implemented the constitutional decision readily, accepting, from 1975 onwards, the task of reviewing the consistency of statutes with the Convention.[21] Yet the Conseil d'Etat continued to invoke the conditions mentioned in Article 55 in order to deny primacy to international law and conventional review. It was only in the *Nicolo* case (1989)[22] that the administrative courts admitted the priority of international law by applying conventional review. Henceforth, the conditions for the development of conventional review existed.

C. The Ordinary Courts and the Protection of Conventional Rights: The Development of Conventional Review

The period 1981–2009 proved to be one of contrasts. Many scholars[23] celebrated conventional review and the Convention's implementation. However, the courts,

[18] In the case of *Mlle Deprez et M Baillard* (CE, 5 January 2005) No 257341, Rec 1, the Conseil d'Etat referred explicitly to the idea of conflict of laws in order to assert the superiority of treaties over Acts of Parliament.

[19] CE ass, 30 October 1998, *Sarran et Levacher*, No 200286 and 200287, Rec, 369; Cass ass, 2 June 2000, *Mlle Fraisse*, No 99-60274, Bull 2000, No 4, 7; the Conseil Constitutionnel confirmed this analysis in its decision relating to the Constitution for Europe (CC decision No 2004-505 DC, 19 November 2004, point 10) in the following terms: 'The name given to this new Treaty does not require as such any ruling as to its constitutionality; Article l-5 thereof, pertaining to the relations between the European Union and the Member States thereof, shows that the title of said treaty has no effect upon the existence of the French Constitution and the place of the latter at the summit of the domestic legal order.'

[20] See generally E Lambert, Le gouvernement des juges et la lutte contre la législation sociale aux Etats-Unis : l'expérience américaine du contrôle judiciaire de la constitutionnalité des lois (Paris, Dalloz, 2005); see especially the judgments of the Cour de Cassation (Cass, 2e civ, 20 December 1956, Bull 1956, No 714, 464) and the Conseil d'Etat (CE, 6 November 1936, Arrighi, Rec, 966) recalling the prohibition to control or quash a law.

[21] Cass ch mixte, No 73-13556, 24 May 1975, *Société des Cafés Jacques Vabre*, Bull 1975, No 4, 6.

[22] CE ass No 108243, 20 October 1989, *Nicolo*, Rec 190.

[23] See especially F Sudre, 'Existe-t-il un ordre public européen?' in P Tavernier (ed), *Quelle Europe pour les droits de l'homme?* (Brussels, Bruylant, 1996) 39; JF Flauss (ed), 'Vers un droit constitutionnel européen? Quel droit constitutionnel européen?' [1995] *Revue universelle des droits de l'homme* 357;

and later the administrative tribunals, went through a range of (conflicting) reactions: after readily expanding conventional review, a significant crisis vis-a-vis the European Court of Human Rights (ECtHR) occurred, followed in turn by a period of peaceful evolution. These reactions operated not only separately and successively but also simultaneously. I will analyse first the negative and then the positive attitudes of the courts, and illustrate these with some statistical data.

The statistics on French violations reflect the late acceptance of the individual petition procedure. The first judgment against France was delivered in 1986.[24] Between 1986 and 1998, the ECtHR held France responsible for 62 violations.[25] By 1998, the number of judgments against France had increased significantly. Thus, between 1999 and 2009, violations were found in 514 cases against France.[26] Within the same timeframe, the ECtHR found only 77 violations by Germany[27] and 201 by the UK.[28] While it fared better than Italy[29] and Turkey,[30] France was among the countries that contributed most to the case overload of the Strasbourg Court in this period. This reveals the relative ignorance about the ECHR and its case law in France and, at the same time, the beginnings of tension between the national and European courts.

With the case of *Poitrimol* (1993),[31] which concerned procedure in criminal matters before the Cour de Cassation, a shockwave ran through the French judiciary.[32] The result was that the judiciary's willingness to make domestic law conform to the ECtHR's case law suddenly decreased significantly. It was often the case that several condemnations were necessary before ECtHR judgments were implemented. *Kress*, a judgment delivered in 2001, revived the crisis.[33] This particularly sensitive application related to the position of the then so-called 'Government Commissioner' (commissaire du gouvernement). This was a member of the administrative courts who intervened at the end of a public hearing to present an opinion on the most legally appropriate solution for a case, and who afterwards attended the deliberations of the trial bench. The parties to the proceedings were not informed in advance about the submissions of the Government Commissioner and were prevented from answering his points or contradicting him. The ECtHR[34] held that this, together with

F Sudre (ed), *L'interprétation de la Convention européenne des droits de l'homme* (Brussels, Bruylant, 1998); P Wachsmann, 'Les méthodes d'interprétation des conventions internationales relatives à la protection des droits de l'homme' in SFDI, Colloque de Strasbourg, *La protection internationale des droits de l'homme* (Paris, Pedone, 1998) 157; M Delmas-Marty, H Muir-Watt and H Ruiz Fabri (eds), *Variations autour d'un droit commun: premières rencontres de l'UMR de droit comparé de Paris* (Paris, Société de Législation comparée, 2002); H Ruiz Fabri (ed), *Procès équitable et enchevêtrement des espaces normatifs* (Paris, Société de Législation comparée, 2003).

[24] *Bozano v France* (1986) 9 EHRR 297.

[25] J Vailhé, La France face aux exigences de la Convention européenne des droits de l'homme (La Documentation française, Paris 2001) 45.

[26] *Annual Report of the ECtHR 2008*, 140 and *Annual Report of the ECtHR 2009*, 147, www.echr.coe.int/Pages/home.aspx?p=echrpublications&c=#newComponent_1345118680892_pointer.

[27] Annual Report of the ECtHR 2008, 140 and Annual Report of the ECtHR 2009, 146; see ibid.

[28] Annual Report of the ECtHR 2008, 141 and Annual Report of the ECtHR 2009, 147; see ibid.

[29] 1,455 violations: *Report 2008*, 140 and *Report 2009*, 146; see ibid.

[30] 1,993 violations: *Report 2008*, 141 and *Report 2009*, 147, see ibid.

[31] *Poitrimol v France* (1994) 18 EHRR 130.

[32] J Vailhé, La France face aux exigences de la Convention européenne des droits de l'homme (La Documentation française, Paris, 2001) 102 ff.

[33] *Kress v France* App no 39594/98, ECHR 2001-VI.

[34] The ECtHR had to repeat its disagreement: *Martinie v France* App no 58675/00, ECHR 2006-VI.

his presence during the court's deliberations, amounted to a violation of the right to a fair trial. In France, the controversy surrounding this issue was considerable—akin to the British debates on prisoners' voting rights. There have been truly hysterical discourses about the interference of a 'foreign' court in domestic concerns undermining core institutions of the French legal tradition.[35]

Nonetheless, over the course of several years, procedures before the administrative courts were modified and parties were authorised to contest the conclusions of the Commissioner, henceforth called the 'Reporting Judge' (rapporteur public).[36] It must be noted that from today's perspective, in spite of the outcry at the time, the judiciary, and especially the Conseil d'Etat, find this state of the law to be very satisfactory, even presenting it as an example of the French judiciary's 'appropriation' of the Convention.[37] This underlines the change in attitude, which is also noticeable with regard to the length of judicial proceedings—the excessive nature of which was responsible for a large proportion of the French violations. In this respect, cooperation between Parliament, the Conseil d'Etat and the government from 2000 onwards resulted in the requirement that compensation be sought in domestic courts before bringing proceedings in Strasbourg.[38]

More generally, the courts increasingly applied the Convention[39] and parties to proceedings became used to invoking it. In several areas of law, such as the status of prisoners and foreigners, especially in deportation cases, reference to the ECHR

[35] See for instance the government's position in *Kress* (n 33) para 62, and the summary presented by R de Gouttes, *Cahiers du CREDHO* No 8, case law of 2000–01; see also D Chabanol, 'Théorie de l'apparence ou apparence de théorie? Humeurs autour de l'arrêt Kress' (2002) *Actualité juridique droit administratif* 9; T Paris, 'Le juge administratif français et la Convention européenne de sauvegarde des droits de l'homme et des libertés fondamentales: du droit international au droit interne?', International Conference on Human Rights Education, Yekaterinburg, Russia, 21–22 October 2013) 5.

[36] The reform has taken a long time to complete. In a first stage, Decree No 2005-1586 of 19 December 2005 stipulated the presence of the government's commissioner at the deliberations, yet without his participation. In a second stage, Decree No 2006-964 of 1 August 2006 excluded his presence during the deliberations before the administrative tribunals but not before the Conseil d'Etat. Finally, in a third stage, Decree No 2009-14 of 7 January 2009 proceeded to a larger modification, including a change of the institution's name and a prohibition on the ex-commissioner attending any deliberations in any administrative courts. This reform has been approved by the ECtHR: *François Marc Antoine v France* App no 54984/09 (4 June 2013).

[37] See J-M Sauvé, 'Le principe de subsidiarité et la protection européenne des droits de l'homme' in Conseil d'Etat (ed), *Le droit européen des droits de l'homme* (Paris, La Documentation française, 2011) 35; J-P Michel and P Gélard, *Report of the Sénat on the European Court of Human Rights*, No 705, 2011–12, 39.

[38] According to Ordinance No 2006-673 of 8 June 2006 (*JORF* 9 June 2006) codified by Art L 141-1 of the Code of Judicial Organisation, the State is responsible for the malfunctioning of the judiciary. The amended law expanded the possibility of claiming compensation for violations of human rights before French courts by providing for exceptions to the principle that liability requires gross negligence, which had previously severely limited the possibility of seeking compensation. Before the administrative courts, the Conseil d'Etat reversed its case law in the same way by CE 28 June 2002, *Magiera* (No 239575, Rec 248). Following a decree of 28 July 2005, inserted into Art R 311-1 of the Administrative Justice Code, the Conseil d'Etat is competent to decide on state liability in the case of excessively lengthy proceedings.

[39] See the French reports of various international conferences: IXth Conference of the European Constitutional Courts, 'Protection constitutionnelle et protection internationale des droits de l'homme: concurrence ou complémentarité?' [1995] *Revue universelle des droits de l'homme* 217; Cour de Cassation, *Les principes communs d'une justice des Etats de l'Union européenne. Actes du colloque des 4 et 5 décembre 2000* (Paris, La Documentation française, 2001). See especially, concerning the Conseil d'Etat, O Duteillet de Lamothe, 'Contrôle de constitutionnalité et contrôle de conventionalité' in *Mélanges en l'honneur de Daniel Labetoulle* (Paris, Dalloz, 2007) 315, 323 f.

has become a sort of reflex. In particular, the Conseil d'Etat has accepted control over matters that were previously deemed 'measures of internal order' (*mesures d'ordre intérieur*), that is, decisions taken principally by prisons or psychiatric hospital authorities, such as isolation, disciplinary punishments and transfers. For a long time, these measures had been excluded from judicial review because they had not been recognised as administrative acts.[40] Under the influence of the ECtHR, the Conseil d'Etat has greatly increased the number of cases where the impact of these 'internal measures' on the situation of the person concerned, particularly on their rights and freedoms, is held to be so serious as to merit judicial review.[41] Similarly, the Cour de Cassation has progressively accepted a number of the European standards.[42] ECHR case law concerning family life,[43] privacy, including the rights of transsexuals,[44] property and the notion of 'possession'[45] is particularly significant in this respect. French judges have even dared to give preference to the Convention over national law.[46]

To sum up, the situation in 2009 seemed to be quite satisfactory: French violations had diminished; the ordinary courts, now better versed in European case law, increasingly practised conventional review; and the Conseil Constitutionnel had developed its constitutional review procedure, but this remained separate from conventional review and limited to a preliminary abstract review. This was the moment chosen for a constitutional amendment introducing a new constitutional procedure—the 'priority preliminary ruling on the issue of constitutionality', known as *QPC* in French.[47] This reform led to major changes throughout the system; it is thus worth surveying its impact on the implementation of the ECHR.

---

[40] See generally J Rivero, *Les mesures d'ordre intérieur administratives: essai sur les caractères juridiques de la vie intérieure des services publics* (Paris, Thèse, 1934).

[41] The case of *Marie* (CE, 17 February 1995 No 97754, Rec 83) is in this respect a turning point, following which the right to contest an 'internal' measure depends on the nature and the severity of the administrative decision and its impact on the concrete individual situation. As acceptance of judicial review depends henceforth on the concrete situation, there is no longer a homogeneous category of internal measures. The cases *Garde des Sceaux, ministre de la justice c/ Boussouar, Planchenault* and *Payet* (CE ass, 14 December 2007, Rec 476, 474 and 498) aim at further reducing the scope of unchallengeable decisions and at systematising the case law on this subject.

[42] D Richet, 'L'interprétation conforme à la Convention européenne des droits de l'homme' [2007] *Cahiers de l'IDEDH* (Institut de droit européen des droits de l'homme) 11, 101.

[43] Concerning the law on parentage see eg Cass 1ère civ, 29 January 2002, *Rolland c/ Fourtier, Bull* civ I, No 32.

[44] Cass ass, 11 December 1992, *René X et Marc X, Bull* Ass plén 1992, no 13, 27.

[45] Henceforth social benefits, the right to a pension and the right to benefit from a well-established case law are considered to be possessions. See the three judgments of the Cour de Cassation dated 24 January 2006: Cass 1ère civ, *Franck X et al c/ Pol Z et al*; Cass 1ère civ, FS P+B, *CPAM de Loir et Cher c/ Sté Le Sou médical et al*; Cass 1ère civ, FS P+B, *Fondation Bagatelle et al c/ SHAM et a, Bull* 2006 I No 30, 28; No 29, 26 and No 31, 29. The Conseil d'Etat's case law has evolved in the same sense: CE ass, 30 November 2001 *Ministre de la défense c/ M Diop*, No 212179, Rec 605 and CE ass, Avis 6 December 2002, *Epoux Draon*, No 250704, Rec 423.

[46] See especially Cass crim, 4 September 2001, No 00-85329 *Bull* 2001, No 170, where the court set aside the law prohibiting the publication and diffusion of opinion polls in the week before elections on the ground that such a limitation on freedom of expression is not necessary for the protection of the legitimate interests mentioned in Art 10(2) ECHR. Since this judgment was delivered shortly before the presidential elections, on 19 February 2002 Parliament adopted a law (No 2002-214) prohibiting the publication of opinion polls the day before and on the day of electoral scrutiny. See also the judgments concerning the police custody of illegally resident foreigners (n 71).

[47] See above, n 1.

III. IMPACT OF THE CONSTITUTIONAL REFORM INTRODUCING THE *QPC* (2010–14)

Accepting a preliminary ruling on the issue of constitutionality indisputably represents progress for the constitutional review of laws,[48] especially regarding their compatibility with constitutional rights. Importantly, it is possible henceforth to challenge a law after its entry into force, provided there is a violation of a constitutional right. The party to proceedings alleging such a violation brings a request for review before the competent tribunal, which may transmit it to one of the high courts—the Cour de Cassation for 'private' law claims[49] and the Conseil d'Etat for administrative law.[50] If the court holds the claim to be 'new' or 'serious',[51] it refers the question to the Conseil Constitutionnel, which must make a decision within three months. After the latter has delivered its judgment, the ordinary proceedings can continue on the basis of the constitutional decision.

In order to underline the precedence and thus the importance of this referral process, the constitutional legislator has chosen the designation '*priority* preliminary ruling on the issue of constitutionality'. This constitutional priority has provoked heated debate, especially regarding the question of whether the new constitutional procedure would undermine conventional review by the ordinary courts. So far, the contribution of this new procedure to the Convention's implementation remains questionable. Thus, it will be argued that, on the one hand, priority referral seems to strengthen the Conseil Constitutionnel and constitutional review to the possible detriment of the ordinary courts and conventional review (A). Indeed, the separation between the two kinds of review implies the possibility of conflicting interpretation of constitutional and conventional rights. But on the other hand, experience since 2009 shows how crucial a role is played by the Cour de Cassation and Conseil d'Etat, because of their involvement in both constitutional and conventional review (B).

A. Constitutional Case Law: Dissociation from or Harmony with ECHR Rights?

The reform has been intensely discussed among scholars. Significantly, constitutionalists and specialists in private law and the ECHR oppose one another: the former are in favour of the Conseil Constitutionnel, while the latter are in favour of the ordinary courts and the Convention. Giving priority to constitutional preliminary rulings refocuses control regarding fundamental rights towards the constitutional

---

[48] Between 28 May 2010 and 25 April 2014 there were 339 applications.

[49] Which in France includes the criminal law.

[50] The new Art 61-1 stipulates: 'If, during proceedings in progress before a court of law, it is claimed that a legislative provision infringes the rights and freedoms guaranteed by the Constitution, the matter may be referred by the Conseil d'Etat or by the Cour de Cassation to the Conseil Constitutionnel which shall rule within a determined period. An Institutional Act shall determine the conditions for the application of the present article.' (Translation: Conseil Constitutionnel.)

[51] The conditions for referring the question to the Conseil Constitutionnel are indicated in Organic Law No 2009-1523 of 10 December 2009 on the application of Art 61-1 of the Constitution, *JORF* of 11 December 2009, p 21379, no 1, section 23-1 to 23-12; see also below, III.B.i.

judge, thereby reducing the role played by the ordinary tribunals. So has the battle been won by the constitutionalists, or could it be a pyrrhic victory? Three remarks are made by way of reply.

First, the formal absence in the Conseil Constitutionnel's decisions of any reference to the Convention may be noted.[52] When compared to the judgments of the German Constitutional Court, which is not always a supporter of the Convention, this response lacks transparency and intelligibility. Not only does this silence prevent the Conseil Constitutionnel from bringing its own arguments before the ECtHR,[53] thereby rejecting dialogue, it also implies that the position taken with regard to the law of the ECHR is never clearly expressed.

The second response concerns the ECHR's legal status with regard to the interpretive power of the Conseil Constitutionnel. As the Convention has merely sub-constitutional status,[54] it is not binding on the latter. This position in the normative hierarchy gives, on the contrary, the choice to the Conseil Constitutionnel to interpret *constitutional* rights in a way that is identical, equivalent or different to interpretations of the ECtHR regarding *conventional* rights. This is true even if the formulation of the two kinds of rights proves to be quite similar. Therefore, the choice between dissociation and harmony of constitutional and conventional rights rests entirely with the Conseil Constitutionnel. Whether the Constitution's interpretation should conform more or less to the Convention amounts to a matter of judicial policy. While the Spanish Constitution prescribes that national fundamental rights must be interpreted according to international norms,[55] no such order exists in the French Constitution.

The third remark relates to the content of constitutional case law. The Conseil Constitutionnel's case law remains characterised by ambiguity, oscillating between a purely national-constitutional and a more European Convention-friendly interpretation.

On the one hand, harmonising constitutional law with conventional law is a stated aim. The decision relating to the pensions of soldiers from the French ex-colonies may be mentioned here.[56] The Conseil Constitutionnel in this case applied the principle of non-discrimination on the ground of nationality, finding that Algerians holding civil or military pensions were treated differently from French nationals with the same place of residence. In its decision concerning maritime commercial tribunals,[57] the Conseil Constitutionnel interpreted the principle of judicial independence in line with the ECtHR. The fact that two or three out of the five members of these courts were civil servants or employees of the State was held to demonstrate the lack of

---

[52] On the motivation, see D Baranger, 'Sur la manière française de rendre la justice constitutionnelle: motivations et raisons politiques dans la jurisprudence du Conseil constitutionnel' (2012) IV *Jus politicum* 13.

[53] D Szymczak, 'Question prioritaire de constitutionnalité et Convention européenne des droits de l'homme: l'européanisation « heurtée » du Conseil constitutionnel français' (2012) IV *Jus politicum* 205, describing this attitude as 'silent dialogue' (216–27).

[54] See above, II.B.

[55] Spanish Constitution, Art 10-2.

[56] CC decision No 2010-1 QPC, 28 May 2010, *Consorts L.*

[57] CC decision No 2010-10 QPC, 2 July 2010, *Consorts C.*

appropriate guarantees of independence. The first decision on police custody[58] also belongs in this category, since the Conseil Constitutionnel struck down the legal regulation of police custody because it guaranteed neither the effective assistance of a lawyer nor information on the right to remain silent. The ECtHR had criticised this several times.[59] Other aspects of this decision seem more problematic, especially the fact that prosecutors were considered to belong to the judicial authority and the fact that the entry into force of this decision was postponed. The Conseil Constitutionnel took this position in order to prevent any interference with the legislative power. However, not only was the appellant deprived of the benefit of the unconstitutionality, as when British courts make declarations of incompatibility under the Human Rights Act 1998, but this postponement, as we will see below,[60] also created some problems for the Cour de Cassation. Later on, the Council tried to avoid such difficulties by declaring that unconstitutionality could be 'invoked by the parties', thus sidestepping the established distinction between justiciability of an issue and the possibility of parties invoking (and benefiting from) unconstitutionality.[61]

On the other hand, the objective of safeguarding constitutional law's autonomy with regard to the European Convention is obvious. This is demonstrated by decisions in which compliance with the Convention is doubtful or even non-existent. So, for instance, the compliance of the decision dealing with the non-disclosure of defence secrets[62] might appear disputable. In this case, the Conseil Constitutionnel, whilst having reduced the scope of secrecy, has maintained the principle according to which, within the scope of secrecy, *judicial* investigations need *administrative* authorisation. Neither the separation of powers nor judicial independence seems to be guaranteed by this decision. Furthermore, concerning discrimination between children born in or out of wedlock, a strong line of case law from the ECtHR exists. Despite this case law, French constitutional judges have found discrimination resulting from the effects of filiation on nationality to be justified.[63] They have also treated as justified discrimination regarding the eviction of travelling communities from parking areas[64] and their special administrative regime.[65] In particular, the Council distinguishes between the situation of such persons who have chosen to live in mobile homes or caravans and adopt an itinerant lifestyle and those who have opted to live in a sedentary, settled manner based on 'objective and rational

---

[58] CC decision No 2010-14/22 QPC, 30 July 2010, *M Daniel W et autres*. The entry into force of this decision had been postponed for a year in order to make it possible for the legislator to modify the legal situation. The final decision on the reform of custody, CC decision No 2011-191/194/195/196/197 QPC, 18 November 2011, *Mme Élise A et autres [Garde à vue II]*, raises doubts again in respect of its conventionality. See C Grewe, 'Les outils dans le cadre de la Convention européenne des droits de l'homme' in D d'Ambra (ed), *Le rééquilibrage du pouvoir juridictionnel* (Paris, Dalloz, 2013), 101.

[59] *Salduz v Turkey* (2009) 49 EHRR 19; *Dayanan v Turkey* App no 7377/03 (13 October 2009).

[60] See below, III.B.ii.

[61] So, for instance, in CC decision No 2013-360 QPC, 9 January 2014, *Mme Jalila K*, the judge distinguished between the justiciability (*erga omnes*) of rights and the possibility of *the parties* invoking them.

[62] CC decision No 2011-192 QPC, 10 November 2011, *Mme Ekaterina B, épouse D, et autres*.

[63] CC decision No 2011-186/187/188/189 QPC, 21 October 2011, *Mlle Fazia C et autres*.

[64] CC decision No 2010-13 QPC, 9 July 2010, *M Orient O et autre*.

[65] CC decision No 2012-279 QPC, 5 October 2012, *M Jean-Claude P*: several inequalities are declared unconstitutional but the principle of the special status of Travellers remains.

criteria'.[66] Thus, this is not treated as discrimination based on ethnic origin. These different situations also explain the verdict of constitutional conformity of the following statutory provision:

> Individuals who have not had a fixed place of abode or residence within a Member State of the European Union for more than six months must carry a circulation book which shall be issued by the administrative authorities.[67]

Accordingly, the judge considered that

> in requiring the individuals concerned to obtain a circulation permit, the legislature did not breach the principle of equality; ... the resulting violation of the freedom of movement is justified by the need to protect public order and is proportional with this objective.[68]

Finally, in an application relating to undocumented migrants in France,[69] the Conseil Constitutionnel was asked to state that their imprisonment was unnecessary, as the Court of Justice of the European Union (CJEU)[70] had held this sanction to be inconsistent with the directive on 'Return'. Accordingly, the Cour de Cassation[71] had removed the option of keeping undocumented migrants in police custody. Nevertheless, the Conseil Constitutionnel maintains the aforementioned[72] strict separation between constitutionality and conventionality, stating that a French law incompatible with European or EU law does not for this reason become unconstitutional.

The future development of this case law seems quite unpredictable. However, it should be noted that the President of the Conseil Constitutionnel has declared that it examines in each case the relevant case law of the ECtHR and that the decisions affirming the constitutionality of a law have also to be understood as a presumption of conventionality.[73] In fact, there are some recent decisions which, although not referring explicitly to the ECHR, use identical wording to that employed by the ECtHR in a judgment concerning France.[74] This is undoubtedly a positive sign, likely to illustrate that constitutional review is not intended to replace conventional review.

---

[66] ibid, Point 18.

[67] ibid, Art 2 of the Law of 3 January 1969 quoted in the decision.

[68] ibid, Point 18.

[69] CC decision No 2011-217 QPC, 3 February 2012, *M Mohammed Alki B*; see for more detail C Lafont, 'Exemples de la garde à vue et de la juridiction pour enfants' in D d'Ambra (ed), *Le rééquilibrage du pouvoir juridictionnel* (Paris, Dalloz, 2013) 119, 126 f.

[70] Case C-61/11 PPU *El Dridi* [2011] ECR I-3015; Case C-329/11 *Achughbabian* [2011] ECR I-12695. Later case law is more tolerant vis-a-vis penal sanctions for illegal stay: Case C-430/11 *Sagor*, ECLI:EU:C:2012:777; Case C-146/14 PPU *Mahdi*, ECLI:EU:C:2014:1320.

[71] The advisory opinion of the Cour de Cassation (Cass crim, avis No 9002, 5 June 2012) has been followed by three judgments dated 5 July 2012: Cass 1ère civ, No 959, pourvoi No 11-30.371; Cass 1ère civ, No 965, pourvoi No 11-30.530; Cass 1ère civ, No 960, pourvoi No 11-19.250.

[72] See above, II.B, and below in the concluding remarks.

[73] This speech, delivered on 4 April 2013, can be found on the website of the Conseil Constitutionnel: www.conseil-constitutionnel.fr. The president declared: 'En revanche si le Conseil la [la loi] juge conforme à la Constitution, cette décision comme la prise en compte de la jurisprudence de la CEDH doivent créer une présomption de conventionalité. Seuls de très sérieux motifs peuvent conduire à envisager de les renverser pour opposer protections constitutionnelle et conventionnelle.'

[74] This concerns first of all the practice of validating by means of law an illegal administrative or judicial decision. In the case of *Zielinski et al v France* (2001) 31 EHRR 19, the ECtHR had already highlighted the conditions under which such a practice could be held conventional; among these criteria is the existence of 'an imperative ground of general interest'. The Conseil Constitutionnel had adapted its case law to the other conditions required by the ECtHR but was satisfied with the presence of 'a sufficient

B. Impact of the Priority Constitutional Ruling on Conventional Review by the Ordinary Courts

The impact of *QPC* on conventional review is much more important than the radical separation between constitutional and conventional review operated by the Conseil Constitutionnel suggests. In this respect it is notable, first, that the high courts are involved in the new procedure of priority constitutional ruling. Secondly, the consequences for conventional review are remarkable in terms of improving implementation of the ECHR.

(i) The High Courts' Involvement in the New Constitutional Review

In the new *QPC* procedure the high courts are invested with responsibility for filtering constitutional questions. Indeed, when a first-instance court or a court of appeal is confronted with a party referral asking for a preliminary constitutional ruling,[75] the competent judge transmits the application—if it meets the necessary conditions[76]—to his/her high court. It is up to the Cour de Cassation or the Conseil d'Etat to decide whether or not the question fulfils the legal conditions[77] and has to be submitted to the Conseil Constitutionnel in order to be decided. In most other legal orders where such a procedure exists, this filtering function is exercised either by the lower judge or by the constitutional court itself. Conferring on the high courts a separate filtering function is quite an unusual solution.

As a result, the Cour de Cassation and the Conseil d'Etat play a decisive role in the distribution between constitutional and conventional review. As there is a sort of competition between the ordinary jurisdictions and the Conseil Constitutionnel concerning the review of laws, it is clear that in this competition the high courts are given a much more active role than constitutional judges. This is all the more true as the priority constitutional ruling may, in addition, conflict with a preliminary referral before the CJEU. This argument was raised by the Cour de Cassation

---

general interest'. After a new violation found by the ECtHR in *Lilly v France (No 2)* App no 20429/07 (25 November 2010), the Conseil Constitutionnel changed its formulation and henceforth requires the existence of 'an imperative ground of general interest': CC decision No 2013-366 QPC, 14 February 2014, *SELARL PJA, ès qualités de liquidateur de la société Maflow France*.

[75] According to section 23-1 of the Ordinance on the Conseil Constitutionnel, in order to challenge a legislative provision the party concerned has to submit a separate and reasoned document. The constitutional argument can be raised at any instance but not by the judge. Special rules are provided for criminal proceedings.

[76] Pursuant to section 23-2, the lower judge has to decide 'without delay' on the question of transmission to the Conseil d'Etat or the Cour de Cassation. The transmission is subject to three conditions: '1. The challenged provision is applicable to the litigation or proceedings underway, or is the grounds for said proceedings; 2. Said provision has not previously been found to be constitutional in the holding of a decision of the Conseil Constitutionnel, except in the event of a change of circumstances; 3. The matter is not deprived of seriousness.'

[77] According to section 23-4, the Cour de Cassation and the Conseil d'Etat have to decide within three months on submission to the Conseil Constitutionnel. They have to observe conditions 1 and 2 required from the lower judges and in addition must prove that 'the issue raised is new or of a serious nature'.

in a reference to the CJEU[78] which has been sharply criticised.[79] In its judgment the CJEU held that the question was not devoid of seriousness and delimited the scope of this 'priority'[80] in relying on the interpretation given by the Conseil Constitutionnel and the Conseil d'Etat.[81] Accordingly, the ordinary courts are not prevented from referring questions to the CJEU.

Besides these difficulties encountered when the *QPC* was introduced, the high courts' involvement in the *QPC* procedure has pushed the latter to rethink their reasoning on human rights. Both courts have felt obliged to increasingly examine, consider and reflect on fundamental rights protection. As a result, sensitivity to human rights has been heightened.[82] In particular, when considering whether a question is new or serious in order to decide whether it should be submitted to the Conseil Constitutionnel, the high courts are led to anticipate the approach of the Conseil Constitutionnel,[83] pointing out possible violations of the Convention or the Constitution and elaborating the best strategy. Thus the collaboration between the high courts within constitutional review proves to be quite beneficial for conventional review.[84]

(ii) Improvements in the ECHR's Implementation

The crisis of the 1990s[85] has been overcome, as illustrated by the decreasing number of French violations, which numbered 98[86] between 2010 and 2013. Both of the

---

[78] Cass QPC No 10-40002, 16 April 2010, [2010] *Revue française de droit administratif* 445. However, following the CJEU's judgment, the Cour de Cassation refused to implement the QPC procedure and did not refer the question to the Conseil Constitutionnel: Cass QPC, No 12132 and 12133, 29 June 2010, pourvoi No 10-40001 and 10-40002, www.courdecassation.fr/jurisprudence_2/questions_prioritaires_constitutionnalite_3396/12111_25_16741.html.

[79] See G Carcassonne and N Molfessis, 'La Cour de Cassation à l'assaut de la question prioritaire de constitutionnalité' *Le Monde* (Paris, 23 April 2010); D Rousseau and D Lévy, 'La Cour de Cassation et la question prioritaire de constitutionnalité: pourquoi tant de méfiance?' *Gazette du Palais* (Paris, 25–27 April 2010); D Simon and A Rigaux, 'Drôle de drame: la Cour de Cassation et la question prioritaire de constitutionnalité' (May 2010) *Europe* 5.

[80] Cases C-188/10 and C-189/10 *Melki and Abdeli* [2010] ECR I-5667. This interpretation had been suggested by the aforementioned decisions of the Conseil Constitutionnel and the Conseil d'Etat.

[81] Just before the CJEU delivered its judgment, the Conseil d'Etat and the Conseil constitutionnel rejected the Cour de Cassation's reasoning: CE 14 May 2010 *Rujovic* No 312 305, Rec 165; CC Decision No 2010-605 DC, 12 May 2010 on the law pertaining to opening up to competition and the regulation of online betting and gambling.

[82] Before the private law courts, see D Guérin, 'L'autorité judiciaire et le nouveau paysage institutionnel français'; concerning the administrative courts, see P Wachsmann, 'Les consequences du rééquilibrage devant la justice administrative', both in D d'Ambra (ed), *Le rééquilibrage du pouvoir juridictionnel* (Paris, Dalloz, 2013).

[83] This could also imply refusing to submit a constitutional question when the High Court can find remedies by itself. For examples see D d'Ambra, 'Le contentieux privé: remous et lames de fond' in d'Ambra, ibid, 137.

[84] See A Roblot-Troizier, 'La QPC, le Conseil d'Etat et la Cour de Cassation' [2013] *Les nouveaux cahiers du Conseil Constitutionnel* 40, 49; D Guérin, 'L'autorité judiciaire et le nouveau paysage institutionnel français' and C Lafont, 'Exemples de la garde à vue et de la juridiction pour enfants', both in d'Ambra (n 82).

[85] See above, II.C.

[86] *Annual Report of the ECtHR 2010*, 150; *Annual Report of the ECtHR 2011*, 160; *Annual Report of the ECtHR 2012*, 158; *Annual Report of the ECtHR 2013*, 204. In 2013, France was found to have committed 28 violations, Germany three and the UK eight. See www.echr.coe.int/Pages/home.aspx?p=echrpublications&c=#newComponent_1345118680892_pointer.

high courts have intensified the evolution that began in the 1990s. More precisely, the Conseil d'Etat has extended its conventional review to all administrative subject matters and deepened its control. The law of aliens, responsibility in certain medical matters, city planning, and administrative and fiscal sanctions are particularly affected.[87]

As to the Cour de Cassation, it has adopted a more protective position with regard to fundamental rights than the Conseil constitutionnel[88] in respect of rights of defence in police custody. In a first move, shortly after a judgment of the ECtHR against France,[89] the criminal chamber of the Cour de Cassation held police custody to be inconsistent with Article 6(1) ECHR but, considering the requirement of legal certainty, postponed the effects of its judgment, like the Conseil Constitutionnel.[90] The civil chamber of the Court, which also had to decide on this subject matter, transmitted the question to the plenary assembly, which not only affirmed the incompatibility of police custody with the ECHR but also announced the immediate entry into force of this judgment.[91] The main argument was that the Convention's implementation cannot be postponed because the right to a fair trial prevails over considerations of legal certainty. Thus, in this case, conventional review proved to be more efficient than constitutional review. More generally, conventional review has been deepened by extending the proportionality test, the Court sometimes examining in a very concrete manner the circumstances of the case before it.[92] Noteworthy too are the efforts of the Court to acknowledge the interpretive authority of the ECtHR's judgments. Thus the Court affirms that States Parties are obliged, even before being challenged in Strasbourg or having their legislation modified, to respect the ECtHR's judgments.[93]

Nevertheless, some difficulties and divergences relating to the Convention's interpretation undoubtedly remain. For instance, regarding the very sensitive problem

---

[87] For the viewpoint of judges, see J-M Sauvé, 'L'examen de la constitutionnalité de la loi par le Conseil d'État', Journée d'étude du Centre de recherche en droit constitutionnel de l'Université de Paris I, 1 April 2011; J-M Sauvé, 'La dynamique de protection des droits fondamentaux en droit national et en droit européen', speech delivered at the Jagelone University of Krakow, 22 October 2012; Y Robineau, 'L'application par la France des arrêts de la Cour européenne des droits de l'homme', speech delivered at the Supreme Court of Azerbaijan, 24 October 2014. From the perspective of scholars, see A Roblot-Troizier, 'La QPC, le Conseil d'Etat et la Cour de Cassation' [2013] *Les nouveaux cahiers du Conseil Constitutionnel* 40, 49; P Wachsmann, 'Les conséquences du rééquilibrage devant la justice administrative' in d'Ambra (n 82) 154.

[88] See above, III.A.

[89] *Brusco v France* App no 1466/07 (14 October 2010).

[90] Cass Crim No 5699, 19 October 2010, pourvoi No 10-82.902; Cass Crim No 5700, pourvoi No 10-82.306; Cass Crim, No 5701, pourvoi No 10-85.051.

[91] Cass ass, No 592, 15 April 2011, pourvoi No 10-30.316; No 591, pourvoi No 10-30.313; No 590, pourvoi No 10-30.242; No 589, pourvoi No 10-17.049, BICC No 743, 1 June 2011.

[92] See below, concluding remarks; and see more generally J-F de Montgolfier, 'Le contrôle de la hiérarchie des normes par le juge judiciaire: question prioritaire de constitutionnalité en matière de droits fondamentaux, rapprochements et diversité', *Bulletin d'information de la Cour de Cassation* No 810, 1 November 2014, www.courdecassation.fr/publications_26/bulletin_information_cour_cassation_27/bulletins_information_2014_6090/n_810_6904.

[93] Cass ass, 15 April 2011 (n 91) police custody: 'les États adhérents à cette Convention [CEDH] sont tenus de respecter les décisions de la Cour européenne des droits de l'homme, sans attendre d'être attaqués devant elle ni d'avoir modifié leur législation.'

of gestational surrogacy,[94] the Cour de Cassation has reiterated its reluctance to bring its case law in line with the ECtHR. Since surrogacy is prohibited in France,[95] it can only be practised abroad. When a family that has entered into a surrogacy arrangement abroad wishes to return to France, it is confronted with the problem of the child's recognition. Could filiation be transcribed into the French registers[96] or at least French citizenship be acknowledged?[97] The Cour de Cassation considered first that, given the prohibition on surrogacy, the public order conflicted with a transcription of parentage.[98] It then reinforced its opposition by deeming surrogacy to be a 'fraud against law', which prevents the superior interest of the child from prevailing.[99] Soon after, this position was rejected by the ECtHR as inconsistent with the Convention.[100] The Conseil d'Etat, on the contrary, has not only recognised that the child's superior interest prevails on the basis of the Convention on the Rights of the Child and the ECHR, but has also declared legal a circular issued by the Ministry of Justice which facilitated the issue of French nationality certificates to children born abroad even in cases of surrogacy.[101]

IV. CONCLUDING REMARKS

It may be concluded from the above discussion, first, that the French system has been significantly improved by the ECHR and conventional review (A); second, that, despite these improvements, the separation between conventional and constitutional review compromises the full efficacy of conventional rights (B); and third, that the French Parliament does not seem to be willing to seriously rethink the protection of fundamental rights and the implications of the subsidiarity principle (C).

A. The French System has Improved

Since the ratification of the ECHR, the French legal system has undergone significant changes. Conventional review operated by the ordinary courts has not only

---

[94] See M Doucet, 'La France contrainte de faire primer l'intérêt supérieur de l'enfant issu d'une GPA. Note sous CEDH, 5e sec, 26 juin 2014, *Labassee c. France*, affaire numéro 65941/11 et *Menesson c. France*, affaire numéro 65192/11' [2014] *Revue générale du droit online*, no 17851, www.revuegeneraledudroit.eu/?p=17851.

[95] Law on bio-ethics No 94-653, 29 July 1994, adding Arts 16-7 and 16-9 to the Civil Code and Art 227-13 to the Criminal Code.

[96] This subject matter is regulated by Art 47 of the Civil Code. Recognition of parentage recorded in a foreign country is provided for in this provision.

[97] A circular dated 25 January 2013 (BO Ministère de la Justice, 30 January 2013, No 2013-01) indicates the procedure for delivering certificates of French nationality, even in cases of surrogacy.

[98] Cass 1ère civ, 6 April 2011, pourvoi No 10-19.053 and pourvoi No 09-17.130.

[99] Cass 1ère civ, 13 September 2013, pourvoi No 12-30.138, No 12-18.315 and Cass 1ère civ, 19 March 2014, pourvoi No 13-50.005.

[100] *Labassee v France* App no 65941/11 (26 June 2014); *Menesson v France* App no 65192/11, ECHR 2014. According to this judgment, France may prohibit surrogacy on its territory but cannot deny the identity of children born abroad in this manner.

[101] CE 12 December 2014, *Association Juristes pour l'enfance et autres*, Nos 367324, 366989, 366710, 365779, 367317, 368861.

emerged, but has also acquired a substantial role in the case law of these courts. At the same time, constitutional review under the supervision of the Conseil Constitutionnel, which once completely neglected fundamental rights, became increasingly focused on this aspect. Paradoxically, when both of these procedures had become well developed and the power-sharing between both types of courts more or less settled, the constitutional amendment introducing the QPC, that is, the priority constitutional ruling, was adopted.

The juxtaposition of the two kinds of review risked severe competition being created. This competition, however, has certainly been beneficial for the protection of rights inasmuch as each player was required to perform a protective function. In this regard, a conflict between judges would have had only negative consequences. As a result, the Conseil Constitutionnel, on the one hand, and the Cour de Cassation as well as the Conseil d'Etat, on the other, made great efforts to harmonise their case law, as illustrated first of all by the police custody cases. But are these efforts too high a price to pay?

B. The Separation Between Constitutional and Conventional Review Compromises the System's Efficacy

Not only is the fragmentation of judicial competences with regard to human rights protection a potential cause of conflict, but more specifically the priority ruling, as organised in France, proves to be profoundly ambiguous. Its ambitions show a real antinomy between improving individuals' rights (only the parties can trigger constitutional review and this review concerns only constitutional rights and not other constitutional provisions) and strengthening the Constitution's supremacy and the priority given to constitutional rulings, and therefore the precedence of constitutional over conventional review. Yet QPC is likely to extend significantly the delay in judgments when both procedures have to take place.[102] Nor is it certain that by this the individual's rights are better safeguarded, or that a conventional review following on from a constitutional one will ensure the Constitution's supremacy.

Moreover, this ambivalence has been prolonged by controversies about the abstract or concrete nature of review.[103] In French public law a preference for abstract review has traditionally prevailed—that is, a kind of review that, instead of taking into account the circumstances of the case at hand, is merely confronting two norms in a quite general way. Such a system is very far from the ECHR model of review, which is much more attuned to the particular elements of the case. This can be verified by analysing how the judges approach the proportionality test with regard to the facts of a particular case. The Conseil Constitutionnel prefers

---

[102] M Hunter-Henin, 'Constitutional Developments and Human Rights in France: One Step Forward, Two Steps Back' (2011) 60 *International and Comparative Law Quarterly* 167, 174–77.

[103] See J-F de Montgolfier, 'Le contrôle de la hiérarchie des normes par le juge judiciaire : question prioritaire de constitutionnalité en matière de droits fondamentaux, rapprochements et diversité' *Bulletin d'information de la Cour de Cassation* No 810, 1 November 2014, available at www.courdecassation. fr/publications_26/bulletin_information_cour_cassation_27/bulletins_information_2014_6090 /n_810_6904/.

an abstract approach,[104] whereas the ordinary judges' method of review is situated between these opposite positions, and employs both of them.[105] This is true even of the Cour de Cassation, although its review is limited to purely legal questions.[106] Obviously, review operated by the Conseil Constitutionnel is more likely to diverge from the case law of the ECtHR than that of the Cour de Cassation or the Conseil d'Etat.

Yet, in my opinion, the abstract and the concrete elements of review cannot be dissociated, even in constitutional review.[107] Both must be examined in order to decide on the constitutionality or the conventionality of a statute and/or its implementation. Perhaps it is this artificial distinction between the law and the conditions of its implementation that explains the lack of a procedure aimed at reviewing not only statutory laws but also the judgments of ordinary courts in respect of their compliance with constitutional and/or conventional rights in the French system.

There is no Supreme Court in France—that is, a court with the competence to supervise and harmonise the case law of the ordinary courts. While this is partly done by the two high courts, fundamental rights do not play a significant role in this supervision. As to the Conseil Constitutionnel, it is neither a Supreme Court—as it specialises in constitutional review—nor authorised to directly check the constitutionality of judgments. Its competence for priority constitutional questions can indirectly bypass this limitation, insofar as the submitted questions may concern a law as interpreted by the ordinary tribunals.[108] However, this could in no way become

---

[104] See the exemplary illustration in the decision on police custody (July 2010, point 20): 'It is incumbent upon the Judicial Authorities and those of the Police Criminal Investigation Department to ensure that in all circumstances the remanding of persons in police custody for questioning is carried out with due respect for the dignity of the human being. It is moreover incumbent upon the competent Judicial Authorities, in the framework of the powers vested in them by the Code of Criminal Procedure, and if need be, on the basis of the criminal offences provided for to this end, to prevent and punish behaviour which adversely affects the dignity of the person remanded in police custody and order compensation for injury sustained by reason of such behaviour. Any possible failure to fully comprehend this requirement when applying the statutory provisions referred to hereinabove does not *per se* render said provisions unconstitutional. Although Parliament is at liberty to amend the same, the provisions submitted for review by the Constitutional council do not adversely affect the dignity of the human being'.

[105] See Montgolfier (n 103). See also the public reporter's conclusions in Conseil d'Etat judgments CE, 10 November 2010, *Communes de Palavas-les-Flots et de Lattes*, No 314449 and 314580 [2011] *Revue française de droit administratif* 124 and CE ass, 13 May 2011, *M'Rida*, No 316734 [2011] *Revue française de droit administratif* 789.

[106] The abstract method is in the foreground in Cass crim, 22 October 2013, No 196, pourvoi No 13-81.945, and Cass crim, No 197, pourvoi No 13-81.949. The concrete method prevails in Cass 1ère civ, 9 April 2013, pourvoi No 11-27.071, *Bull* 2013, I, No 66, where the incompatibility with the Convention does not result from unconstitutionality stated by the Conseil Constitutionnel (CC decision No 2012-268 QPC, 27 July 2012) (the effects of which are postponed until 2014), but rather from the fact that the specific appellant has not been informed about the existence of a remedy. See also Cass 1ère civ, 4 December 2013, No 12-26.066 concerning an incestuous marriage.

[107] So, when the Conseil Constitutionnel has to decide when the unconstitutional norm should be repealed and when legislative reform is necessary, it postpones this moment but frequently safeguards the appellant's rights by authorising the latter to invoke the unconstitutionality.

[108] See A Roblot-Troizier, 'La QPC, le Conseil d'Etat et la Cour de Cassation' (2013) 40 *Les nouveaux cahiers du Conseil Constitutionnel* 49; more particularly on the relationship between the Conseil Constitutionnel and the Cour de Cassation, see D d'Ambra, 'Le contentieux privé: remous et lames de fond' in d'Ambra (n 82) 131, 136 f. See also the parliamentary report on the QPC: J-L Warsmann, 'Rapport d'information n° 2838 déposé le 5 octobre 2010 par la Commission des lois constitutionnelles sur l'évaluation de la loi organique n° 2009-1523 du 10 décembre 2009 relative à l'application de l'article 61-1 de la Constitution'.

equivalent to the intense control that exists in, say, Spain or Germany, where a direct application before the Constitutional Court is admitted against judgments likely to infringe fundamental rights. Only such a procedure, being similar to that of the ECtHR, could really improve the subsidiarity principle and decrease the overload of the Strasbourg Court.[109]

C. The Parliament Seems Far from Rethinking the Rights Protection System

It is true that Parliament has initiated manifold procedural and substantive reforms under the influence of the ECtHR's case law. Some of them have brought deep changes, such as conferring on administrative tribunals the power to make interim orders in urgent applications[110] and giving a suspending effect to applications against deportation orders relating to aliens.[111] Amongst the numerous modifications in criminal and family law, it is worth mentioning the law of 15 June 2000, which allows the re-opening of a criminal proceeding after the ECtHR has found a violation committed by France.[112] Yet, it should be highlighted that Parliament still does not systematically check the compliance of draft legislation with the Convention. On the contrary, it continues to adopt incompatible laws. Furthermore, the separation of constitutional and conventional review resulting from the case law of the Conseil Constitutionnel has been confirmed and strengthened by Parliament since it is now part of the constitutional amendment creating the QPC procedure. Clearly, there seems to be no willingness to seriously improve the judicial protection of human rights.

This is not particularly surprising when we consider how modest French public debates on Convention rights have been. On the whole, these debates gained only the attention of specialists as they related to quite technical subjects, such as phone tapping, reporting judges' role, prosecutors' status, especially their independence, and, more recently, reform of police custody. Some serious problems have failed to attract wider public interest. These include the existence of torture or inhuman treatment in French prisons, anti-terrorist policy and its implications for individual rights and freedoms, the extent of data protection in France with regard to data collected by the National Security Agency (NSA) in the United States, and discrimination against Roma. The limits of improving the Convention's implementation in France may well lie in these areas.

---

[109] See C Grewe, 'Quelques spéculations sur la contribution des systèmes internes au désengorgement de la CourEDH' (2002) 7–8 *Revue universelle des droits de l'homme* 296.
[110] Law No 2000-597 of 30 June 2000, *JORF* 1 July 2000 and Art L 511-1 Administrative Justice Code. The judge does not deal with the merits of the case and reaches a decision as quickly as possible.
[111] Law No 90-34 of 10 January 1990 modifying Ordinance No 45-2658 of 2 November 1945 on the entry and the residence of aliens in France, *JORF* No 10, 12 January 1990, 489.
[112] Law No 2000-516 of 15 June 2000 strengthening the protection of the presumption of innocence and the rights of victims, *JORF* No 0138, 16 June 2000, 9038, Art 89.

18

The European Court of Human Rights and the Italian Constitutional Court: No 'Groovy Kind of Love'

ORESTE POLLICINO

I. INTRODUCTION

A FEW YEARS ago I speculated that the 'tale' of the interaction between the Italian Constitutional Court (ICC) and the Court of Justice of the European Union (CJEU) has become, over time, too well known to require a further detailed overview of its evolution (or involution).[1]

If there is one certainty when it comes to investigating the relationship between the ICC and the European Court of Human Rights (ECtHR), where the attitude of the ICC towards Strasbourg remains uncertain, it is that the recent interaction between the ICC and ECtHR could never be considered predictable. Over the past decade, the relevant case law of the ICC has brought many surprises and judicial *coups de théâtre*.

In the present chapter, after exploring the reasons behind the 'surprising' relationship between the two courts (section II and II.A), I will focus on two ICC rulings from 2007 that have, in a way, opened the door to an exercise in creative thinking on the part of the Italian constitutional judges with regard to their relationship with the ECtHR (section III). Next, I will consider the implications of those rulings and the subsequent case law from, on the one hand, a sources-of-law-based perspective (section III.A) and, on the other, an interpretive perspective. In the concluding remarks (section IV), I will ask whether the ICC could have followed a different path.

---

[1] O Pollicino, 'The Italian Constitutional Court and the European Court of Justice: A Progressive Overlapping between the Supranational and the Domestic Dimensions' in M Claes, M de Visser, P Popelier and C Van de Heyning (eds), *Constitutional Conversations in Europe: Actors, Topics and Procedures* (Cambridge, Intersentia, 2012) 101.

II. THE (ALMOST) 'ORIGINAL SIN'

Perhaps the main reason for the dynamic interaction between the ICC and the ECtHR is the (almost) 'original sin' of the Italian constitutional revision of 2001.

More precisely, the 'original sin' that negatively influenced the relationship between the European Community and the Italian legal order from the beginning was the incorporation of the Treaty of Rome into the national legal system through legislation with the status of ordinary law, rather than constitutional law. By contrast, with regard to the relationship between the domestic legal order and the European Convention on Human Rights (ECHR), the original problem seems to lie in a provision which, while constitutional in status (adopted with the constitutional revision of 2001), is not terribly enlightening in terms of its content. The constitutional revision of 2001, which was meant to deal exclusively with the relationship between state and regions, added a new provision to the Italian Constitution. According to Article 117(1), 'legislative powers shall be vested in the State and the Regions subject to the Constitution and with the constraints deriving from the EU legal order and international obligations'.

The provision, coming as it did rather out of the blue, fragmented scholarly interpretation. There have in fact been at least three main readings of it by Italian constitutional scholars. According to the first thesis, nothing much thereby changed in the relationship between the Italian legal order and sources of international law.[2] According to this view, Article 117(1) refers only to the relationship between State and regional statutes, its purpose being restricted to governing the relationship between the domestic and international orders.

Other scholars, as recently noted,[3] have emphasised the importance of the constitutional status given to the primacy of EU law, and asserted that Article 117(1) paved the way for the acceptance of the Italian monist thesis.[4] In other words, according to the second thesis, pursuant to Article 117(1), all international treaties to which Italy is a party, and the ECHR in particular, enjoy the same special status within the national legal order as that accorded to general norms of international law by Article 10 of the Italian Constitution.

A third thesis argues for a 'middle way'.[5] The constitutional provision would grant immunity to abrogation by subsequent domestic law to international treaties

---

[2] C Pinelli, 'I limiti generali alla potestà legislativa statale e regionale e i rapporti con l'ordinamento comunitario' (2001) 5 *Foro italiano* 145, 194; A D'Atena, 'Il nuovo Titolo V della parte II della Costituzione—Primi problemi della sua attuazione' para 5, www.rivistaaic.it.

[3] G Martinico and O Pollicino, 'The Impact of the Protection of Human Rights by the European Courts on the Italian Constitutional Court' in P Popelier, C Van De Heyning and P Van Nuffel (eds), *Human Rights Protection in the European Legal Order: The Interaction between the European and the National Courts* (Cambridge, Intersentia, 2011) 261, 265.

[4] F Paterniti, 'La riforma dell'art. 117, 1 co. della Costituzione e le nuove prospettive dei rapporti tra ordinamento giuridico nazionale e Unione Europea' (2004) 3 *Giurisprudenza Costituzionale* 2101.

[5] See, inter alia, M Luciani, 'Le nuove competenze legislative delle regioni e statuto ordinario' www. rivistaaic.it, and, more recently, M Cartabia, 'La Cedu e l'ordinamento italiano, rapporto tra fonti, rapporti tra giurisdizioni' in R Bin, G Brunelli, A Pugiotto and P Veronesi (eds), *All'incrocio tra costituzione e Cedu. Il rango delle norme della Convenzione e l'efficacia interna delle sentenze di Strasburgo* (Turin, Giappichelli, 2007).

that have been incorporated into the Italian legal order by an Act of Parliament. On this view, the dualistic matrix of the Italian legal system would be preserved. The consequence of this approach is that an ordinary law in conflict with the ECHR would be subject to review by the Constitutional Court for any potential violation of Article 117(1) of the Constitution.

In any case, clearly something was going to change after the entry into force of Article 117(1) with regard to the relationship between the ECHR and the domestic legal order. It was from that moment, in fact, that it became very difficult, if not impossible, for the ICC to maintain its position that, despite significant scholars' efforts to find a constitutional basis for the ECHR, the latter was to be ranked among ordinary statutes.

More precisely, according to a first group of authors, the constitutional basis for the incorporation of the ECHR could have been identified in Article 10[6] of the Italian Constitution, whereas according to a second group that basis resides in Article 11,[7] and a third group believe that it lies in Article 2.[8] This debate is of all but historic interest since the constitutional amendment, but it brings to light the various views behind the incorporation of the ECHR into the domestic legal system.

According to the first thesis, the ECHR includes general rules that are part of the generally recognised tenets of international law to which Article 10 attributes a special status. This would imply that the provisions enshrined in the ECHR, regardless of any formal incorporation into domestic law, could enter into the Italian legal system with constitutional status through the obligation, based on the Article 10, to conform to the tenets of international law. According to the second group of authors, the constitutional foundation of the ECHR can be found in Article 11 of the Constitution, which allows for restrictions on sovereignty that are 'necessary for an order that ensures peace and justice among nations'. With regard to the third view, the reference to the inviolable rights recognised and guaranteed by Article 2 of the Constitution is a key point. This clause affords constitutional protection to the 'new fundamental rights' that emerged after the adoption of the Constitution of 1948. Among these rights, those provided by the ECHR would find a (constitutional) basis.

As demonstrated in its case law, the ICC has not viewed these attempts to give special constitutional protection to the ECHR favourably. In relation to Article 10 of the Constitution, the Constitutional Court has specified that the privileged constitutional status enjoyed by the tenets of international law as generally recognised rules cannot extend to international obligations—such as the ECHR—entered into by the State under an international treaty.[9]

---

[6] Art 10(1) prescribes that 'The Italian legal order complies with the norms of international law generally recognized'.

[7] Art 11 provides that 'Italy rejects war as an instrument of aggression against the freedoms of other peoples and as a means for settling international controversies; it agrees, on conditions of equality with other states, to the limitations of sovereignty necessary for an order that ensures peace and justice among Nations; it promotes and encourages international organizations having such ends in view'.

[8] Art 2 provides that 'The Republic recognizes and guarantees the inviolable rights of the person, as an individual and in the social groups where human personality is expressed. The Republic expects that the fundamental duties of political, economic and social solidarity be fulfilled'.

[9] Constitutional Court, judgments no 48/79, no 32/60, no 104/69, no 14/64 and no 323/1989.

Regarding Article 11, the ICC, treating the issue as though it were beyond dispute,[10] affirmed that no international treaty—irrespective of its subject area—can entail a limitation on sovereignty in the terms provided by Article 11 of the Constitution. With respect to the possible interpretation of Article 2 of the Constitution as an open clause likely to afford constitutional protection to new fundamental rights, the Constitutional Court has never tackled this issue with specific regard to the ECHR. In more general terms, it has clarified that the guarantee provided by Article 2 is intended to refer only to the rights expressly laid down by the Constitution and to those directly connected thereto.[11]

By rejecting attempts to find a constitutional basis for the ECHR, the Constitutional Court has de facto confirmed the dualistic approach behind the Italian legal system. In particular, it has argued that the ECHR, as well as all the international treaties ratified by Italy, has the same rank in the hierarchy of the sources of law as mandated by the statute through which it has been incorporated into the domestic legal order.[12]

Since the ECHR, like other international treaties, was implemented via an ordinary statute,[13] prior to its landmark rulings of 2007 the ICC (apart from in one isolated decision)[14] attributed to the ECHR the status of ordinary statutory law. To put it simply, according to the ICC, the provisions of the ECHR could have been repealed by any successive statutory law in conflict with them. The abrogative effect, in the absence of any constitutional protection for the ECHR, would have resulted in the rule of *lex posterior derogat legi priori* being applied in order to solve any conflict between two statutes placed in the same position on the scale of sources of law.

From the end of the 1990s, however, the Constitutional Court's position began to soften: without changing its opinion about the place occupied by the ECHR in the Italian sources of law hierarchy, the ICC began looking at the relationship between the Italian constitutional legal system and the ECHR in a different and complementary way. In particular, in decision no 388 of 1999, the court seems to have drawn a distinction, in relation to the sources of international law, between the 'content' and its 'container', namely the ordinary statute which converts the international source into a national law. In this regard, it has been argued by the Constitutional Court that, where the content is characterised by the aim to protect human rights, those rights should enjoy a constitutional guarantee notwithstanding the legal status of their 'container'. In other words, since this decision, the Constitutional Court has seemed less interested in looking from a formal(istic) point of view at the static position of the ECHR in the hierarchy of the sources of law, and more interested, from a substantial and axiological point of view, and by reason of its fundamental

---

[10] Constitutional Court, judgment no 188/1980.
[11] Constitutional Court, judgment no 98/1979.
[12] Constitutional Court, judgments no 188/1980, no 153/1987, no 323/1989 and no 315/1990.
[13] Law of 4 August 1955, no 848.
[14] See judgment no 10/1993, in which, in relation to the ECHR and its ratification by ordinary law, the Constitutional Court speaks in terms of an 'atypical source of law'. This special status of the ECHR, according to this judgment, would place it in a higher position in the hierarchy of sources of law with respect to the ordinary legal order.

rights-based content, in its suitability to complement the recognition of inviolable fundamental rights protected by Article 2 of the Constitution.

These developments were integrated with and, in a way, overturned by the adoption of the new Article 117(1) in 2001, as discussed in greater detail below.

Meanwhile, at the beginning of the new millennium, some ordinary judges started to look at the relationship between the ECHR and the national legal order in a surprising (if not revolutionary) way, making almost no reference to 'new' Article 117(1) of the Constitution.

For example, in order to solve a conflict between ordinary national laws and ECHR principles, the Tribunale of Genoa[15] started to apply the solution according to which, since the historic decision of the Constitutional Court in *Granital* in 1984,[16] ordinary judges have applied the priority of EU law in cases of conflict between national law and EU law. It was followed in this position by other courts of first and second instance. This approach, supported by the highest ordinary and administrative courts,[17] has mainly relied on the consideration that, due to the incorporation of the ECHR into the EU dimension by the bridge provided by the general principles of EU law mentioned in former (but also in the present) Article 6 of the Treaty on European Union, it seems a necessary consequence to provide the same constitutional protection to EU and ECHR law. In other words, this brave new judicial approach interpreted the well-known paragraph 16 of the landmark decision of the ECJ in *Simmenthal*[18] as applying to ECHR law as well.

Based on how the constitutional judges reacted when they had the opportunity, in 2007, to enter into this debate, there is no doubt, as will be seen in the next section, that the ICC was not exactly enthusiastic about this new, 'revolutionary' ordinary judges' approach.

III. THE LANDMARK DECISIONS OF 2007

Two decisions handed down by the ICC at the end of October 2007 seemed finally to have an impact on one of the fundamental principles of the Italian Constitution: the notion of openness to international law, embodied in Articles 10 and 11, and above all in Article 117(1) which was added by the constitutional revision of 2001. The latter was the provision considered by the Constitutional Court in the two judgments examined in this section that focus on the relationship between the Italian constitutional legal order and the ECHR.

---

[15] See eg Court of Genoa, 23 November 2000; Court of Appeals of Rome, 11 April 2002; Court of Appeals of Florence, 20 January 2005.

[16] Constitutional Court, judgment no 170/1984.

[17] Supreme Court of Cassation, 19 July 2002, no 10542; 11 June 2004, no 11096; 23 December 2005, no 28507. Council of State, 9 April 2003, no 1926.

[18] Case C-106/77 *Simmenthal* [1977] ECR I-62, para 21, according to which: 'Every national Court must in a case within its jurisdiction, apply Community law in its entirety and protect rights which the latter confers on individuals and must accordingly set aside any provision of national law which may conflict with Community law, whether prior or subsequent to the Community rule.'

The final outcome of the two decisions in question may be summarised as follows:

(a)   Article 117(1) of the Constitution was identified by the constitutional judges as the basis that endows the ECHR with a higher status than ordinary legislation. This means that in case of conflict between the ECHR and a national statute subsequent to the internal legislation (Law No 848 of 1955) that gave the ECHR effect in the domestic legal system, the ordinary hearing the case must suspend it and request a decision of the Constitutional Court. This does not imply that the ECHR has a constitutional rank; on the contrary, the ECHR itself has to be consistent with all constitutional provisions, and not just with its fundamental principles (which is the effect of the '*controlimiti*' doctrine applied to EU law). The ICC adopts a two-stage assessment. The first stage is to assess whether a conflict exists between the relevant ECHR provision and the Italian Constitution. If no such conflict exists, the ICC will move to the second stage: to ascertain the possible incompatibility of the domestic legislation in question with the Convention. If a conflict is found to exist, the domestic legislation is struck down because it violates Article 117(1) of the Italian Constitution;

(b)   The Constitutional Court specified that the exact meaning of the ECHR can be ascertained only as it is interpreted by the ECtHR. That is why, according to the ICC, the content of the Convention is essentially that which may be inferred from the Court's case law.

These two points deserve separate analysis because they form the basis of the subsequent creative ICC case law regarding the relationship between the Italian constitutional order and the Strasbourg order.

A. Implications of the Judgments of 2007 from a 'Sources of Law'-Based Perspective

With regard to the first conclusion reached by the ICC in decisions no 348 and 349 of 2007, it is evident that, by identifying Article 117(1) as the constitutional provision that enables the Constitutional Court to ascertain a possible violation of the ECHR by a subsequently enacted domestic statute, the Court has managed to halt the activist approach adopted by the ordinary courts in recent years. This approach required the statutory law conflicting with the ECHR to be put aside by applying the analogy that the Constitutional Court has finally authorised ordinary judges to deal with statutes in violation of Community law after 20 years of 'bloody war' with the European Court of Justice.[19]

In other words, with regard to the interpretation of the ECHR, the Constitutional Court, as we will see in more detail below, is not willing to be unsurped by the ordinary courts.

In the light of the foregoing, there is no doubt that the ICC wanted to make clear, once and for all, that no exceptions would be tolerated to its constitutional mandate to assess the constitutionality of national legislation.

---

[19] Constitutional Court, judgment no 170/1984.

What seems worth adding, in connection with the analysis of the ICC judicial techniques specifically coined with regard to its relationship with the ECtHR, is that, in order to make their point clear, the constitutional judges relied, in a rhetorical sense, upon an argument connected to the relationship between EU law and the domestic legal order.

In particular, the constitutional judges recognised that the well-established case law of the CJEU has affirmed that the fundamental rights protected by the ECHR are part of the general principles of European law, and that this view has been codified in (former) Article 6 of the Treaty on European Union and extensively in the provisions of the European Charter of Fundamental Rights. Directly challenging the main grounds of reasoning used by the 'subversive' common judges, the ICC argued, however, that it is nonetheless impossible to apply by analogy to the ECHR the same treatment reserved to EU law.

The reason behind this approach is that, according to the constitutional judges, the ECHR legal system has distinct structural and functional legal features compared to the EU legal order. This difference is confirmed, in the view of the constitutional judges, by the language of Article 117(1), which distinguishes between the constraints deriving 'from the European legal order' and those deriving—only—from 'international obligations'. On this point, the ICC drew an unconvincing distinction between

the EC provisions, which have direct effect, and the ECHR provisions, which are international law sources binding only States, without providing any direct effect in the internal legal order such as to make the national judges competent to put aside the national provisions in conflict with them.[20]

The peculiarities of the ECHR legal system, starting with the very intrusive powers granted to the ECtHR and the possibility for individuals to have direct access to the Court, are not 'peculiar' enough, according to the Italian constitutional judges, to amount to any transfer of sovereignty in the terms provided by Article 11 of the Constitution. Furthermore, the Constitutional Court added, quoting the relevant case law of the CJEU,[21] that the fundamental rights of the ECHR enjoy the status of general principles of EU law only in relation to national rules that are within the scope of Community law. In other words, according to the Constitutional Court, in the situation under discussion, which was characterised by an exclusively domestic relevance, the CJEU would have denied its jurisdiction to ascertain the possible violation by national law of ECHR fundamental rights in their role of general principles of EU law.[22]

By thwarting attempts by the common judges to set aside any national law in conflict with the ECHR, the ICC clearly specified that, on the one hand, the provision of the 'new' Article 117(1) determined the ECHR's passive strength[23] with respect

---

[20] Constitutional Court, judgment no 348/2007, para 3.3.

[21] Case C-159/90 *Society for the Protection of Unborn Children* [1991] ECR I-4685; Case C-299/95 *Kremzow* [1998] ECR I-2629.

[22] Constitutional Court, judgment no 349/2007, para 6.1.

[23] In the sense that the ECHR no longer runs the risk of being abrogated by a subsequent national statute law.

to national ordinary statutes, but, on the other hand, it had the effect of giving the Constitutional Court competence to ascertain any possible conflict between the ECHR and national law.

We saw above that scholars have proposed three possible interpretations in this regard: Article 10, Article 11 and Article 2 of the Constitution as the constitutional basis for the ECHR. In relation to the first interpretation, in judgment no 349/2007, the Constitutional Court confirmed its previous case law by arguing that the privileged constitutional status enjoyed by the tenets EU international law, as generally recognised, does not extend to international obligations based on an international treaty such as the ECHR. According to the constitutional judges, however, a different conclusion is possible when, against reasoning dominated by a formal hierarchical approach, the international treaty in question 'reproduces general consuetudinary principles of international law'.[24]

With regard to the second interpretive option, the Constitutional Court stated that the European legal system has the nature of an autonomous legal order, which implies the transfer of a portion of sovereignty from the national to the supranational dimension under Article 11 of the Constitution. In order to support this statement, the constitutional judges emphasised the constitutional parameter (Article 11) used by the ordinary judges to provide constitutional protection to EU law and noted that it is not apt to obtain the same effect for the ECHR, referring to the established precedent discussed above.[25] Moreover, considering that the ECHR, like other international treaties (irrespective of subject matter), cannot entail a limitation on sovereignty under Article 11, the constitutional judges held that 'the ECHR is "only" a multilateral international public law treaty that does not entail and cannot entail any limitation on sovereignty in the terms provided by Article 11 of the Constitution'.[26]

With respect to the possible identification of a constitutional basis for the ECHR in Article 2 of the Constitution, and with reference to inviolable, constitutionally protected rights, the hope had been expressed that after a long silence on this subject, the Constitutional Court would have finally followed the thesis of the special nature *ratione materiae* of human rights treaties compared to all other international treaties.[27] By basing the priority of the ECHR over conflicting national law on Article 2, the Constitutional Court would have shifted from a formal hierarchy to a substantive one. Accordingly, this shift would have legitimated the judicial trend, started by the ordinary judges, of setting aside domestic national legislation that conflicts with the ECHR. This is exactly what the Constitutional Court wished to avoid. The silence of the ICC in relation to Article 2 of the Constitution, then, is not surprising.[28]

---

[24] Constitutional Court, judgment no 349/2007, para 6.1.

[25] Constitutional Court, judgment no 188/1980, quoted in judgment no 349/2007.

[26] Constitutional Court, judgment no 348/2007, para 6.1.

[27] C Pinelli, 'Sul trattamento giurisdizionale della CEDU e delle leggi con essa configgenti' (2007) *Giurisprudenza costituzionale* 3518.

[28] See, for a deeper analysis of the abovementioned decisions, and more generally, for a general framework of the impact of the EU and ECHR laws on the domestic jurisdictions of EU Member States, G Martinico and O Pollicino (eds), *National Judges and Supranational Laws: On the Effective Application of the EC Law and the ECHR* (Groningen, Europa Law Publishing, 2010); O Pollicino, *Allargamento dell'Europa ad est e rapporti tra Corti costituzionali e Corti europee. Verso una teoria generale dell'impatto interordinamentale del diritto sovranazionale?* (Milan, Giuffrè, 2010).

It has been mentioned above that in decisions no 348 and 349 of 2007, the ICC's main goal was to stop the judicial activism of the ordinary judges prior to the entry into force of the Lisbon Treaty. In contrast, in 2011, the constitutional judges needed to react to the assault of the administrative judges on the ICC's privileged position as the guardian of the constitutionality of supranational law (with the famous exception carved out with regard to EU law).

In particular, with regard to the abovementioned judicial assault, the reference is, first of all, to decision no 1220/2010, in which the Council of State declared that, after the entry into force of Article 6 of the Lisbon Treaty, 'the ECHR provisions which protect the same rights protected also by the European Charter of Fundamental Rights, have become directly applicable in the domestic legal order'.[29]

The highest administrative tribunal seems[30] to have based its assumption on a special emphasis given to the binding value of the European Charter, relying upon Article 6(1) TEU and to the obligation, now expressly envisaged by Article 6(2) TEU, to join the Convention.

The second decision of an administrative judge to which the ICC reacted was judgment no 11984/2010 of the Lazio Regional Administrative Tribunal. According to this decision, with the entry in force of Article 6(3) of the Lisbon Treaty,[31] the fundamental rights protected by the ECHR have become, in all respects, part of EU law and, accordingly, should avail of the same constitutional parameters (Article 11) and the same conflict settlement rules that apply in case of a contrast between national law and EU law (that is, disapplication by the common judge and not centralised assessment of the constitutionality of the domestic provision by the ICC).

The ICC started its counter-reaction to the brave new judicial assault by highlighting that the change in the wording of the new Article 6(3) TEU with respect the corresponding provision, in force until the end of November 2010, added by Article F2 of the Treaty of Maastricht,[32] had no substantial implications for the difference in treatment of EU law and the ECHR.

With regard to decision no 1220/2010 of the Council of State, relating to the alleged direct applicability of the ECHR provisions, the ICC could not have been more clear. In particular, in relation to the first argument—according to which the binding effect now recognised to the EU Charter of Fundamental Rights would have given a different status, by means of Article 52(3)[33] of the Charter, to the provisions of the ECHR protecting the same rights—the ICC recalled, first of all, that Article 6(2)

---

[29] Council of State, judgment no 1220/2010, para 5.

[30] A Schillaci, 'Il Consiglio di Stato e la CEDU' www.diritticomparati.it.

[31] According to which 'Fundamental rights, as guaranteed by the European Convention for the Protection of Human Rights and Fundamental Freedoms and as they result from the constitutional traditions common to the Member States, shall constitute general principles of the Union's law'.

[32] According to which 'The Union shall respect fundamental rights, as guaranteed by the European Convention for the Protection of Human Rights and Fundamental Freedoms signed in Rome on 4 November 1950 and as they result from the constitutional traditions common to the Member States, as general principles of Community law'.

[33] According to which 'In so far as this Charter contains rights which correspond to rights guaranteed by the Convention for the Protection of Human Rights and Fundamental Freedoms, the meaning and scope of those rights shall be the same as those laid down by the said Convention. This provision shall not prevent Union law providing more extensive protection.'

establishes that 'The provisions of the Charter shall not extend in any way the competences of the Union as defined in the Treaties'. The ICC continued by denying that the European Charter of Fundamental Rights could represent an instrument of protection of fundamental rights beyond the competence of the European Union, quoting, in this respect, the relevant case law of the CJEU prior to[34] and after[35] the entry into force of the Treaty of Lisbon.

The persistence of the ICC on this point reveals how crucial it is. In this case, in fact, the ICC used the EU-based argument not only to preserve, as has been seen in relation to judgments no 348 and 349 of 2007, its privileged position as judge of the constitutionality of supranational law, but also, more drastically, to keep its position as judge of fundamental rights within the national legal order itself. More precisely, in relation to the latter concern, the ICC felt the need to clarify that the trend towards a decentralised system of constitutionality emerging in the CJEU case law could not put in discussion, in purely domestic cases, its role as the judge of rights encapsulated in the system of centralised justice.

In particular, the real fear of the Constitutional Court seems to be that the ordinary judges could start to prefer a direct application of the provisions of the European Charter of Fundamental Rights (and the consequent disapplication of conflicting national law) over raising questions of constitutionality in relation to any conflict between the national law and the constitutional provision safeguarding the same fundamental rights envisaged by the abovementioned provision of the Charter.[36]

That fear is even more pressing in light of the case law of the Luxembourg Court that seems to foster a progressive margin of intervention for the common judge and, consequently, to reduce the room for centralised evaluation by the Member States' constitutional courts. The reference here is to the *Mangold*[37] and *Kücükdeveci*[38] judgments,[39] in which the CJEU established the direct application of non-self-executing directives because those directives gave specific expression to a general principle of EU law (the principle of non-discrimination on grounds of age).[40]

---

[34] Case C-217/08 *Mariano* [2009] ECR I-35.

[35] Case C-400/10 *PPU McB* [2010] ECR I-8965.

[36] See V Sciarabba, 'La tutela europea dei diritti fondamentali e il giudice italiano' www.european-rights.eu.

[37] Case C-144/04 *Mangold v Helm* [2005] ECR I-9981.

[38] Case C-555/07 *Kücükdeveci v Swedex* [2010] ECR I-365.

[39] See V Sciarabba, 'Dopo Mangold la Corte di giustizia torna sul rapporto tra principi generali, direttive e norme interne' (2010) 2 *Diritto pubblico comparato ed europeo* 376; V Sciarabba, 'La sentenza Kücükdeveci e le prospettive della giustizia costituzionale europea' www.astrid-online.it.

[40] More precisely, in Case C-144/04 *Mangold*, the Court of Justice stated that 'It is the responsibility of the national court to guarantee the full effectiveness of the general principle of non-discrimination in respect of age, setting aside any provision of national law which may conflict with Community law, even where the period prescribed for transposition of that directive has not yet expired' (para 78). In Case C-555/07 *Kücükdeveci*, the Court of Justice, as well as referring to the general principle of non-discrimination, also expressly referred to the directive by stating that 'that it is for the national court, hearing proceedings between individuals, to ensure that the principle of non-discrimination on grounds of age, as given expression in Directive 2000/78, is complied with, disapplying if need be any contrary provision of national legislation, independently of whether it makes use of its entitlement, in the cases referred to in the second paragraph of Article 267 TFEU, to ask the Court for a preliminary ruling on the interpretation of that principle' (para 56).

If this trend, in a way, risks weakening the role of the Constitutional Court as adjudicator of rights, the same role would certainly be irreversibly undermined if the same judicial attitude were extended, as in the abovementioned decisions of the administrative judges, to situations of purely domestic relevance, in which there is no connection with EU law.

In light of the above and in light of the envisaged future EU accession to the ECHR, it is possible to agree with the view that

> the inclusion of the European Charter of Fundamental Rights and, in the near future, of the ECHR in the material scope of application of EU law represents the most dangerous attack ever faced by the Italian Constitutional Court.[41]

At the basis of the said assumption there is, as should have emerged from the case law discussed above, the risk of a further[42] step toward a consolidation, despite the ICC's constitutional mandate, of a decentralised constitutional judicial review caused by a possible direct application, by the ordinary judges, of the provisions of the European Charter which protect the same rights enshrined in the Italian Constitution.

B. The Implications of the Judgments of 2007 from an Interpretive Perspective

With regard to the second crucial element of the 2007 decisions, related to the self-imposed unconditional obligation for all judges to give to the Convention only the meaning given to it by the ECtHR in its case law, the first impression is that the said obligation originated as an attempt at some kind of 'judicial compensation'. More precisely, the ICC's goal seems to have been to compensate for the downgrading of the Convention with regard to its 'formal' status after the revision of 2001, at least in connection with the literal interpretation of Article 117(1), according to which the duty to respect, on the one hand, the Constitution and, on the other, the obligations stemming from international law would be of the same ranking.

In other words, the ICC tried to compensate for the downgrading of the ECHR to an intermediate source below the Constitution and above primary law by attaching a special consideration to the ECHR in relation to interpretation of the rights contained therein.

Regardless of the real reasons behind this approach, it seems that the constitutional judges realised almost immediately that such an interpretive constraint, interpreted in a radical and absolute way, gave them too little room for *manoeuvre* with regard to the ECtHR case law, and within two years they had developed the first of (at least) three judicial techniques aimed at departing from that kind of constraint without, at least explicitly, abnegating it.

---

[41] M Bignami, 'Costituzione, Carta di Nizza, CEDU e Legge nazionale: una metodologia operativa per il giudice comune impegnato nella tutela dei diritti fondamentali' www.rivistaaic.it.

[42] V Ferreres Comella, 'The European Model of Constitutional Review of Legislation: Toward Decentralization?' (2004) 2 *International Journal of Constitutional Law* 461.

The first technique consists in adopting reasoning according to which the case law of Strasbourg would be binding for the Constitutional Court only in its substance (or in its essence).

Strangely enough, the said judicial technique emerged for the first time in the very judgment in which the constitutional judges drew the most radical implications from the self-imposed obligation to be bound by the ECtHR's case law. More precisely, in decision no 317/2009, the ICC, on the one hand, affirmed that

> this Court cannot substitute its own interpretation of a provision of the ECHR for that of the Strasbourg Court, thereby exceeding the bounds of its own powers, and violating a precise commitment made by the Italian state through signature and ratification of the Convention without any derogations.[43]

In other words, the ICC is of the view that departing from the ECtHR's interpretation of the ECHR would breach Italy's obligations under international law. On the other hand, the ICC added that it

> goes without saying that the assessment of the European case law established regarding the relevant Convention provision must be carried out in a manner that respects the essence (or the substance) of case law of the European Court of Human Rights.[44]

It is not clear what the basis for such a limitation would be: why should only the essence of the case law of the ECtHR be binding when, in contrast, the case law of the CJEU is binding in all its elements? In order to explain this difference it is not enough to point out that while, according to the landmark decisions of 2007, the ECHR should respect the entire Constitution, by contrast, the well-known case law of the Constitutional Court relating to the relationship between the EU legal order and the national one identifies only the fundamental principles of the Constitution as an obstacle to the national enforcement of EU law. Furthermore, and even more problematically, according to which criteria would it be possible to distinguish between the essence (that is, the substance) of ECtHR case law and the non-essential or non-substantive part of it?

No clear answers to these questions emerge in the case law of the ICC. Instead, in 2011, the Court endorsed a second judicial technique with the same aim of departing from the (self-imposed) obligation to consider entirely binding the case law of the Strasbourg Court. In decision no 236/2011, the ICC considered a reference concerning national legislation which provided that a reduction of the statute of limitation for certain offences would not apply retroactively to the benefit of defendants in proceedings that were already pending before the Court of Appeals or before the Supreme Court of Cassation. The Court found the question to be groundless, drawing away in its judgment from the case law of the ECtHR in a quite original way. The constitutional judges conceded that, if they were to conclude that the principle of the retroactivity of more favourable criminal legislation were to be held more severe than that already recognised in the case law of the Court, this would have constituted, of course, a departure from the case law of the Strasbourg Court.

---

[43] Constitutional Court, judgment no 317/2009, para 7.
[44] Constitutional Court, judgment no 311/2009, para 6.

However, the ICC, making concrete use of the distinguishing judicial technique and manipulating the relevant case law of the Strasbourg Court, added that

> no such novel characteristic is apparent from the judgment of the European Court of 17 September 2009 (Scoppola v Italy). There is nothing in the Court's judgment which can preclude the possibility that, in special circumstances, the principle of retroactivity in mitius may be subject to exceptions or restrictions: this is an aspect which the ECtHR did not consider, and which it had no reason to consider, given the characteristics of the case upon which it was deciding.[45]

In other words, according to the second judicial technique, the ICC distinguished between the case at hand and the relevant case law of the Strasbourg Court.

The two judicial techniques explored so far tried to avoid a direct clash between the ICC and the ECtHR and a direct and explicit *revirement* of what has been formally declared in the 'twin' decisions of 2007 with regard to the self-imposed obligation to follow the ECtHR's interpretation of the Convention.

By contrast, with the third judicial technique under investigation, the ICC, focusing on a more substantial criterion in order to gain more room for manoeuvre with respect to the Strasbourg case law, has managed to achieve the second goal (that is, to avoid an explicit *revirement* of the principle adopted in 2007), but not necessarily the first one (that is, to prevent a direct departure from the case law of the Strasbourg Court).

As mentioned above, this time the ICC relied on substantive-based criteria according to which, regardless of the 'formal' status of the sources of law that enter into conflict, the aim of the constitutional judges is to achieve two main goals: first, to make it clear that, when it comes to fundamental rights, respect for international law obligations cannot constitute grounds for lesser protection compared to that already available under national law, but on the contrary, must constitute an effective instrument for expanding that protection; and secondly, and consequently, to achieve, in balancing between conflicting rights, 'the greatest expansion of protection', in the words of the Constitutional Court.

The same court, in decision no 317/2009, explained the meaning that should be given to this expression by adding that the

> greatest expansion of protection must include a requirement to weigh up the right against other constitutionally protected interests, that is with other constitutional rules which in turn guarantee the fundamental rights which may be affected by the expansion of one individual protection. This balancing is to be carried out primarily by the legislature, but it is also a matter for this Court when interpreting constitutional law.[46]

The last sentence, concerned with identifying the body best placed to carry out the necessary balance where fundamental rights conflict, deserves further analysis because it goes along with another important element of the same decision, in which the constitutional judges made express reference to the margin of appreciation doctrine. More precisely, according to the ICC,

---

[45] Constitutional Court, judgment no 236/2011, para 13.
[46] Constitutional Court, judgment no 311/2009, para 7.

The reference to the national 'margin of appreciation'—elaborated by the Strasbourg Court in order to soften the rigidity of the principles formulated on European level—is primarily manifested through the legislative function of Parliament, though it must always be present in the assessments of this Court, which is not unaware that the protection of fundamental rights must be systematic and not broken down into a series of provisions that are uncoordinated and potentially in conflict with one another. Naturally, it is for the European Court to decide on the individual case and the individual fundamental right, whilst the national authorities have a duty to prevent the protection of certain fundamental rights—including from the general and unitary perspective of Article 2 of the Constitution—from developing in an unbalanced manner to the detriment of other rights also protected by the Constitution and by the European Convention.[47]

It is clear that the reference to the margin of appreciation becomes a rhetorical tool, in the reasoning of the ICC, in order to distinguish between the individual justice mandate, which, according to the Italian constitutional judges, should be the exclusive mission of the European Court of Human Rights, and the constitutional justice mandate, which by contrast should be the prerogative of the Constitutional Court.

In connection with the identified *summa divisio*, another important distinction between the roles and competences of the two courts stems from the reasoning of the ICC. While the balancing carried out by the Strasbourg Court would be 'broken down into a series of provisions that are uncoordinated and potentially in conflict with one another', the assessment which characterises the activity of the Constitutional Court would instead be 'systematic' and 'coordinated' because it includes a 'check and balance' approach to the different values at the heart of a constitutional legal order.

This implies, in other words, that the same case, in Strasbourg and in Rome, could be decided in different ways because of the different context and the different nature of the adjudication—a difference that was in fact exemplified in decision no 264/2012.

In this case the ICC considered a challenge to legislation modifying the arrangements applicable to the calculation of pensions for workers who have spent all or part of their working life in Switzerland. Whereas under the previous interpretation of the legislation, payment of contributions in Switzerland established entitlement to a pension in Italy on the basis of Italian contributions at equivalent salary, irrespective of the fact that the contribution levels in Switzerland were significantly lower, following an enactment providing for an 'authentic interpretation' the Italian pension was to be calculated on the basis of the actual level of Swiss contributions, thus resulting in lower pensions. The court considered the case in the light of ECHR case law, with specific reference to the *Maggio* case, in which the ECtHR had held that it was 'not persuaded' of the fact that the general interest was compelling enough to overcome the dangers inherent in the use of retrospective legislation and thus concluded that Italy infringed the applicants' rights under Article 6(1) by intervening in a decisive manner to ensure that the outcome of proceedings to which it was a party were favourable to it.[48]

---

[47] ibid.
[48] *Maggio v Italy*, App 46286/09, judgment of 31 May 2011.

Despite the relevant case law of the ECtHR clearly pointing to the annulment of the Italian legislation, the ICC concluded, instead, that there was a compelling general interest in justifying the recourse to retrospective legislation. Indeed, according to the ICC,

> the effects of the said provision are felt within the context of a pension system which seeks to strike a balance between the available resources and benefits paid, in accordance also with the requirement laid down by Article 81(4) of the Constitution, and the need to ensure that the overall system is rational (judgment no 172 of 2008), thus preventing changes to financial payments to the detriment of some contributors and to the benefit of others.[49]

It is not difficult to identify the application, in a concrete case, of the dichotomy—individual justice versus constitutional justice—that the ICC theoretically developed in decision no 311/2011.[50]

IV. FINAL REMARKS: AN ALTERNATIVE JUDICIAL PATH FOR THE CONSTITUTIONAL COURT?

The Constitutional Court, following the line emerging from the then latest precedent (judgment no 388/1999), could maybe have taken a different, value-based approach in its landmark decisions of 2007. Further, by recognising the constitutional nature of the ECHR, it could also have distinguished its status from that of 'ordinary' international treaties. Instead, as we have seen, the ICC decided to follow an interpretation-based approach, relying on a formal view within the perspective of a hierarchy of sources of law according to which all international treaties, including the ECHR, are a step higher in that hierarchy. They no longer have the same status as ordinary laws, but, as the Constitutional Court pointed out, 'they are to a degree subordinated to the Constitution, but are intermediate between the Constitution and ordinary status'.[51] This upgrade applies, as we have seen, to *all* international treaties ratified by Italy. Subject to the condition that they are not in conflict with the Constitution, they can thus lead to the annulment by the Constitutional Court of *all* subsequent ordinary statutes in conflict with them.

Unfortunately, the clarity of this formal, hierarchically based approach has a number of drawbacks. The first is the one that has already been brought to light: the exclusion of any power for ordinary judges to set aside national legislation in conflict with ECHR and the connected risk of undermining the effectiveness of ECHR law. It would be naive to think that *effet utile* is an exclusive prerogative of

---

[49] Constitutional Court, judgment no 264/2012, para 5.3.

[50] It should be added that a year later the ICC (in judgment no 170/2013) partially revised its radically contrasting position with the Strasbourg Court in relation to the admissibility of retrospective legislation. In this case the Court heard a referral from a bankruptcy judge challenging legislation which enabled certain amounts due to the State in respect of tax to be granted priority ranking in bankruptcy proceedings, notwithstanding their otherwise unsecured status, and stipulated that such arrangements were to apply with retroactive effect to bankruptcy proceedings that had already been initiated when the legislation came into force. The ICC held, referring also to the ECHR, that whilst retroactive legislation in the area of private law was permitted as a matter of constitutional law, it must be justified by 'compelling reasons of general interest', which, according to the same Court, were not present in that case.

[51] Constitutional Court, judgment no 348/2007, para 4.5.

EU law. If it were possible to agree that the protection of fundamental rights must be assured in the domestic legal order in the most direct way, then the same logic seems, *a fortiori*, applicable to domestic legislation conflicting with ECHR law. The second drawback is the unavoidable generalisation that every judicial approach based on a certain degree of simplification implies. Is it not confusing to put the ECHR and, for example, the Treaty on Principles Governing the Activities of States in the Exploration and Use of Outer Space, Including the Moon and Other Celestial Bodies, on the same level simply because they are formally both international treaties ratified by Italy?

More problematically, the choice of putting all international agreements on the same level has serious consequences. For example, a hypothetical international treaty ratified by Italy which is supposedly in conflict with the ECHR's stricter guarantee of the freedom of expression will have to be considered, by the mere application of the chronological criterion, as prevailing over the protection afforded by Article 10 ECHR.

Even more problematic is the fact that equating all treaties results in ranking international treaties concluded by governments in the so-called simplified form similarly to ordinary treaties. These treaties in simplified form are binding on the State when they are concluded at the international level, notwithstanding the absence of parliamentary approval and ratification by the president.

Following the interpretation of the Constitutional Court, these treaties will be on the same level as ordinary treaties and will equally limit the normative powers of the legislator, with the detail that, unlike the former, the latter have never received parliamentary approval.

Indeed, behind the formal dress, there is the substance, and in the case of the EHCR the latter has a constitutional character, as the Constitutional Court itself has de facto acknowledged. This admission came about when the Constitutional Court noticed the 'substantial coincidence' between the principles contained in the EHCR and those set out in the Constitution.[52]

The emphasis on the aforementioned differentiation between the obligations stemming from the EU legal order and those deriving from the ECHR is perhaps the weakest point of the case law that has been explored. Instead of equating ECHR law with any other sources of international law (under Article 117), the Constitutional Court could have looked, not at the end, but at the beginning of the Constitution in order to find in Article 11 the appropriate constitutional parameters for the ECHR, as it has done in the past with regard to EU law. The benefit of this method is that it would adopt a substantial approach aimed at underlining the constitutional nature of the ECHR provisions. The reasons why the Court excluded the relevance of Article 11 are not completely convincing. The formalistic approach to the ECHR, 'as every international Treaty cannot entail any limitation on sovereignty in the terms provided by Article 11 of the Constitution', seems to forget several key 'small details'.[53] When the Constitution was drafted, the Founding Fathers who wrote about the limitations of sovereignty in Article 11 had Italy's entry into the United

---

[52] Constitutional Court, judgment no 388/1999, no 129/1967 and no 7/1967.

[53] GF Ferrari and O Pollicino, 'The Impact of the Supranational Laws on the National Sovereignty of Member States, with Particular Regard to the Judicial Reaction of UK and Italy to the New Aggressive

Nations in mind. In this respect, it is possible to argue that, especially in light of the latest reforms in judicial procedures under the ECHR, the latter has a greater impact on the limitation of national sovereignty than accession to the United Nations. Moreover, the Constitutional Court's qualification of the ECHR as a 'multilateral international public law Treaty' could be put in question, since the ECtHR has remarked on the peculiar nature of the ECHR in relation to other treaties,[54] defining it as 'a constitutional instrument of European public order (*ordre public*)'.[55] Apart from this 'self-qualification argument', it should be objectively noted that it does not seem enough to cite, as the constitutional judges did, a 27-year-old precedent,[56] pursuant to which the ECHR may not entail any limitations on sovereignty in the terms provided by Article 11 of the Constitution to justify the exclusion of the constitutional protection provided by the said constitutional provision.

In 27 years, many things have changed, mainly due to Protocol 11. These changes, which in 1998 gave the ECtHR compulsory jurisdiction over individual complaints, had far-reaching effects, from removing the jurisdiction of the Council of Ministers to decide complaints on their merits to suppressing the role of the Commission to filter claims. It also made the hearing procedure entirely public (previously, 95 per cent of complaints were decided confidentially).

In this sense, the Constitutional Court seems to forget that ECHR law, more than a merely a static legal provision, is a dynamic process or a constitutional work in progress that is continuously emerging, mainly thanks to the growing constitutional character of the ECtHR case law.

Another 'historical' component undervalued by the Constitutional Court is the fact that Italy's participation in the system of protection of fundamental rights provided by the ECHR may be considered more functional to the achievement of constitutional goals, as embodied in Article 11, to guarantee peace and justice among nations, than was the European Economic Community originally, as it was oriented, at least directly, to economic-based goals.

As clearly emerges from the above analysis, in the last seven years the ECHR has moved from being an almost unknown walk-on character in the case law of the ICC to being one of its central protagonists. This increasing role has necessitated the elaboration, as we have seen, of new judicial techniques by the ICC in order to achieve a balance between, on the one hand, the need for fidelity to its judgments of 2007 and, on the other hand, the imperative not to lose its privileged position as arbiter of fundamental rights at the crossroads between the domestic and the international legal orders. This is a balance that has probably not yet been achieved, and consequently the relationship between the ICC and the ECtHR is destined to remain, for the moment, strained.

Approach of the European Court of Human Rights', speech delivered at the conference 'Sovereignty in Question', London, 29 June 2011.

[54] In *Ireland v UK* [1978] 2 EHRR 25, 239, the ECtHR clarified that 'unlike international Treaties of the classic kind, the Convention comprises more than mere reciprocal engagements between contracting States. It creates, over and above a network of mutual, bilateral undertakings, objective obligations which, in the words of the Preamble, benefit from a "collective enforcement"'.

[55] *Loizidou v Turkey* [1998] 20 EHRR 99, 75.

[56] Constitutional Court, judgment no 188/1980, quoted in decision no 349/2007.

19

From Conflict to Cooperation: The Relationship Between Karlsruhe and Strasbourg

JULIA RACKOW

I. INTRODUCTION

THIS CHAPTER EXAMINES the relationship between the European Court of Human Rights (ECtHR) in Strasbourg and the German Federal Constitutional Court (FCC) in Karlsruhe in order to assess some of the factors underlying the relatively harmonious cooperation between the two courts. Following a few brief remarks on the status of the European Convention on Human Rights (ECHR) in the German legal system, some landmark cases in which conflicts between Strasbourg and Karlsruhe fell to be resolved will be presented (II). I will then assess the potential for future conflicts in the area of religious freedom (III). In the final section I will show how controversies that arise are resolved at the judicial level between the courts based on the FCC's cooperative vision of subsidiarity, and how the factors determining the relationship between the Convention and the German legal order go beyond judicial dialogue and subsidiarity (IV). Certain legal areas are especially sensitive in the German constitutional context, and the German constitutional culture arguably determines how such issues are handled.

In the German legal system, the Convention only has the status of a federal statute, ranking below the Basic Law.[1] The German courts must observe and apply the guarantees of the Convention, as well as the jurisprudence of the ECtHR, but they are not considered a direct constitutional standard of review.[2] The hierarchy of norms established in the Basic Law makes federal statutes subject to judicial review. The standard of review must be a norm with constitutional status. Only the guarantees and principles of the Basic Law have constitutional status. Consequently, from a formalistic point of view, in case of a conflict between the Basic Law and a Convention right, the Basic Law must prevail.

---

[1] *cf* Art 59 (2) of the Basic Law.
[2] *Entscheidungen des Bundesverfassungsgerichts* (Reports of the Federal Constitutional Court, *BVerfGE*) 111, 307; 128, 326.

Still, there are only a few cases of conflict. In general terms, the German Basic Law's fundamental rights catalogue (in Articles 1–19 of the Basic Law) and the Convention were drafted in a similar historical context, using a similar structure and parallel guarantees. The Universal Declaration of Human Rights served as a model for both charters of fundamental rights. Furthermore, the Basic Law provides the individual constitutional complaint, which prevents many cases from going to the ECtHR.[3] The constitutional complaint must be based on the allegation of a violation of the fundamental rights established by the Basic Law. The constitutional framework alone does not, however, determine the relationship between Strasbourg and Karlsruhe—as the following frequently discussed cases show.

II. THREE LANDMARK CASES

For a long time the relationship between the ECtHR and the German jurisdiction seemed harmonious. At least, it was not subject to debate. Conflicts occurred—especially diverging judicial decisions—but they were not expressly treated as conflicts and so went unnoticed.[4] The facts of these cases did not attract much attention and the differences between the Basic Law and the Convention were minor. The FCC did not elaborate on the position of the Convention in the German legal system in these judgments, but simply adapted its jurisprudence to the Convention and the jurisprudence of the ECtHR without further explanation.[5]

Both courts have addressed divergence in three landmark cases. We will see below that these cases raised some concerns about a serious confrontation between the two courts and how the FCC in Karlsruhe defined the relationship with the ECtHR in its subsequent judgments.

A. Caroline von Hannover

The relationship between the ECtHR and the FCC became complicated in *Caroline von Hannover*, the first notable case leading to a direct discrepancy between the Convention and domestic German law.

Princess Caroline von Hannover took legal action against the publication of various photos taken of her in public places in private life situations. After her claims were dismissed by the German courts, she filed an individual complaint to the FCC arguing that her general right of personality under the Basic Law, which includes the right to privacy, had been violated by the publication of the pictures. In order

---

[3] C Tomuschat, 'The Effects of the Judgments of the European Court of Human Rights According to the German Constitutional Court' (2010) 11 *German Law Journal* 513, 514 f.

[4] U Volkmann, 'Fremdbestimmung—Selbstbehauptung—Befreiung, Das BVerfG in der Frage der Sicherungsverwahrung' (2011) 66 *JuristenZeitung* 835, 837, with reference to *BVerfGE* 13, 167, reversed by *BVerfGE* 92, 91 (Baden-württembergische Feuerwehrabgabe) after *Karlheinz Schmidt v Germany* (1994) 18 EHRR 513; also BVerfG, Order of 7 August 1990—2 BvR 2034/89; *Vogt v Germany* (1996) 21 EHRR 205.

[5] Volkmann (n 4) 837.

to balance her general right of personality and the freedom of the press, the FCC applied a proportionality test developed by the German courts. This jurisprudence restricted the scope of privacy of persons who are permanently subject to public interest because of their job or position (absolute persons of contemporary history), such as politicians or celebrities, as opposed to persons whose newsworthiness is tied to an event (relative persons of contemporary history) or mere private individuals.[6] The degree of privacy they are entitled to depends on the degree of public interest in them. A person like Caroline von Hannover, as an 'absolute person of contemporary history', had to tolerate the publication of pictures taken in private life situations in public places according to the FCC, while she could legally prevent the publication of pictures taken of her in her home or other places of local seclusion to which she recognisably retreated in order to be protected from the public.[7]

Karlsruhe also considered entertainment to be covered by the protection that freedom of the press provides: 'The press should be allowed to decide according to its own publishing standards what it regards as being worthy of public interest and what it does not deem to be worthy of such interest.'[8] In applying this test, the FCC struck a balance in favour of freedom of the press in its 1999 judgment, and the complaint was partly dismissed. Caroline von Hannover subsequently filed an individual application to the ECtHR. In 2004 the ECtHR struck a balance in favour of privacy rights.[9] The proportionality test applied by the ECtHR considered that Caroline was not exercising official functions in the published photographs.[10] That she was a member of a royal family did not justify a public interest in publication because photographs depicting her private life did not contribute to a debate of general public interest in a democratic society.[11]

Many German scholars criticised the ECtHR's decision, especially with regard to the principle of subsidiarity, arguing that the Court merely modified the proportionality test.[12] It was questioned whether the details of the balance between privacy rights and freedom of the press in the case of every picture affected the common European minimum standard laid out in the Convention or whether the balance in some cases should have belonged to the margin of appreciation of the Member State.[13] The ECtHR had to define the margin within which cases of privacy infringements could be decided differently in every Member State, while the ECtHR's jurisprudence

---

[6] *BVerfGE* 101, 361 (*Caroline II*), official English translation available at www.bundesverfassungsgericht.de/entscheidungen/rs19991215_1bvr065396en.html, paras 68 ff.

[7] ibid, para 72.

[8] ibid, para 59.

[9] *Von Hannover v Germany* (2005) 40 EHRR 1.

[10] ibid, para 63.

[11] ibid, para 64.

[12] C Grabenwarter, 'Schutz der Privatsphäre versus Pressefreiheit—Europäische Korrektur eines deutschen Sonderwegs?' (2004) 4 *Archiv für Presserecht* 309, 315 f; K Ziegler, 'The Princess and the Press: Privacy after Caroline *von Hannover v Germany*' in K Ziegler (ed), *Human Rights and Private Law: Privacy as Autonomy* (Oxford, Hart Publishing, 2007) 189–209.

[13] Proposing a 'corridor solution' ('*Korridorlösung*'): G Lübbe-Wolff, 'Der Grundrechtsschutz nach der Europäischen Menschenrechtskonvention bei konfligierenden Individualrechten—Plädoyer für eine Korridorlösung' in M Hochhuth (ed), *Nachdenken über Staat und Recht: Kolloquium zum 60. Geburtstag von Dietrich Murswiek* (Berlin, Duncker & Humblot, 2010) 193 ff.

decided that cases outside this margin were justified or unjustified by the freedom of the press.[14] Some argued that the ECtHR had violated Article 53 ECHR[15] in this situation, which presented a conflict of rights, giving preference to privacy rights to the detriment of freedom of the press guaranteed by the Basic Law.[16]

Nevertheless, in its decision on Caroline's subsequent constitutional complaint in 2008, the FCC left the final say to the ECtHR, demonstrating its desire to cooperate. Again, photos taken of her and her husband in public places whilst on holiday were the subject of this complaint. This time, the pictures were accompanied by a report on the illness of her father, who was then head of the State of Monaco. The FCC acknowledged the ECtHR's jurisprudence and modified the proportionality test according to Strasbourg's standards.[17] No reference was made to the former German jurisprudence and its degrees of public interest and privacy. Instead, the FCC based its decision on the public interest reasoning of the ECtHR, which distinguished between public figures and ordinary persons.[18] The general question, however, about the effect of the ECtHR's judgments in German constitutional law was not discussed in this decision.

Von Hannover (No 2) (2012)[19] was perceived as a piece of 'appeasement politics'[20] conducted by the ECtHR. Caroline brought the FCC's 2008 judgment to the ECtHR. Although the depicted scenes from the Princess's private holiday did not appear to differ from the photos that were the subject of *Von Hannover* (2004), the Court emphasised the margin of appreciation of the Contracting States and remarked on this issue quite extensively:

> The Court reiterates that the choice of the means calculated to secure compliance with Article 8 of the Convention in the sphere of the relations of individuals between themselves is in principle a matter that falls within the Contracting States' margin of appreciation, whether the obligations on the State are positive or negative … Likewise, under Article 10 of the Convention, the Contracting States have a certain margin of appreciation in assessing whether and to what extent an interference with the freedom of expression protected by this provision is necessary … However, this margin goes hand in hand with European

---

[14] ibid, 200.

[15] Art 53 ECHR determines that the Convention must never limit the fundamental freedoms guaranteed under domestic constitutional law.

[16] A Nußberger, 'Die Straßburger Sicht' in RT Baus, M Borchard, K Gelinsky and G Krings (eds), *60 Jahre Bundesverfassungsgericht—Grenzüberschreitende Herausforderungen für Karlsruhe* (Berlin, Konrad Adenauer Stiftung, 2012) 95, 100; W Hoffmann-Riem, 'Kontrolldichte und Kontrollfolgen beim nationalen und europäischen Schutz von Freiheitsrechten in mehrpoligen Rechtsverhältnissen—aus der Sicht des Bundesverfassungsgerichts' (2006) *Europäische Grundrechte—Zeitschrift* 492, 499; Lübbe-Wolff (n 13).

[17] BVerfG, 1 BvR 1602/07, 26 February 2008, *BVerfGE* 120, 180 (*Caroline III*), paras 52 ff, 98 ff, English translation available at www.bundesverfassungsgericht.de/entscheidungen/rs20080226_1bvr160207en.html.

[18] ibid, paras 99–101.

[19] *Von Hannover v Germany (No 2)* (2012) 55 EHRR 15.

[20] H Fenwick, 'An Appeasement Approach in the European Court of Human Rights?' UK Human Rights Blog, 17 April 2012, ukhumanrightsblog.com; E Bates, 'Analysing the Prisoner Voting Saga and the British Challenge to Strasbourg' (2014) 14 *Human Rights Law Review* 1, 31. *cf* H Fenwick, 'Enhanced Subsidiarity and a Dialogic Approach—or Appeasement in Recent Cases on Criminal Justice, Public Order and Counter-Terrorism in Strasbourg against the UK?' (ch 10), this volume.

supervision, embracing both the legislation and the decisions applying it, even those delivered by an independent court.[21]

The ECtHR restricted its own role '[w]here the balancing exercise has been undertaken by the national authorities in conformity with the criteria laid down in the Court's case-law'.[22] In these cases 'the Court would require strong reasons to substitute its view for that of the domestic courts'.[23]

Finally, the ECtHR also made reference to the dialogue with the national courts in the development of the *Von Hannover* jurisprudence, observing that 'the national courts explicitly took account of the Court's relevant case-law'.[24] This observation was followed by a detailed description of how Strasbourg's jurisprudence had been received:

> Whilst the Federal Court of Justice had changed its approach following the Von Hannover judgment, the Federal Constitutional Court, for its part, had not only confirmed that approach, but also undertaken a detailed analysis of the Court's case-law in response to the applicants' complaints that the Federal Court of Justice had disregarded the Convention and the Court's case-law.[25]

President Spielmann confirmed this observation of a new approach adopted by the ECtHR expressly in his speech at the Yeravan Pan-European Conference, when he pointed out 'a trend towards judicial self-restraint when it is clear that the superior national courts have, at the domestic level, examined the case in light of the relevant Convention provision and case-law principles'.[26]

B. Görgülü

A serious crisis in the relationship between the courts became apparent in *Görgülü*. This complaint was decided in Strasbourg in 2004 shortly before *Von Hannover*. The FCC's decision followed that same year. On this occasion the FCC made its first fundamental statement on the effect of the ECtHR's decisions in German law.

The applicant in *Görgülü* sought custody and a right of access to his child, who had been born out of wedlock. The mother gave the child up for adoption after the birth in 1999. After that, the child lived with foster parents. As the natural father, the complainant initiated a number of judicial proceedings, including a constitutional complaint, for custody and a right of access. After all of them were unsuccessful, he filed an individual application to the ECtHR. The Court held unanimously that the decision on custody and the exclusion of the right of access violated the right to respect for family life under Article 8.[27] The duty of the State to enable contact

---

[21] *Von Hannover v Germany (No 2)* (n 19) paras 104 f.
[22] ibid, para 107.
[23] ibid.
[24] ibid, para 125.
[25] ibid.
[26] D Spielmann, Speech at Yeravan Pan-European Conference, 3 July 2013, www.echr.coe.int.
[27] *Görgülü v Germany* App no 74969/01 (26 February 2004).

between natural parents and their children required that, in the best interests of the child, the father and his child should be reunited.[28] Therefore the father should at least have a right of access to his child.[29]

The local German court consequently granted custody and a right of access to the complainant.[30] The higher regional court overruled this decision, arguing that it was only the State of Germany that was bound by the ECtHR's jurisprudence in international law, not the German courts.[31]

Upon Görgülü's subsequent complaint in 2004, the FCC overruled the higher regional court's decision because it violated the right to family life under Article 6 of the Constitution in conjunction with the principle of the rule of law.[32] The FCC also held that, under the Constitution, German public authorities are not directly bound by the Convention and the ECtHR's judgments; however, they are required to take them into account. The Convention and Strasbourg's case law serve as guides to interpretation in determining the content and scope of fundamental rights of the Constitution.[33] This requirement results from the Constitution's commitment to international law, the so-called *Völkerrechtsfreundlichkeit* ('comity to international law').[34]

According to the FCC, in cases of conflict, courts had to justify why they could not follow the jurisprudence of the ECtHR.[35] Scholars of international law criticised this as a mere formal requirement to provide motives for the failure to implement the Convention.[36] But this was not the intention of the judgment. The obligation to take the ECtHR's jurisprudence into account as defined by the FCC goes further than the interpretation of section 2 of the Human Rights Act 1998 (HRA) and the English courts' subsequent development of the mirror doctrine.[37] While English courts point out that 'taking into account' means that the jurisprudence of the ECtHR is not binding,[38] the FCC clarifies that the reasons for dissenting from the ECtHR must be important. And significantly, the affected individual can submit a

---

[28] ibid, para 45.

[29] ibid, para 64.

[30] *Amtsgericht* (Local Court) Wittenberg, Order of 19 March 2004—5 F 463/02 UG.

[31] *Oberlandesgericht* (Higher Regional Court) Naumburg, Order of 30 June 2004—14 WF 64/04; Order of 30 March 2004—14 WF 64/04.

[32] *BVerfGE* 111, 307, official English translation available at www.bundesverfassungsgericht.de/entscheidungen/rs20041014_2bvr148104en.html.

[33] *BVerfGE* 111, 307, English translation at para 32.

[34] cf *BVerfGE* 111, 307, English translation at para 33; *Völkerrechtsfreundlichkeit* is to be distinguished from *Konventionskonformität* (Convention conformity): see T Giegerich, 'Wirkung und Rang der EMRK in den Rechtsordnungen der Mitgliedstaaten' in O Dörr, R Grote and T Marauhn (eds), *EMRK/GG. Konkordanzkommentar*, 2nd edn (Tübingen, Mohr Siebeck, 2013) para 76.

[35] *BVerfGE* 111, 307, English translation at para 62.

[36] A Zimmermann, *Grundrechtsschutz zwischen Karlsruhe und Straßburg* (Berlin, De Gruyter, 2012) 30; H Sauer, 'Die neue Schlagkraft der gemeineuropäischen Grundrechtsjudikatur' (2005) 65 *Zeitschrift für ausländisches öffentliches Recht und Völkerrecht* 35, 45.

[37] G Lübbe-Wolff, 'The ECtHR and National Jurisdiction: The Görgülü Case' [2006] *Humboldt Forum Recht* 138, 145.

[38] B Hale, '*Argentoratum Locutum:* Is Strasbourg or the Supreme Court Supreme?' (2012) 12 *Human Rights Law Review*, 65, 68.

constitutional complaint based on the principle of the rule of law where a national state body has failed to take into account a decision of the ECtHR.[39]

Nevertheless, the FCC's judgment received rather harsh criticism for its emphasis on the 'sovereignty contained in the last instance in the German constitution'.[40] This emphasis raised concerns that the FCC might choose a German *Sonderweg* in relation to the ECtHR—a reservation to exercise a review of the ECtHR's decisions according to the standard of the Basic Law or an ultra vires review, similar to the former EU law jurisprudence of the FCC.[41] This could set a negative example for other Member States.[42] There was talk of a 'Bermuda triangle' between Strasbourg, Karlsruhe and Luxembourg, and 'dark clouds'.[43] It is important to note that the conflict was conducted exclusively in the courts and analysed solely by scholars. The government did not comment on the issue. However, some judges of the FCC declared the beginning of a discourse between Strasbourg and Karlsruhe, and a 'constitutional alliance'.[44] While the critics stressed the part of the judgment that insisted on the sovereignty of the German Constitution and the status of the Convention in German law, which is not a direct standard of review, the judges emphasised the openness of the German Constitution to international law, which made the Convention an indirect standard of review and the failure to take the ECtHR's judgments into account subject to judicial review.[45] Over a decade later, *Görgülü* and *Von Hannover* can indeed be considered the beginning of a dialogue. Both courts demonstrated their willingness to reconsider their positions in *Von Hannover*. *Görgülü* contained the first statement on the relationship between the courts in general terms. The subsequent preventive detention cases confirm this observation.

C. Preventive Detention

Any fundamental conflict that might have been indicated in *Görgülü* seems to have been eased in the *Preventive Detention* cases. These cases, unlike the previous ones, caused some controversy among the general public. Until this time, the debate about the nature of the relationship between the ECtHR and the German courts had only taken place between scholars and judges. The prospect of the release of

---

[39] *BVerfGE* 111, 307, English translation at para 63.

[40] *BVerfGE* 111, 307, English translation at para 35.

[41] *BVerfGE* 37, 271 (*Solange I*); this approach was modified in: *BVerfGE* 73, 339 (*Solange II*); *BVerfGE* 102, 147 (*Bananenmarkt*); BVerfG 126, 286 (*Honeywell*).

[42] Tomuschat (n 3) 522 ff, esp 525; A von Bogdandy, 'Pluralism, Direct Effect, and the Ultimate Say: On the Relationship between International and Domestic Constitutional Law' (2008) 6 *International Journal of Constitutional Law* 397, 403.

[43] Sauer (n 36) 63 f; O Klein, 'Straßburger Wolken am Karlsruher Himmel—Zum geänderten Verhältnis zwischen Bundesverfassungsgericht und Europäischem Gerichtshof für Menschenrechte seit 1998' (2010) 29 *Neue Zeitschrift für Verwaltungsrecht* 221.

[44] A Voßkuhle, 'Der europäische Verfassungsgerichtsverbund' (2010) 29 *Neue Zeitschrift für Verwaltungsrecht* 1, 8; Lübbe-Wolff (n 37) 146.

[45] *cf* the critical assessment by Tomuschat (n 3) 526; Voßkuhle, 'Der europäische Verfassungsgerichtsverbund' 4 stresses the openness to international law; Lübbe-Wolff (n 37) 146.

several persons still considered a public danger after having served sentences for murder, rape and child abuse was discussed in political forums as well as in the media.[46] The FCC had previously held that the dual sanction system of the German Criminal Code distinguishing between penalty and preventive detention was in accordance with constitutional law in a decision of 2004.[47] Preventive detention is ordered by the sentencing courts and is generally executed after the person concerned has served their prison sentence according to section 66 StGB (German Criminal Code). The level of danger that the detainee poses is reviewed on a periodic basis and they are released on probation if they are no longer dangerous to the public.

When the applicant in *M v Germany* committed the offence in question and was convicted, the version of section 67d of the Criminal Code then in force stipulated a maximum detention of 10 years, after which the detainee had to be released.[48] This provision was amended by the Combating of Sexual Offences and Other Dangerous Offences Act (Gesetz zur Bekämpfung von Sexualdelikten und anderen gefährlichen Straftaten) of 26 January 1998,[49] which entered into force while the applicant was in preventive detention.[50] According to the amended provision, the detainee was to be released after 10 years only if he was no longer considered dangerous to the public.[51] The maximum duration was thus extended to a potentially unlimited period of time. The applicant's subsequent requests for review of his continued preventive detention were refused on the grounds of the modified provision.[52]

In *M v Germany*,[53] as well as in several other individual complaints filed by detainees under the preventive detention rule, the ECtHR considered preventive detention to be a penalty that had to fulfil the requirements of the prohibition on retrospective punishment. Based on this determination, the ECtHR decided that

---

[46] eg 'Sicherungsverwahrung verfassungswidrig—Kommen bald 500 Mörder und Vergewaltiger auf freien Fuß?' *Bild Zeitung* (Berlin, 5 May 2011); J Jüttner, 'Urteil zur Sicherungsverwahrung: "Ein unerträglicher Zustand"' *Der Spiegel* (Hamburg, 5 May 2011); D Hoffmann, 'Zwischen Mahn- und Polizeiwache' *Süddeutsche Zeitung* (Munich, 27 July 2010).

[47] *BVerfGE* 109, 133.

[48] s 67d (old version) provided: '1. Detention in a detoxification facility may not exceed two years and *the first period of preventive detention may not exceed ten years* ... 2. If there is no provision for a maximum duration or if the time-limit has not yet expired, the court shall suspend further execution of the detention order on probation as soon as there are justifiable reasons for testing whether the detainee can be released without committing further unlawful acts. Suspension shall automatically entail supervision of the conduct of the offender. 3. *If the maximum duration has expired, the detainee shall be released.* The measure shall thereby be terminated.' (Emphasis added.)

[49] (1998) *Bundesgesetzblatt* I Nr 6, 160.

[50] *M v Germany* (2009) 51 EHRR 976, para 53.

[51] Section 67d (amended version 1998) was worded: '1. Detention in a detoxification facility may not exceed two years ... 2. If there is no provision for a maximum duration or if the time-limit has not yet expired, the court shall suspend on probation further execution of the detention order as soon as it is to be expected that the person concerned will not commit any further unlawful acts on his or her release. Suspension shall automatically entail supervision of the conduct of the offender. 3. If a person has spent ten years in preventive detention, the court shall declare the measure terminated *if there is no danger that the detainee will, owing to his criminal tendencies, commit serious offences* resulting in considerable psychological or physical harm to the victims. Termination shall automatically entail supervision of the conduct of the offender.' (Emphasis added.)

[52] *M v Germany* (n 50) paras 17 ff.

[53] ibid.

the retrospective imposition and the extension of preventive detention stipulated in section 67d of the German Criminal Code violated Articles 5 and 7 ECHR (the right to liberty and the prohibition of punishment without law).

Following this decision, German courts handled the implementation of the ECtHR's jurisprudence regarding preventive detention in a variety of ways. Some applied the decisions, some expressly refused to apply the ECtHR's jurisprudence, and some referred the question to the FCC.[54] However, a public debate questioning whether or not *M v Germany* should be implemented did not take place. Despite previous comments during the legislative process on preventive detention,[55] no public figure from any part of the political spectrum questioned the authority of the ECtHR's decision. Public protest against the release of prisoners under the preventive detention rule took place in some prominent cases, accompanied by warnings from prison and police authorities of the danger that some of the detainees posed.[56] But the public uproar and media campaign was not directed against the ECtHR in any way that could be compared to the reaction to the decision in *Hirst*[57] or *Othman*[58] in the UK. If anyone was to blame for the release of the detainees who were considered a public danger, it was the German Parliament. Instead of blaming Strasbourg, the weekly magazine *Der Spiegel* explained that although the ECtHR and the FCC had warned the German legislature on several occasions that the preventive detention rule violated the Convention and the Constitution, it had failed to introduce a law that would pass the test of these two courts.[59] However, Andreas Voßkuhle, President of the FCC, stated in the oral hearing before the 2011 judgment on preventive detention that the ECtHR had only marginally considered the security interest of the population.[60] This statement shows that the preventive detention rule—apart from its legal aspects—was a sensitive issue in Germany. Interestingly, it is also in accordance with the German constitutional context that it was the President of the FCC who voiced criticism of the ECtHR's decision. He mentioned not only legal aspects but also the political interests behind the preventive detention rule, while politicians did not question the ECtHR's decision. It is not contemplated in the German constitutional context that representatives from other constitutional branches than the judiciary criticise or even defy a judicial decision. The ECtHR belongs to the judiciary. Therefore the FCC is the only organ with the authority to voice such criticism.

---

[54] Zimmermann (n 36) 27.

[55] D Hoffmann, 'Zwischen Mahn- und Polizeiwache' *Süddeutsche Zeitung* (Munich, 27 July 2010) quoting former Chancellor Gerhard Schröder, '*Wegsperren—und zwar für immer*' ('Lock away—forever') in 2001, when the legislation on retrospective preventive detention was passed.

[56] *cf* 'Sicherungsverwahrung verfassungswidrig—Kommen bald 500 Mörder und Vergewaltiger auf freien Fuß?' *Bild Zeitung* (Berlin, 5 May 2011); Jüttner (n 46).

[57] *Hirst v UK (No 2)* (2005) 42 EHRR 41 (GC).

[58] *Othman (Abu Qatada) v UK* (2012) 55 EHRR 1.

[59] Jüttner (n 46): '*Diese Entscheidung hat der Gesetzgeber provoziert*' ('The legislature provoked this decision').

[60] D Hipp, 'Streit über die Sicherungsverwahrung: Im Zweifel für die Dauerhaft' *Der Spiegel* (Hamburg, 8 February 2011) quoting Voßkuhle: 'The security interests of the population' were only considered by the ECtHR 'in a rather marginal way' (translation by the author).

In 2011, the FCC reversed its earlier decision but sustained the sanction system that does not consider preventive detention a penalty.[61] In effect, it fitted the ECtHR's jurisprudence into the context of the German constitutional order. Without the quality of a penalty, there could not be punishment without law in the sense of Article 7 ECHR. But the FCC declared the preventive detention regime as it stood at the time a disproportional infringement on the right to liberty and the rule of law established in the Basic Law. The evaluations of the Convention's Article 7 required the careful definition of the qualitative difference between penalty and preventive measures according to the FCC.[62] Penalty and preventive detention were legitimate on different constitutional grounds. This also required a qualitative distance between the two measures. The provisions of the Criminal Code concerning preventive detention were held unconstitutional, not on the grounds of retrospective punishment as the ECtHR had decided, but based on a violation of the so-called distance requirement (*Abstandsgebot*). As the distance requirement results from the fundamentally different objectives and basis of legitimation of prison sentences and preventive detention, the deprivation of liberty effected by preventive detention must keep a marked distance from the execution of a prison sentence.[63]

On this occasion, the FCC made its second fundamental statement on the status of the Convention and the decisions of the ECtHR in German law. The parameters laid out in *Görgülü* were reaffirmed.[64] However, the FCC now seemed to take openness to international law and the 'taking into account of Strasbourg's judgments' further. It stated that the 'factual precedent' (*faktische Präzedenzwirkung*) laid down by the ECtHR's jurisprudence in all cases—not only those to which Germany was a party— required the avoidance of conflicts, and thus breaches of international law.[65] Under the condition that the Convention would not restrict the protection of rights under the Basic Law (also enshrined in Article 53 ECHR), and within the limits of recognised methods of constitutional interpretation, the Convention must be given effect by all public authorities.[66] It appears that—indirectly—the Convention becomes a mandatory standard of review in spite of its formal status as a federal law, as mentioned at the beginning of this chapter. The FCC ensures the fulfilment of this obligation by accepting constitutional complaints based on violations of the Convention—not directly but in conjunction with constitutional fundamental rights.[67]

International lawyers appreciated the more cooperative approach.[68] Upon receiving the complaint of another detainee under the preventive detention rule in *Schmitz v Germany*,[69] the ECtHR itself expressly took note of the reversal of the FCC's case law concerning preventive detention and welcomed

---

[61] *BVerfGE* 128, 326, press release in English available at www.bundesverfassungsgericht.de/ pressemitteilungen/bvg11-031en.html.

[62] *BVerfGE* 128, 326, para 100.

[63] Federal Constitutional Court, press release no 31/2011 of 4 May 2011.

[64] *BVerfGE* 128, 326, paras 87 f.

[65] ibid, paras 89, 91.

[66] ibid, para 93.

[67] ibid, para 87.

[68] Zimmermann (n 36) 27.

[69] *Schmitz v Germany* App no 30493/04 (9 June 2011), para 41.

the Federal Constitutional Court's approach of interpreting the provisions of the Basic Law also in the light of the Convention and this Court's case-law, which demonstrates that court's continuing commitment to the protection of fundamental rights not only on a national, but also on a European level.

Harmony between Karlsruhe and Strasbourg was restored. Has the conflict been resolved once and for all?

The answer in the context of the German legal order must be that conflicts will occur but are to be avoided according to the FCC's approach. The preventive detention decision is an encouraging signal in the context of a continued dialogue. In the words of the FCC:

> An interpretation that is open to international law does not require the Basic Law's statements to be schematically aligned with those of the Convention but requires its valuations to be taken on to the extent that this is methodically justifiable and compatible with the Basic Law's standards.[70]

It remains to be seen how the FCC will deal with future cases of conflict, but one area in particular—that of religious freedom—presents considerable potential for conflicts between domestic fundamental rights and the Convention, and the ECtHR's jurisprudence respectively. The issue of religious freedom bears potential for judicial conflict not only between the FCC and the ECtHR but also in other Member States. Switzerland, France and Turkey, for instance, have dealt with the issue of headscarves in public places; the crucifix in Italian public schools was also brought before the ECtHR.

III. POTENTIAL CONFLICTS

Religious freedom in public spaces is an issue that could become controversial between Karlsruhe and Strasbourg. Both the FCC and the ECtHR have already had to decide on issues concerning the wearing of headscarves as well as on crucifixes in public schools. Both issues were controversial and the debate on this issue is far from over in Germany. The FCC declared the crucifix in public schools to be incompatible with religious freedom[71]—a decision that was unusually unpopular in Germany—[72] while the ECtHR decided the contrary in the Grand Chamber judgment in *Lautsi*, reversing the Chamber judgment.[73] In the headscarf case the FCC decided in 2003 that the ban without a statutory legal basis violated religious freedom, but left it to the *Länder* to adopt such a statutory regulation.[74] This decision

---

[70] Federal Constitutional Court, press release no 31/2011 of 4 May 2011 concerning Judgment of 4 May 2011, *Preventive Detention I*, 2 BvR 2365/09, 2 BvR 740/10, *Preventive Detention II*, 2 BvR 2333/08, 2 BvR 1152/10, 2 BvR 571/10, www.bundesverfassungsgericht.de/pressemitteilungen/bvg11-031en.html.
[71] *BVerfGE* 93, 1.
[72] O Bruttel and N Abaza-Uhrberg, 'Die Sicht der Bevölkerung auf Grundgesetz und Bundesverfassungsgericht' (2014) *Die öffentliche Verwaltung* 510, 516.
[73] *Lautsi v Italy* (2011) 50 EHRR 42.
[74] *BVerfGE* 108, 282.

was highly supported by public opinion.[75] On 27 January 2015 the FCC overruled such a statutory regulation partly and a judgment applying it.[76] The ECtHR, on the other hand, clearly stated that the headscarf ban in Turkey and Switzerland as well as the recent burqa ban in France were justified.[77]

A. The Headscarf Debate in Germany

On 27 January 2015 the FCC delivered an order in a second headscarf case concerning a regulation in Nordrhein-Westfalen[78] which prohibits teaching staff from expressing their religious beliefs by wearing religious symbols.[79] The complainants, two female Muslim public schoolteachers, filed constitutional complaints against the imposition of sanctions under employment law for wearing a headscarf or a hat covering the hair contrary to the ban on religious symbols at public schools. The employment tribunals had dismissed both of their claims.[80] The Federal Employment Tribunal did not find a breach of fundamental rights in the contested provisions. It also considered the jurisprudence of the ECtHR but concluded that no violation of Article 9 ECHR could be found.[81] The ECtHR's rulings on headscarf bans for teachers at public schools in Switzerland[82] and for teachers and students at public universities in Turkey[83] left a margin of appreciation to Contracting States to restrict religious manifestations in order to guarantee the neutrality of education according to this ruling. This did not amount to discrimination of women, as men and women were equally forbidden to wear religious symbols.[84]

When deciding on these cases, the FCC had to balance conflicting rights. The approach to such situations[85] has been established in the aforementioned cases: while all public authorities are obliged to take the ECtHR's jurisprudence into account, these situations have precisely been named as possible triggers for divergences. The religious freedom of the teacher guaranteed in Article 4(1) of the Basic Law as well as her occupational freedom (Article 12(1) of the Basic Law) and the prohibition on discrimination because of her faith (Article 3(2) and (3) of the Basic Law) must be balanced against the (passive) religious freedom of students guaranteed in Article 4(1)

---

[75] Bruttel and Abaza-Uhrberg (n 72) 515.

[76] BVerfG, order of 27 January 2015, 1 BvR 471/10; 1 BvR 1181/10, available in German at: www.bundesverfassungsgericht.de.

[77] *Dahlab v Switzerland* App no 42393/98, ECHR 2001-V; *Sahin v Turkey* (2005) 44 EHRR 99; *SAS v France* App no 43835/11, ECHR 2014 (GC).

[78] § 57 IV Schulgesetz Nordrhein-Westfalen.

[79] BVerfG, order of 27 January 2015, 1 BvR 471/10; 1 BvR 1181/10, available in German at: www.bundesverfassungsgericht.de.

[80] Bundesarbeitsgericht (Federal Employment Tribunal, BAG), judgment of 20 August 2009—2 AZR 499/08—juris; judgment of 10 December 2009—2 AZR 55/09—juris.

[81] BAG, judgment of 20 August 2009—2 AZR 499/08—juris, para 25; judgment of 10 December 2009—2 AZR 55/09—juris, para 26.

[82] ibid, with reference to *Dahlab v Switzerland* (n 77).

[83] ibid, with reference to *Sahin v Turkey* (n 77).

[84] BAG (n 81).

[85] Balancing two rights, as in *Von Hannover*, inevitably leads to the restriction of one right. In this situation the FCC exceptionally stipulates the possibility of departing from the ECtHR's jurisprudence.

of the Basic Law, parents' right to the care and upbringing of their children (Article 6(2) of the Basic Law), and the religious neutrality of public education.

In its first ruling on a headscarf ban in 2003, the FCC considered that without a specific statutory regulation teachers were allowed to wear headscarves at school, but left the federal states (*Länder*) a 'margin of appreciation' to pass legislation if they wished to ban religious symbols.[86] In the meantime, several *Länder* banned religious symbols that posed a danger to neutrality or peace at school.[87] The provision for Baden-Württemberg was drafted with a general and abstract prohibition, establishing a presumption that religious symbols implied such a danger regardless of the circumstances at the particular school and the particular conduct of the teacher concerned, thus amounting to a blanket ban. At the same time, it excluded symbols representing Christian and Western educational and cultural values from the ban.[88] The Federal Administrative Tribunal held this to be in accordance with constitutional law.[89] This decision was widely criticised, especially with regard to discrimination, although the ECtHR jurisprudence left a wide margin of appreciation.[90] It was argued that the decision was probably also incompatible with EU law.[91] Directive 2000/78/EC[92] prohibits direct discrimination on the grounds of religion under Article 2(2) *lit* a and indirect discrimination under Article 2(2) *lit* b. The stakes for justification in Article 2(5) and Article 4 of the Directive are higher than in Article 14 ECHR. The question of whether the Court of Justice of the European Union (CJEU) would demand the stricter standards of the Directive or follow the jurisprudence of the ECtHR is still open.[93] The headscarf ban from Nordrhein-Westfalen that had reached the FCC contains an identical provision prohibiting religious symbols with the exception of those representing Christian and Western educational and cultural values. There is a strong argument that the blanket ban on headscarves for all teachers regardless of their personal beliefs, the age of the students and the actual existence of ideological conflicts at the particular school infringes religious freedom in a manner that cannot be justified.[94] Some

---

[86] *BVerfGE* 108, 282, 309 f.

[87] Eight Länder currently have regulations on religious symbols: § 38(2) Schulgesetz für das Land Baden-Württemberg (as amended 9 November 2010)—the provision was first introduced by Gesetz zur Änderung des Schulgesetzes of 1 April 2004, GVBl 178; § 57(4) Schulgesetz für das Land Nordrhein-Westfalen (as amended 27 June 2006)—the provision was first introduced by Erstes Gesetz zur Änderung des Schulgesetzes für das Land Nordrhein-Westfalen of 13 June 2006, GVBl S 270, Nr 15. Other Länder with headscarf regulations: Niedersachsen, Saarland, Hessen, Bayern, Bremen, Berlin; three Länder have draft laws on a ban: Schleswig-Holstein, Rheinland-Pfalz, Brandenburg; five do not plan a ban: Hamburg, Mecklenburg-Vorpommern, Thüringen, Sachsen, Sachsen-Anhalt.

[88] *cf* § 38(2) Schulgesetz Baden-Württemberg; § 57(4) Schulgesetz Nordrhein-Westfalen.

[89] Bundesverwaltungsgericht (Federal Administrative Court, BVerwG), judgment of 24 June 2004—2 C 45.03—*BVerGE* 121, 140, (2004) 57 *Neue Juristische Wochenschrift* 3581.

[90] S Baer and M Wrase, 'Staatliche Neutralität und Toleranz in der "christlich-abendländischen Wertewelt"' [2005] *Die Öffentliche Verwaltung* 243, 249 ff.

[91] ibid, 251.

[92] Council Directive 2000/78/EC of 27 November 2000 establishing a general framework for equal treatment in employment and occupation, [2002] OJ L303, 16–22.

[93] Baer and Wrase (n 90) 251.

[94] C Walter and A von Ungern-Sternberg, 'Verfassungswidrigkeit des nordrhein-westfälischen Kopftuchverbots für Lehrerinnen' [2008] *Die Öffentliche Verwaltung* 488, 491 f.

argued that the provision is therefore unconstitutional;[95] others thought it was possible to interpret the provision in a way that is compatible with the Constitution by implying that the individual circumstances must be evaluated or that symbols of all religions are treated equally.[96]

Additionally, some regarded the exception for symbols representing Christian and Western educational and cultural values as direct discrimination. Allowing them may imply a presumption that certain religions do not pose a threat to the principle of neutrality of the State established in the Basic Law and the maintenance of peace at schools, while others do pose a threat.[97] Others argued that religious freedom—especially as it is guaranteed in international human rights law—requires tolerance towards other religions, but not necessarily equal treatment of all religions.[98] The Federal Administrative Tribunal did not even find unequal treatment of different religions in this provision, because it could be interpreted as a reference not to a religion, but to a 'set of values derived from the tradition of occidental culture which is also fundamental to the Basic Law independently of its religious origin'.[99] This interpretation, however, is difficult to reconcile with the FCC's approach, which expressly required strict equality between religions.[100] The provision leaves no room for interpretation without overlooking the explicit intention of Parliament to spare nuns' habits and *kippas* from the ban.[101]

Strong arguments were presented by scholars for a violation of religious freedom and the prohibition of discrimination for religious motives, while the German courts have declared the contested provisions constitutional. In its decision of 27 January 2015 however, the FCC found a violation of religious freedom and a case of discrimination in the court decisions that were subject to the complaint.[102] It also held the statutory provision which exempts symbols representing Christian and Western values unconstitutional and thus null and void.[103] The statutory ban of religious symbols posing a threat to neutrality at school remains in force as the provision can be interpreted in accordance with the Basic Law.[104] A headscarf ban could be justified in specific situations where a danger of religious conflicts has been

---

[95] ibid, 494.

[96] Baer and Wrase (n 90) 248.

[97] Walter and von Ungern-Sternberg (n 91) 493.

[98] J Kokott, 'Laizismus und Religionsfreiheit im öffentlichen Raum' [2005] *Der Staat* 343, 359.

[99] BVerwG, [2004] *Neue Juristische Wochenschrift* 3581, 3584: '[Der hier verwendete Begriff des "Christlichen"] bezeichnet ungeachtet seiner Herkunft aus dem religiösen Bereich—eine von Glaubensinhalten losgelöste, aus der Tradition der christlich-abendländischen Kultur hervorgegangene Wertewelt, die erkennbar auch dem Grundgesetz zu Grunde liegt und unabhängig von ihrer religiösen Fundierung Geltung beansprucht.'

[100] Baer and Wrase (n 90) 249 with reference to: *BVerfGE* 108, 282 (318); Kokott (n 98) points out that the FCC's approach in this judgment is ambiguous, as it leaves room for different regulations according to regional differences in religious tradition, but, on the other hand, requires strict equality between religions ('*Gebot strikter Gleichbehandlung*').

[101] NRW LT-Drs 14/569, 31 October 2005, 8 f.

[102] ibid, paras 80 ff.

[103] ibid, paras 123 ff.

[104] ibid, para 116.

demonstrated and must be resolved. However, in the cases of the applicants no such danger became manifest.[105]

The FCC arrived at the conclusion that there was no violation of the Convention as it is interpreted by the ECtHR by leaving a wide margin of appreciation to the Contracting States.[106] At the same time, it made an important and progressive point with regard to the status of the Convention in the German legal system in this decision: According to the formula from *Görgülü* and *Preventive Detention*, the Convention is not considered a direct standard of review, but only serves as a guide to interpretation. In principle, the FCC stands by that formula. But a different situation in this case allowed the FCC to introduce a new approach. Since in the present case the complaint is indirectly directed against a statute of a *Land*, rather than merely taking Articles 9 and 14 of the Convention and the jurisprudence of the ECtHR into account, the Convention does become a standard of review. The reason for this is Article 31 of the Basic Law which provides that federal law shall take precedence over the law of the *Länder*. It had been mentioned in *Preventive Detention* that the Convention has the status of a federal law. It follows, then, that it takes precedence over the law of the *Länder* and therefore becomes direct standard of review.[107]

This decision will not be the last word on the headscarf issue. The FCC's first senate did not only reverse the lower courts' judgements, it also diverged substantially from the decision of the FCC's second senate in 2003, as the two dissenting judges pointed out.[108] According to the second senate's decision a general prohibition could be justified as long as the legislator provided a legal basis. This is one reason why this might not be the final decision on the issue. The decision raises further questions of constitutional law, such as the binding force of FCC judgments for the FCC itself and for the legislator, as well as all other public authorities.[109]

B. The ECtHR's Approach to Headscarf Bans

Since the applicants were successful, and this case will not become subject to a complaint at the ECtHR, a conflict between Karlsruhe and Strasbourg was avoided. But the headscarf issue is still unresolved in Germany. It is possible that the provisions on religious clothing from other *Länder* will reach the FCC since the decision only directly concerns the case of *Nordrhein-Westfalen* while other *Länder* have adopted

---

[105] ibid, paras 101, 121.
[106] ibid, paras 148 ff.
[107] ibid, para 149.
[108] Dissenting opinion by judges Schluckebier and Hermanns, paras 2, 6, 7.
[109] On the duty to submit the case to the plenum of both senates according to § 16 (1) BVerfGG: C Möllers, 'A Tale of two Courts', VerfBlog, 14 March 2015, www.verfassungsblog.de/a-tale-of-two-courts; M Hong, 'Two Tales of Two Courts: zum Kopftuch-Beschluss und dem „horror pleni"', VerfBlog, 27 March 2015, www.verfassungsblog.de/two-tales-of-two-courts-zum-kopftuch-beschluss-und-dem-horror-pleni/.

different regulations. There will be legislative changes, but again different provisions are conceivable because the FCC's decision not only leaves room for the legislator, but also diverges from the 2003 judgment. Future complaints against statutes of the *Länder* would in any event have to be examined according to the new approach applying the Convention as standard of review.

Considering its recent jurisprudence, the ECtHR would probably not object to the headscarf ban. The recent jurisprudence of the ECtHR—especially its judgment of 1 July 2014 on the so-called French *burqa* ban[110]—suggests a cautious approach and could be said to confirm the Court's current tendency to self-restraint.[111] It has been observed that the criticism, especially from UK politicians and judges,[112] has had some effect on the ECtHR in such a way that national public interests are considered more carefully.[113] Thus, the ECtHR might have avoided possible conflicts in this judgment, not only regarding France but also other States Parties such as Germany, where the issue of religious symbols in public places has been controversial in jurisprudence and legislation.

The Federal Employment Tribunal's and the FCC's view that the ECtHR's rulings in *Dahlab v Switzerland* and *Leyla Sahin v Turkey* left a margin of appreciation to the Contracting States must be agreed with in principle. A closer look, however, reveals that the ECtHR examined the particular situation in these cases. The ECtHR's ruling in *Dahlab v Switzerland* relied especially on the young age of the students, in that they could be easily influenced.[114] This could support the aforementioned view that a blanket ban on headscarves violates the Convention, because it considers certain religious expressions a public danger in general without any requirement for the State to prove an actual danger in the particular situation.[115] However, the ECtHR also found that the headscarf ban was difficult to reconcile with the principle of gender equality.[116] This was confirmed in *Leyla Sahin v Turkey*.[117] In this ruling the ECtHR stressed the fact that the State took this measure in order to take a stance against extremist political movements based on its historical experience.[118] It considered in particular the Turkish context, where 'it must be borne in mind the impact which wearing such a symbol, which is presented or perceived as a compulsory religious duty, may have on those who choose not to wear it'.[119] In Turkey 'the majority of the population, while professing a strong attachment to the rights

---

[110] *SAS v France* (n 77).

[111] As noted above at II.A.

[112] Lord Hoffmann, 'The Universality of Human Rights' (2009) 125 *Law Quarterly Review* 416; M Pinto-Duschinsky, *Bringing Rights Back Home: Making Human Rights Compatible with Parliamentary Democracy in the UK* (London, Policy Exchange, 2011); David Cameron, 'The European Court of Human Rights', speech delivered 25 January 2012, www.gov.uk/government/speeches/speech-on-the-european-court-of-human-rights.

[113] See nn 15, 16 and 20.

[114] *Dahlab v Switzerland* (n 77).

[115] Walter and von Ungern-Sternberg (n 94) 492.

[116] *Dahlab v Switzerland* (n 77).

[117] *Sahin v Turkey* (n 77) para 111.

[118] ibid, para 115 with reference to paras 107–09 of the Chamber judgment.

[119] ibid.

of women and a secular way of life, adhere to the Islamic faith'. In this situation a headscarf ban could be regarded as 'a pressing social need by seeking to achieve those two legitimate aims, especially since, as the Turkish courts stated ..., this religious symbol has taken on political significance in Turkey in recent years'.[120]

In *SAS v France* the ECtHR modified the *Dahlab* jurisprudence and held that gender equality was not a legitimate aim 'in order to ban a practice that is defended by women—such as the applicant—in the context of the exercise of the rights enshrined in those provisions, unless it were to be understood that individuals could be protected on that basis from the exercise of their own fundamental rights and freedoms'.[121] Neither was human dignity accepted as a legitimate aim.[122] The claim was however rejected on the basis of a new legitimate aim: a concept of 'living together'.[123] In this case, unlike in the previous decision, the ECtHR required the State to provide evidence of the necessity of the ban, especially a blanket ban.[124]

The ECtHR is consistent in granting a wide margin of appreciation to the States Parties when restricting religious symbols. It has, however, departed from previous value judgments on religious clothing. Therefore, the ECtHR may well have found the headscarf ban—with the discriminating exception of symbols representing Christian and Western cultural values in schools in Nordrhein-Westfalen—as contrary to the Convention.

In a case like this one, the definition of the margin of appreciation would be particularly interesting. Firstly, the complaint was directed against a court decision and indirectly against a statutory provision. It has been demanded in the prisoners voting rights debate that the ECtHR should be especially careful to respect the margin of appreciation of the legislator.[125] Secondly, the margin of appreciation in rights conflict situations, such as the religious freedom of the teacher and the students, applies to both rights. Consequently, the ECtHR would have had to solve the same dilemma as in the balance between privacy rights and the freedom of the press. In the headscarf case, however, there is not as much room for a 'corridor solution' as was suggested in *Von Hannover*.[126] The headscarf is considered a compulsory religious duty by a significant part of the Muslim community. A headscarf ban would therefore be a severe infringement of religious freedom in any event. And the religious freedom of the students leaves just as little room for balancing.

IV. CONCLUDING REMARKS: FACTORS DETERMINING THE RELATIONSHIP

Some factors concern the relationship between the two courts; some go beyond judicial aspects. The question of why the ECtHR's judgments are generally received

---

[120] ibid.

[121] *SAS v France* (n 77) para 119.

[122] ibid, para 120.

[123] The dissenting judges criticised this approach, along with many scholars.

[124] *SAS v France* (n 77) para 139.

[125] Bates (n 20) 6, 11.

[126] See above at II.A.

differently in Germany and the UK is not necessarily answered by the nature of the relationship between the courts. The general reception is related to the public perception of the two courts and the general constitutional culture in Germany.

A. The Relationship Between the Courts

The above analysis of the cases that led to conflicts reveals some of the purely 'technical' judicial difficulties to be overcome in the relationship between the ECtHR and the FCC.

(i) Basic Law Rights and Convention Rights: Almost Congruent

Conflicts occur where there are differences, but the structural similarity should make it easier for the ECtHR to take national peculiarities into account. The German Constitution contains a bill of rights that is very similar to the Convention. The conflict in the preventive detention cases, for example, was partly based on a difference between the right to liberty in the Convention and that set out in the German Constitution.[127]

Pursuant to Article 2(2), second sentence of the Basic Law, the liberty of the person is inviolable. Article 2(2), third sentence of the Basic Law allows restrictions on liberty by law in general terms.[128] Further parameters are stipulated in the Basic Law.[129] This permitted more far-reaching restrictions than the Convention. Article 5(1) ECHR guarantees the right to liberty and security of the person and provides an exhaustive list of permissible grounds for deprivation of liberty.[130] The ECtHR found that the preventive detention rule could not be reconciled with any of the permissible grounds under Article 5 ECHR.[131]

(ii) Conflict of Rights Situations

Where rights conflict emerges there is a potential site of disagreement with regard to the appropriate balance. Article 53 ECHR stipulates that the Convention must

---

[127] Nußberger (n 16) 104.

[128] Art 2(2), third sentence of the Basic Law provides: 'These rights may be interfered with only pursuant to a law.'

[129] Pursuant to Art 20(3) of the Basic Law, the legislature is bound by the constitutional order, the executive and the judiciary by law and justice. Pursuant to Art 101(1) of the Basic Law, no one may be removed from the jurisdiction of the lawful judge. Under Art 103(2) of the Basic Law, an act may be punished only if the fact of its being punishable was determined by law before the act was committed.

[130] Art 5(1) ECHR, insofar as it is relevant, provides: 'Everyone has the right to liberty and security of person. No one shall be deprived of his liberty save in the following cases and in accordance with a procedure prescribed by law: (a) the lawful detention of a person after conviction by a competent court; ... (c) the lawful arrest or detention of a person effected for the purpose of bringing him before the competent legal authority on reasonable suspicion of having committed an offence or when it is reasonably considered necessary to prevent his committing an offence or fleeing after having done so; ... (e) the lawful detention of persons for the prevention of the spreading of infectious diseases, of persons of unsound mind, alcoholics or drug addicts or vagrants.'

[131] *M v Germany* (n 39) para 92.

never limit the rights guaranteed under domestic law. But in conflict of rights situations, giving way to one right inevitably brings about the limitation of the other right. Therefore, in these situations the ECtHR must take a cautious approach in order to give enough room to the scope of domestic rights. Even if, as was argued in *Von Hannover*, the ECtHR does not respect subsidiarity sufficiently, the FCC's implicit approach seems to be: once Strasbourg hands down a judgment, it must be applied—maybe for the sake of the Convention system as a whole.[132] After all, accession to the Convention means accepting that the national point of view cannot always prevail.[133] The concept of *Völkerrechtsfreundlichkeit* (comity to international law), as introduced by the FCC, demands that this approach be adopted.

(iii) The FCC's Approach: Substantive Subsidiarity

The FCC understands subsidiarity not only in a formal way that obliges the ECtHR to respect the national legal orders; the dialogue between courts is also an expression of subsidiarity.[134] It takes two to enter into a dialogue. The FCC seems to accept its own responsibility for making subsidiarity work, yet some scholars have called for an even stronger commitment. Giegerich proposes an interpretation of the Basic Law that raises Convention rights to the rank of the Constitution, which, he argues, would leave the traditional idea of sovereignty behind.[135] It would make Convention rights a direct standard of review and the jurisprudence of the ECtHR binding in the interpretation of domestic law. On the other hand, the Basic Law already provides this possibility, as it allows the transfer of sovereign powers in Article 24(1). Zimmermann argues that the FCC should adopt the same approach towards the ECtHR as the approach it has developed towards the CJEU.[136] The current UK debate, however, raises the question of whether a progressive approach is viable with regard to the Convention system as a whole.[137] Protocol 15,[138] which inter alia includes the principle of subsidiarity expressly in the preamble to the Convention, can also be interpreted as a call for more self-restraint.[139] When some States express strong objections to the ECtHR's activism, it might be advisable to consolidate the current relationship between the ECtHR and the Contracting States before postulating an even stronger position of the Court.

---

[132] Volkmann (n 4) 841 f.

[133] G Lübbe-Wolff, 'How Can the European Court of Human Rights Reinforce the Role of National Courts in the Convention System?' (2012) *Dialogue between Judges* 11, 15, www.echr.coe.int/Pages/home.aspx?p=echrpublications/seminar&c=#n1347971225809_pointer.

[134] Lübbe-Wolff, ibid.

[135] Giegerich (n 34) para 77 f.

[136] Zimmermann (n 36) 32 ff.

[137] In this sense, see G Nolte, 'Grenzen der Politik—am Beispiel der Menschenrechte' in C Franzius and FC Mayer (eds), *Grenzen der europäischen Integration* (Baden-Baden, Nomos, 2014) 145–48.

[138] Protocol No 15 amending the Convention on the Protection of Human Rights and Fundamental Freedoms, 24 June 2013.

[139] Bates (n 20).

B. Cultural Aspects

The UK debate has revealed certain contested areas underlying the conflict with the ECtHR. In the same manner, sensitive issues can be identified in the ECtHR case law concerning Germany. However, the way in which the UK debate developed does not mirror any debate on the ECtHR in Germany so far. As an attempt to explain the difference, the German 'constitutional review culture' is proposed as a determining factor for the development of the debate.

(i) Sensitive Issues

Whether certain issues are a source of conflict between the ECtHR and a Member State seems to depend partly on the public sensitivity of the issue at hand. While prisoners' voting rights and counter-terrorism action give rise to serious debate in the UK, the issue of preventive detention or headscarves at school receives considerably more attention than other cases in Germany. The issue of religious freedom is likely to remain controversial. According to polls from 2013 69 per cent are in favor of the FCC's 2003 judgment, interpreted as allowing headscarf bans for school teachers.[140] 55 per cent did not agree with the decision against the crucifix at school.[141] Lieve Gies explains in her contribution to this volume[142] that the ECtHR is criticised in the UK only in certain areas while other decisions do not lead to any controversies. Where Convention rights appear to protect criminals or suspected terrorists they are perceived as a threat to security interests, whereas the protection of traditional 'British' liberties—in the area of DNA retention for instance—is generally welcomed.[143] The tensions between the UK government and the ECtHR have demonstrated the difficult task of identifying issues of fundamental importance while preserving the Court's independence.[144] The ECtHR's recent self-restraining approach shows its ability to identify these fundamental issues.

   Certain issues become controversial because human rights are cultural products.[145] Not only are rights in their substantive dimension cultural products: the way they are enforced depends not just on institutional frameworks, but also on a certain constitutional culture, which is connected to this constitutional framework. Having identified certain issues with conflict potential it remains to be seen why these cases—although quite controversial—were not followed by a general debate in Germany as has occurred in the UK.

---

[140] Bruttel and Abaza-Uhrberg (n 72) 515.
[141] Bruttel and Abaza-Uhrberg (n 72) 516.
[142] L Gies, 'Human Rights, the British Press and the Deserving Claimant' (ch 24), this volume.
[143] ibid.
[144] D Feldman, 'Sovereignties in Strasbourg' in R Rawlings, P Leyland and AL Young (eds), *Sovereignty and the Law* (Oxford, Oxford University Press, 2013) 213, 235.
[145] Lübbe-Wolff (n 133) 16.

(ii) 'A Constitutional Review Culture'

Here, German constitutional review is presented not as an institutional safeguard to prevent conflicts, but as part of a constitutional culture that protects the ECtHR from open hostility. The ECtHR receives little public attention in Germany. One reason for this might be that the aforementioned decisions are attributed to the FCC in the perception of the general public. The public did not manifest concerns about the ECtHR's decisions in these cases. If it was an issue at all, this was only in the sense that it was asked how the FCC would resolve the dilemma. An additional aspect of this public image is that the FCC currently enjoys wide acceptance and popularity in Germany. 75[146] to 86[147] per cent of the population trust in Karlsruhe; no other public authority is more popular.[148] The German public accepts a great deal of 'judicial government' and welcomes the judicial control of legislation. The ECtHR's legitimacy seems to be tied to the (currently high) legitimacy of the FCC. Hence it can be regarded as a protective shield for the ECtHR in the German constitutional order. Interestingly, the German government tends to wait for a decision from the FCC, even though some of the aforementioned cases clearly called for legislative intervention. In the preventive detention cases it was apparent that the legislature had to modify the provisions of the Criminal Code that breached the Convention. And finally, it is the German constitutional culture behind these developments that prevents the ECtHR from coming into open conflict with German institutions.

There is a distinction between constitutional framework and constitutional culture when determining the relationship between the ECtHR and domestic institutions. It has been argued that the concept of parliamentary sovereignty in the UK is not compatible with the ECtHR's review.[149] A parliamentary committee, however, has found that parliamentary sovereignty was 'not an argument against giving effect to' an ECtHR judgment.[150] Similarly, in the case of Germany, it is not (only) the institution of judicial review accepting individual constitutional complaints itself that prevents conflicts between the ECtHR and the German government. The German government could have refused to change its legislation in the preventive detention cases, just as the UK government could have introduced a bill on prisoners' voting rights. It is because of a general agreement in Germany that these questions are to be resolved between the courts that the government abstains from voicing open disagreement with the ECtHR's decisions. The relationship with Strasbourg remains a matter for the courts in Germany.

---

[146] R Köcher, 'Das Bollwerk' *Frankfurter Allgemeine Zeitung* (Frankfurt, 21 August 2012), www.faz. net/aktuell/politik/inland/bundesverfassungsgericht-das-bollwerk-11863396.html.

[147] Bruttel and Abaza-Uhrberg (n 72) 510.

[148] Bruttel and Abaza-Uhrberg (n 72) 510; R Köcher, 'Das Bollwerk' *Frankfurter Allgemeine Zeitung* (Frankfurt, 21 August 2012), www.faz.net/aktuell/politik/inland/bundesverfassungsgericht-das-bollwerk-11863396.html.

[149] Pinto-Duschinsky (n 112).

[150] Joint Select Committee on the Draft Voting Eligibility (Prisoners) Bill, *Draft Voting Eligibility (Prisoners) Bill: Report*, 2013, para 112 f; Bates (n 20).

20

Russia's Response to the European Court of Human Rights' Systemic Findings: Words or Actions?

OLGA CHERNISHOVA[*]

I. INTRODUCTION

R USSIA HAS BEEN a special client of the European Court of Human Rights (ECtHR).[1] For 10 years, between 2002 and 2012, it assumed the greatest national annual share of new cases lodged. Only in 2013 was it displaced by Ukraine—a development explained by the growing number of applications against that country rather than by a drop in the number of applications against Russia. For a long time Russia was also country number one in terms of applications pending with the Court. In November 2011, at its peak, there were about 42,000 complaints against Russia at the Court—more than a quarter of the total number at the time (153,850). As with new applications, this trend was reversed in 2013, and by May 2014 Russia had, for the first time in years, descended to third place behind Ukraine and Italy, with about 14,000 applications pending (about 15 per cent of the total of 93,500 applications).[2] About half of these cases have been identified by the Registry as potentially inadmissible, under the criteria contained in Articles 34 and 35 of the European Convention on Human Rights (ECHR),[3] and are destined to be processed by a single judge in simplified fashion under the procedure introduced by Protocol 14 to the Convention. Still, about 7,500 pending cases appear to raise sufficiently serious questions under the Convention to be allocated for examination to one of the Court's collegial bodies—a committee of three judges or chamber of seven judges.

Not surprisingly, this impressive flow of individual complaints has resulted in a significant output of judgments. Between May 2002, when the first judgment was

---

[*] This paper reflects the author's personal views and ideas.

[1] For an up-to-date overview of some of the issues, see House of Commons Library Standard Note of 31 July 2014, SN/IA/6953, 'Russia and the Council of Europe', www.parliament.uk/briefing-papers/SN06953/russia-and-the-council-of-europe.

[2] See the Court's monthly statistics for 2014, www.echr.coe.int/Pages/home.aspx?p=reports&c=#n1347956867932_pointer.

[3] See the Court's general statistics for 2013, 49, www.echr.coe.int/Documents/Stats_analysis_2013_ENG.pdf.

rendered in the case of *Burdov v Russia*,[4] and May 2014 the Court issued about 1,600 judgments against Russia, most of them finding at least one violation of the Convention's provisions.[5] The implementation of these judgments in the most limited sense, that is, ensuring the payment of just satisfaction awards, has not encountered any serious obstacles, and the sums due were paid as ordered by the Court. This is true even for those judgments greeted with some sort of public display of official disagreement, such as when Russia was found responsible for the violations occurring in the so-called 'Moldovan Republic of Transnistria'—an unrecognised entity situated at the border between Ukraine and Moldova.[6]

At the same time, the Court's conclusions often reach beyond the situation of individual applicants, be it with the pilot cases of *Burdov v Russia (No 2)*[7] and *Ananyev v Russia*,[8] or others seen in the context of numerous similar individual violations—for example, the absence of effective investigations into enforced disappearances in the Northern Caucasus in 1999–2006,[9] extra-judicial renditions of foreign nationals,[10] or structural deficiencies of the legislative and practical framework governing the examination of entrapment pleas in criminal proceedings.[11]

Fifteen years after the entry of the Convention into force for Russia, how can we evaluate and measure the impact of those judgments on the Russian legal system? Which steps are genuinely aimed at implementing the European human rights standards, and which are just words that mask the absence of real change? Might the Russian experience be, in some way, useful for the current UK debate on the Convention and the Court?

Without pretending to give an exhaustive answer to these questions, let me try to trace at least some of the most important developments, while of course not forgetting the areas where such changes are still most welcome. My attention will be primarily focused on the steps taken by the highest judicial authorities of Russia, which serve as sort of general measure in response to the ECtHR's findings of a systemic nature.

II. STRUCTURAL DEVELOPMENTS

National courts are the primary guardians of the rights enshrined in the Convention (and in the Russian Constitution), and their work lies at the heart of the subsidiarity

---

[4] *Burdov v Russia* (2004) 38 EHRR 29.
[5] See the Court's statistics on violations by country and by State, www.echr.coe.int/Documents/Stats_violation_1959_2013_ENG.pdf.
[6] See Interim Resolution ResDH (2005) 42 concerning the judgment of the European Court of Human Rights of 8 July 2004 (Grand Chamber) in the case of *Ilaşcu v Moldova and the Russian Federation*.
[7] *Burdov v Russia (No 2)* (2009) 49 EHRR 2.
[8] *Ananyev v Russia* (2012) 55 EHRR 18.
[9] *Aslakhanova v Russia* nos 2944/06, 8300/07, 50184/07, 332/08 and 42509/10, §§ 217, 219 (18 December 2012).
[10] *Savriddin Dzhurayev v Russia* (2013) 57 EHRR 22.
[11] *Lagutin v Russia* nos 6228/09, 19123/09, 19678/07, 52340/08 and 7451/09, § 134 (24 April 2014): 'The Court has already highlighted the structural nature of the problem [failure to conduct an effective judicial review of the entrapment plea], indicating that in the absence of a clear and foreseeable procedure for authorising test purchases and operational experiments the system was in principle inadequate and prone to abuse (see paragraphs 93 and 115 above with further references).'

principle. They are confronted with the same questions as those brought to the Court in Strasbourg, first in the process of exhaustion of domestic remedies before the application is lodged, and later, if a violation has been found, at the execution stage. These questions are in no way alien to them, even if the analysis applied or the conclusions drawn by the European judges differ from that which national judges are used to. The courts in Russia are also well aware of the external layer of control that the supranational court represents. Understanding this, the top level of the Russian judiciary has played an important role in promoting structural changes to the traditionally closed legal system.

Before describing the relevant rulings of the highest courts, let me say a few words about the nature and value of these judicial acts. The rulings of the Constitutional Court arise out of questions raised by individuals or certain State organs, including courts, about the conformity of the applicable statutory provision to the Russian Constitution.

The non-judicial rulings of the Supreme Court require, perhaps, more insight for a British reader. Historically, in Soviet legal thought the idea that the court's decision could extend beyond the case under examination was something of a blasphemy. An exception was made for non-judicial rulings issued by the Supreme Court in order to harmonise the lower courts' practice in a given field.

The Plenary of the Supreme Court issues between 20 and 50 resolutions each year, which are published in the official sources. While the Russian doctrine does not formally recognise precedent as a source of law, lower courts are expected to follow these resolutions. A senior judge of the Supreme Court and then secretary to its Plenary defined the aim of resolutions as

> *not just drawing the courts' attention to the need of correct application of the laws, but obliging them to resolve cases in strict conformity with the applicable federal legislation, generally recognized principles and norms of international law ... The explanations of judicial practice contained in the resolutions of the Plenary are obligatory for the courts.*[12]

W Butler, a well-known scholar of Russian law, remarked that

> *although for the most part these 'explanations' interpret rather than create legal norms, the line is no less difficult to draw in Russian law than in other legal systems; many Russian jurists believe that in some instances the Plenum of the Russian Supreme Court has stepped across the line into law-creation.*[13]

Below I set out some notable examples of the developments brought about by the highest courts which have shaped the system of implementation of the ECtHR's judgments in Russia.

As the first example, on October 2003 the Plenary of the Russian Supreme Court adopted a Resolution 'On the application by ordinary courts of the universally recognized principles and norms of international law and the international treaties

---

[12] Interview with the judge of the Supreme Court, Secretary of the Plenary V Demidov; *Advokatskiye Vesti* No 1, 2004 (in Russian).

[13] WE Butler, *Russian Law*, 3rd edn (Oxford, Oxford University Press, 2009). Cited in precedent.hse. ru/data/2013/07/31/1288279458/WE_Butler_Russian_Law.doc.

of the Russian Federation'.[14] In that Resolution the Supreme Court dispelled the often-cited suggestion that the ECtHR's judgments bore only 'the strength of recommendations'. It stated that 'pursuant to Article 46(1) of the Convention, final judgments adopted in respect of the Russian Federation are binding on all authorities of the Russian Federation, including courts'. It thus called on the courts to 'have regard to the practice of the European Court of Human Rights so as to avoid any infringement of the Convention'. The courts were called upon to act 'within their competence so as to ensure fulfilment of the obligations of the State' arising from the status of the Russian Federation as a State Party to the European Convention. The Supreme Court then took steps to explain to the lower courts the practical implications of the ECtHR's judgments that had been delivered against Russia, such as treating non-enforcement of domestic judicial decisions as an integral part of a 'fair trial' within the meaning of Article 6 of the Convention.[15] This prepared the ground for further actions aimed at combating non-enforcement of domestic decisions (see below).

My second example dates back to 2010, when the Russian Constitutional Court examined whether final judgments in civil matters could be re-opened following the finding of a violation by the ECtHR, despite the absence of a direct legislative provision permitting such re-opening. On the nature and legal value of the ECtHR's judgments, the Constitutional Court stated:

> The Russian Federation, having ratified the European Convention on human rights, has recognised ipso facto and without any special agreement the jurisdiction of the [ECtHR] as binding in so far as it concerns the questions of interpretation and application of the Convention and its protocols ... Therefore ... not only the Convention ... but also the judgments of the [ECtHR]—in so far as they, in line with the generally recognised principles and norms of international law, interpret the meaning of the rights and freedoms enshrined in the Convention, including the right to access to court and fair trial—are an integral part of the Russian legal system and must be taken into account by the federal legislator in regulation of social relationships and by the law-enforcement bodies when they apply the relevant legal norms.

As to the fact that no legal norm directly provided for the re-opening of a civil case following the finding of a violation by the ECtHR, the Constitutional Court insisted that such a mechanism should exist, drawing a direct parallel between its own judgments and those of the ECtHR:

> [T]he rights and freedoms guaranteed by the Convention are, in substance, the same as those guaranteed by the Russian Constitution; and the finding of violations of these rights, accordingly, by the [ECtHR] and the Constitutional Court—in view of the common legal nature of these bodies and their ultimate purpose—calls for the existence of a single institutional mechanism to implement their judgments.[16]

---

[14] Plenary of the Supreme Court, Resolution no 5, 10 October 2003. English translation published in (2004) 25 *Human Rights Law Journal* 108.

[15] ibid, point 12.

[16] Constitutional Court of the Russian Federation, judgment no 4-P concerning the constitutionality of Section 392 part 2 of the Code of Civil Procedure, based on complaints by A Doroshok, A Kot and E Fedotov, 26 February 2010.

Following that ruling, changes were introduced into the Civil Procedural Code, and the ECtHR's judgments have been listed as one of the grounds for the re-opening of final domestic judgments.[17]

To provide a full picture of the stance of the Constitutional Court, we must mention its most recent position[18] taken in the wake of the Grand Chamber's judgment *Konstantin Markin v Russia*, which is discussed in detail in Professor Bowring's chapter.[19] Briefly, the Constitutional Court addressed a situation where its own case law was in conflict with that of the ECtHR, and attempted to create a mechanism for resolving such conflicts. It explained that the domestic court should re-open proceedings after the finding of a violation by the ECtHR, notwithstanding the previous finding by the Constitutional Court of the constitutionality of the norm applied. The ECtHR's new interpretation of the provision in question raises matters of constitutionality, and thus the case should be returned to the Constitutional Court. When re-examining the norm in question, the Constitutional Court could still find it constitutional, and thus confirm its disagreement with the ECtHR's interpretation; in such cases it would 'determine possible constitutional mechanisms for the realisation of the ECtHR's judgment'.[20]

In June 2014, the Federal Law on the Constitutional Court was changed accordingly.[21] Thus, Article 43 of the Law added the issuing of a final judgment by the ECtHR as an exception to the rule that the Constitutional Court may not examine for a second time the constitutionality of a legal provision. This change appears to be aimed at creating a mechanism to resolve conflicts of interpretation between the Constitutional Court and the ECtHR, wherever they exist, and avoid the confusion that might arise from the co-existence of two final and contradictory judgments. This mechanism could potentially be used in respect of a number of such pending conflicts.

However, the changes went further than the demands of judgment no 27-P. Articles 85 and 101 of the Federal Law on the Constitutional Court now stipulate that any judgment of an 'international tribunal in the area of human rights and freedoms'—that is, even where there is no conflicting interpretation—can be submitted to the Constitutional Court where an ordinary court in the process of executing such judgment determines that the domestic legal norm lying at the origin of the violation in question should still be subject to constitutional review.[22] While this could be viewed as an attempt to bring about legislative change wherever general

---

[17] s 392 of the Civil Procedural Code was amended in December 2010 to take into account this judgment and listed the findings of the ECtHR as one of the grounds for the re-opening of final judgments.

[18] Constitutional Court of the Russian Federation, judgment no 27-P, concerning the constitutionality of Sections 11 and 392 parts 3 and 4 of the Code of Civil Procedure, based on the referral by the Presidium of the Leningrad Military Circuit, 6 December 2013.

[19] *Konstantin Markin v Russia* (2013) 56 EHRR 8 (GC). See B Bowring, 'The Russian Federation and the Strasbourg Court: The Illegitimacy of Sovereignty?' (ch 21), this volume.

[20] For more on this, see G Vaypan, 'Acquiescence Affirmed, its Limits Left Undefined: Russian Constitutional Court has Ruled on its Relationship with European Court of Human Rights' www.cjicl.org.uk/2013/12/26/acquiescence-affirmed/.

[21] Federal Constitutional Law N 9 FKZ, 9 June 2014.

[22] ibid.

measures are necessary to implement a judgment from the ECtHR, the possibility of creating conflicting interpretations remains very real.

In September 2014, in a judgment concerning controversial legislative provisions imposing administrative sanctions for the so-called 'propaganda of non-traditional sexual relations among minors', the Constitutional Court came back to the question of conflicting interpretations.[23] In response to a plea that the case be adjourned pending examination by the ECtHR, it noted that the complaint at the ECtHR was still pending and that potential 'collisions' of interpretation between the two courts could be overcome by relying on the procedural mechanisms as set out in the judgment 27-P.[24] The court has not so far had a chance to test the limits of such interpretation in practice, or what would happen in case of a failure to find a reconciliatory reading. But we can be certain that such conflicts would be very difficult to overcome, in view of the final and binding nature of the Constitutional Court's ruling, accorded to it by the Russian Constitution and the relevant legislation.[25]

My final example is the Resolution of the Plenary of the Russian Supreme Court no 21 of 27 June 2013.[26] This Resolution is intended to draw the attention of all courts of general jurisdiction to the jurisprudence of the ECtHR and attempts to synthesise the most important positions expressed by the ECtHR in respect of Russia. It addresses three principal groups of questions. The first group concerns general questions of how the Convention and the ECtHR's judgments can be relied upon in the adjudication of cases by ordinary courts. The Supreme Court effectively accorded to the ECtHR's judgments *erga omnes* effect, saying that they should be taken into account in their entirety and that the courts should bear in mind all judgments adopted by the Court, and not just those brought against Russia. Secondly, the Supreme Court addressed a non-exhaustive list of recurrent problems, mostly 'procedural' rights under Articles 5 and 6 of the Convention, which have been raised in several applications against Russia.[27] For example, point 14 stresses the need to comply with the deadlines set for appellate review of complaints against detention orders.[28] The Supreme Court also noted, in point 16, the recurrent situation where the civil courts resolve cases in the absence of claimants who serve prison terms, and instructed the judges to change this practice.[29] Finally, the third group of questions concerns the execution of the ECtHR's judgments in which violations have been

---

[23] Constitutional Court of the Russian Federation, judgment no No 24-P, concerning constitutionality of Section 6.21 part 1 of the Russian Federation Code of administrative offences, based on complaints by N Alekseyev, Ya Yevtushenko and D Isakov, 23 September 2014.

[24] See n 19.

[25] Art 125 §§ 5 and 6 Russian Constitution; Art 79 Federal Constitutional Law on the Constitutional Court of the Russian Federation.

[26] For the English translation of the Resolution and further discussion of it, see O Chernishova and A Kovler, 'The June 2013 Resolution No 21 of the Russian Supreme Court: A Move towards the Implementation of the Judgments of the European Court of Human Rights' (2013) 33 *Human Rights Law Journal* 7.

[27] See Resolution of the Plenary of the Russian Supreme Court no 21 of 27 June 2013, pp 5, 8, and 10–16.

[28] For the corresponding findings of the ECtHR see, eg, *Idalov v Russia* App no 5826/03, § 157 (GC, 22 May 2012).

[29] For corresponding findings of the ECtHR see, eg, *Larin v Russia* App no 15034/02, § 56 (20 May 2010).

found, insofar as the courts are required to take individual measures aimed at the restitution of applicants' rights. This aspect appears to be the least developed in current Russian doctrine and the jurisprudence of the higher courts, and consequently the directions contained in points 17–24 of the Resolution are of great importance.

III. RESPONSE TO SYSTEMIC PROBLEMS

While the rulings of the Plenary of the Supreme Court and the Constitutional Court are a source of law for the lower courts, they create no more than a general framework for implementing the ECtHR's judgments. The question remains of how this framework is implemented in practice. Below I will describe the progress achieved in four areas identified by the ECtHR as posing systemic problems under the Convention. Let me start with the most visible developments that followed the two pilot judgments adopted against Russia.

In the first years after Russia ratified the Convention, the problem of non-enforcement of domestic judgments was the single most important group of complaints. In 2009 the Court adopted its first pilot judgment against Russia, *Burdov No 2*,[30] calling for the adoption of a number of general measures to address the systemic problem. The authorities' reaction to this judgment can be described as a successful example of implementation of the pilot judgment through large-scale reforms.[31] The adoption of Federal Law no 68 in May 2010 allowed domestic courts to award pecuniary damages for delays in the enforcement of judicial decisions concerning the State's monetary obligations, as well as some other groups of cases, such as excessively lengthy judicial proceedings. The Federal Law refers directly to the practice of the ECtHR as one of the criteria that should be used to determine whether delays are reasonable and also the amount of the compensation to be awarded. The execution of this group of cases was closed by the Council of Europe's Committee of Ministers in 2011, after an effective domestic remedy had been introduced and the domestic courts had awarded compensation to the claimants.[32] The Committee of Ministers, in particular, welcomed the fact that this remedy was actively implemented in judicial practice; it took note of the 'wide set of measures adopted by the Russian authorities, in particular by the federal Supreme Court, by the Supreme Commercial Court, and by the Ministry of Finance and Federal Treasury, in order to guarantee the effectiveness of the new compensation remedy at domestic level'; and noted 'with great satisfaction that appropriate budgetary arrangements have been made in order to guarantee effective and timely execution of judicial decisions delivered in accordance with the Compensation Act'.[33]

---

[30] See n 8.

[31] See M Isayeva, I Sergeyeva and M Suchkova, 'Enforcement of the Judgments of the European Court of Human Rights in Russia: Recent Developments and Current Challenges' (2011) 8(15) *SUR— International Journal on Human Rights*, www.surjournal.org/eng/conteudos/pdf/15/04.pdf.

[32] Interim Resolution CM/ResDH(2011)293 Execution of the judgment of the European Court of Human Rights Burdov No 2 against the Russian Federation regarding failure or serious delay in abiding by final domestic judicial decisions delivered against the State and its entities as well as the absence of an effective remedy.

[33] ibid.

In response to this development, about 200 cases before the ECtHR were settled by the government, and hundreds of similar cases lodged after the pilot judgment were dismissed in view of the existence of an effective domestic remedy.[34] The Federal Law continues to be applied, and in 2013 the courts of general jurisdiction awarded compensation in about 1,500 cases for excessive length of judicial proceedings and over 50 cases of non-enforcement.[35] It might be added that the enforcement of non-pecuniary awards was not covered by this Federal Law. The need to resolve this issue has recently been illustrated by the adoption of another corresponding pilot judgment by the Court.[36]

The second pilot judgment that, under Article 46 of the Convention, obliged Russia to take steps of a general nature within a certain timeframe—*Ananyev v Russia*[37]—confirmed the existence of the well-known structural problems of overcrowding of pre-trial detention centres and insufficient legal and administrative safeguards against resulting inhuman treatment in breach of Article 3. The Court abstained from indicating specific reforms, but suggested a number of possible avenues and identified two issues that should be addressed in particular: excessive length of pre-trial detention; and further ways of combating overcrowding in prisons. In addition to the proposal to settle about 200 similar pending cases, the Russian government has drawn up a wide range of measures, including: training programmes for officials; translation and dissemination of relevant ECtHR judgments; wider access of public monitoring committees to the places of detention; proposed changes to ensure easier access for detainees' lawyers and relatives; and proposals to legislate for a minimum standard of 4 square metres per person for prison cells.[38] In December 2012 the Criminal Procedural Code was changed to the effect that persons accused of crimes carrying a sentence of less than three years (previously two) are no longer subject to pre-trial arrest. The government has also adopted technical guidelines on the use of electronic surveillance devices for those placed under house arrest.[39]

Of particular interest is the Russian Supreme Court's response to the first underlying problem of overcrowding—the length of pre-trial detention—since traditionally the Russian courts rely heavily on pre-trial detention as a measure of restraint for criminal suspects. The Supreme Court summarised its position on the use of pre-trial detention in two consecutive Plenary Resolutions adopted in October 2009 and December 2013. Both are entitled 'On the application by courts of measures of restraint: pre-trial detention, bail and house arrest'.[40] Already in 2009 the Supreme

---

[34] See *Nagovitsyn and Nalgiyev v Russia* (2011) 52 EHRR SE4.

[35] Figures published by the Judicial Department at the Russian Supreme Court, www.cdep.ru/index.php?id=79&item=1775.

[36] *Gerasimov v Russia* App nos 29920/05, 3553/06, 18876/10, 61186/10, 21176/11, 36112/11, 36426/11, 40841/11, 45381/11, 55929/11 and 60822/11 (1 July 2014).

[37] *Ananyev v Russia* (n 8).

[38] Interim Report/Action Plan for the execution of the pilot judgment of the European Court of Human Rights on applications *Ananyev v Russia*, DD(2014)580, May 2014.

[39] ibid.

[40] Plenary of the Russian Supreme Court, Resolutions no 22, 29 October 2009, and no 41, 22 December 2013. The latter repealed and replaced the former.

Court required the lower courts to take into account the individual characteristics of each suspect or accused, rather than to invoke mechanically the three 'classic' criteria: the seriousness of the charges, the risk of escape and of the obstruction of justice. In the Resolution of December 2013 it further stressed that while these criteria were a prerequisite *sine qua non* for the initial decision to place the person in detention, after a certain amount of time they would no longer suffice. It also explained, in some detail, the procedure of applying alternative preventive measures of restraint. In September 2013 the Supreme Court placed on its website a collection of translations of relevant paragraphs from the judgments of the ECtHR directed against Russia and criticising various aspects of existing judicial practice.[41] Published under the auspices of the Supreme Court, the document opens with a strongly critical passage from the judgment in *Dirdizov v Russia*, in which the ECtHR recalled its numerous previous findings about 'the fragility of the reasoning employed by the Russian courts to authorise an applicant's remaining in custody'.[42] By editing and placing this compilation on its internet portal, the Supreme Court sent a strong message to judges to apply the ECtHR's standards. Has the message been received? In 2012 the Russian courts granted 90 per cent of all requests lodged by investigators to place suspects in custody and 98 per cent of requests to extend such detention. By 2013 the figures had hardly changed: 90 per cent of initial requests were granted, as were about 95 per cent of extension requests. Overall, the total number of persons in pre-trial detention has not decreased. On a positive note, the use of house arrest as a measure of restraint in criminal proceedings keeps growing steadily (about 5,800 cases in 2013 as compared to 4,450 cases in 2012), while the use of bail remains relatively rare (fewer than 400 cases). In 2013 pre-trial arrest was applied in 133,300 instances (132,900 in 2012).[43]

In addition to the two pilot judgments, two more examples are worth mentioning. First, in view of a steady number of cases concerning extradition and expulsion of foreign nationals, mostly to Central Asian States,[44] in June 2012 the Supreme Court issued a resolution containing guidelines for courts dealing with extradition requests and appeals against decisions to extradite.[45] The Supreme Court pointed out that a request for extradition should not be granted if there are serious reasons to believe that the person might be subjected to torture or inhuman or degrading treatment in the requesting country. Extradition can also be refused if it might entail a danger to the person's life or health. Courts were reminded to look at both the individual's personal circumstances and the general situation in countries where there exists a high risk of prescribed treatment, as attested by the relevant national and international sources. As a result of this and previous resolutions of the Supreme

[41] www.vsrf.ru/search.php?page=2&searchf=%E5%E2%F0%EE%EF%E5%E9%F1%EA%E8%E9%20%F1%F3%E4.

[42] *Dirdizov v Russia* App no 41461/10, § 108 (27 November 2012).

[43] Figures published by the Judicial Department with the Russian Supreme Court, www.cdep.ru/index.php?id=79&item=1775.

[44] See eg *Garabayev v Russia* App no 38411/02 (7 June 2007); *Muminov v Russia* (2011) 52 EHRR 23; *Abdulazhon Isakov v Russia* App no 14049/08 (8 July 2010); *Savriddin Dzhurayev v Russia* (n 10).

[45] Plenary of the Russian Supreme Court, Resolution no 11 on the adjudication of cases relating to extradition of persons for criminal prosecution or execution of sentences, or transfer of convicted prisoners for the serving of sentences, 14 June 2012.

Court, the situation of applicants detained pending extradition has improved. In its latest judgments the Court has systematically found no breaches of Article 5(1) ECHR, or did so only in respect of those periods of detention preceding the said resolution.[46] In the words of the members of the European Court, '[t]he Supreme Court has accordingly demonstrated its willingness to secure the implementation of general measures in execution of Strasbourg judgments'.[47]

The situation with regard to Article 3 in such claims remains more complex. A number of recent regional courts judgments directly cite the ECtHR's position as a part of their reasoning leading to a positive evaluation of the applicants' claims in this respect.[48] In some recent cases, the ECtHR also endorsed the findings of the national authorities.[49] In others it regretted that they had failed to properly evaluate the pleas of potential ill-treatment and the insufficiency of official assurances, even if the applicant's extradition had eventually been refused for more 'technical' reasons.[50]

However, there is one extremely worrying development in this area which threatens to overshadow any positive ones: a surge in illegal renditions of persons in breach of interim measures of the Court under Rule 39 of the Rules of Court.[51] In July 2013 the Committee of Ministers expressed grave concern over another incident involving allegations of kidnapping and illegal transfer of an applicant protected by an interim measures order under Rule 39 of the Rules of Court.[52] Nine cases had been recorded by the Parliamentary Assembly of the Council of Europe (PACE) by April 2014. Unfortunately, no tangible progress has been reported in the domestic investigation into most of these cases.[53]

My final example concerns insufficient legal safeguards over police-controlled covert operations, most commonly used to combat the traffic of illegal substances, but also other crimes, such as corruption. The problem is huge—roughly, about every seventh criminal conviction in Russia concerns drug-related crime—and in

---

[46] *Ermakov v Russia* App no 43165/10, §§ 254, 274 (7 November 2013); *Akram Karimov v Russia* App no 62892/12, § 151 (28 May 2014).

[47] See Dialogue between Judges 2014, 'Implementation of the Judgments of the European Court of Human Rights: A Shared Judicial Responsibility?' Seminar background paper prepared by the Organising Committee, www.echr.coe.int/Documents/Dialogue_2014_ENG.pdf.

[48] For example, in August 2014 the Kurgan regional and Moscow regional courts quashed administrative decisions to remove Ukrainian nationals for breach of immigration rules, referring to the rights under Art 3 of the Convention, its interpretation by the European Court and Resolution no 11 (n 45), europeancourt.ru/2014/10/13/17302/#more-17302.

[49] *Oshlakov v Russia* App no 56662/09, § 89 (3 April 2014); *Latipov v Russia* App no 776/11, § 94 (12 December 2013); *Yefimova v Russia* App no 39786/09, § 199 (19 February 2013).

[50] *Zokhidov v Russia* App no 67286/10, § 129 (5 February 2013).

[51] Rule 39 of the Rules of Court provides for a possibility to apply interim measures and is often used to stay extradition/deportation/expulsion of persons claiming a potential breach of Art 2 or 3 of the Convention in the country of destination.

[52] CM/Del/Dec(2013)1176/H46-2E adopted at the 1176th meeting of the Ministers' Deputies on 10 July 2013.

[53] See PACE Resolution 1991 (2014), adopted on 10 April 2014 (17th Sitting), 'Urgent need to deal with new failures to co-operate with the European Court of Human Rights'. See also the similarly named Report of the Committee on Legal Affairs and Human Rights (rapporteur Mr Kimmo Sasi) (doc 13435) and PACE Recommendation 2043 (2014) of 10 April 2014.

order to prosecute, the police often rely on so-called 'controlled purchases', where the police employ 'cooperating witnesses' or undercover agents in order to procure illegal substances and obtain the materials for prosecution. The latest judgments of the ECtHR against Russia offer a detailed overview of the problems related to the authorisation of police-controlled operations in the first place and, second, to the evaluation of entrapment arguments by the trial courts.[54] The Court had previously found that the Russian police were virtually unaccountable for the conduct of their undercover agents and informants because of the absence of a clear and foreseeable procedure for authorising test purchases.[55] In such circumstances, the Court emphasised the courts' role in examining criminal cases where the accused alleged that he had been incited by a police agent to commit an offence. Any arguable plea of entrapment places the courts under an obligation to examine it in a manner compatible with the right to a fair hearing. The procedure to be followed must be adversarial, thorough, comprehensive and conclusive on the issue of entrapment, with the burden of proof on the prosecution to demonstrate that there was no incitement. The scope of review must include the reasons why the covert operation was mounted, the extent of police involvement in the offence, and the nature of any incitement or pressure to which the applicant was subjected.[56] The Court has found that the Russian criminal courts had capacity to effectively examine such pleas, in particular under the procedure for the exclusion of evidence.[57]

The Russian Supreme Court's position in respect of this problem is basically consistent with the ECtHR's requirements. The Plenary of the Supreme Court set out the following conditions on which the results of the test purchase can be admitted as evidence in criminal trials: (i) they must have been obtained in accordance with the law; (ii) they must demonstrate that the defendant's intention to engage in trafficking of illegal substances had developed independently of the undercover agent's acts; and (iii) they must demonstrate that the defendant had carried out all the preparatory steps necessary for the commission of the offence.[58] The lower courts are systematically called to examine each of these claims if they are raised by the defendants. In 2012 the Presidium of the Supreme Court prepared an overview of the relevant judicial practice. Addressing the courts' evaluation of the operative experiments—police controlled purchase of drugs—the Supreme Court referred directly to the standards of review established by the ECtHR. Perhaps more importantly, it also cited domestic practice where convictions had been quashed by higher courts for failure by the trial courts to properly address defendants' pleas of entrapment.[59] The Supreme Court also quashes such sentences, both as a measure of execution of

---

[54] See *Veselov v Russia* nos 23200/10, 24009/07 and 556/10 (2 October 2012); *Lagutin v Russia* nos 6228/09, 19123/09, 19678/07, 52340/08 and 7451/09 (24 April 2014).

[55] *Vanyan v Russia* App no 53203/99, §§ 46 and 47 (15 December 2005); *Khudobin v Russia* (2009) 48 EHRR 22; *Bannikova v Russia* App no 18757/06, §§ 49–50 (4 November 2010); *Veselov* (n 54) §§ 106, 126–27.

[56] *Ramanauskas v Lithuania* (2010) 51 EHRR 11 (GC).

[57] *Khudobin* (n 55) §§ 133–35.

[58] Plenary of the Supreme Court, Resolution no 14 on jurisprudence in criminal cases involving narcotic drugs or psychotropic, strong or toxic substances, 15 June 2006.

[59] Presidium of the Russian Supreme Court, Overview of Jurisprudence in Criminal Cases Involving Narcotic Drugs or Psychotropic, Strong or Toxic Substances, 27 June 2012, p 7.

the ECtHR's judgments and on appeal, straining to bring the practice of the lower courts to a more acceptable standard.[60] Unfortunately, in the absence of a proper system of authorisation of undercover police operations and in view of the large number of such cases, the scope for judicial correction remains wide.[61]

IV. CONCLUSION

When describing the relationship between the ECtHR and Russia it would certainly be wrong to mention only those areas where progress has been palpable. In many respects, the responses of the national authorities remain manifestly insufficient considering the gravity and scale of violations found by the Court. The largest gap is the absence of investigations into grave human rights violations in the North Caucasus, principally Chechnya, which concerns issues such as the disproportionate use of force and enforced disappearances. Other major problems include ill-treatment of suspects and detainees by the police, suffering of persons with serious health problems in detention, various aspects of criminal fairness, restrictions on the right to freedom of assembly and freedom of religion—the list could be continued. Even where the heaviest burden of tackling these problems does not lie with the courts, they certainly bear a varying share of responsibility for the failures to find an adequate response to victims' claims at the national level.

Nevertheless, one can reasonably conclude that the efforts made by the highest judicial authorities, including the Supreme Court and the Constitutional Court, have resulted in a set of instruments which should allow the Russian judiciary to follow the ECtHR's approach in much of their work. Whether and to what extent they do so depends on the nature of the problems; social and economic matters appear easier to solve than those concerning political rights. Undoubtedly, the national courts are also benefiting from participating in the Convention system, because, among other things, international supervision results in greater respect on the part of the traditionally powerful executive branch of the Russian State towards its own judiciary. Judges are becoming aware of the ECtHR's standards, and the new generation of lawyers feel confident about relying on ECHR case law in domestic proceedings. This gives hope that the bridge from words to actions can be successfully crossed.

---

[60] See eg DH-DD(2014)485E, *Communication from the Russian Federation concerning the case of Veselov against Russian Federation*, App no 23200/10 (10 April 2014) p 2 concerning the quashing of convictions of the three applicants in this case. See also decision no 46-D13-23, 5 November 2013, by which the Supreme Court, acting in supervisory capacity quashed a person's conviction and closed criminal proceedings because of the trial courts' failure to properly take into account the accused's plea of entrapment. See www.vsrf.ru/stor_pdf.php?id=564798.

[61] In the judgment in *Lagutin* (n 54), Judge Pinto de Albuquerque, joined by the Russian Judge Dedov, argued in a Separate Opinion that the Court should have given proper guidance to the Russian authorities on amending legislation governing undercover police operations, in order to introduce proper safeguards for the planning and carrying out of such operations, in addition to the assessment of evidence during trial.

It is clear, however, that this can happen only if the mechanism of human rights protection in Europe, as it stands today, remains solid and credible and is backed up by the joint political will of the countries sharing a common 'belief in those fundamental freedoms which are the foundation of justice and peace in the world'. I fully share the concerns expressed by many authoritative figures of the risk of 'contagion' of the negative attitude, or even defiance, towards this system that can sometimes be witnessed today in the UK.[62] As rightly noted by the leading UK experts in the field, the public demonstration of such extremely negative attitudes remains quite unprecedented elsewhere in Europe.[63] In Russia, not many examples of such public defiance can be found: in the recent statement issued in relation to the ECtHR's record-setting award of almost two billion euros in the *Yukos* case,[64] the Ministry of Justice—the only official body to issue a public statement—dryly doubted the 'fairness of the Court's finding' and expressed its intention to seek review in the Grand Chamber.[65]

An interesting 2012 study compared Russia's and UK's responses to the implementation of ECtHR judgments.[66] The two countries remain very different in terms of the nature of cases brought against them. They are also quite far apart on a comparative scale of the strength of democratic institutions and the general legal climate, including the culture of implementation of international tribunals' rulings. The author of the study suggested that despite these differences, two factors were nevertheless critical for compliance: robust domestic institutions with the capacity and willingness to implement the Court's rulings, and the place of ECtHR jurisprudence within a larger culture of rights. And while Russia's compliance has been described as 'half-hearted' and 'a la carte',[67] only domestic institutions can change this situation for the better, with guidance and support from international bodies.

The judiciary is the most natural ally in this process, and, as I have tried to demonstrate in this chapter, judges have already shown themselves willing to accept responsibility for the protection of rights wherever possible. Unfortunately, the Russian democratic institutions remain weak, and the culture of rights is not so deeply rooted in a society traditionally dominated by the authoritative State. The UK, on the other hand, is one of the founding members of the Council of Europe and seen worldwide as a champion of human rights. Its strong domestic institutions committed to safeguarding and protecting rights and freedoms have long served

---

[62] See P Leach and A Donald, 'Hostility to the European Court and the Risks of Contagion' UK Human Rights Blog (21 November 2013), ukhumanrightsblog.com/2013/11/21/hostility-to-the-european-court-and-the-risks-of-contagion-philip-leach-and-alice-donald/.

[63] See D Harris, M O'Boyle, E Bates and C Buckley, 'UK Withdrawal from the Convention? A Broader View' UK Constitutional Law Blog (24 July 2014), ukconstitutionallaw.org/2014/07/24/david-harris-michael-oboyle-ed-bates-and-carla-buckley-uk-withdrawal-from-the-convention-a-broader-view/.

[64] *OAO Neftyanaya Kompaniya Yukos v Russia* (just satisfaction) (2014) 59 EHRR SE12.

[65] See the Ministry's press release of 31 July 2014, minjust.ru/ru/press/news/o-postanovlenii-evropey-skogo-suda-po-pravam-cheloveka-po-delu-oao-nk-yukos-protiv-rossii.

[66] See C Hillebrecht, 'Implementing International Human Rights Law at Home: Domestic Politics and the European Court of Human Rights' (2012) 13 *Human Rights Review* 279.

[67] ibid.

as examples to others. The echo of the findings of the UK mechanisms ensuring implementation, such as the Joint Committee on Human Rights and the application by the judiciary of the Human Rights Act, continues to resonate well beyond its borders.

Whatever short-term aims may be pursued by the politicians today, the shared responsibility for the survival and success of the existing Convention system has to be borne in mind if we want to use it tomorrow as a tool to achieve common goals. Its demise would not make our continent a better place.

21

The Russian Federation and the Strasbourg Court: The Illegitimacy of Sovereignty?

BILL BOWRING

I. INTRODUCTION

THIS CHAPTER CONCERNS what could have been, but turned out not to be, the Russian *Hirst*: the case of *Konstantin Markin v Russia*.[1] The 2010 Chamber judgment against Russia caused a storm of protest, especially in the Constitutional Court of the Russian Federation (CCRF), which had been subjected to severe criticism by Strasbourg. The Chairman of the CCRF, Judge Valery Zorkin, responded to the judgment with a plethora of references to Russia's sovereignty and threats to it. But in a classic case of a 'meaningful dialogue'[2] with the CCRF, the Grand Chamber, while finding against Russia, refrained from criticising the CCRF, to which the case returned. Instead of the expected confrontation, the CCRF produced a judgment of pragmatism, following the example, in part, of the German Constitutional Court.

In order to explore these issues, I first point to remarkable parallels in the histories, imperial and legal, of the UK, including England and Scotland, and Russia. Second, I examine the paradoxical, if not hypocritical, approach of the USSR to international human rights—an approach that underlies the complexities of Russia's present-day legal culture. Third, I analyse the history and role of the CCRF, as one of the protagonists in this story. Fourth, I discuss the surprising complexities surrounding Russia's accession to the Council of Europe, and its ratification of the European Convention on Human Rights (ECHR). Fifth, I explain what is meant by 'sovereignty' in today's Russia, and why it weighs so heavily on the mind of Judge Zorkin. Sixth, I come to the fascinating history of the *Markin* case and the 'judicial conversation' between Strasbourg and St Petersburg. I conclude by borrowing the

---

[1] *Konstantin Markin v Russia*, no 30078/06, Chamber (First Section) Judgment of 7 October 2010; Grand Chamber Judgment of 22 March 2012, 56 EHRR 8.

[2] This concept is put forward by Lady Hale in her lecture 'What's the Point of Human Rights?' (28 November 2013), www.supremecourt.uk/docs/speech-131128.pdf.

analysis of a brilliant young Russian colleague, Grigory Vaipan.[3] He notes that commentators feel a sense of relief that the CCRF has refrained from asserting Russian 'national sovereignty' or its own 'monopoly of interpretation' as against the European Court of Human Rights (ECtHR). However, in his view there is no guarantee that the CCRF will not in future cases seek to assert itself through the back door rather than through a direct confrontation.

II. RUSSIA AND BRITAIN—A SHARED HISTORY

Russia and Britain have more in common than might at first glance appear to be the case. Both became the centres of great empires—maritime in the case of Britain and continental in the case of Russia. Both of these empires had their origins in the sixteenth century. Britain's empire started with the possessions of England under Elizabeth I (1533–1603), in whose reign Spain was defeated with the destruction of the Spanish armada in 1588, and the basis was laid for American colonies: the 'First British Empire'. Russia, as Moscow, began to expand under Ivan IV 'Grozniy' (1530–84), crushing Boyar resistance and conquering the Khanates of Kazan in 1552 and Astrakhan in 1556. Relations between Moscow and England began in 1553, with correspondence and even a marriage proposal from Ivan.[4] A letter has been discovered in which Ivan reacted in strong terms to what he saw as a rejection by Elizabeth.[5] But diplomatic relations have continued ever since.

The British and Russian Empires saw their greatest expansion in the eighteenth century. Britain defeated France in the Seven Years War (1754–63) and, despite losing the American War of Independence and the North American colonies, won Canada and pursued the start of her Empire in India. Russia under Catherine II (1729–96), assisted by Prince Potemkin, moved decisively into Asia and seized Crimea in 1783. Russia became a multi-national empire with a large Muslim population, and Catherine created the world's first State Islamic structure.[6] The foundations of the academic discipline of law in Russia were laid by Semyon Yefimovich Desnitsky, who was sent by the Russian government to study for six years (1761–67) at the University of Glasgow, where he was awarded a doctorate in civil law, and attended Adam Smith's lectures on constitutional law. He was the first professor of law to teach in Russian, translated Blackstone's *Commentaries on the Laws of England* into Russian, and wrote the first legal textbooks. The introduction of jury trial and justices of the peace in the Russian Empire in 1864 were in part a consequence of Desnitsky's work.[7]

---

[3] Grigory Vaipan, 'Acquiescence Affirmed, its Limits Left Undefined: Russian Constitutional Court has Ruled on its Relationship with European Court of Human Rights' [2013] *Cambridge Journal of International and Comparative Law*, cjicl.org.uk/2013/12/26/acquiescence-affirmed/.

[4] I Lubimenko, 'The Correspondence of Queen Elizabeth with the Russian Czars' (1914) 19(3) *American Historical Review* 525.

[5] J Vincent, 'Ivan the Terribly Rude' *The Telegraph* (London, 2 January 2004), www.telegraph.co.uk/news/worldnews/europe/russia/1450732/Ivan-the-terribly-rude.html.

[6] AW Fisher, 'Enlightened Despotism and Islam Under Catherine II' (1968) 27(4) *Slavic Review* 542.

[7] See B Bowring, *Law, Rights and Ideology in Russia: Landmarks in the Destiny of a Great Power* (Oxford, Routledge, 2013) 21–32.

Britain and Russia were on the same side in the war against Napoleon, and fought on the same side in World Wars I and II. There was remarkably little conflict between the great maritime and continental empires from the sixteenth to the twentieth centuries, with the exception of the Crimean War (1853–56).

My students can never give an answer when I ask them what the Crimean War was about. Russians may have read Lev Tolstoy's patriotic *Sevastopol Sketches* (1855), which tell the reader nothing about the *casus belli*. British students may have heard of the 'Charge of the Light Brigade', the heroically quixotic British cavalry attack on Russian guns, immortalised by the Poet Laureate, Alfred Lord Tennyson, and of the nurse Florence Nightingale who revolutionised the care of wounded British soldiers. And the English language gained the phrase 'balaclava helmets'.[8]

Russia's devastating defeat in the Crimean War precipitated action by the new Tsar, Aleksandr II (1855–81). Aleksandr, who was no liberal or reformist by nature, brought about the abolition of serfdom in 1861, several years before the US abolition of slavery, as well as the Great Reforms of 1864, which introduced jury trial, a fighting Bar and independent judges to the Russian Empire.[9]

In the twentieth century both Britain and Russia suffered the trauma of the loss of empire, a process that has not yet run its course. Britain's continued occupation of the Falkland Islands, Gibraltar and the Chagos Islands (Diego Garcia) in the British Indian Ocean Territory, a colony created in 1965, are all hugely controversial. Russia's latest incidents were the war with Georgia in 2008[10] and the illegal annexation of Crimea in 2014.

Both countries suffer existential crises, and agonise over what each stands for— what are their missions—without empire. Hence Britain's unwillingness to accept the status of member of the EU and the judgments of the Strasbourg Court, and the tensions between Moscow and Strasbourg which are the subject-matter of this chapter. Neither Britain nor Russia is able to reconcile itself to the status of ordinary, albeit powerful, members of the 47-State Council of Europe.

III. THE SOVIET UNION AND HUMAN RIGHTS

What was the USSR's attitude to contemporary human rights?[11] The short answer is that the USSR, having abstained from the vote on the Universal Declaration of Human Rights in 1948, ratified almost all UN human rights treaties, but, in accordance with the twin pillars of the Soviet approach to international law—state

---

[8] These were hand-knitted and sent to British troops in Crimea to protect them from extreme cold, in the absence of official equipment. The name derives from the battle of Balaclava (a small town near Sevastopol) on 25 October 1854.

[9] See Bowring (n 7) 33–47.

[10] B Bowring, 'Georgia, Russia and the Crisis of the Council of Europe: Inter-State Applications, Individual Complaints, and the Future of the Strasbourg Model of Human Rights Litigation' in J Green and C Waters (eds), *Conflict in the Caucasus: Implications for International Legal Order* (London, Palgrave Macmillan, 2010).

[11] See B Bowring, 'Human Rights in Russia: A Discourse of Emancipation or Just Another Mirage?' in I Pogany (ed), *Human Rights in Eastern Europe* (Cheltenham, Edward Elgar, 1995), from which much of the material in this section is drawn.

sovereignty and non-interference in internal affairs—the reality was quite different, as I show in this section. There was never any intention that the content of these treaties would be implemented within the USSR. For example, in 1974 Sergei Kovalyov was convicted of 'anti-Soviet agitation and propaganda' and served seven years in labour camps in the Perm region and Chistopol prison, and later three years in internal exile at Kolyma. His crime was his attempt to establish the first branch of Amnesty International in the USSR. He had been a member of the small group of activists who in 1969 created the Action Group for the Defence of Human Rights in the USSR. He was released in 1984, and later became the first Human Rights Ombudsman under President Yeltsin.[12]

The first Constitution of the USSR was adopted on 31 January 1924, and regulated relations between the 'union republics'.[13] A new Soviet Constitution with, for the first time, a chapter on human rights was unanimously approved on 5 December 1933. In September 1934 the USSR joined the League of Nations, and was elected a permanent member of the League's Council. According to Andrey Vyshinsky, notorious as prosecutor of the Moscow show trials, the 1936 (Stalin) Constitution reflected the following changes:

> The complete triumph of the socialist system in all branches of the national economy, the fundamental realisation of socialism, the liquidation of the exploiter classes, the annihilation of man's exploitation by man … all these factors evoked the necessity of changing the Constitution of the USSR so that the new Constitution should reflect all the changes … since 1924.[14]

Nikolai Bukharin, one of the most sophisticated and intellectually attractive members of the Bolshevik leadership, was a member of the drafting Commission of the 1936 Constitution, and later boasted that he had written the document from the first word to the last. He was reported as saying that the new Constitution was a document 'which would make it impossible for the people any longer to be pushed aside'.[15]

The Stalin Constitution[16] contained Chapter X, 'Fundamental Rights and Duties of Citizens'. Naturally the first right guaranteed was the right to work (Article 118): 'Citizens of the U.S.S.R. have the right to work, that is, are guaranteed the right to employment and payment for their work in accordance with its quantity and quality.' This was followed by other social and economic rights: rest and leisure (Article 119); old age pensions and social security (Article 120); education free of charge (Article 121); equal rights for women (Article 122); non-discrimination (Article 123); and freedom of conscience and religious belief (Article 124).

---

[12] See B Bowring, 'Sergei Kovalyov: The First Russian Human Rights Ombudsman—and the Last?' in R Mullerson, M Fitzmaurice and M Andenas (eds), *Constitutional Reform and International Law in Central and Eastern Europe* (Dordrecht, Kluwer Law International, 1998) 235–56.

[13] See http://constitution.garant.ru/science-work/modern/4096920/.

[14] A Vyshinsky, *The Law of the Soviet State* (New York, Macmillan, 1948) 120.

[15] L Kochan and R Abraham, *The Making of Modern Russia*, 2nd edn (Harmondsworth, Penguin, 1990) 377.

[16] English translation at www.departments.bucknell.edu/russian/const/1936toc.html.

Freedom of speech, freedom of the press, freedom of assembly and freedom of demonstrations were all guaranteed in the following highly qualified form: 'In conformity with the interests of the working people, and in order to strengthen the socialist system' (Article 125). Freedom of association and self-organisation were similarly qualified: 'In conformity with the interests of the working people, and in order to develop the organizational initiative and political activity of the masses of the people' (Article 126).

The Constitution gave guarantees without qualification of freedom from arbitrary arrest (Article 127), and inviolability of the home and secrecy of correspondence (Article 128)—two rights which were violated every day during Stalin's repression. Bukharin believed sincerely that the Constitution would be respected, and convinced himself that a genuine relaxation of repression would take place.[17] But the last months of 1936 were only a lull in the Great Purge of 1934–38, in which at least 10 to 15 million people died. The rights enshrined in the new Constitution were unenforceable: there were no remedies. Vyshinsky was not at all embarrassed by this: Proletarian declarations of rights frankly manifest their class essence, reflecting nothing of the desire of bourgeois declarations to shake off and mask the class character of the rights they proclaim.[18] Bukharin was tried in the Trial of the Twenty-One in March 1938, and was executed on the 15th of that month.

The USSR was a founder member of the United Nations, and is a permanent member of the Security Council. The very same Vyshinsky became Foreign Minister of the USSR in March 1949,[19] having attended the Third Session of the UN General Assembly at the end of 1948. In March 1953, following Stalin's death, he was appointed as the USSR's permanent delegate to the United Nations. That was the session in which, on 10 December 1948, the Universal Declaration of Human Rights was adopted. Forty-eight States voted in favour of the Declaration, while eight, including the USSR, abstained.

In the introduction to a collection of Russian translations of major human rights instruments published in the last year of the USSR, Lev Shestakov[20] asked why the USSR abstained. He gave three reasons,[21] which were also the reasons Vyshinsky gave. First, in the opinion of the Soviet delegation, the draft Declaration had limited itself to fixing only formal rights, and did not contain measures for the material and legislative guaranteeing of those rights. Second, the draft failed to enshrine the right of peoples to self-determination, on which the USSR had insisted, as a principled question. Third, Articles 19 and 20 (freedom of expression and freedom

---

[17] R Conquest, *The Great Terror* (Harmondsworth, Penguin, 1971) 134.

[18] Vyshinsky (n 14) 554.

[19] A Vaksberg, The Prosecutor and the Prey: Vyshinsky and the 1930s Moscow Show Trials (London, Weidenfeld, 1990) 279.

[20] 26 March 1937—31 May 2009, Head of the Department of International Law at Moscow State University until his death. I met him in 1993, with Grigoriy Tunkin (30 September 1906—23 August 1993).

[21] L Shestakov, *Prava Cheloveka: sbornik universalnikh i regionalnikh mezhdunarodnikh dokumentov* (Human rights: collection of universal and regional international documents) (Moscow, Moscow University Press, 1990) 6–7.

of association) had been drafted in such a way as to permit fascist propaganda; the USSR wished to include in Article 19 the words 'the inalienable right of every human being is ... the fight against fascism in the field of ideology, politics, state and social life'.

Despite this abstention, the USSR later ratified every one of the UN human rights treaties. As I have already indicated, the principle of non-interference in internal affairs meant that these treaties would have no effect within the USSR. And the Brezhnev Constitution of 1977 followed the same model as the 1936 Constitution in Chapter 7, entitled 'The Basic Rights, Freedoms and Obligations of Citizens of the USSR'.

There were dramatic changes in the last years of the USSR. On 11 March 1985 the Politburo of the Communist Party of the Soviet Union elected Mikhail Gorbachev General Secretary. He was 54 years old. At the 27th Congress of the CPSU in February 1986 he announced new policies of *glasnost* ('openness'), *perestroika* ('restructuring'), *demokratizatsiya* ('democratisation'), and *uskoreniye* ('acceleration' of economic development). In place of Marxism-Leninism, there was a turn to 'common human values'.[22] Watching TV in Krasnodar in the summer of 1986, I saw Gorbachev addressing a conference of party officials in Khabarovsk, in the far east of Russia, declaring: 'Comrades, there will be a revolution!' They looked aghast.

Decisive steps were taken towards a greater respect for international law. On 10 February 1989 the Presidium of the Supreme Soviet passed a decree recognising the compulsory jurisdiction of the UN's International Court of Justice with respect to six human rights treaties, including the 1948 Genocide Convention and the 1984 Convention against Torture.[23] This decree reversed the reservation entered by the USSR when ratifying the Genocide Convention, refusing the compulsory jurisdiction of the International Court of Justice (ICJ), which led to one of the most important early advisory opinions of the ICJ—the *Reservations to the Convention on the Prevention and Punishment of the Crime of Genocide* Opinion of 28 May 1951.[24] Schweisfurth commented that 'this move marked a positive shift in the previously negative attitude of the Soviet Union towards the Principal judicial organ of the United Nations'.[25]

He saw, rightly I think, these developments as exemplifying a farewell to the strict, traditional, positivistic approach to human rights.[26]

---

[22] M Gorbachev, '*Perestroika i novoye mishleniye dlya nashei strany i dlya vsevo mira* (Perestroika and new thinking for our country and the whole world) (Moscow, Politizdat, 1987).

[23] Reported in (1989) 4 *Interights Bulletin* 3. The other treaties were: the 1949 Convention for the Suppression of Traffic in Persons; the 1952 Convention on the Political Rights of Women; the 1965 Convention on the Elimination of Racial Discrimination; and the 1979 Convention on the Elimination of Discrimination against Women.

[24] www.icj-cij.org/docket/files/12/4283.pdf.

[25] T Schweisfurth, 'The Acceptance by the Soviet Union of the Compulsory Jurisdiction of the ICJ for Six Human Rights Conventions' (1990) 2 *European Journal of International Law* 110, 111.

[26] See B Bowring, 'Positivism versus Self-Determination: The Contradictions of Soviet International Law' in S Marks (ed), *International Law on the Left: Re-Examining Marxist Legacies* (Cambridge, Cambridge University Press, 2008).

Further significant steps taken before the collapse of the USSR included the publication of a strategy document, *The Conception of Judicial Reform*, published on 24 October 1991 (after several years' work) by Sergei Pashin,[27] Sergei Vitsin,[28] Tamara Morshchakova[29] and others, and the enactment on 22 November 1991 of the Declaration of the Rights and Freedoms of the Person and Citizen by the Supreme Soviet of the Russian Soviet Federative Socialist Republic (RSFSR).

On 8 December 1991, Russian president Boris Yeltsin, Ukrainian president Leonid Kravchuk and Belarusian parliament chairman Stanislau Shushkevich signed the Belavezha Accords which declared the Soviet Union effectively dissolved and established the Commonwealth of Independent States (CIS) in its place.

IV. THE CONSTITUTIONAL COURT OF THE RUSSIAN FEDERATION

The collapse of the USSR was preceded by another momentous event—the creation of a constitutional court for Russia. The Law of the RSFSR on the Constitutional Court of the RSFSR, drafted by Sergei Pashin, was signed by President Yeltsin on 12 July 1991.[30] Pashin was only 29 years of age.

Thirteen justices were elected by the Congress of People's Deputies of the RSFSR on 30 October 1991. The justices elected Valery Zorkin (b 1943) as their chairman. Zorkin has proved to be a great survivor: on 10 February 2012 the then president Medvedev appointed Zorkin to a further six-year term.[31] Zorkin was chairman of the court from 1991 to 1993, and again from 2003–06 and 2006–09. Justices Gadis Gadzhiev (b 1953) and Yuriy Rudkin (b 1951) are also still members of the court. Tamara Morshchakova (b 1936), a leading proponent of human rights, was vice-chairman of the court from 1995 to 2002, but was forced to retire upon reaching the age of 65 in 2001. She remains one of the most critical commentators on the Russian constitution and court, and trenchant critics of the Putin regime.

The Constitutional Court started work in January 1992. Pashin commented that the Law represented 'an important guarantee of the right of the citizen to

---

[27] He was born in 1962 and was from 1990 to 1996 the leading expert on judicial reform in the legal department of the President's Administration, and introduced the first experiment in jury trial in nine regions of Russia in 1993. Following his fall from grace and dismissal, he was twice (being once dismissed and reinstated) dismissed, and is now a leading scholar and critic of Russian constitutionalism and the Constitutional Court.

[28] Born in 1929, for many years Professor and General of Police at the Moscow University of the Ministry of the Interior; one of the most respected reformers in Russia.

[29] Born 28 March 1936. From 1958 to 1991 she was a senior legal researcher and professor. She was elected a Justice of the Constitutional Court on 29 October 1991, and from February 1995 to April 2002 she was Deputy Chairman of the Court. An amendment to the Law on the Constitutional Court enacted in January 2001 forced her to retire by reason of age. Many consider that this was a deliberate ploy to remove her, in view of her independent and principled stance.

[30] For a complete history see A Trochev, Judging Russia: Constitutional Court in Russian Politics, 1990–2006 (Cambridge, Cambridge University Press, 2008); see also J Henderson, The Constitution of the Russian Federation: A Contextual Analysis (Oxford, Hart Publishing, 2011).

[31] W Partlett, 'Valery Zorkin's State and Revolution' *Brookings* (13 February 2012), www.brookings.edu/opinions/2012/0213_russia_zorkin_partlett.aspx.

judicial protection'.[32] He wrote that the provisions of the new law were based on Chapter 4, Article 93 of the German Constitution, which provides that the Federal Constitutional Court considers cases 'by way of petition on constitutionality, which may be laid by any person considering that one of his basic rights has been infringed by state power'. Article 32 of the Constitution of the RSFSR, as amended in April 1992, stated that universally accepted human rights norms take precedence over the laws of the RSFSR, and have direct effect.

From 6 July 1992 to 30 November 1992 the Court was occupied by the *Case of the Communist Party*,[33] which did not produce the hoped-for (by the applicants) definitive condemnation of the Communist Party, a Russian Nuremberg. Instead, in a compromise decision, the Court ruled that President Yeltsin had rightly dissolved the highest bodies of the Party, but also ruled that the Party could continue to exist at the local level.[34] The Communist Party of the Russian Federation is to this day the only significant opposition party organised in every region of Russia.

In its work during 1992 and 1993 the Court focused on social and economic rights. In the *Age Discrimination Case* (4 February 1992)[35] it set aside the dismissal of two workers for having reached pensionable age, and ordered an amendment to the Labour Code. It applied not only the Declaration of Rights and Freedoms (not by then incorporated into the Constitution), but also the UN's 1966 International Covenant on Economic, Social and Cultural Rights and a range of International Labour Organization conventions ratified by the USSR. In *Time Limits for Challenging Unfair Dismissal*, a number of workers filed petitions complaining of the unconstitutionality of amended legislation providing for two-year time limits. The Court held, on 23 June 1992,[36] that the amendments violated five norms of international law and 14 articles of the Constitution.

The Court sat all night following President Yeltsin's decree of 21 September 1993 which tore up the 1978 Constitution and disbanded Parliament, and held, having decided of their own motion to sit and adjudicate, that his actions violated the Constitution. Yeltsin shelled the White House, the seat of the Parliament, and on 6 October 1993 suspended the Court itself. The Court did not sit again until February 1995. To Yeltsin's credit, Valery Zorkin and his colleagues continued to sit in the reconstituted court, but the number of judges was increased from 13 to 19.

---

[32] S Pashin, *Konstitutsionnii sud Rossii: obrashchatsya mogut vsye* (The Constitutional Court of Russia: all may apply) *Sovetskaya Iustitsiya* (2 January 1992).

[33] See J Henderson, 'The Russian Constitutional Court and the Communist Party Case: Watershed or Whitewash?' (2007) 40(1) *Communist and Post-Communist Studies* 1.

[34] Постановление Конституционного Суда Российской Федерации от 30 ноября 1992 г. № 9-П «По делу о проверке конституционности Указов Президента Российской Федерации от 23 августа 1991 г. № 79 «О приостановлении деятельности коммунистической партии РСФСР», от 25 августа 1991 г. № 90 «Об имуществе КПСС и коммунистической партии РСФСР» и от 6 ноября 1991 г. № 169 «О деятельности КПСС и КП РСФСР», а также о проверке конституционности КПСС и КП РСФСР» (Order of the CCRF of 30 November 1992 No. 9-P 'The case of the constitutionality of the Decrees of the President of 23 August 1991 No.79 'On cessation of the activity of the Communist Party of the RSFSR' and other decrees).

[35] Vedomosti Verkhovnovo Soveta RSFSR No 13, Art 669.

[36] ibid, Art 1809.

An initial test of the renewed Constitutional Court was presented by the First Chechen War. On 31 July 1995, the Constitutional Court of the Russian Federation delivered its judgment on the constitutionality of President Yeltsin's decrees sending federal forces into Chechnya.[37] The Court was obliged in particular to consider the consequences of Russia's participation in the 1977 Additional Protocol II to the 1949 Geneva Conventions.[38] As Gaeta pointed out:

> The Court determined that at the international level the provisions of Protocol II were binding on both parties to the armed conflict and that the actions of the Russian armed forces in the conduct of the Chechen conflict violated Russia's international obligations under Additional Protocol II to the 1949 Geneva Conventions. Nonetheless, the Court sought to excuse this non-compliance because Protocol II had not been incorporated into the Russian legal system.[39]

Despite the order of the Court, incorporation has still not taken place. And Chechnya was de facto independent for two years from 1997 to 1999, having defeated the federal forces, although it was not recognised by any State.

V. ACCESSION TO THE COUNCIL OF EUROPE[40]

Russia applied to join the Council of Europe on 7 May 1992, at a time when, as noted above, there were a number of progressive developments, both legislative and in the work of the Constitutional Court. Russia was allowed to become a full member of the Council of Europe on 28 February 1996, despite the fact that it was by then engaged in bitter internal armed conflict in Chechnya. The Council now has 47 Member States, including nine of the former 'Union Republics' of the USSR.[41] The process has been completed whereby the Council of Europe, which began life in 1949 as (in the words of Ian Brownlie and Guy Goodwin-Gill) 'a sort of social and ideological counterpart to the military aspects of European co-operation represented in the North Atlantic Treaty Organisation ... inspired partly by interests in promotion of European unity and partly by the political desire for solidarity in the face of the ideology of Communism',[42] now includes almost all of the formerly 'communist' States. This is an extraordinary 'irony of destiny', to poach the title of the ever-popular Soviet film *Ironiya sudby, ili s lyogkim parom!* (1975).

---

[37] An unofficial English translation of this judgment was published by the European Commission for Democracy through Law (Venice Commission) of the Council of Europe, CDL-INF (96) 1.

[38] The Russian Federation is a party to the 1949 Geneva Conventions. The Soviet Union ratified both of the 1977 Additional Protocols on 29 September 1989 to become effective on 29 March 1990. The Russian Federation deposited a notification of continuation on 13 January 1992.

[39] P Gaeta, 'The Armed Conflict in Chechnya before the Russian Constitutional Court' (1996) 7(4) *European Journal of International Law* 563, 568.

[40] See B Bowring, 'Russia's Accession to the Council of Europe and Human Rights: Compliance or Cross-Purposes?' (1997) 6 *European Human Rights Law Review* 628. This has been translated into Russian, and appears in (1998) 10 *Rossiiskii Byulleten po Prava Cheloveka* (Russian Bulletin on Human Rights) 12. The material presented in this section is drawn from these publications.

[41] Armenia, Azerbaijan, Estonia, Georgia, Latvia, Lithuania, Moldova, Russia, Ukraine.

[42] I Brownlie and G Goodwin-Gill, *Brownlie's Documents on Human Rights*, 6th edn (Oxford, Oxford University Press, 2010).

On 21 February 1996, the Russian State Duma approved membership of the Council of Europe by 204 votes to 18, by adopting the Federal Law 'On the Russian Federation joining the Council of Europe'. First Deputy Foreign Minister Igor Ivanov told the Duma that joining the Council was in Russia's national interest. He added that membership would permit Russia to better defend the interests of ethnic Russians living abroad, particularly in the Baltic republics. The Chair of the Duma's International Affairs Committee, Vladimir Lukin, assured deputies that the benefits of Council membership would more than justify the $25 million a year dues that Russia must pay. The upper house, the Federation Council, unanimously approved the Duma's two bills on the subject and they were signed by the President on 23 February 1996.

The debate that took place in the State Duma[43] showed that most members understood the many 'obligations' to which Russian committed itself upon joining the Council of Europe not to be obligations at all, but simply recommendations, a number of which were to be taken as provocative attempts to keep Russia out of the Council of Europe, and which could be adopted or discarded at will. It is not surprising, then, that the veteran human rights campaigner Sergei Kovalyov had already on 26 January 1996 expressed deep ambivalence about membership, saying, 'I fear the Council does not realise the responsibility it bears ...'.[44]

The scholar SA Glotov, himself a Deputy of the State Duma and member of the 'Narodovlastiye' (People's Power) faction, gave the following reasons why the Council of Europe should wish to have Russia as a member,[45] on the basis, of course, that Russia had fulfilled most of the demands of the Council of Europe, namely: the holding of new elections to Parliament; the abolition of the Congress of People's Deputies of the RSFSR; and the promulgation of an extensive report on the state of law and order and perspectives for improving it. First, the acceptance of Russia gave the Council of Europe a 'second wind', as well as the opportunity to encourage the spread of Western European values and norms in this country of millions of people. Second, European security was likely to be better safeguarded. Third, Russia's accession significantly strengthened a more united Europe in its rivalry with the United States and Japan. Fourth, the Council of Europe was able to give further support to Russia's 'reformers', which in Glotov's view serves the interests of major Western financial companies and political groups. Fifth, failure to accept Russia could tend to support the growth of terrorism in Russia.

Why should Russia wish to join the Council of Europe? First, because Russia would have a sound international tribune from which to express its interests and help form public opinion. In particular, this tribune could be used for the protection of the Russian-speaking populations in the Baltic States (Estonia, Latvia and Lithuania), and for the purpose of expressing Russia's negative attitude towards the expansion of NATO. Second, joining would help with the establishment of legal and social reform. Third, Russia's joining the Council of Europe would permit

---

[43] These debates are set out in detail in SA Glotov, *Pravo Soveta Yevropi i Rossii* (The Law of the Council of Europe and Russia) (Krasnodar, Yug, 1996).
[44] S Parish, *OMRI Daily Digest* (26 January 1996).
[45] Glotov (n 43) 11.

the organisation of international humanitarian cooperation. Fourth, although this appears paradoxical, the Council of Europe would provide an arena for promoting integration between Russia and States of the former USSR. Fifth, membership of the Council of Europe would permit direct cooperation (within the Congress of Local and Regional Authorities) between regions of other Member States and the republics, *krais* and *oblasts* of the CIS. Sixth, the long experience of European States in the political struggle of various parties and groups supplies the basis for norms which guarantee the functioning of the opposition, and the handing over of power.[46]

At a ceremony held in Strasbourg on 28 February 1996 to mark Russia's entry into the Council of Europe, the Russian Foreign Minister, Yevgeniy Primakov, handed over the documents affirming Russia's adherence to the Council's Charter. He also signed the European Convention on Human Rights, the European Convention Against Torture, the European Charter on Local Self-Government and the Framework Convention on Protection of National Minorities. He did this pursuant to the obligations placed upon Russia in Parliamentary Assembly Opinion 193 (1996) of 25 January 1996,[47] confirmed in Committee of Ministers Resolution No 96/2.

Point 7 of the Opinion set out a number of respects in which Russia was already seeking to conform with the fundamental principles of the Council of Europe (more precisely, as set out in Article 3):

> Every Member of the Council of Europe must accept the principles of the rule of law and the enjoyment by all persons within its jurisdiction of human rights and fundamental freedoms, and collaborate sincerely and effectively in the realisation of the aim of the Council.

Russia's compliance in the first year after accession was far from complete. The death penalty is a prime example. The Council of Europe's Committee on Legal Affairs and Human Rights received official confirmation that in the first half year of 1996, at least 53 executions were carried out in Russia, in flagrant violation of the commitment entered into by the country upon accession to the Council to put into place an immediate moratorium on executions.[48] Despite the fact that the Clemency Commission regularly recommends clemency, Amnesty International received information that President Yeltsin had granted clemency in only five cases in 1995. Seven hundred prisoners remained on death row. On 3 October 1996, Amnesty International issued a statement claiming that Russia was treating its Council of Europe commitments with contempt.[49] This was followed by a resolution of the Parliamentary Assembly on 29 January 1997, calling upon Russia to honour the obligations it had undertaken to end executions, and threatening to exclude Russian delegates unless a moratorium was quickly imposed.[50] On 19 November 2009 the Constitutional Court noted that Russia had signed Protocol 6 to the ECHR on 16 April 1997 and is therefore obliged, by virtue of Article 18 of the Vienna

---

[46] ibid.

[47] This is set out ibid, 82–89.

[48] See http://assembly.coe.int/ASP/Doc/XrefViewHTML.asp?FileID=7677&Language=EN#Footref3.

[49] Amnesty International, AI Index: EUR 46/43/96, 3 October 1996.

[50] P Morvant, *OMRI Daily Digest* (30 January 1997).

Convention on the Law of Treaties 1969, 'to refrain from acts which would defeat the object and purpose' of the Protocol. Thus, the moratorium presently in place continues until ratification by Russia of the Protocol.[51]

On 6 March 1997 the then General Secretary of the Council of Europe, Daniel Tarschys, visited Moscow with a view to reviewing Russia's progress in fulfilling its obligations.[52] According to research carried out by journalist Svetlana Sukhova,[53] Russia had done a great deal in the space of a year. The list is impressive, and worth setting out in full:

(1)   The European Convention on Human Rights was signed on February 29, 1996. A draft law entrenching the right of individual petition was to be presented to the State Duma in spring 1997.

(2)   The new Criminal Code entered into force on January 1, 1997.[54] A draft law has been prepared on the introduction of a moratorium on the death penalty. On February 28, 1997 President Yeltsin instructed the Russian Foreign Ministry to sign Protocol 6 of the ECHR, and the Ministry of Justice to prepare a scheme for its implementation.

(3)   The following instruments had been signed, but not yet ratified:
   (a)   The European Convention on Prevention of Torture and Inhuman and Degrading Treatment;
   (b)   The Framework Convention on the Protection of National Minorities;
   (c)   The European Charter on Local Self-Government;
   (d)   The Charter on Regional or Minority Languages.

(4)   Two parts of the Civil Code had been enacted,[55] and the third, concerned with rights of inheritance, is in the process of drafting.

(5)   The working out of the Criminal Procedural Code had not yet started.

(6)   The Law on Advocates received its first reading in November 1996.

(7)   The Law on the Human Rights Ombudsman had been enacted and signed by the President,[56] although a new Ombudsman to replace Sergei Kovalyov had not yet been appointed, at the time of writing.

(8)   The Law on Freedom of Association had received readings in the State Duma and the Federation Council, but had been returned by the President.

(9)   The Law on National-Cultural Autonomy was being drafted.

(10)   On 7 November 1996 the European Conventions on Reciprocal Assistance in the Criminal Justice Field, and on the Transfer of Prisoners, had been signed.

(11)   In connection with the Russian Government's review of the question 'On the state and measures for securing the conditions of persons in custody in the Investigating Isolators and prisons of the Russian Interior Ministry', a proposal has been made for

---

[51] See Bowring (n 7) 174–92.

[52] S Sukhova, '*Rossiya stala na god blizhe k Evrope*' (In a year Russia has come closer to Europe) *Sevodnya* (7 March 1997).

[53] ibid.

[54] Adopted by the State Duma on 24 May 1996, approved by the Council of the Federation on 5 June 1996, and signed by President Yeltsin on 13 June 1996. A commentary was published by the journal *Yuridicheskiy Biulletien Predprinimatelya* (Moscow, 1996).

[55] Part 1 came into force on 1 January 1995, while Part 2 came into force on 1 March 1996.

[56] The Bill was passed by the Duma on 25 December 1996 and by the Federation Council on 12 February 1997. It was signed by President Yeltsin on 26 February 1997. See P Morvant, *OMRI Daily Digest* (27 February 1997).

amendments to the law 'On the Organs of the Federal Security Service', as well as an analysis of measures previously taken for their adoption in a series of Investigative Isolators (SIZOs—remand prisons).

(12)   The Law on Alternative Military Service had received its first reading in the State Duma on 14 December 1994.

On 28 February 1998, the State Duma of the Russian Federation voted to ratify the ECHR. A total of 294 (65.3 per cent) deputies voted for, with only 11 (2.4 per cent) against and two (0.4 per cent) abstentions. Thus, 307 of the deputies voted, but many members failed to vote at all. The upper chamber of the Russian Parliament, the Federation Council, approved this decision on 13 March 1998, and the Federal Law of the Russian Federation 'On Ratification of the Convention for the Protection of Human Rights and Fundamental Freedoms and the Protocols to it' entered into force on 30 March 1998. The ECHR itself entered into force for Russia on 1 November 1998.[57] In this way, Russia fulfilled one of the most important commitments it had made on accession to the Council of Europe.

From 2000 to 2003 President Putin expressly referred to himself as following in the footsteps of the great reforming Tsar, Aleksandr II, and his law reforms of 1864. Putin too presided over the creation of a system of justices of the peace; the installation of jury trial throughout Russia with the exception of Chechnya; enhanced judicial status; and a much reduced role for the prosecutor in criminal and civil trials.[58] The reforms of 2001–03 were driven through the Russian Parliament by Dmitriy Kozak of the President's Administration. These included the three new procedural codes enacted from 2001 to 2003, Criminal, Arbitrazh (Commercial), and Civil, as well as the radical improvements to Yeltsin's Criminal Code of 1996, 257 amendments in all, which were enacted on 8 December 2003. The Council of Europe had substantial expert input into all of this new legislation.[59] However, the initial phase of legal reform from 2000, which included enactment of the new procedural codes referred to in the next paragraph, came to a definitive end in late 2003, simultaneously with Putin's declaration that he would 'liquidate the oligarchs as a class', the arrest of Mr Mikhail Khodorkovsky and the destruction of his highly successful oil company YUKOS.[60]

---

[57] It should be noted that on the same day the State Duma voted, by an even larger majority, to ratify the European Convention for the Prevention of Torture and Inhuman and Degrading Treatment (CPT).

[58] B Bowring, 'Russia in a Common European Legal Space: Developing Effective Remedies for the Violations of Rights by Public Bodies. Compliance with the European Convention on Human Rights' in Kaj Hober (ed), *The Uppsala Yearbook of East European Law 2004* (London, Wildy, Simmonds and Hill, 2005) ed.

[59] I was one of the Council of Europe's experts engaged alongside Mr Kozak, Judge Radchenko and others in preparing the final draft of the Criminal Procedural Code.

[60] Mr Khodorkovsky spent 10 years in prison, was put on trial twice, and according to the Permanent Court of Arbitration in The Hague, in its decision of 28 July 2014, YUKOS was expropriated by the Russian State—see www.reuters.com/article/2014/07/28/us-russia-yukos-idUSKBN0FW0TP20140728.

However, simultaneously with the speeches reported above, Putin was prosecuting with unprecedented ruthlessness a new conflict in Chechnya.

Following from the decision of the CCS referred to above, and in accordance with the 1993 Constitution, generally recognised principles and norms of international law and international treaties of the Russian Federation shall be an integral part of its legal system. If other rules have been established by an international treaty of the Russian federation than provided for by law, the rules of the international treaty shall apply. The apotheosis of this new relationship seemed to have truly arrived with the Resolution of the Plenum of the Supreme Court of the Russian Federation of 10 October 2003. The Resolution was entitled 'On application by courts of general jurisdiction of the commonly recognized principles and norms of the international law and the international treaties of the Russian Federation'.[61] The Supreme Court consulted widely in composing this Resolution: participants in discussion included justices of the RCC, Justice Kovler, and other experts.

However, Russia began to lose a number of high-profile cases in the Strasbourg Court. In May 2004, in *Gusinskiy v Russia*[62] the Court held that Russia had acted in bad faith in using the criminal justice system to force a commercial deal by arresting a TV magnate. In July 2004, in *Ilaşcu v Moldova and Russia*[63] the majority of the Grand Chamber of the Court found in a controversial ruling that Russia had rendered support to Transdniestria, which had broken away from Moldova, amounting to 'effective control'.[64] The first six Chechen applicants against Russia won their applications to Strasbourg in February 2005.[65] In April 2005 in *Shamayev and 12 others v Russia and Georgia*,[66] the Court condemned Russia for deliberately refusing to cooperate with the Court despite diplomatic assurances.

Under Putin, Medvedev, and now Putin again, the human rights situation in Russia has continued to deteriorate. Russia has found itself subject to the new 'pilot judgment' procedure of the European Court of Human Rights. On 10 January 2012 the Court delivered a pilot judgment against Russia in the case of *Ananyev v Russia*.[67] Mr Ananyev was held in the Smolensk remand prison IZ-67/1 from 20 January to 23 March 2007. During his two-month stay he was accommodated in a cell that measured 15 square metres and included 13 sleeping places. He had less than 1.25 square metres of personal space and the number of detainees significantly exceeded the number of sleeping places available. This was, the Court held, inhuman and degrading treatment, violating Article 3 of the Convention.

The Council of Europe has continued to monitor Russia's progress, or lack of it, in complying with the undertakings it gave on accession in 1996. On 14 September 2012 the Parliamentary Assembly of the Council of Europe published the latest

---

[61] In English at www.supcourt.ru/catalog.php?c1=English&c2=Documents&c3=&id=6801.

[62] *Gusinskiy v Russia* (2004) 41 EHRR 17.

[63] *Ilaşcu v Moldova and Russia* (2004) 40 EHRR 1030.

[64] See, for a discussion of this and later judgments, B Bowring, 'Geopolitics and the Right to Education, and Why "No Person" is in Fact a Child' (2014) 26(2) *Child and Family Law Quarterly* 196.

[65] *Isayeva, Yusupova and Bazayeva v Russia* (2005) 41 EHRR 847. These applicants were represented, from 2000, by me and my colleagues at the European Human Rights Advocacy Centre, which I founded, in partnership with the Russian human rights NGO 'Memorial', with €1 million EU funding in 2002.

[66] *Shamayev and 12 others v Russia and Georgia* App no 36378/02, ECHR 2005-III.

[67] *Ananyev v Russia* (2012) 55 EHRR 18.

report of its Rapporteurs, Mr György Frunda (Romanian) and Mr Andreas Gross (Swiss), on *The Honouring of Obligations and Commitments by the Russian Federation*,[68] covering the previous seven years from 2005. The Rapporteurs considered that lack of independence and the interconnected matter of the public's lack of confidence in the judiciary were the main problems in the Russian judicial system. These problems have deep roots in the legal and political culture, as in Soviet times judges were often seen not as arbiters, but rather as defenders of the interests of the State. They reported:

317. The poor state of judicial independence is clearly facilitated by a legislative and administrative framework that fails to protect judges from undue influence by State or private interests. The way the judiciary operates puts pressure on judges through a complex system which is not always apparent or visible and includes not only external pressure, but also internal mechanisms and bureaucracy.

318. These internal mechanisms have become more significant as a result of the government's drive to strengthen the powers of the executive, known in Russia as 'strengthening the vertical power'. Political interference has increased under laws brought into force in the wake of the Beslan siege, allegedly for 'counter-terrorism' purposes.

The Rapporteurs were particularly struck by events at the Constitutional Court:

327. In a 2009 interview with the Spanish newspaper, El País, Constitutional Court Judge Vladimir Yaroslavtsev claimed that the presidential executive office and security services had undermined judicial independence in Russia. In October 2009, the Constitutional Court, in an unprecedented motion, accused Mr Yaroslavtsev of 'undermining the authority of the judiciary' in violation of the judicial code and forced him to resign from the Council of Judges.

328. Judge Anatoly Kononov, who has frequently dissented from decisions taken by the majority of the court, in his interview to *Sobesednik*, supported Mr Yaroslavtsev, claiming that there was no independent judiciary in Russia. Mr Kononov was forced to step down from the Constitutional Court on 1 January 2010, seven years ahead of schedule.

These were two of the most hard-working, intelligent and independent judges sitting in the Constitutional Court.

The European Parliament of the European Union has also expressed grave concern. On 13 September 2012 a Plenary Sitting of the European Parliament passed a Resolution on 'The political use of justice in Russia'.[69] The preamble to the Resolution noted as follows:

C. ... the human rights situation in Russia has deteriorated drastically in the last few months and the Russian authorities have recently adopted a series of laws which contain ambiguous provisions and could be used to further restrict opposition and civil society actors and hinder freedom of expression and assembly.

The Parliament highlighted a number of examples of deterioration of the human rights situation in Russia.

---

[68] Doc 13018, at assembly.coe.int/ASP/Doc/XrefViewHTML.asp?FileID=18998&Language=EN.

[69] See www.europarl.europa.eu/document/activities/cont/201209/20120924ATT52181/20120924ATT52181EN.pdf.

First, it referred to the failure of the Russian authorities to find and prosecute the real perpetrators of some horrifying cases: the murder outside her apartment of the investigative journalist Anna Politkovsakaya on 7 October 2006; the shooting of the lawyer, my colleague Stanislas Markelov and the journalist Anastasia Baburova in central Moscow on 19 January 2009; the abduction and murder in Grozny of my colleague the human rights activist Natasha Estemirova on 15 July 2009; and the death in custody of the young lawyer Sergei Magnitsky on 16 November 2009. And the perpetrator of the murder of the British citizen Alexander Litvinenko on 23 November 2006 has never been brought to trial; on 11 February 2014 the British Court of Appeal allowed his widow the right to a public inquiry into his murder.[70]

Second, the Parliament commented that the guilty verdict in the second trial of Mr Khodorkovsky and his colleague Mr Lebedev for allege fraud was politically motivated.

Third, it pointed to the use by law enforcement agencies of politically constructed reasons to eliminate political competition and to threaten civil society, and to dis-proportionate sentencing, such as the two-year term of imprisonment imposed on members of Pussy Riot for their protest against Mr Putin in the main Orthodox cathedral of Moscow.

Finally, it raised serious concerns about the 'Foreign agent law' enacted in July 2012, under which a very large number of Russian human rights and ecological NGOs are being persecuted. On 6 February 2013 my European Human Rights Advocacy Centre (EHRAC) litigation project lodged an application at the ECtHR on behalf of 11 leading Russian NGOs, complaining that the law violates their rights to freedom of association and expression.[71] And on 1 December 2014 in Moscow the Secretary General of the Council of Europe, Mr Thorbjørn Jagland, expressed his opinion that the label 'foreign agent' had no place in modern Europe, and said he was opposed to the term 'foreign agent' being imposed on organisations which receive funding from abroad. The law could lead to organisations funded by the Council of Europe being declared 'foreign agents'.[72]

As at the time of writing this chapter, it is plain that on the one hand many signifi-cant changes have been made in Russia since its accession to the Council of Europe from 1996, and it will be impossible to put the clock back. Russia now regularly accepts a level of interference which would have been quite unthinkable in Soviet times. The fact that so many of the reforms were in effect restorations of Aleksandr II's Great Reforms has made the process more complex but also more eduring. On the other hand, the current regime in Russia, while paying respect to Aleksandr's reforms, is also strongly influenced by anti-Western and anti-Liberal thinking. Not

---

[70] www.theguardian.com/world/2014/feb/11/alexander-litvinenko-widow-court-victory-inquiry. I am representing Marina Carter (as she now is) in her application which is pending at the European Court of Human Rights.

[71] www.mdx.ac.uk/__data/assets/pdf_file/0007/58651/EHRAC-Press-release-97-NGO-Foreign-Agent-Law_website.pdf.

[72] http://hro.rightsinrussia.info/hro-org/foreignagents-153.

only has Russia's government taken an increasingly conservative and even national-ist course in policy and action, there is now evidence that Russia is giving support to the far right in Western Europe.[73]

VI. SOVEREIGNTY

One symptom of Russia's sharp turn to the right in the last decade is the frequent invocation of 'sovereignty' as a decisive factor in the ideology of the regime. This is not only reminiscent of the Soviet approach to international law, but also draws from the legal theorist of the Nazi Party, Carl Schmitt. The concepts of sovereignty and 'sovereign democracy' became prominent in the discourse of the Russian elite in the early years of the twenty-first century. This was primarily the initiative of Vladislav Surkov, the Kremlin's 'grey cardinal', although one of the most important authors of the discourse was Valery Zorkin, whose role in the Constitutional Court since 1991 I outlined above.[74]

On 22 August 2004 Zorkin published a long article in the official daily news-paper *Rossisskaya Gazeta* entitled 'Apology for the Westphalian System' in which he insisted that 'From this point of view Russian democracy—is sovereign, and the sovereignty of the Russian state—is democratic'.[75] In November 2004 he participated in a discussion on 'The Sovereign State in Conditions of Globalisation: Democracy and National Identity'.[76] In 2006 the collection *Sovereignty* appeared,[77] with contributions from Surkov, Dmitry Medvedev and Vladimir Putin, and a key chapter, featuring many quotations from Carl Schmitt, entitled 'Sovereignty as a Political Choice'.[78] These were therefore publications by the most senior officials of the Russian Federation, aimed at a mass audience.

As I outlined above, state sovereignty and non-interference in the internal affairs of States were the twin pillars of the Soviet approach to international law. So the accession of Russia to the Council of Europe in 1996, when Russia subjected itself to a list of legally binding obligations, and ratification of the European Convention on Human Rights in 1998, represented a fundamental change of policy, and a vol-untary loss of sovereignty.

---

[73] See Luke Harding, 'We should beware Russia's links with Europe's right. Moscow is handing cash to the Front National and others in order to exploit popular dissent against the European Union' *The Guardian* (London, 8 December 2014), www.theguardian.com/commentisfree/2014/dec/08/russia-europe-right-putin-front-national-eu.

[74] See the analysis of this phenomenon in Bill Bowring, *Law, Rights and Ideology in Russia: Land-marks in the Destiny of a Great Power* (Abingdon, Routledge, 2013), esp ch 10 'Sovereign Democracy', 193–205.

[75] Valery Zorkin, *Apologiya Westfalskoi sistemy* (Apology for the Westphalian system) *Rossiiskaya Gazeta* (13 July 2004), www.rg.ru/2004/07/13/zorkin.html.

[76] Valery Zorkin, *Suverennoye gosudarstvo v usloviyakh globalizoatsii: demokratiya i natsionalnaya identichnost* (Sovereign State in conditions of globalisation: democracy and national identity) in Vladislav Surkov (ed), *Teksty 1997–2007* (Moscow, Yevropa, 2008).

[77] Nikita Garadja (ed), *Suverenitet* (Sovereignty) (Moscow, Yevropa, 2006).

[78] A Filippov, *Suverenitet kak politicheskiy vybor* (Sovereignty as a political choice) in Garadja, ibid, 80–94; Filippov has translated many works of Schmitt into Russian.

Russia has a 'monist' approach to international law, and Article 15(4) of the 1993 Constitution provides that treaties take priority over domestic law. On ratification, the ECHR became an integral part of Russian law. On 10 October 2003 the Supreme Court adopted a Resolution 'On application by courts of general jurisdiction of the commonly recognized principles and norms of the international law and the international treaties of the Russian Federation',[79] and on 27 June 2013 a Ruling 'On application of the ECHR by the courts of general jurisdiction.'[80]

There have been many judgments against Russia since 1998, and Russia has always paid sums of just satisfaction (compensation) ordered by the European Court of Human Rights (ECtHR), and has engaged with more or less tangible results with the Committee of Ministers on questions of enforcement and implementation. Indeed, Russian judge Anatolii Kovler was one of the best judges at Strasbourg from 1999 to 2012.

VII. *KONSTANTIN MARKIN v RUSSIA*

On 7 October 2010 the Chamber of the ECtHR gave judgment in the case of *Konstantin Markin v Russia*, a controversial case concerning violations of Article 14 (discrimination) and Article 8 (respect for family and private life), where a serving male officer was denied leave to look after his children, which would have been available to a female officer.[81] The Chamber strongly criticised the ruling of 15 January 2009 of the Constitutional Court of the Russian Federation (CCRF).

On 29 October 2010 Judge Zorkin wrote another long article in the *Rossiisskaya Gazeta* entitled 'Limits of Compromise', stating that 'Like any other European State, Russia must fight as much for the preservation of its sovereignty, as for the careful relationship with the European Convention, and defence of its sovereignty against inadequate, doubtful decisions'.[82] He added:

> The principles of state *sovereignty* and the supremacy of the Constitution in the legal system of Russia lie at the foundation of its constitutional system. The Convention as an international treaty of Russia is a component part of its legal system, but it is not higher than the Constitution … Each decision of the European Court is not only a legal but a political act. When such a decision is taken in the interests of the protection of the rights and freedoms of the citizen and the development of our country, Russia will always precisely obey it. But when it or another decision of the Strasbourg court is doubtful from the point of view of

---

[79] Ruling of the Plenary session of the Supreme Court of the Russian Federation No 5 'On application by courts of general jurisdiction of the commonly recognised principles and norms of the international law and the international treaties of the Russian Federation' (10 October 2003), www.supcourt.ru/catalog.php?c1=English&c2=Documents&c3=&id=6801.

[80] Ruling of the Plenary session of the Supreme Court of the Russian Federation No 21 'On application of the Convention for the Protection of Human Rights and Fundamental Freedoms of 4 November 1950 and Protocols thereto by the Courts of General Jurisdiction' (27 June 2013), www.supcourt.ru/catalog.php?c1=English&c2=Documents&c3=&id=9155.

[81] *Konstantin Markin v Russia* (n 1).

[82] V Zorkin, *Predel ustupchivosti* (The limits of compromise) *Rossiiskaya Gazeta* (29 October 2010), www.rg.ru/2010/10/29/zorkin.html (emphasis added).

the goal of the European Convention on Human Rights and moreover in a direct fashion concerns national *sovereignty*, and fundamental constitutional principles, Russia has the right to work out a defence mechanism against such decisions.

Precisely through the prism of the Constitution the problem of the relationship between orders of the CC and the ECtHR must also be worked out ... Like any other European state, Russia must fight as much for the preservation of its *sovereignty*, as for the careful relationship with the European Convention, and defence of its *sovereignty* against inadequate, doubtful decisions.

On 18 November 2010, the Strasbourg Court communicated to Russia the *United Opposition* case,[83] in which complaints were made about the 2003 elections. Judge Zorkin complained that the Court's decision was 'connected with political reasons' and said: 'Not all decisions of the ECtHR are obligatory for execution, in particular, those concerning sovereignty'. This was followed by heated exchanges with Jean-Paul Costa, the ECtHR's then President, and others at the Thirteenth International Constitutional Justice Forum in St Petersburg in November 2010.[84] At this forum Zorkin declared that Russia could even leave the ECHR because of the threat posed to its sovereignty.[85]

Mr Zorkin sought juridical support from the judgment of the German Constitutional Court in its 2004 *Görgülü* judgment,[86] which at the time had been a cause for concern for the then president of the ECtHR, Lucius Wildhaber, who had interpreted the decision as denying binding force to ECtHR judgments and setting a bad example with counterproductive effects in other countries.[87] Gertrude Lübbe-Wolff, on the contrary, sought to show that:

As the Constitutional Court puts it, the Basic Law—the German Constitution—has not taken the greatest possible steps in opening itself to international-law connections. The greatest possible step would have been to endow international agreements and other international law with the status of constitutional law—or an even higher status—and thereby to reduce to a minimum or even exclude the possibility of conflict between national and international law. This step has not been taken in Germany—neither generally nor with respect to the Convention in particular. The Convention has only been given the status of a normal federal statute. Accordingly, there is the possibility of conflict between the Convention and higher-ranking domestic law, and the Constitutional Court has made it clear that in the event of such a conflict, it is the Constitution—not the conflicting international agreement—which German Courts would have to apply.

The *Görgülü* decision dwells on the issue of conflict at some length and insists on the national sovereignty which the German state has reserved by not submitting to international law unconditionally. On an atmospherical level, this has probably contributed to the impression that the Constitutional Court is questioning the authority of the Convention or even seeking conflict with the ECtHR. Sticking to the hard legal doctrines set out in the

---

[83] www.newsru.com/arch/russia/18nov2010/zorkin.html.
[84] www.loc.gov/lawweb/servlet/lloc_news?disp3_l205402410_text.
[85] www.ej.ru/?a=note&id=10609#.
[86] Decision of 14 October 2004, 2 BvR 1481/04, www.bverfg.de/entscheidungen/rs20041014_2bvr 148104e.html.
[87] 'Im Ausland mißverstandlich' *Der Spiegel* (15 November 2004).

decision, however, you will find that there is little to worry about. By stressing the obligation of all German Courts, including the Constitutional Court, to interpret not only ordinary law, but also constitutional law in accordance with the Convention as read by the ECtHR, and by stating that in a case of failure by a court of ordinary jurisdiction to take due account of a decision of the ECtHR, the party concerned may take this to the Constitutional Court as a violation of the relevant constitutional right, the decision even enhances and strengthens the role of the Convention in German Law.[88]

This was also the position taken by the German judge at Strasbourg, Angelika Nussberger, in her response to Zorkin at the St Petersburg Forum in November 2010.[89]

On 11 December 2010, at a meeting at former President Medvedev's residence with judges of the CCRF, Judge Zorkin referred to the St Petersburg discussions of the previous month.[90] Mr Medvedev took up the theme of sovereignty and replied to Zorkin:

> But as I see it, we have never handed over any part of sovereignty that would give any international or foreign court the right to make decisions changing our national legislation. Many European countries much more closely integrated into European institutions follow this same principle.

Judge Zorkin and his fellow thinkers were further outraged by the Strasbourg Court's judgment of 12 April 2011 in *Republican Party v Russia*, in which the ECtHR held that the dissolution of the party in 2007 violated its rights under Article 11.[91]

However, before the confrontation between Strasbourg and St Petersburg had the chance to really come to a head, the *Markin* case was referred at Russia's request to the Grand Chamber of the ECtHR, and on 22 March 2012 the Chamber's judgment was upheld, but this time with no overt criticism of the Constitutional Court.[92]

Armed with the Grand Chamber judgment, Mr Markin returned to the Russian courts, and on 30 January 2013 the Leningrad Okrug Military Court applied to the CCRF to decide the issue arising from the fact that in Russian law the judgments of the CCRF and the ECtHR appeared to be of equal status. The CCRF gave judgment on 6 December 2013;[93] Judge Sergei Mavrin, a participant in the debates, was Judge Rapporteur.[94]

---

[88] G Lübbe-Wolff, 'ECtHR and National Jurisdiction: The Görgülü Case' (2006) 12 *Humboldt Forum Recht*, www.humboldt-forum-recht.de/druckansicht/druckansicht.php?artikelid=135, para 9.

[89] www.ej.ru/?a=note&id=10609.

[90] eng.news.kremlin.ru/news/1464/print.

[91] *Republican Party v Russia* App no 12976/07 (judgment of 12 April 2011).

[92] *Konstantin Markin v Russia* (n 1).

[93] Published in the *Russian Gazette* on 18 December 2013 at www.rg.ru/2013/12/18/ks-dok.html.

[94] See commentary on the website of the Constitutional Court, www.ksrf.ru/ru/News/Pages/ViewItem. aspx?ParamId=3137.

My EHRAC colleague Kirill Koroteev commented that this was 'the conflict which never was'.[95] He observed:

> [T]here is definitely not a conflict between the Russian Constitutional Court and the ECtHR, there is only a violation of the Convention, as correctly interpreted by the ECtHR. I note that the Russian government at the hearing before the Grand Chamber wholly reasonably did not put forward arguments as to 'interference with internal affairs' or 'violation of sovereignty': such arguments would have been rejected.[96]

Koroteev highlighted four recent cases in which the Constitutional Court had violated the Convention, and concluded:

> [I]n view of the unreserved support for the legislative and executive authorities given by the judges in the building of the Senate and the Synod[97] only the ECtHR will exercise judicial control of the constitutionality and compliance with the Convention of Russian laws.[98]

Ekaterina Mishina[99] in turn described the judgment as 'A Rubik's Cube from the CCRF' 'that can be turned any way you like it: You want a green side? You got it. You want a red one? You can have that, too.'[100] After turning the cube, the CCRF had come out on top. She referred to the justices' meeting with President Putin on 12 December 2013[101] in which he said:

> In my opinion, the Russian Constitutional Court chose optimal solutions and very appropriate ones, as I have already said, from a legal point of view. You suggested an appropriate way of implementing decisions of the European Court, which will not lead to distortion of provisions of the Russian Constitution.

Like the German Constitutional Court, the CCRF had taken a pragmatic approach. It held that if provisions of Russian law impeached by the ECtHR are found to be consistent with the Constitution, then the issue must be referred to the CCRF, which will determine possible constitutional means of implementation of the judgment of the ECtHR. Outright refusal to obey the judgment of the ECtHR was ruled out. As Mishina added:

> Good for you, dear judges. You masterfully avoided an open confrontation with the ECtHR and at the same time made it clear who the boss is and who will decide whether to implement decisions of the European Court of Human Rights on Russian territory.[102]

---

[95] Kirill Koroteev, 'Konflikt, kotorovo net. Kommentarii k resheniyu Yevropeiskovo suda po delu "Markin protiv Rossii"' (The conflict which never was. Commentary on the decision of the European Court in 'Markin v Russia') (28 January 2014), roseurosud.org/stati-i-knigi-o-evropejskom-sude/51-kommentariy-po-delu-markin-protiv-rossii.

[96] ibid.

[97] The Constitutional Court of the Russian Federation is now housed in the magnificently reconstructed building for the Senate and Synod, the highest judicial instances of the Russian Empire.

[98] Koroteev (n 95).

[99] She worked for the Constitutional Court, teaches at the National Research University—Higher School of Economics, and has been a visiting professor at the University of Michigan.

[100] E Mishina, 'A Rubik's Cube from the Russian Constitutional Court' (30 December 2013), imrussia.org/en/rule-of-law/633-a-rubiks-cube-from-russias-constitutional-court.

[101] www.kremlin.ru/transcripts/19832.

[102] Mishina (n 100).

Judge Zorkin's long articles 'The Civilisation of Law', published on 13 March 2014, and 'Law and Economics', published on 22 May 2014, did not mention either the *Markin* case or sovereignty.[103] On 23 May 2014, the State Duma passed at second and third reading a law amending the law 'On the Constitutional Court' so as to implement the CCRF's judgment. And Markin got his leave, and was paid compensation.

VIII. CONCLUSION

I agree with the conclusion of a brilliant young colleague, Grigory Vaipan.[104] He wrote under the title 'Acquiescence Affirmed, its Limits Left Undefined'[105] that the CCRF had entirely avoided the 'purely dogmatic question of supremacy' between the national court and the international one. However, the CCRF had not followed other European courts in developing balancing tests, as, for example, the German Constitutional Court in the *Görgülü* case already referred to, and the UK Supreme Court in *Pinnock*,[106] which held that UK courts should implement

> a clear and constant line of [ECtHR] decisions whose effect is not inconsistent with some fundamental substantive or procedural aspect of [British] law, and whose reasoning does not appear to overlook or misunderstand some argument or point of principle.[107]

For Vaipan, the judgment of the CCRF had avoided laying down such guidelines, and had simply noted that

> if ... challenged legal provisions are found to be consistent with the Constitution, the Constitutional Court ... within the limits of its competence will determine possible constitutional means of implementation of the judgment of [the ECtHR].[108]

As Vaipan observes, this approach is completely ad hoc. However, despite its lack of clarity, or perhaps because of deliberate unclarity, the CCRF has left open the continued possibility of a 'meaningful dialogue' (in the words of Baroness Hale of the UK Supreme Court)[109] between the St Petersburg and Strasbourg courts.

Russia has not followed the UK's 'continuing prevarication, and even defiance, over the implementation of the Strasbourg pilot judgment on prisoner voting rights', in the words of Professor Philip Leach and Alice Donald, who warn of a 'risk of

---

[103] V Zorkin, 'Tsivilizatsiya prava: Yesli provo pogibaet, to mir okazhetsya u kraya bezdny' (The civilization of law: if law dies, then the world will find itself in a catastrophe) *Russian Gazette* (13 March 2014), www.rg.ru/2014/03/12/zorkin.html.

[104] He was a member of the Moscow State University team that won the international rounds of the Jessup International Law Moot Court Competition in Washington, DC in 2012, and now leads a project on litigation at the Constitutional Court, for which I serve as an expert.

[105] Vaipan (n 3).

[106] *Manchester City Council v Pinnock* [2010] UKSC 45, www.bailii.org/uk/cases/UKSC/2010/45. html.

[107] ibid, para 48.

[108] Vaipan (n 3).

[109] www.supremecourt.uk/docs/speech-131128.pdf.

contagion'.[110] It will be recalled that following the Strasbourg judgment in *Hirst v UK (No 2)*[111] the UK was given until 22 November 2012 to repeal its blanket ban on prisoner voting. The UK failed to comply, resulting in a reprimand from the Council of Europe's Committee of Ministers,[112] but no sanctions.

Russia has not (yet) defied the Strasbourg Court. And the CCRF has decided to pursue a path of pragmatism, whilst at the same time reserving the right to exercise its unique power to interpret and enforce the Russian Constitution. In my view the omens to that extent are good for Russia's continued membership of the Council of Europe and engagement with the Strasbourg Court.

However, Russia's illegal annexation of Crimea and intervention in eastern Ukraine have given rise to legal proceedings. On 13 March 2014, Ukraine lodged an interstate application under Article 33 ECHR (Inter-State cases) against Russia, and on the same day the Court granted interim measures.[113] This is not the first such case. The parties are awaiting the judgment of the Grand Chamber in *Georgia v Russia (No 2)*,[114] which concerns the August war of 2008 between Russia and Georgia. An oral hearing took place on 22 September 2011. Furthermore, on 31 July 2014 a Chamber of the ECtHR ordered Russia to pay €1,866,104,634 to shareholders of YUKOS,[115] and Russia has requested a referral to the Grand Chamber. The potential effect of adverse judgments in these cases would be far more damaging and aggravating to Russia than has been the case in any of the adverse judgments against the UK, and these have been relatively small in number. Russia could yet denounce the ECHR, and leave the Council of Europe.

---

[110] P Leach and A Donald, 'Hostility to the European Court and the Risks of Contagion' UK Human Rights Blog (21 November 2013), ukhumanrightsblog.com/2013/11/21/hostility-to-the-european-court-and-the-risks-of-contagion-philip-leach-and-alice-donald/.

[111] *Hirst v UK (No 2)* (2005) 42 EHRR 41.

[112] www.theguardian.com/politics/2012/dec/10/votes-for-prisoners-uk-delaying-tactics.

[113] *Ukraine v Russia* App no 20958/14. See the press release at hudoc.echr.coe.int/webservices/content/pdf/003-4699472-5703982.

[114] *Georgia v Russia (No 2)* App no 38263/08 (13 December 2011).

[115] *OAO Neftyanaya Kompaniya Yukos v Russia* App No 14902/04 (29 January 2009).

Part V

The Role of the Media in Shaping the Relationship

22

Public Watchdogs and Democratic Society: The Role of the Media and of the Strasbourg Court

ROBERT UERPMANN-WITTZACK

I. INTRODUCTION

ACCORDING TO ARTICLE 16 of the French Declaration of the Rights of Man and of the Citizen (1789), '[t]oute Société dans laquelle la garantie des Droits n'est pas assurée, ni la séparation des Pouvoirs déterminée, n'a point de Constitution':[1] 'Any society in which no provision is made for guaranteeing rights or for the separation of powers has no Constitution.'[2] There must be checks and balances, and any exercise of power needs oversight: 'Madness in great ones must not unwatch'd go.'[3]

In a democratic society, such oversight functions are manifold. They are mostly attributed to state organs such as parliaments and courts. In fact, judicial review is an important element of public oversight. This is true both for domestic and for international courts. In a system of Nation States, control is essentially a domestic concern, but in Europe, domestic control has been complemented by a form of external review, which is exercised by the European Court of Human Rights (ECtHR).[4] However, scrutinising the powerful is not only incumbent on state and interstate bodies such as parliaments and courts. Rather, such scrutiny is also a task of the press and other media, which the ECtHR has dubbed 'public watchdog[s]'.[5] So both the judiciary and the media exercise watchdog functions. The watchdogs

---

[1] Déclaration des Droits de l'Homme et du Citoyen, 26 August 1789, www.legifrance.gouv.fr/Droit-francais/Constitution/Declaration-des-Droits-de-l-Homme-et-du-Citoyen-de-1789.

[2] English translation available at www.conseil-constitutionnel.fr/conseil-constitutionnel/root/bank_mm/anglais/cst2.pdf.

[3] W Shakespeare, 'Hamlet', 3.1.197, in *Complete Works* (Oxford, Oxford University Press, 1984) 870, 887.

[4] For an emphatic view of this see E Myjer and P Kempees, *Jack and the Solemn Promise* (Nijmegen, Wolf Legal Publishers, 2010) 7 ff.

[5] The term was first used in *Barthold v Germany* (1985) 7 EHRR 383, para 58, and has been constantly repeated since; see eg *Observer and Guardian v UK* (1992) 14 EHRR 153, para 59; *Max Mosley v UK* (2011) 53 EHRR 30, para 114; *von Hannover v Germany (No 2)* (2012) 55 EHRR 15 (GC), paras 102, 110; all ECtHR judgments are available on the HUDOC database at hudoc.echr.coe.int.

may themselves be powerful. The British media certainly are, and so is the ECtHR. So, *quis custodiet ipsos custodes*—who watches the watchdogs? In fact, there is mutual oversight. Whilst the ECtHR has taken great care to help elucidate the scope and the limits of media freedom, the media are called upon to watch on all exercise of public powers, including that of the judiciary and the ECtHR.

In dealing with this mutual relationship, this chapter will rely on the abundant case law of the ECtHR. In fact, Strasbourg decisions on freedom of the press have two different layers. On the one hand, the Court is called upon to determine the watchdog role of the press and its boundaries. Whereas the press are expected to scrutinise political or other public affairs, a fair balance must be struck between freedom of the press and competing interests such as the protection of the judiciary or, more often, protection of the private lives of celebrities such as Naomi Campbell[6] or Caroline von Hannover,[7] to mention just two famous cases. Section II will deal with the scope of the public watchdog role of the media and Strasbourg's judicial watchdog role with regard to the media. On the other hand, the ECtHR's own role vis-a-vis domestic courts is at stake. Is it up to the 'European watchdog'—that is, the ECtHR—to balance competing interests such as media freedom and respect for private life, or should the ECtHR respect the decisions taken by domestic courts? This question will be addressed in Section III.

II. WHAT ROLE FOR THE MEDIA?

A. The Media as Public Watchdog

Although Article 10 of the European Convention on Human Rights (ECHR) does not mention the media as such, or the press, the ECtHR has recognised the special role of the press as a 'public watchdog', and it has extended this protection to other media.

This protection relies on an approach which has its origin in the wording of Article 10(2) ECHR. According to this paragraph, any interference with freedom of expression must be 'necessary in a democratic society'. According to the ECtHR, such a society is characterised by 'pluralism, tolerance and broadmindedness', and it follows from this that Article 10 'is applicable not only to "information" or "ideas" that are favourably received or regarded as inoffensive or as a matter of indifference, but also to those that offend, shock or disturb the State or any sector of the population'.[8] This reasoning goes back to the *Handyside* judgment[9] of 1976, and has been constantly reaffirmed since.[10]

---

[6] See *MGN v UK* (2011) 53 EHRR 5.

[7] See *von Hannover v Germany (No 1)* (2004) 40 EHRR 1; *von Hannover v Germany (No 2)* (n 5); *von Hannover v Germany (No 3)* App no 8772/10 (ECtHR, 19 September 2013).

[8] *Handyside v UK* (1979–80) 1 EHRR 737, para 49.

[9] ibid; for an appraisal of this landmark decision see S Dollé and C Ovey, 'Handyside, 35 Years Down the Road' in J Casadevall, E Myjer and M O'Boyle (eds), *Freedom of Expression: Essays in Honour of Nicolas Bratza* (Nijmegen, Wolf Legal Publishers, 2012) 541 ff.

[10] See, inter alia, *Hertel v Switzerland* (1999) 28 EHRR 534, para 46; *von Hannover v Germany (No 2)* (n 5) para 101; *Mouvement Raëlien Suisse v Switzerland* (2013) 56 EHRR 14 (GC), para 48.

Freedom of expression has a broad scope. The media may entertain, and they may also exaggerate or even provoke.[11] If freedom of expression enters into conflict with other rights or interests, however, courts have to strike a balance. Therefore, they have to determine the relative weight of freedom of expression in a given case. This is done with reference to the concept of democratic society laid down in Article 10(2) ECHR. In order to function, a democracy requires free public debate on political issues and other questions of public interest. In this respect, 'freedom of the press and other news media affords the public one of the best means of discovering and forming an opinion of the ideas and attitudes of political leaders'.[12]

Generally speaking, any expression of information or ideas which contributes to such public debate needs strong protection, whilst the level of protection may be reduced where no such issue is concerned. When the press take up topics of public interest, they fulfil a 'protection and warning role'[13] which the ECtHR has labelled a 'public watchdog' function.[14] This is a functional approach to freedom of expression: the press are granted special protection if and because they fulfil a vital role for democracy. In fact, Article 10 ECHR is founded on two different arguments. For the individual, freedom of expression is a core element of one's self-fulfilment,[15] and in this respect expression must be protected regardless of its usefulness for society. For the media, however, which may not avail themselves of a right to self-fulfilment, the democratic rationale becomes crucial. Media coverage is protected because and insofar as freedom of expression is 'one of the essential foundations of a democratic society and one of the basic conditions for its progress'.[16] The special protection that follows from this role is not limited to the press *sensu stricto*—it has been extended to audio-visual media.[17]

In order to define the public watchdog role of the press, the ECtHR usually refers to the concept of public interest. In some recent cases, the Court synonymously used the notion of general interest.[18] Certainly, the public interest, which triggers the public watchdog role of the media, is quite broad. In fact, it must be determined with regard to the role of the media 'in a democratic society'. According to a non-exhaustive enumeration given by the ECtHR in *von Hannover (No 2)*, it covers political issues and crimes as well as sporting issues and performing artists.[19] On the other hand, there is no public interest in media coverage where the media indulge in 'idle gossip'[20] and where reporting has 'the sole aim of satisfying public

---

[11] *Kurier Zeitungsverlag und Druckerei v Austria (No 2)* App no 1593/06 (ECtHR 19 June 2012), para 42.

[12] *Animal Defenders International v UK* (2013) 57 EHRR 21 (GC), para 102.

[13] *Kurier Zeitungsverlag und Druckerei v Austria (No 2)* (n 11) para 42.

[14] See n 4.

[15] *Handyside v UK* (n 8) para 49; *Lingens v Austria* (1986) 8 EHRR 407, para 41; *von Hannover v Germany (No 2)* (n 5) para 101.

[16] *Lingens v Austria* (1986) 8 EHRR 407, para 41; *von Hannover v Germany (No 2)* (n 5) para 101.

[17] *Jersild v Denmark* (1995) 19 EHRR 1 (GC), para 31; *Centro Europa 7 Srl and Di Stefano v Italy* App no 38433/09 (GC), paras 131–32; see also E Komorek, 'Is Media Pluralism a Human Right?' (2009) *European Human Rights Law Review* 395, 400.

[18] *von Hannover v Germany (No 2)* (n 5) paras 109, 117–18, 124 (general interest) against paras 102, 110, 118 (public interest).

[19] ibid, para 109.

[20] *Standard Verlags GmbH v Austria (No 2)* App no 21477/05 (ECtHR, 4 June 2009), para 52.

curiosity'[21] or the 'curiosity of a certain readership'.[22] It has also been emphasised that the mere fact that the public is interested in a certain subject does not constitute a public interest in this subject.[23] The media are prima facie free to report what satisfies public curiosity and even to participate in idle gossip. However, if that media coverage collides with other rights or interests, the latter will prevail unless there is a specific public interest in media coverage with regard to the case at hand.[24]

B. The Special Role of the Judiciary

In a democratic society, it is particularly important to closely watch the conduct of political leaders and the action taken by governmental or parliamentary bodies. Nevertheless, the need for public scrutiny extends to all kind of state authority and also to the judiciary. In judgments against Austria, the ECtHR rightly stated that the public watchdog role of the media

> undoubtedly includes questions concerning the functioning of the system of justice, an institution that is essential for any democratic society. The press is one of the means by which politicians and public opinion can verify that judges are discharging their heavy responsibilities in a manner that is in conformity with the aim which is the basis of the task entrusted to them.[25]

This has led the ECtHR to state that judges acting in their official capacity may be subject to more severe criticism than ordinary citizens.[26] While scrutinising the judiciary is important, Article 10 ECHR specifically addresses the limits of such a watchdog role. According to Article 10(2) ECHR, it is legitimate to restrict freedom of expression in order to maintain 'the authority and impartiality of the judiciary'. This implies that judges enjoy a stronger protection against the press in the exercise of their judicial functions than politicians.[27] The ECtHR had the occasion to address this in *Sunday Times (No 1)*. According to the Court:

> The phrase 'authority of the judiciary' includes, in particular, the notion that the courts are, and are accepted by the public at large as being, the proper forum for the ascertainment of legal rights and obligations and the settlement of disputes relative thereto; further, that the public at large have respect for and confidence in the courts' capacity to fulfil that function.[28]

---

[21] *von Hannover v Germany (No 2)* (n 5) para 110.

[22] *Standard Verlags* (n 20) para 52.

[23] *Mosley v UK* (n 5) para 114.

[24] See also G Phillipson, 'Leveson, the Public Interest and Press Freedom' (2013) 5 *Journal of Media Law* 220, 231.

[25] *Prager and Oberschlick v Austria* (1996) 21 EHRR 1, para 34; *Kobenter and Standard Verlags GmbH v Austria* (2010) 50 EHRR 16, para 29 (ii); see also *Mustafa Erdoğan et al v Turkey* App nos 346/04, 39779/04 (ECtHR, 27 May 2014), para 41.

[26] *Mustafa Erdoğan et al v Turkey*, ibid, para 42.

[27] ibid.

[28] *Sunday Times v UK (No 1)* (1979–80) 2 EHRR 245, para 55.

In later judgments, the ECtHR specified the 'special role of the judiciary in society'.[29] Two aspects are important. First of all, the judiciary must enjoy public confidence if it is to successfully fulfil its role as a guarantor of justice. Moreover, with a view to maintaining their authority and impartiality, judges are subject to a particular duty of discretion which hinders them from replying where politicians could defend themselves in public speech.[30] Therefore, States may shield judges from exaggerated criticism where politicians would have to expose themselves even to severe verbal attacks, and it may be necessary to defend judges 'against destructive attacks that are essentially unfounded'.[31] Whilst even offensive criticism may be legitimate, pure insults and gratuitous personal attacks are not.[32] The same standards that the ECtHR has developed in cases concerning judges in the United Kingdom and Austria should likewise apply in favour of European judges in Strasbourg. One may wonder whether certain media attacks on the ECtHR and its former President, Nicolas Bratza, are still acceptable according to these standards.[33] Characterising ECtHR judges as 'Europe's court jesters' and its British President Bratza as the 'son of a Serbian concert violinist' who had 'never held a senior judicial position in Britain', as *The Times* did on 19 April 2012,[34] ridicules and decries the members of the Court in general and its President in particular. This comes at least close to a gratuitous personal attack, which goes beyond the public watchdog role of the press.[35]

However, the task of the ECtHR as a human rights court is not to impose restrictions on media freedom in favour of the judiciary but to assess protective measures imposed by domestic authorities. Within the limits drawn by Article 10 ECHR, it is up to the States Parties to decide to what extent the judiciary actually need to be protected. It seems, in fact, that so far no State has prosecuted verbal attacks on the ECtHR through its domestic authorities. This inaction might contribute to a loss of respect for and confidence in the Strasbourg Court. On the other hand, at least, no chilling effects occur that might discourage the media from fulfilling their public watchdog role vis-a-vis the Court.

C. Professional Duties and the Ethics of Journalism

Whilst the public watchdog role of the media is essential for the good functioning of a democratic society, the media themselves have thereby gained a power which must not be exercised without control. Thus, Article 10(2) ECHR recognises that the exercise of freedom of expression goes hand in hand with 'duties and responsibilities'. This formula is unique within the Convention system, and

---

[29] *Prager* (n 25) para 34; *Kobenter* (n 25) para 29 (ii).
[30] See also JP Costa, 'La liberté d'expression des juges de la Cour européenne des droits de l'homme' and Lord Neuberger of Abbotsbury, 'Where Angels Fear to Tread', both in Casadevall, Myjer and O'Boyle (n 9).
[31] *Prager* (n 25) para 34; *Kobenter* (n 25) para 29 (ii); *Mustafa Erdoğan* (n 25) para 42.
[32] *Mustafa Erdoğan* (n 25) paras 44–45.
[33] See E Myjer, 'About Court Jesters: Freedom of Expression and Duties and Responsibilities of Journalists' in Casadevall, Myjer and O'Boyle (n 9) 111.
[34] Reprinted in Myjer, ibid, 112.
[35] *Mustafa Erdoğan* (n 25) paras 44–45.

it emphasises the need to protect other rights and interests against excessive and unfair media coverage. The private lives of celebrities and other individuals must be respected, just as the authority and impartiality of the judiciary must be protected against undue interference. The ECtHR has referred to these duties and responsibilities in order to explain that the media must act 'in good faith and on an accurate factual basis and providing reliable and precise information in accordance with the ethics of journalism …'[36] While it is up to the media itself to choose the technique of reporting they deem appropriate in a given case, they must respect certain professional standards.[37] However, as the media are expected to fulfil their watchdog role with regard to the exercise of public authority, public authorities are not in a good position to set professional standards for the media. Parliament and public administration might be tempted to rule out inconvenient criticism. In order to avoid the risks of public authority press regulation, European human rights law gives preference to a system of self-regulation. The Resolution on Indicators for Media in a Democracy adopted by the Parliamentary Assembly of the Council of Europe in 2008 spells out this concept:

> [T]here should be a system of media self-regulation including a right of reply and correction or voluntary apologies by journalists. Media should set up their own self-regulatory bodies, such as complaints commissions or ombudspersons, and decisions of such bodies should be implemented. These measures should be recognised legally by the courts; … journalists should set up their own professional codes of conduct and they should be applied.[38]

The ECtHR has likewise referred to such systems of self-regulation. In *Stoll v Switzerland* the judges willingly endorsed the careful opinion given by the Swiss Press Council when ruling that Swiss authorities had rightly prosecuted journalists for disclosing a confidential diplomatic paper.[39] When it came to analysing whether the form of the incriminated articles met the standards of journalistic ethics, the Court made it clear that 'the opinion of the Press Council, a specialised and independent body, [was] of particular importance'.[40] In *Max Mosley v UK*, self-regulation again played an important role. The ECtHR noted, inter alia, that a system of press self-regulation had been established in the UK before it concluded that Article 10 ECHR did not require a pre-notification procedure, which would go beyond the existing standards of the Editors' Code of Practice and UK law.[41] This preference for self-regulation reflects the public watchdog role of the media. As the media are expected to scrutinise and, if necessary, criticise parliamentary, governmental and judicial state authorities, any state control over the media might discourage

---

[36] *Kurier Zeitungsverlag und Druckerei v Austria* App no 1593/06 (19 June 2012), para 48; see also *Stoll v Switzerland* (2008) 47 EHRR 59 (GC), para 103; *Mosley v UK* (n 5) para 113.

[37] *Jersild v Denmark* (n 17) para 31; *Mosley v UK* (n 5) para 113.

[38] Council of Europe, Parliamentary Assembly, Resolution 1636 (2008) of 3 October 2008 on indicators for media in a democracy, 8.25–8.26 (available at semantic-pace.net); for an overview of existing systems of self-regulation see L Fielden, 'A Royal Charter for the Press: Lessons from Overseas' (2013) 5 *Journal of Media Law* 172.

[39] *Stoll v Switzerland* (n 36) paras 22–24, 122, 126–28, 133, 135, 145, 147, 150–51.

[40] ibid, para 145.

[41] *Mosley v UK* (n 5) esp para 119.

them from fulfilling their public watchdog role.[42] Therefore, State control over the media should be reduced to a minimum. This is possible if the media establishes a system of self-regulation, which will enable state authorities to confine themselves to a subsidiary control.[43] Unfortunately, the ECtHR has not further developed this idea. So, it is up to the States Parties to decide on an appropriate framework for self-regulation and on the necessary degree of state supervision in their respective countries.

III. WHAT ROLE FOR THE ECtHR?

A. The Margin of Appreciation after *MGN* and *von Hannover (No 2)*

The ECtHR held quite early on in its jurisprudence that state authorities may enjoy a certain margin of appreciation when a balance must be struck between competing rights and interests.[44] It has held that the margin of appreciation is particularly wide where morals are at stake.[45] The lack of a consensus among European States may be another reason for granting a wide margin of appreciation.[46] However, the case law has hardly been consistent in this respect. In more recent years, it has become clear that the margin of appreciation doctrine is an essential element of substantive subsidiarity.[47] Without the principle of subsidiarity, the high-level protection of human rights granted by the ECtHR might in fact harmonise legal human rights cultures throughout Europe. Ultimately, the common European minimum standard guaranteed by the ECHR could evolve into a uniform high-quality standard which leaves no room for diverging domestic standards. Thus, integrating European human rights law would equalise existing European cultures and legal traditions to the detriment of the current richness. Moreover, domestic constitutional courts would lose their innovative capacity if they were reduced to implementing ECtHR standards. European governments clearly rebutted the idea of uniform European standards when they recently adopted Protocol No 15 to the ECHR.[48] Article 1 of Protocol No 15 shall add to the Convention Preamble a reference to the principle of subsidiarity and to the margin of appreciation. Whilst the new recital recognises the 'supervisory jurisdiction' of the ECtHR, it emphasises that States bear 'the primary responsibility to secure' human rights.

---

[42] See A White, 'Ethical Journalism and Human Rights' in T Hammarberg, D Mijatović et al, *Human Rights and a Changing Media Landscape* (Strasbourg, Council of Europe Publishing, 2011) 47, 57–59 with regard to threats posed by defamation laws.

[43] See also T Hammarberg, 'Media Freedom and Human Rights in Europe' in Casadevall, Myjer and O'Boyle (n 9) 43, 48–49.

[44] See *Young, James and Webster v UK* (1982) 4 EHRR 38, para 65, with reference to *Sunday Times v UK (No 1)* (n 28) para 59; for a recent confirmation see *Eweida et al v UK* (2013) 57 EHRR 8, para 84.

[45] *Handyside v UK* (n 8) para 48; *Müller et al v Switzerland* (1991) 13 EHRR 212, paras 35–36.

[46] *SH et al v Austria* App no 57813/00, 31 BHRC 443 (GC), para 94.

[47] See also G Lübbe-Wolff, 'How Can the European Court of Human Rights Reinforce the Role of National Courts in the Convention System?' (2012) 32 *Human Rights Law Journal* 11, 14.

[48] Protocol No 15 amending the Convention on the Protection of Human Rights and Fundamental Freedoms of 24 June 2013, CETS No 213.

If the risk of full harmonisation is to be avoided, the ECtHR must give leeway to national solutions by granting a wide margin of appreciation. Although the principle of subsidiarity applies to the European Convention as a whole, it has gained specific importance in cases involving the role of the media. In *MGN Limited*, the ECtHR was faced with a judgment of the House of Lords that had been adopted by a narrow majority of 3:2.[49] The ECtHR highlighted that the High Court, the Court of Appeal and especially the five members of the House of Lords had carefully examined the case and that the different judges had given detailed analyses.[50] In this situation, the ECtHR considered

> that, having regard to the margin of appreciation accorded to decisions of national courts in this context, the Court would require strong reasons to substitute its view for that of the final decision of the House of Lords or, indeed, to prefer the decision of the minority to that of the majority of that court, as the applicant urged the Court to do.[51]

As the ECtHR could not find such reasons, it accepted the majority view of the House of Lord which saw Naomi Campbell's private life violated by publishing details of her treatment for drug addiction and showing photos of her allegedly leaving a Narcotics Anonymous meeting,[52] although the fact that Naomi Campbell had previously publicly denied being a drug addict had in principle justified the media's interest.[53] Two years later, the Grand Chamber affirmed this approach in *von Hannover (No 2)*:

> Where the balancing exercise has been undertaken by the national authorities in conformity with the criteria laid down in the Court's case-law, the Court would require strong reasons to substitute its view for that of the domestic courts.[54]

In this case, the ECtHR agreed with the German Federal Constitutional Court in accepting the view of the German Federal Court of Justice that a report on the illness of the then reigning Prince of Monaco provided sufficient reason to publish photos of his daughter and son-in-law on a skiing holiday at this time.[55] At first glance, *MGN Limited* was decided in favour of the celebrity's private life, whilst *von Hannover (No 2)* was decided in favour of the press. In reality, however, both cases were decided in favour of the domestic judiciary. Although both were 'borderline case[s]',[56] the ECtHR accepted the solutions reached in the domestic proceedings because they were based on a careful examination of the cases at hand and of the criteria developed by the ECtHR.

---

[49] *Campbell v MGN* [2004] UKHL 22, [2004] 2 AC 457.
[50] *MGN v UK* (2011) 53 EHRR 5, para 149.
[51] ibid, para 150.
[52] ibid, paras 6 ff; see also *Campbell v MGN* (n 49) paras 88, 125, 160, 170.
[53] See Lord Hoffmann in *Campbell v MGN* (n 49) paras 36, 63, 66.
[54] *von Hannover v Germany (No 2)* (n 5) para 107.
[55] ibid, paras 117–18.
[56] See Arden LJ, 'Media Intrusion and Human Rights: Striking the Balance' in Casadevall, Myjer and O'Boyle (n 9) 69, 77 with regard to *von Hannover v Germany (No 2)*; for *MGN* see R Walker, 'When Is there a Public Interest in Private Life?' in Casadevall, Myjer and O'Boyle (n 9) 61, 64–65.

It is true that the ECtHR was criticised for disregarding the margin of appreciation in *Axel Springer AG*, which was decided on the same day as *von Hannover (No 2)*.[57] In fact, it seems that it remains difficult for the Court to accept its limited role as a European watchdog—a role that follows from the principle of subsidiarity. Two Chamber judgments handed down in the first half of 2014 confirm this view. In *Couderc and Hachette Filipacchi Associés*, the Strasbourg Court held by four votes to three that the French Cour de Cassation had erred in restricting freedom of the press.[58] Although both the majority judgment and the Dissenting Opinion referred to the margin of appreciation, the Court entered into a detailed analysis of the criteria relevant to balancing media freedom and respect for private life without further developing the concept of a margin of appreciation to be accorded to domestic courts.[59] In *Lillo-Stenberg and Sæther*, by contrast, the ECtHR clearly reaffirmed *MGN Limited* and *von Hannover (No 2)*. The ECtHR had to review a Norwegian Supreme Court judgment[60] which had been rendered by the same majority of three votes to two as the House of Lords judgment in *MGN Limited*. The ECtHR stated that

> both the majority and the minority of the Norwegian Supreme Court carefully balanced the right of freedom of expression with the right to respect for private life, and explicitly took into account the criteria set out in the Court's case-law which existed at the relevant time.[61]

As a consequence, it accepted the press-friendly solution reached by the Supreme Court because it did not find sufficient reason to substitute the majority view with that of the minority or with its own view.[62]

Comparing *Couderc* with *Lillo-Stenberg*, *MGN Limited* and *von Hannover (No 2)*, one might be inclined to put the different attitude adopted in *Couderc* down to different domestic legal cultures. In *MGN Limited* and *Lillo-Stenberg*, both the majorities and the minorities of the domestic supreme courts gave detailed legal analyses of the case.[63] Whilst German legal procedure does not allow Dissenting Opinions in ordinary courts, the Federal Court of Justice equally rendered a carefully reasoned judgment in *von Hannover (No 2)*.[64] In *Couderc*, by contrast, the Cour de Cassation merely gave a short summary of relevant aspects.[65] It seems that the new margin of appreciation approach taken by ECtHR privileges legal systems where judicial decisions are carefully reasoned. When domestic judges are willing to adopt the balancing test developed under the ECHR seriously, they enjoy a wide

---

[57] See *Axel Springer AG v Germany* (2012) 55 EHRR 6 (GC), Dissenting Opinion of Judge López Guerra joined by Judges Jungwiert, Jaeger, Villiger and Poalelungi; M Pellonpää, 'Some Thoughts on the Principle of Subsidiarity and Margin of Appreciation in the Context of Freedom of Expression' in Casadevall, Myjer and O'Boyle (n 9) 519, 537.

[58] *Couderc and Hachette Filipacchi Associés v France* App no 40454/07 (ECtHR, 12 June 2014).

[59] ibid, paras 47–48, 74 and Dissenting Opinion of Judges Villiger, Zupančič and Lemmens.

[60] *Lillo-Stenberg and Sæther v Norway* App no 13258/09 (16 January 2014), para 12.

[61] ibid, para 44.

[62] ibid, paras 44–45; for a critique of the Supreme Court's majority view see E Weinert, 'European Court of Human Rights Sanctions Long-Lens Photography of Celebrity Wedding: *Lillo-Stenberg v Norway* (No 13258/09) (16 January 2014)' (2014) 25 *Entertainment Law Review* 183, 186.

[63] See *MGN v UK* (n 50) paras 26–54; *Lillo-Stenberg* (n 60) paras 13–14.

[64] See *von Hannover v Germany (No 2)* (n 5) paras 29–39.

[65] See *Couderc and Hachette Filipacchi Associés v France* (n 58) para 24.

margin of appreciation with regard to the outcome of a given case.[66] However, if domestic courts barely spell out their reasoning, in accordance with French legal tradition, they may not avail themselves of a margin of appreciation.

There is another possible explanation. In *Lillo-Stenberg* and *von Hannover (No 2)* the ECtHR accepted domestic judgments which favoured the press,[67] while in *Couderc* and *Axel Springer AG* the ECtHR criticised domestic courts for not having decided in favour of the press. Ultimately, in all of these cases, freedom of the media prevailed. *MGN Limited* is not only the oldest case in this line, but it is also the only one in which the media lost both before domestic courts and in Strasbourg. So, beyond commitments to the margin of appreciation, ECtHR case law might be revealing an implicit press-friendly attitude since the 2012 Grand Chamber judgments against Germany in *von Hannover (No 2)* and *Axel Springer AG*.

B. The Role of an Advisory Opinion Procedure

Protocol No 16,[68] which has not yet entered into force, is to introduce an advisory opinion procedure with a view to strengthening the dialogue between domestic courts and Strasbourg.[69] Under this protocol, the highest domestic courts would be able to ask the ECtHR to deliver an advisory opinion on questions of ECHR guarantees which have been posed in pending proceedings. The advisory opinion procedure resembles the preliminary rulings procedure under Article 267 TFEU. Under this provision, any domestic court may request a preliminary ruling by the Court of Justice of the European Union if the interpretation of EU law or the validity of secondary EU law is at stake in a given case. In both cases, domestic courts suspend their proceedings in order to seek the advice of a European court. However, the aim of the two procedures is quite different. While the advisory opinion procedure should respect the principle of subsidiarity,[70] the preliminary rulings procedure is an essential means of guaranteeing the uniform interpretation and application of EU law throughout EU Member States.[71] This quest for uniformity, which is the rationale of Article 267 TFEU, runs counter to the very idea of substantive subsidiarity. While preliminary references guarantee the uniform application of European law, a margin of appreciation signifies that divergent solutions found by domestic judges may equally conform to common European standards. If domestic courts use

---

[66] See also A Bårdsen, 'The Norwegian Supreme Court and Strasbourg: The Case of *Lillo-Stenberg and Sæther v Norway*' (2014) 15 *German Law Journal* 1293, 1305.

[67] *von Hannover v Germany (No 3)* (n 7) also enters into this line.

[68] Protocol No 16 to the Convention on the Protection of Human Rights and Fundamental Freedoms of 2 October 2013, CETS No 214.

[69] See Council of Europe, Explanatory Report to Protocol No 16, para 1, conventions.coe.int/Treaty/EN/Reports/Html/214.htm; Parliamentary Assembly, Opinion 285 (2013) of 28 June 2013, 2.1 (available at semantic-pace.net).

[70] See the third recital of the Preamble to Protocol No 16.

[71] See Case 166/73 *Rheinmühlen-Düsseldorf v Einfuhr- und Vorratsstelle für Getreide und Futtermittel* [1974] ECR 33, para 2; Case 107/76 *Hoffmann-La Roche v Centrafarm Vertriebsgesellschaft Pharmazeutischer Erzeugnisse mbH* [1977] ECR 957, para 5.

the advisory opinion procedure under Protocol 16 and ask the ECtHR about the parameters for a balancing test before they have completed their own assessment of the case and then simply implement the Opinion of the ECtHR, their own margin of appreciation is curtailed. This illustrates the danger of an advisory opinion procedure where domestic courts should have a margin for decisions that are not predetermined by European standards.[72]

In fact, in *MGN Limited, von Hannover (No 2)* and *Lillo-Stenberg and Sæther*, subsidiarity has been realised without an advisory opinion procedure. Quite to the contrary, a request for an advisory opinion might have induced the ECtHR to go into the details of the cases and to strike a balance between the competing interests involved where it was up to the domestic courts to strike this balance.[73] If Protocol No 16 had been in force 10 years ago, the German Federal Court of Justice might have requested an advisory opinion after the 2004 Chamber judgment in *von Hannover (No 1)* in order to challenge the Chamber's very restrictive concept of public figures which excluded celebrities like Caroline von Hannover who assumed no official functions.[74] In its request, the Federal Court of Justice could have exposed why the Chamber was wrong, and this would have given the ECtHR the chance to rectify its position and to adopt a broader concept of public figures. However, the same result has been attained even in the absence of an advisory opinion procedure. German courts simply refused to follow exactly the narrow approach taken by the Chamber in *von Hannover (No 1)*. In *von Hannover (No 2)*, the Grand Chamber had the opportunity to revisit the question and corrected the Chamber's restrictive view by stating that Caroline von Hannover was a public figure irrespective of any official functions.[75]

These examples show that domestic courts and the ECtHR may enter into a fruitful dialogue without having an advisory opinion procedure at their disposal. At the same time, the advisory opinion procedure, which comes close to the EU preliminary rulings procedure, might foster the unifying impetus of ECtHR case law if domestic courts ask the ECtHR to assess a specific situation. So Protocol No 16 may even harm the principle of subsidiarity unless requests under this Protocol are handled with utmost care. Domestic courts should only use the advisory opinion procedure in order to challenge Strasbourg case law. In this case, the request, which has to be reasoned according to Article 1(3) of Protocol No 16, must explain why the ECtHR should modify its jurisprudence. If these requirements are not met, the Panel of the Grand Chamber established under Article 2(1) of Protocol No 16 should refuse to accept the request. After all, the risk that Protocol No 16 might turn into a means of unifying human rights standards throughout Europe[76] remains high.

[72] See also Pellonpää (n 57) 538.
[73] See ibid, 538–39.
[74] See *von Hannover v Germany (No 1)* (n 7) para 72.
[75] See *von Hannover v Germany (No 2)* (n 5) para 120.
[76] See above, III.A.

IV. CONCLUSION

In conclusion, the media play a prominent public watchdog role in all debates of public interest. This has been recognised by the ECtHR, and it is also true of any discussion on the proper role of the ECtHR. However, like any other powerful body, the media must be themselves controlled. Over the years, the ECtHR has developed a series of criteria which help in assessing the relevance of media freedom in a given case. Starting from the idea of a democratic society enshrined in Article 10(2) ECHR, which is associated with 'pluralism, tolerance and broadmindedness', the ECtHR has held that freedom of expression extends to information and ideas that 'offend, shock or disturb'.[77] Given the public watchdog function of the press, protection is particularly strong where a debate of public interest is at stake, whereas pure entertainment or 'idle gossip'[78] will rarely be able to justify an interference with other interests such as the protection of private life.[79] The judiciary deserve particular protection in order to uphold their authority and public confidence in their impartiality. Judges need greater protection than politicians because judicial neutrality and discretion hinder them from defending themselves against public attacks in the same way that politicians are able to.[80] While ECtHR judges should also be protected from 'destructive attacks that are essentially unfounded'[81] and from gratuitous personal attacks, such protection may not come from the ECtHR. Rather, protecting the domestic and the European judiciary falls within the competence of States Parties.

Within this framework, it is up to self-regulatory bodies and domestic authorities to control the media. European human rights law gives a certain preference to self-regulation in order to shield the media from state interference that might compromise their public watchdog role. Nevertheless, the specific regulatory regime is left to political choice.[82] As long as control is carefully and effectively realised at the domestic level, the European watchdog should not intervene.[83] Properly handled, the margin of appreciation doctrine is a powerful tool for realising the substantial subsidiarity of the Convention system. In this context, Protocol No 15 is to be welcomed because it reminds the ECtHR of its subsidiary role, whereas Protocol No 16 might have the adverse effect of fostering the unification of human rights standards throughout Europe unless the advisory opinion procedure is used with utmost prudence and with the sole aim of challenging existing Strasbourg case law.[84]

---

[77] *Handyside v UK* (n 8) para 49.
[78] See *Standard Verlags GmbH v Austria (No 2)* (n 20) para 52.
[79] See above, II.A.
[80] See above, II.B.
[81] See Prager (n 25) para 34; *Kobenter and Standard Verlags GmbH v Austria* (n 25) para 29(ii); *Mustafa Erdoğan* (n 25) para 42.
[82] See above, II.C.
[83] See above, III.A.
[84] See above, III.B.

23

'You Couldn't Make it Up': Some Narratives of the Media's Coverage of Human Rights'

DAVID MEAD

I. INTRODUCTION

It is a sign of a healthy democracy that there are different views within society and that the outcome of individual cases, and the balance struck between individual rights, can be vigorously debated. But such debates must be based on fact, not misconception, deliberate or otherwise. Persuasion should be based on truth rather than propaganda.[1]

T HIS CHAPTER MOVES away from the easy comfort of doctrinal study. Its focus is the misreporting of human rights stories in the British media or—perhaps more accurately—in sections of it. Such a phenomenon will become of pivotal importance as we move towards repeal of the Human Rights Act 1998 (HRA) and replacement with a British Bill of Rights, and loosening of ties to Strasbourg, following the Conservative election victory in May 2015. It was prompted in part by my own experiences of making a complaint to the Press Complaints Commission (PCC) about newspaper coverage of publicly funded immigration cases, specifically a piece in the *Daily Mail* on 1 July 2013 entitled 'Legal Aid Lawyers Milking Pointless Migrant Appeals: Nine in Ten Cases are Thrown Out as Number of Reviews Soars to 10,000 a Year'.[2] The claim was brought under clause 1(i) of the Editors' Code of Practice: publishing inaccurate, misleading or distorted information. It is simply untrue that 90 per cent of legally

---

[1] Lord Neuberger MR giving the annual Judicial Studies Board lecture 'Open Justice Unbound', 16 March 2011. The speech was previously available at www.judiciary.gov.uk/Resources/JCO/Documents/Speeches/mr-speech-jsb-lecture-march-2011.pdf but has since been removed. Reference from author's own notes.

[2] J Doyle and J Slack, 'Legal Aid Lawyers Milking Pointless Migrant Appeals: Nine in Ten Cases are Thrown Out as Number of Reviews Soars to 10,000 a Year' *Daily Mail* (London, 1 July 2013), www.dailymail.co.uk/news/article-2352107/Legal-aid-lawyers-milking-pointless-migrant-appeals-Nine-cases-thrown-number-reviews-soars-10-000-year.html. Noting without judging that the *Daily Mail* was responsible for 36% of complaints to the PCC in 2013 while accepting that the stories are not solely about legal, let alone human rights reporting, nor always about accuracy: Brian Cathcart, 'The Table of Statistics the Press Complaints Commission Would Rather You Didn't See' *Huffington Post* (31 January 2014), www.huffingtonpost.co.uk/professor-brian-cathcart/pcc-complaint-statistics_b_4701685.html.

aided immigration judicial reviews fail at the first hurdle—that is, are refused permission. Data from the Bingham Centre supplied to the Ministry of Justice consultation on judicial review in 2013[3] provides evidence that a legally aided applicant is about five times more likely to be given permission than a privately funded one. Ultimately I 'succeeded': following informal resolution, the *Mail* agreed to publish a clarification. The matter took over five months to be resolved, by which time of course much damage had been done, and any clarification was somewhat stale. Two lessons result from this. First, procuring a PCC (or, I suppose, an Independent Press Standards Organisation (IPSO)) resolution takes a great deal of time, energy and resilience. Few of us have enough of all three. Many hours were invested in making a case, analysing the Ministry of Justice (MoJ) data to counter the *Mail*'s repeated assertions in correspondence. Second, many articles must, therefore, pass into the public domain without correction. No one can remain eagle-eyed and vigilant all the time. It is this that led to my interest in human rights reporting in the media.

This chapter will proceed in three main parts: what types of misreporting do we see? (II); how is this misreporting achieved? (III); and what narratives do we pick up, and what wider ramifications might there be (IV)? It will conclude (V) that large numbers of us in the UK, simply through our choice of daily newspaper, may have an understanding of human rights—and their protection—that is greatly at odds with reality. There is a real skew in the sorts of stories that are reported and the sorts of people portrayed as worthy rights-holders, as well as a misrepresentation of the frequency with which human rights claims succeed and with which they are even asserted. Such stories, or many of them, play into a narrative of fear and security— how many stories can we think of about terrorism/terrorists and security, linked to human rights claims?—and a narrative of Englishness, and of European 'otherness' and invasion. In short, newspaper articles and headlines frame, in the sense used by George Lakoff,[4] the debate about human rights and political entitlement and portray a very narrow, partial conception of what it means to say, and to claim, that something is 'against human rights'.

It ought to be added, lest it be thought otherwise, that such a conclusion is not especially new, not in some circles anyway. There was a section on myths and misunderstandings in the review of the working of the Human Rights Act by the Department for Constitutional Affairs (DCA), as long ago as 2006.[5] We might think too of the work done by the Human Rights Futures project at the London School of Economics (in June 2011)[6] and especially of the sterling efforts of barrister Adam

---

[3] Response to Ministry of Justice Consultation Paper CP 14/2013, *Transforming Legal Aid: Delivering a More Credible and Efficient System*, 7, www.biicl.org/files/6419_bingham_centre_legal_aid_response_june_2013.pdf.

[4] G Lakoff, *Don't Think of an Elephant: Know your Values and Frame the Debate* (White River Junction, Chelsea Green Publishing, 2004).

[5] Department for Constitutional Affairs Review into the Implementation of the Human Rights Act (July 2006).

[6] *Human Rights Act Reporting in the Media: Corrections and Clarifications*, www.lse.ac.uk/human-Rights/documents/2011/KlugHRAMedia.pdf.

Wagner, editor of the UK Human Rights blog.[7] There is much in what follows that would have escaped me had he not written about it. Further, it has to be added that this chapter is not to any extent informed by any sort of communications theory, although it might be developed in this direction in the future. That said, this chapter offers something new, or some insights at least, first by bringing together much of what has been written on this topic before, alongside some recent examples, and then by providing a limited framework within which we might view it all.

II. TYPES OF MISREPORTING

This section sets out a simple typology, identifying the ways in which the daily copy produced by journalists might fail accurately to convey either the full or proper human rights dimension of any story. In turn, we shall consider what we will term 'clearly misleading' reporting—reporting that wrongly locates the story within a human rights context, and a scapegoating or undermining narrative of a human rights story. There is no hard and fast distinction between any and each of these three. None of them necessarily speaks either to journalistic intention—does the writer or editor seek to mislead or is it simply an ignorance of the basic facts or legal situation?—or to a wider hidden agenda. That said, one would clearly have to be very benevolent indeed to assume that in none of the instances that follows was there anything but—at worst—a sloppiness of research or simply the unquestioned repetition of journalistic assumptions about law.

A. Misleading Human Rights Stories

The most obvious, best-known and constantly asserted—by those critical of media reporting of human rights issues—is the tendency to conflate the 'two Europes'. This is amply demonstrated by each of the two following headlines, chosen as exemplars of each side of the coin. The *Sun*, in the first example,[8] seeks to convey the thrust of the Court of Appeal's decision upholding a challenge on Article 8 grounds to the system of enhanced criminal records checks.[9] Yet, readers would be left with the view that this was another matter of EU meddling, alongside the apocryphal supposed ban on bent bananas.[10] Whether this was deliberate on the part of the newspaper or simply sloppiness, who can say? The report led to a PCC complaint

---

[7] ukhumanrightsblog.com.

[8] A Lazzeri 'Inhuman Rights' *The Sun* (London, 10 February 2013), www.thesun.co.uk/sol/homepage/news/4787497/Youngsters-at-risk-after-EU-ruling.html. The online version has now been amended.

[9] *R (oao T) v Chief Constable of Greater Manchester Police* [2013] EWCA Civ 25, upheld recently by the Supreme Court: [2014] UKSC 35.

[10] The *Sun* reported the relevant Commission Regulation (EC) 2257/94 as 'Brussels bureaucrats proved yesterday what a barmy bunch they are—by outlawing curved bananas' (London, 21 September 1994), on which see the European Commission's own site on Euromyths: ec.europa.eu/unitedkingdom/blog/index_en.htm.

by barrister Adam Wagner and a finding against the paper. However, the eventual correction was hidden in the last column of page two.

By contrast, the second example, taken from the *Daily Telegraph*,[11] reporting the fact that Learco Chindamo, the killer of a London schoolteacher in the 1990s, could not be deported, was in general portrayed as being the result of human rights laws, specifically the HRA, whereas in truth the key reason was the role played by EU freedom of movement law, as codified in the 2004 Citizens' Rights Directive.[12] In short, the media narrative here is one of both Europes being the same. 'What does it matter?', the narrative suggests. 'Let's get out of all them.'

There are countless other examples of sloppy reporting, whether this is the fault of the journalist, an overzealous sub-editor or some other agent or factor in the production of news from event to copy to publication. One example which occurred in late 2013 led to a severe public rebuke from the European Court of Human Rights (ECtHR) itself. It concerned what the Court typified as 'seriously misleading' reports of the amounts of compensation due to be paid by the UK government and, of course, the *Daily Mail* implied, by 'us', that is, the UK taxpayer.

Under the headline 'Human Right to Make a Killing',[13] the *Daily Mail* asserted that murderers, terrorists and traitors had received compensation totalling £4.4m since 1998, making a sum of '£22,000 for each taxpayer-funded criminal'. What the story did not reveal was, first, that the sum of £4.4m was for both costs and compensation, with the former comprising just under 40 per cent of the total, and, secondly, that the sums covered all those who succeeded before the ECtHR. This included, as the Court's release made clear,[14] those who had been blacklisted on grounds that they were Catholic (*Tinnelly*),[15] and a disabled mother and her son (*Glass*[16]). The damage, which we may infer was intended, was done. Readers of the *Daily Mail* will have had a choice of two narratives, perhaps combined: human rights suck money from hard-working families, and human rights are not for the likes of us. We shall revert to this below. The story was corrected, over a month later, noting that '[i]n fact, the money went to a range of claimants and only £1.7million

[11] C Hope, 'Learco Chindamo: The Deportation Debate' *Daily Telegraph* (London, 23 August 2007), www.telegraph.co.uk/news/uknews/1561081/Learco-Chindamo-The-deportation-debate.html.

[12] European Parliament and Council Directive 2004/38/EC of 29 April 2004 on the right of citizens of the Union and their family members to move and reside freely within the territory of the Member States [2004] OJ L158/77.

[13] 'Human Right to Make a Killing' *Daily Mail* (London, 8 October 2013), www.dailymail.co.uk/news/article-2449256/Human-right-make-killing-Damning-dossier-reveals-taxpayers-European-court-payouts-murderers-terrorists-traitors.html.

[14] Council of Europe, 'Court Concern at "Seriously Misleading" UK News Articles' (11 October 2013), www.humanrightseurope.org/2013/10/court-concern-at-seriously-misleading-uk-news-articles.

[15] *Tinnelly v UK* (1998) 27 EHRR 24.

[16] *Glass v UK* (2004) 39 EHRR 15.

was compensation; legal costs accounted for the rest'.[17] As Adam Wagner pointed out on the UK Human Rights blog,

> the damage is already done. A month has passed, which in social media time might as well be a million years. People have moved on. Another human rights myth is implanted in the collective consciousness, and no sad little correction is going to dislodge a front page headline.[18]

There is much work to be done, beyond the confines of this paper, to consider the differential impact, and thus differential problems associated with reporting—whether of legal stories or more generally—in traditional and reporting in new media, online. One is obviously longevity or durability, another searchability or retrievability, and another, as we shall see below, the linking of supposedly similar stories algorithmically.

Another newspaper report, on similar lines, again ignoring the legal reality, was a report in the *Times* that 'tens of thousands of prisoners are in line for compensation because they have been denied the right to vote'.[19] This assertion was made even though in none of the prisoner cases so far has the ECtHR awarded any damages and even though the Court had noted that in any future cases it was unlikely even to award costs, as was pointed out on the Council of Europe's own HumanRightsEurope blog.[20] Since the publication of that story, of course, that has been proved correct: in *Firth v UK* there was no award of either compensation or even costs, with the Court holding that judgment itself was satisfaction enough.[21]

B. Overemphasising the Human Rights Elements

This is the second example of misreporting—a criticism that seems counter-intuitive: instinctively, we might well think that newspaper stories that give prominence to human rights concerns and explain outcomes of legal decisions in terms of human rights should be lauded as adding to public knowledge and as contributing to an informed debate. Generally this would indeed be the case, but in the illustrative examples selected below, a different analysis is offered. These are cases or situations where we can identify newspapers as having tended to overplay the critical role of human rights doctrine in decision-making, where the narrative subtext being created is one that is suggestive of human rights marginalising more 'traditional values', or defeating what would be a common sense outcome. In short, the blame for the

---

[17] *Daily Mail* (10 November 2013), www.dailymail.co.uk/home/article-2498733/Clarifications-corrections-European-Court-Human-Rights.html.

[18] A Wagner, 'Too Little Too Late as Daily Mail "Corrects" Bogus Human Rights Splash' UK Human Rights Blog (12 November 2013), ukhumanrightsblog.com/2013/11/12/too-little-too-late-as-daily-mail-corrects-bogus-human-rights-splash.

[19] R Ford, 'Prisoners Denied Vote Could Win Damages' *The Times* (London, 25 October 2013), www.thetimes.co.uk/tto/law/article3903856.ece (paywall).

[20] Council of Europe, 'Court: UK Media Guns Take Aim Again' (25 October 2013), www.humanrightseurope.org/2013/10/court-uk-media-guns-take-aim-again.

[21] *Firth v UK* [2014] ECHR 874 (GC).

'wrong' result can, and should, be placed squarely at the door of European human rights law. There are two subtly different forms of this. The first, which can be seen most often in immigration decisions, are those decisions which are frequently made on grounds other than the Human Rights Act 1998 (HRA) yet where the HRA is placed at the forefront of the story. Secondly, and at one stage removed, is the practice of imposing a damning human rights narrative where simply there was none, again (implicitly or explicitly) to confound what should otherwise have been the 'right' result. Perhaps the best known in this category are what have become known apocryphally as the 'KFC prisoner' and police wanted posters.

Turning to the first, on 12 May 2014 readers of the *Daily Telegraph* were presented with the following headline: 'Immigration Judges Block Foreign Killer's Deportation on "Human Rights" Grounds'.[22] A close reading of the decision referred to, that of Judge Renton in the Upper Tribunal in *MAI v Secretary of State for the Home Department*,[23] shows that one key factor in the Upper Tribunal reaching a different view to that of the Panel was ultimately a different evaluation of the threat of persecution if MAI were returned. The Upper Tribunal considered that the Panel had erred in law in concluding that MAI would not face persecution if returned, since the Panel '[did] not deal with the evidence given by the Appellant and members of his family concerning relevant events in the UK and the nature of the Somali clan system which would allow information to be transmitted from the UK to Somalia of the Appellant's movements'. The reader of this *Telegraph* piece would have no idea that there was this alternative, more 'traditional' common law basis to the appeal being upheld. The only reference to this in the paper was its report that 'MAI also claimed that he would be the target of a "blood feud" by the family of FA, whom he killed in Cardiff in 1997'. Without indicating that this claim also formed part of the judge's reasoning, while quoting at length from the judgment those aspects pertaining to Article 8, this way of reporting leaves readers with a skewed view of the relevance and weight attached to the ECHR. It would be fair to say the *Telegraph* has 'form' on this, as Adam Wagner documents well.[24] On 16 June 2012, it reported that of 184 deportation appeals brought in the preceding year on, or including, Article 8 grounds, a little over half (96) were successful, but the paper did not indicate how many were successful solely or primarily, or only, on Article 8 grounds.[25] As Adam Wagner has pointed out, they could be successfully appealed on grounds of error of law, rationality or even for procedural flaws as well as, or instead of, Article 8.[26]

---

[22] D Barrett, 'Immigration Judges Block Foreign Killer's Deportation on "Human Rights" Grounds' *Daily Telegraph* (London, 12 May 2014), www.telegraph.co.uk/news/uknews/immigration/10824715/Immigration-judges-block-foreign-killers-deportation-on-human-rights-grounds.html.

[23] Case DA/01641/2013 and IA/18986/2012, 16 April 2014, tribunalsdecisions.service.gov.uk/utiac/da-01641-2013-ia-18986-2012.

[24] A Wagner, 'Immigration Judges Named and Shamed by *Sunday Telegraph*' UK Human Rights Blog (17 June 2012), ukhumanrightsblog.com/2012/06/17/immigration-judges-named-and-shamed-by-sunday-telegraph.

[25] D Barrett, 'Judges who Allow Foreign Criminals to Stay in Britain' *Daily Telegraph* (London, 16 June 2012), www.telegraph.co.uk/news/uknews/immigration/9335689/Judges-who-allow-foreign-criminals-to-stay-in-Britain.html.

[26] Wagner (n 24).

In the second category, imposing human rights in a non-human rights issue, it was widely reported in 2006 that a prisoner staging a rooftop protest was given fast food because his human rights demanded it: the *Sun* reported this story with the headline 'Finger-nickin' good' and reported it thus:

> A YOB who spent all day on a roof lobbing bricks at cops was rewarded with a KFC take-away. Police gave him the meal because of his HUMAN RIGHTS as the suspected car thief staged his second rooftop siege in seven months.[27]

Yet this myth was soon debunked. The police conceded that he was given a KFC meal, but this was part of an overall negotiating strategy, not because of some hitherto unknown arcanity of the ECHR.[28] On similar lines, it has passed into journalistic folklore that human rights are to blame for the police being unable to publicise details of suspects. At the Conservative Party conference in October 2009, the then Shadow Justice Secretary was reported thus: 'How many times have we seen police or probation officers say they can't disclose the identity of a criminal because of his privacy under the Human Rights Act—police in Derbyshire refused to disclose photos of fugitive murderers. That's complete nonsense and we'll end it straight away.'[29] Yet the local force—Derbyshire—released an official statement in response saying it had never refused to release photos on human rights grounds.[30] The danger is all too obvious: either journalists enter into 'groupthink' and do not check the accuracy of what they are reporting; or, even though this does not seem to be the case in this example, those on the ground, here the police officers, come to accept the reflected and reported 'truth', which gains lifeblood and a foothold of its own, and simply procreates unless corrected.

C. Undermining Human Rights Law

Closely linked to this is the third way in which the media misreport human rights issues: heaping blame on the HRA for what in fact are administrative or similar failings. To be fair, this is not generally the fault of the media alone or in isolation, but is symptomatic of a more far-reaching malaise. This is the worrying practice, adopted in the years since 1998 by certain senior politicians, of setting up the HRA as a scapegoat. The media play their role, though, by unquestioningly reporting and repeating these exculpatory claims. We might conclude that this can only be because of a failure of separate journalistic investigation, or we might conclude that it is because the narrative accords with a particular newspaper's *weltanschaung*. The first fits with the criticism aired by *Guardian* journalist Nick Davies in *Flat Earth News*[31]—the reduction in media copy produced by journalists, and the growing trend simply to lift, recycle or regurgitate PR or similar press releases, a practice typified as 'churnalism'. It fits too with the significant reduction on newspaper

---

[27] *The Sun* (London, 7 June 2006).
[28] See DCA Review (n 5) 31 for the rebuttal.
[29] Quoted in LSE Human Rights Futures Project report (n 6) p 1
[30] ibid.
[31] N Davies, *Flat Earth News* (London, Chatto and Windus, 2008).

payrolls of dedicated legal editors.[32] It is, we might think, a strange position for the Fourth Estate to adopt—founded, as media enterprises continue to remind us, most recently and most dramatically in light of the Charlie Hebdo shootings in Paris, on the critical role they play in exposing, criticising and speaking truth to power. All that being so, and media freedom being so highly revered by the media, should we then assume that there must be an alternative explanation for reinforcing these false claims about human rights protections? One can far more easily understand why cabinet ministers would seek to highlight the supposed shortcomings of domestic human rights law, even if we do not accept such excuses as valid. Instead of the fault being (say) limited funds or poorly thought-through policies, it locates blame with the judges and the independent legal system. We all have, after all, a vested interest in portraying ourselves in our best light. It is not the task of independent journalists, though, to be complicit in that venture.

Again, the coverage of a specific single decision, usually known colloquially as the Afghan hijackers case, makes the point. The Joint Committee on Human Rights in its report on the DCA's 2006 review[33] documented all this very well.[34] Both the Prime Minister and the then Home Secretary, John Reid, made public their ire at the High Court decision (by Sullivan J) ordering that a group of Afghanis (who had some time earlier hijacked a plane at Stansted and then claimed asylum) be given discretionary leave to remain.[35] Yet all the High Court had decided was that it was an abuse of power for the Home Secretary to ignore an earlier decision by three Immigration Adjudicators when he had not exhausted all routes of appeal and review. That decision, taken some two years earlier, which had been made after taking extensive (eight days of) evidence, held that returning the applicants to Afghanistan would violate Article 3. In other words, it was unlawful for the executive to seek to usurp and sideline the judicial process by a two-year delay of its own making. Despite the fact that the government itself had accepted prior to that earlier Adjudicators' hearing that none of the hijackers posed a security risk or public danger, the then Home Secretary was reported as saying:

> When decisions are taken which appear inexplicable or bizarre to the general public, it only reinforces the perception that the system is not working to protect or in favour of the vast majority of ordinary decent hard-working citizens in this country.[36]

The Prime Minister himself had voiced similar exasperation: '[I]t's not an abuse of justice for us to order their deportation, it's an abuse of common sense frankly to be in a position where we can't do this.'[37] Yet within 24 hours of John Reid's words

[32] A Wagner, 'The Monstering of Human Rights', speech delivered at the University of Liverpool, 19 September 2014, p 11, author's own personal copy.

[33] See above, n 5.

[34] *The Human Rights Act: The DCA and Home Office Reviews*, 32nd report of session 2005/6, HC 1716/HL 278 (14 November 2006).

[35] *S v Secretary of State for the Home Department* [2006] EWHC 1111 Admin.

[36] 'Government Appeal over Hijackers' BBC News (11 May 2006), news.bbc.co.uk/1/hi/uk_politics/4760873.stm.

[37] Press Conference with the French Prime Minister, 10 May 2006, reported in the DCA Review (n 5) 9.

being uttered, and within 48 hours of the High Court judgment, the *Sun*'s campaign to 'rip up' the HRA had begun. This in turn led to David Cameron's pledge in that same paper to replace the HRA with a British bill of rights—number 3 in a list of 10[38]—and from there we can plot a direct line to the Conservative's policy announcement, in October 2014, with which we are all familiar, and thence their manifesto pledge in the same terms. We might also think here of how the failure by the Home Office to deport several hundred foreign national criminals at the end of their sentences played out in the press, again in 2006. John Reid was interviewed by the *News of the World* and said this:

> [T]he vast majority of decent, law-abiding people ... believe that it is wrong if court judgments put the human rights of foreign prisoners ahead of the safety of UK citizens. They believe that the Government and their wishes are often thwarted by the courts. They want the deportation for foreign nationals [sic] to be considered early in their sentence, and are aware that this was overruled by the courts.[39]

Yet, just a few weeks later his evidence before the Home Affairs Select Committee was very different. It was clear that the reason so many had escaped and thus evaded deportation was as much to do with administrative culture, technological and systems defects and managerial/leadership failings as it was with Article 8 ECHR.[40]

III. THE TECHNIQUES OF MISREPORTING

The previous section identified various types of misreporting. This next part attempts to sketch the ways in which newspaper reporting of the kind described above might mislead readers and leave them without a full or accurate picture. This is not, to repeat a point made above, grounded in communications theory. That said, it is clear that matters such as selective (non-)reporting, and how (that is, positioning vis-a-vis other material) and where (in the paper) a report is presented, as well as the context and the language in which it is written, will also be relevant for the conclusions readers will draw, prompting them one way or another. The same is true for selective (non-)reporting of cases and opinions about specific case law and human rights more broadly. We shall address in turn selectivity—what we might term a sin of omission—and turn then to considering the presentation of a story, or the sins of commission. Specifically, here, we shall consider four factors at play: prominence, phrasing, pre-emption and partiality.

As important to any analysis of human rights reporting as the way in which a news item is constructed is to bear in mind the fact that many human rights cases

---

[38] *The Sun* (London, 3 October 2009).

[39] 'No More Cock-Ups Home Secretary' *News of the World* (London, 7 May 2006).

[40] Home Affairs Select Committee, *Immigration Control* (HC 775, 23 July 2006), oral evidence, 23 May 2006, www.publications.parliament.uk/pa/cm200506/cmselect/cmhaff/775/6052301.htm. Matters have not improved. It is far likelier that structural, fiscal and systemic failings continue to account for the mismanagement of foreign criminals than human rights law: see Public Accounts Committee 29th report 2014/15, *Managing and Removing Foreign National Offenders*, HC 708 (20 January 2015), www. publications.parliament.uk/pa/cm201415/cmselect/cmpubacc/708/70802.htm.

do not even make it into the newspapers. This is trite, but we can only judge what we read—unless we are very well versed in domestic human rights matters, in which case we will probably not be swayed by what is being written in the press in any event. The following are the results of some basic, limited empirical research which tried to ascertain the extent and depth of reporting of recent Strasbourg judgments in the UK. I searched the Nexis database for the names of applicants in cases against the UK in Strasbourg decided between 1 January and 15 May 2014[41] (in the database category for 'UK Newspapers'), alongside general Google searches on the assumption that if a paper were to report anything, it would use the name of the person bringing the case. I think it would be fair to say that readers of newspapers in the UK have an interest in the outcome of such cases. There were four cases against the UK in that period which reached the ECtHR for formal disposal on the merits.

Only readers of the *Daily Telegraph* would know that the UK lost the case brought by an Iborian, in the UK with a false passport, who was claiming recovery of wages confiscated as part of his criminal punishment.[42] Though he succeeded in claiming that this was disproportionate and, therefore, a breach of Article 1 of the First Protocol, he was awarded just £1,630 despite the confiscation of £22,000 in wages. It is easy to see how this could have fitted within a particular media framing: a narrative that is critical of those whom European judges consider to be fitting beneficiaries of protection. It is hard to see why this was not latched onto by the *Daily Mail*, but it seems not to have appeared on its radar. That narrative is all the more visible when we see the related articles, listed in the online version of the *Telegraph*.[43] This opens us up to considering the ductility of readership through hyperlinks and the role played by algorithmic selection, an aspect of media/communications theory that is beyond the remit of this paper.

There was not a single mention in any newspaper of the Court holding, in favour of the government, that the UK's legislation on secondary picketing did not constitute a disproportionate restriction on the right to strike and on trade union activity in Article 11.[44] Similarly, there was no mention of the government winning in the case brought against it by the Mormon Church, which argued that failure to allow it to claim a rate reduction for its two temples violated Article 9 in conjunction with Article 14.[45] By contrast, widely reported was the government's victory in a challenge to the State Immunity Act 1978 over allegations of torture by Saudi Arabia. The ECtHR held that there was not a breach of the right to a fair trial in

---

[41] And so does not cover reporting of *McDonald v UK* [2014] ECHR 492.

[42] *Paulet v UK* [2014] ECHR 477.

[43] These include 'Immigration Judges Block Foreign Killer's Deportation on "Human Rights" Grounds'; '102 Criminals We Can't Deport'; and 'The Foreign Rioters We Cannot Deport Because of their "Right to Family Life"': David Barrett and Bruno Waterfield, 'Strasbourg Awards Damages to Foreign Criminal who Used Fake Passport to Work in Britain' *Daily Telegraph* (London, 13 May 2014), www.telegraph. co.uk/news/uknews/crime/10826941/Strasbourg-awards-damages-to-foreign-criminal-who-used-fake-passport-to-work-in-Britain.html.

[44] *National Union of Rail, Maritime and Transport Workers v UK* App no 31045/10 (ECtHR 2014).

[45] *Church of the Latter-Day Saints v UK* App no 7552/09 (4 March 2014).

Article 6. The case was covered by both the *Guardian* and the *Evening Standard*, although the reach of the latter is limited to London.[46]

It seems likely—let us put it no higher than that, given the limited evidence base above—that readers of certain newspapers will have rather a skewed view of both the Court's caseload, and thus of the reach of human rights protection, and of the likelihood of the Court finding there to be no breach, simply by dint of what is not published rather than what is. We might note by contrast, and again this feeds the same media narrative, that the challenge to whole-life sentences in *Vinter v UK*[47] made all the main national papers. It was covered on the front pages of the *Daily Mail*, *Daily Mirror* and *Daily Telegraph*, there was a double-page spread on pages six to seven of the *Sun*, it made page nine of both the *Guardian* and the *Daily Express*, and a full page on page five of the *Times*, but it was only a short item on page 25 of the *Independent*. Again, as the Court itself pointed out in its rebuke in 2013 to the *Daily Mail*,[48] presenting the 'truth' of the number of government losses since 1998, put at 202, tells a very incomplete story of the cases and case law against the UK unless readers also know that over 13,000 claims against the UK were lodged in that period, making a loss rate of 1.5 per cent![49]

As was noted above, where and how a story is presented—rather than being omitted entirely—can be critical to the views formed of any event. Let us now consider four factors at play: prominence, phrasing, pre-emption and partiality. The prominence of a report on a human rights concern, such as the front-page spread for *Vinter*, is designed to inform the reader of something quite apart from the substance of the story itself. It indicates editorial choice concerning the significance of the story and is of course the only part of a newspaper on general display— the only part that will be seen by those browsing in the newsagent or queuing at the supermarket checkout. While it might not be the best example in many ways, the front-page headline in the *Daily Mail* 'Truth about Tory Catfight'[50] is instructive.

The piece is interesting because it seeks to (re)take some of the moral high ground thought to have been lost in the reporting of what became known in the UK as 'Catgate', arising from the Home Secretary's speech to the Tory Party conference in 2011. The Home Secretary sought to undermine the HRA by referring to a case in which a gay Bolivian man had supposedly avoided deportation because he and his partner (in her words) 'and I am not making this up—had a pet cat', and followed this immediately with, 'This is why I remain of the view that the Human Rights Act needs to go'.[51] The speech, not surprisingly, was widely reported in the

[46] *Jones v UK* [2014] ECHR 32.

[47] *Vinter v UK* [2013] ECHR 645.

[48] Council of Europe (n 14).

[49] Although not the statistics used by the Council in its rebuke, we can see the broad picture in terms of success rate in the Overview 1959–2013: www.echr.coe.int/Pages/home.aspx?p=reports&c= #n1347956867932_pointer. They show (at 7–8) 497 judgments against the UK, of which the government lost 299, but that is in the context of a total number of 19,310 applications decided.

[50] J Doyle et al, 'Truth about Tory Catfight' *Daily Mail* (London, 6 October 2011), www.dailymail. co.uk/news/article-2045794/Theresa-May-cat-claim-Truth-Tory-cat-gate-row.html.

[51] The full speech can be found at www.politics.co.uk/comment-analysis/2011/10/04/theresa-may-speech-in-full.

mainstream media with a very clear focus and skew. The story was not new. The *Daily Mail* itself had reported the original case in 2009 under the headline 'Migrant Facing Deportation Wins Right to Stay in Britain ... Because He's Got a Cat'.[52] The problem was that the judgment did not quite say that, yet it gained a currency all of its own. Thus, with its 'Truth about Catgate' story, the *Daily Mail* entered the fray, seeking to gainsay the deniers. In truth, however, that story, which sought to confirm the correctness of its earlier approach in 2009, is not supported by the judgment. It is stretching the truth to claim, as the subheadline proclaims, that the judge 'DID rule migrant's pet was a reason he shouldn't be deported'.[53] A host of reasons are given in the judgment as to why the man should not be deported, at the end of which Judge Devittie actually says: '[T]he evidence concerning the joint acquisition of Maya by the appellant and his partner *reinforce[d] my conclusion* on the strength and quality of the family life that the appellant and his partner enjoy.'[54] In other words, he had already decided and the cat was simply evidence of the bond, not the reason. It was disingenuous of the *Daily Mail* to claim otherwise, yet this front-page placing not only re-tells the story but seeks to reinforce—and to render unmissable—two of its own pre-existing narratives, both of which would likely accord with its readers' convictions. The first is one that belittles the HRA, implicitly offering readers the view that genuine human rights protection is being undermined by trivial claims. This has clear echoes of the sort of undermining that we witnessed above when we looked at the case of the Afghan hijackers. Second are its implicit preconceptions of who should and who should not be worthy recipients of that protection. Here, it is clear that gay Bolivian men should fall outwith the scope of human rights guarantees.

Next, let us consider the phrasing and language used by the press—something that is crucial in framing discourse. It comes as no surprise that *Daily Mail* readers might not be the most enthusiastic supporters of human rights if the editor of the paper insists on talking of '"human rights" of prisoners',[55] making us think of the semiotics of Saussure and Barthes.[56] It is beyond doubt that prisoners have human rights and, doctrinally speaking, beyond doubt too that they have the human right to vote. While that latter aspect of the full human rights menu might be subject to normative contestation, the use of quotation marks is designed to signify that we should doubt the generality, with punctuation symbolising the phrase 'so-called'.

[52] *Daily Mail* (London, 19 October 2009), www.dailymail.co.uk/news/article-1221353/Youve-got-cat-OK-stay-Britain-officials-tell-Bolivian-immigrant.html—a web address that is itself illustrative.

[53] Doyle et al (n 50).

[54] Available at personal.crocodoc.com/ombGOOP#redirect, para 15 (emphasis added).

[55] J Slack, 'Terrorists and Murderers "Should Get the Vote" ... But Only Six Months Before Release: Plans to Protect "Human Rights" of Prisoners' *Daily Mail* (London, 18 December 2013), www.dailymail.co.uk/news/article-2525566/Terrorists-murderers-vote-months-release-Plans-protect-human-rights-prisoners.html.

[56] Semiotics—that part of the study of language that looks at the meaning of signs and symbols rather than the words themselves—is thought to have begun with the Swiss writer Ferdinand de Saussure and his work on the signifier and the signified (whereby the former (the actual text) connotes a separate meaning), developed by, inter alia, Roland Barthes in works such as *Mythologies* (trans Annette Lavers) (New York, Hill and Wang, 1972) in which, for example, he offers an interpretation of wrestling as a spectacle that satisfies our conceptions of good and evil rather than as a sport per se.

We start to get the feeling that human rights might not be, and, importantly, should not be, thought to be quite as universal and inalienable. It offers us an alternative conception of human rights for prisoners, one where such rights per se are both contested and contestable.

Our next technique is what we might term pre-emptive reporting, where newspapers lull and mislead us by reporting stories out of all proportion to their precedential value. It is not that the reports are false—and we may here think back to the conflation of the EU and the ECHR; rather they simply do not present an accurate or full picture. We might identify two slightly different approaches. First are those reports of court cases that do not make it completely clear that it was but a claim, not a decided outcome. The best-known example remains that of serial killer Dennis Nilsen who, the *Sun* reported on 13 May 2006, 'received hardcore gay porn in jail thanks to human rights law'.[57] The reality, shown in the DCA 2006 review,[58] is that he applied for judicial review to challenge the prison governor's refusal, but permission was refused—in other words, it was rejected at the earliest possible stage. Yet readers were never told this, so into folklore it passed. Alternatively, newspapers report on cases as they percolate through the legal system but leave readers in the dark as to the final outcome. This is especially problematic where a case is reversed on appeal but that is never reported, or where the actual legal outcome was different to the prediction made by the newspaper. The *Daily Mail* did this with the *Animal Defenders* case[59] at Strasbourg, with the following headline the day before the case was decided: 'Britain faces threat of US-style political TV "attack adverts"'.[60] The paper also averred that 'insiders fear the verdict will go against the government, meaning any political group can buy time on British television'. We might here note, as another technique of misreporting, the skewed selection in the *Mail* report of likely beneficiaries of any change—the single Tory fear identified in the subheading was that 'defeat could pave way for union barons to use adverts to drum up support for strikes'.[61] The government won. The case thus did not, as the paper hinted, 'spark fresh controversy over whether the ECHR has the right to overrule MPs at Westminster', yet readers of the *Daily Mail* would have no idea that it did not.[62] For a newspaper so keen to defend free speech, it does seem baffling that the eventual outcome—on a matter, let us be clear, going to the heart of freedom of expression and media regulation—did not make it into the pages of the *Daily Mail* anywhere.[63] It rather defeats the very purpose of such a right, leaving its readers not simply in the dark and poorly informed but in all likelihood under a serious misapprehension

---

[57] *The Sun* (London, 13 May 2006).

[58] See above, n 5.

[59] *Animal Defenders International v* UK App no 48876/08, ECHR 2013 (extracts).

[60] Simon Walters and Brendan Carlin, 'Britain Faces Threat of US-Style Political TV "Attack" Adverts' *Daily Mail* (London, 21 April 2013), www.dailymail.co.uk/news/article-2312350/Britain-faces-threat-US-style-political-TV-attack-adverts.html.

[61] Though the full piece reported that 'organisations and individuals ranging from rich businessmen with outspoken views to unions, animal rights groups and campaigners on both sides in the abortion and climate change debates could win air time to promote their views, win votes or change the law'.

[62] See Walters and Carlin (n 60).

[63] According to a *Nexis* search conducted on 15 May 2014.

about the scope of free speech in Britain, as well as thinking it to be yet one more defeat at the hands of the unelected Euro-bureaucrats.

The last way in which newspapers are apt to mislead is in the partiality they display in, for example, the selection of sources or data or evidence. I do not mean by this the party allegiances (supposed or actual) or socio-economic leanings of most newspapers (or perhaps their owners?) and journals such as the *Economist*. These are usually well known to readers, and made clear in editorials and banner headlines on election day, such as the front page of the *Sun* on 9 April 1992, 'If Kinnock wins today will the last person to leave Britain please turn out the lights', in turn leading to the infamous headline two days later, 'It's The Sun Wot Won It'. Those sorts of examples are about more obvious political (im)partiality, not inaccuracy, misreporting and hidden bias. While there is no duty on newspapers to provide balance, as there is on the much more tightly regulated broadcast media, partiality in the provision of information by newspapers laying claim to a public interest in journalistic freedom cannot in the long term lead to a healthy democracy. This must be all the more so when it comes to reporting the political or constitutional fundamentals at the heart of the system, the opening up of which newspapers are so keen to claim as their role. We can see this in two ways, namely the provision of information either out of context or without counter. On 16 April 2012, the *Daily Mail* reported the results of a YouGov poll that 72 per cent either strongly agreed or tended to agree with the statement 'Human rights have become a charter for criminals and the undeserving'. So far as I can see, the results of opposing polls have never featured in that paper.[64] Neither a public perception poll by the Equality and Human Rights Commission in 2009 (as part of its Human Rights Inquiry), reporting that 81 per cent agreed or strongly agreed with the statement 'Human rights are important for creating a fairer society in the UK',[65] nor a Liberty/Com Res poll of October 2010,[66] which saw 96 per cent support for a law that protects rights and freedoms in Britain, was reported. Secondly, partiality is also evident in the selection of those asked to provide 'expert opinion'. The following is not empirically sound, but from reading the various articles in the course of preparing this chapter, readers of the *Daily Mail* are regularly offered insights from *Policy Exchange* or from Dominic Raab MP, with his catchphrase 'the Mickey Mouse Court at Strasbourg', or from interest groups usually identifying with victims, such as Peter Saunders, chief executive of the National Association for People Abused in Childhood. It is very rare for the views of anyone left of centre to be published, and certainly rare indeed for anyone to be quoted with even lukewarm support for the ECHR, the HRA or human rights generally.

---

[64] Searching *Daily Mail Online* on 15 May 2014: www.dailymail.co.uk/home/index.html.

[65] 'Public Perceptions of Human Rights', www.equalityhumanrights.com/publication/public-perceptions-human-rights.

[66] 'Britain Agrees: What's Not to Love about the Human Rights Act?' (2 October 2010), www.liberty-human-rights.org.uk/news/press-releases/britain-agrees-what%E2%80%99s-not-love-about-human-rights-act.

IV. WIDER NARRATIVES

What views, then, might regular readers of the *Daily Mail* or the *Daily Telegraph* have on human rights? Several thoughts and messages manifest here.

First, and this is by no means limited to those newspapers or to reporting of the HRA generally, the protection of human rights is a very juris-centric exercise. Inevitably, it is the reporting of court cases, actual or putative, that makes the news. There is little or no insight into human rights culture, or the protection of human rights in practice by everyday decision makers in social services departments, head-teachers, prison governors and the like.[67] We see protection as, if not only then at least best, realised through courts, and barristers, and legal rulings, with the attendant costs, individualisation and arbitrariness of judicial process. We do not conceive of protection of human rights at source and on the ground, for example by virtue of policies being rewritten or decisions being taken that give due weight to competing rights and social interests. As Sanchita Hosali said at a British Institute of Human Rights session in 2014—and this is recalled and paraphrased, not a ver-batim quotation—it's just not newsworthy to print "man in Leeds has human rights respected by council"'.[68] It is far from ideal to have such a representation of how human rights have been brought home. We might add to this the lesser point that reporting of human rights stories is all and always about the substance and scope of rights—or some selected ones anyway—and almost never about the modalities: readers may well be reaching the conclusion that British judges are striking down legislation, with headlines like 'Supreme Court Finds Violation of Right to Private Life'—and so may well be reaching imperfect views on the relative balance of power between politicians and judges. While I am not arguing for detailed exegesis on sections 3 and 4 HRA, good journalism would require the limitations of any judgment to be spelled out. This is not always the case.

Next, regular readers would, I suggest, largely be thinking first that the govern-ment in the main loses human rights cases brought against it, certainly in the con-text of European Court of Human Rights (ECtHR) applications, when the truth, as we all know, is very far removed from that.[69] Secondly, they are led to think that human rights are concerned with certain sorts of claims by certain sorts of people or groups. Again, a search against the *Daily Mail Online* with the term 'European Court of Human Rights' produces a skew towards prisoners, either voting or sen-tencing, towards immigration decisions, and towards criminals and terrorists, groups known colloquially as FPTs (foreigners, paedophiles and terrorists), in other words, a framing of security not equality. We certainly see nothing approaching the full panoply of human rights cases or issues. We thus see a narrative that undermines the universality of human rights, with some groups seen as less worthy and as less

---

[67] D Mead, 'Outcomes Aren't All: Defending Process-Based Review of Public Authority Decisions under the Human Rights Act' [2012] *Public Law* 63.

[68] British Institute of Human Rights seminar, 'Human Rights beneath the Headlines', 8 May 2014.

[69] See above, n 49.

deserving of protection (recall the '"human rights" of prisoners' headline), with newspapers offering moral judgement on the character of individual recipients. We might contrast this anecdotally with the portrayal of human rights abuses abroad, in Ukraine, Syria or Nigeria. Might it be the case that the implicit message of such reports is that these are 'real' or 'true' human rights? It is also fairly clear, thirdly, that human rights are not about protecting victims but are a 'criminal's charter'. I have done some empirical research on this.[70] Regular readers of the *Daily Mail*, from the frequency with which such stories are reported, would think that the success rate of foreign nationals escaping deportation on human rights—usually Article 8—grounds (that is, how often the Home Secretary loses a judicial review) is about 92 per cent. In reality, though there is some dispute, even on the *Daily Mail*'s figures for another story it is about 66 per cent, and the Home Office data puts it at about 24 per cent. Quite a difference to thinking that fewer than one in ten are ever deported. Let us consider another piece in the *Daily Mail*.[71] Its spotlight is the ECtHR case brought by the alleged Omagh bombers claiming that the domestic civil proceedings for damages, brought by the families of their victims, breached Article 6. The small problem was that the case at that point was merely at the stage of a communication to the government; it has not yet been declared admissible, and may never be, but it would be a very well-informed reader that would realise the rather precipitate nature of this report. This is another example of the pre-emptive reporting that we considered above. Yet, as we saw earlier, the editor chose not to mention even in passing several key judgments of the Court or even Grand Chamber which were handed down around the same time, highlighting instead this one at almost its earliest possible stage.

To be fair, it is not always the case that victims are presented as being short-changed.[72] The recent decision of the High Court holding the police liable for failing properly to investigate the so-called black cab rapist, John Warboys,[73] and thus prevent his committing further offences, was presented in both the *Daily Mail*[74] and the *Daily Telegraph*[75] (though nothing appeared in the *Daily Express*) in human

---

[70] D Mead, 'They Offer You a Feature on Stockings and Suspenders Next to a Call for Stiffer Penalties for Sex Offenders: Do We Learn More about the Media than about Human Rights from Tabloid Coverage of Human Rights?' (22 September 2014), protestmatters.wordpress.com/2014/09/22/they-offer-you-a-feature-on-stockings-and-suspenders-next-to-a-call-for-stiffer-penalties-for-sex-offenders-do-we-learn-more-about-the-media-than-about-human-rights-from-tabloid-coverage-of-human-r.

[71] C Greenwood, 'After Terrorists Go to European Court … Human Rights Law Helps Murderers Not Victims, Say Omagh Families' *Daily Mail* (London, 20 April 2014), www.dailymail.co.uk/news/article-2609088/After-terrorists-European-court-Human-rights-law-helps-murderers-not-victims-say-Omagh-families.html.

[72] On the tabloids' selective approach towards victims of human rights violations see further Liev Gies, 'Human Rights, the British Press and the Deserving Claimant' (ch 24), this volume.

[73] *DSD and NBV v Commissioner of Police for the Metropolis* [2014] EWHC 436 (QB).

[74] M de Graaf, 'More than 100 Victims of "Black Cab Rapist" John Worboys Could Sue after Two Women Successfully Win their Bid for Compensation' *Daily Mail* (London, 28 February 2014), www.dailymail.co.uk/news/article-2570459/More-100-victims-black-cab-rapist-John-Worboys-sue-two-women-successfully-win-bid-compensation.html.

[75] D Barrett, '100 Victims Could Sue in "Black Cab Rapist" John Worboys Case' *Daily Telegraph* (online, 28 February 2014), www.telegraph.co.uk/news/uknews/crime/10667340/100-victims-could-sue-in-black-cab-rapist-John-Worboys-case.html.

rights terms, with an explanation that the judgment was founded on a violation of Article 3 for the serious and persistent systemic failings.

The next message to take from all this reporting is that Englishness is best. A certain form of chauvinism pervades the discourse. It is rare—but not unheard of—for readers to be made aware of the crucial role the UK played in drawing up the ECHR after the War. Where this does occur, certainly in recent times, it is generally in the context of what is asserted as the mass deviation from its historic roots, as in 'After 60 Years, Bring Back Britain's Rights'.[76] In general, rights and rights-holders are seen as alien entities, as 'other,' in contrast with traditional English liberties. We might think here of the *Daily Mail*'s longstanding opposition to identity cards and more recently to secret trials (such as the campaigns by Conservative civil libertarians such as David Davis MP), and this headline in relation to the attempt to extradite Gary McKinnon: 'A Great Day for Gary—and British Justice: after a 3-year *Mail* campaign bitterly opposed by America, British courts and civil servants, Theresa May yesterday courageously decided Asperger's sufferer Gary McKinnon will NOT be extradited for hacking Pentagon computers in pursuit of little green men'.[77]

We might fruitfully consider here the reports of the recent whole-life prison sentence cases both at the ECtHR and before the Court of Appeal.[78] There is not a great divergence between the two courts. The Court of Appeal, on one reading, simply ensured that ministerial discretion under section 30 of the Crime Sentences Act 1997 was exercised compatibly with Article 3, the very matter on which the ECtHR was not convinced and which founded the basis of the violation. To portray this as UK judges 'defy[ing] Europe to say "life means life" ... leaving our courts free to order serial killers, paedophiles and terrorists to die behind bars'[79] seeks to create a plank-sized gap where the reality was a cigarette paper. The Grand Chamber in *Vinter* itself could not have been clearer:

> Contracting States must also remain free to impose life sentences on adult offenders for especially serious crimes such as murder: the imposition of such a sentence on an adult offender is not in itself prohibited by or incompatible with Article 3 or any other Article of the Convention ... This is particularly so when such a sentence is not mandatory but is imposed

[76] 'After 60 Years, Bring Back Britain's Human Rights' *Daily Mail* (London, 3 September 2013), www.dailymail.co.uk/debate/article-2410491/Daily-Mail-Comment-After-60-years-bring-Britains-rights.html.

[77] J Slack, 'A Great Day for Gary—and British Justice: after a 3-year *Mail* campaign bitterly opposed by America, British courts and civil servants, Theresa May yesterday courageously decided Asperger's sufferer Gary McKinnon will NOT be extradited for hacking Pentagon computers in pursuit of little green men' *Daily Mail* (London, 16 October 2012), www.dailymail.co.uk/news/article-2218786/Gary-McKinnon-Theresa-May-courageously-decides-Aspergers-sufferer-NOT-extradited.html. One might cynically add that there was not such an outcry at the extradition of Babar Ahmad around the same time. For more detail see Gies, this volume.

[78] *R v McLoughlin* [2014] EWCA Crim 188.

[79] J Slack, 'I Deserve to Die behind Bars, Admits Triple Killer whose 40-Year Sentence was Deemed Too Lenient by UK Judges as they Defy Europe to Say "Life Means Life"' *Daily Mail* (London, 18 February 2014), www.dailymail.co.uk/news/article-2561876/UK-judges-defy-Europe-say-life-prison-sentences-mean-life.html.

by an independent judge after he or she has considered all of the mitigating and aggravating factors which are present in any given case.[80]

It is hard to see how the Court of Appeal escaped the full fury that had earlier been directed at the ECtHR, when the *Daily Mail*'s front page proclaimed that 'Meddling European judges rule even Britain's most evil killers have human right to seek freedom'.[81] The UK review regime already in place required that review be exercised compatibly with the human right not to subject someone to inhuman treatment and punishment, in other words when it can no longer be justified on legitimate penological grounds, the very issue in *Vinter*, and would only arise in exceptional circumstances justifying release on compassionate grounds. This was accepted in *Vinter*, too. Indeed, the ECtHR itself had presaged this: 'reading of s. 30 [compatibly with Article 3] ensuring some prospects under the law for release of whole life prisoners would, in principle, be consistent with this Court's judgment [in earlier cases].'[82] The narrative put out by the *Daily Mail* could not be clearer: if it wasn't for those pesky Europeans ...

V. CONCLUSION

This short chapter has shed some light on how the media—or, more accurately, certain sections of it—cover human rights, and more importantly what that reporting tells its readers, and thus tells us more widely: what matters are important, what 'proper' human rights are, and who should properly be claiming them. It chimes with other reporting—on the human rights gravy train, on fat cat legal aid lawyers, and the more Europhobic elements of the British press and polity. This chapter has not covered how the media has reported privacy cases under the HRA, though *Daily Mail* editor Paul Dacre's spat with Mr Justice Eady should not go unremarked. We can perhaps see another reason why certain segments of the media stand foursquare against what they would portray as the incoming tide. Is it any surprise that his newspaper titles are among the most vitriolic in their opposition to the Human Rights Act *in toto* when his professed view is that

> thanks to the wretched Human Rights Act, one judge with a subjective and highly relativist moral sense can [create a privacy law] with a stroke of his pen ... Since time immemorial public shaming has been a vital element in defending the parameters of what are considered acceptable standards of social behaviour, helping ensure that citizens—rich and poor—adhere to them for the good of the greater community. For hundreds of years, the press has played a role in that process. It has the freedom to identify those who have offended public

---

[80] *Vinter* (n 47) para 106.
[81] J Doyle et al, 'What about the Victims' Rights' *Daily Mail* (London, 10 July 2013), www.dailymail. co.uk/news/article-2359071/What-victims-rights-Meddling-European-judges-rule-Britains-evil-killers-human-right-seek-freedom.html.
[82] *Vinter* (n 47) para 125.

standards of decency—the very standards its readers believe in—and hold the transgressors up to public condemnation.[83]

On 2 October 2014, the Lord Chancellor and Justice Secretary, Chris Grayling, announced that the Conservatives would scrap the HRA and introduce a British bill of rights so as to 'break the formal link between British courts and the European Court of Human Rights', should they win the General Election in 2015. This became a firm manifesto commitment and, having won a 12-seat majority, the Conservative Government is set to implement that policy. Interestingly, in the context of this chapter, this pledge was contained in two sections of the manifesto: the one dealing with crime and victims of crime, and the one on foreign relations and the EU, not in that part of the manifesto on constitutional matters or matters relating to the citizen and the state.

Newspaper reporting of the eight-page Autumn 2014 policy document was to some extent as we might expect. The *Daily Mail* reported it thus on its front page: 'End of Human Rights Farce', with the sub-heading reading 'In a triumphant week for British values, Tories unveil plans to give Parliament and judges power to ignore the European Court and its crazy decision-making'.[84] The *Daily Express* weighed in with 'Human Rights Madness to End: Europe's Judges to be Stopped Meddling in our Affairs'.[85] The *Sun* headlined with 'PM Adopts Our Manifesto', one element of which was emblazoned 'Axe Hated Human Rights Act'.[86] There was very little, if any, critical comment on the plans. Readers would not have known, for example, that the Conservative document misrepresented the whole-life tariff decision in *Vinter* as the ECtHR ruling 'that murderers cannot be sentenced to prison for life', which was not the case at all. Nor did any newspaper challenge Grayling's assertion that the ECtHR should 'no longer be binding over the UK Supreme Court' as something that was simply not legally the case; Article 34 ECHR simply binds the UK to implement Strasbourg judgments as a matter of international law. To that extent, the reporting was skewed and thus mis-informative, but that claim can be made against most media outlets in this case. Even the left-of-centre *Guardian* contained, within its front-page story headed 'Conservatives pledge powers to ignore European Court of Human Rights rulings', very little by way of detailed unpicking of the

---

[83] Speech given by Paul Dacre to the Society of Editors, 9 November 2008, www.pressgazette.co.uk/node/42394.

[84] *Daily Mail* (London, 3 October 2014). An online piece—'Tory Plans to Shackle Human Rights Judges REJECTED by Europe, Leaving Britain's Membership of Court Hanging by a Thread' *Daily Mail* (3 October 2014), www.dailymail.co.uk/news/article-2779401/Tory-plans-shackle-European-human-rights-judges-REJECTED-Strasbourg-court-row-intensifies.html—provides in fact a far more balanced assessment. It gives several column inches to those who opposed the plans—including Grayling's predecessor Dominic Grieve who asserted that the documents contained several howlers, and his then opposite number, Emily Thornberry, as well as several senior Lib Dems. It also highlighted the Council of Europe's position, that a proposal to render judgment advisory only was inconsistent with the Treaty, in the first paragraph. It did nonetheless give much greater prominence to explaining the details of the government's position.

[85] *Daily Express* (London, 3 October 2014).

[86] *The Sun* (London, 2 October 2014).

proposals, focusing instead on what might be termed the bigger picture: the British role in drafting the Convention and the patchwork that would result from UK withdrawal. In fact, the *Daily Mail* online piece[87] provided readers with a greater critique of the plans than did the *Daily Telegraph*.[88] Its readers learnt only that 'Labour said the plans have been "cobbled together on the back on an envelope"' without any further explanation, and reported Dominic Grieve describing the plans as 'a recipe for anarchy', again without more. It reported without question the fact that the plans 'would enable Parliament to block controversial European plans to give prisoners the vote, and to ban whole-life tariffs', the latter of course never having been banned and the former turning the judgment in *Hirst* on its head; Strasbourg does not require that prisoners vote, simply that the absolute ban on all prisoners voting be lifted.[89]

Of course, there are arguments to be had here on human rights protection in the UK and in Europe, and on the future of the Human Rights Act—on the scope of the rights protected, on its mechanism, on Member States' relationship with a supranational court amongst other things—but at least let us start on a level playing field, one untainted by misreporting and mischief, or a parochial focus on egregious cases.[90]

---

[87] See above, n 84.

[88] P Dominiczak, 'Conservatives Set Out Plans to Allow Judges to "Ignore" European Court of Human Rights' *Daily Telegraph* (London, 2 October 2014), www.telegraph.co.uk/news/politics/conservative/11139943/Conservatives-set-out-plans-to-allow-judges-to-ignore-European-Court-of-Human-Rights.html.

[89] *Hirst v UK (No 2)* (2004) 28 EHRR 40.

[90] The front page of the *Times* (London, 20 January 2015) set out the views of Lord David Pannick, who was quoted as saying how striking it was that 'all the significant departures from the European Convention and the Human Rights Act were grounded in parochial disputes about particular cases'.

24

Human Rights, the British Press and the Deserving Claimant*

LIEVE GIES

I. INTRODUCTION

THE UK'S HUMAN Rights Act 1998 (HRA) is routinely excoriated in sections of the press. Newspaper headlines such as 'Rip up the INhuman Rights Act',[1] 'Good for crooks, bad for human rights'[2] and 'Heroin ... it's my yuman rights, Mr Mackay, innit'[3] are typical of the inflammatory rhetoric targeted at the HRA. According to Klug, 'the tabloids have effectively created a subtitle to the Act in the public's mind which reads: human rights for FTPs: foreigners, terrorists, and paedophiles—law abiding citizens need not apply'.[4] Amos has suggested that national newspapers are a contributory factor in 'the climate of disrespect which often surrounds the HRA'.[5] The former Lord Chancellor, Lord Falconer, and the Joint Committee on Human Rights (JCHR) have expressed similar misgivings about press treatment of the HRA.[6]

In this chapter I will discuss a variety of elements that have shaped the HRA's media image. My main aim, however, is to look in depth at an issue that is rendering the current human rights regime especially unpalatable to sceptical audiences: the notion that wrongdoers are just as deserving of human rights as other individuals. The mere suggestion that sex offenders, murderers and terrorists enjoy basic rights

---

* The discussion in this chapter is drawn from 'Extradition, Human Rights Abuse and the Sufferer Nearby', ch 5 in L Gies, *Mediating Human Rights: Media, Culture and Human Rights Law* (London, Routledge, 2015).

[1] T Kavanagh, 'Rip Up the INhuman Rights Act' *The Sun* (London, 3 July 2007), www.thesun.co.uk/sol/homepage/news/justice/241588/Rip-up-the-INhuman-Rights-Act.html.

[2] Editorial, 'Good for Crooks, Bad for Human Rights' *Daily Telegraph* (London, 16 November 2006), 26.

[3] R Littlejohn, 'Heroin ... it's my yuman rights, Mr Mackay, innit?' *Daily Mail* (London, 14 November 2006), 15.

[4] F Klug, 'A Bill of Rights: Do We Need One or Do We Already Have One?' [2007] *Public Law* 701.

[5] M Amos, 'Problems with the Human Rights Act 1998 and How to Remedy Them: Is a Bill of Rights the Answer?' (2009) 72 *Modern Law Review* 883.

[6] C Falconer, 'Human Rights Are Majority Rights' The Lord Morris of Borth-y-Gest Memorial Lecture, Bangor University, 23 March 2007, www.britishpoliticalspeech.org/speech-archive.htm?speech=297; JCHR, *The Work of the Committee in 2007 and the State of Human Rights in the UK*, 2007–08 session, 6th report.

in spite of their criminality is sufficient to create a tabloid frenzy. What is rendering the HRA objectionable to detractors is the perception that the least deserving in society have benefited disproportionately from the legislation. One of the stock narratives in media discourse revolves around the idea that affording rights protection to those who find themselves on the wrong side of the law is tantamount to eroding the rights and interests of the law-abiding majority. 'What about our rights?' howl the tabloids with indignation whenever it is claimed that wrongdoers deserve dignity and should have their humanity recognised in law. The most punitive media commentaries will readily imply that offenders should be regarded as having forfeited their rights as a form of retribution or just deserts.[7]

The question of how the media separate out the deserving and the undeserving in relation to human rights claims, constructing what are effectively victim hierarchies, forms the main focus of analysis in this chapter. Scholars of humanitarian journalism have long been concerned about the issue of distant suffering and the lack of empathy shown by the media and their audiences to victims of humanitarian crises. Distance in this regard means not only physical or geographical distance but also distance in the sense of difference and otherness attributed to victims who live in relative proximity to media audiences. Cohen defines this as the state of 'internal bystanders' or 'knowing about atrocities and suffering within your own society'.[8]

The case at the centre of this chapter is that of the British internet hacker Gary McKinnon, who was accused of cyberterrorism by US authorities. The reason for choosing this particular case is that its treatment by the media stands in marked contrast to the representation of other terrorism cases. Unusually for a terrorism suspect, McKinnon attracted considerable levels of positive media coverage, portraying him as a victim of a serious injustice. He fought a lengthy and ultimately successful legal battle against his extradition to the US on terrorism charges relating to an alleged break-in into military and NASA computer systems in 2001 and 2002. US authorities described the security breach as 'the biggest military computer hack of all time',[9] resulting in a shutdown of parts of the military's network.

McKinnon readily admitted the offences but he always denied any malicious intent, claiming that he was merely searching for evidence of extraterrestrial life. He gained many prominent supporters in the course of his legal fight against extradition, assembling a powerful alliance. A public relations agency reportedly provided its services to his campaign on a pro bono basis.[10] The Daily Mail actively championed his case, endorsing supporters' claim that McKinnon, who was diagnosed with Asperger syndrome, a form of autism, was a vulnerable person who would fall victim to serious rights abuses if he were extradited. The Home

---

[7] A Mooney, 'Human Rights: Law, Language and the Bare Human Being' (2012) 32 *Language and Communication* 169.

[8] S Cohen, *States of Denial: Knowing about Atrocities and Suffering* (Cambridge, Polity Press, 2001) 142.

[9] J Ronson, 'Game Over' *The Guardian* (London, 9 July 2005), www.theguardian.com/theguardian/2005/jul/09/weekend7.weekend2.

[10] C McClatchey, 'How Gary McKinnon Became a Cause Celebre' BBC News, 4 August 2009, news.bbc.co.uk/1/hi/magazine/8181100.stm.

Secretary, Theresa May, finally agreed in 2012 that extraditing McKinnon to the US where he faced a very long prison sentence would be a violation of his human rights, in particular his right not to be subjected to degrading treatment (Article 3 of the European Convention on Human Rights (ECHR)) and his right to respect for private and family life (Article 8 ECHR).

II. THE UNPOPULARITY OF HUMAN RIGHTS IN THE ERA OF THE HRA

There are undoubtedly several reasons why the HRA and domestic human rights protections tend to attract negative media coverage. The idea that human rights as a concept compares unfavourably to 'ancient' civil liberties is an important undercurrent in the media reporting. The headline 'indefinite detention breaches human rights' is more likely to encode negative meaning than one that reads 'indefinite detention breaches civil liberties'.[11] Individuals who complain that their human rights have been violated are likely to be given a less sympathetic hearing in the media than if they were to complain about a restriction of civil liberties in an otherwise identical case. To understand the media polemic surrounding the UK's current human rights regime, the distinction between human rights and civil liberties is of crucial importance.

Rights and liberties have, to use a marketing term, very different brand identities. Put simply, civil liberties stand for brand Britain while human rights represent brand Europe. The former signify a solid, homegrown product that has stood the test of time, while the latter stand for an inferior foreign surrogate which failed to impress Bentham and Dicey in their time and is still struggling to convince today's media commentators. In the space of just a few years, rights have become a metaphor for an overbearing and interfering State while liberties nostalgically evoke an era when government did as little as possible, its principal duty being to refrain from interfering with individual liberty. Although the fault lines between liberties and rights are not a matter of ideology alone, ideological differences nevertheless matter in the debate: the right, most notably the Conservative Party, which has made abolition of the HRA its official agenda,[12] is keen to be seen to be championing civil liberties. The position of the left is comparatively more fragmented: while some sections are ideologically more favourably disposed to the current human rights regime, there are also sceptical voices expressing doubt about the current state of human rights law.[13] In the eyes of detractors, the HRA and the ECHR do not bolster individual freedom; they place unacceptable fetters on it. They argue that while human rights advocates busied themselves transforming minor social aches—typically involving the misrecognition of specific minorities—into full-blown rights

---

[11] See Gies (n *) ch 2.

[12] Conservative Party, *The Conservatives' Proposals for Changing Britain's Human Rights Laws*, news.bbc.co.uk/1/shared/bsp/hi/pdfs/03_10_14_humanrights.pdf.

[13] T Campbell, KD Ewing and A Tomkins (eds), *The Legal Protection of Human Rights: Sceptical Essays* (Oxford, Oxford University Press, 2011).

issues, a Janus-faced Labour government introduced draconian anti-terrorism laws undermining genuine liberty.[14]

A further aggravating factor in the HRA's lack of popular appeal is that the image of human rights is inevitably bound up with that of the European Union (EU). The reader does not need reminding that the institutions of the EU are distinct from the institutional framework of the ECHR, principally the Council of Europe and the European Court of Human Rights (ECtHR). However, to many in the British media, Europe would appear such a faraway place that the distinctions between these different institutions are blurred to the point of being non-existent. The strong eurosceptic stance of the right-leaning press and the perceived alienness of human rights have created a climate in which distrust of Europe infects anything that is directly or even indirectly associated with human rights in a European context, most prominently the ECHR and the HRA.

The Head of the European Commission Representation in the United Kingdom once wrote of a 'wilful ignorance' on the part of the British press which

> is never more apparent than when the EU is taken as a generic term to cover anything vaguely European or based in Brussels ... A mantra oft repeated by my staff is that the European Court of Human Rights is a body of the Council of Europe, an intergovernmental organisation entirely separate from the EU. Eight years on and this same distortion of fact to implicate the EU in stories with which it has no connection remains steadfastly employed by journalists.[15]

Media stories about Europe tend to be overwhelmingly negative, and this is no different for coverage involving human rights in a European setting. One only has to think of the controversy involving prisoners' voting rights[16] to realise that the image of human rights has suffered because of its inevitable association with the controversial political project that Europe represents in British media.

Media framing of rights as predominantly an instrument of international law further emphasises their perceived foreignness. Human rights are often mentioned in the same breath as military juntas and dictatorships. They conjure up images of torture, genocide and oppression in far-flung places, reaching their nadir in Tiananmen Square, Srebrenica and more recently Syria and Iraq. Human rights only tend to be in the news when they are brutally violated, not when they are upheld by governments. The exotic image of human rights and their near-exclusive association with the wrongful behaviour of foreign regimes render it difficult for Western audiences to envisage that they are also relevant in keeping government at home in check. Thus, for example, Cottle points out that while Western media have over time

---

[14] See D Raab, *The Assault on Liberty: What Went Wrong With Rights* (London, Fourth Estate, 2007); KD Ewing, *Bonfire of the Liberties: New Labour, Human Rights, and the Rule of Law* (Oxford, Oxford University Press, 2010).

[15] J Dougal, 'Living with Press Eurotrash' (2003) 14 *British Journalism Review* 29, 32.

[16] T Newton Dunn, '2,000 Perverts and Thugs Will Get the Vote: Fury Looms over PM's Plans After EU Ruling' *The Sun* (London, 29 January 2011), www.thesun.co.uk/sol/homepage/news/3378673/2000-perverts-and-thugs-will-get-vote-under-government-plans.html; T Shipman, '6,000 Perverts and Thugs to Get the Vote: Tory Rebels' Fury at Plans to Let Inmates Cast a Ballot' *Daily Mail* (London, 6 January 2011), www.dailymail.co.uk/news/article-1344508/6-000-perverts-thugs-vote-elections.html.

increased their coverage of international human rights, there has paradoxically also been a growing media hostility to asylum seekers, among whom are many victims fleeing human rights abuse elsewhere. He observes that 'the news media are generally disposed to conceive and compartmentalize human rights in a way that leave them blind to human rights abuses committed in their own countries'.[17]

It would be impossible to ignore the role of the war on terror in the hardening of public attitudes to human rights. Considering the profound impact of the events of 11 September 2001, the media's ambivalent relationship with domestic human rights law would appear to be the inevitable by-product of the prevailing security climate. In this febrile atmosphere, politicians and sections of the press blamed judges' interpretation of the HRA for hampering the effort to combat terrorism.[18] It seems reasonable to suggest that had it not been for the war on terror, it would have been much easier for the HRA to establish itself and gain public acceptance. Thus, in an assessment of the first decade of the HRA, the former Senior Labour Minister Jack Straw wrote that:

> Without one event when the statute [the HRA] was still in its infancy, its subsequent development would, I believe, have been smooth and unremarkable. But the atrocities of September 11, 2001 happened. That not only led, directly or indirectly, to two wars but also to conditions which tested close to destruction some of the key foundations of any liberal democracy—of which the HRA was the best and most recent exemplar. It is hard to exaggerate the pressures which those with responsibility encounter when a population, or part of it, is scared. Many sections of the public, and the media on their behalf, put the necessary balance between ends and means to one side, and simply demand to know why they had not been kept safe and what we were doing to keep them safer.[19]

Straw's comments appear to endorse the notion that there were fundamental tensions between rights and security and that restricting civil liberties was a necessary sacrifice to safeguard and protect the nation from terrorism. This frame no doubt gained considerable currency in UK media, just as it did, for example, in US media during the war on terror era.[20] The circumstances to which the terrorism threat gave rise were undeniably significant as they put the new human rights regime to the test very early on in its existence and activated media prejudices towards specific minorities. Nevertheless, the anti-terror climate is but one of many elements that have shaped media attitudes to domestic human rights law. The perceived threat from terrorism may have given journalists and editors cause to criticise judges' interpretation of the HRA, but it should also be noted that many already opposed the Bill before it had become law and crucially before the terrorism threat had become an overriding concern. Many in the media were apprehensive that the HRA would

---

[17] S Cottle, *Global Crisis Reporting: Journalism in the Global Age* (Milton Keynes, Open University Press, 2009) 103.

[18] For the discussion of some high-profile examples see JCHR, *The Human Rights Act: The DCA and Home Office Reviews*, 2005–06 session, 32nd report.

[19] J Straw, 'The Human Rights Act—Ten Years On' (2010) 6 *European Human Rights Law Review* 576, 578.

[20] DL Altheide, 'The Mass Media and Terrorism' (2007) 1 *Discourse and Communication* 287.

inexorably lead to the development of a privacy law notably lacking in the common law prior to the HRA, an apprehension that was not without cause.[21]

In order to make sense of the press industry's long-standing opposition to the HRA, which first surfaced when the Bill was still making its way through Parliament back in 1997, one needs to take account of the deep-rooted misgivings in the press industry concerning the HRA's inherent capacity to protect privacy at the expense of freedom of expression. The conflict between press freedom and privacy reached something of an apotheosis recently with the judicial inquiry led by Lord Justice Leveson.[22] The inquiry involved a wide-ranging examination of press standards and conduct which originated in the phone hacking at the News of the World, part of the News International arm of Rupert Murdoch's News Corp. On several occasions, witnesses testified that their privacy had been invaded in the pursuit of commercial gain rather than the pursuit of the public interest enshrined in the press's own code of ethics. The wrangling over what kind of regulator the press requires post-Leveson is further evidence of the deep unease of the press concerning privacy and the balance to be struck with freedom of expression.

Although the Leveson Inquiry also heard from non-celebrity victims of press intrusion, it prominently featured celebrity campaigners whose privacy had been invaded by reporters. There has been strong criticism in the press that the HRA predominantly favours celebrities with something to hide.[23] This criticism forms part of the wider invective that the UK's domestic human rights regime almost systematically protects the wrong type of victims, which is most strikingly reflected in the media framing of the HRA as a 'villains' charter'. Fundamentally, such misgivings touch on the unpalatable truth that wrongdoers too enjoy the protection afforded by human rights on a universal basis. Furthermore, they reveal how victims of rights abuses tend to be ranked in media discourse according to their perceived worthiness. Some victims fail to arouse any public concern, or worse even encounter outright hostility, while others more readily succeed in mobilising public support. In the UK's domestic human rights context, the question of who can legitimately claim to be a victim of rights abuse therefore goes to the heart of the political debate about the scope and extent of rights protection under the HRA.

---

[21] A Rusbridger, editor of *The Guardian*, noted in 2001: 'The reality is dawning on newspaper lawyers and editors that the courts are—with some degree of relish—about to embark on a process of establishing and developing a right to privacy, as enshrined within Article Eight of the European Convention on Human Rights ... [Y]ou currently have a lot of editors and lawyers extremely concerned about the gradual erosion of press freedom in this country. The challenge facing the press is whether it is prepared to see these issues as in any way connected and whether editors can see a way of forming a common cause to fight these threats together.' A Rusbridger, 'Courting disaster: a supermodel and a former police clerk are just two people currently bringing court cases which may ultimately threaten press freedom. But why do these, and a slew of other actions, pose such a menace to the future of British newspapers? Alan Rusbridger explains' *The Guardian* (London, 19 March 2001), 2.

[22] Leveson Inquiry, webarchive.nationalarchives.gov.uk/20140122145147/http:/www.levesoninquiry.org.uk.

[23] P Morgan, then editor of the *Mirror*, famously commented on the model Naomi Campbell's legal victory in the privacy case of *Campbell v Mirror Group Newspapers* [2004] UKHL 22: 'This is a very good day for lying, drug-abusing prima donnas who want to have their cake with the media and the right to then shamelessly guzzle it with their Cristal champagne' (quoted in F Gibb and A Sherwin, 'Campbell's Win over *Mirror* May Become Model for Privacy Rules' *The Times* (London, 7 May 2004), 9).

III. THE POLITICS OF PITY AND DISTANT SUFFERING

The ability of media audiences to relate to distant suffering is instrumental in bringing human rights violations to the world's attention and creating the necessary scope for political intervention. Boltanski draws an important distinction between compassion and pity: while compassion is characteristic of the Good Samaritan who comes face to face with suffering and is able to intervene personally to help the victim, physically distant suffering can only be acted upon through a politics of pity whereby the spectator's scope for intervention is contingent on the actions undertaken by intermediaries such as governments and NGOs.[24] Thus, Boltanski argues that 'to arouse pity, suffering and wretched bodies must be conveyed in such a way as to affect the sensibility of those more fortunate'.[25] The spectacle of suffering, often harrowing and undignified from the victims' perspective, can only be ethically justified on the condition that the exposure and publicity will result in some form of intervention in aid of sufferers.[26] However, while acute humanitarian crises may command the attention of the media and their audiences for a limited period of time, the media's default position towards human rights abuse is largely one of indifference and neglect. Public and media interest are unlikely to be sustained in the long term, succumbing to what is known as 'compassion fatigue'.[27] Humanitarian causes face a near-permanent threat of delegitimisation in which 'no manner of representing distant others as a cause of public action seems to do justice to the moral claim of suffering'.[28]

While it is important that audiences should feel a moral obligation towards the victim, this is by no means the sole component of a regime of pity. Seu identifies three potentially very critical obstacles in converting the spectacle of suffering into concrete political action: how the media represent the suffering or the calamity, how these representations are received by audiences, and how willing audiences are to act on their knowledge of the suffering.[29] Identifying media representations as an important factor in the emergence of a collective willingness to alleviate distant suffering, Cottle uses the term 'mediated ethics of care':

> Depending on how journalists craft their news packages, involve different voices and narratives and reproduce scenes of human suffering, so the viewing and reading audience is variously invited to assume a position of felt connection and possible obligation to the news represented subject.[30]

[24] L Boltanski, *Distant Suffering: Morality, Media and Politics* (Cambridge, Cambridge University Press, 1999).

[25] ibid, 11.

[26] ibid, 172.

[27] S Moeller, *Compassion Fatigue: How the Media Sell Disease, Famine, War and Death* (London, Routledge, 1999).

[28] L Chouliaraki, 'Post-Humanitarianism: Humanitarian Communication beyond a Politics of Pity' (2010) 13 *International Journal of Cultural Studies* 107, 107.

[29] IB Seu, '"Doing Denial": Audience Reaction to Human Rights Appeals' (2010) 21 *Discourse and Society* 438.

[30] Cottle (n 17) 101.

Depending on the form and tone of the reporting, for example, different 'regimes of pity'[31] may be evoked, structuring the spectator's relationship with mediated suffering. The extent to which victims' suffering is the subject of concerned media coverage therefore plays a potentially significant role in any claim-making about the rights-worthiness of victims.

If audiences fail to identify with victims or tire of the suffering on display, it would appear at least in part to be the result of the way in which humanitarian crises and human rights abuses are packaged for audience consumption. According to Boltanski, the distance between the victim and the spectator somehow has to be mediated without being cancelled out altogether (a collapse of distance which Chouliaraki refers to as 'ecstatic news'):[32] the viewer must be touched but empathy should not turn into the kind of intensely personal identification normally reserved for people to whom one is very close.[33] The individual victim serves as a mere representative of general suffering and deserves pity by virtue of his or her humanity, not because of any personal ties with the spectator. Silverstone argues that the ability to identify with the Other without eliminating difference altogether is a matter of maintaining 'proper distance'.[34] Voice and access, being able to speak and to be heard as a victim, are crucial in the creation of this equilibrium between sameness and otherness: 'hospitality to the stranger in the symbolic space of media representation is a precondition for media justice.'[35]

Much of the analysis of the media's attitudes to distant suffering is premised on the idea that the victim is a faraway stranger who is subjected to the gaze of a remote spectator who is not in any personal or direct danger. However, the emphasis on distant calamities should not mask the difficulties of conveying any suffering occurring in close proximity to the spectator, such as—as in the specific case studied in this chapter—human rights violations at home as opposed to abuses taking place in far-flung corners of the globe. The position of spectators is arguably less sheltered when there is an awareness that a similar fate may well befall them, for example when there is a realisation that anti-terrorism legislation ostensibly targeting terrorists may also be used against other individuals. This is not to say, however, that there is no metaphorical distance to be mediated in order to convince the media and their audiences of the rights-worthiness of victims, especially when the latter are strongly associated with an unpopular minority. Sufferers may be in close physical proximity to media audiences, but in cultural and social terms the unique nature of their suffering or oppression may also render them very distant from mainstream society.

In his work on suffering and denial, Cohen draws a distinction between 'internal bystanding' and 'external bystanding', the former involving awareness and knowledge of suffering taking place in the bystander's own immediate environment.[36] While he suggests that most people in contemporary Western societies mainly

---

[31] L Chouliaraki, *The Spectatorship of Suffering* (London, Sage, 2006).
[32] ibid, 9.
[33] Boltanski (n 24) 12.
[34] R Silverstone, *Media and Morality: On the Rise of the Mediapolis* (Cambridge, Polity, 2007) 47.
[35] ibid, 139.
[36] Cohen (n 8) 140.

have 'mediated knowledge' of atrocities, making them remote bystanders, his analysis also engages with the long and problematic history of immediate bystanders ignoring great suffering occurring on their own doorstep. The war on terror has brought human rights abuses closer to home for Western audiences, perhaps not in a geographical sense but at least in a political sense, requiring them to face up to accusations that their own governments have been involved in torture and other human rights violations. Knowledge and denial of such accusations are still heavily mediated; however, the fact that Western governments are involved narrows the gap between internal and external bystanding, making it harder still to deny responsibility for acts that are more commonly associated with States with a poor human rights record.

Margalit's concepts of 'thick' and 'thin' relations categorise victims not so much on the basis of their physical distance to the public, whose display of pity is required to trigger political intervention, as on the basis of differing degrees of closeness in human relations.[37] With thick relations involving the closest of human bonds, typically in the guise of kinship, friendship and nationality—bonds that are firmly rooted in shared memories—thin relations are between strangers who have nothing more than their humanity in common. It is the latter which arguably constitute the proper terrain of human rights. As Oliver, drawing on Margalit's work, observes, 'the human rights regime, on a theoretical level at least, seeks to construct a moral community based upon universal abstract humanity rather than upon specific inter-subjective relations'.[38]

According to Ignatieff, '[p]ity is a complex emotion, mingling compassion and contempt'.[39] It places the spectator or bystander in a position of superiority, leaving the question of whether the sufferer is somehow to blame inevitably lingering at the back of the observer's mind. In the case of terrorism suspects who claim that their human rights have been infringed by the State, the tone of media reports may imply that the wrongs they have committed are a just cause for their ill treatment. Analysing newspaper coverage of human rights in the US and the UK, Mooney detects

a particular construction of human rights as transactional and only available to the worthy ... The logic underlying this position is that human rights are earned, that they are 'payback' for good citizens and hence can be taken away from bad citizens.[40]

The perception that those who commit wrongs forfeit their rights may therefore make it exceedingly hard to generate positive media publicity for many victims of rights abuse. To be worthy of pity, the victim needs to be seen as morally innocent—that is, as having no hand in his or her own misfortune, which is why children, the elderly and women more easily attract global compassion as 'bona fide' victims.[41]

---

[37] A Margalit, *The Ethics of Memory* (Cambridge, MA, Harvard University Press, 2002).

[38] S Oliver, 'Simulating the Ethical Community: Interactive Game Media and Engaging Human Rights Claims' (2010) 51 *Culture, Theory and Critique* 93, 96.

[39] M Ignatieff, *The Needs of Strangers* (London, Vintage, 1994) 43.

[40] Mooney (n 7) 175.

[41] Moeller (n 27).

By contrast, as has been noted in relation to victims of famine: 'Men associated with violent political factions can starve by the thousands without creating a flutter of interest in their victim status.'[42] Because of a presumption of culpability, terrorism suspects are more likely to be labelled 'evil' in the media than to be treated as worthy of human rights protection.

The rhetoric of evil, which looms large at times of serious political and social crisis,[43] has as its very purpose to separate the rights-worthy from the rights-unworthy. To be demonised as evil is to be expelled from the realm of rights protection and ultimately from humanity itself: indeed, as Silverstone observes, 'to ascribe evil to the other is to place him or her beyond the pale of understanding; the other is incomprehensible and, in a world supposedly governed by reason, the other is dispensable.'[44] Such sentiments are also echoed by Agamben, who detects the unmistakable figure of homo sacer in the security rhetoric of the war on terror.[45] Homo sacer is the subject who, stripped of all rights, is reduced to bare life—that is, life that can be taken with impunity because it is considered to be without value. Bauman, furthermore, talks of 'wasted lives', redundant humans who are deemed a threat to the hygiene of society: refugees, prisoners and asylum seekers often find themselves at the margins of humanity.[46] He considers how the war on terror enabled the tabloids to inject the old fear of 'spongers' and 'welfare scroungers' with a 'new, indomitable weapon of mass intimidation' and a 'new brand of officially inspired and whipped-up collective fear'.[47] One of the preconditions of a politics of pity being that the victim or sufferer of harm should be properly humanised,[48] the demonisation of terrorism suspects in the years following 11 September 2001 made it more difficult to categorise them as rights-bearing subjects—something that was amply demonstrated in the erosion of human rights standards in some well-documented cases.[49]

At first glance, the campaign against Gary McKinnon's extradition seems to defy the notion that terrorism suspects are not regarded as worthy of rights protection by the media and their audiences: here is someone who, despite an obvious susceptibility to being deemed 'beyond the pale', found wide-ranging support among media commentators, civil liberties campaigners, celebrities and politicians. What facilitated the favourable media representations of McKinnon's cause is examined in the remainder of this chapter. There was arguably an element of self-interest underpinning public concern about McKinnon's possible extradition, making him anything but a distant sufferer, but importantly his story was also consistently told in such a way by his supporters as to reject the central premise of the extradition proceedings that he was a terrorist. The sense of obligation which audiences were

---

[42] ibid, 107.

[43] Silverstone (n 34) 75.

[44] ibid.

[45] G Agamben, *State of Exception* (Chicago, Chicago University Press, 2005).

[46] Z Bauman, *Wasted Lives: Modernity and its Outcasts* (Cambridge, Polity, 2004).

[47] ibid, 54.

[48] L Chouliaraki, 'Towards an Analytics of Mediation' (2006) 3 *Critical Discourse Studies* 153.

[49] Senate Select Committee on Intelligence, *Committee Study of the Central Intelligence Agency's Detention and Interrogation Program* (3 December 2014), www.intelligence.senate.gov/study2014/sscistudy1.pdf.

invited to experience in his case mainly originated in a perception that he was one 'one of us' and moreover a vulnerable member of society who was more properly the subject of community solidarity (or thick relations) than one who should be subjected to the vagaries of the politics of pity. However, it is important to bear in mind that McKinnon's story could have been framed in an entirely different way, casting him as a distant figure with whom audiences might have found it hard to identify: his UFO obsession and mental disability resonate with trope of the loner,[50] which exhibits the traits of a more menacing masculinity associated, for example, with the paedophile and the violent tearaway that is the suicide bomber.

IV. DISABILITY AND INNOCENCE

McKinnon's supporters have always maintained that he was a harmless eccentric who was merely interested in the existence of 'little green men'. They claimed that when he hacked into the Pentagon and NASA computer systems, he was not even remotely driven by terrorist intent. In the words of Boris Johnson, the Conservative London Mayor, McKinnon was 'a classic British nut job'.[51] Adopting a typical 'reportage frame', which distinguishes itself from the standard mode of news reporting in that it actively encourages identification and empathy,[52] the Daily Mail journalist Allison Pearson described McKinnon in similar terms as 'a gentle sci-fi nut' and a 'mild-mannered UFO nut'.[53] His supporters insisted that McKinnon's eccentric interests were the result of his autism. His 'odd' or 'strange' behaviour was thus relabelled as a psychiatric condition, casting a different light on his obsession with UFOs.

Disability was a key part of McKinnon's human rights claim. For supporters, his condition provided an entirely rational explanation for his hacking activities. At the same time, they also regarded his autism as a potent argument against his extradition, his vulnerability rendering him deserving of the public's pity and the State's mercy. Indeed, the recognition that someone is vulnerable is a core aspect of human rights communication: Turner argues that it is the shared experience of vulnerability that provides the basis for a common humanity.[54] He identifies embodiment (and everything it entails in terms of the body's precariousness and susceptibility to injury) as foundational of universal rights and describes it as 'the real source of our common sociability'.[55] A sufferer must be perceived as sufficiently vulnerable and injurable in order to gain public sympathy and understanding. In McKinnon's

---

[50] R Collier, *Masculinities, Crime and Criminology: Men, Heterosexuality and the Criminal(ised) Other* (London, Sage, 1998).
[51] McClatchey (n 10).
[52] Cottle (n 17) 144.
[53] A Pearson, 'They Let Real Terrorists Stay Here But Send My Boy—Who's too Timid to Use the Tube—to a Terrible US Jail' *Daily Mail* (London, 3 July 2009), www.dailymail.co.uk/news/article-1197190/They-let-terrorists-stay-send-boy--whos-timid-use-Tube--terrible-U-S-jail.html.
[54] BS Turner, *Vulnerability and Human Rights* (Pennsylvania, Pennsylvania State University, 2006).
[55] ibid, 25.

case, medical experts submitted evidence that there was a very high chance of a serious deterioration of his mental health if he were extradited. While learning difficulties are commonly the target of very negative media stereotypes, fuelling social stigma,[56] McKinnon's Asperger was presented as a mitigating factor which rendered him incapable of committing any terrorist offences, a view supported by various psychiatric assessments. Professor Baron-Cohen opined in evidence submitted to the Administrative Court that 'McKinnon's motivation was unrelated to any terrorist agenda, nor did he have any wish to cause harm, damage, or loss to the US as a nation or any individual'.[57]

These explanatory factors, backed up by medical evidence, amounted to a powerful narrative of vulnerability and incapacity to commit harm. Its success as a frame was founded on a clear logic, the authority of its sponsors and its powerful political message. However, the frame's persuasiveness also hinged on its ability to mobilise a particular image of the male computer geek. It has been noted that there appears to be a much higher incidence of Asperger syndrome among computer geeks—individuals who take an almost obsessive interest in technology—the explanation being that sufferers of the syndrome tend to prefer the neatly ordered world of machines to the unpredictable environment of humans and real-life social interaction.[58] Geeks are considered brilliant with technology but severely lacking in social skills, which sees them both celebrated and derided in popular culture. Moreover, such a portrayal also chimes with the stereotypical media image of 'the autistic savant who has exceptional talent in a particular area'.[59]

The image of geeks as nerdy but harmless individuals is also reflected in the way in which hacking is perceived as a crime. There is a growing realisation that hacking can cause significant harm to society (one only need think of the phone hacking scandal in Britain) but there is also great ambivalence involving 'vacillating responses to the maverick qualities that seem to be at a premium in the hard-to-adapt-to hi-tech world of constant change'.[60] The hacker's reputation as a genius who is able to crack sophisticated corporate security barriers persists, contributing to the belief that hacking is an achievement to be celebrated rather than something to be prosecuted and punished. When a young computer hacker who suffered from Asperger syndrome was put on trial in New Zealand in 2008, the Crown Prosecutor suggested that the police should consider employing him while the judge discharging the offender was moved to 'wish him well'.[61] An Israeli hacker wanted for an attempted intrusion of Pentagon computers was described by Prime Minister

[56] P Corrigan, V Thompson, D Lambert et al, 'Perceptions of Discrimination among Persons with Serious Mental Illness' (2003) 54 *Psychiatric Services* 1105.

[57] *R (McKinnon) v Secretary of State for Home Affairs* [2009] EWHC 2021 (Admin), para 18.

[58] A Hunter, 'High-Tech Rascality: Asperger's Syndrome, Hackers, Geeks, and Personality Types in the ICT Industry' (2009) 24 *New Zealand Sociology* 39.

[59] CS Jones and V Harwood, 'Representations of Autism in Australian Print Media' (2009) 24 *Disability and Society* 5, 15.

[60] PA Taylor, 'Hackers: Cyberpunks or Microserfs?' (1998) 1 *Information, Communication and Culture* 401, 416.

[61] Quoted in Hunter (n 58) 41.

Netanyahu in 1998 as 'damn good', while the hacker's lawyer suggested that his client had done the US a favour and should be rewarded instead of punished.[62]

Echoing such views, McKinnon's supporters argued that rather than prosecuting him, the authorities should consider employing him so as to put his intelligence and extraordinary skills to good use. For example, the senior Labour politician Keith Vaz, chairman of the Home Affairs Committee, was quoted as saying that '[a]nyone who can hack into the computer system of the Pentagon should not actually be sent to trial—I believe he should be offered a job'.[63] Similarly, Baroness Browning opined in Parliament that 'the Pentagon would do well to employ Gary McKinnon to sort out the weaknesses in their computer system'.[64] Having conducted a survey among its users, the information technology analysis and news website ITPRO reported that the response had been overwhelmingly that McKinnon should be employed by officials as 'a classic case of poacher turned gamekeeper'.[65]

V. GEOPOLITICS AND EXTRADITION

The legal basis for the extradition request concerning McKinnon can be found in the Extradition Act 2003. The Act implemented the European Framework Decision on the European Arrest Warrant, creating a fast-track procedure for extradition requests from EU Member States. The legislation also extends to a number of other countries, designated as 'category 2 territories' which by virtue of an order made under the 2003 Act include the US.[66] The fast-track procedure, which applies to 32 different types of crime, including computer-related criminality as per Schedule 2 to the Act,[67] does not require the requesting country to produce any prima facie evidence of the alleged crime (ss 71(4) and 73(5)). According to the Act's critics, this means that suspects are deprived of the opportunity to challenge evidence against them in a UK court.[68] One further element of controversy concerns the lack of reciprocity in the extradition arrangements between the UK and the US. Under the Extradition Treaty signed by the US and the UK in March 2003, no prima facie evidence is required when the US is requesting a suspect's extradition, while extradition requests by the UK are subject to more stringent evidential safeguards (demonstrating 'probable cause') in line with the US Constitution.[69]

Critics of the extradition arrangements believe that there is ample evidence to support their argument that the Treaty is effectively generating a lopsided

---

[62] Taylor (n 60) 614.

[63] D Martin, 'Ministers Should Give Gary McKinnon a Job, Says Senior Labour MP Keith Vaz' *Daily Mail* (London, 19 November 2009), www.dailymail.co.uk/news/article-1229403/Ministers-Gary-McKinnon-job-says-senior-Labour-MP-Keith-Vaz.html.

[64] HL Deb 16 December 2010, vol 723, col 729.

[65] N Kobie, 'Your Views: Gary McKinnon' ITPRO (17 July 2009), www.itpro.co.uk/612898/your-views-gary-mckinnon.

[66] S Broadbridge, *The UK/US Extradition Treaty*, House of Commons Library, Standard Note SN/HA/2204 (2009), 4.

[67] 'Extradition: Processes and Review', www.gov.uk/extradition-processes-and-review.

[68] Broadbridge (n 66).

[69] ibid, 1.

effect.[70] The secrecy of the agreement with the US and the manner in which Parliament was bypassed have been heavily criticised by politicians and some media commentators.[71] Former Home Secretary David Blunkett, who signed the Extradition Treaty, commented on the radio in September 2010 that 'there is there is still a debate—and I'm prepared to concede this—about whether we gave away too much'.[72] Lord Lester, a Liberal Democrat peer and a human rights barrister, has commented that the extradition arrangements are 'part of an imperial trend in United States foreign and legal policy in seeking to extend US jurisdiction beyond its territory without being prepared for reciprocity with other friendly states'.[73]

The newly formed coalition government of Conservatives and Liberal Democrats announced a review of relevant extradition arrangements in September 2010, led by former Court of Appeal judge Sir Scott Baker.[74] The remit of the review was to examine whether the arrangements of the UK/US Extradition Treaty were unbalanced. The Baker Report, published in October 2011, concluded that this was not the case.[75] The Joint Committee on Human Rights (JCHR) reported the findings of its own inquiry into the European Arrest Warrant in June 2011, calling for a number of changes, including the requirement that an extradition request be supported by prima facie evidence.[76] The Home Affairs Committee also conducted an inquiry, publishing its report in March 2012 in which it urged the government to renegotiate its Extradition Treaty with the US.[77] Theresa May's decision in October 2012 not to extradite McKinnon was accompanied by the announcement that a 'forum bar' would be introduced, meaning that 'where prosecution is possible in both the UK and in another State, the British courts will be able to bar prosecution overseas, if they believe it is in the interests of justice to do so'.[78]

Geopolitics undoubtedly played a significant role in McKinnon's fight against extradition. His perceived vulnerability was compounded by the imputed unfairness of a Treaty which according to critics poses a significant risk to the civil liberties of everyone in the UK. Unease about the Extradition Act and the Extradition Treaty with the US in particular demonstrated serious concerns that essential legal safeguards had been sacrificed in the name of security and counter-terrorism. McKinnon's case drove home the indiscriminateness of extradition laws: the absence of prima facie evidence in court meant that his predicament was one which could easily befall anyone. Critics of the Extradition Treaty claim that there was a

---

[70] Liberty, 'Extradition Act 2003 Undermines Fundamental Rights' (30 November 2006), www.liberty-human-rights.org.uk/news/press-releases/extradition-act-2003-undermines-fundamental-rights.

[71] Broadbridge (n 66).

[72] 'Extradition', BBC Radio 4, 2 September 2010, www.bbc.co.uk/programmes/b00tjrp6.

[73] Quoted in Broadbridge (n 66) 15.

[74] BBC News, 'Extradition Law Review to Consider US-UK Treatment', www.bbc.co.uk/programmes/b00tjrp6.

[75] S Baker, *A Review of the United Kingdom's Extradition Arrangements* (30 September 2011), www.gov.uk/government/uploads/system/uploads/attachment_data/file/117673/extradition-review.pdf.

[76] Joint Committee on Human Rights, *The Human Rights Implications of UK Extradition Policy*, 15th Report (2010–12, HL 156, HC 767).

[77] Home Affairs Committee, *The US-UK Extradition Treaty*, vol 1, 20th report (2010–12, HC 644).

[78] A Horne, Extradition and the European Arrest Warrant: Recent Developments (House of Commons Library SN/HA/6105, 2013).

profound betrayal of citizens by a British State eager to please its most trusted ally and too weak to resist demands which infringe fundamental freedoms. The basic contract between governed and government was seen to have been violated, leading Boris Johnson to ask on his blog: 'How can the British government be so proto-plasmic, so pathetic, so heedless of the well-being of its own people, as to sign the warrant for his [McKinnon's] extradition?'[79]

McKinnon figured as the sacrificial lamb on the altar of interstate security. Not only was he one of 'us'; he could be any one of 'us'. As noted above, this shifted the focus from the distant stranger suffering a fate which is too remote to pose a threat to the spectator who was exposed to the same risk on an equally random basis, one of the classic cases of internal bystanding described by Cohen.[80] It is at this point in the McKinnon story that the politics of pity gave way to the much less selfless, tribal consideration that anyone could find themselves in the same position as the victim. Indeed, in an adjournment debate in 2006 the then Solicitor-General Mike O'Brien disabused parliamentarians of the notion that the Extradition Act 2003—and by extension the new extradition treaty with the US—was aimed solely at terrorists.[81] While US authorities insisted that McKinnon had committed serious offences, his public image was that of the blameless victim caught up in the geopolitical web of the war on terror. McKinnon's case may have been the most high profile, but it has certainly not been the only one of its kind. There have been several other extradition cases which have also caused public controversy. For example, the case of the so-called NatWest Three, three British bankers extradited to the US on fraud charges in 2005 in connection with the collapse of the US energy firm Enron, also sparked criticism about the extradition arrangements between the UK and the US.[82]

However, it is perhaps more instructive to compare the publicity surrounding McKinnon's case with extradition cases involving Muslim terrorism suspects whose legal struggles, though similar, failed to mobilise elite support. There have been accusations of double standards in respect of the very different political decisions that were reached in the case of McKinnon and those affecting Muslim terrorism suspects.[83] A particularly high-profile case is that of Abu Hamza, a Muslim cleric who was extradited to the US for various offences, including sponsorship of terrorist activities and the attempt to establish a terrorist training camp in Oregon.[84] He unsuccessfully fought a lengthy battle against extradition, with his lawyers arguing that his transfer to the US would violate his right not to be subjected to degrading treatment which life-long imprisonment in a US maximum-security prison would

---

[79] B Johnson, 'Quest to Extradite Harmless Hacker, Gary McKinnon' (27 January 2009), www.boris-johnson.com/2009/01/27/quest-to-extradite-harmless-hacker-gary-mckinnon.

[80] Cohen (n 8) 141.

[81] HL Deb 16 December 2010, vol 723, col 729.

[82] Broadbridge (n 66) 16.

[83] S Walshe, 'Britain's Double Standard on Extradition to US Prison Abuse' *The Guardian* (London, 8 November 2012), www.theguardian.com/commentisfree/2012/nov/08/britain-double-standard-extradition-us-prison-abuse.

[84] V Dodd, 'Abu Hamza Extradition to US Blocked by European Court' *The Guardian* (London, 8 July 2010), www.theguardian.com/uk/2010/jul/08/abu-hamza-human-rights-ruling.

represent. Hamza suffers from physical disability, having lost his hands and an eye. While McKinnon's disability was an important factor in his portrayal as a vulnerable and morally innocent individual, Hamza's very visible physical impairments played a significant part in the hostile media response his case attracted. Poole observed in relation to Hamza's overwhelming media presence in the British press that 'his demonisation parallels that of the media's global Islamic monster, Osama Bin Laden'.[85] Dubbed 'Captain Hook' by British tabloids on account of the metal, hook-shaped prostheses attached to his arms, Abu Hamza has been routinely caricatured as a pantomime villain, a grotesque and almost comical character who is physically repulsive and morally 'beyond the pale'.

Cybersecurity does not impinge on the public's awareness of security in the same way as Islamic terrorism does, and herein lies a crucial difference between McKinnon's case and that of Hamza. The media frames applied to Hamza put him squarely in the realm of Islamic fundamentalism. To quote from the Daily Mail's sympathetic portrait of McKinnon, while 'no one encountering Gary McKinnon for the first time is going to think: "Oooh, here's an evil terrorist"', there could be no doubt that Hamza, described as 'the hook-handed hate preacher' in the same article, is the real deal as far as 'evil' terrorists go.[86] However, it would be hard to resist the idea that race and religion have equally played a significant part in the public debate on extradition and human rights. McKinnon was perceived as 'one of us' who is at worst an 'Ordinary Decent Criminal'[87] and thus not a terrorist, while Hamza's public persona is that of a terrorist monster.

While Abu Hamza's story generated many lurid headlines, adding to the concerns of British Muslims that the media are only interested in the extremist fringes of their communities,[88] the case of the IT worker Babar Ahmad, who has also unsuccessfully fought extradition to the US, received markedly less publicity. Yet, it was the parallel circumstances with McKinnon's case that caused his family to accuse the Home Secretary of 'double standards' in halting McKinnon's extradition just weeks after extraditing Ahmad along with Talha Ahsan, another British-born terrorism suspect who also happened to suffer from Asperger syndrome, leading his supporters to argue that he was as vulnerable an individual as McKinnon was.[89] The relative obscurity of Ahmad and Ahsan provides a further illustration of asymmetries in the recognition shown by the media towards victims of human rights breaches. Indeed, the Independent newspaper called Ahmad 'the forgotten victim of the war on terror'.[90]

---

[85] L Poole, 'The Effects of September 11 and the War in Iraq on British Newspaper Coverage' in E Poole and JE Richardson (eds), *Muslims and the News Media* (London, IB Tauris, 2006).

[86] Pearson (n 53).

[87] C Pantazis and S Pemberton, 'From the "Old" To the "New" Suspect Community' (2009) 49 *British Journal of Criminology* 646, 654.

[88] F Ahmad, 'British Muslim Perceptions and Opinions on News Coverage of September 11' (2006) 32 *Journal of Ethnic and Migration Studies* 961.

[89] M Shafiq, 'Gary McKinnon Extradition and Double Standards' (16 October 2012), ramadhanfoundation.com/home/gary-mckinnon-extradition-and-double-standards.

[90] 'Six Years in Jail, No Charge: The War on Terror's Forgotten Victim Speaks' *The Independent* (London, 8 July 2010), www.independent.co.uk/news/uk/home-news/six-years-in-jail-no-charge-the-war-on-terrors-forgotten-victim-speaks-2021138.html.

Ahmad, a British Muslim of Pakistani origins, was arrested in 2003 by anti-terrorism police and suffered serious abuse at their hands, including religious abuse, which resulted in 73 physical injuries. He was awarded £60,000 in compensation in 2009. Although he was released without charge in 2003, he was arrested again in 2004 and was soon transferred to a high-security prison, where he remained until his extradition to the US in late 2012.[91] The reason for his re-arrest was an extradition request from US authorities which accused him of involvement in terrorist activities. He was indicted on the basis of allegations that he had provided material support to terrorists through websites supporting Taliban and Chechen fighters. Another allegation, which was based on Ahmad's alleged possession of classified US navy plans, involved a conspiracy to kill, kidnap, maim or injure persons or damage property in a foreign country. As in McKinnon's case, the CPS declared to have insufficient evidence to prosecute Ahmad in the UK. Ahmad has described himself as a devout Muslim and he has complained about the sensationalist media response to his alleged crimes.[92]

The apparent similarities between McKinnon and Ahmad are striking: both are British-born citizens and in both cases the US requested their extradition on cyber-terrorism-related charges. Mirroring McKinnon's fears, Ahmad argued that he too might be imprisoned for life in circumstances which would breach his human rights if he were convicted in the US. Both suspects claimed that they were suffering from the consequences of an extradition law branded lopsided by politicians, media commentators and human rights campaigners. Nevertheless, significantly fewer column inches were devoted to Babar Ahmad's case. While the Daily Mail ran a campaign in order to lift the threat of extradition for McKinnon, it has published only a handful of articles on Ahmad's case.[93] The coverage may be somewhat more balanced in other news outlets,[94] but Ahmad's plight was largely ignored by the media. While there may well have been a sound basis for the very different decisions reached in extradition cases involving Muslim suspects, an inability to identify with the plight of Ahmad and the others would at least in part explain a media indifference which stands in stark contrast with the public validation of McKinnon's status as a victim of serious human rights infringements.

VI. BRINGING THE DISTANT SUFFERER CLOSER

In order to be able to relate to the suffering of another person, there has to be a recognition that the Other is human and therefore worthy of pity. Humanisation

---

[91] ibid.
[92] ibid.
[93] To be specific, a *Lexis* search of the *Daily Mail/Mail on Sunday* shows that a total of 23 articles making reference to Babar Ahmad were published in the period 7 August 2004—26 August 2010. This compares with a total of 161 articles referring to McKinnon in the period 14 November 2002—7 September 2010.
[94] A comparison using *Lexis*: *The Guardian*: 50 articles referring to Ahmad in the period 6 August 2004—13 August 2010; 93 articles referring to McKinnon in the period 13 November 2002—17 September 2010. *The Independent*: 20 articles referring to Ahmad in the period 6 August 2004—13 August 2010; 54 articles referring to McKinnon in the period 13 November 2002—9 September 2010.

requires that victims of rights abuse are not simply talked about in news reports as passive objects but are given their own voice in public debate. In Chouliaraki's words:

> [H]umanization is a process of identity construction that endows the sufferer with the power to say or do something about her condition, even if this power is simply the power to evoke and receive the beneficiary action of others. The human sufferer is the sufferer who acts.[95]

Gary McKinnon was an active participant in the public debate about his extradition, as was, crucially, his mother, Janis Sharp, who campaigned tirelessly on his behalf. She acted as his chief spokesperson, giving countless media interviews and running a Twitter feed, and she also stood as a candidate in the 2010 parliamentary election. Her involvement appeared to have been instrumental in getting the Daily Mail to back McKinnon's fight against extradition. According to McClatchey, 'the story appeals to mothers in Middle England, the Mail's readership base'.[96] Sharp also found her own voice in the press, writing an impassioned plea to David Cameron and Theresa May in an open letter in the Guardian in which she said of her son that '[a] boy who cycled, swam, composed music and sang, now sits in the dark with his cats and never wants to see or speak to anyone'.[97] Those who struggled to relate to the adult McKinnon as a primary victim may have found it easier to identify and empathise with a mother who was set to lose her child through a contested extradition treaty.

McKinnon's plight was therefore not just viewed through the lens of the alien hunter or geeky character; Sharp's description of him as a 'boy' in her open letter implored the public to see him as the child of a mother who was deserving of pity. It is the strong bond with his family and the perceived ordinariness of the main protagonists that were arguably vital in constructing McKinnon as a worthy recipient of human rights protection. Maternal activism is not new in human rights movements, the most famous example being the campaign of the Mothers and Grandmothers of the Plaza de Mayo in Argentina generating worldwide attention for the Disappeared. Indeed, such has been the power of kinship activism in this particular setting that it has tended to marginalise survivors of torture in Argentina, the so-called 'Ex-Disappeared' whose plight has been obscured through the disproportionate publicity given to those who are still disappeared.[98] While Janis Sharp's campaign was not on the same scale, it too showed the capacity of maternal blood ties to act as a key focus in media attitudes to victims of human rights abuse.

McKinnon's media access, facilitated by his mother's tireless campaigning, stood in marked contrast to the lack of voice for Muslim terrorism suspects who

---

[95] Chouliaraki (n 48) 169.

[96] McClatchey (n 10).

[97] J Sharp, 'An Open Letter about my Son, Gary McKinnon, to Theresa May and David Cameron' *The Guardian* (London, 7 September 2012), www.theguardian.com/commentisfree/2012/sep/07/open-letter-gary-mckinnon.

[98] A Gandsman, 'The Limits of Kinship Mobilizations and the (A)politics of Human Rights in Argentina' (2012) 17 *Journal of Latin American and Caribbean Anthropology* 193.

similarly claimed that their rights were at serious risk of being violated. Hamza's comprehensive demonisation meant that precious few rights organisations voiced concerns about the lack of legal safeguards as regards his extradition, despite the fact that it raised issues that were ostensibly very similar to those raised by the McKinnon case. The plight of Babar Ahmad was largely overlooked by news media, as was that of other Muslim terrorism suspects fighting extradition to the US. Talha Ahsan's brother pleaded that 'compassion should be extended to our family too', but this fell on deaf ears, as he pointed out: 'The Daily Mail spearheads a campaign against British citizens being extradited and it refers to Talha Ahsan and Babar Ahmad as unwanted guests. No government of the day wants to upset the Daily Mail.'[99] Harb and Bessaio have noted that '[t]he ongoing "othering" of Muslims and their concomitant sense of exclusion from Britishness deepened after the September 11 atrocities when Islam was demonized as the enemy within'.[100]

While global and national media have an important responsibility for the intensification of Islamophobia, the political rhetoric deployed in the war on terror was equally instrumental in the depiction of Muslims as a fundamental threat to Western values and liberties.[101] Indeed, following Hillyard's original thesis concerning the status of the UK's Irish population as a 'suspect community', Muslims have been identified as the 'new suspect community' whereby 'suspicion is primarily linked to an individual's perceived membership of a sub-group and not to suspected wrongdoing'.[102] The claim that Gary McKinnon was a terrorist, as US prosecutors maintained, was easily discounted because he simply did not fit the default cultural frame of the male dark-skinned bearded Muslim. McKinnon easily passed as 'one of us': as we have seen, his public image was that of the quintessential British eccentric looking for ET on US military servers. His alleged crimes were made light of as a harmless pastime to be celebrated for its Britishness, a rationalisation which was largely unavailable in respect of Muslim suspects.

VII. CONCLUSION

It would be difficult to give a definitive explanation for the HRA's negative media image. Despite trenchant criticism of the Act by media commentators and leading politicians, it is important to bear in mind that the principles of human rights are not at issue as these are widely considered to be the cornerstone of a democratic society. However, the human rights doctrine is at its most challenging when it is applied and requires difficult decisions which are likely to be unpalatable to media audiences. This chapter has sought to highlight that there is a stubborn us/them distinction in

---

[99] D Rickman, 'Gary McKinnon Extradition Block Sees Government Accused of "Double Standards" over Human Rights' *Huffington Post* (16 October 2012), www.huffingtonpost.co.uk/2012/10/16/gary-mckinnon-talha-ahsan-babar-ahmad_n_1969651.html.

[100] Z Harb and E Bessaio, 'British Arab Muslim Audiences and Television after September 11' (2006) 32 *Journal of Ethnic and Migration Studies* 1063, 1064.

[101] Ahmad (n 88).

[102] Pantazis and Pemberton (n 87) 649.

frames suggesting that human rights protections are proper and legitimate for the dominant majority but are problematic when claims involve specific minorities. To make the claim that terrorism suspects are human too is often seen as bordering on the subversive. Nevertheless, McKinnon's human rights claim did not cause the predictable public outcry and did not encounter the hostility that similar claims by terrorism suspects normally attract. It could be said that McKinnon's good fortune was that he was the subject of thick relations involving solidarity and concern for a victim of rights infringements who was considered 'one of us' and who was therefore very much like 'us'. Witnessing his suffering from the perspective of the majority of the British audience was a matter of internal bystanding. The publicity given to McKinnon's potential extradition reflected a growing anxiety that extradition laws, and by extension anti-terrorism laws, potentially affect everyone, as opposed to simply singling out the evil terrorist who is deemed beyond the pale.

Despite this being a very instructive case when studying media framing of human rights claims, media discourse in this instance was hardly an endorsement of the domestic human rights regime. Critics found plenty of ammunition in the McKinnon case to argue that many security measures were misguided, victimising the 'good' citizen instead of targeting the 'real' terrorist and consequently also that the current human rights regime tends to protect the wrong people. What on the surface appeared to be a principled stance which challenged the excesses of security in support of human rights, including the much beleaguered HRA, may instead have confirmed and further entrenched hierarchies of rights-worthiness, weakening the inclusivity principle according to which human rights exist to protect all human beings regardless of who they are.

Conclusions

25

The UK and European Human Rights: Some Reflections

ELIZABETH WICKS, KATJA S ZIEGLER AND LOVEDAY HODSON

F OLLOWING THE MANY detailed explorations of the issues encountered in the relationship between the UK and European human rights is a difficult task. This conclusion seeks to reflect upon, and emphasise, some of the major points identified in this collection, as well as offer a limited analysis of what we view as one of the most pressing issues on the current political agenda in the UK: the future of human rights protection.

I. THE COMPLEXITY OF THE 'STRAINED' RELATIONSHIP

The relationship between the United Kingdom and European human rights is a multi-faceted one. It operates on many different levels and, it appears, with varied degrees of 'strain':

— between courts at different levels;
— between layers of standards (domestic/international), with the added difficulty of the unclear separation of the two in the UK;
— between the courts (including the European Court of Human Rights (ECtHR)) and Parliament;
— between government (executive) and the courts (including the ECtHR);
— between the UK and the two Europes: the European Union (EU) and its Charter of Fundamental Rights and Freedoms in addition to the European Convention on Human Rights (ECHR) system;
— between (parts of) the public/media and human rights.

At one level, the relationship operates between different judicial bodies, most notably between the UK Supreme Court and the ECtHR. This is the relationship introduced so authoritatively by Lord Kerr and Judge Mahoney in the first two chapters of this collection. It is a working relationship, with an explicit judicial and extra-judicial dialogue, and yet it increasingly shows signs of strain. A number of senior British judges have recently spoken out publicly against decisions, and indeed the broader ethos of the judges in Strasbourg.[1] For better or worse, the judges in both courts are at the front line of the relationship between the UK and European human rights. Strasbourg judges are frequently required to review decisions of the domestic courts for compliance with the Convention, albeit subject to a margin of appreciation, while domestic judges are explicitly required by the Human Rights Act 1998 (HRA), which is today at the core of the constitutional protection of human rights in the UK, to 'take into account' Strasbourg judgments—a deceptively simple instruction.

In addition to the relationship between the ECtHR and the domestic courts, there is an additional layer of complexity in the UK which results from the closely-entwined identity of international and domestic human rights standards following the constitutional solution adopted under the HRA. The UK is not unique in tying the domestic protection of rights to international standards, as the example of Austria demonstrates; and while a multi-layered system of human rights protection is never without complexity, the duality of the ECHR as both the basis of national human rights protection (through the HRA) and international human rights protection adds to the complexity of the relationship between the UK and European human rights when defining the standard of protection at the domestic level. It is thus not just a relationship between courts at national and international levels, each applying their own sets of rights, with the international court and standard providing a minimum safeguard. While that basic relationship certainly also exists for the UK, there is a further layer and complicating factor relating to the need to untangle (or even develop) the domestic standard of protection from the international minimum standard. The approach of the UK courts, perhaps in light of the relative novelty of the specific task since the HRA came into force in 2000, has been searching in this regard, and the situation has been a source of potential confusion.

There has therefore been some interesting agonising by some UK judges, not just on specific issues of human rights protection but also about the general relationship between the two systems. One example is the debate as to whether the ECHR provides a floor and/or a ceiling for the interpretation of the ECHR through the HRA by UK judges, culminating in the 'mirror' doctrine, expertly explained in Richard Clayton's chapter. It is now accepted that the ECHR cannot prevent UK judges from affording greater protection of human rights at domestic level than the protection required by the Convention at international level (in line with practice elsewhere in Europe and Article 53 ECHR). However, the debates within the UK demonstrate the difficulties that may arise from a conceptually complex situation in which the domestic system of human rights protection is largely achieved

---

[1] See eg 'Lord Sumption gives the 27th Sultan Azlan Shah Lecture, Kuala Lumpur, The Limits of Law, 20 November 2013', www.supremecourt.uk/docs/speech-131120.pdf; Lord Mance, 'Destruction or Metamorphosis of the Legal Order?', speech delivered at the World Policy Conference, Monaco, 14 December 2013, www.supremecourt.uk/docs/speech-131214.pdf; Lord Justice Laws, 'Lecture III: The Common Law and Europe', Hamlyn Lectures 2013, 27 November 2013, www.judiciary.gov.uk/wp-content/uploads/JCO/Documents/Speeches/laws-lj-speech-hamlyn-lecture-2013.pdf; The Rt Hon Lord Judge, 'Constitutional Change: Unfinished Business', speech delivered at University College London, 4 December 2013, www.ucl.ac.uk/constitution-unit/constitution-unit-news/constitution-unit/research/judicial-independence/lordjudgelecture041213/.

through incorporation of the ECHR in domestic law without a separate domestic codification. The (questionable) 'mirror' doctrine was designed by domestic judges so as to avoid the UK leaping ahead of Strasbourg in the protection of human rights. This was perhaps out of a sense of responsibility—a desire not to fragment the Convention system at the international level, particularly given the hope that the HRA might have the effect of increasing the influence of UK jurisprudence on the ECHR in Strasbourg, but it was nevertheless misguided with regard to domestic human rights protection, as pointed out by Lord Kerr in his chapter. The possibility that UK jurisprudence might carry particular weight at Strasbourg results from the symbiotic way in which rights are protected in the UK, which means that UK courts routinely interpret and apply provisions of the ECHR, and in doing so are at least seen to apply the same standard as that applied by the ECtHR.[2] This in turn may have at least an indirect influence on the interpretation of the ECHR in Strasbourg: where national case law applies the ECHR as the national standard, it may be easier to map onto a Convention case at international level. Therefore, (unintentionally) decisions from those States might be looked at more than national case law that applies a differently worded standard.

A recent example of domestic agonising over the relationship between the ECHR and the national courts by Supreme Court judges is the case of *Nicklinson*.[3] In this case, the Supreme Court framed for itself a question of whether it remains open to a domestic court to declare that a statutory provision which the Strasbourg Court has held to be within the UK's margin of appreciation and hence compatible with the ECHR at international level nonetheless infringes Convention rights as applied in the UK. The Supreme Court clarified that the 'mirror' principle does not necessarily assist with the question of whether a statutory provision, in this case the universal prohibition of assisted suicide,[4] which is within the UK's permitted margin, is nonetheless a violation of a Convention right at the domestic level. After much (arguably unnecessary) analysis, the Supreme Court judges in *Nicklinson* agreed that it remained open to find such a provision incompatible under the HRA. (The majority chose not to formally declare such incompatibility, for reasons that were more to do with the court's relationship with the Westminster Parliament than with the ECtHR.)[5] That domestic courts must ultimately 'form their own view as to whether or not there is an infringement of Convention rights for domestic purposes'[6] is a timely reminder that domestic judges retain an essential role in protecting and developing human rights in the UK—a role that is independent of, albeit related to, the ECtHR's protection of rights within the UK. Many controversial rights issues will fall within the UK's margin of appreciation at a regional level, as the UK

---

[2] *R (Ullah) v Special Adjudicator* [2004] UKHL 26, para 20, per Lord Bingham (pointing to the need to interpret the Convention uniformly across the States party to it).
[3] *R (Nicklinson) v Ministry of Justice; R (AM) v Director of Public Prosecutions* [2014] UKSC 38.
[4] s 2 Suicide Act 1961, as amended by the Coroners and Justice Act 2009.
[5] This has been discussed more fully elsewhere: E Wicks, 'The Supreme Court Judgment in Nicklinson: One Step Forward on Assisted Dying; Two Steps Back on Human Rights' (2014) 23 *Medical Law Review* (online).
[6] *Nicklinson* (n 3) para 74 per Lord Neuberger.

government was so keen to assert at the High Level Conference in Brighton, and which is now explicit in the Convention's Preamble, but this will not, and could not, preclude the UK's own judiciary from examining those issues for compatibility with domestic HRA rights.

Despite some provocative speeches from senior British judges, the relationship between domestic and Strasbourg judges is one of dialogue and respect. Where it faces strain, there are formal and informal mechanisms for relief (discussed more fully below). This relationship is but the tip of the iceberg, however, because the relationship between the UK and European human rights also encompasses the relationship between the Westminster Parliament and the ECtHR, and here the strain seems to be increasing. The most obvious example of this is the prisoner voting saga, which remains unsettled at the time of writing. As discussed in the chapter by Ruvi Ziegler and elsewhere,[7] the focus of the disagreement between many UK MPs and Strasbourg judges is the weight to be given to a majority decision of an elected representative legislature. While the UK clearly has a margin to decide how to regulate this area, and the demands of the ECtHR are much more minimal than many opponents are prepared to acknowledge,[8] the political conflict has built around an assertion that a relevant majority decision by the Westminster Parliament should be the final word on compatibility with the Convention. From this perspective, the breaking point could have been on a variety of issues: prisoner voting, rather than, say, the extradition of suspected terrorists or deportation of immigrants, has been the rallying cry for opposition to the ECHR because the prisoner voting decisions require explicit revision of an Act of Parliament, and thus majority support within Westminster. The battle for supremacy between Westminster and Strasbourg plays out against a backdrop of the margin of appreciation, the principle of subsidiarity, and debates about judicial supremacy. It is, perhaps, the relationship most directly connected to the 'strain' discussed in Section II below.

Related to the relationship between Westminster and Strasbourg is that between UK government ministers and the ECtHR. It is not new for government ministers to criticise a Strasbourg judgment: the domestic response to the first finding of a violation of the right to life (Article 2 ECHR) in the *McCann* case reminds us of that.[9] In recent years, however, the language has become heightened. Prime Minister David Cameron, for example, famously claimed that it made him 'physically ill even to contemplate having to give the vote to anyone who is in prison'.[10] Following the

---

[7] See also E Bates, 'Analysing the Prisoner Voting Saga and the British Challenge to Strasbourg' (2014) 14 *Human Rights Law Review* 503.

[8] It is the absolute nature of the ban that has been found incompatible with the Convention.

[9] Nicholas Bonsor, the Minister of State for Foreign and Commonwealth Affairs, in reply to a question on *McCann*, said: 'The judgement of the majority, based on no new evidence and defying common sense, has done nothing for the standing of the court in the United Kingdom' (HC Deb 30 October 1995, vol 265, col 60, written answers). Sir Nicholas Lyell, the Attorney-General, gratefully pointed out in Parliament, however, that the judgment had 'no effect in our law save in relation to costs' (HC Deb 30 October 1995, vol 265, col 13). Thus, unlike in relation to the prisoner voting cases, there was no need for majority support at Westminster in order for the UK to comply with the Strasbourg judgment.

[10] A Hough, 'Prisoner Vote: What MPs Said in Heated Debate' *Daily Telegraph* (London, 11 February 2011), www.telegraph.co.uk/news/politics/8317485/Prisoner-vote-what-MPs-said-in-heated-debate.html.

2015 general election, in which a Conservative Party with a manifesto commitment to repeal the HRA and potentially withdraw from the ECHR gained a majority of seats in Westminster, it seems likely that the relationship between government ministers and the ECtHR will continue to be a focus of attention. More ominous than political rhetoric are the concrete steps already taken by governments, led by the UK, to seek to restrict the judicial powers of the ECtHR. As discussed by Noreen O'Meara in her chapter, Protocol 15 will add explicit recognition of the margin of appreciation and the principle of subsidiarity to the Preamble of the Convention, two principles which had until now been regarded as mere interpretive tools. Indeed, the Declarations from the High Level Conferences at Interlaken, Izmir and Brighton all focus on clarification of the relationship between national authorities and the Court (a focus which somewhat overshadows the Court's workload issue). The Brighton Declaration, for example, encourages the ECtHR to give 'great prominence to and apply consistently' the principles of subsidiarity and the margin of appreciation. This is a reminder that the contracting States' governments, and especially that of the UK, feel free to try to influence the overall direction and approach of the judicial body charged with enforcing the Convention. Such tendencies can be observed not just at the political level but also judicially, in particular through the use of third-party interventions. For example, the UK government has intervened not just in order to indirectly 're-open' the litigation against the UK in the prisoner voting context, but also in an attempt to change the approach of the Court of upholding the absolute prohibition on torture under Article 3 ECHR.[11] Clearly it is open to States to make use of procedural tools available. However, in light of the fundamental nature of the protection of Article 3 ECHR in the Convention system, an approach of 'silent' erosion seems not only inappropriate, but also conflicts with the conscious responsibility at times demonstrated by UK judges in dealing with the Convention. Efforts to restrict the extraterritorial application of the Convention, as discussed in Clare Ovey's chapter in this collection, also form part of this 'silent' erosion.

While the voluntary nature of the ECHR as an international treaty does give contracting parties a residual influence over its future, the Convention's role of ensuring protection for human rights across Europe, including protecting individuals from their own governments, cautions against such governmental interference. Threats such as those seen in the Conservative Party's proposal of 3 October 2014 which envisage withdrawal from the system unless the system changes to suit that political party's priorities, not only belittle and deprecate the position of human rights throughout Europe, they also reflect a fundamental misunderstanding of the function and significance of an external human rights control—for any State.

It would be a mistake to focus solely upon external relationships when considering the UK and European human rights. Some of the most problematic and

---

[11] Following *Chahal v UK* (1997) 23 EHRR 413, paras 76 and 79 ff (submission of the UK government and the ECtHR's response, respectively). See in particular: *Saadi v Italy* (2009) 49 EHRR 30, paras 117 ff; *Othman (Abu Qatada) v UK* (2012) 55 EHRR 1. See also H Fenwick, 'Enhanced Subsidiarity and a Dialogic Approach—or Appeasement in Recent Cases on Criminal Justice, Public Order and Counter-Terrorism at Strasbourg against the UK?' (ch 10), this volume.

strained relations are entirely internal to the UK. Under the HRA, the Westminster Parliament gave a clear instruction to domestic courts to interpret legislation in a way that is compatible with Convention rights so far as it is possible to do so, together with a power to issue a declaration of incompatibility where such interpretation is not possible. It also, and this may be the most significant element in the present context, ensured that courts and tribunals were themselves bound by the Convention rights, meaning that it would be unlawful for a court to reach a decision that is incompatible with the Convention rights. Despite this, the role of domestic courts in upholding Convention rights can bring them into conflict with the UK's Parliament and executive branches. Thus, for example, the declaration of incompatibility issued in the *Belmarsh Detainees* case[12] met with severe criticism from senior members of government, and in *Nicklinson*, discussed above, we see a majority of the Supreme Court supremely cautious about issues of constitutional propriety and not overstepping the appropriate boundaries between the courts and Parliament.[13] Mark Ockelton's chapter also reveals some of the controversies in the domestic enforcement of Convention rights which can arise independently of the ECtHR.

So far, the relationships outlined between UK institutions of government and the ECtHR have assumed a homogenous 'UK' approach. That, of course, is not an accurate reflection of the United Kingdom at the start of the twenty-first century. There are well-established devolved regimes in Scotland, Wales and Northern Ireland, and the relationships of those devolved legislatures/executives with Strasbourg are far more positive than those based in London. The Convention rights are a fundamental part of the devolution settlements and there is far less support for a denigration of these rights, or the role of the ECtHR, in the UK nations and regions beyond England. Indeed, the Conservative Party's proposals on human rights met with a significant outcry north of the border.[14] The future evolution of the UK, and the nature and extent of devolution, remains on the political agenda. The state is not symmetrical, but it never was, and dealing with complexities and asymmetries is unavoidable. This all suggests that relations between each of the devolved regions and Strasbourg will continue to develop in their own right, and any settlement of the current controversies between England and Strasbourg will not necessarily be replicated elsewhere in the UK.

As many chapters in this collection have emphasised, the very concept of 'European human rights' is broad and encompasses the EU and its Charter of Fundamental Rights and Freedoms in addition to the ECHR system. Thus, when considering the relationship between the UK and European human rights, it is impossible to disregard the UK's relationship with the EU as such and EU human rights more specifically. As with its relationship with the ECHR system, the UK's relationship with the EU is multifaceted, including relations between domestic courts, the Court of Justice of the European Union (CJEU), the Westminster Parliament, the UK executive, and

---

[12] *A v Secretary of State for the Home Department* [2005] 3 All ER 169.

[13] *Nicklinson* (n 3). Lord Kerr's and Lady Hale's dissenting judgments take a less cautious approach.

[14] See eg 'Tory Human Rights Plan Provokes Holyrood Rebellion' *The Scotsman* (Edinburgh, 4 October 2014), www.scotsman.com/news/uk/tory-human-rights-plan-provokes-holyrood-rebellion-1-3562556.

the other institutions of the EU. The supremacy of EU law within the domestic law of the UK, as well as the wide-ranging scope of EU influence, raises particularly challenging issues for these relationships. Furthermore, the possibility of EU accession to the ECHR would further strengthen the link between the two Europes in the area of fundamental rights and add further potential strain and sources of confusion to the relationship ('euroscepticism meets ECHR-scepticism and rights scepticism'?). In the unexpected outcome of Opinion 2/13, in which the draft accession agreement was held to be incompatible with the Union Treaties,[15] the CJEU may have expressed its own version of ECHR-scepticism (besides or as part of pursuing an institutional interest). In light of this recent development, the evolving relationship between the CJEU and the ECtHR as well as the EU and Council of Europe Member States will continue to be debated, with repercussions for the UK's own relationship with European human rights.

Finally, it should be noted that any evaluation of the relationship between the UK and European human rights should focus not only on the viewpoint adopted by the three branches of UK government, but also more broadly on the views of the British people towards the ECtHR, influenced greatly by the relationship between the British media and the Court. The chapters by Lieve Gies and David Mead expertly demonstrate the influence and negative impact that press reporting has upon public perceptions of human rights.[16] Indeed, it might even be claimed that a significant reason for any strained relationship between the UK and European human rights is the nature of media reporting on the latter.[17] Responses to judgments of the ECtHR and domestic judgments under the HRA are often misleading, uninformed and one-sided. This not just an issue with the media, and is particularly harmful when resorted to by those in power. When the government mirrors the popular press in adopting sceptical positions, it can alienate large sectors of the public from judicial decision making both in the UK and in Strasbourg. However, as has also been shown by these chapters, the role of the media is also multi-faceted: it may motivate government to take a particular stand, but it may also be used *by* government to further its agenda; and it may also shape whom the public perceive as 'deserving' of human rights protection. In all these ways it is doubtless a 'fourth power', but that power also depends on the freedom of expression itself (as discussed by Robert Uerpmann-Wittzack).

Thus, the relationship between the UK and European human rights has many strings to it. Some are strained to breaking point; others remain in a condition conducive to productive dialogue. Having outlined these different types of relations, we will now consider why some are under strain.

---

[15] Opinion 2/13, *EU Accession to the ECHR* [2014] ECR I-0000.

[16] Adam Wagner has recently made a number of contributions on the UK Human Rights Blog to expose and fight misreporting by the media. See eg ukhumanrightsblog.com/2014/09/29/is-this-the-best-human-rights-correction-ever-or-the-worst/ with links to other incidents. See also A Wagner, 'The Monstering of Human Rights', ukhumanrightsblog.com/2014/09/22/the-monstering-of-human-rights/.

[17] Notably, the relationship between courts and the media was a topic of discussion between judges of the ECtHR and judges of the German Federal Constitutional Court on the occasion of the visit of a Strasbourg delegation to Karlsruhe on 2 February 2015, www.bundesverfassungsgericht.de/SharedDocs/Pressemitteilungen/DE/2015/bvg15-007.html.

II. WHY THE 'STRAIN'?

The strain identified and discussed throughout the chapters in this collection seems to arise from a number of distinct issues, albeit issues that are interrelated and frequently fudged beyond recognition—which, in itself, is part of the problem. These issues are:

— the 'sovereignty' element(s);
— the 'rights' element;
— the 'foreign' (or 'Europe') element and the externalisation of rights; and
— the nature of the debate in the UK.

A. The 'Sovereignty' Element(s)

In many ways, the UK's relationship with European human rights is largely influenced by the 'European' element—or, in other words, perceived 'sovereignty' issues. This in itself breaks down into two distinct concepts. First, there are issues of the UK's national sovereignty (state sovereignty) and the manner in which it is reduced by membership of the EU and also arguably, although less obviously, by ratification of the ECHR. Second, there is the Westminster Parliament's parliamentary sovereignty which is often confused or conflated with the first notion of sovereignty.

National, or state, sovereignty is a defining feature of statehood and refers, in brief, to a range of relevant characteristics which include the existence of an internal body with authority to rule the State and the effectiveness of the exercise of its control throughout the territory, and an ability to make decisions on action to be taken on the international plane, including the degree of freedom of decision and action from external restraints and influences, as well as the ability of the State to influence other States. In its internal dimension, relevant in our context, sovereignty entails the right of a State to be free from intervention in internal affairs, which overlaps with the expression of the right to self-determination of its population. The right to choose its own constitution and form of government fall into this category. State sovereignty is not absolute. It operates within the limits of international law and may also be limited factually. Legal limitations, amongst others, result from entering into treaties by means of which States limit their sovereignty. Thus international cooperation, integration, and political, economic and military interdependence are possible, whilst equally recognising that such factors may affect the degree of sovereignty which a State enjoys. The UK's sovereignty is reduced by collaboration within Europe, and especially by membership of the EU. But it remains a sovereign State, and any reduction in sovereignty is counterbalanced by an increase in legal protection for human rights.

There is another important sense of sovereignty in the present context, however, which is often confused with the former, in particular in the debates about 'Europe'. This is the Westminster Parliament's sovereignty. The UK's constitutional framework prioritises a Diceyan concept of parliamentary sovereignty.[18] Traditionally this has meant that the UK Parliament is legally unlimited and indeed cannot be limited by any legal constraints. More recently, it has been acknowledged that such an absolute conception (owing much to Austin's nineteenth-century positivist view of the sovereign) is 'out of place in the modern United Kingdom'.[19] Those are the words of Lord Steyn; Lord Hope has further explained that

> Parliamentary sovereignty is no longer, if it ever was, absolute. It is not uncontrolled ... It is no longer right to say that its freedom to legislate admits of no qualification whatever. Step by step, gradually but surely, the English principle of the absolute legislative sovereignty of Parliament which Dicey derived from Coke and Blackstone is being qualified.[20]

Crucially, however, both of these senior judges make very clear that they still regard parliamentary sovereignty as an important principle of the constitution.[21] Therefore, while membership of the EU, devolution, and even the HRA may have chipped away at the Diceyan tradition, the UK's constitution continues to elevate a (if not 'the') principle of parliamentary sovereignty to the very centre of its workings. Such a view is unique in Europe. It is also less than ideal for encompassing external influences (from European bodies) or issues of legality (in relation to legally enforceable human rights).

Thus, while all Member States have concerns about sovereignty and all have certain sacrosanct constitutional concepts, the UK's preoccupation with a supreme legislature which is not and cannot be legally restricted in its freedom to legislate does present particular conceptual and practical difficulties when considering the implementation of European human rights. While it may, at first glance, seem ironic that a State with such obstacles to the acceptance of external restraints should rely upon the Convention rights (that is, rights drafted and originally implemented externally) within its domestic scheme of protection for human rights, it is in fact entirely understandable because of an absence of home-grown rights. As Brice Dickson fully explains in his chapter, the home-grown element of rights protection (namely common law rights) remains underdeveloped. And this is for the very reason identified above: the idea of a court imposing legal restraints upon Parliament is anathema to the UK constitution, or at least has been so for hundreds of years.

However, it must also be said that the 'flexible' UK constitution has been able to accommodate European influences much more easily than some continental systems, which are corseted into observing non-derogable constitutional principles. For example, it can be said that parliamentary sovereignty has been able to accommodate supremacy of EU law as a formal concept—on a formal construction of Parliament limiting itself but not legally irreversible—much more easily than other States in Europe which are tied by substantive clauses in their constitution. However, even under this more evolved version of parliamentary sovereignty in the

---

[18] AV Dicey, *The Law of the Constitution*, 10th edn (London, Macmillan, 1959).
[19] *R (Jackson) v Attorney-General* [2005] UKHL 56, [2006] 1 AC 262, para 102 (per Lord Steyn).
[20] ibid, para 104 (per Lord Hope).
[21] Lord Hope, for example, claims that the constitution is 'dominated by the sovereignty of Parliament' (ibid).

UK, human rights are exactly such a substantive limit which it is more difficult to accommodate within the UK's constitutional framework.

B. The 'Rights' Element

This leads on to the second element in the UK's relationship with European human rights, namely the growing scepticism about the very concept of human rights. This is not just a rejection of a particular European mechanism for protection of rights, but a broader distrust of human rights in general. Indeed the phrase 'human rights' is increasingly used as a shorthand for meddling bureaucracy, in a similar way to the denigration of 'health and safety' from something that should be overwhelmingly positive to something that carries with it an implicit pejorative sense.

There is some history of rights scepticism within the UK, partially linked to scepticism towards courts, which historically were extremely conservative in the era of establishing labour rights. There is also an increasing move towards rights scepticism in academic literature.[22] However, times and paradigms have changed. The scepticism about rights within our current context of European human rights seems far removed from these other movements.

So, what exactly are the objections to human rights today? One obvious objection, evident in most newspaper reports critical of 'human rights' (and in many casual conversations as well), is that they protect the wrong people. This perception is analysed by Lieve Gies in her chapter on the media, which highlights the media's selective portrayal of who is considered 'deserving' of rights protection . The idea that there are people who deserve human rights and other people who have forfeited them is simply irreconcilable with the concept and function of human rights, based as it is upon inherent values of equality and human dignity and the functional rationale of limiting those in government.

Such popular hostility towards human rights is frequently based on a lack of understanding of how human rights operate. It should also be remembered that very few rights (especially the Convention rights) are absolute in nature. The fact that every single human being is entitled to the protection of all of the rights does not mean that those rights cannot be legitimately limited on the basis of conflicting interests within a democratic society. Human rights law (at least in its current manifestation within Europe at this time) does not prioritise the individual's right over all other considerations; it simply requires, in general terms, that any limitation of such a right is non-arbitrary and pursues a legitimate aim in a proportionate manner. To draw from a commonly discussed scenario: the fact that an immigrant has a family life within the UK does not preclude deportation if that is a proportionate response to the need to protect society from crime, but it does require a sensitive balancing of those potentially conflicting interests, rather than a knee-jerk reaction.

---

[22] See eg T Campbell, KD Ewing and A Tomkins, *The Legal Protection of Human Rights: Sceptical Essays* (Oxford, Oxford University Press, 2011).

A second common objection to human rights at the present time, especially in the context of European human rights, is the claim that those rights are being expanded. This is seen particularly in the context of the right to respect for private life in Article 8 ECHR. Consider, for example, the comments of Lord Sumption made in November 2013:

> The text of Article 8 protects private and family life, the privacy of the home and of personal correspondence. This perfectly straightforward provision was originally devised as a protection against the surveillance state by totalitarian governments. But in the hands of the Strasbourg court it has been extended to cover the legal status of illegitimate children, immigration and deportation, extradition, aspects of criminal sentencing, abortion, homosexuality, assisted suicide, child abduction, the law of landlord and tenant, and a great deal else besides. None of these extensions are warranted by the express language of the Convention, nor in most cases are they necessary implications.[23]

This criticism of the ECtHR is misconceived. It assumes that any specific issues not mentioned within the terms of Article 8 must be an unwarranted extension of that provision, and yet a vague notion such as 'respect for private life' will inevitably require interpretation on a case-by-case basis. And what was regarded a part of private life in the late 1940s may well be different from what we would so regard today. The ECtHR has long used a 'living instrument' doctrine to help it to interpret the Convention. This means that the Convention is interpreted in the light of present-day conditions.[24] The approach encourages the Court to recognise new aspects and applications of the rights expressed in the text, and this invariably proves to be controversial. However, to argue, as Lord Sumption appears to, that there is, for example, no right to abortion in the Convention misses the point that abortion is an aspect of a woman's private life, dynamically interpreted, to which the Contracting Parties undoubtedly owe an obligation of respect. The Court's use of this evolutive interpretation not only responds to scientific advances and social changes, but can also serve as a response to the higher standards of compliance with human rights expected of today's state governments. This latter point can, of course, prove particularly controversial, and perhaps there are occasions on which the Court's application of the 'living instrument' doctrine could be explained more fully by the Court. Indeed, as Mowbray has pointed out, a 'greater willingness to elaborate upon the application of the doctrine in specific cases would help to alleviate potential fears that it is simply a cover for subjective ad-hockery'.[25] There are certainly substantive debates to be had about the scope and application of specific rights. Constructive criticism and debate are acceptable and important, for they invariably lead to better reasoning. But a constructive engagement with the interpretation of a particular right is far removed from a sweeping rejection of the very concept of rights under the ECHR.

The two distinct elements of European human rights identified so far—the sovereignty element and the human rights element—although distinct, also crucially

---

[23] 'Lord Sumption' (n 1) 7–8.

[24] *Tyrer v UK* (1979–80) 12 EHRR 1

[25] A Mowbray, 'The Creativity of the European Court of Human Rights' (2005) 5 *Human Rights Law Review* 57, 71.

overlap within the UK. This is because the UK's constitutional commitment to parliamentary sovereignty leads to a distrust of judicial restraints on Parliament's freedom to make laws which feeds into and enhances the distrust of legally enforceable 'rights', as these, by their very nature, impinge on Parliament's sovereignty. Thus, the UK's constitutional framework has traditionally prioritised democratic accountability and civil liberties, based around a concept of residual freedom whereby we are free to do anything provided that it is not prohibited by the law—a very limited idea of 'freedom'. Legal rights in codified documents are new and thus seen as 'foreign' (even when found in a domestic Act of Parliament such as the HRA). This conjunction of the two elements discussed above partially explains the strained nature of the relationship between the UK and European human rights, in the form of the issue of 'human rights law'. The role of a court, whether based in London or Strasbourg, in telling the elected branches of government what to do is part of a broader constitutional debate about the role of judges and the nature of the constitution. It is the legal enforcement of European human rights—as foreign 'impositions' (see below), a question thus closely linked to the sovereignty element—that causes concern for some. In particular, there is the question of who should have the final say on 'our' rights: a judge who is at least widely perceived to be unelected and unaccountable (and maybe even foreign) or an elected, and thus removable, politician? Broader constitutional debates about political or legal constitutionalism are a backdrop to this question, but it should also be remembered that the UK constitution is an evolving one, and in recent years senior judges have expressed the view that it is the 'rule of law enforced by the courts [which] is the ultimate controlling factor on which our constitution is based'.[26] This change, from the absolute power of the sovereign to a constitutional democracy, suggests that a gradual recognition of the acceptability of judicial enforcement of rights (even perhaps against a supreme legislature) might also be evolving.

C. The 'Foreign' (or 'Europe'?) Element: Externalisation of Rights

As mentioned above, it is the legal enforcement of European human rights as foreign 'impositions' that causes concern for some. The 'foreign' element entails significant consequences. It allows for externalisation, disowning human rights as foreign 'grafts', and scapegoating or instrumental use of human rights, in particular in political discourse. The 'foreign' influence element is not only visible in the context of human rights but informs much of the eurosceptic discourse (as in EU-scepticism). One aspect is the lack of care in differentiating the EU and the ECHR, fudging 'Europe' so that it becomes an amorphous, huge, almost omnipresent beast and object onto which all sorts of scepticisms are transferred. Wherever the centre of gravity of scepticism and hostility is seen to lie today (it used to be clearly the EU, but the tide in the UK has turned also against the ECtHR), fudging the 'two Europes' into a collective 'Other' does not help either Europe.

---

[26] *Jackson* (n 19) para 107 (per Lord Hope).

A culmination of fudging even to the point of contradiction can be seen in the combination of rights scepticism and euroscepticism directed against the EU Charter of Fundamental Rights—with contradictory arguments (as a eurosceptic could be expected to welcome rights to limit 'Europe', but that clashes with a rights scepticism) and debates verging on the absurd (as Sionaidh Douglas-Scott exposes).

Related to this UK-centric distrust of legal rights, at a more detailed level of substantive analysis of rights there may also be elements of clashes of legal cultures (bluntly: common law meets codification, or parliamentary sovereignty meets constitutional rights) which may add to the strain. Helen Fenwick and Brice Dickson discuss the example of the more flexible approaches to 'overall fairness' of trials under the common law in the UK versus strict review of rights of defence with regard to specific evidence. The dividing line between whether there is a violation of the Convention or just a different legal culture with a different solution is a thin one and not easy to decide, and there is an inherent risk of watering down the protection of the Convention in order to accommodate specific 'traditions' of legal culture of whatever origin (together with a risk of oversimplification and overemphasising differences). However, with the necessary sensitivity to the coming together of a wide variety of legal cultures, such issues should be dealt with at the level of interpretation of rights and the margin of appreciation doctrine should provide the appropriate tool to resolve such questions.

D. The Nature of the Debate in the UK

The debates about European human rights in the UK reflect some characteristics which distinguish them from debates in other European States. The chapters in this collection that address other countries' relationships with European human rights indicate that the British debates appear to be more extreme, both in the sense of elevating a specific issue to a reason to criticise the entire system, and perhaps also in the sense of the vitriol of the language used, especially by the media, in contributing to the debate.

It appears to be a particularly British approach to adopt an all-or-nothing stance and to readily and repeatedly discuss an exit from the EU and ECHR. Other European countries, even when encountering their own culture clashes with the ECtHR, do not seem to resort so quickly to exit scare scenarios, as we can see in the comparative chapters in this collection. For example, France, as described by Constance Grewe in her chapter, experienced some severe conflicts going to the structure of government institutions and the organisation of the judiciary (in relation to the participation of the *commissaire du gouvernement* in deliberations of judges in administrative proceedings, which conflicts with Article 6 ECHR)[27] which was met with an outcry. However, criticism was discussed in a subject-matter-oriented way and even segued—over time—into an acknowledgment of an overall improvement of human rights protection in France.

---

[27] *Kress v France* App no 39594/98, ECHR 2001-VI.

Similarly, as Julia Rackow demonstrates in her chapter on the German perspective, while there is some criticism of the ECtHR in legal and political circles, and among public opinion, such criticism tends to be issue-oriented rather than, as in the UK, fundamentally challenging the legitimacy of the entire ECHR system. Rackow also notes that, in Germany, issues concerning adverse judgments of the ECtHR tend to be viewed as judicial matters, for resolution by the courts, and not matters on which the legislative or executive branches of government would generally seek to intervene. This again stands in stark contrast to the approach in the UK, where the question of the appropriate role of the courts and Parliament is central.

In Russia, constructive judicial engagement with the Convention has made a direct contribution towards ensuring that confrontation has been avoided. As Bill Bowring explains in his chapter, an issue which had the potential to be as politically sensitive in Russia as the prisoner voting saga is in the UK did not result in the level of outrage experienced in the UK when dialogue and pragmatism won out. Growing confidence in the use of language of rights among the legal profession, Chernishova further suggests, is rooting the Convention increasingly firmly in Russian law. What is particularly striking is the demonstrable way in which such engagement can occur without undue concern on the part of the judiciary about the diminution of their constitutional role or the legitimacy of Strasbourg. Yet it is clear that an established legal rights culture alone is not always sufficient to protect against even the more serious rights violations.

In relation to Italy, Oreste Pollicino identifies a strained relationship between the ECtHR and the Italian Constitutional Court (ICC), but this seems largely based on potential conflicts between a constitutional system of fundamental rights and the ECHR system. In Italy, review for conformity with the ECHR has become part of domestic constitutional review, going beyond a mere 'taking into account' of the ECHR. Pollicino notes that the ECHR has progressed from being 'an almost unknown walk-on character in the case law of ICC to being one of its central protagonists',[28] but this has also necessitated the elaboration of new judicial techniques by the ICC in order to achieve a balance between Italy's constitutional system of fundamental rights and the ECHR system.

A similar struggle can be identified in France and Germany. However, it must be noted that although the German Federal Constitutional Court (FCC) has rejected the ECHR as its formal standard of review in favour of German constitutional rights (on the basis of a dualist approach to unincorporated treaties), it would be too simplistic to present this as an inward-looking reliance on the own bill of rights and possibly even 'constitutional identity'. The FCC is required to take the ECHR and ECtHR decisions into account, and only departs from them if important reasons warrant it. Moreover, the German Constitutional Court recently developed its cooperative approach further in declaring decisions of the ECtHR (against whatever State Party) as 'factual precedent', as Julia Rackow points out in her chapter.

---

[28] O Pollicino, 'The ECtHR and the Italian Constitutional Court: No "Groovy Kind of Love"' (ch 18), this volume.

Austria is perhaps the country most comparable to the UK, given that the domestic fundamental rights regime in both countries relies heavily on the ECHR. Andreas Th Müller's chapter in this collection is therefore illuminating in illustrating the additional complexity that results both from multiple sources of human rights within one constitutional setting and from relying on an external source domestically. It shows that a multiplicity of sources of domestic human rights protection may be manageable. There may even be additional benefits for the continuous evolution of a modern system of human rights protection. Müller also highlights the potential for courts to use such complexities not just for judicially activist human rights protection but to further their own institutional interests.

The public and media response to judgments of the ECtHR is of a very different order in other European countries. For example, as Constance Grewe makes clear, some adverse judgments by the ECtHR in relation to serious problems concerning French prisons and anti-terrorism policy have simply failed to attract wider public interest. In Russia, which between 2002–12 had the greatest number of new cases lodged at the ECtHR, there is (as yet) no sign of the vitriol unleashed against the ECtHR in the UK. As Olga Chernishova argues in her chapter, robust domestic institutions with the capacity and willingness to implement the Court's rulings are needed in any contracting State if the ECtHR's judgments are to make a difference, and alongside that capacity (and no doubt an inspiration for it) is a secure position for the ECtHR jurisprudence within a larger domestic culture of rights.

Significantly, the two chapters in this collection on the Russian perspective both express concern at the risk of 'contagion' of the negative attitude towards the ECHR system from within the UK. There is genuine concern that the UK might lead a trend towards non-cooperation in the face of unpalatable judgments, and even to 'exit talk' from the ECHR. Any act of defiance by the UK government against a judgment of the ECtHR is therefore a dangerous precedent. As Bill Bowring notes, adverse judgments against Russia in the context of Georgia and/or Ukraine carry the potential to lead to outright defiance, or even denouncement, of the ECHR. It is a terrible time for the UK to be setting such a bad example.

III. RELIEVING THE STRAIN?

Having considered the different types of relationships between the UK and European human rights, and analysed some possible causes of strain in (at least some of) those relationships, it is now necessary to consider how that strain might be relieved.

Before doing so, it is worthwhile noting that the two contributors to this volume with the most direct experience of 'living' the relationship are inclined to deny the existence of strain, at least within the judicial context. While there are certainly some signs of strain in the extra-judicial pronouncements of other senior judges, it may be that the dialogue that already undoubtedly exists between senior domestic courts and the ECtHR plays a key role in relieving that strain. As such it may be a lesson to draw upon.

A. Dialogue

Dialogue will have a vital role in increasing understanding. It can take many forms, including within court judgments (whether UK judges explaining their reasoning in ways that Strasbourg judges can subsequently take into account, or Strasbourg judges sending judicial messages to domestic judges). Dialogue is already written into the HRA and thus a declaration of incompatibility is the start of a dialogue with Parliament, informing it that the legislation in question is not compatible with a Convention right, but leaving Parliament to determine how best, if at all, to remedy that incompatibility. Dialogue between UK politicians and Strasbourg judges tends to take a political rhetoric approach (and be driven by ulterior agendas) that may not be conducive to improving relationships. There is, however, scope for behind-the-scenes dialogue that can avoid this danger. The British media also contribute to dialogue with Strasbourg—and not always in a productive manner. As Robert Uerpmann-Wittack explains in his chapter, a free press is essential in order that it can play a watchdog role, but with that role should also come some responsibilities to present accurate information and informed comment (which is not currently always the case, as noted by David Mead in his chapter). The British people are part of the dialogue too, not least at elections when their choice of politicians will have long-term influences on the future relationship between the UK and European human rights.

Dialogue may relieve the strain, but at what price? Dialogue might present some dangers to the effective protection of European human rights. Dialogue could amount to appeasement; a concession to the political priorities of a government of the day, rather than a neutral application of human rights norms. Could such appeasing dialogue have the result of watering down human rights protection (perhaps in order to rescue the overall Convention system from the threat of a UK exit)? Such dialogue might present one solution, as discussed by Helen Fenwick, but what impact will a lower level of European human rights protection have on other European States, and what message does the UK's negative approach to human rights send within and even beyond Europe? Kenyan President Uhuru Kenyatta, facing charges of war crimes in The Hague, recently made a speech in which he drew support from the UK Prime Minister in his efforts to assert Kenyan supremacy: 'The push to defend sovereignty is not unique to Kenya or Africa. Recently, the Prime Minister of the United Kingdom committed to reasserting the sovereign primacy of his Parliament over the decisions of the European Human Rights Court. He even threatened to quit the court.'[29] The manner in which the UK redefines its relationship with the ECtHR, if it seeks to do so, will have implications not only within the EU and the Council of Europe, but across the world.

---

[29] U Kenyatta, 'Ruto the Acting President as I attend ICC case' Capital FM (6 October 2014), www.capitalfm.co.ke/eblog/2014/10/06/ruto-the-acting-president-as-i-attend-icc-case. See also Adam Wagner, 'Kenyan President Uses Tory Human Rights Plans to Defend War Crimes Charges' UK Human Rights Blog (24 October 2014), ukhumanrightsblog.com/2014/10/24/kenyan-president-uses-tory-human-rights-plans-to-defend-war-crimes-charges.

B. Strengthening the Institutional Aspect of Human Rights Protection in the UK

Other means of relieving the strain in the relationship between the UK and European human rights might involve a strengthening of the independence of judges, or at least, as a start, more sensitivity towards the fact that the independence of the judiciary is even a relevant issue in the circumstances. Such an awareness amongst government might help to alleviate the worst forms of 'scolding' of courts and lead to a shared appreciation of the importance of a convention that it is not acceptable for government to scold judges for the content of their judgments.[30] In other words, criticism by other branches of government should not go significantly beyond what the constitutional division of power provides to correct judicial mistakes and to protect the independence of judges where they are prevented from 'talking back' (as Mark Ockelton demonstrates in his chapter).

Approaching the perceived problem from a contrasting angle, it could be asked whether a unique UK solution might be to add and strengthen a majoritarian overlay to human rights, by entrusting Parliament with the final word on human rights issues. Alice Donald explores the possibilities that lie in this direction. Clearly, ultimately a tension will remain, as the very rationale of human rights lies between majority decisions and minority protection. However, such tensions can be reduced by adhering to the UK's constitutional tradition of open and informed debate of human rights issues within the parliamentary process.

C. Home-Grown Human Rights

More optimistically, further development in 'owning' human rights or developing *home-grown human rights* would be a positive move, and may relieve the strain both on the two sovereignty elements and on the foreign/European elements of this relationship. By home-grown human rights we do not mean home-grown rights designed to lower the standards set by the Convention, to emphasise a traditional notion of sovereignty, or to provide a stronger bargaining chip in the relationship with Strasbourg (by providing opportunities to rely on a newly created national constitutional identity in order to bypass international human rights obligations— or even worse: water them down throughout Europe). A domestic bill of rights is unlikely to be a recipe for giving the government more leeway in human rights issues, as the tensions between the courts and the government will remain even under a domestic bill of rights. A domestic bill of rights will allow a clearer distinction to be drawn between the international and the domestic layers of human rights (and thus end any debate about the 'mirror' principle), but its mere existence will not automatically and immediately embed a human rights culture. Rackow, for example, points out that in Germany the human rights culture is closely linked to

---

[30] The erosion of the existing convention was recently discussed by the Master of the Rolls, Lord Dyson: 'Criticising Judges: Fair Game Or Off-Limits?', Third Annual Bailii Lecture, 27 November 2014, www.judiciary.gov.uk/wp-content/uploads/2014/11/bailii-critising-judges.pdf.

a 'constitutional review culture'. But what becomes apparent is that the dwindling acceptance of and consensus regarding human rights in the UK may be part of the problem, and exacerbated by the 'foreign' element. As law as a social construct depends ultimately on its acceptance, drastic debates are deeply concerning and must be taken seriously. Ultimately the significance of human rights and their persuasiveness must speak for themselves—that is, under the proverbial Rawlsian veil of ignorance, abstracting from specific situations. However, the development of a basic social consensus may be supported by the existence and development of home-grown human rights, their institutional embeddedness, be it in the powers of review by the courts or institutions such as the JCHR, and a more widespread human rights education, leading, so it is hoped, to more informed public debate, responsible engagement with human rights by those in power and the development of a more principled human rights jurisprudence by the courts.

The HRA may have been designed to 'bring rights home', but many in the UK do not yet accept them—and they are not 'forced' to because the 'foreign' element discussed above always provides a convenient reason to reject them (ie externalisation of human rights). Home-grown human rights could be developed in a variety of ways, such as through the common law or through domestic codification. A written domestic bill of rights may be a faster, more structured and overall more appropriate way of developing domestic constitutional principles and human rights, as argued by Sionaidh Douglas-Scott in her chapter, but the common law can be used more to assist in the task of developing a coherent body of human rights law in the UK, and maybe the answer is to pursue both alleys in a complementary, mutually supporting way.

The common law has the potential to do far more than it currently does to protect human rights. Indeed, there is a history of common law rights dating back to Coke CJ in the seventeenth century which was briefly revived pre-HRA in an extra-judicial capacity in the 1990s. The HRA seemed to negate the need for common law protection and, as Brice Dickson discusses, the courts have turned their back on earlier attempts to develop common law rights to work alongside the rights set out in the ECHR. However, the failure of the public to engage with the Convention rights within the HRA suggests that, whether the HRA survives after the election of a Conservative government in May 2015 or not, there is an important role to be played by the common law in protecting home-grown rights at a domestic level. Questions will remain to be answered, of course, as to how such rights might be effective against a sovereign Parliament, and it is clear that they could not alone provide a sufficient replacement for the HRA.

Leaving the common law to develop UK human rights (not even mentioning the slow, haphazard nature of such a process) would not in all likelihood significantly engender public debate and education in human rights—they would remain a technocratic matter confined to the judicial process. Embarking on a codification exercise has at least the potential, if linked to a widespread consultation, to promote wider discussion, and provide more opportunity for the development of a human rights 'culture' within and outwith the courts. It could also be used to fundamentally debate the relationship between parliamentary sovereignty and the rule of law, and the relative weight of these principles in a modern constitution of the United Kingdom. Such an codification exercise—along the lines of the experiences of Canada in 1982, New Zealand in 1990, at territory level in Australia (ACT 2004, Victoria 2006) and the EU Charter of Fundamental Rights 2000—could also provide a modern impetus to the development of human rights and put the UK back into the position of a forerunner on this issue. It may be asked, however, whether untangling domestic human rights protection from the ECHR in the UK would decrease the influence of the UK jurisprudence in Strasbourg, which results largely (but not only) from the direct application of the ECHR and the volume of jurisprudence generated by UK courts (recalling that this an important potential benefit of the HRA). But this would merely put the UK on an equal footing with virtually all other States in Europe. Moreover, the influence it would be able to exert would depend on a number of factors which would either continue to exist or are in the hands of the UK anyway, such as whether the ECHR would continue to be directly applicable in the UK (a feature that distinguishes it from some continental jurisdictions, including Germany where the ECHR only informs the interpretation of domestic law); the quality of human rights reasoning; and, last but not least, the accessibility of domestic judgments: undoubtedly the UK enjoys the huge advantage of using a *lingua franca*.[31]

D. Developing a Human Rights 'Culture'

Despite being one of the intentions underlying the 'bringing rights home' ethos of the HRA in the late 1990s, there is still a lack of human rights culture in the UK, where the scepticism about human rights has only increased in the intervening years. Education of the public, media, politicians and lawyers about the nature and function of human rights would inevitably lead to better informed debates and better judgments at all levels. By human rights 'culture', we mean an informed approach to human rights, both by those in power and by ordinary citizens, an 'owning' of human rights as a valuable achievement of the polity and citizens, and good-quality human rights reasoning in the legal sphere, derived from principle. In other words, we are seeking a culture of substantive and constructive debate rather than an a priori dismissal of human rights as foreign, insidious and self-serving; an environment where scapegoating of human rights is not acceptable.

One persistent obstacle to building a constructive rights dialogue in the UK is the conflation of the two Europes. While historically the EU and the Council of Europe share a common overall goal—the preservation of peace and liberal democracy in Europe—they are distinct organisations. They are two different 'clubs' with overlapping membership but significantly different rules. This does not seem to be a difficult concept to grasp, and yet it seems to elude many interested parties—from members of the press to members of the government, to a significant proportion of first-year law students.

---

[31] The importance of accessibility of their judgments in order to contribute to European or international debates is not lost on higher national courts as it becomes increasingly common for courts outside the English-speaking world to provide English translations or summaries of some of their judgments.

In part because of this coalescing of the two Europes in public perceptions, it would be extremely useful to distinguish the rights issue from other 'Europe' issues. Whatever one's position on the UK's place and role in 'Europe', an effective guarantee of individual rights necessitates external oversight. That oversight does not have to come from Strasbourg, and indeed there may be scope for reform there, but it has to come from somewhere outside the UK. The Strasbourg system is by far the most advanced and successful of human rights regimes, and it would be unfortunate and short-sighted were that success to alienate the UK, one of its founding parties. But the need for external oversight on human rights issues is not inevitably linked to the UK participating in 'Europe' (much less the EU) and the two debates would both benefit from being untangled from the other.

Finally, and related to the above issue, it is important to emphasise that public fears and misgivings about 'European judges' telling 'us' what to do are entirely misplaced in the human rights arena. In cases against the UK, the ECtHR judges are informing the UK government where the limits of its powers lie. Similarly, the CJEU in this context will inform the EU where the limits of its powers lie. It is the job of these courts to protect the people of Europe from their governments and the institutions of the EU respectively. Without such protection, there would be inadequate legal remedies when a public body kills, tortures, degrades, or infringes freedom, nor would there be the same incentive to prevent these actions. The UK government does infringe rights, as does every other government to a greater or lesser extent, and it will not always just be the rights of other people that are infringed.

IV. THE FUTURE RELATIONSHIP

At the time of writing, the future relationship between the UK and European human rights looks undeniably bleak. The Conservative Party's proposals to repeal the HRA, rewrite, so as to limit the application of, the Convention rights and even potentially withdraw from the ECHR entirely are a sobering reflection on what is likely to be the nature of the debate about human rights in the UK following the May 2015 election . Perhaps it is only in the UK, with its unique combination of a constitutional commitment to an outdated concept of parliamentary sovereignty, a eurosceptic tabloid press, and a distinctly British island mentality, that a proposal to repeal the only domestic legal protection for human rights is likely to be seen as a political asset ahead of an election.

From a number of perspectives (historical, institutional interest, perhaps even political), it is not in the least bit surprising that a political party which hopes to form a government would wish to remove the legal restraints upon its powers imposed by human rights laws; yet, from the perspective of a modern constitutional state and considering that those campaigning for the removal of such restrictions aspire to hold government office, it is utterly surprising. For those of who believe in, and support the application of, human rights, the task is to change the perception of human rights amongst the public so that it is no longer considered to be a vote-winner to promise to remove them. Common sense speaks to this: human rights have their strongest instinctive appeal when they are viewed as benefits for us as individuals against the exercise of public power; they have a weaker appeal for many when seen only as benefits for other (often 'undeserving') people. It is, of course, no surprise that most human rights cases involve the least popular members of society (prisoners, suspected terrorists, mental health patients, immigrants) because it is they who are most likely to have their rights infringed. But a government unrestrained by human rights law puts us all at risk. The ECHR system is currently the best means of ensuring that the UK government respects the rights of everyone within the UK's jurisdiction, and future developments within the EU are likely to strengthen that protection. There is room for debate on how specific rights are interpreted, how proportionality is determined, what measures are needed to remedy violations, and many other important issues on which even human rights experts are divided, but if the UK wishes to contribute to answering these questions, it needs to be an active participant in the protection of European human rights. The multi-faceted relationship between the UK and European human rights has to be worked upon at all levels in the hope that one day 'human rights' will not have a more negative connotation in the UK than in the rest of Europe and the world beyond.

Index

Lightning Source UK Ltd.
Milton Keynes UK
UKOW04n2356211216

290581UK00002B/4/P